The WTO as an
International Organization

The WTO as an International Organization

Edited by **Anne O. Krueger**

with the assistance of Chonira Aturupane

The University of Chicago Press

Chicago and London

The University of Chicago Press, Chicago 60637
The University of Chicago Press, Ltd., London
© 1998 by The University of Chicago
All rights reserved. Published 1998
Paperback edition 2000
Printed in the United States of America
07 06 05 04 03 02 01 00   2 3 4 5
ISBN: 0-226-45487-8 (cloth)
ISBN: 0-226-45449-5 (paperback)

Library of Congress Cataloging-in-Publication Data

The WTO as an international organization / edited by Anne O. Krueger
  with the assistance of Chonira Aturupane.
      p.   cm.
  Papers presented at the Conference on the World Trade Organization
as an International Institution held in Singapore in Dec. 1996.
  Includes bibliographical references and index.
  ISBN 0-226-45487-8 (cloth : alk. paper)
  1. World Trade Organization—Congresses.   2. International trade—
Congresses.   3. Free trade—Congresses.   4. Commercial policy—
Congresses.   5. Free trade—Developing countries—Congresses.
I. Krueger, Anne O.   II. Aturupane, Chonira.   III. Conference on the
World Trade Organization as an International Institution (1996 : Singa-
pore)
HF1385.W78   1998
382'.06'01—dc21   97-33584
                                                              CIP

Contents

*

Foreword

As Singapore's ambassador to the GATT, and then to the WTO, from December 1991 to February 1997, I had long felt the need for increased "interaction" between the communities of international trade officials, academics, and policymakers. With increasing globalization, a well-functioning open multilateral trading system is of crucial importance for us all. Understanding that system well, and making it function smoothly, is a challenging task for which the skills and insights of academics and policymakers alike are greatly needed. Indeed, the latter are dependent on scholars for dispassionate, objective analysis of the critical issues facing the world of trade.

I was very pleased, therefore, when the Conference on the World Trade Organization as an International Institution was organized, and when I was invited to participate. The conference brought together national policymakers, officials from the trade community, and academics from a variety of disciplines. The stimulating papers provided an excellent backdrop for discussion of the challenges and issues facing the WTO. I believe that all participants were enriched by the excellent dialogue that took place at the conference.

Held only about two months before the inaugural WTO ministerial meeting in Singapore in December 1996, the conference had special significance. The results of the deliberations provided input for defining the agenda of the Singapore meeting.

The papers and discussion at the conference continue to have great relevance for the WTO as it grapples with new and increasingly complex issues. Apart from trade and trade-related issues, the WTO, in concert with the IMF and the World Bank, also has to take into account other issues such as development, environment, and the impact of technology on the global trading system. The authors of the papers have given us much food for thought. Even though we may not agree with all of their conclusions, the relevance of the issues addressed and the quality of the discussion that the papers generated make all the contributions important. It is my belief that the outcome of the proceedings of the conference will be of interest and benefit to all those interested in international economic issues and the maintenance of an open multilateral trading system.

I hope that this volume represents only the first step toward closer interactions and interchange between the academic and policymaking communities concerned with global issues of trade.

K. KESAVAPANY

Acknowledgments

With any edited volume, the primary acknowledgment must be to the contributors to the volume. In the case of this volume, the debt to contributors is even greater than usual: the authors gathered at a conference in Palo Alto in September 1996 and the interactions were highly productive and stimulated all in the revisions of these papers. In addition to those whose contributions are included in the volume there were many others (included in the list of participants) whose comments and analyses were stimulating and invaluable.

In turn, neither the paper preparation nor the conference would have been possible without the support of Richard Blackhurst and Gary Sampson of the WTO and of Seamus O'Clearicain of the Ford Foundation. Deborah Carvalho, administrator of the Center for Economic Policy Research at Stanford, provided excellent organization and arrangements for the conference, with the able assistance of Christy Drexel. Evren Ergin, Jess Gasper, and Calgar Ozden, all then graduate students at Stanford, were excellent research assistants.

Financial support for the project was provided by the Ford Foundation, and is gratefully acknowledged.

Abbreviations

AD antidumping
APEC Asia-Pacific Economic Cooperation
ASEAN Association of Southeast Asian Nations
CAP Common Agricultural Policy
CEA Council of Economic Advisers
CFCs chlorofluorocarbons
CG.18 Consultative Group of Eighteen
CGE computable general equilibrium
COMECON Council for Mutual Economic Assistance
CU customs union
CVD countervailing duty
DSB Dispute Settlement Body
DSU dispute settlement understanding
EC European Community
EDF European Development Fund
EEC European Economic Community
EFTA European Free Trade Area
EPG Eminent Persons Group
EPU European Payments Union
EU European Union
FOGS functioning of the GATT system
FTA free trade area
G7 Group of Seven
GATS General Agreement on Trade in Services
GATT General Agreement on Tariffs and Trade
GCC Gulf Cooperation Council
GSP Generalized System of Preferences

IBRD International Bank for Reconstruction and Development
IDA International Development Association
IDB Integrated Data Base
IFC International Finance Corporation
ILO International Labor Organization
IMF International Monetary Fund
ITC International Trade Commission
ITO International Trade Organization
LAFTA Latin American Free Trade Association
LAIA Latin American Integration Association
MAI Multilateral Agreement on Investment
MFA Multifiber Arrangement
MFN most favored nation
MTN multilateral trade negotiations
NAFTA North American Free Trade Agreement
NAM National Association of Manufacturers
NATO North Atlantic Treaty Organization
NFTC National Foreign Trade Council
NGO nongovernmental organization
NIRA National Industrial Recovery Act
NT national treatment
NTB nontariff barrier
OECD Organization for Economic Cooperation and Development
PPP purchasing-power parity

PTA preferential trading arrangement
ROO rules of origin
RTAA Reciprocal Trade Agreements Act
STR special trade representative
TAA Trade Agreements Act
TAFTA Transatlantic Free Trade Area
TBT technical barriers to trade
TPRM Trade Policy Review Mechanism
TRIM trade-related investment measure

UNCTAD United Nations Conference on Trade and Development
UNDP United Nations Development Programme
USTR U.S. trade representative
VER voluntary export restraint
WHO World Health Organization
WIPO World Intellectual Property Organization
WPS working paper series
WTO World Trade Organization

Chronology

1944	Bretton Woods Conference.
1946	The IMF and IBRD open for business.
1947	Drawing up of the GATT.
1947	First round of multilateral tariff reductions negotiated in Geneva.
1947	Start of the Marshall Plan and the establishment of the Organization for European Economic Cooperation.
1948	Adoption of the ITO charter by the International Conference on Trade and Employment in Havana.
1949	Second round of multilateral tariff negotiations at Annecy.
1951	Third round of multilateral tariff negotiations at Torquay.
1956	Fourth round of multilateral trade negotiations at Geneva.
1957	Signing of Treaty of Rome establishing the European Common Market.
1957	Establishment of the Commission of the European Communities.
1960	Creation of LAFTA.
1960–61	Fifth round of tariff negotiations under the GATT: Dillon Round.
1961	The Organization for European Economic Cooperation becomes the OECD.
1964–67	Sixth round of multilateral tariff negotiations under the GATT: Kennedy Round. The first multilateral tariff negotiations round to deal with nontariff measures.
1967	Establishment of ASEAN.
1973–79	Seventh round of multilateral tariff negotiations under the GATT: Tokyo Round.
July 1975	Establishment of the CG.18 by the GATT Council.
1979	The enabling clause: The Decision on Differential and More Favorable Treatment, Reciprocity, and Fuller Participation of Developing Countries.
1979	Declaration on Trade Measures taken for Balance of Payments Purposes by GATT contracting parties.
1983	Establishment of a formal office of legal affairs for the GATT Secretariat.

1986–92	Eighth round of multilateral tariff negotiations under the GATT: Uruguay Round.
1989	The Canada-U.S. Free Trade Agreement goes into effect.
1989	Trade Policy Review Mechanism (TPRM) introduced into the GATT following the midterm review of the Uruguay Round.
1989	Formation of APEC.
April 1990	Proposal to create a WTO by Canada's trade minister, John Crosbie.
February 1992	Signing of the Treaty of Maastricht.
1 January 1994	NAFTA goes into effect.
15 April 1994	Signing of the Final Act embodying the results of the Uruguay Round of multilateral trade negotiations and establishing the WTO in Marrakesh, Morocco.
1 January 1995	Birth of the WTO.
28 July 1995	Conclusion of negotiations on the *Financial Services Agreement*.
28 July 1995	Conclusion of negotiations on *Movement of Natural Persons*.
November 1996	Formal agreements concerning cooperation reached between the WTO and the IMF and World Bank.
December 1996	WTO Ministerial Conference in Singapore.
February 1997	Conclusion of negotiations on *Basic Telecommunications:* the telecommunication agreement.
26 March 1997	Agreement by forty governments to implement the ministerial Declaration on Trade in Informational Technology Products.

Introduction

Anne O. Krueger

Until the end of 1994, there was no multilateral or international organization that dealt with trade issues between countries. For almost fifty years, the international trading system had functioned without such an organization: under the aegis of the General Agreement on Tariffs and Trade, rules of the game had been developed and respected. But the GATT was created through agreement among trading nations: it did not have the international standing of the International Monetary Fund (IMF) or the World Bank, both of which were international organizations. Instead, the GATT Secretariat, as its name implied, served the signatories to the GATT.

All of that changed suddenly in 1994, when, contradicting earlier gloomy forecasts, the Uruguay Round of trade negotiations under the GATT ended not only with considerable progress in strengthening the international trading system, but also with an agreement to found the World Trade Organization.

The WTO now has the same legal and organizational standing as the Fund and the Bank. The WTO came into being on 1 January 1995, without much fanfare. The staff of the WTO was the same as that of the former GATT, although it was subsequently expanded by about 10 percent to 400, contrasted with the Fund's approximate 3,000 and the World Bank's 6,000 employees! The WTO was housed in the same building as the GATT had been, and the director general of the GATT became director general of the WTO.

A casual observer might well have asked whether anything had changed. The answer was a qualified yes. On one hand, the WTO was assigned responsibilities additional to those earlier carried out by the GATT. On the other hand,

Anne O. Krueger is the Herald L. and Caroline L. Ritch Professor in Humanities and Sciences and director of the Center for Research on Economic Development and Policy Reform at Stanford University.

the fact that the WTO was an organization provided potential and opportunities for the institution to alter its role in the international trading system, at least to some extent, relative to the passive "instrument of the GATT signatories" that the GATT Secretariat had earlier, necessarily, taken.

While considerable attention was given to the substantive achievements and challenges arising out of the Uruguay Round agreement, little attention was paid to the challenges facing the WTO as an international organization.

It was therefore deemed worthwhile to focus attention on the fledgling international organization. To that end, a conference was organized by the Program in International Economics of the Center for Economic Policy Research at Stanford University on the WTO as an international institution.

To provide the reader with some helpful background for the papers that follow, this introduction provides a short history of those aspects of the evolution of the international trading system since the Second World War that are pertinent to consideration of the WTO and its effectiveness. An initial section points out the irony of the weakness of the institutional structure underlying trading relations compared to the enormous success in liberalizing international trade. A second section reviews the key principles of the open multilateral trading system as they are embodied in the WTO. A third section briefly sketches some of the threats arising out of protectionist pressures that many observers believe constitute major challenges for the WTO. A fourth section introduces some of the key problems with which the WTO will have to deal: policies toward preferential trading arrangements, establishing agreements for trade in services, pressures for environmental and labor standards, and liberalization of agriculture. A fifth section focuses on the need for a strengthened and effective international organization. A final section overviews the individual papers that follow.

The papers cover many aspects of the issues outlined in this introduction. Chapter 15 synthesizes the key results, bringing together some of the crucial insights from individual papers. It starts with a "communiqué" that paper givers agreed to at the conference, enumerating those areas where they believed that progress might be made at the Singapore ministerial meeting in December 1995. The actual results of the Singapore ministerial and the challenges ahead for the WTO are then synthesized.

Ironies in the Evolution of the International Trading System

The evolution of the multilateral trading system since the Second World War has been replete with ironies. A first irony is that the growth and liberalization of the international trading system has been the most prominent success of the postwar period, even though the nations participating in deliberations over the postwar international economic system were unable to produce a charter for an international trade organization that was acceptable to key governments.[1] Hence, the great liberalization of tariffs and trade in the postwar period was achieved under the auspices of the GATT, which did not even have the legal status of an international economic organization.[2]

A second irony is that the very success of the multilateral tariff negotiations conducted under the aegis of the GATT was so remarkable that the world has become interdependent at an unprecedented rate. That interdependence in itself has generated a number of new challenges for the international trading system. As transport costs and tariff barriers have fallen and the ease of communication has increased, trade in services is booming, while foreign investment is rising sharply, treatment of intellectual property rights in other countries matters as it never did before, and there is increasing concern about a "level playing field" for all competitors.

A third irony is that concerns over the ramifications of increased interdependence gave rise to great gloominess over the prospects for a successful outcome of the Uruguay Round, yet the round achieved far more than those instigating it anticipated. The pessimism regarding the outcome of the round was well founded, given the complexities of the issues with which negotiators were dealing, and the round was far longer than any preceding one, beginning in 1987 and concluding only in 1994.[3] However, the outcome included not only a framework agreement on services, agreements on intellectual property rights and trade-related investment measures, a timetable for phasing out all quantitative restrictions on trade, and first steps toward bringing agriculture more firmly under a multilateral discipline, but also the establishment of the WTO, giving that body the same international status as the International Monetary Fund and the World Bank.

A fourth irony is that the United States provided strong leadership for an open multilateral system and its very success has resulted in its retreat from

1. As is well known, the International Trade Organization (ITO) was envisaged as a third pillar—along with the IMF and International Bank for Reconstruction and Development (later the World Bank)—of the postwar economic order. In deliberations about the postwar arrangements, however, there was a significant divide between those who anticipated a postwar return to depression as in the 1930s, and those who expected a return to more "normal" economic conditions. The former group pushed for a number of provisions in the ITO Charter that effectively permitted signatories to undertake virtually any trade policy they desired if it was done to pursue domestic "employment objectives." There were sufficient objections to this in the U.S. Congress that the ITO Charter was not submitted for ratification, and other major countries did not ratify the charter, pending U.S. action.

While work was progressing on the ITO Charter, the United States undertook an initiative for a first multilateral round of trade negotiations. In order to make the round meaningful, the GATT was formulated and accepted. At the time it was anticipated that the GATT articles would become part of the charter of the ITO, but in the absence of the ITO, the GATT articles became the basis for governance of the international trading system.

2. See Dam (1970) for an account.

3. There had been seven rounds of multilateral tariff negotiations: the Geneva Round in 1947, the Annecy Round in 1949, the Torquay Round in 1951, another round in Geneva in 1956, the Dillon Round in 1960–61, the Kennedy Round in 1964–67, and the Tokyo Round in 1973–79. For a chronology of major events in GATT history, see Hoekman and Kostecki (1995).

open multilateralism. That retreat has taken place when the United States is no longer as dominant economically as it was yet when trade liberalization is probably even more in U.S. economic self-interest than it was in the first quarter century after the Second World War. U.S. support for the GATT and for the successive rounds of multilateral tariff negotiations at a time when it was simultaneously economically dominant was clearly an important factor in permitting the cooperative dismantling of trade barriers.[4] Its very success in fostering the open multilateral trading system led to a reduction in its share of world GDP and world trade. Increased competition from abroad has, in turn, increased protectionist pressures in the United States and led Americans to see themselves more as a competitor in, rather than as a protector of, the open multilateral trading system. Yet even the United States is more "globalized" than it was, as its percentages of GDP in exports and imports have risen and its businesses are increasingly global in scope.

Thus, the history of international trade since the Second World War has been one of "accidental success," where plans (such as the International Trade Organization [ITO]) were not realized and the outcome (i.e., liberalization under the GATT) far exceeded what any of those planning the system could have reasonably hoped for.

That track record should be borne in mind, as this volume focuses on future challenges. The major challenges that are currently facing the open multilateral trading system and the WTO as an international organization arise to a fair degree out of past successes and the increased globalization of economic activity. As will be seen, however, increased interdependence has raised to the forefront difficult and complex issues. A simple litany of those issues is enough to persuade even the most optimistic that continued liberalization and economic integration will require not only commitment and attention on the part of the world's key policymakers, but also an appreciation of the importance of maintaining the open multilateral system.

Principles Underlying the GATT and WTO

The key principle to which the GATT contracting parties subscribed was an open and nondiscriminatory trade, thus giving rise to the term "open multilateral system."[5] Except for provisions in article XXIV, which governs preferential trading arrangements,[6] signatories undertook to treat all other GATT signatories equally in applying whatever tariffs they imposed on imports from

4. Another contributing factor was the memories of the 1930s and the fear that competitive "beggar thy neighbor" policies might result once again in worldwide depression.

5. The GATT articles were incorporated into the WTO. Nonetheless, the WTO encompasses a number of additional issues, and hence I shall refer to the GATT principles to designate that set of commitments that have prevailed in the GATT articles since 1947.

6. See the discussion of preferential trading arrangements and article XXIV in the next section.

abroad.[7] GATT articles precluded export subsidies and quantitative restrictions on trade (with the exception of some provisions for grandfathering existing quantitative restrictions).[8]

GATT contracting parties *did not* commit to free trade with zero tariffs. Under GATT auspices, however, it was anticipated that they would undertake a series of negotiating rounds in which "tariff concessions" would be exchanged. As took place in the first round in 1947 (where the articles were simultaneously drafted), contracting parties negotiated with their key trading partners for reductions of tariffs on items they exported in return for "concessions" on items of interest to their trading partners.[9] Once tariff concessions were agreed, they extended to all contracting parties (the most-favored-nation, or nondiscrimination, clause). The tariff rates were subsequently "bound" so that tariffs could not be raised unless the "escape clause" was invoked.

The principle that each country should offer "concessions" on its own tariffs in order to gain something (tariff reductions from its trading partners) flew right in the face of international trade theory, which demonstrated that, in most circumstances, tariffs hurt most the countries that impose them. However, for purposes of analyzing some of the challenges facing the international system, it is useful to note that the principle of reciprocal concessions has important political economy implications that require stressing. That is, when bargaining is reciprocal, the interests of exporters in a given country will support the agreement and make it politically more acceptable than would be the case if unilateral tariff reduction were to be undertaken by a country. When, for example, in the Uruguay Round the United States and other developed countries undertook to dismantle the Multifiber Arrangement over the next decade, that commitment was politically easier because American exporters of goods such as machinery supported the agreement because of promised reductions in tariffs in importing countries. While the GATT articles may not represent "good economics," in the sense that reducing a tariff unilaterally normally helps the

7. In the 1960s, the GATT articles were revised to permit, among other things, the Generalized System of Preferences for developing countries. This permitted unilateral discrimination, in the form of tariff remissions, for developing countries. The Multifiber Arrangement (MFA), which was administered under the GATT, permitted individual country quotas and was clearly discriminatory.

8. The MFA, which is a series of quantitative restrictions on imports of textiles and apparel administered by exporters, is administered under the GATT despite the obvious inconsistency with the GATT principles. Under the Uruguay Round agreement, however, the MFA is to be phased out within ten years, and nations have agreed to refrain from entering any new "voluntary export restraints" or other arrangements involving quantitative restrictions.

9. Bargaining was relatively simpler in early rounds when the United States, Canada, key European countries, and Japan were the key trading nations. Normally, exchanges of "concessions" took place between "principal suppliers," with a balancing out at the end of the round for third parties who would benefit from the negotiated reductions when it was deemed that they had not themselves "given enough." Of course, until the Uruguay Round, developing countries did not participate actively in the negotiations, but were "free riders" benefiting from whatever tariff reductions were negotiated because of the most-favored-nation principle embedded in the GATT.

trade-liberalizing country,[10] those arrangements do represent good politics, in tying export interests to political support for trade liberalization. I return to this point below in considering the scope for advances of liberalization through sectoral bargaining.

The open multilateral trading system has served the world well, as has the system of multilateral tariff negotiations. Indeed, as early as 1970, it was possible to argue that the GATT had been so successful that tariffs among the major industrialized countries were no longer a problem, and that remaining barriers to trade were virtually all nontariff barriers (see Baldwin 1970). World merchandise trade in volume terms had grown at an average annual rate of around 8 percent between 1950 and 1974, while world output had grown at around 5 percent. There was no question that trade was, at least to some extent, an "engine of growth," and that trade liberalization had contributed to that growth.

Growth in both trade and output slowed down after 1974. From 1974 to 1994, the volume of world trade grew at an average annual rate of about 4 percent while growth of world output averaged about 2 percent.[11] A number of factors accounted for slower growth, although again the volume of international trade grew more rapidly than output. Removing nontariff barriers to trade, especially nontraditional trade in services and related items, became paramount once tariffs had successfully been dismantled, and the pace of liberalization was clearly slower.

Before turning to the challenges to the system, it should be noted that two major exceptions were made to the "open multilateral" aspect of the international trading system. One concerned centrally planned economies, and the other related to developing countries.

The provisions governing trade with centrally planned economies were never of great importance under the GATT because those economies were to a very great degree cut off from world trade. With the abandonment of central planning and the emergence of economies in transition, one challenge for the WTO is to devise terms of entry for those economies. For the economies in transition that are embracing market principles, the challenge is minimal. For Chinese entry, however, serious issues are raised. Not only is China still far from a market economy, it is sufficiently large so that concerns regarding possible decisions that might adversely impact international markets cannot be entirely dismissed. Clearly, China is too large to remain outside the WTO and to be entitled to the exceptions that developing countries had in the past (but that are now being abandoned in any event).

10. It is significant that, in the "new" trade theory dealing with imperfectly competitive markets, tariff reductions may not be in the interests of a country if undertaken unilaterally, but a cooperative solution may be vastly preferable to a noncooperative tariff equilibrium. On this point, see Irwin (1996, 216ff.).

11. WTO 1995a, data from chart 1.6, p. 16. It should be noted that the WTO measure of output growth is below that of real GDP because of the more rapid growth of services than of goods. The same is probably true, however, for trade in services, and as such, the comparison figures may still be valid.

Developing countries' attitudes and trade policies during the 1950s and 1960s generally resulted in heightened walls of protection as industrialization through "import substitution" was attempted. That generally meant that developing countries were not benefiting as much as they might have from the growth of the world economy, while the "balance-of-payments" provisions of the GATT were liberally interpreted to enable developing countries to maintain quantitative restrictions, often including import prohibitions, on their imports. Moreover, the GATT articles were amended in the early 1960s to provide nonreciprocal preferential treatment of imports from those countries. One consequence was that developing countries (the East Asian newly industrializing countries being a prominent exception) were losing shares of their world markets (see Krueger 1990). Until the 1980s, therefore, it appeared that the world was divided into three major trading areas: the industrialized countries and the newly industrializing countries, the other developing countries, and the centrally planned economies.

Interestingly, the developing countries' leaders themselves began recognizing the economic costs of their failure to integrate with the international economy, and policies began shifting during the 1980s. Many developing countries participated in the Uruguay Round, agreeing to items such as the treatment of intellectual property rights and rules governing trade-related investment measures, but also seeking and achieving agreement for liberalization of trade in agricultural products and in textiles and apparel. By the early 1990s, the centrally planned economies began shifting toward market-oriented economies, and they, too, therefore began integrating with the rest of the world. Thus, one "challenge" that faced the international economy as of the late 1970s and early 1980s in fact was resolved without international action.[12]

Increasing Protectionist Pressures and Bilateralism

Increased interdependence and globalization has necessarily made producers in many countries much more sensitive to small changes in their competitors' situations than was earlier the case. After all, when merchandise from Hong Kong can be air freighted overnight to New York for transport costs equal to about 5 percent of cif value, U.S. producers are much more concerned with that competition than when ocean shipments used to take three weeks and cost 20 percent or more of cif prices.

While the benefits of globalization are widely recognized, the sensitivity to foreign competition has increased pressures for protection in a number of industrialized countries. When the United States was a dominant economy and simultaneously had a strong political consensus for free trade,[13] protectionist

12. To be sure, the economies in transition needed to achieve membership in the WTO.

13. It is now often forgotten that, until the late 1960s, even the American labor unions supported free trade, and there was little opposition to it. Even the protection then granted to textiles, apparel, and footwear was insufficient to prevent large increases in imports at that time.

pressures were held at bay in other countries and, in any event, U.S. pressures to remove quantitative restrictions in Europe and Japan, and subsequent rounds of multilateral tariff negotiations, resulted in bound tariffs that were very low.

Over time, however, those seeking protection have found other remedies, and simultaneously, protectionist pressures in the United States have increased dangerously. Moreover, the United States has increased its willingness to exert pressure bilaterally on its trading partners.

Administered Protection

Each of these two trends is dangerous. One alternative to protection through tariffs was voluntary export restraints, but those measures were outlawed by the Uruguay Round. The other alternative was and is administered protection. Antidumping (AD) and countervailing-duty (CVD) measures are sanctioned under the GATT articles. AD duties may be imposed when it is determined that producers are selling below cost of production or that their selling price in the importing country's market is below that at other destinations. CVDs are used when it is determined that a government has subsidized its exports of a particular product.

In theory, a case can be made for AD and CVD when the exporting firm intends to use predatory pricing to obtain monopoly control in a given market. In fact, however, the test for AD and CVD cases is much weaker. In the United States, for example, a foreign firm can be found to be dumping even if it is selling well above marginal cost or if it fails to provide adequate information in the time stipulated by the American authorities. Even different timing of the recording of sales in the home and the foreign market could result in a finding of dumping when sales prices were, in fact, identical.[14]

The harassment value of an AD or CVD suit may be considerable for the foreign firm against which the complaint is filed, as is evidenced by the number of times countries have agreed to voluntary export restraints to avoid AD or CVD proceedings and penalties.[15] Moreover, the AD and CVD provisions of U.S. law permit GATT-consistent discrimination in tariff rates between countries on imports of identical goods, regardless of whether tariff rates were bound during GATT negotiations. The average U.S. tariff on imports for which AD and CVD tariffs were in effect in the early 1990s was several times higher than the average tariffs on other goods. To make matters still worse, there is no automatic sunset provision or mechanism by which AD or CVD duties are removed or reconsidered after any specified period of time.

There is no doubt that, in the United States, administered protection has become a major barrier to trade and a vehicle by which protectionist pressures can be satisfied. Given the importance of the United States as a trading nation, that in itself is reason enough to be concerned about administered protection.

---

14. See Boltuck and Litan (1991) for a full analysis.
15. See Krueger (1993, chap. 3) for a discussion.

But, in fact, a number of other countries are emulating U.S. law with respect to AD and CVD provisions and increasingly using those weapons as protectionist instruments.

One of the challenges facing the WTO, as an international organization, and the world trading system will be to find means to contain the protectionist content of AD provisions in domestic legislation.

Bilateral Trade Negotiations

In addition to administered protection, the tendency to negotiate bilaterally has increased, again especially by the United States. Since the mid-1980s, U.S. trade policy has become increasingly aggressive and bilateral.[16]

"Voluntary import expansions" have become frequent, as negotiations have resulted in stipulated shares of the market for U.S. products.[17] In some instances, such as Korean insurance and Japanese semiconductors, the United States has obtained preferential treatment for itself. In others, there has been market opening, and the United States has defended the practice by pointing to those results.

The problems with bilateral dealings are several, however: large countries are able to pinpoint the economic activities about which they wish to negotiate and understandably choose those of greatest concern to themselves; their exports receive preferential treatment sometimes as a direct outcome of the negotiations and sometimes because foreign governments are attempting to avoid further pressure; and, perhaps even more important, the political economy of GATT (and, in the future, WTO) negotiations, under which export interests were harnessed to the pursuit of trade liberalization, is undone. Exporters can seek, and have obtained, more favorable terms by pressuring for direct negotiations on issues of concern to them, and as such have been less supportive of multilateral activities.

Even if bilateralism were confined to the United States (and it is inherently a process that will gain more favor in large countries), there would be cause for concern as such dealings further undermine support for the open multilateral system. However, as the United States resorts increasingly to bilateral measures, the tendency to move away from open multilateralism, toward regional preferential arrangements or other mechanisms for protecting one's producers from the vagaries of administered protection and bilateral pressures, will necessarily become stronger.

Finding ways to contain, and if possible greatly restrict, resort to administered protection and bilateralism is clearly a challenge for the open multilateral trading system, and for the WTO. It should be of concern for all trading nations, not only because they may become the objects of administered

16. This is not to say that there were no bilateral dealings before that date; but until then, they were infrequent and seen to be exceptions to general practice. Since the mid-1980s, they have been considered standard practice in the United States.

17. See Irwin (1994) for an account.

protection or bilateral pressures, but also because of the erosion of support for the WTO and open multilateralism that results from these measures.

Substantive Challenges to the System

Regional Trading Arrangements

Preferential trading arrangements, under article XXIV, were to be permitted only when (1) the arrangement was to consist of complete tariff removal for countries within the arrangement; (2) it was to cover "substantially all" trade; and (3) it had to go into effect on a predetermined and fixed timetable.[18] Until the 1980s, however, little attention was paid to article XXIV, in large part because the only successful preferential trading arrangement appeared to be the European Union (EU), which had begun as a customs union with the Treaty of Rome in the 1950s, and gradually moved toward increasing integration.

The EU, in turn, had been reducing its external tariffs (in line with the various rounds of multilateral tariff negotiations) at the same time as it was integrating internally. As such, trade with the rest of the world had been expanding rapidly because of rapid European growth and the magnitude of preferences was dropping because of lower tariffs. Hence, until the 1980s, attention to preferential trading arrangements was generally diminishing, although when preferential arrangements were taken to GATT panels for approval, very few were found to meet the article XXIV requirements.[19] To a considerable extent, the very rapid expansion (and liberalization) of world trade obscured any potential "trade diverting" effects that future preferential arrangements might have. Adding to that the fact that preferential trading arrangements other than the EU were generally failing to integrate the countries entering into them, it is little wonder that the issue of preferences did not arise in more serious form.

The situation changed in the 1980s, however, when the United States abandoned its long-standing policy of multilateralism and began entering into preferential trading arrangements.[20] While most observers viewed the initial U.S. forays into preferential arrangements as being idiosyncratic and not indicative of a trend,[21] the decision to negotiate an extension of the Canada-U.S. Free Trade Agreement into the North American Free Trade Agreement (NAFTA)

18. In light of the U.S. position of the late 1980s and 1990s, it is ironic that the United States opposed any preferential trading arrangements in the negotiations leading up to Bretton Woods and the ITO, while the United Kingdom insisted upon permissible preferences.

19. This is not to say that they were found to be inconsistent: rather, panels failed to reach a conclusion. See World Trade Organization (1995b).

20. The first such arrangement (other than the Generalized System of Preferences, which the United States had reluctantly joined in 1976 and which was GATT-sanctioned) was the Caribbean Basin Initiative under which the United States unilaterally extended duty-free status to a large number of imports from Caribbean countries. See Krueger (1993, chap. 7) for a discussion.

21. Even the Canada-U.S. Free Trade Agreement had been preceded by the auto parts agreement between those two countries. The auto parts agreement was a sectoral preferential arrangement and clearly would have been GATT-illegal had it been tested.

with Mexican accession changed the situation rapidly. At about the same time, the U.S. administration announced its intention to seek a Western Hemisphere Free Trade Agreement, and subsequently the Western Hemisphere nations declared their intention of achieving regional free trade by 2005. The Asia-Pacific Economic Cooperation (APEC) group of nations has also declared its intention to achieve regional free trade by 2010 for developed countries and by 2020 for developing countries.[22]

Meanwhile, with the transition to market economies of the countries of eastern Europe, the EU seems set to expand to include at least the Czech Republic, Hungary, Poland, the Baltic states, and probably Romania and Bulgaria, and it has already entered into customs union (not including agricultural products) with Turkey.[23]

There are a number of reasons for concern about proliferating preferential arrangements. Use of rules of origin and other protectionist measures within trading blocs has considerable potential for trade diversion, and can therefore result in the establishment of yet more opposition to multilateral trade liberalization.[24] And there are issues arising from individual countries' membership in overlapping free trade agreements.[25] Different rules of origin can apply to each individual member country; addition of new members can "dilute" the value of concessions obtained by existing members.[26]

The strong move toward increased preferential trading arrangements therefore presents a challenge for the WTO to ensure not only that these arrangements are compatible with an open multilateral system, but also that members of preferential arrangements will not divert their support from the WTO and multilateral arrangements. The key issue is whether and how preferential trading arrangements can be structured so as to be conducive to further multilateral liberalization.

Trade in Services

As is well known, trade in services is increasing as a percentage of all international trade in goods and services. The WTO estimates that, by 1994, world

---

22. It remains unclear whether the APEC intention is for free trade policies for countries within the region or for a preferential trading arrangement.

23. There are also preferential arrangements, through the Lomé convention, with a number of African countries.

24. The U.S. negotiations with Mexico centered, at the end, on rules of origin for textiles and apparel and autos. In each instance, U.S. domestic producers were seeking protection from East Asian exporters by requiring sufficient North American content to handicap their competitors.

25. A country could not belong to more than one customs union since membership, by definition, requires a common external tariff. Membership in multiple free trade agreements, however, is not only theoretically possible but is already a practice. Mexico, for example, has free trade agreements with several countries, including Chile, Venezuela, and Colombia, as well as the United States and Canada.

26. See, for example, the discussion by Snape (1989, 194) of the difficulties that might result for the Caribbean Basin Initiative countries and Canada were Australia to negotiate a free trade agreement with the United States involving sugar and beef. Difficulties have already been reported in Caribbean countries as some trade and foreign investment has been diverted to Mexico now that it has a free trade agreement with the United States.

trade in *commercial* services had reached U.S. $1.1 trillion and was growing at an average annual rate of 8 percent (WTO 1995a).

Since many services are location-specific in either their production or their consumption, barriers to trade in services tend to vary with the nature of the service. In some instances (e.g., software via satellite), it is virtually impossible to erect barriers. In many instances, domestic regulations of activities such as banking and insurance raise questions as to how liberalization might be achieved. In still other cases, issues of migration (of professional workers on temporary assignment, of construction workers, and so on) raise other issues.

Yet very clearly, liberalization of trade in services is vital to the continued integration of the international economy. The General Agreement on Trade in Services (GATS) in the Uruguay Round provided a framework for notification of existing rules governing trade in services, and for negotiations in specific sectors, most notably financial services and maritime products. In both of these latter instances, however, a multilateral agreement was not reached. On financial services, an agreement was reached without the United States, and no agreement was reached on maritime services. The challenge is to structure the WTO's functions, to find mechanisms to bring about agreements, and in particular, to enable bargaining across sectors.

Agriculture

Whereas the GATS provided little more than a framework, the agreements covering agriculture were a major step in beginning to dismantle economic inefficiencies in the world's agricultural activities. Even after the Uruguay Round agreements are fully implemented, however, rates of protection (and their producer subsidy equivalents) will remain very high. In contrast to trade in services, where there is not yet a comprehensive framework for measuring protection or the value of "concessions," the framework for further liberalization of production and trade in agricultural commodities exists. It will be important, however, to ensure that further cuts are forthcoming, for the world as a whole and especially for economies currently in transition and for exporters of temperate agricultural commodities.

Concerns about Labor and the Environment

Increasing globalization has been accompanied by increased global awareness and concern about the global commons. To a great extent, that heightened awareness has been healthy and beneficial, but it has had some side effects on multilateral trade issues that need to be addressed.

Two of these issues have sufficiently serious implications for the open multilateral trade policy to warrant discussion here. In each instance, the political imperative to do something is strong enough to constitute a major challenge to the open multilateral trading system to find a response that will ease concerns without significantly damaging the efficiency of resource allocation in the world economy. This is especially so since those seeking protection have no hesitation in cloaking their aspirations with the legitimacy of other issues.

The two key issues focus on the environment and labor standards. In each instance, there are calls for resort to trade measures as a mechanism for enforcing, or at least attempting to enforce, the labor or environmental standards deemed appropriate by those concerned. The issues are similar in that each is essentially unrelated to trade, yet the pressure groups behind each issue call for trade measures as a remedy for the perceived problems.

The issues are different, however, in that there are significant environmental "spillovers," where the negative externality of environmental despoliation in one country can affect the rest of the world, whereas labor standards are inherently domestic matters.[27] Despite those differences, however, the two issues have one major characteristic in common: genuine supporters, whose motives may be entirely altruistic, are joined by those seeking protection for the usual reasons of self-interest. The challenge, in each instance, is to find policies that will address the legitimate concerns in such a way that self-interested seekers of protection cannot use the issue to promote their own selfish ends. The substance of the issues are different, however. Each issue, and the challenge it poses to the WTO, is therefore considered separately.

Strengthening the Organization

In 1947, the GATT was intended as a stopgap arrangement until the ITO was ratified. Although the successes achieved under the GATT were remarkable, the shift to the WTO with a formal status as a multilateral institution alongside the World Bank and the IMF is highly significant.

The challenge for the WTO is one of perception and one of reality. On one hand, the perceptions of the GATT as a weak, Geneva-based, small organization must be altered. On the other hand, reality must change as dispute settlement, trade policy surveillance, and other related activities increase their importance and impact in the world.

Perception is important, especially when the same people, housed in the same place, are undertaking much the same jobs. For the WTO, this challenge is enormous as the budgetary and staff expansion permitted to date have been small contrasted with the enormity of the challenges facing the WTO.

The World Bank, IMF, and WTO are instructed by their governments to achieve "coherence" in economic policies between trade, financial, and

---

27. It has sometimes been argued that people find it offensive to consider people working at "substandard" wages or in a workplace that fails to meet their standards. One can argue that a great deal of the "offense" comes from lack of awareness of the alternatives that poor people face. It is also, of course, true that when individuals find practices offensive, they are free to choose products made under other circumstances. Carrying the "offensive" argument to its logical conclusion would imply that people in a Muslim country could, for instance, adopt trade sanctions against countries where pork is eaten, or that those in monogamous societies could use trade sanctions in countries where polygamy is permitted.

developmental issues, and the WTO has a mandate in this direction. However, while the Bank and the Fund have their own financial base (generated by paid-up capital), the WTO does not. Moreover, while the Bank and the Fund have considerable influence by virtue of their resources and of their dealing predominantly with developing countries, the GATT is dealing with relations between countries, and inherently must be concerned with the trade practices of the most powerful.

There is thus a major challenge confronting the WTO as an institution to buy its way into the game with the Bank and the Fund. Clearly, finding mechanisms that increase coherence is important in reality. But for the WTO it is doubly important because it needs to raise perceptions of its standing as the third of the global international economic institutions.

Contributions in the Present Volume

The papers in this volume focus on some of the key challenges that confront the WTO as it evolves. These challenges range from concerns about its capacity to undertake its currently assigned tasks to issues surrounding the ways in which the Uruguay Round agreements can be carried out.

Papers in part 1 examine the WTO's institutional capacity. Richard Blackhurst describes the organization and functioning of the secretariat. David Vines considers how the WTO's mandate and organizational capabilities differ from those of the IMF and the World Bank, and the ways that those considerations will affect the WTO's capacity. David Henderson proceeds to analyze the functioning of six international organizations to see what can be learned about their scope for independent action. Judith Goldstein examines the extent to which international rules and organizations can override domestic political concerns.

John Jackson examines one of the more controversial aspects of the WTO—the newly strengthened dispute settlement mechanism, and how that may affect the functioning of the international trading system in the context of national political constraints.

Given the importance of the politics in individual countries, it is clear that the support for international institutions by the dominant players is crucial. To that end, John Odell and Barry Eichengreen consider the determinants of U.S. support for the GATT and now the WTO.

Part 2 addresses some of the substantive challenges the WTO faces. Frieder Roessler examines the problems arising out of the tendency to assert "linkages" between trade and other issues, while Kym Anderson considers the problem specifically from the viewpoint of labor standards and environmental issues.

The next several papers consider "new issues" that arise because of the Uruguay Round agreements and the changing international economic environment. The first concerns coherence: the WTO is charged with finding means to achieve more coordination in the realms of international finance, international capital flows, and development and trade. Gary Sampson addresses the issues raised by that mandate in his paper. Richard Snape analyzes the incorporation of trade in services into the WTO discipline. Another issue growing in importance is the increased use of AD and CVDs. Robert Baldwin addresses the issue and considers how the WTO could reduce the negative consequences of this trend. T. N. Srinivasan addresses the growing resort to preferential trading arrangements in the context of an open multilateral system. A new issue not addressed in these chapters, but considered in chapter 15, is agricultural protection.

Part 3 considers the role of the WTO from the perspective of two groups of countries: economies in transition and developing countries. Jaroslaw Pietras considers how the international trading system and the WTO affected the ease of transition from centrally planned economies to market-oriented economies with special emphasis on the eastern European countries. In his comment, Constantine Michalopoulos considers differences between the circumstances of those economies and the countries in transition that were not members of the WTO as transition started.

Michael Finger and Alan Winters likewise consider key provisions of the WTO as they affect developing countries. In his comment, Alan Hirsch suggests how some of these, and other, considerations played out in the case of South Africa.

In chapter 1, Richard Blackhurst addresses some of the institutional issues associated with the mandate of the WTO and the capacity of its secretariat to carry out that mandate. He first examines the nature of the WTO as an institution, distinguishing between what he terms "best endeavors" organizations (where members are obliged to try to achieve objectives) and sanction-based organizations such as the WTO. He focuses on the ways in which the WTO, as a rules-making and rules-enforcing organization, differs from the World Bank and the IMF in its mandate, and the ways in which those differences affect the desired relationship of the members to the secretariat and its functions.

Blackhurst then explains the mandate of the WTO, and the ways in which that mandate has enlarged since the GATT Secretariat began functioning in the late 1940s. From the evidence he presents, there can be little doubt that the secretariat and the delegations to Geneva are carrying a very large workload. In the final section, Blackhurst considers whether the WTO Secretariat is equipped to carry out the functions assigned to it under the Uruguay Round agreement. He concludes that more efficient use of existing resources will not permit the secretariat to carry out the mandate, and puts forward the case for increased resources. He contrasts the size of the budget and the staff of the WTO Secretariat with that of other international organizations: fourteen international organizations (including the International Labor Organization, the United Nations Population Fund, the International Telecommunications Union, and the World Intellectual Property Organization) had larger staffs than did the WTO in 1996. Similarly, the WTO's 1996 budget of $101 million contrasted with the United Nations Development Programme's $1,840 million, and even the United Nations Office for Project Services' budget of $403 million. Blackhurst provides a strong case for a shift of some resources from other international organizations toward the WTO, given the tasks assigned to it, but notes that the interests of ministers of agriculture and commerce and others will probably prevent such a shift.

David Vines addresses the question of the international organizations, the ways in which they can be effective, and the capacity of the WTO to carry out its mandate effectively. He also analyzes the need for coordination ("coherence") among the institutions. He notes that organizations, to be effective, need (1) an analytical capacity in an area where there is a need that cannot be met by individual nations or the private market, (2) a way of achieving agreement among their members and implementing those agreements, and (3) sanctions that can be applied if the agreement is violated. He argues that both the IMF and the World Bank have those capabilities and that, to a significant degree, their activities reinforce each other in generating their capability. Analytical capacity provides greater force for policy advice; policy advice is listened to in part because of lending capacity but also because of the strength of analytical capacity; and sanctions are present in the form of the ability to withhold lending.

In Vines's analysis, the WTO is an entirely different organization, focusing as it does on setting rules *between* its members and then, to a degree, enforcing them in its dispute settlement mechanism. As of now, Vines does not see the WTO's analytical capacity as being sufficient to give it the clout it would need to strengthen its role. It is also lacking sufficient resources, with a very small staff. Vines believes that cooperation with the Bank and the Fund can play a useful role if it enables the WTO to acquire the capacity and resources to meet the challenges it faces. But he does not believe that, simply because issues of trade, finance, and capital flows overlap, formal coordination mechanisms are necessarily called for.

David Henderson considers the role of six international agencies—the Organization for Economic Cooperation and Development (OECD), IMF, World Bank, Commission of the European Communities, GATT/WTO, and United Nations Conference on Trade and Development (UNCTAD)—in influencing cross-border liberalization. He seeks to understand how each agency has influenced events, particularly external liberalization. In the process, some hypotheses emerge about the determinants of international institutions' effectiveness.

Henderson starts by considering the structure of each of the six, focusing on the size, the role and status of their staffs, their relations with member governments, and the channels through which they can exert an independent influence. Henderson distinguishes between agencies such as the WTO and the OECD, which are intergovernmental, and agencies that are international, such as the World Bank and the IMF. He also notes that intergovernmental agencies' size is an ambiguous concept, because of the role played by the national delegations to the institution. This is a point that Richard Blackhurst notes in his paper, as well.

A number of dimensions can be used to characterize the six agencies. Among those noted by Henderson are size, the mandate of the institution, the universality of its membership and its governing structure, the degree to which it must depend on national governments for budgetary resources, and, related to that, the autonomy of its staff.

Channels of influence include budgetary resources, the extent of research undertaken (which itself is a function of the willingness of governments to permit analytical leadership on the part of the agency), and interactions with national government representatives. The effectiveness of the heads of the organizations is also very important.

Henderson then considers the past effectiveness of international agencies and reaches some tentative conclusions for the future. He starts by pointing out that decisions governing cross-border liberalization have always been, and will continue to be, taken by national governments. However, governments may be more willing to do so when they are acting simultaneously with other governments. Moreover, governments consist of many different actors and ministries, and international agencies can influence the outcome in intragovernmental decision making. Moreover, as governments are more willing to embrace liberalization, the effectiveness of international agencies supporting liberalization will likely increase. Henderson also points to the qualifications of staff of international institutions as an important determinant of their effectiveness.

He concludes by considering some aspects of the future roles of the WTO, UNCTAD, and the OECD in light of his earlier analysis. He considers that the WTO is much better situated to influence events by virtue of its being much more thoroughly accepted after the Uruguay Round, but notes that the small size of the secretariat and its limited role may inhibit its ability to do so. He also considers the role of the WTO Secretariat in research, and rejects the notion that the OECD should become the "research arm" of the WTO, both because the law-and-economics competency of the WTO is not available at the OECD, and because the OECD's wide-ranging competence can better serve the WTO in other dimensions. He advocates the continued reliance on the OECD for developing new ideas as they become politically acceptable, such as agricultural policies in the 1980s and an investment code in the mid-1990s.[28]

Whereas Henderson's assignment was to consider how international agencies can be effective, Judith Goldstein focuses on the ways in which domestic

28. Many of the participants at the conference questioned the wisdom of the OECD's development of an investment code. They believed that such a code, relating as it does to cross-border flows, more properly belonged with the WTO, and that its initial development at the OECD ran the risk of alienating developing countries who are not members of the OECD, but who nonetheless would be asked to subscribe to the resulting doctrine when it as "handed over" to the WTO.

politics affect the role national governments play in international institutions. On one hand, when there is a fragile majority for something such as free trade, developing international institutions can legitimize and support that majority, both by expanding the size of the coalition supporting it, via the bundling of issues and by using agenda-setting authority. In that sense, the GATT enabled politicians to hide from their constituents and thus to mute the pressures that came from individual lobbying interests. At the same time, GATT bargaining enabled politicians to seek support from export interests and thus blunt protectionist pressures.

On the other hand, in a democratic society, pressures from powerful constituents cannot be ignored. Goldstein considers how these elements play out in the trade arena. She worries that the more formal rules under the WTO, and the proscription against using voluntary export restraints and other informal measures, may prevent political leaders from taking the protectionist actions for a few vested interests that would enable free trade principles to prevail over most activities.

Goldstein also notes the importance of ideas in circumscribing what politicians and international institutions can do. International regimes can legitimate and disseminate ideas and norms. Moreover, as ideas regarding the importance of a liberal trade regime for economic efficiency and growth have gained ascendency, that too has helped keep protectionist pressures at bay and may strengthen the role of the WTO.

John Jackson considers a related aspect of the WTO: the extent to which the expanded dispute settlement functions mandated to the organization will affect the international trading system. Whereas nations were earlier able to block the results of a dispute settlement procedure against themselves, this can no longer happen.

This raised a number of questions, many of which can be grouped under the heading of "sovereignty," which was raised once the new dispute settlement procedures were agreed upon. Jackson reviews these procedures and some of the key questions that arise.

After considering some of the "birth defects" of the GATT as an institution, Jackson turns to the automaticity of dispute settlement procedures, as established in the WTO. In particular, he notes the virtues of the legal authority behind binding decisions, as contrasted with the earlier procedure. He argues that legally binding findings in international law do influence governments, even of large countries that could arguably ignore these findings.

However, Jackson notes a number of key issues regarding the new procedures. First is whether the system is overloaded. By the end of February 1997, sixty-eight complaints had been initiated under the new dispute settlement process, two to three times the normal rate of application. Jackson notes that, despite additional WTO resources given to the dispute settlement procedure, there is a significant danger that the very willingness of countries to use these processes makes the system vulnerable to overload.

Although the situation is not entirely clear-cut, Jackson believes that the entire history of GATT and now WTO findings is to make the procedure more and more "rules-oriented" and less and less a negotiating session between sovereign governments. He points to the evidence on both sides of this issue, but believes that the weight of evidence, history, and interpretation is preponderantly on the side of increasingly rules-oriented procedures. This entails an obligation to perform when there is a finding against a party. Jackson believes that this means that "compensation" is not a substitute for conforming to GATT/WTO rules, and is intended instead as a temporizing remedy until conformity is achieved. Yet another issue is the standard of review, and the latitude the panels give governments to interpret WTO agreements as they see fit. Here, Jackson believes that panels will continue to give fairly wide latitude to individual governments' interpretations of their obligations, but he notes that this interpretation does not entirely resolve the problem, as there is still a question as to how far governments may go. There are also questions as to the extent to which panels will in effect be restraining governments when they "go too far," as contrasted with being judicially activist in interpreting WTO agreements and rules.

On these and other issues analyzed in the paper, Jackson is essentially optimistic, although he points to many issues that need clarification. Nonetheless, he concludes that already the dispute settlement procedure is gaining acceptance, and that "it is likely to be seen in the future as one of the most important, and perhaps even watershed, developments of international economic relations in the twentieth century."

As Goldstein makes clear in her paper, the WTO can only do what its members want it to do. Moreover, important members' support is crucial for the ability of the organization to carry out its mandate. In their paper, Odell and Eichengreen focus on the role of the United States as a dominant player in the WTO. Because the United States is so large, its behavior toward the WTO will be crucial in affecting the effectiveness of the organization. Yet, as they point out, a number of aspects of U.S. trade policy seem to indicate a lack of commitment to the multilateral system. Not only has the United States exerted bilateral pressures on its key trading partners such as Japan and Korea without resort to the multilateral trading system, it has also adopted measures such as Super-301 and the Helms-Burton bill, which blatantly violate WTO principles. At the same time, the United States was a key instigator of the Uruguay Round and pushed for trade liberalization and its extension to noncommodity issues such as intellectual property rights.

Odell and Eichengreen provide a framework for understanding the determinants of U.S. trade policy by examining the differences in the U.S. situation in the 1940s and the 1990s. In the 1940s, after a charter for an International Trade Organization had been agreed upon in Havana (under U.S. leadership), the United States failed to ratify that agreement, and the ITO never came into being. In 1994, by contrast, the United States did ratify the Uruguay Round agreement, although there was opposition to it.

Odell and Eichengreen consider the differences between the 1940s and the

1990s: in the 1940s, the United States had no alternative to the open multilateral system, whereas the Europeans did have alternatives: in the case of the United Kingdom, Commonwealth trading ties were seen as an exit option, and in the case of continental Europe, a fallback arrangement was clearly a preferential trading arrangement.

Ironically, the weaker bargaining position of the United States in the 1940s meant that its negotiators gave in on points that were objectionable to the American public and Congress. In the 1990s, Europe and Japan did not have such credible exit options, and as a result the Uruguay Round agreement was closer to the American desires, incorporating new areas such as trade in services, intellectual property rights, trade-related investment measures, and bringing agriculture more fully under WTO disciplines.

Odell and Eichengreen also consider the role of other factors: the willingness of the president to lend his authority to support the agreement, the extent to which there was close contact between the agents bargaining in the round and those in Washington on whose behalf they were acting, and so on. Their conclusion is fairly optimistic: the United States has no alternative but to support the open multilateral trading system, and hence the WTO; and, barring the arrival of an agreement requiring ratification at the time of other major problems requiring the leadership's full attention, the prospects for continued U.S. support of the open multilateral trading system, and therefore the WTO, are good.

Another challenge for the WTO arises out of the desire of many to link trade issues with other issues of concern internationally. In his paper, Frieder Roessler considers the WTO's role (and that of other international organizations) in linking trade and other issues in multilateral agreements between nations. Roessler points to some of the linkages that were used under the GATT for balance-of-payments exceptions for developing countries (which linked trade policy to monetary objectives) and shows how these linkages undermined both the trade regime under the GATT and the monetary regime under the IMF.

He then notes the number of linkages that were proposed for the WTO—including labor standards, environmental issues, and investment conditions, to name just a few. Only environmental standards were incorporated into the wording of the final agreement, although working groups were set up on investment and labor standards. Roessler therefore addresses the question of whether international objectives for the environment can be served through linkages with trade issues.

He essentially argues that they cannot. On one hand, if trade bargains can be undone at any time because of a breakdown in the environmental regime, the trading system will be subject to greater uncertainty. Moreover, the environmental regime is put at risk whenever the trade regime is under threat, and conversely. Roessler argues that this has happened with past linkages, and is likely to happen with future ones. He concludes that the WTO has responsibility for trade issues, and that the international regimes governing trade and those governing other issues can be most effective when they are separate. When they are together, he believes that the linkages and the resulting exemptions from trade policy disciplines free protectionist forces to use these linkages to achieve their objectives.

Whereas Roessler considers the general issue of linkages with attention to environmental and labor standards issues, Anderson directly addresses the challenges that environmental- and labor-standards issues create for the WTO. Anderson starts by considering the various pressures that have arisen to link trade with these issues, noting that, while some advocates of use of the trade stick (or carrot) are genuinely concerned with the environment or with labor standards, protectionist groups use these issues to further their own agenda.

Anderson then considers some of the problems that arise from these concerns for the WTO. One major problem is that rich and poor countries have different levels of concern with the environment in part because they are at different stages of development. The same holds even more for labor standards, where low-wage countries have low living standards. Because of this "natural" divide, efforts to enforce either environmental or labor standards through the trading system are likely to increase trade conflicts and tensions between the industrialized countries and poorer countries. There is certainly evidence that, when incomes have risen sufficiently, people choose to allocate more resources to their environment; similarly, labor standards become closer to those in richer industrialized countries. At a minimum, a north-south conflict over these issues may lead to less open trade regimes in the south (perhaps because of fear of vulnerability to trade sanctions) and that, in turn, would significantly slow down growth. Such an outcome might in fact result in a net deterioration of the environment or of labor standards, the opposite result from the original objective.

Anderson also notes that, in the case of labor standards, efforts to impose them by rich countries inevitably reduces poor countries' comparative advantage in labor-intensive goods insofar as those standards raise costs of hiring unskilled workers. As such, either the quantity of unskilled labor employed or the take-home wages of workers would fall. To that extent, overall labor conditions for the affected workers would deteriorate.

Anderson points to what he considers first-best policies—which are not trade-based policies—to deal with environmental concerns, especially when spillovers are present. He thus concludes that first-best policy to meet legitimate concerns would not resort to trade sanctions.

However, Anderson notes that the failure of the WTO to address environmental and labor issues is dangerous. In part, this is because the relatively new environmental groups may underestimate the damage that can be caused by use of trade sanctions and in their zeal harm the trading system more than might be the case if the WTO were involved. Anderson believes that part of the solution must lie in better communication to the public and to policymakers in industrialized countries about why proposed labor and environmental standards could cause significant difficulties for them.

When policymakers were considering the architecture of the postwar international economic system, it was envisaged that there would be three international organizations:[29] one for international finance (the IMF), one for capital flows (the World Bank), and one for trade. Even in the IMF charter, coordination between the IMF and the ITO was envisaged, as the preamble states that the purpose of a well-functioning international monetary system is to facilitate international trade.

With the signing of the Uruguay Round agreement, ministers called for the WTO to assume a role in achieving "coherence" among the three key international economic organizations. Gary Sampson considers the issues that arise in attempting to achieve greater coherence.

Sampson starts by pointing out that, although there was some formal coordination between the GATT and the IMF, its scope was relatively limited. Sampson's paper describes the mandate for coherence, and discusses some of the difficulties that arise in achieving coordination. Aside from the fact that the WTO has far fewer staff and monetary resources than either the Bank or the Fund, major obstacles arise. In particular, the WTO is generally within the responsibility of trade ministers, while the Fund and the Bank are generally governed by ministers of finance or governors of central banks.[30] Finding ways to achieve coordination internationally is extremely difficult in a context where the cognizant ministers do not necessarily even coordinate among themselves in national governments. As Sampson notes, the way to achieve greater coherence is likely to involve the staffs of the three institutions achieving cooperative arrangements, primarily informally.

In the first several decades of the GATT, the most-favored-nation (MFN) provisions of the articles became increasingly dominant, and except for the EU, preferential trading arrangements such as Commonwealth preferences receded in importance.

Since the mid-1980s, however, preferential trading arrangements, especially among regional groupings of countries, have been formed in increasing numbers. Under the WTO, nations are committed to an open *multilateral* trading system. Increasing reliance on preferential trading arrangements therefore raises important questions as to their compatibility with the WTO principles.

In his paper, T. N. Srinivasan considers the evolution of preferential trading arrangements and their treatment under article XXIV of the GATT and documents the increase in importance of such arrangements. He points to the difficulty GATT panels had in finding that customs unions and free trade areas that were notified to the GATT were consistent with article XXIV—in most cases, panels terminated their work without finding either in the affirmative or in the negative.

29. Initially, Keynes's proposal was for four international organizations. The fourth, which was never developed into a formal proposal, was an institution to stabilize world primary commodity prices.

30. Foreign ministers or aid ministers are sometimes the relevant national authority for the World Bank.

He considers the argument, made by some, that preferential trading arrangements may be steps on the way to greater multilateral liberalization, and reviews the various models that have been developed that are consistent with that view. He shows that most of these models require very special assumptions and gives a number of reasons for skepticism as to this view.

He next asks whether the concept of "open regionalism," as developed in defense of APEC, can resolve the dilemmas inherent in preferential arrangements. He concludes that it "is not a particularly fruitful new concept in the arena of trade liberalization."

Srinivasan suggests ways in which the WTO processes relating to acceptance of preferential arrangements might be strengthened to become more consistent with the open multilateral system. He proposes that any preferential trading arrangement be required to lay down a timetable under which the arrangements will be extended to all WTO members, and that any customs union that results in the raising of any external tariff should be required, within five years, to rescind the increase.

He considers other proposals, including Bhagwati's proposal that any customs union should adopt the lowest tariff for each commodity that was found in any of the partner countries preunion, and implementation of the Kemp-Wan criterion that trade volumes with nonpartner countries should be higher after the formation of a customs union than they were preunion.

Srinivasan concludes that preferential trading arrangements entail so many difficulties that the best hope for the WTO would be to rule them out entirely. This view was not unanimously endorsed by conference participants, as is discussed in chapter 15. However, there was unanimous agreement that preferential trading arrangements and their proliferation present major challenges for the WTO.

Alongside increasing resort to preferential trading arrangements, another disturbing trend in the international trading system over the past two decades has been the increased resort to "administered protection" under which countries have established legal procedures for determining when firms have exported to them "unfairly" by selling below cost (dumping) or receiving government subsidies. The administered protection consists of remedies for these practices by imposition of AD or CVDs.

As Finger and Winters also note in their paper, the imposition of these duties constitutes a unilateral retrogression from WTO rules. As AD and CVD procedures have increasingly been used, analysts have sought to find ways of strengthening the rules to avoid their protectionist component. Baldwin reviews these proposals, focusing on finding ways to achieve agreement on competition policy as a substitute for AD measures, which would subject domestic firms to the same discipline as foreign ones.

In his paper, Robert Baldwin considers the existing WTO rules governing the use of AD and CVDs. He concludes that AD and CVD laws are conferring protection for reasons that were not intended. He analyzes the extent to which

AD and CVD procedures actually result in the attainment of greater "fairness," as is said to be their objective, and the extent to which instead they result in greater protection to those in the industry seeking it. In particular, recent studies show that AD laws have enabled collusion between domestic and foreign firms and thereby increased monopoly power of those firms.

Baldwin believes that the adoption of international rules on competition policy is the solution to this problem in the long run, but proposes restraints on AD and CVD rules in the short run to prevent some of the unintended side effects of these measures.

Among the major challenges for, and achievements of, the Uruguay Round was the agreement to bring trade in services under an international discipline, parallel to that for goods. Richard Snape analyzes the agreement with respect to services, and assesses the challenges for the GATS as part of the WTO.

There are some inherent differences between trade in services and trade in goods, as Snape notes. While goods transactions can mostly be undertaken at arm's length, there are many services that can be provided only with physical proximity. In some instances, "commercial presence" is required, and in other instances, people have to be sent by service providers to the customers.

Some of these issues are covered in the GATS and some are not. But there are many ways in which barriers to market access can be imposed, as Snape points out. Moreover, barriers may exist for all entrants, not only foreigners. The fact that there are many modes of delivery and many types of barriers makes negotiating services agreements difficult. And the GATS in effect established a framework within which agreements could be reached on a sector-by-sector basis. Snape points out that the sector-specific aspect of services, while perhaps driven by differences in their nature and in the barriers facing them, prevents the sort of cross-sectoral trade-offs in negotiations for barrier reduction that has characterized the lowering of tariffs on trade in goods.

The financial services agreement, in Snape's judgment, was unsatisfactory, and failed to result in significant market opening. By contrast, the Telecoms Agreement resulted in significantly increased market opening, with the agreement between sixty-nine countries covering over 90 percent of basic telecommunications trade.

However, there are varying degrees of difficulty in reaching agreements in other services sectors. There has been no progress in maritime transport services, for example, and negotiations have been suspended until 2000.

Snape argues that the GATS is probably too general in its attempt to cover all modes of delivery and forms of barriers to access, and not general enough with respect to obligations of countries under services agreements. He believes that movement of people, investment, and competition policy are not linked only to services, and that tying those issues to services negotiations may be retarding progress. If instead only cross-border trade and measures discriminating between domestic and foreign suppliers were covered, further agreements might be secured more quickly. Snape believes that separate agreements covering other issues could meet the same objectives while posing fewer obstacles to services agreements.

However, Snape also believes that the current ability of countries to take MFN and national-treatment exceptions is arguably undesirable, and that the services disciplines could be strengthened to embrace the MFN and national-treatment principles of trade in goods under the GATT.

In his discussion of Snape's paper, Robert Baldwin questions whether the delinking of investment treatment and related issues from services is feasible, since many of the complaints by service providers focused on barriers of those types as inhibiting their ability to sell overseas. Snape agreed that these issues needed coverage, but believed that they could better be addressed on a stand-alone basis.

Two groups of countries face special problems with the international trading system: the countries in transition from centrally planned economies to market-oriented economies, and developing countries. Jaroslaw Pietras considered the WTO's role in relation to economies in transition, and Michael Finger and Alan Winters assessed the WTO's role with respect to developing countries.

Just at the time when the WTO Secretariat was faced with the new challenges arising from the creation of the WTO and implementation of the Uruguay Round, it was also challenged by the emergence of the economies in transition. In his paper, Pietras considers the situations of the eastern European countries that are members of the WTO and assesses how the WTO has affected their transition.

Pietras points out the difficulties involved in the transition, and the necessity for reorienting the trade regime completely—away from the ties with the other centrally planned economies' large enterprises, and toward the world market. These challenges were, of course, only part of the overall effort, as the need to privatize, to develop viable commercial codes, and to remove the monetary overhang and develop new tax structures, and a host of other pressing issues competed for policymakers' time and attention.

The needs of these economies from the international trading system were, of course, access to their markets, and assurance of a stable international environment in which they could reorient their trade. In making the transition, the existence of international rules and norms were very helpful, and the eastern European economies in transition initially embraced very open trading systems.

However, Pietras notes a few dimensions in which the international system, especially as practiced, has made it more difficult for policymakers. On one hand, as time has passed, domestic pressure groups have gained influence in the eastern European countries. And they have been able to point to protectionist measures in their major trading partners as a rationale for seeking more protection. The fact of these practices elsewhere has made it difficult to convince the public and politicians that open trading policies are most conducive to rapid transition and growth.

On the other hand, the importance of the EU for the eastern European countries as natural trading partners is undeniable. Given that, eastern European countries are under pressure not to lower (or at least not to bind) their tariffs "too much" because their entry into the EU would require compensation to third countries if their tariffs then increased. Pietras points to this concern as a significant issue.

In his comment on Pietras's paper, Constantine Michalopoulos considers the additional problems that have arisen for countries in transition desiring entry into the WTO. Partly because of limited secretariat resources, progress has been slow, and that in itself leaves those countries vulnerable to the withdrawal of MFN treatment until they become WTO members. Similarly, they are still being treated as state trading countries for purposes of AD processes in some of their major trading partners, although many of them have made great progress in privatization. While rapid entry into the WTO would not automatically solve that problem, it would reduce its severity.

Michalopoulos also notes that a problem arises for the economies in transition with regard to their tariffs: they are reluctant to bind them at their prevailing low levels both because of the EU pressures that Pietras notes and because they believe they will need to be able to make offers of binding in future rounds of trade negotiations. Michalopoulos believes that these countries have little bargaining power anyway, small as they are in international trade, and that it is in their self-interest to bind unilaterally. Nonetheless, the negotiating framework of the WTO makes this appear less attractive to them.

Finger and Winters consider the WTO as it can affect developing countries. They take as their starting point that developing countries that have successfully integrated with the international economy have achieved their economic objectives more satisfactorily than those that have not. They therefore focus their analysis on ways in which the WTO can or could better affect that integration. They point out that all multilateral tariff negotiations that result in tariff reductions benefit developing countries both by the resulting lower tariff rates and by the increased certainty that rates cannot be increased. But they focus their attention on the ways in which GATT/WTO rules, which serve as guidelines to what trade policy should be, affect developing countries, noting that international rules can serve as bulwarks against domestic political pressures.

After reviewing the tariff reductions made by developing countries in the Uruguay Round, Finger and Winters proceed to examine three sets of rules: AD and other rules that permit countries to restrict imports unilaterally; regional arrangements; and special and differential treatment. They argue that AD rules under the WTO permit too much latitude to developing countries, and are not guidelines for good trade policy. With respect to regional arrangements, they argue for augmenting the existing provisions for those arrangements within the WTO. Finally, they examine those aspects of special and differential treatment for developing countries that remain in the WTO.

In the discussion of the Finger-Winters paper, Alan Hirsch analyzes the ways in which the existence of WTO rules and the international economy has affected South Africa as it has reoriented its economic policies. He concurs with much of the Finger-Winters analysis, but notes that there are also problems of implementation of WTO rules, and that developing countries could benefit from more technical assistance with these.

Chapter 15 sums up the WTO's challenges and constraints as informed by these papers.

References

Baldwin, Robert E. 1970. *Nontariff Distortions of International Trade.* Washington, DC: Brookings Institution.

Boltuck, Richard, and Robert E. Litan. 1991. *Down in the Dumps.* Washington, DC: Brookings Institution.

Dam, Kenneth W. 1970. *The GATT: Law and the International Economic Organization.* Chicago: University of Chicago.

Hoekman, Bernard, and Michel Kostecki. 1995. *The Political Economy of the World Trading System: From GATT to WTO.* Oxford: Oxford University Press.

Irwin, Douglas. 1994. *Voluntary Import Expansions: Another Bad Trade Idea.* Washington, DC: American Enterprise Institute.

————. 1996. *Against the Tide: An Intellectual History of Free Trade.* Princeton, NJ: Princeton University Press.

Krueger, Anne O. 1990. Trends in the Trade Policies of Developing Countries. In *The Direction of Trade Policy,* ed. Charles S. Pearson and James Riedel, 87–107. Cambridge, MA: Basil Blackwell.

————. 1993. *Economic Policies at Cross-Purposes: The United States and Developing Countries.* Washington, DC: Brookings Institution.

Snape, Richard. 1989. A Free Trade Agreement with Australia? In *Free Trade Areas and U.S. Trade Policy,* ed. Jeffrey Schott, 167–96. Washington, DC: Institute for International Economics.

World Trade Organization. 1995a. *International Trade: Trends and Statistics.* Geneva: WTO.

————. 1995b. *Regionalism and the World Trading System.* Geneva: WTO.

I   The WTO's Institutional Capacity

1   The Capacity of the WTO to Fulfill Its Mandate

Richard Blackhurst

The first two parts of this paper deal principally with questions that flow directly from the title. Section 1.1 begins with a very brief look at the nature of the World Trade Organization as an institution, then considers in more detail the resources currently available to the WTO to carry out its mandate. While there is necessarily a large descriptive element, an understanding of how the institution functions is crucial to most, if not all, of the topics considered in this conference volume. This is especially true given that, in many respects, the WTO functions very differently from other international economic organizations.

Section 1.2 attempts to identify the evolving mandate given by the member countries, first to the GATT and now to the WTO. There is a core set of tasks on which there is a consensus among the members, and which is relatively easy to describe. The future evolution of the WTO's mandate is a more difficult question. As is evident from the December 1996 Ministerial Conference in Singapore, there is both considerable pressure to expand the mandate and widely divergent views among the member countries about whether it should be expanded and, if so, in what direction(s). In essence, the question is, what does the ongoing integration of the global economy imply for the mandate that WTO member countries should give to themselves and to the secretariat for the first part of the twenty-first century?

In certain respects, it would have been more logical to examine the mandate

Richard Blackhurst is adjunct professor of economics at the Graduate Institute of International Studies in Geneva. He joined the GATT/WTO Secretariat in 1974, and from 1985 until April 1997 was director of Economic Research and Analysis.

This paper benefited considerably from comments by Doug Irwin, Judith Goldstein, and others at the conference, as well as from suggestions from anonymous referees. Several WTO colleagues provided excellent suggestions, as did some delegates. Maika Oshikawa was very helpful with many of the statistics.

first, and then to consider the resources available to carry out the mandate. The decision to begin with an examination of the resources, and the way the WTO functions, was based on a belief that a knowledge of these aspects of the WTO will make it easier to understand the nature of the evolving mandate.

In section 1.3, the analysis turns to a consideration of two options for enhancing the WTO's ability to fulfill its mandate. One involves using existing resources more efficiently. The second is to increase the amount of resources available to the WTO through some combination of additional permanent delegates in Geneva, additional backup staff in capitals, and an enlarged secretariat.

1.1   The WTO and Its Resources

1.1.1   The WTO as a Binding Legal Agreement

The WTO is the legal and institutional foundation of the multilateral trading system. It is *not* a "best endeavors" organization. Although there are a limited number of examples where other international economic institutions place legally binding (contractual) obligations on their members, the WTO is unique both in the extent of its contractual obligations (including policy bindings contained in each member's schedules) and in the enforcement mechanism built into its system for resolving disputes.[1] At the end of an integrated dispute settlement process that covers a wide range of trade-related policies in the areas of goods, services, and the protection of intellectual property, there lies— if all else fails—multilaterally authorized trade sanctions. This was true with the GATT and, as a result of major changes agreed to in the Uruguay Round that make the dispute settlement process much more automatic (individual countries can no longer block the process), it is even more true with the WTO. *It is a critically important feature of the WTO and, just as it did with the GATT, it colors virtually everything that occurs in the WTO context.*

The obligations of WTO members are contained in *The Results of the Uruguay Round of Multilateral Trade Negotiations,* formally adopted in Marrakesh in April 1994 and comprising twenty-nine individual legal texts and twenty-eight additional ministerial declarations, decisions, and understandings that spell out further obligations and commitments (altogether 558 pages in the English version), together with approximately 26,000 pages of computer printout detailing each member's schedule of tariff concessions and schedule of services commitments. In contrast to the GATT, every WTO member must

---

1. For example, for much of the 1960s, when International Monetary Fund regulations required member countries to peg their currencies either to gold or to the U.S. dollar, Canada maintained a floating exchange rate. Since Canada did not ask to borrow from the IMF, there was no enforcement mechanism, and all the IMF could do was annually admonish the Canadian government to return to a fixed exchange rate as soon as possible.

submit schedules on tariff concessions and services commitments, and—with only *very* limited exceptions, mainly for the least-developed countries—every member accepts in its entirety a common set of rules and disciplines covering goods, services, and intellectual property (the so-called single undertaking).

1.1.2   The Council and Committee Structure

Figure 1.1 provides an overview of the institutional structure of the WTO. Between meetings of the Ministerial Conference (no less frequently than once every two years), the main governing body is the General Council.[2] The council also meets in two other forms—as the Dispute Settlement Body, to oversee the dispute settlement procedures, and as the Trade Policy Review Body, which conducts regular reviews of WTO members' trade policies and practices. The main bodies that report to the General Council are the Council for Trade in Goods, the Council for Trade in Services, and the Council for Trade-Related Aspects of Intellectual Property Rights. Under these three councils are various committees, each responsible for administering specific agreements and preparing and adopting decisions for approval by the respective council. Two aspects of the council and committee structure are relevant to the current discussion.

Composition. All of the WTO councils and committees are open to all members, and in practice the membership is virtually identical on all the ones considered important. This is in contrast to an institutional arrangement in which the body that meets regularly is composed of a subgroup of members, with the entire membership meeting only to decide matters that require action by all members.

Thus there is nothing in the WTO that corresponds to the International Monetary Fund's (IMF's) or World Bank's executive boards or interim and development committees. The closest the GATT came to such a body was the Consultative Group of Eighteen (CG.18), established on a temporary basis in 1975 and made a permanent body in 1979. The group's report to the GATT Council, in which it recommended that it become a permanent body, states, "It is strongly believed in the Group that the GATT should have at its disposal a small but representative group which would permit existing and emerging trade policy issues to be discussed in confidence among responsible officials from capitals, and thus facilitate an effective concertation of policies in the trade field."[3] The number of annual meetings ranged from two to four. One of the most important

2. The General Council also supervises four plurilateral agreements—indicated in figure 1.1 by the broken line—to which some but not all WTO members are signatories.

3. GATT 1980, 285. The CG.18 included nine alternate members who participated fully in the group's discussions; the main formal difference between full members and alternate members was that the former are provided with two seats, one to be used by an adviser, while alternate members had only one.

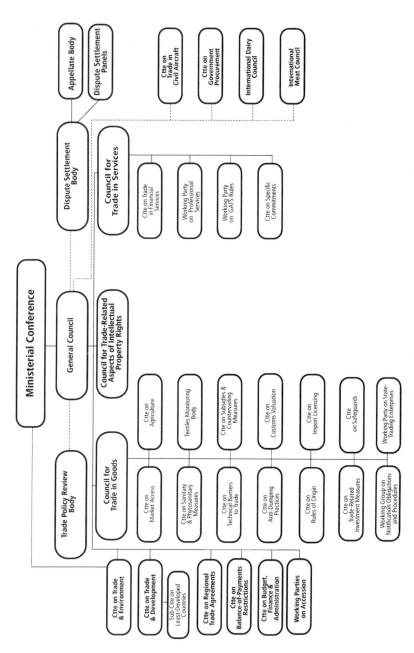

Fig. 1.1   WTO structure

Source: WTO Secretariat.

Note: The chart does not include three working groups—on investment, competition policy, and transparency in government procurement practices—which will be established in response to decisions taken at the Singapore Ministerial Conference.

features of the group's work was that it was able to bring together high officials from a number of capitals. This greatly increased the value of its discussions and the force of its recommendations (it was not a decision-making body).

In November 1985, it was decided that the membership of the CG.18 should be enlarged to twenty-two full members.[4] The group's last meeting was in 1987, and in December 1988 the contracting parties agreed to the director general's suggestion that the group "remain in suspense" for 1989. To a very limited extent, the gap created by the demise of the CG.18 has been filled by a number of ad hoc groups such as the de la Paix Group (self-selected, composed of Geneva ambassadors) during the Uruguay Round, and the current Invisibles Group (participation based on consultations among the Quad countries and a guarantee of capital-based participants, and *not* limited to services issues).

Voting. Unlike the IMF and the World Bank, which have weighted voting (related to countries' relative contributions to the two organizations' capital funds), the GATT and now the WTO is a "one country, one vote" organization.[5] Except for waivers and accessions, where mail ballots were used, voting very rarely occurred in the GATT, there being a strong preference among members to operate on the basis of consensus, and there is no obvious reason to expect the situation to be very different in the WTO.[6] Article IX on decision making states: "The WTO shall continue the practice of decision-making by consensus followed under GATT 1947. Except as otherwise provided, where a decision cannot be arrived at by consensus, the matter at issue shall be decided by voting." The provisions on voting, which were revised in the Uruguay Round, are detailed in the appendix.

1.1.3   Resources to Carry Out the Mandate

Three main categories of resources are available to carry out the WTO's mandate: the member country delegations in Geneva, their support staff in national capitals, and the WTO Secretariat. Because it is not always clear whether the term "the WTO" refers to all three or to just the secretariat, I use the term "WTO family" to refer to all three whenever it is not completely clear from the context that the reference is to an aggregate of the delegates, support staff in capitals, and the secretariat. A fourth category of resources, which traditionally has not been important in GATT/WTO work but which shows signs of perhaps becoming more important in the future, involves cooperation with

4. The IMF Executive Board began with sixteen members. It was subsequently increased to twenty-two, and then two years ago—with the addition of Russia and Switzerland—to twenty-four.

5. Contributions to the WTO's 1996 budget ranged from the minimum of 0.03 percent or 33,990 Swiss francs (forty-one members) to 17,980,710 Swiss francs for the United States. The fifteen members of the European Union (individual WTO members) contributed a total of 51,324,900 Swiss francs, or 45 percent of the total.

6. Voting was necessary because the GATT Council did not have the authority to approve waivers and accessions.

other intergovernmental organizations and nongovernmental organizations (NGOs).

National Delegations in Geneva

One of the most important distinguishing features of GATT and now the WTO, relative to other international organizations, is the much more active role the delegates from member countries play in the WTO's day-to-day activities.[7] In other words, Geneva-based delegations are a very important part of the WTO's resources. Indeed, a number of delegations like to stress that the WTO is a "member-driven" organization, presumably in contrast to other unnamed international organizations. Thus such considerations as the number of members with permanent delegations resident in Geneva, the size of those delegations, the extent of the individuals' professional experience with GATT/WTO activities, the support they receive from capitals, and the frequency of ministerial-level meetings are all important for the operation of the WTO.

As of April 1997, the WTO had 131 members (accession working parties have been established to consider applications from another 28 governments, including China, Chinese Taipei, the Russian Federation, Saudi Arabia, and Vietnam). Of those 131 members, 97 have one or more full-time representatives resident in Geneva, but in many instances they also have to cover other international organizations headquartered in Geneva (UNCTAD, ILO, WHO, WIPO, and so forth). The remaining 34 governments (one quarter of the membership) are represented either by staff at embassies elsewhere in Europe or by staff in the national capital. Many of these countries are small in terms of population (15 had a population under one million in 1995), but 8 of the members without a resident representative in Geneva have populations ranging from 6 1/2 to 17 1/2 million (in ascending order, Chad, Guinea, Rwanda, Niger, Malawi, Burkina Faso, Mali, and Mozambique).

Among the 97 WTO members with representation in Geneva in June 1997, the size of the WTO delegation ranged from one professional (in many instances, almost certainly part-time on WTO matters) to twenty-two, with an average of just under five professionals per delegation. Six members reported WTO delegations with more than ten professionals: Brazil, the European Community, and the United States (eleven each), Thailand (fifteen), the Republic of Korea (seventeen), and Japan (twenty-two).[8] In interpreting these figures, and keeping in mind the description of the WTO as a "member-driven" organization, it is helpful first to recall that all WTO councils, committees, and working groups are open to all members, and second to keep in mind the workload implicit in figure 1.1 with its four councils, eighteen committees, one negotiating group, and two working parties on services, the Textiles Monitoring Body,

7. As is evident from David Henderson's paper (chap. 3 in this volume), delegates from OECD member countries also play a major role in that organization's day-to-day activities.

8. Statistics on WTO delegations are based on information reported to the WTO Secretariat by WTO members, as reported in the June 1997 WTO directory. The figure for the EC does *not* include staff in the delegations of the 15 individual EC members (seventy-nine in total).

and the Trade Policy Review Body (plus other bodies not shown in figure 1.1, including the three new working groups on investment, competition, and government procurement agreed to at the Singapore Ministerial Conference, twenty-eight accession working parties, "heads of delegations" meetings, meetings of the several informal regional groups, and meetings of various ad hoc discussion and negotiating groups).

In 1995, there were 454 meetings in the WTO that used interpreters (down from 561 in 1994). Allowing for approximately ten weeks a year during which few, if any, meetings take place, those 454 meetings meant an average of nearly 11 meetings a week on various issues. And, of course, the meeting schedule is often more intense in certain periods. In the first half of 1996 alone, the number was 415; if this 47 percent increase over the first half of 1995 is applied to the 1995 total, the estimated figure for 1996 is 667 meetings with interpretation, or nearly 16 a week. For meetings of all kinds, including those with interpretation, the 1995 figure was 1,650 (39 per week), with the number of such meetings in the first half of 1996 (46 per week) running 17 percent ahead of the first half of 1995.[9] And it is not simply an increase in the number of meetings, but also in the level of specialized knowledge required by the expanded mandate agreed to in the Uruguay Round. While officials from capitals participate in certain WTO meetings, the workload is carried primarily by the Geneva delegations, with the assistance of the secretariat staff that services the meetings.

Backup Support in Capitals

Obtaining plausible estimates of the amount of backup resources available to the delegations in their respective capitals would be very difficult, for at least two reasons. First, much of the assistance undoubtedly is provided by staff who do not work full-time on WTO matters. Second, it would not be enough to consider only staff at the trade ministry. Staff from ministries and other government agencies dealing with foreign relations, agriculture, health and safety standards, customs revenue, banking, insurance, telecommunications, patents and trademarks, competition laws, and other trade-related policies will, to varying degrees, provide support to colleagues in Geneva.

When considering the extent to which the amount of backup support from capitals varies among the delegations, it is not unreasonable to assume that in most instances the degree of variation is roughly similar to the degree of variation in the size of the delegations in Geneva. The amount of resources a country devotes to the WTO is determined by the importance it attaches to WTO activities, by how much it believes WTO activities require, and by what it feels it can afford. For many countries, the cost of maintaining an official and his or

9. One factor behind the increase in meetings in the WTO building may have been the increase in meeting rooms when the WTO took over that part of Centre William Rappard previously occupied by the UN High Commissioner for Refugees, and a resulting shift of meetings from delegation offices to the WTO building. However, the widespread concern among delegations over the increase in meetings suggests that this was, at most, a relatively minor factor.

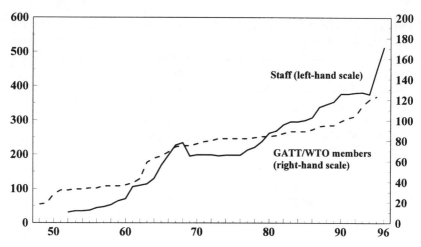

Fig. 1.2   Number of secretariat staff (1952–96) and of GATT contracting parties/WTO members (1948–96)

Source: GATT and WTO Secretariat data.

Note: Beginning in 1987, the staff figure includes Uruguay Round staff, and beginning in 1989, it includes Trade Policy Review Mechanism staff. In contrast, temporary assistance positions, which averaged about 64 during the Uruguay Round and reached 93 in 1994, are included only for 1995 and 1996.

her family in Geneva is higher than in the national capital, and this factor may weigh more heavily on some delegations than others. But, aside from this, there is no obvious reason why the relative division of the resources devoted to WTO activities, between Geneva and the national capital, should vary greatly between countries. In other words, small delegations in Geneva are likely to have limited backup support from capital, and vice versa for the big delegations in Geneva.

The Secretariat

The evolution of the combined number of professional and general service positions in the GATT Secretariat during 1952–94, and in the WTO Secretariat for 1995 and 1996, is shown in figure 1.2, together with the evolution of GATT/WTO membership.[10] This is *not* meant to imply that there is (or should be) any kind of mechanical link between the two. Economies of scale in supplying secretariat services, for example, would argue for less than proportionate increases in staff, while an expanding mandate and/or expanding secretariat responsibilities would argue for more than proportionate increases in staff.

There was a sharp increase during the Dillon and Kennedy Rounds, with the staff more than tripling between 1960 and 1968, from 71 to 234. After declining in 1969 to 195, the number of staff was virtually constant for six years, before beginning to increase gradually in the final years of the Tokyo Round

10. GATT Secretariat staff were employed by the Interim Commission for the International Trade Organization (ICITO) and GATT. As of July 1997 the WTO, which still does not have its own staff, was operating with a staff on loan from the ICITO.

negotiations, a trend that continued until the late 1980s, when the total was boosted by the additional staff hired to help with the Uruguay Round negotiations and to carry out the trade policy reviews (virtually all of those positions, as well as most of the nearly one hundred temporary assistance positions, were converted into permanent positions in 1995). The figure for 1996 of 513 also reflects 47 new positions provided for in the 1996 budget.[11]

The resources available to the WTO Secretariat can be put in perspective by comparing the staff and budget with those of other international economic organizations. Table 1.1 provides data for 1996 on the size of the staff and the annual budget for seventeen such organizations. *The figures obviously indicate only very rough orders of magnitude, in particular because it is difficult to put the figures for each institution onto a common, fully comparable basis (some budgets are a mixture of operating expenses and grants/loans, temporary staff and consultants are accounted for in different ways, and so forth).* Granting this, it is very difficult not to conclude that, relative to the secretariats of other international economic organizations, the GATT had and the WTO has a very small secretariat.

- The WTO budget is only slightly more than 1 percent of the combined budget of the seventeen international economic organizations.
- If the WTO Secretariat's annual budget were *doubled,* there would still be eleven international economic organizations with larger budgets.
- If the WTO Secretariat staff *doubled* in size, there would still be eight international economic organizations with larger staffs than the WTO.
- Recalling the "member-driven" description of the WTO, a rough estimate would put the number of delegates resident in Geneva and working more or less full-time on WTO activities at around 460. If this figure is added to the secretariat staff, giving a figure of 973, there are still eight international economic organizations in table 1.1 with larger staffs.

Clearly budgetary stringency in national capitals has very little, if anything, to do with the size of the GATT/WTO Secretariat staff and budget. The explanation involves not money, but rather (1) the nature of the mandate that the WTO

11. Between 1948 and 1996, the GATT/WTO Secretariat's budget increased from $89,000 a year to $94 million, but the postwar inflation makes this a completely uninteresting comparison. A not entirely frivolous way of "deflating" the annual budget figures is to express them in relation to the annual value of world merchandise trade (the evolution of both the budget and trade series is a composite of volume changes—staff increases in the case of the GATT—and inflation), that is, in minutes of world merchandise trade in that year. Early in the GATT's existence, there was a sharp increase, from less than 1 minute to 3 minutes, after which it was virtually unchanged for a decade. Then between 1960 and 1968—when, as mentioned above, the number of staff more than tripled—it jumped to 7.5 minutes (an increase of 170 percent in seven years). During the next two decades there were sharp ups and downs, but the trend was essentially flat (in minutes of world trade, the 1989 budget was smaller than the 1968 budget). In 1996, the WTO budget was equivalent to about 9.5 minutes of the value of world merchandise trade in 1995 (a 27 percent increase in the twenty-six years since 1968), and to a little more than 7.5 minutes of 1995 world trade in goods and services combined.

Table 1.1   **Staff and Annual Budget of Selected International Economic Organizations**

Organization	Number of Staff in 1996	Annual Budget in 1996 (millions of U.S. dollars)
World Bank	6,781[a]	1,375
Food and Agriculture Organization of the United Nations	5,100	600[b]
United Nations Development Programme	4,914[c]	1,400[c]
International Monetary Fund	2,577[d]	475
Organization for Economic Cooperation and Development	2,322[e]	330
International Labour Organisation	2,286	290
World Food Programme	2,069[f]	1,200
United Nations Industrial Development Organization	1,758	193
United Nations Office for Project Services	941[g]	403[h]
United Nations Population Fund	919	305
International Civil Aviation Organization	759	60
European Bank for Reconstruction and Development	753	213
United Nations Environment Programme	745	99[i]
International Telecommunication Union	726[g]	139[g]
World Intellectual Property Organization	630	121
World Trade Organization	513	94[j]
United Nations Conference on Trade and Development	443	78

Sources: The figures in this table were compiled from a variety of sources, including WTO budget documents, *Yearbook of International Organizations 1996/1997* (K. G. Saur, Munich), descriptive material published by the organizations, websites, and personal communications.

[a]The staff figure includes an estimated 1,100 long-term consultants.

[b]Sum of regular budget ($325 million) and field program expenditure (mainly technical assistance).

[c]1995; the budget figure incorporates the core program, support budget, and extra-budgetary items.

[d]In terms of effective staff years.

[e]Includes 350 consultants, experts, fellows, and temporary staff.

[f]Plus 2,178 temporary staff employed mainly in emergency operations.

[g]1995.

[h]1994.

[i]Includes contributions to Environment Fund, Trust Fund, Counterpart Fund, and regular budget.

[j]Includes $3.7 million for the Appellate Body. The figure of 513 for the staff includes the staff servicing the Appellate Body, but not the seven members of the Body.

members give to the WTO Secretariat and (2) a flawed budget-setting process (more on this below).

As regards the role of the secretariat in implementing the WTO's mandate, it is possible to imagine a spectrum at one end of which is a secretariat limited to scheduling meeting rooms, reproducing documents, and providing interpreters (the "pencil-sharpening" model), and at the other end of which is a proactive, assertive secretariat that not only plays a high-profile public role in promoting multilateral rules and freer nondiscriminatory trade, but also an independent and high-profile role in decisions about the evolution of the multilateral trading system (the "cutting-edge" model). While it would be incorrect to say that many delegations want a secretariat at the pencil-sharpening end, it would be no exaggeration to say that a large majority—including all of the delegations from the larger countries—do not want a secretariat that is even remotely near the cutting-edge end. Thus the emphasis on the WTO being a "member-driven" organization. Consider, for example, the following points:

- The secretariat staff and budget are small relative to other international economic organizations.

- The director general does not have the authority to initiate a dispute settlement case, no matter how blatant the violation of the rules. This, together with no tradition of third-party complaints in the GATT, was an important factor behind the proliferation of voluntary export restraints (VERs) and similar GATT-illegal measures, which posed an increasingly serious threat to the GATT's credibility and effectiveness from the late 1960s until the end of the Uruguay Round.

- The secretariat is not empowered to interpret GATT rules (only dispute settlement panels, which are advised by but never include members of the secretariat, can do so).

- Even in situations outside the dispute settlement process—such as the committee that examines countries that have invoked one of the GATT's balance-of-payments provisions to justify an otherwise-illegal increase in trade barriers, or the working parties that examine free trade area and customs union agreements—it is the member countries, not the secretariat, that pass judgment on the conformity of the actions with GATT obligations.

- With certain very rare exceptions, secretariat staff are not allowed to chair WTO committees, working parties, and so forth, even though article VI of the agreement establishing the WTO states that "the responsibilities of the Director-General and of the staff of the Secretariat shall be exclusively international in character"—in other words, that they should represent the multilateral interest and not the interests of individual WTO members.

In addition to being subjected to these five constraints, the GATT Secretariat faced two other constraints for much of its existence.

- It was not until 1977—nearly thirty years after its creation—that the secretariat was allowed to begin regularly reporting on trade policy developments in the member countries.[12]

- The GATT Secretariat—although it serviced a rules-based agreement involving *contractual* obligations—was not allowed to have a formal Office of Legal Affairs (or a formal legal adviser) until 1983, thirty-five years after it was established. The IMF, in contrast, had a General Counsel and a Legal Division from the day it opened for business.

These various limitations do not mean the secretariat is powerless. Secretariat staff are actively involved in providing legal, economic, and policy advice to individual delegations in Geneva, to support staff in capitals, and on missions to member countries. They interact with delegations in developing approaches on particular issues, helping to resolve differences, and assisting with the implementation of WTO obligations. During the Uruguay Round, the director general was chairman of the Trade Negotiations Committee, which had overall responsibility for managing the negotiations, and he played an important role during the final phase of the round. The same was true in the run-up to the Singapore Ministerial Conference, when the director general was chairman of the informal meetings of the heads of delegation.

Activities such as public speeches by the director general and other members of the secretariat and the preparation of background papers also provide opportunities to influence the course of the members' work. Another channel is through secretariat publications. Here it is important to note that the member countries allow the secretariat to publish material on its own authority without prior clearance by them. These publications include the secretariat's annual report (previously *International Trade,* now entitled the *WTO Annual Report*), and one-off studies such as the April 1995 *Regionalism and Multilateralism in the World Economy.*

At the December 1988 midterm review of the Uruguay Round, the contracting parties increased the secretariat's responsibilities by agreeing to set up the Trade Policy Review Mechanism (TPRM). The focus of this activity is periodic reviews of individual country trade regimes, prepared by the secretariat. It also includes an annual overview of developments in the international trading environment that are having an impact on the multilateral trading system, assisted by an annual report by the director general "highlighting significant policy issues affecting the trading system."

Granting these various points, it is still relevant to ask why the member countries keep the WTO Secretariat relatively small and give it such a limited

---

12. The twice-a-year publication initially was entitled *Survey of Developments in Commercial Policy* and then, beginning November 1983, the title was changed to *Review of Developments in the Trading System.* This publication, the last one of which covered September 1988 to February 1989, stopped when the TPRM was introduced in 1989.

role in fulfilling the WTO mandate.[13] Undoubtably the principal explanation is that trade policy is so highly politicized at the national level. Governments are afraid of the political consequences at home of any step in the direction of giving the secretariat more authority and a bigger role. As is described below, this does not mean they never take such steps, but they do so very cautiously and only infrequently.

There is, it should be added, a range of views on this point among the member countries. Many of the smaller countries apparently would be prepared to accept a larger and more activist secretariat because they believe it would help them in protecting and promoting their trading interests. The larger countries, in contrast, have two incentives for keeping the secretariat small (aside from a possible uneasiness about any step that might enhance the ability of smaller countries to protect and promote their trading interests). One is budgetary. Each member's contribution to the secretariat's budget is based on its share of world trade. This means that increases in the budget are paid for primarily by the larger traders, while many of the benefits from increased secretariat activities would go to the smaller traders (more on this below). The other incentive stems from the one-country, one-vote nature of the WTO, and the resulting incentive for the large countries to see to it that the delegations (that is, themselves) hold on to the bulk of the authority and influence over the nature and direction of WTO activities.

Cooperation with Intergovernmental Organizations and NGOs

The IMF is the only international organization explicitly mentioned in the original GATT (in connection with the invocation of the balance-of-payments provisions). In contrast, the Uruguay Round agreements mention not only the IMF, but—among others—the World Bank, World Intellectual Property Organization, World Customs Organization, International Organization for Standardization, Codex Alimentarius Commission, International Office of Epizootics, and International Plant Protection Convention. Moreover, article V:1 of the WTO agreement states, "The General Council *shall* make appropriate arrangements for *effective cooperation* with other intergovernmental organizations that have responsibilities related to those of the WTO" (emphasis added).

Equally interesting is the provision—a first for the GATT/WTO system—for cooperation with NGOs. WTO article V:2 states, "The General Council *may* make appropriate arrangements for *consultation and cooperation* with nongovernmental organizations concerned with matters related to those of the WTO" (emphasis added).[14] To date, there has been only one formal arrangement

13. To describe the GATT or WTO Secretariat as being relatively small and having a narrow role does *not* mean that it is unimportant, ineffective, or inefficient. It is an important, effective, and efficient secretariat. The question is whether it could or should play an even more important and effective role in helping the WTO family to fulfill its mandate.

14. See WTO document WT/L/162 (23 July 1996), "Guidelines for Arrangements on Relations with Non-governmental Organizations."

for cooperation between the WTO and NGOs, namely in connection with the Agreement on Preshipment Inspection, involving the International Federation of Inspection Agencies and the International Chamber of Commerce. On a less formal level, the secretariat has organized seminars with NGOs interested in trade and environment issues, and an NGO center (meeting rooms and other facilities) was made available in Singapore during the Ministerial Conference.

Cooperation with other intergovernmental organizations and NGOs is not just about additional resources (for example, in the form of technical expertise), but equally or more importantly about bringing new views and arguments to bear on the wide range of issues covered by the WTO's rules and procedures.

1.2   The GATT/WTO Mandates

In the GATT/WTO context, "mandate" is not a well-defined term. The goals laid down in the preamble to the Marrakesh agreement are too broad to be analytically useful. On the other hand, any attempt to list the multitude of specific tasks specified in each of the many agreements would soon get bogged down in a mass of detail of the kind found in detailed work programs. In what follows, I have tried to find a middle ground where the definition of the GATT/ WTO mandate is simultaneously broad enough to be manageable and detailed enough to be operationally useful. The approach is to define the mandate to include two elements: one is the fundamental goals of the GATT/WTO system, and the other is a set of "instructions" specifying which sectors of the economy and which policies are to be covered in the pursuit of those goals.

1.2.1   The Mandate under GATT 1947

The GATT system originally had two fundamental goals or functions: (1) To reduce policy-related uncertainty surrounding the exchange of goods across national frontiers, by providing a set of rules and procedures governing countries' trade-related policies. These multilateral disciplines, together with reductions in trade barriers, promoted trade-related investment at home and abroad and brought the gains that come from increased international specialization. (2) To provide a forum for dispute settlement, and for negotiations both to strengthen and extend the rules and procedures, and to further liberalize trade-related policies. As for the sectors and policies to be covered in pursuit of these goals, the instructions were simple: the GATT covered trade in goods, and the policy coverage was limited to measures applied at the border, in particular, tariffs and quantitative restrictions.[15]

---

15. The "national treatment" provision in article III of the GATT can be viewed as covering domestic measures, but only in the particular sense of requiring that imports "into the territory of any other contracting party shall be accorded treatment no less favourable than that accorded to like products of national origin in respect of all laws, regulations and requirements affecting their internal sale, offering for sale, purchase, transportation, distribution or use." More to the point,

Under the above definition of the mandate, member countries can alter the mandate in any of three ways. (1) They can add to or subtract from the basic goals. An example of this was the midterm review decision to establish the TPRM, which required adding "regular surveillance of members' policies" to the second goal. (2) They can add to the list of sectors covered by the rules. An example of this is the Uruguay Round agreement to bring traded services under GATT/WTO rules. (3) They can add to the list of policies covered by the rules. An example of this was the Code on Technical Barriers negotiated in the Tokyo Round. These three ways of revising or expanding the mandate are not entirely independent. For example, because firms producing and exporting services often need a physical presence in the foreign market, the decision in the Uruguay Round to expand the *sectoral coverage* to include traded services also involved extending the *policy coverage* to include policies governing foreign direct investment in services.

The original mandate—to pursue the two fundamental goals through a near-exclusive focus on border measures applied to trade in goods—guided work through the GATT's first two decades and the first six rounds of multilateral negotiations (the Kennedy Round, held during 1964–67, was the sixth). Although the Tokyo Round (1973–79) is not renowned for the increases in market access that it achieved, it marked an exceptionally important turning point in the GATT's history. For the first time in an important way, the GATT's rules and procedures formally "moved inside the border," in this instance to cover technical standards, production subsidies, and government procurement. True, the new rules took the form of "codes" to which only subgroups of contracting parties (including all of the Organization for Economic Cooperation and Development [OECD] countries) subscribed, but they were formally a part of the GATT system.

In 1975 and again in 1989, the contracting parties also expanded the mandate by adding to the basic goals in two ways (the first of which proved to be temporary). One was the previously mentioned creation (on a provisional basis) in 1975 of the CG.18 as a forum for discussion of "existing and emerging trade policy issues . . . among responsible officials from capitals." The other was the decision, taken initially at the December 1988 midterm review of the Uruguay Round, to establish (on a provisional basis) the TPRM, under which the trade regimes of individual members would be collectively reviewed and evaluated by the other GATT members.

To sum up, and recalling the three sources of possible change in the GATT's mandate, between 1947 and 1994 the mandate was enlarged (1) by expanding the goals to include providing a forum for discussing existing and emerging policy (a change that lapsed with the demise of the CG.18), and a forum for the regular surveillance of members' policies (the TPRM), and (2) by adding

---

there were no GATT negotiations on those internal measures, and no rules on their use beyond the need to be nondiscriminatory.

technical barriers to trade, domestic subsidies, and government procurement to the list of policies covered by the rules.

1.2.2 The WTO's Current Mandate

In the Uruguay Round, the member countries used all three ways of changing the mandate to give the WTO a mandate that expands in important ways on the GATT's mandate. To begin with, the fundamental goals described above are expanded in article III of the WTO agreement, which spells out the five functions of the WTO: (1) administer and implement the multilateral and plurilateral trade agreements that together make up the WTO; (2) act as a forum for multilateral trade negotiations; (3) administer arrangements for the settlement of disputes; (4) review national trade policies; and (5) cooperate with the IMF and the World Bank with a view to achieving greater coherence in global economic policymaking. The GATT's original mandate included the first three functions, and the fourth was provisionally added in 1989 and made permanent under the WTO. The fifth function is the only completely new addition.

Another change, which it is premature to describe as a new goal (as that term is used in this paper), but which nevertheless could have important implications for the WTO's mandate in coming years, is the reference to "sustainable development" in the preamble to the WTO. This provided, for example, a rationale for the formal creation of the WTO Committee on Trade and Environment.

As everyone knows, an expansion of the basic goals of the GATT was not the most important change in the mandate to come out of the Uruguay Round. Much more important were the expansion to a major new sector and to major new policy areas. The list of sectors covered by the multilateral rules expanded to include services. As noted above, the addition of this sector expanded the list of national policies covered by the multilateral rules to include investment policies in the services area. The list of national policies covered by the multilateral rules expanded; in particular, it includes national laws for the protection of intellectual property. Other new policy areas subject to WTO rules include sanitary and phytosanitary regulations, and regulations for preshipment inspection.

1.2.3 Future Evolution of the WTO's Mandate

There have been several suggestions for a further expansion of the WTO's current mandate. Four would involve an expansion of the types of ostensibly domestic policies covered by multilateral trade rules—that is, a further move inside the border—to include investment policies, competition policies, policies toward corruption in government procurement, and core labor standards. In addition, some delegations have suggested that the WTO should be not just a negotiating forum, but also a forum for "analysis and discussion" (which, if realized, would be an addition to the second of the two fundamental goals described above).

The ongoing integration of the world economy—globalization—is a key force pushing for an expansion of the WTO's mandate, particularly in the policy-coverage dimension. A growing share of domestic output is being traded internationally. Not only multinational enterprises, but also small and medium-sized enterprises in both developed and developing countries alike, increasingly spread their activities such as sourcing, marketing, and investment across national boundaries. There is a need to ensure that the multilateral WTO rules—designed to reduce the uncertainty surrounding transactions across national frontiers—reflect these and other modern commercial realities. In addition, as countries' "economic lives" become more intertwined, there is an increased risk that trading partners will perceive "spillovers" from ostensibly domestic policies, for example, competition policies. The GATT's success in bringing down many conventional border protection measures is also a factor, as existing nonborder restrictions on market access become more visible to trading partners (for example, domestic regulations) and as countries are tempted to compensate for reduced border protection by introducing new nonborder protection.

Another factor behind certain proposals for expanding the WTO's mandate—and one that should be a concern as regards possible future expansions—is the previously mentioned fact that the WTO, in contrast to other international economic organizations, has an effective enforcement mechanism—that is, an effective way of sanctioning member countries that are found to be in violation of the institution's rules and that refuse to change the illegal behavior. At the end of the WTO dispute settlement procedures, if all else fails, lie multilaterally approved trade sanctions. A desire to gain access to this enforcement mechanism is the main reason that the WTO mandate was expanded to include the protection of intellectual property (despite the existence of the World Intellectual Property Organization), and it was the main motivation behind proposals to expand the mandate to include the protection of core labor standards (despite the existence of the International Labour Organisation [ILO]). It should be added, however, that the existence of an effective enforcement mechanism also makes it harder to achieve agreement to expand WTO rules into new subject areas (if the WTO were a "best endeavors" organization, it almost certainly would have a much more extensive mandate).

1.3 Improving the Capacity of the WTO to Fulfill Its Mandate

There is a widespread perception that the WTO has, thus far, encountered no major problems in fulfilling its mandate. Implementation of the Uruguay Round agreement is progressing, by and large, on schedule. The revised dispute settlement procedures are working very well, both in creating a strong incentive for countries to resolve disputes before they reach the panel stage, and in demonstrating their ability to overturn policies even in sensitive areas. The Singapore Ministerial Conference was an important success, as was the telecommunications agreement signed in February 1997, and the ministerial

Declaration on Trade in Informational Technology Products (announced at Singapore, followed by the 26 March 1997 agreement by forty governments to implement the declaration).[16] Other work, such as the many accession working parties, the examination of a large number of article XXIV agreements, the trade policy reviews, is being carried out competently and largely on schedule (see WTO 1996). As with any institution, however, there are always questions concerning the possibilities for using the *existing resources* more efficiently, and the WTO family is no exception. This is the first of the two options examined in this section for improving the WTO's capacity to fulfill its mandate.

The second option, in contrast, involves an increase in resources in view of the increased demands on the WTO. Is it possible that the resources currently available to the WTO family fall short—perhaps considerably short—of what is needed to fulfill the current and likely future mandate? With ongoing globalization and the creation of the WTO, has the multilateral trading system entered an era that is very different and much more demanding than the GATT era, while the member countries remain wedded to budgetary attitudes appropriate to the GATT of ten or twenty years ago? An affirmative answer would mean that a substantial increase in the amount of resources that the member countries devote to the WTO is needed, through an increase in the number of permanent delegates in Geneva, an increase in backup support in capitals, an increase in the secretariat's staff and budget (and perhaps authority), or some combination of all three.

1.3.1   Using Existing Resources More Efficiently

It is widely accepted that the single most important step that could be taken to use existing resources more efficiently would be to streamline certain categories of work that ordinarily take place in large meetings.[17] The unwieldy nature, in certain circumstances, of meetings with a large number of delegates in the room (if only half the delegations participate with an average of two delegates each, there are 130) means the solution will involve a greater reliance on one or more groups (fora) composed of a relatively small subset of WTO members.[18] Since there is no prospect of the WTO adopting weighted voting,

16. In his fascinating book on the implications of digitization, Negroponte (1996) makes a distinction between bits and atoms, and states that "GATT is about atoms." In the next edition, in addition to correcting this sentence by putting it in the past tense, he can add that, thanks to the Telecoms Agreement, the WTO is about bits as well as atoms. More seriously, the book predicts a number of profound changes that could have profound implications for the WTO's future mandate.

17. Among other efforts to improve the use of existing resources, the work of the Working Group on Notification Obligations and Procedures should be mentioned, where efforts center on trying to rationalize and reduce the burden on members of the more than two hundred notifications currently required under the WTO.

18. It should be noted that no one is talking about a need to streamline specific market access negotiations—that is, negotiations aimed at specific reductions in specific import barriers. Consensus is not an issue in such cases. For example, in the case of both the negotiations on informational technology products and the telecom negotiations, the participation was determined implicitly by the need to achieve a "critical mass." Given that the reductions in barriers had to be done

such a group or groups would not—in contrast to the UN Security Council and the executive boards of the IMF and World Bank—take decisions binding on all the members.

Such a group would provide a forum for discussing and debating cross-cutting management issues, important trade issues, and new policy areas. Depending on the topic, the group might also attempt to reach a consensus that would then be presented to the entire membership for approval. This was the approach used in Singapore to reach a consensus on the final communiqué: a group of thirty-four members discussed, debated, and eventually reached a consensus, which was then presented to all the members for acceptance. It worked, but was widely criticized, particularly by many of the ninety-four members who were not part of the core group and felt they were presented with a series of faits accomplis. It was this experience, in particular, that triggered the latest search for ways to improve WTO decision making.

As was noted above, several informal "discussion" groups, which meet more or less regularly, already exist (an ad hoc response to a felt need). The issue, therefore, is whether to create a more formal group/forum, whose activities would be fully transparent and whose membership would be representative of the entire WTO membership. Two competing models are currently on the table. One involves a formally structured group similar to the CG.18, which was active for a decade preceding the launching of the Uruguay Round. The advantages of such a group would include its relatively small size (not necessarily limited to eighteen members) and its ability to attract representatives from capitals. It would also provide an opportunity for the smaller traders (well over half the WTO membership) to participate—albeit on a rotating basis—in a high-prestige, small inner circle of WTO members.[19]

Critics are quick to point out what they view as important disadvantages of the CG.18 model. These include the likelihood that the already considerable influence of the three or four largest traders would be increased by virtue of their permanent seats, and the problems created by asking a body with a fixed membership (for any given period) to deal with a variety of issues that include some of little or no interest to some of the participants. Under the CG.18, there were also complaints about a lack of transparency.

The second option, introduced during the Uruguay Round negotiations and used at the Singapore Ministerial Conference, is often described as the "concentric circles" model. An inner circle of countries, whose number has varied from eight in specific subject areas to thirty-four when a broad range of issues

---

on a most-favored-nation basis—that is, extended to all WTO members—the goal was to minimize "free riding" by making the agreement contingent on the participation of members that have shares of world trade in the good or service above a certain threshold and that collectively account for a "significant" share of world trade in the good or service.

19. Any formula for a new CG.18-type group would need to anticipate the entry into the WTO of China and Russia.

were being discussed, serves as the basic discussion, debate, and (when necessary) negotiating group. The results are then provided to a larger circle or to all the other members, frequently with a recommendation that a consensus decision be taken on the issue(s) under consideration.

A key distinction from the CG.18 model is flexibility in the membership of the inner circle. Countries that care strongly about an issue generally can gain membership in the inner circle. In effect, this allows custom-designed inner circles that ensure the participation of all the members with a strong stake in the outcome on a particular issue. Supporters of the concentric-circle model like to link this feature with the GATT/WTO "consensus" method of decision making, which enables delegations to adopt a position of not opposing the consensus without actually having to cast an affirmative vote. Those not involved in the negotiating process are always likely to be unhappy, but under the informal concentric-circle model they will know it was up to them to have made their claim for involvement earlier rather than to block the consensus.

These advantages—which tend to be emphasized by the thirty or so midsized countries that are large enough to demand inclusion in, for example, the group of thirty-four members that worked on the Singapore communiqué, but not large enough to demand an individual permanent seat in a new CG.18-type group—are not sufficient to have prevented the kind of widespread unhappiness with the concentric-circle model that was very much in evidence at Singapore. It remains to be seen if reforms in use of this model are feasible and, if so, if they would be sufficient to give it a wider acceptability. Such reforms include giving the countries in the outer circle(s) more time to reflect on results received from the inner circle and taking their views into account to a greater extent than in the past, increasing transparency and communication, and increasing the participation of senior officials from capitals.

Although it is not clear in which direction efforts to find a better forum for discussion, debate, and consensus building are likely to go, pressure for a change is bound to continue to build, as the membership grows from today's 130 to more than 160 and as WTO decision making is faced with a widening range of increasingly more complex issues.

1.3.2   Does the WTO Need More Resources?

When the member countries faced this question during the transition from the GATT to the WTO, they answered it affirmatively, at least as regards the secretariat. Over the course of the Uruguay Round negotiations, there was a separate budget for Uruguay Round staff and related expenses and, beginning in 1989, a separate budget for staff and other expenses associated with the TPRM. For 1994, the *regular* GATT budget and staff—in effect, the pre–Uruguay Round secretariat—were, respectively, $48 million and 313. Through a consolidation of the Uruguay Round and TPRM staffs and budgets, plus some additional increases, the 1996 WTO budget and staff stood at $94 million and 513.[20] Relative to the pre–Uruguay Round era, there has also been some increase in the size of many delegations resident in Geneva.

In contrast, if the question of whether additional resources are needed is posed today (mid-1997), the answer from the member countries is no. The Budget Committee insisted on a zero-growth budget for the secretariat in 1997 (no additional staff), and current indications for 1998 point to another zero-growth budget.

This section offers a *preliminary* examination of the question of whether the current level of aggregate resources available to the WTO—delegations in Geneva, backup support in capitals, the secretariat, and intergovernmental organizations and NGOs—is sufficient for the WTO to fulfill its mandate. Although there is some discussion below of a possible need for additional resources in particular categories—for example, in the delegations or in the secretariat—there is no attempt at a rigorous analysis of the optimal (or at least a desirable) distribution of resources *among* the four categories.

It would be helpful if it were possible to begin by summarizing conclusions from the academic literature on the question of the optimal size of an international organization. Unfortunately, there appears to be virtually nothing in the existing literature that has any practical relevance to answering that question.

One way to introduce an element of rigor into an analysis of the budget-setting process for the WTO is to pose the question in a context loosely analogous to an "efficient markets" approach.[21] If the "market" for international organizations operates efficiently, the member countries get the size of organization (in terms of resources) they want. If the organization is not the correct size, it must be the result of one or more market failures. More specifically, granted the clear preference of the leading delegations to keep the WTO Secretariat small, it is still possible for the secretariat's budget—as well as those of the resident delegations and support staff in capitals—to be "too small," that is, smaller than it would be if the budget process were not flawed. Are there any sources of market failure that might support the view that the WTO family is being underfinanced?

It can be argued that the nature of the budget-setting process for the WTO is flawed, so much so that it almost certainly creates such a market failure. In capitals, instructions to WTO Budget Committee participants are formulated with substantive inputs from agencies and individuals with no firsthand experience with the WTO's work program, through a process frequently characterized by confusion and conflicting interests regarding not only the budgets of

---

20. It should be noted that at the same time the GATT/WTO budget was being increased, member countries were freezing or cutting the budgets of several other international organizations.

21. This approach was suggested to me by Robert Baldwin. The main reason it is only loosely analogous to an efficient-markets analysis is that the WTO family is principally a coalition or grouping of countries with different interests and different goals, rather than a single entity with a well-defined objective function.

individual international organizations, but also the country's overall budget for these organizations. Moreover, as the WTO's mandate expands beyond goods and beyond traditional border measures, the interest in and familiarity with the WTO's work is increasingly dispersed among the many different ministries now involved in WTO activities. It is increasingly difficult for any one minister—or, indeed, for the government as a whole—to grasp the full implications of the WTO's new role in international commercial relations (even supposing that any one of the ministers had the incentive to assume that responsibility). "Turf" considerations almost certainly also play a role. Ministries already jealous of the trade minister's expanding portfolio will be, at best, unenthusiastic about giving even incremental increases in resources to the WTO family. Their likely attitude toward proposals for nonincremental increases is even easier to predict.

One way of appeasing finance officials by keeping the country's overall budget for international organization activities constant (or even on a *declining* trend), while increasing the resources provided to the WTO, would be to shift resources from other international economic organizations to the WTO family. The problem, of course, is that turf considerations and entrenched interests would make this politically very difficult (as just noted, the turf problem is already very much in evidence as the WTO assumes responsibility for important activities in such areas as intellectual property protection, telecommunications, and financial services). It is not difficult, for example, to predict the reaction of the labor minister to a proposal to shift funds from the ILO to the WTO, or of the agriculture minister to a proposal to shift funds from the Food and Agriculture Organization or the World Food Programme to the WTO. This raises the question, whose answer goes beyond the scope of this paper, of whether the configuration of international economic organizations in table 1.1, including the allocation of resources among them, is the best one for fulfilling the world community's needs as we approach and enter the twenty-first century.

Other evidence and arguments in support of the view that the WTO family is being underfinanced tend to be mainly of a practical nature. Consider, for example, the following points.

Number of Meetings and Work Program. In the first half of 1996 there was an average of forty-six meetings a week in the WTO building. As for paperwork, in 1996 the secretariat issued 81 million pages of documents (combined total for three languages), an increase of 18 percent over 1995. The considerable difficulty this is creating for all delegations, but in particular for those with small permanent staffs in Geneva—that is, for the vast majority of WTO members—is now openly discussed.[22] One suggestion for improving the situation

---

22. One result of the large number of meetings is that some medium-sized countries and most of the smaller countries "free ride" in many WTO activities, in the knowledge that other countries are participating and there is full transparency, making it possible for them to concentrate their

is to encourage groups of countries (for example, from the same region) to cooperate by dividing up the responsibility for covering various meetings, but so far there has been a marked lack of interest among most delegations for such arrangements. The great risk, of course, is that the member countries will continue to view the problem as one of too many meetings, rather than as one of insufficient resources to meet new obligations and responsibilities.

Behind the large number of meetings is an ambitious work program, the magnitude of which is not easy to convey in a few sentences. The broad categories of activity include implementation of the Uruguay Round results, surveillance activities, dispute settlement, a large number of accession working parties, the examination of twenty-seven free trade area and customs union agreements, and other standard WTO day-to-day activities. Chapter 5 in the *1996 WTO Annual Report* provides a good introduction to the activities at a reasonably detailed level (it is seventy-six pages long).[23] As regards additional activities in the near future, there are the three new working groups agreed to at Singapore (on investment, competition, and transparency in government procurement), plus the beginning of preparations for the next round of negotiations on (at least) agriculture and on services that are mandated to begin before the year 2000.

What is not evident from the WTO annual report is the work that would have been done if more resources—in the delegations and in the secretariat—had been available. To take just one example, following the 1994 Marrakesh meeting, where ministers formally signed the Uruguay Round agreements, the Services Division and the delegations prepared a "GATS work program" for the next two years or so. Prominent on the work program were the continuing negotiations on financial services, basic telecommunications, maritime transport services, and movement of natural persons, but it also included many activities related to the implementation and operation of the new agreement. Because of limitations of staff in the delegations and in the secretariat, relatively little progress was made on the more routine (but important) activities that compose the last category.

An inability to complete planned work is part of a larger category that might be called missed opportunities, and that includes a number of activities and initiatives that would advance the WTO mandate, but that are not even considered because everyone assumes the resources to do them will not be available. Examples of such initiatives include (1) the establishment of WTO regional

---

limited staff on those meetings in which they have a key stake. While perhaps understandable on a pragmatic level, this is hardly an approach that is consistent with the long-run effectiveness and credibility of a member-driven organization.

23. Other sources include WTO document WT/L/88, entitled "Provisions for Review, Future Work, or Negotiations in the WTO Agreement and Related Decisions and Declarations"; the annual report of the WTO bodies compiled in WTO document WT/MIN(96)/2; and the declaration issued at the end of the December 1996 Ministerial Conference in Singapore. All three documents are available from the secretariat, as well as on the WTO Web site, <http://www.unicc.org/wto>.

offices in sub-Saharan Africa, the former Soviet Union, Latin America, and Asia to help with the critical technical assistance needs of countries in those regions; (2) much more frequent trade policy reviews of the least-developed countries and other lower-income developing countries in the WTO (as a way of stimulating the reform process); and (3) the financing, out of the WTO's regular budget, of a minimum number of full-time WTO delegates resident in Geneva (say three) for *every* WTO member (see Blackhurst forthcoming).

Dispute Settlement. The major revision of the dispute settlement system was one of the most significant achievements in the Uruguay Round. The new "automaticity," the increased use of the dispute settlement system by non-OECD countries, and the growing complexity of trade relations have led to a significant increase in the number of cases. Cases brought to the Dispute Settlement Body (DSB), particularly those that progress through the panel process, are very time-consuming for the delegations involved and for the WTO Secretariat, not the least because their very tight and strict timetables limit flexibility. In the case of the secretariat, panels generally involve not just professionals from the Legal Affairs Division, but also from the relevant operational divisions. This trend is already creating problems for the secretariat staff—problems that will become critical if the trend continues.

In the first two years of its operation, the DSB received sixty-four formal requests for consultation, and in twenty-six of those cases there was a request to establish a panel. In contrast, during the last two years of the previous GATT dispute settlement system, there were forty-one requests for consultations, but only eight requests to establish panels. It is perhaps not out of place to note that the 1997 budget and staff of the International Court of Justice in The Hague, which heard an average of two cases a year over the past fifty years and which in April 1997 had nine cases pending, was $10.3 million and eighty employees (including the fifteen judges).[24] The WTO caseload as of mid-July 1997 is eleven panels and two appeals in progress. For 1997, the budget and staff of the WTO Legal Affairs Division is $1.8 million and twelve, while that of the Appellate Body is $4.4 million and fourteen (the seven members plus supporting staff). It should be kept in mind (1) that the Legal Affairs Division is responsible for a significant amount of nonpanel work, and (2) that, as was noted above, staff from other divisions (agriculture and commodities, rules, and so forth) frequently are heavily involved in panel work.

New Policy Areas. As the WTO moves into new and often more technically complex policy areas—services, intellectual property protection, sanitary and phytosanitary measures, and environment, and now investment and competition policies—there is not only an increased need for staff in the delegations, back in capitals and in the secretariat, but for more technically specialized

24. These figures do *not* include the budget and staff of the International Criminal Tribunal for Former Yugoslavia.

staff. The days when a relatively small delegation in Geneva would suffice, because each delegate could adequately master several of the topics discussed each week, are long gone.

Technical Assistance. Membership in the GATT/WTO has expanded sharply in recent years, for example from 85 at the beginning of the Uruguay Round in September 1986 to 127 ten years later (and to 131 in April 1997). Another 28 countries are at various stages of the accession process. What many of the new members, and virtually all of the acceding countries, have in common is a critical and urgent need—that is, a *way-above-average* need relative to anything seen under the GATT—for technical assistance. For those already in the WTO, this means assistance to help them implement their WTO obligations, defend their WTO rights, participate adequately in the WTO's day-to-day activities (recall the "member-driven" nature of the WTO), and prepare for the next round of multilateral negotiations (at a minimum on agriculture and services) by 2000. Those in the accession process need assistance in negotiating their accession, after which they will join the group needing the more general kind of technical assistance.

The ability of the WTO Secretariat staff to fulfill these growing needs is severely limited. There are currently thirteen professionals (plus the director) in the Technical Cooperation and Training Division (three of whom are involved full-time in the training courses that the secretariat provides in Geneva for delegates from developing and transition economies). Professional staff from other divisions are often responsible for the more specialized technical assistance missions, but this cannot be an important source of additional staff because of the pressure of work in those other divisions. There are efforts to stretch resources by improving cooperation between the WTO and other international economic organizations—in particular, with the United Nations Conference on Trade and Development and the Geneva-based International Trade Centre. But both of those institutions are relatively small, have budgets that are under pressure from member countries, and are not especially well endowed with staff capable of providing technical assistance on the wide range of technically complex issues covered by the WTO (such as antidumping rules and procedures, to name only one). In short, while increased cooperation and rationalization of technical assistance activities is desirable and will offer some help, the current and likely future resource gaps are so large that these actions are not a solution to the technical assistance challenge facing the WTO.

The first three points just mentioned—number of meetings and work programs, dispute settlement, and new policy areas—argue for an increase in resources for the WTO family as a whole. The point about technical assistance, in contrast, argues for an increase in staff available in the secretariat.

In thinking about the issue of whether the WTO Secretariat is short of staff, it is helpful to divide the 513 staff members into three broad groups. One consists of staff providing basic support services, such as interpretation, translation, documentation, personnel, finance, and so forth; approximately 271 staff, or 53 percent of the total, are in this category. The member countries generally are responsive to the need for additional staff in these activities, which is not too surprising given that shortages of staff in these areas can have an immediate and obvious impact on the work of the delegations.

To a degree, many of the same considerations apply to requests for additional staff in the second broad group, which consists of staff in the operational divisions—that is, in the divisions whose staff interacts with delegates and support staff in capitals on a daily basis, servicing meetings, providing advice, and so forth. Still, this has not prevented the emergence of staff shortages, as is evident from the above remark regarding the inability to complete the initial planned GATS work program. Another example is the division responsible for carrying out the trade policy reviews, which continues to be seriously understaffed.[25] Approximately 183 staff, or 36 percent of the total, are in this second broad group.

The remaining 58 staff members (33 professionals and 25 general service, together accounting for 11 percent of the secretariat) are in the three divisions whose size the member countries (or at least the large ones) treat as being highly discretionary: Technical Co-operation and Training, Information and Media Relations, and Economic Research and Analysis. More so than for the other divisions in the WTO Secretariat, the amount of resources available to these three divisions—and in particular to the latter two—is heavily influenced by the member countries' desire to keep the secretariat far away from the cutting-edge end of the spectrum described above.[26]

Another common trait linking the activities of these three divisions is economies of scale in providing services of value to, if not all, at least a majority of the delegations. For technical assistance, there are obvious advantages to having it centralized in the secretariat, rather than having each country seek such services bilaterally from the OECD countries or from private consultants. Similarly for research and media relations. Each member country could commission economic studies on issues on the WTO agenda, and each country could contract with private firms to prepare modern, sophisticated media material designed to introduce and explain the WTO to groups in their respective societies. But again it would be much less expensive to centralize such activities in the WTO Secretariat. This has happened, but to date only on a very limited basis.

Much more could be done in all three areas. In the case of technical assistance, the need is obvious. As for economic research and media relations, it is more a matter of missed opportunities.

---

25. Keesing (forthcoming) documents in some detail the view that the resources available for trade policy reviews should be increased substantially.

26. Outsiders concerned by the very limited staff and budget of the Economic Research and Analysis Division have suggested that additional funds be raised from outside sources—individual governments or foundations—and used to supplement ERAD's regular budget. However, given that the reason behind the limited ERAD staff and budget is *not* budget stringency in capitals, it is quite possible that such a move would be strongly resisted by the WTO Budget Committee (which could, for example, simply reduce ERAD's regular budget by whatever amount of funds came from the outside).

By way of summing up, it seems likely that the amount of resources available to the WTO family is likely to continue growing incrementally, as the mandate grows in size and complexity, just as it did under the GATT. The interesting question, therefore, is whether there is a need for a more than incremental increase. A convincing answer would require a more detailed analysis of current and likely future needs than is possible in this paper. That being said, the analysis suggests, at a minimum, that the question warrants careful further analysis, with a close look at missed opportunities being a particularly important part of that analysis. My view is that incremental increases in resources will not be sufficient to permit the WTO to play the role it should be playing as the emerging preeminent international economic organization in a progressively more integrated global economy.

Appendix

Table 1A.1   **Decision Making in the World Trade Organization**

Rule	Decision	Provision
Majority of votes cast	All decisions except those listed below	Article IX:1
Two-thirds majority comprising more than one-half of members	Financial regulations and budget estimates	Article VII:3
Two-thirds majority of members	Entry into force of amendments	Article X:3
	Approval of terms of accession	Article XII:2
Three-quarters majority of members	Waiver of obligations	Article IX:3
	Amendments effective for all members[a]	Article X:1–5
	Adoption of interpretations	Article IX:2
Consensus as a rule[b]	Decisions of the Dispute Settlement Body	Article IX:1 and article 2:4 of the dispute settlement understanding
	Waiver of obligations subject to transition period	Note to article IX:3
	Addition of a plurilateral trade agreement	Article X:9
Unanimity[c]	Entry into force of certain amendments	Article X:2

[a]Decision that (1) an amendment is of such a nature that any member that has not accepted it may remain a member only with the consent of the Ministerial Conference, or that (2) an amendment does not change rights and obligations and shall therefore be effective also for those WTO members that have not accepted it.

[b]At the meeting where a decision is taken, no member present formally objects to the proposed decision.

[c]Formal acceptance by all members.

References

Blackhurst, R. Forthcoming. The WTO and the Global Economy. *The World Economy.*
General Agreement on Tariffs and Trade. 1980. *Basic Instruments and Selected Documents.* 26th supplement. Geneva: GATT Secretariat, March.
————. 1994. *The Results of the Uruguay Round of Multilateral Trade Negotiations: The Legal Texts.* Geneva: GATT Secretariat.
Keesing, D. B. Forthcoming. *Trade Practices Laid Bare: Improving the WTO Trade Policy Review Mechanism.* Washington, DC: Institute for International Economics.
Negroponte, N. 1996. *Being Digital.* New York: Vintage Books.
World Trade Organization. 1996. *World Trade Organization Annual Report 1996.* Geneva: WTO Secretariat.

2 The WTO in Relation to the Fund and the Bank: Competencies, Agendas, and Linkages

David Vines

2.1 Introduction

"Linkages" between global economic institutions are on the agenda. At the inauguration of the World Trade Organization (WTO) in 1994, the WTO's director general was required to "review with the Managing Director of the International Monetary Fund, and the President of the World Bank, the implications of the WTO's responsibilities for its cooperation with the Bretton Woods Institutions, as well as the forms such cooperation might take, with a view to achieving greater coherence in global economic policy-making."[1] As a consequence of this mandate, formal cooperation agreements have recently been signed between the WTO and the Fund and the Bank.

This paper examines what one can expect from linkages and cooperation between the WTO and the Fund and the Bank.

I argue that it is not possible to understand how the WTO should be "linked" to the Fund and the Bank without a rather clear idea of (1) what all of these institutions are for and what they now do, and (2) what their respective future agendas are. In my paper I therefore first analyze three questions.

David Vines is fellow and tutor in economics at Balliol College, Oxford; adjunct professor of economics in the Research School of Pacific Studies at the Australian National University; director of the Research Programme into Global Economic Institutions of the Economic and Social Research Council of Great Britain; and a research fellow of the Centre for Economic Policy Research in London.

The author is indebted to participants at the Stanford conference for many helpful remarks on the paper, and to Julio Nogués for an exceptionally detailed set of written comments which he sent to the conference. The ideas in the paper were initially presented at a seminar at the Australian National University on 17 September 1996, at which the author also received extremely useful comments. He has also benefited from suggestions by Heinz Arndt, John Braithwaite, Geoffrey Brennan, Paul David, and David Robertson, and from general discussions with Anne Krueger and Barry Eichengreen. This paper was in proof before the author saw Krueger (1997), which presents related and similar arguments on the IMF and the World Bank in more detail.

1. See chapter 9 by Gary Sampson in this volume for a very useful review of how this "global coherence" agenda has developed.

1. What are the functions of the Fund, the World Bank, and the WTO—that is, what problems do these institutions exist to solve?

2. In what way do these three institutions now pursue their objectives—that is, what are their competencies?

3. What are the respective future agendas of these institutions?[2]

Only then do I consider the linkage question. I focus, given the emphasis of volume, on the issue of linkages between the WTO and the Fund and between the WTO and the Bank, and I discuss the effect of such linkages on the WTO's mission. I attempt to discuss explicitly the connections between, on the one hand, functions, competencies, and agendas and, on the other hand, potentials for linkages.

My argument is simple, and my conclusion, in a way, skeptical. The IMF and the World Bank exist to do very different sorts of things from what the WTO does, and they have different sorts of agendas. They are also very different kinds of organizations, whose competencies are different from those of the WTO. Explicit cooperation between the WTO and the Fund and the Bank will, I argue, be valuable to the WTO in the pursuit of its objectives only *if* (1) the Fund and the Bank possess competencies relevant to the WTO's objectives, which (2) they would not use in the required manner without such formal cooperation. I argue that this is not the case. Instead I argue, paradoxically, that such formal cooperation may turn out to be very valuable if it helps the WTO in its own organizational development—if, in fact, it helps the WTO to become more like the Fund and the Bank as an organization. I suggest ways in which this might happen.

This argument is developed as follows. In section 2.2 I present a framework of analysis for examining organizations. In sections 2.3 and 2.4 I use this framework to describe and contrast the activities and competencies, the organizational structures, and the agendas, of the IMF, the World Bank, and—in more detail—the WTO. In section 2.5 I consider the implications of this discussion for cooperation and linkages between the WTO and the Fund and the Bank. Section 2.6 offers conclusions.

2.2   The Roles of Institutions

2.2.1   Regimes, Organizations, and Agency

It is important to clarify the meaning of the word *institution.* According to one common usage, the term *institution* is of broad scope: "a way of thought or action of some prevalence or permanence, which is embedded in the habits of a group or the customs of a people" (*Encyclopaedia of Social Sciences* 1937). In this paper, to avoid confusion, I will instead use the word *regime.*

---

2. There is a large amount of material relevant for this analysis, including a wealth of empirical detail in chapter 3 in this volume by David Henderson.

Examples of global economic regimes are international financial stability and global free trade.[3]

It is useful to distinguish the broad meaning of the word *institution* (which I will call regime) from a narrow meaning, namely, the organizations that are embedded within these regimes. In this paper, again for clarity, I will use the word *organization* to stand for *institution* in this narrow sense. Thus I will call the IMF, the World Bank, and the WTO "global economic organizations," rather than "global economic institutions."

Two ideas central to the paper flow from this distinction.

The first idea is that global economic organizations are needed to achieve and oversee global regimes: "organisations are required to overcome the transactions, implementation and enforcement costs that otherwise create problems of co-ordination and collective action and frustrate policymakers' good intentions" (Eichengreen and Ghironi 1996, 3). In more detail this argument will have two parts. First, it is costly to *achieve* solutions to global collective action problems: it is costly to assemble relevant information about the nature of the problem, costly to evaluate alternative responses, and difficult to reach consensus on the appropriate responses.[4] It is then costly to *oversee* these solutions: costly to implement agreed solutions, costly to monitor compliance with agreed solutions, and also costly to enforce them. This is a kind of Coase-theorem argument as to why these organizations are necessary.

The second idea is that these global economic organizations are not just black boxes: how they carry out their tasks is related in a complex way to both what these tasks are and what competencies the organizations have. Although the Coase theorem says why organizations are needed, the obverse to the Coase theorem is agency theory. This suggests that it is never a trivial task to ensure that those who work in an organization actually support its objectives. This appears especially true of global economic organizations whose objectives are complex and subtle.

2.2.2   Implications for Understanding Organizations

These two ideas give us criteria for understanding organizations and for discussing their effectiveness (see also Vines 1998).

Focus: The Right-Sized Sphere of Action

The question of focus of an organization is central, both focus in the range of aspects of a regime with which it is concerned, and focus in the range of activities that it carries out.

---

3. A regime is not intrinsically benign; thus the approximate opposites of the above regimes are globally unstable currency and asset markets, and global protectionism with bilaterally managed trade.

4. When discussing the difficulties of international macroeconomic policy coordination, Richard Cooper produced a now famous example about the difficulties of creating international cooperation over global public health issues. This was not obtained until there was scientific agreement about how, for example, disease is transmitted.

There may be economies of scale and scope in assembling and evaluating information, and in monitoring and enforcing solutions. There may also be advantages of issue linkage in reaching solutions, and in enforcement (where sanctions in one domain may be used against transgressions in another). These considerations point toward organizations with broad mandates, which carry out a wide range of activities, or toward the importance of explicit linkages between them.

Pointing in the opposite direction, the existence of multiple objectives can lead to incentive problems. Dixit (1996) argues persuasively that organizations need a tight focus, so that the incentives on those within them are sharp. Using a principal-agent framework, he shows, roughly speaking, that the discipline that a governance system can impose on its agent is inversely proportional to the number of different tasks that the agent is asked to fulfill. There is thus a significant trade-off here.

Competencies

Research Capacity and Policy Advice Capabilities. If they are to succeed in their tasks, organizations such as the Fund, the Bank, and the WTO may need (1) research capabilities and capacity for intellectual leadership and (2) ability to give policy advice and the capacity to advocate that this advice be adopted. Such competencies are, in fact, essential if the organization operates with significant discretion in solving the day-to-day coordination problems that are presented to it. Entrepreneurship may also be needed in dynamically mapping out the territory in which the organization attempts to solve problems, and in discovering the techniques to be used. Leadership may be essential in ensuring that the organization adapts in the required direction.

Sanctions. The ability to monitor compliance with agreed solutions, to enforce, and, if necessary, to punish deviations must be central to an organization whose purpose is to achieve and support a regime.

Resourcing

There must be adequate resources available for an organization to meet the relevant costs of achieving and overseeing solutions to collective action problems. More than this, organizations can easily dissipate the coordination gains that they are designed to promote, either if their members become engaged in distributional quarrels, or if the organization itself absorbs as rents the benefits that are to be created.

Credibility

The credibility of an organization relates to its ability in all of the dimensions referred to above: to be appropriately focused, with the appropriate capabilities, possessing sanctions, and adequately resourced. A credible organization is one that appears likely to go on doing its task well, and it calls forth a commitment of effort from its members. Since the solution of many collective action problems takes time, such commitment is likely to enhance effectiveness and to build future credibility.

2.2.3   Global Economic Organizations

The IMF, the World Bank, and the WTO are located within what appear to be three rather different regimes within the world economy.[5] These three regimes can be broadly called (1) the international monetary and financial system, (2) the global development policy regime, and (3) the global trading system.

Table 2.1 provides a summary of these regimes and organizations, and the differences between them. The points to which it draws attention are examined in detail in sections 2.3 and 2.4. It will be argued that the Fund and the Bank on the one hand and the WTO on the other hand are very different types of organizations concerning whether the global regime to which they relate is implicit (the Fund and the Bank) or explicit (the WTO); whether they are primarily involved in regime management (the Fund and the Bank) or regime construction (the WTO); whether they have research and policy advice capabilities; what kind of sanctions they have; and, finally, whether they have access to their own resources.

2.3   The IMF and the World Bank

2.3.1   The IMF and the International Monetary System

The IMF's Core Activities

The IMF began its life as a multilateral organization that administered the *international monetary system.*[6] Thus it was an organization that managed what we might call an explicit macroeconomic policy regime: a specified system of rules about fixed exchange rates explicitly constraining the policies of member governments, in the global interest.

The IMF now has a very different role, in the carrying out of which there are two core activities (see Rodrik 1995; Fischer 1995). First, it has become essentially an organization that conducts research and offers advice on macroeconomic policies for individual—primarily less developed—countries. Second, the Fund makes loans: because it was initially established to administer a system of fixed exchange rates, it was given at its birth the ability to lend in the defense of such fixed exchange rates, and this ability has been transformed into a more general capability to lend at a time of balance-of-payments crisis, whatever the exchange rate regime. The Fund's organizational structure is tightly focused on these two aspects: preparation of confidential internal

---

5. Of course this simplifies, and there are overlaps.
6. See Vines (1997) for an extended version of the arguments in this section.

Table 2.1   Global Economic Regimes and Organizations: A Sketch Map

Regime and Organization	Aspect of Regime and Activity of Organization	Type of Influence Wielded by Organization	Type of Sanctions That Support Influence	Organization Has Intellectual Leadership Capability?	Organization Has Policy Advice and Advocacy Capability?	Organization Has Access to Own Resources?
International financial and monetary system: IMF	Macroeconomic stability (1) Research and policy assistance	Constraint on national policies		Yes	Yes	Yes
	(2) Lending		Conditionality			
	International exchange rate regime	International surveillance (very loose)	Informal only			
	Solution to sovereign debt problems	Constraint on national policies				
	(1) Lending		Conditionality			
	(2) Debt restructuring?					
Development policy: World Bank	Development assistance (1) Research and policy assistance	Constraint on national policies		Yes	Yes	Yes
	(2) Lending		Conditionality			
	"Other" development issues	?	?			
Global trading system: WTO	Solving collective action problems in trade (1) Constraining domestic rent seeking	Global rules	Dispute settlement "Civil law" type	Not yet	Not yet	No
	(2) "Strategic trade"	Regulatory structure	May become more difficult			

macroeconomic analyses of its members' economies, and carrying out missions that negotiate lending programmes (IMF adjustment programmes).

The usefulness of an organization with these two capabilities results from the inability of many developing countries to satisfactorily formulate and implement macroeconomic policy, and the difficulties that may exist in convincing markets that macroeconomic adjustment is under way when it is. The Fund's two core activities, directed toward addressing these problems, contain a mutually reinforcing set of features, of the kind discussed in section 2.2, which give it strength and effectiveness as an organization. Its ability to attach "conditionality" to its loans depends fundamentally on its research, and policy analysis and advice functions: the research function gives the Fund a competitive advantage in the provision of such information. Conditionality means that the advice will be taken, and that the money will be repaid: sanctions are available in that the nonrepayment of multilateral international debt carries a heavy penalty. And the fact that the money will be repaid means that the research function can be afforded out of the seigniorage associated with the loan. This package of competencies thus contains its own resourcing. This is an extraordinarily coherent package: it is possible to argue that, as a result of bringing them together, the Fund has become the most effective international organization in history.

Note that this package of activities relates to the failure or potential failure of national macroeconomic policies. They are *not* intrinsically activities of international coordination. They are administered bilaterally between the Fund and the nation concerned. And they are *not* carried out under the banner of the kind of explicit rules that the WTO writes.

Nevertheless, there are important senses in which the IMF does sustain a global macroeconomic policy regime. First, its existence enables rich countries to assist in the solution of macroeconomic problems in the poorer countries while enabling these richer countries to hold back from direct bilateral political power relations with the poorer countries; we might say that by doing this the Fund sustains what is, in effect, an implicit regime. Second, considerable effort in the Fund is devoted to the review of country programs by functional departments to ensure consistency of treatment of countries in similar circumstances (for example, by the Fiscal Affairs Department and, in particular, the Policy Development and Review Department). Many observers have commented on the coherence and consistency of the internal IMF intellectual tradition, which underpins its advice (see Clark 1996c; Eichengreen and Kenen 1994). This state of affairs was well summed up recently by the current managing director: "intellectual discipline will be maintained while I am here—we deal with crises and we cannot have our troops rethinking strategy on the field of battle" (quoted in Clark 1996a, 23). Even if the Fund does not administer a regime of codified substantive rules, its research and policy advice functions produce very strong procedural rules that lay down broadly what is appropriate to do in what circumstances, even if a large and important degree of discretion is required in the operation of these rules.[7] Thus—in the sense that the same rules are applied everywhere—what results can be called a global regime.

Agenda Issues and Organizational Challenges

One can argue that there are at least two major items on the future agenda for the IMF. Both are difficult. Why this is so contains important messages for organizational effectiveness.

The first case is that of international macroeconomic policy coordination. Ever since the collapse of the Bretton Woods fixed exchange rate system in 1971, it has been unclear just what role the Fund should play in the process of *global* surveillance of macroeconomic policies. There are good reasons for this. Group of Seven (G7) countries are now committed to the operation of their monetary policies in the pursuit of anti-inflation objectives in a way that is inconsistent with commitments to fixed, or semifixed, exchange rates: independent use of national monetary policy in controlling inflation implies continuous relative movements in interest rates, as different inflationary shocks hit different countries in different ways and so require different interest rate movements. These interest rate movements would lead to unmanageable movements of international capital between countries, so large as to make it impossible to defend a fixed exchange rate system. As a consequence, it would be a mistake for the Fund as an organization to become involved in the policing of a semifixed exchange rate regime.[8] As a senior IMF official has said to me, any attempt by the Fund to become involved in this policing in such circumstances would not only fail, but also bring the organization into disrepute.

It is true that there appears to be a need for more coordination of macroeconomic policies internationally than currently exists. In terms of the analysis of section 2.2, however, the IMF currently lacks the relevant competencies: there are deep problems as to agreement on appropriate policies, on monitoring, on enforcement, and on sanctions. It is important for the Fund as an organization not to commit itself to this activity if it cannot do it properly.

The second area is that of international sovereign debt negotiations. Without the adoption of some reforms, the following appears to be a likely outcome of a future debt crisis: borrower will not pay (and politically cannot pay); a liquidity injection is not available (unlike the Mexican case); and lenders cannot agree on how to write the debts down. That would leave the borrower country financially crippled for an extended period. It would most likely be more difficult to resolve than were the sovereign debt problems of the 1980s, because borrowing is now not from a few large, easy-to-negotiate-with banks, but from a vast number of anonymous, unorganized, and probably litigious bondholders: the collective action problem is very great.

---

7. I am using the distinction between substantive and procedural rules in a different way from that proposed by Kahler (1995), to characterize the rules that describe how a regime is operated, rather than to characterize the rules that govern how it is established.

8. For advocacy of such target zones, see Williamson 1985, 1994; Williamson and Miller 1987; Bergsten and Williamson 1994; Mundell 1993; and McKinnon 1988, 1993.

The details of the possible reforms need not concern us here.[9]

Our concern is, however, with the role for the IMF as an organization; of relevance to this is that not only are the collective action problems in this area large but also agreement on the creation of the required new international regime would be hard to achieve, much harder than for agreement concerning the Fund's "core activities." Indeed, as the analysis of section 2.2 suggests, agreement may be well nigh impossible when there is not a shared view on the appropriate policies.[10] Furthermore, there are very significant legal obstacles to obtaining a collective action solution, since these would require overturning the current legal rights of bondholders (see Eichengreen and Portes 1995). Finally, it is not even clear that the Fund is the right organization to oversee such a regime, since the Fund might face a conflict of interest that makes it unacceptable as the broker of the collective action solution: it might be required both to oversee the write-down procedure and to advise the defaulting country as to appropriate policies.

The resolution of sovereign debt problems is a genuinely international problem, and it appears to require the construction of a new international regime appropriate to new forms of international intermediation through bonds. The important point to notice here is the difficulties in the way of the Fund as an organization taking the lead in solving them. The Fund as an organization will be ill-advised to try, if a way cannot be seen through these difficulties.

2.3.2 The World Bank and the Global Development Policy Regime

The World Bank's Core Activities

The World Bank began as an organization for funneling capital to the wartorn global periphery in the face of liquidity-constrained capital markets; it was never an organization managing an explicit global regime.[11] With the integration of global capital markets that has taken place in the past thirty years, the initial conception of the Bank now makes little sense. The World Bank now owes its strength and distinctiveness to bringing together into one organization

9. The following list, taken from Portes and Vines (1997), is what appears necessary: (1) contractual provisions, to be broadly incorporated in international debt contracts, which would help to facilitate debtholders' decision making and hence make decisions on balance sheet write-down possible; (2) provisions for a debtor government to impose a stay, supported by stopping payments, assisted by IMF lending into arrears; (3) enforced bondholder representation in any sovereign debt "bankruptcy" procedures; (4) qualified majority voting on any write-down; and (5) enforced sharing procedures for the proceeds from such a write-down.

10. "The Clinton Administration is likely to support expanded financial resources for the IMF, since the United States is the leading source of portfolio capital to emerging markets and the country which underwrote the largest share of the Mexican bailout. . . . But other high-income countries may not agree. . . . The most prosperous and financially secure developing countries, not consulted by the G-10, may be suspicious of innovations that acknowledge the possibility, however slight, that debts might one day have to be restructured. Thus, as was the case during the Mexican meltdown in 1995, it will be difficult for the international community to achieve consensus" (Portes and Vines 1997, 41).

11. See also Gilbert 1997; Gilbert et al. 1997; and House and Vines 1997. I am grateful to Chris Gilbert for many helpful discussions about the material in this section.

a number of activities. The core International Bank for Reconstruction and Development (IBRD) function bundles together lending, development research, and development assistance—all glued together by the Bank's ability to exercise conditionality. The International Development Association (IDA) function is similar except that the lending is "concessional" and is effectively aid. The Bank is now best thought of as a multilateral organization that enables richer countries to assist with the development problems of the poorer countries without entering into direct bilateral political power relations with them; we might say that by doing this the Bank sustains what is an implicit "global development policy" regime.

The importance of the World Bank as an organization arises, I would argue, for reasons that are similar to those advanced above for the IMF: it can capture some of the gains from its conditionality. The Bank does this by borrowing funds from private capital markets (at a AAA rating) and charging a markup on these funds when it lends them out to clients (at much lower rates than they could obtain on the private markets because such loans—if available at all— would carry a high risk premium). It uses this markup both to support aid and to fund its research and its development-promotion functions. The strength of those functions in creating an organizational capacity and oral tradition of knowledge within the Bank, in turn, makes it possible for the Bank to impose conditionality in a manner that actually does add value to the projects for which it lends. Such an argument suggests that, if the Bank did not exist or it were privatized, then neither the research nor the development-promotion functions would survive, since they both support, and are supported by, the imposition of conditionality, which could not itself survive. The Bank would become like any other moderately large international bank.

Notice that such conditionality will not only raise expected repayments to the World Bank, as the enforcer of conditionality, but in forcing the adoption of good policies, it will increase returns to private-sector banks who lend alongside it. The World Bank can therefore generate an externality, which further promotes development by encouraging the inflow of private funds into its client states. In due course the supply of funds to its borrowing clients will increase, both as development proceeds and as funds are attracted as a result of the Bank's own actions. This, in turn, will mean that the Bank's clients will be able to obtain funds from private markets without paying the markup to the World Bank that it uses to support its research and development-promotion function, and without the need to submit to the Bank's conditionality. These countries can, and should, *graduate* from borrowing from the Bank.

In sum, this view of the World Bank is driven by the analysis of section 2.2: its distinctiveness and strength derive from the way it bundles together three functions: lending, development research, and development assistance. By lending for approved development projects, it is able to assist governments to benefit from its development experience. That experience—together with the sanctions made possible by conditionality—ensures a higher success rate on loans than might otherwise be attained. This success pays for the research, which underpins the assistance.

Agenda Issues and Organizational Challenges

One can argue that there are, for the Bank as for the Fund, major items on the agenda that contain important messages for organizational effectiveness.

The new president of the World Bank, James Wolfensohn, has conducted a review of the Bank's activities, which was presented to the Bank's executive board under the banner of a new "Strategic Compact" on 13 March 1997. This review identified two strategic issues. First, its IBRD lending now appears to be problematic. At a time when capital flows to developing countries are booming, the IBRD is only lending at 55 percent of its capacity. The high-growth "middle income" developing countries no longer need or want the World Bank; they dislike the conditions attached to its loans—about policies that the country should pursue (for example, about the environment)—and have little difficulty in borrowing from other sources. One view is that the Bank's core activity is outdated product. Second, too many of the Bank's projects and programs appear to fail or to underperform, notwithstanding the fact that the Bank's lending is supported by conditionality.[12]

It can be argued that these difficulties arise from a loss of focus by the Bank on its core activity; to overcome this the bank needs to reestablish its purpose with greater coherence. It should not be denied that the bundle of competencies brought together in the Bank's core activities are more complex, diffuse, and "difficult" to manage than those of the IMF (Naïm 1994). This is partly because the Bank's mission to lend can conflict with its concern for microeconomic development. But it is especially because "development" contains a much more complex agenda than something like macroeconomic stabilization: "development" is interconnected with concerns about, for example, gender and the environment, which are exceedingly difficult to integrate into an overall framework. In a revealing contrast, Arnold Harberger recently suggested that "while [the image] of the Fund is like a commercial bank in that there is a single corporate line in dealing with the outside world," that of the Bank "is something like a traveling seminar" (quoted in Clark 1996a, 23).

This could be changed. In his comments on this paper Julio Nogués documents the contribution made by the transformation of the Bank's intellectual thinking in the early 1980s toward open, liberal trade policies, and concludes that the Bank made a fundamental contribution to the understanding in the third world of the importance of trade liberalization. Extraordinarily valuable though this work has been, the Bank could now do more. I completely agree with his comments that "trade and trade liberalization topics have to be

---

12. Press reports emanating from the Bank at the time of the release of the Strategic Compact suggested that "34 percent of projects were failing to meet their objectives, including expected return on investments."

resurrected from where they are standing now in the hierarchy of the Bank's objectives and come to occupy, once again, a predominant role." Nogués argues that this should be done (1) because promoting the long-range balanced growth of international trade is one of the main purposes of the Bank and (2) because the goal of universal free trade has never been so close. I would simply add that we know so much more than we did fifteen years ago about the benefits of openness. It is around this objective that the core research and policy-advice functions of the Bank could be focused, sharpened, and strengthened,[13] and its organizational effectiveness greatly strengthened.

2.4   The WTO and the Global Trade Regime

2.4.1   The WTO's Core Activities: Rule Writing and Enforcement

The core activity of the WTO relates to the negotiation and implementation of explicit *global rules* on government policies relating to cross-border trade. This activity is explicitly international; it relates to the treatment by one government of internationally traded goods and services produced in other states, relative to those produced in third states and within its own state.

Quite unlike the Fund, whose primary output is adjustment assistance (advice and loans) to individual countries, or the Bank, whose primary output is development assistance (advice and loans) to individual countries, the primary output of the WTO is rule writing and enforcement of an explicit global regime. It is an organization that *writes rules* and, in so doing, makes laws with which its contracting parties agree to abide. Unlike the Fund and the Bank, whose effectiveness ultimately stems from a combination of an internal knowledge base and an ability to exert conditionality on individual countries, the effectiveness of the WTO rests upon its combination of a global forum in which rules can be brokered and a dispute settlement process in which they can be enforced.

2.4.2   Reciprocity

Neoclassical trade theory argues that free trade is first-best for individual nations considered separately, so that unilateral trade liberalization is desirable for individual countries. Much of the worldwide drive to liberalization in the past ten years has indeed been genuinely unilateral (and the World Bank has played a critical part in encouraging this process). But if this were all that there was to liberalization then there would be no collective action problem for an international organization to solve.

The collective action problem that the WTO addresses arises from the need

---

13. For an excellent summary of the evidence and advocacy of the relevant measures, see World Bank (1996). For more technical and persuasive evidence on the "convergence" issue, see Sachs and Warner (1995).

for reciprocity in trade liberalization: the fact is that there are kinds of trade liberalization that individual states will not pursue unilaterally (see, for example, Arndt 1994; Johnson 1976; Bhagwati and Irwin 1987). For such liberalization to occur, states must "trade concessions": state A, desiring liberalization of a particular kind from state B, must make an offer of liberalization itself, which it would not do otherwise. When there is a need for reciprocity, trade negotiations take on the nature of a prisoner's dilemma, in which only cooperative solutions can yield liberalization outcomes.

There are three reasons why this is important, relating to three different kinds of departures from standard neoclassical competitive-markets case for free trade.

National Market Power

The first case for reciprocity arises when nations have market power, even if no producers or consumers do, so that the structure of all individual markets remains internationally competitive. In this case trade liberalization leads to a shift in national demands toward imports, which if the country is large, will raise their price.[14] In this case the unilateral "optimal tariff" is not zero.

To use global reciprocity negotiations in order to remedy optimal tariff resistance to unilateral liberalization is, in principle, simple. It requires simply to widen the group of countries enough, and to widen the agenda of trade liberalization enough, so that there are sufficient net benefits for all the individual participants to offset any remaining terms of trade deterioration. However, protection undertaken explicitly to exploit national market power in the global economy is rare: this is the least important form of protectionism.

Rent Seeking in National Polities

The second case for reciprocity relates to the determination of trade policies by national governments subject to rent seeking. When products are intensive in the use of factors of production whose political support is important for election, protection can be a device for increasing governmental welfare, even if it does not raise national welfare.

To use global reciprocity negotiations in order to remedy rent-seeking resistance to liberalization at the national level is also, in principle, simple. It requires simply to widen the group of countries, and the agenda of liberalization, enough so that rent seekers perceive sufficient additional rents from market access abroad to drop their opposition to liberalization.[15]

14. Put another way, to pay for the extra imports associated with trade liberalization, exports must be increased; if the nation is of nonnegligible size in export markets, then the extra export volumes will require lower prices.

15. There is a puzzle. Unilateral liberalization also creates (potential) rents for the exports, which will be stimulated by the real currency depreciation associated with the liberalization. If global reciprocity negotiations can buy off opposition to protectionism, why cannot the domestic politics of unilateral liberalization? Is it that, in the latter, possibly different industries are involved? Or is it that the rent-seeking polity does not understand the macroeconomics of the real depreciation that will follow in the wake of unilateral liberalization?

Trade under Imperfect Competition

The third, and much more difficult, reason for reciprocity relates to international trade in markets that are imperfectly competitive. In this case "strategic protectionism" considerations arise from the interaction of two features. When there are large economies of scale, or where there are large gains from R&D and from learning economies, prices need to be set above marginal costs. And where there are entry barriers, because products are imperfect substitutes, or because of network externalities, or because of the threat of predatory pricing, prices can also be above average costs. In this case there are rents that a nation as a whole can earn from protection: protecting production that might not otherwise exist, or ensuring a larger level of output than would take place under free trade, can raise national welfare. It could even, in some circumstances, raise global welfare.

Reciprocity negotiations concerning this area are exceptionally complex to carry out. It is also not at all clear that there are good easy-to-write, easy-to-enforce rules available in this area. But this area is increasingly where the important questions lie.

2.4.3   The WTO as a Very Particular Form of Organization

The conventional view of the GATT as an institution may be put in the following way. First, the GATT was a contract signed by governments that became contracting parties to it. They undertook obligations and acquired rights. Second, it was clearly understood that the GATT was an institution in which the secretariat intrinsically had no power: only contracting parties could interpret the contract; should differences arise in the interpretation, a dispute settlement panel and other elements of a dispute settlement mechanism would come into play (see Sampson 1996; Jackson, chap. 5 in this volume; Quraishi 1996). This dispute settlement process has been strengthened in an important way in the establishment of the WTO, for example, by removing the offending party's veto of the establishment of a panel and the adoption of a panel's report. Nevertheless, this process operates in a way analogous to the civil law—aggrieved parties must bring suits against offending parties; there are no sanctions possessed by the institution itself.

The WTO is gradually evolving away from this original GATT model. It is becoming much more a legal framework of regulatory review. This is a move into a constitutional structure, or a rule-based governance system, away from a mere structure as a contract. Quraishi (1996) discusses the possible range of techniques for implementation in this less clearly defined, but richer organizational structure. These range from preemptive measures that create a disposition to conform from within (such as international consultation, or the secretariat's persuasion of national representatives to act effectively as conduits of the WTO code), to procedures that ensure compliance (such as notification procedures and collection of information by the WTO), to surveillance mechanisms, to, finally, procedures for correcting noncompliance, which would make possible proceedings by the WTO itself against its members.

Nevertheless, this evolution is in its early stages; the WTO remains, like the GATT before it, a very peculiar organization. Its structure consists of a Ministerial Conference beneath which sits the General Council, particular councils, and a proliferation of committees—all bodies of national delegates. The role of the secretariat, beneath the director general, is essentially to service these committees. This arrangement is ad hoc, and the relationships between the committees are extremely unstructured. Some have argued that this structure of the WTO is unworkable. The origins can be found in the way in which the WTO is the sum total of a series of negotiations, which were pursued along a series of separate tracks. The end result was, and is, a series of understandings rather than, yet, a real organization.

2.4.4   Agenda Issues: The New Imperfect Competition Environment

When the original GATT was established, its ambitions in relation to reciprocity benefits were essentially limited to the first two kinds described above—agreements to constrain "optimal" tariff setting and agreements by policymakers to place constraints on rent seeking. It concerned itself essentially with tariff reductions, on goods alone (not on services), and excluded agriculture. It pursued its work through a series of rounds of negotiations of tariff cuts. But gradually these extended beyond tariffs, first to a consideration of nontariff barriers (especially initially "voluntary" export restraints) and then into complex imperfect competition issues (especially, initially, antidumping). That widening of the agenda continued apace in the Uruguay Round and in the creation of the WTO with the liberalization of markets for services (which is intrinsically an imperfect-competition area) and with the tightening of the global regime on intellectual property (also an intrinsically imperfect-competition area).

Difficulties are likely to grow, with the increasing attention that is being given to the integration of rules against restrictive practices into the multilateral trading system, and with the need for and prospects of regulating regulatory regimes. These are all set to involve, in some way or another, moves away from a "code-type" approach to dealing with specific problems, from "shallow integration" to "deep integration."

Such dealing with specific problems is bound to undermine the "core canons" of the code approach.

In getting to where it has, the WTO has so far paid allegiance to four core canons. These are the most-favored-nation (MFN) principle (article 1); the national treatment obligation (article 9, designed to ensure that border commitments are not circumvented by nonborder measures); the principle that the WTO places restraints only on its governmental contracting parties and not on private-sector actors; and the no-process-measures principle. These principles have constrained and defined the nature of the reciprocity deals and the rules that the GATT/WTO has written. All of these principles appear to be there because of what the WTO *is,* namely, a contract among governments, having rather limited leadership, research, and interpretive capacity, and without the normal organizational processes of governance exercised by a board over its constituent parts. It is essentially a fragile body, and the rule-writing process and the rule-enforcing process seem unlikely to survive in the face of sustained pressure to break down these principles. Yet as the arguments for reciprocity move into the area of imperfect competition, it seems intrinsically likely that these canons will come under increasing strain.

The MFN principle is at risk when negotiations turn from simple border measures to more complex trade facilitation issues. One paradigm example is standards setting in high-tech industries with strong network characteristics, such as telecommunications and computing. Agreement on standards may be essential for coordination reasons. But compatibility standards can become a means of leveraging the control of one or other component of the emerging global information infrastructure into a position of market power in delivery of services (see David and Steinmuller 1996; David and Shurmer 1996). Given that an agreement will favor one standard at the expense of another, an MFN requirement may present difficulties. Hoekman and Mavroidis (1995) outline two basic issues that arise. First, foreign firms may want to participate in the development of national standards, but domestic firms may not favor this and may seek to keep them out. Second, procedures used to determine conformity of foreign goods to national standards may be used to restrict market access. In both of these areas there is room for bilateral and possibly significant log-rolling deals that clearly deviate from a broadly construed MFN principle. The trade regime may therefore need to begin to regulate the standards-setting process in an ongoing manner, in the interest of the MFN principle. This is an awesome thought.

National treatment is under threat due to, for example, subsidies in relation to R&D. A characteristic of high-tech industries is that governments tend to support "precompetitive" and "basic" R&D, and this was allowed in the Uruguay Round agreement. But drawing the line between this and "ordinary" subsidies is likely to prove increasingly difficult and require the administration of a regime that requires case-by-case interpretation (see the long and thoughtful discussion in Hoekman and Mavroidis 1995).

The "constrain only the contracting parties" requirement is under threat for two reasons. First, there are inexorable pressures toward the internationalization of competition policy. The globalization of many markets that are traditionally highly regulated—for example, telecommunications, transport (including air transport), and utilities such as water and power—will see pressures to globalize regulation. The growth of other markets in which there are prospects of global market dominance—for example, computing (and information generally) and very large equipment (such as aircraft)—will give rise to related pressures. Antidumping practice already violates this "constrain only

the contracting parties" requirement; even a resolution of antidumping para-
doxes will require large moves toward a managed international competition
regime (see Holmes 1995 for a brief discussion). Second, the new global intellectual property regime—although in principle requiring only that the contracting parties themselves carry out enforcement in their domestic courts—
may well see the WTO become involved in the administration of constraints
on offending private-sector parties.

The "no-process-measures" principle is under serious threat from the trade
and the environment and trade and labor standards agendas discussed by Kym
Anderson (chap. 8 in this volume). Frieder Roessler (chap. 7 in this volume)
argues persuasively that significant damage has also been done to this principle
by incorporating the intellectual property regime within WTO rules.

2.4.5   Organizational Challenges

In terms of the categories discussed in section 2.2, there are very many challenges facing the WTO. As an organization, it now appears to be severely overburdened (see Woolcock 1996). Faced with the huge range of issues identified
above, and in the Uruguay Round (see Krueger's introduction in this volume),
how is its focus to be achieved? It is at present dependent on the emergence of
sufficient enthusiasm from its Ministerial Conference meetings, and the evidence suggests that it has been difficult to maintain a degree of enthusiasm
proportionate to the vast size of its work program. This is true both for implementing the decisions made in the Uruguay Round and for developing a sufficiently innovative approach to the "new trade issues" that the WTO will be
required to deal with. The WTO appears to need a different kind of leadership,
more research capability, and the structure to solve more of the day-to-day
coordination problems that will be presented to it, and to give policy advice
arising from these solutions. Where will the resourcing necessary for this come
from? How will its sanctions, freedom from rent seeking, and overall credibility be preserved?

2.5   Global Economic Organizations, the Global Agenda, and Linkages

I have now completed my survey of the core activities and competencies and
the organizational structures of the IMF, the World Bank, and the WTO. I have
also considered their most important problematic agenda areas: for the Fund,
finding a role in global macroeconomic policy coordination and sovereign debt
issues; for the Bank, creating a sharper intellectual focus on the trade liberalization and trade agenda; and for the WTO, finding the capacities and organizational competencies to deal with the new trade-under-imperfect-competition
agenda.

I now consider the issue of cooperation and linkage between the WTO and
the Fund and the Bank. I argue that such linkages and cooperation may well
help to bring progress in the WTO's problematic agenda area, the objective of

dealing with the new trade-under-imperfect-competition agenda. However, I argue that they may do this most effectively by helping the WTO to acquire the capacity and resources that it needs to meet its challenges.

2.5.1   Coordination versus Competence

It is natural to argue that, although "the task of international institutions [organizations] is coordination among countries . . . the effective governance of the system requires coordination among institutions [organizations]" (Clark 1996b). In this section I query whether this presumption necessarily points to the desirability of formal coordination mechanisms between international organizations.

Coordination among countries has been extensively analyzed. The case for it rests upon spillovers from the policy actions of one country onto the policy targets of another country: cooperation between countries can help to internalize these externalities. Analysis of such spillovers underpins, for example, the discussions of multilateral trade liberalization in section 2.4. But, at the same time, the analysis of macroeconomic policy coordination in section 2.3 also showed why such coordination might not be pursued—even when at first sight it appears potentially desirable—because of the manner in which it infringes on the ability of the policy authorities to pursue key objectives (in that case inflation).

The latter type of coordination—among international organizations—has been much less extensively analyzed by economists. The case for it rests upon spillovers from the policy actions of one organization onto the policy targets of another organization: cooperation between organizations can help to internalize these externalities. A good example of the kinds of issues involved comes from relations between the IMF and the World Bank in the 1980s.[16] There were, first of all, complaints at the time that IMF macroeconomic adjustment programs were having damaging effects on investment and longer-term growth in developing countries. Second, there were complaints that the investment spending on development projects supported by the World Bank led to macroeconomic outcomes that jeopardized IMF adjustment programs.

There can be no *presumption* that the latter kind of cooperation really *is* needed for the effective governance of the international system. The issue has been studied by political scientists under the heading of "overlapping games" (see Hoekman 1989; Roessler, chap. 7 in this volume). There are two diametrically opposed concerns. Clearly, without cooperation, the negative spillovers from the pursuit of its own objectives by one organization might impact negatively on the objectives of the other organization. This is a feature of the above IMF/World Bank example. Conversely, concern by each organization with the objectives of the other organization might hamper its ability to achieve not just its own objective, but any objective at all. "Goal overload" might result, caus-

---

16. The issues that follow are discussed extensively in Corbo et al. (1989).

ing the organization to cease to be competent at *whatever* it does; as already discussed, "focus" is important.

2.5.2   An Example: Linkages between the IMF and the World Bank

The example of the Fund and the Bank just given provides an interesting insight into the conflict between cooperation and competence. The initial response of the Fund and the Bank was for each organization to accept some responsibility for the objectives of the other organization. The first set of concerns led to IMF programs that were designed to promote "adjustment with growth." The second set of concerns led to the explicit imposition of macroeconomic conditionality by the World Bank.

But the ultimate solutions to these spillover problems were very different. (1) The Fund retreated from explicit concern with longer-term growth issues, in order to avoid blunting its concentration on macroeconomic stability, the issue about which (as we have said) it has knowledge and skills, and in the pursuit of which (through lending coupled with conditionality) it has sanctions.[17] (2) In order to stop imposing macroeconomic conditionality that was, at times, at variance with that imposed by the Fund, the Bank retreated from the area of macroeconomic conditionality (in which it possessed neither the knowledge or the skills of the Fund). To this end it entered into a formal agreement with the Fund, according to which it now entrusts the assessment of macroeconomic performance of borrowing countries to the Fund. Since 1989, when this agreement was reached, the approval of certain types of loan disbursement by the World Bank has had to receive the approval of the Fund.

Notice that these two outcomes are the kinds that might be suggested by the work by Dixit (1996) on "focus," already cited. In the first case, one can argue that the Fund's need to focus on areas in which it had competence overrode its giving explicit concern to the objectives of the Bank, and thus that the goal of competence overruled the goal of explicit cooperation. In the second case, the outcome was different: the Bank's focus on its area of competence was preserved, yet explicit cooperation with the objectives of the Fund was maintained, by means of a specific agreement. That agreement formally delegates to the Fund the responsibility for an aspect of the Bank's imposition of sanctions (namely, the analysis necessary for the imposition of macroeconomic conditionality, and the monitoring of compliance with it).

2.5.3   Cooperation, Competence, and the WTO's Linkage Agreements with the IMF and the World Bank

Formal agreements concerning cooperation were reached between the WTO and the IMF and the World Bank in November 1996 (WTO 1996). These

---

17. Of course there are always elements of a trade-off between short-term stabilization and long-term growth in macroeconomic policy. This trade-off is most obvious in relation to fiscal policy. For an extensive formal analysis, see Weale et al. 1989.

agreements essentially provide for (1) the granting of observer status to the secretariat of the WTO at relevant meetings of the Fund and the Bank (and vice versa for Fund and Bank staff at relevant meetings of the WTO); and (2) consultation between the secretariat of the WTO and the staff of the Fund and the Bank concerning matters of mutual interest (essentially trade-policy-related issues).

Taken at face value, these agreements might, in themselves, help to resolve spillovers between the policy actions of the WTO and the Bank and the Fund. Gary Sampson (chap. 9 in this volume), for example, presents these agreements as directed toward underlying contradictions and inconsistencies between monetary, finance, and trade policies in the world economy. And one can indeed point to the kind of problems that he identifies: the damaging effect of currency fluctuations on international trade, or the contradiction in working to solve the debt problems of developing countries through promoting export expansion, while advanced countries have in place trade measures that block this export expansion.

However, these problems do not appear to me to be things that formal WTO agreements with the Fund and the Bank are likely to help eradicate. As we have already seen, all of these issues—currency fluctuations, debt, export expansion, market access—are now on the separate agendas of the Fund, the Bank, and the WTO. What is not yet clear is how an agreement among these organizations would bring competence by one organization to help achieve the objectives of the other. Thus the case is very different from the example of the formal agreement between the Fund and the Bank discussed above.

Nevertheless, even if these agreements do not lead to formal coordination mechanisms, it may be that they operate at the level of "community creation." Geneva is a long way from Washington, and it is easy to imagine that WTO staff can feel isolated from those other organizations, thousands of miles away, which are dedicated to promoting the "Washington consensus" of sound money and free trade. These agreements may well—through meetings and consultations to which they give rise—reinforce a sense of common general commitment to the same elements of this consensus amongst the professional staff of all of the WTO, the Fund and the Bank. They can nurture a shared epistemic community.

A further, more substantive possibility is that these agreements might serve essentially as "framework agreements," making possible subsequent precise and formal forms of collaboration between the WTO and the Fund and the Bank. If these present agreements make that possible, when needed in the future—and especially if they make that possible in ways that would not have been possible without them—then they will have been valuable. To enhance the capacities of organizations to cooperate with each other, in order to enable them to deal collectively with (as yet unseen) contingencies is prudent.

Finally, it may be that the real significance of these agreements is that they play an important part in the necessary process of strengthening the organization competencies of the WTO. Because the WTO Secretariat is now charged with helping to achieve greater coherence in global economic policymaking, this could well strengthen the hand of those who would endow the secretariat with stronger research and intellectual leadership functions, greater capacities for giving policy advice and greater freedom to advocate policy positions, and greater resourcing. All these things have been identified above as missing.

This last possibility enables one to take an imaginative view of the call for the WTO to be involved in overseeing the development of coherence in global policy-making, and about the cooperative agreements with the Fund and the Bank that have emerged from this call. As discussed in the previous section, the WTO is at present immensely overburdened. The call for the WTO to be thus involved appears to arise in part from the imperative for the organization both to be better resourced and to have more entrepreneurial freedom with which to push forward its tasks.

2.6   Conclusions

The WTO is an organization devoted to developing and administering rules to counter protectionism in the global trading system. It is thus par excellence an organization whose function relates to an explicit global regime. But the WTO is more devoted to the construction than to the detailed management of this global set of rules. Although the WTO's Disputes Settlement Procedure is concerned explicitly with the function of rule observance, by far the greatest amount of energy within the WTO is devoted to rule making. I have thus claimed that what the WTO *does* as an organization is very different in character from the Fund and the Bank. And I trace the central difference in what the WTO *is* as an organization in comparison to the Fund and the Bank—its lack of research leadership, its lack of policy advice capability, and its lack of resourcing—back to these differences between it and the Fund and the Bank as to what it *does*. (It is of course partly also because of its history.)

I have also argued that the nature of the problems of protectionism that the WTO needs to solve is changing, partly as a result of its own success with straightforward tariff-reduction issues. Increasingly, as the WTO moves into dealing with the difficult problems relating to the liberalization of trade under imperfect competition (in networked quasi-monopolies, in services, in areas in which intellectual property is important), it will need to write rules about regulatory regimes. This will require that the nature of the WTO as an organization change—it must inevitably take on more of the leadership, research, and advice capability that one associates with the Fund and the Bank. This will then put it in a position as a global-resource organization about trade policies, in the same way as the Fund now is about macroeconomic policies and the Bank is about microeconomic policies generally.

All of this will inevitably require resourcing issues to be addressed. And it will certainly take time, maybe a very long time.

In the face of this imperative, the WTO as an organization has needed bargaining tools (1) to get the decisions that are required in relation to these "new issues" work programs to be taken more seriously, and (2) to get sufficient staff resources to enable it to take the lead on these new issues (while also processing the existing work program arising from the Uruguay Round). The call for the WTO to be involved in overseeing the development of coherence in global policymaking appears to arise in part from this imperative for the organization both to be better resourced and to have more entrepreneurial freedom with which to push forward its tasks.

If formal cooperation between the WTO and the Bank can help lead to required development of the WTO's organizational competencies then that will be a highly beneficial—if perhaps initially unintended—outcome.

In the meantime the World Bank provides advice about and development assistance with unilateral trade liberalization policies for individual countries, quite independently of the progress of the WTO's multilateral trade agenda. The Bank is now deeply committed to liberalization as a core component of its policy advice (as is evident, for example, from its 1996 *Global Economic Prospects* report). And in terms of the organizational analysis at the beginning of the paper, the Bank has the capacity to focus on this set of issues, to research and lead it, to resource it, and to give policy advice to individual countries. Bank advocacy of trade policy liberalization and Bank assistance in trade policy management provides all of what, in this area, the WTO is at present organizationally incapable of providing.

There is no need for a formal agreement with the WTO to push the Bank in this direction—it is going there already. But as I argue above, it could go faster. If the agreements between the WTO and the Bank can help spur the Bank in this direction, then this will be a beneficial outcome.

References

Arndt, H. 1994. The Political Economy of Reciprocity. *Banca Nazionale Quarterly Review* 188 (September): 259–69.

Bergsten, F., and J. Williamson 1994. Is the Time Right for Target Zones or the Blueprint. In Bretton Woods Commission, *Bretton Woods: Looking to the Future.* Washington, DC: Group of Thirty.

Bhagwati, J., and D. Irwin. 1987. The Return of the Reciprocitarians: US Trade Policy Today. *World Economy* 10, no. 2: 109–30.

Clark, I. 1996a. Inside the IMF: Comparisons with Policy-Making Organisations in Canadian Governments." Photocopy.

———. 1996b. Orchestrating Governance of the International System. Talk given at a conference organized by the Reinventing Bretton Woods Committee, Paris, May.

———. 1996c. Should the IMF Become More Adaptive? Working Paper WP/96/11. Washington, DC: International Monetary Fund.

Corbo, V., M. Goldstein, and M. Khan. 1987. *Growth Oriented Adjustment Programmes.* Washington, DC: International Monetary Fund and World Bank.

David, P., and M. Shurmer. 1996. Formal Standards Setting for Global Telecommunications and Information Services: Towards Institutional Renovation or Collapse? *Telecommunications Policy* 20, no. 10: 789–816.

David, P., and E. Steinmuller. 1996. Standards, Trade, and Competition in the Emerging Global Information Infrastructure Environment. *Telecommunications Policy* 20, no. 10: 817–30.

Dixit, A. 1996. *The Making of Economic Policy: A Transaction-Cost Politics Perspective.* Cambridge: MIT Press.

Eichengreen, B., and F. Ghironi. 1996. European Monetary Unification and International Monetary Co-operation. University of California at Berkeley, April. Photocopy.

Eichengreen, B., and P. Kenen. 1994. Managing the World Economy under the Bretton Woods System: An Overview. In *Managing the World Economy: Fifty Years after Bretton Woods,* ed. P. Kenen. Washington, DC: Institute for International Economics.

Eichengreen, B., and R. Portes. 1995. *Crisis, What Crisis? Orderly Workouts for Sovereign Debtors.* London: Centre for Economic Policy Research.

Fischer, S. 1995. The World Bank and the IMF at Fifty. Paper presented at the conference "The Future of the International System and Its Institutions," International Centre for Monetary and Banking Studies, Geneva, 2–4 September 1993. Published in *The International Monetary System,* ed. Hans Genberg, 171–200. Heidelberg: Springer Verlag.

Gilbert, C. 1997. Wanted: A Vision for the World Bank. *Newsletter of the ESRC Global Economic Institutions Research Programme* (London: CEPR) no. 5: 2–3.

Gilbert, C., R. Hopkins, A. Powell, and A. Roy. 1997. The World Bank: Its Functions and Its Future. Global Economic Institutions Research Program Discussion Paper no. 15. London: Centre for Economic Policy Research.

Hoekman, B. 1989. Determining the Need for Issue Linkages in Multilateral Trade Negotiations. *International Organization* 43: 693–714.

Hoekman, B., and P. Mavroidis. 1995. Policy Externalities and High-Tech Rivalry: Competition and Multilateral Cooperation beyond the WTO. Geneva: World Trade Organization. Photocopy.

Holmes, P. 1995. International Competition Policy and the WTO. *Newsletter of the ESRC Global Economic Institutions Research Programme* (London: CEPR) no. 2: 2–6.

House, B., and D. Vines. 1997. The Future of the World Bank. *Newsletter of the ESRC Global Economic Institutions Research Programme* (London: CEPR) no. 6: 6–11.

Johnson, H. G. 1976. Trade Negotiations and the New International Monetary System. Geneva: Graduate Institute of International Studies.

Kahler, M. 1995. *International Institutions and the Political Economy of Integration.* Washington, DC: Brookings Institution.

Krueger, A. 1997. Whither the World Bank and the IMF. Stanford University. Photocopy.

McKinnon, R. 1988. Monetary and Exchange Rate Policies for International Stability: A Proposal. *Journal of Economic Perspectives* (winter): 83–103.

———. 1993. The Rules of the Game: International Money in Historical Perspective. *Journal of Economic Literature* 31 (March): 1–44.

Mundell, R. A. 1993. Prospects for International Monetary Reform. Paper presented at the "Conference on the Future of the International Monetary System and Its Institutions," International Centre for Monetary and Banking Studies, Geneva, 2–4 September.

Naïm, M. 1994. The World Bank: Its Role, Governance, and Organizational Culture. In Bretton Woods Commission, Bretton Woods: *Looking to the Future,* C273–86. Washington, DC: Group of Thirty.

Portes, R. and D. Vines. 1997. *Coping with International Capital Flows.* London: Commonwealth Secretariat.

Quraishi, A. 1996. *The World Trade Organisation.* Manchester: Manchester University Press.

Rodrik, D. 1995. Why Is There Multilateral Lending? CEPR Discussion Paper no. 1207. London: Centre for Economic Policy Research.

Sachs, J., and A. Warner. 1995. Economic Reform and the Process of Global Economic Integration. *Brookings Papers on Economic Activity,* no. 1: 1–95.

Sampson, G. 1996. Compatibility of Regional and Multilateral Trading Agreements: Reforming the WTO Process. *American Economic Review* 86 (May): 88–92.

van Doormael, A. 1978. *Bretton Woods: Birth of a Monetary System.* London: Macmillan.

Vines, D. 1997. The Fund, the Bank, and the WTO: Functions, Competencies, and Reform Agendas. Discussion Paper no. 26, Global Economic Institutions Research Programme. London: Centre for Economic Policy Research.

———. 1998. Integrity and the Economy: Consistently Exercised Concernedness and Trust. In A. Montefiore and D. Vines, *Integrity in the Public and the Private Domains.* London: Routledge.

Weale, M., A. Blake, N. Christodoulakis, J. Meade, and D. Vines. 1989. *Macroeconomic Policy: Inflation, Wealth, and the Exchange Rate.* London: Unwin Hyman.

Williamson, J. 1985. *The Exchange Rate System.* Washington, DC: Institute for International Economics.

———. 1994. Reinventing the IMF. Washington, DC: Institute for International Economics, Photocopy.

Williamson, J., and M. Miller. 1987. *Targets and Indicators: A Blueprint for the International Co-ordination of Economic Policy.* Washington, DC: Institute for International Economics.

Woolcock, S. 1996. The New Commercial Policy Agenda: Strengthening or Overburdening the WTO? Paper presented at a conference, "An Agenda for the WTO: Strengthening or Overburdening the System?" Chatham House, London, 29–30 May.

World Bank. 1996. *Global Economic Prospects.* Washington, DC: World Bank.

World Trade Organization. 1996. *WTO Agreements with the Fund and the Bank.* Document WT/L/195. Geneva: WTO.

Comment: The Linkages of the World Bank with the GATT/WTO   Julio J. Nogués

Introduction

In the following comment, I would like to offer some insights that will help the reader to understand better some of the issues involved in an analysis of interactions between global economic organizations. Among the four-way classification groups for which linkages and interactions could be analyzed—between the International Monetary Fund (IMF) and World Bank, the IMF and the World Trade Organization (WTO), and the Bank and the WTO, and among all three of them—my comments will focus mainly on those between the Bank

Julio J. Nogués is alternate executive director for Argentina, Bolivia, Chile, Paraguay, Peru, and Uruguay at the World Bank.

and the WTO because I believe this linkage is central to the objectives of this conference.

The next section highlights the intellectual and operational contribution of the World Bank to trade liberalization; this contribution is of such importance that it helps to understand why the multilateral trading system is where it is today and even, perhaps, why the General Agreement on Tariffs and Trade (GATT) matured into the WTO. I then summarize the nature of the activities that have characterized the informal linkages of the Bank with the GATT/WTO since the early 1980s, and present some brief comments relating to the formal agreement that has recently been signed by the president of the World Bank and the director general of the WTO. I conclude with some remarks about the future role of the Bank in supporting trade liberalization goals.

Contribution of the World Bank to Trade Liberalization: Building and Strengthening the Linkage with the GATT/WTO

Within the World Bank, trade policy and trade liberalization goals became preeminent areas of work during the 1980s when it underwent a historical transformation of its economic thinking. Up to those days, the development paradigm held by the Bank can perhaps be best portrayed by the two-gap model of economic growth developed by, among others, Hollis Chenery, who was the chief economist during the years when Robert McNamara was its president. According to this view, economic growth is essentially a process of overcoming bottlenecks or gaps, and many quite uneconomic investments could be justified by this model. For example, under this paradigm, the Bank had no problems lending to public enterprises as long as it saw that this would help to overcome some development bottleneck. During those days, the Bank did not give much weight to competitive markets, nor to the ability of relative prices in allocating scarce resources. Instead, it had a certain fascination with planning models.

The arrival in 1982 of Anne O. Krueger as the new chief economist of the Bank marked the beginning of what probably has been the most significant and long-lasting shift in its economic thinking away from planning and toward markets. Today it is fair to say that the Bank's management and staff endorse the idea that markets play a crucial role in the economic growth process. It goes without saying that they also hold very different views regarding the economic role of governments than those held during the 1970s and early 1980s. This was an intellectual revolution within the Bank that few remember today, and I must say that at the beginning it was not always a smooth one, as many tried to hold on to old ideas.

This shift of economic thinking is basic to understanding how the linkage of the Bank to the GATT/WTO was built and how it has strengthened over the years. For markets to be able to provide the correct signals for resource allocation, it is crucial that open trade policies be implemented. Providing developing countries sound policy advice on trade liberalization implied a major research effort and the design of new lending instruments, and I would like now to offer some comments on the contribution of the Bank in these areas.

The Intellectual Contribution

There probably has been no single organization around the world, including leading research centers and universities, that has invested as much financial and human resources as the Bank has in measuring the costs of different forms of protection and the benefits of trade liberalization. The Bank used the capital it has in developing countries of being an "honest broker," to disseminate the results of this research. As a consequence, today more than ever before, the leaders of a significant and growing number of developing countries have a much better understanding of (1) the implications of unilateral and non-discriminatory trade liberalization policies, (2) the basic economics underlying the GATT, and (3) the stakes they have in an open multilateral trading system. Industrial countries have also learned quite a lot from this research.

How much the Bank has contributed to the literature on these topics is not easy to assess with precision. An easier question to look at is the allocation of the Bank's resources to the research of the above-mentioned topics. One approximation, the one I have used in preparing these comments, is to quantify what portion of the Bank's working paper series (WPS) has been allocated to trade-related topics. Figure 2C.1 portrays the time path of the total number of papers published in the WPS, as well as those discussing trade-related topics. The papers included in this last category have at least one of the following characteristics: the word "trade" appears in the title, and they have been in-

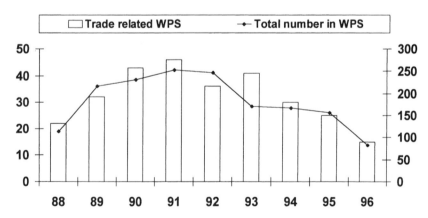

Fig. 2C.1   Trade-related papers published in the World Bank's working paper series

Source: Data from the World Bank.
Note: Data for 1996 are from January through August.

dexed under "international economics" or "trade policy." Out of a total of 1,638 articles published between 1988 when the WPS appeared and August 1996, 290 (i.e., 18 percent) fall into the selected category. The graph also shows that the participation of the trade-related papers in the total has been quite steady.

For any topic, measuring the Bank's intellectual output solely through the contributions to the WPS will provide an underestimation of its true contribution. For example, in the area of trade, some of the significant contributions that are left out of the count include (1) most of the papers prepared for two major research projects financed by the Bank, *Liberalizing Foreign Trade,* published in seven volumes by Basil Blackwell, and *The Political Economy of Agricultural Pricing Policies,* published in five volumes by Johns Hopkins University Press; (2) an important number of contributions on the economic implications for developing countries of the multilateral trade negotiations (MTNs), including the papers published in the *Symposium Issue of the World Bank Economic Review on Multilateral Trade Negotiations and Developing Countries Interests* (September 1987), edited by Jagdish Bhagwati, Anne O. Krueger, and Richard Snape, and the papers published in the *Handbook on Multilateral Trade Negotiations,* edited by J. Michael Finger and Andrezj Olechowski; and (3) other papers produced by Bank staff published in outside journals without passing through the WPS, as well as the numerous country-specific reports prepared in the context of specific operations addressing trade policy issues.

Summing up, during the 1980s, the contribution of the World Bank to the understanding of the impact of unilateral trade liberalization policies was a major one. Likewise, the efforts of the Bank in analyzing the negative impact of several industrial countries' protectionist policies on the export potential, growth, and employment prospects of developing countries were equally significant. Finally, the Bank also made a major contribution to the understanding of the economic dimension of most of the negotiating topics tabled at the Uruguay Round. All this literature was produced precisely at a juncture when many developing countries were also undergoing a significant shift in their economic thinking, away from heavy-handed governments toward market-oriented policies.

The Operational Contribution

The operational efforts made by the Bank in favor of the adoption of trade liberalization policies by developing countries have also been substantial. Nevertheless, in this case, I would like to underline the word "efforts" because unlike its intellectual contribution, although the Bank's operational record is quite good, there have also been some failures. In any case, in order to foster structural adjustment policies including trade liberalization, during the early 1980s the Bank developed what we now know as fast disbursing operations.

Once the research complex of the Bank provided specific meaning to the concept of trade liberalization, it began to be incorporated in several types of fast disbursing operations including trade policy loans, structural adjustment loans, and sectoral adjustment loans. The major difference between these categories is that, while the second type of operations seek to cover a wide range of macroeconomic and structural adjustment policies, the others usually have narrower objectives.

Figure 2C.2 shows the total number of adjustment operations as well as those including trade policy among their conditionality. As we can see, between the fiscal years 1985 and 1996, the share of these operations in adjustment loans has been and still remains quite high, that is, around 70 percent. This is not surprising, given the Bank's objective since the early 1980s in favor of trade liberalization. In terms of value and for these same years, the board has approved loans partially or fully supporting trade policy liberalization measures for a total amount of $34 billion. Nevertheless, as is shown in figure 2C.3, within the total lending of the International Bank for Reconstruction and Development (IBRD) and the International Development Association (IDA), the share of adjustment operations including trade policy component has not been that high, and the reason is simply that the share of adjustment loans in total Bank lending has remained in the 15–20 percent range.

How effective have these Bank-supported trade liberalization programs been? When we look at it country by country, the picture that emerges is mixed, with some operations being very successful and others a failure. In contrast, when we look at the aggregate effects, the progress that has been made is quite significant. Failed projects include, for example, the two trade policy loans approved by the board for Argentina in 1988 for $500 million and in 1989 for $300 million. The trade policy loans failed mainly because they did not support

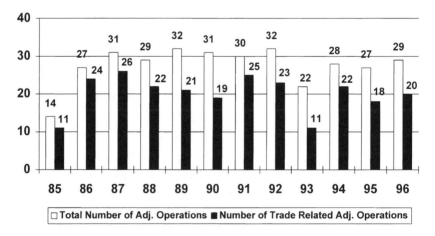

Fig. 2C.2   Annual number of total and trade-related adjustment operations approved by the boards of the IBRD and IDA, fiscal years 1985–96
Source: Data from the World Bank.

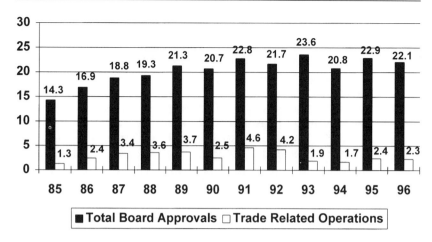

Fig. 2C.3   Annual aggregate and trade-related operations approved by the boards of IBRD and IDA, fiscal years 1985–96 (billions of U.S. dollars)
Source: Data from the World Bank.

what today we would consider to be a strong trade liberalization program backed by a clear political commitment. As a consequence, and starting from a position of very high tariffs and across the board nontariff barriers (NTBs), when all had been said and done, Argentina had somewhat fewer NTBs with an important increase in its debt to the Bank.

The very poor record of the Bank's adjustment loans in Argentina during the 1980s should not overshadow the significant contribution to policy reforms implemented by that country during the 1990s. In relation to trade liberalization, it is of interest to note that the far-reaching measures of recent years were implemented without support from the Bank. This experience reinforces the lesson that what matters the most for success of ambitious reform programs is political commitment.

The poor track record of the Bank in Argentina during the 1980s should also not overshadow the successes in other countries. One important case that comes to mind is Mexico, where the two trade policy loans of the Bank provided critical foreign exchange needed during the country's transition from a very closed economy to a much more open one.

At a more aggregate level, estimates performed by the International Trade Division of the Bank show that the degree of integration into international trade flows of countries that have received financing from the Bank in support of trade policy reforms has been much higher than that of countries that have not received this support. These figures show that, on average between 1981 and 1993, reforming countries' imports from industrial countries grew at 8.3 percent per annum in contrast to the nonreforming, whose imports from the same source grew at only 3.6 percent per annum. A similar picture emerges for imports coming from other developing countries.

In short, on a country-by-country basis, the picture that emerges is one of mixed performance, but when we look at the aggregate result, the performance is good and there is no doubt that it has played a significant role in the trade liberalization progress of many developing countries. I'm quite sure that as a consequence of its operational experience, the Bank would not repeat in other countries the mistakes it made during the 1980s in Argentina. Knowing what we know today, should the Bank do more to foster an increase in the number of developing countries implementing strong trade liberalization programs and/or to assist those that have already introduced these programs to extend these measures to other areas such as trade in services? I will return to this question in the concluding remarks.

The Informal Linkages between the World Bank and the GATT/WTO

The informal linkages that I want to highlight here are those relating to the contribution of the Bank to the MTNs and the accessions of developing countries to the GATT/WTO.

Linkage of the Bank to the GATT/WTO Secretariat and the Multilateral Trade Negotiations

During the early 1980s when trade policy became a prominent area of work for the Bank, the relationship with the GATT Secretariat gathered strength and became very rich and productive. For example, several GATT staff visited Bank headquarters periodically to explain what the agreement was all about. During those early years, the Bank staff's knowledge of the GATT, even among those that were working on trade liberalization programs, was practically non-existent. Likewise, the Bank staff often visited the GATT Secretariat to share their experiences with specific countries and on specific issues.

During the early 1980s, the Bank became a strong supporter of launching a new round of MTNs under the aegis of the GATT. These were the years of the debt crisis, and the early emphasis of the Bank was that increasing worldwide integration of trade and financial flows would provide a conducive environment to the solution of the crisis. This logic explains why the Bank's research complex saw great merits in a new round of MTNs. At that time, the allocation of research resources was primarily directed at showing the tremendous costs imposed on developing countries by several industrial countries' trade policies. For example, major research pieces illustrated the cases of NTBs, agriculture protectionism, textile quotas, policies against unfair trade, unilateral retaliation policies, intellectual property, and international trade in services. Likewise, other contributions argued that, by requesting special and differential treatment, developing countries had missed important opportunities opened by successive rounds of MTNs for enlarging their export markets.

Probably the big initial push from the Bank in favor of the MTNs came through a major conference, "The Role and Interests of the Developing Countries in the Multilateral Trade Negotiation," held in Bangkok, Thailand, in late

1986. The proceedings of this conference were published in the symposium issue of the *World Bank Economic Review, Multilateral Trade Negotiations and Developing Country Interests,* in September 1987. The introductory section to this issue states that "the Bangkok Conference was designed to identify these interests [of the developing countries in the MTNs] within the framework of the sectoral and systematic issues likely to emerge at the MTN." The conference papers showed that important economic rewards to developing countries for taking an active participation in the Uruguay Round were achievable and measurable not only in terms of its effects in helping them to lock in unilateral liberalization measures, but also in the significant opportunities opened up during the MTNs for liberalizing markets, particularly industrial countries' markets of some products that had been protected with high costs to their exports.

For several reasons, the Bank, unlike the GATT/WTO Secretariat, was and still is in a unique position to contribute to a better understanding of international trade policies. First, the secretariat has never had an important research budget. Second, given its nature, it was and still is impossible for the GATT/WTO to produce a piece that is critical of policies that are part of the agreements they administer. Examples of this can be found in areas such as agricultural protectionism, policies against unfair trade, and quotas for balance-of-payments purposes, all of them sanctioned in the GATT. The strong bilateral pressures played by some contracting parties preventing the WTO Secretariat from undertaking critical and independent research on the impact of the policies it monitors is not a minor but a major shortcoming that distinguishes it from the Bank and the IMF. The multilateral character of the WTO will be significantly strengthened the day its members provide the secretariat with the resources to undertake critical and independent research.

Under these circumstances, the Bank seized the opportunity to contribute to developing countries' understanding of the very important role played by their own trade policies and of the significant contribution they could play and the gains they could achieve if they participated actively in a new round of MTNs. The facts have shown that the Uruguay Round was the first MTN where many developing countries accepted the rules of the game imposed by the "reciprocity" principle, and where their historical united stance in favor of the special and differential treatment came to an end. Major examples of this active participation include the collaborative work of developing and industrial countries in the Cairns Group; the increasing number of countries that joined the GATT during the 1980s, most of them with the goal of having an opportunity to negotiate at the round; and perhaps most salient, the significant "offers" tabled during the round with the purpose of obtaining specific market-access objectives from trading partners.

Bank Linkages to Developing Countries' Accession to the GATT and
to Their Tariff Bindings at the Uruguay Round

Table 2C.1 shows that, after 1980 and up to 1995, thirty-one countries acceded to the GATT, of which six had already graduated from the status of

Table 2C.1   **Countries Acceding to the GATT since 1980 and Receiving Trade-Related Adjustment Loans from the World Bank during 1985–96**

Name of Country	Date of Entry	Year of Board Approval of Trade-Related Operations
Antigua and Barbuda[a]	March 1987	—
Bahrain[a]	December 1993	—
Belize[a]	October 1983	—
Bolivia	September 1990	1986, 1992
Botswana	August 1987	—
Brunei[a]	December 1993	—
Colombia	October 1981	1985, 1986, 1989, 1991
Costa Rica	November 1990	1985, 1993
Czech Republic	April 1993	1991
Dominica	April 1993	1987
El Salvador	May 1991	1991, 1994
Fiji	November 1993	—
Guatemala	October 1991	1993
Hong Kong[a]	April 1986	—
Lesotho	January 1988	—
Macao[a]	January 1991	—
Maldives	April 1983	—
Mali	January 1993	1988, 1990, 1991, 1994, 1996
Mexico	August 1986	1987, 1988, 1989
Morocco	June 1987	1986, 1989, 1992, 1996
Mozambique	July 1992	1989, 1992, 1994
Namibia	September 1992	—
Paraguay	January 1993	—
Saint Lucia	April 1993	—
Saint Vincent and Grenadines	May 1993	—
Slovak Republic	April 1993	—
Swaziland	February 1993	—
Thailand	November 1982	—
Tunisia	August 1990	1988, 1989, 1992
Venezuela	August 1990	1989, 1990
Zambia	February 1982	1986, 1991, 1992, 1994, 1996

Sources: GATT/WTO Secretariat and the World Bank.

[a]Graduated from borrowing from the World Bank.

borrowers from the IBRD. The table also shows that fourteen of the twenty-five current IBRD borrowers, or 56 percent, received trade-related adjustment operations after 1985. Therefore, the presumption is that many of these operations assisted these countries in moving their trade regimes to a position that facilitated their accession to the GATT.

Table 2C.2 shows the percentage of imports with bound tariffs as well as the weighted average post–Uruguay Round rates. I list only the developing countries that have reported their statistics to the GATT/WTO Secretariat, in table 2C.2. The figures show that, during the Uruguay Round, the tariff bindings of these countries increased substantially. Table 2C.1 also shows that most of the

Table 2C.2   **Percentage of Imports with Bound Tariff Rates**

	Percent Bounded		Post–Uruguay Round Tariff Rates	
Countries	Pre–Uruguay Round	Post–Uruguay Round	Applied	Bounded
Argentina[a]	17.1	100.0	10.3	31.0
Brazil	16.0	100.0	11.7	29.0
Chile[a]	100.0	100.0	11.0	25.0
Colombia[a]	4.4	100.0	10.9	39.7
Czech and Slovak Republics[a]	96.2	100.0	3.8	4.0
El Salvador[a]	97.8	97.8	10.7	34.2
Hungary[a]	87.1	94.4	6.8	6.6
India[a]	11.6	58.5	30.9	52.2
Indonesia[a]	29.7	93.4	10.7	38.4
Jamaica[a]	0.0	100.0	15.5	56.3
Korea, Republic of	21.3	83.2	7.7	16.4
Malaysia	1.6	77.4	6.4	9.3
Mexico[a]	100.0	100.0	10.4	34.1
Peru[a]	17.1	100.0	14.6	33.7
Poland[a]	0.0	91.3	6.9	12.3
Romania[a]	9.8	100.0	11.7	45.1
Senegal[a]	39.1	58.3	11.8	16.6
Sri Lanka[a]	9.9	26.7	28.6	38.9
Thailand	7.5	64.3	26.1	27.5
Tunisia[a]	0.0	67.9	24.8	48.7
Turkey[a]	35.6	45.1	26.3	33.3
Uruguay[a]	13.3	100.0	14.6	29.4
Venezuela[a]	100.0	100.0	12.4	31.6
Zimbabwe[a]	9.8	14.7	4.5	35.3

Source: The Uruguay Round: Statistics on Tariff Concessions Given and Received, by J. Michael Finger, Merlinda D. Ingco, and Ulrich Reincke.

[a]Countries receiving trade-related adjustment operations after 1986.

countries in this sample received one or more trade-related adjustment loans, raising again the presumption that the Bank played an important role in facilitating the process of extensive tariff bindings. Given the numerous cases of trade policy reversals in developing countries, I stress the importance of these bindings in helping to stabilize their trade policies.

This active participation of developing countries in the Uruguay Round represents a historical breakthrough, and it is my view that the Bank played an important role in it. The informal collaboration with the GATT/WTO Secretariat still continues. For example, the Bank has just published another book on the Uruguay Round, this one presenting an elaboration of the statistics on tariff concessions which will surely be widely used. Also, when preparing their reports for the Trade Policy Review Mechanism, the staff from the GATT/WTO Secretariat maintain very rich but informal contacts with Bank staff.

Summing up, some of the gains to developing countries achieved by the long-lasting and rich but informal linkages between the World Bank and the GATT/WTO include a much better knowledge of the role of the agreement; a much better knowledge by developing countries of what the costs are to them of other countries' protectionist measures, and a more accurate assessment of what the MTNs are all about and what can be realistically expected from an active participation in them. The Bank always worked in close collaboration with the GATT Secretariat, and I view this informal collaboration and the research and operational efforts of the Bank as having had a major positive impact in pushing forward trade liberalization in developing countries and, therefore, in strengthening the multilateral trading system.

The Formal Agreement between the Bank and the WTO

On 3 December 1996 the boards of the IBRD and the IDA approved the contents of the Agreement between the International Bank for Reconstruction and Development, the International Development Association, and the World Trade Organization. On 28 April 1997 the agreement came into force when it was signed by the president of the Bank and the director general of the WTO. The preamble to the agreement mentions the increasing interlinkages between these organizations and the call in the Marrakesh Agreement establishing the WTO for achieving greater coherence among economic policies. The preamble also mentions article V of the Bank's Articles of Agreement, calling for it to "cooperate with any general international organization and with public international organizations having specialized responsibilities in related fields," as an additional justification for the agreement.

The agreement has thirteen paragraphs that deal with several topics including institutional consultation; staff attendance at other organizations' meetings; exchange of documents and information; staff consultation and cooperation; and standard clauses on confidentiality, implementation, review, termination, and approval.

At this stage, the reader may wonder why a formal agreement was necessary, if the informal collaboration between the Bank and the WTO/GATT Secretariat has been so rich and productive. Bank staff explain that, once the WTO was created, its secretariat approached the Bank (and the IMF) to formalize an agreement, and in this sense, it appears to be more profitable to the WTO than to the Bank. During the discussions, some board members expressed fears that the agreement could add unnecessary risks to the relation of some developing countries with the Bank and compromise the independence of the output that had hitherto characterized the research of the Bank. On this second point, management made it very clear to the board that this independence would not be compromised.

Overall, the agreement has been carefully crafted, and except for the issue of staff attendance at each other's meetings, it essentially represents a formalization of most of the consultations and working linkages that had developed informally over the years. In contrast, the issue of staff attendance at each other's meetings is new and poses delicate issues particularly for developing countries working with the Bank.

The meetings of the governing bodies of the WTO and of the executive board of the Bank have each been divided in two tiers: for tier 1 meetings the other organization enjoys standing invitations, while for tier 2 meetings special invitations must be delivered. At the WTO the Bank has a standing invitation to the meetings of all the governing bodies except the Dispute Settlement Body, the Committee on Budget, Finance, and Administration, and dispute settlement panels. An ad hoc invitation (tier 2) to the Bank staff to attend as observer the meetings of the Dispute Settlement Body will be issued by the WTO when it is concluded that it will take up matters of common interest to both organizations.

A standing invitation to the WTO staff for attendance to the board meetings of the Bank is issued when the board addresses general or regional trade policy issues. Bank management is responsible for proposing to the board the meetings where WTO would be invited as an observer, and the invitation would be dispatched on a no-objection basis by each member of the board. At tier 2 meetings the board will discuss a country-specific operation addressing trade policy objectives. On this subject, several executive directors expressed concern that the presence of the WTO should not compromise the Bank's views on trade policy. Bank management was also concerned with this topic, and in its written remarks, it expressed very clearly that, while the WTO's concern is with the country's legal rights and obligations under its agreements, the Bank views trade policy as a critical element of development policy.

A second concern raised by some executive directors relates to the board discussions addressing adjustment operations with trade policy components for countries not yet members of the WTO. Given the much greater bilateral influences on the WTO than on the Bank, it was feared that presence of WTO staff could debilitate the accession negotiations of developing countries. For these cases, it has been agreed that the views of the country under discussion would be given particular weight.

Summing up, except for presence at each other's meetings of the governing bodies, this agreement between the Bank and the WTO could be seen as a formalization of most of the informal linkages that have hitherto characterized their joint work. As has been the case in the past, the agreement does not specify the modalities by which the cooperation will take place, and in this sense, I think it has been carefully crafted. On the other hand, for the time being, access of the WTO staff to the meetings of the Bank's board remains quite restricted. How much this formal agreement will add to the rich and productive collaboration of the Bank staff with the GATT/WTO Secretariat, only time will say. The spirit that guided the past informal collaboration was characterized by trust, openness, and a great concern for not intruding into the mandate of the other organization. In my view, the likelihood of success of this formal agreement will depend on whether this spirit continues to prevail.

Concluding Remarks on Trade Liberalization: Which Way for the World Bank?

The above comments represent my contribution to the understanding of the linkages and interactions between the WB and the GATT/WTO. In this final section I would like to stress David Vines's conclusion that the Bank's most problematic agenda area is "creating a sharper intellectual focus on the trade liberalization and trade agenda." In my view, trade and trade liberalization topics have to be resurrected from where they are standing now in the hierarchy of the Bank's objectives and come to occupy, once again, a predominant role. One reason is that, according to its Articles of Agreement, promoting "the long-range balance growth of international trade" (article 1) is one of the main purposes of the Bank. Another central reason is that there probably has been no other period in the life of the Bretton Woods organizations when the goal of near universal free trade may be achieved. The progress at the Uruguay Round, the major unilateral trade liberalization programs implemented by more than fifty developing countries during the last decade, and the increasing number of regional patches of near free trade are all developments that point to the fact that, in an important and growing number of countries, the forces pushing for more open trade regimes are indeed very strong.

It would be a historical error of major proportions for the Bank to conclude that, because so much has been achieved, there remains no significant progress to be expected from investing additional intellectual and financial resources in this area. Such a conclusion would not take into account that, for all practical purposes, Africa remains a closed continent, nor that, although the countries of central and eastern Europe as well as the newly independent states of the former Soviet Union are making progress, implementing and supporting major trade liberalization programs remains a major challenge for them. It would also be an error to assume that because many countries in Latin America have implemented important reforms to their trade regimes and bound their tariff rates at the Uruguay Round, they run little risk of policy reversals or that they could not do more in the trade liberalization area. The examples could go on to incorporate the major impediments to trade that are still enforced by industrial countries.

The simple but fundamental point is that the multilateral trading system still has a long way to go before reaching a situation close to free trade. When they were created, the Bretton Woods organizations had as one of their major goals to re-create the economic and financial conditions that would facilitate the international flows of capital and goods. At that time, the founding fathers had in mind that the International Trade Organization (ITO) was soon going to come into existence and the joint work of the three organizations would serve as a powerful force in favor of free trade. The ITO never came into existence, and it has been only natural for the Bank to interpret broadly its articles of agreement (article I in particular) and during the 1980s to accept the responsibility and challenge of helping countries to understand better the implications of trade policy reforms, and to provide the financial resources needed during the transitions from closed to open trade economies.

Under the circumstances the World Bank has played this role in a superb way and trade liberalization is one of the areas where it can be proud of a job well done, but much remains to be achieved. In short, the Bank has a moral obligation to seize the opportunity and once again become a major voice in favor of free trade. The vision of the founding fathers was that this can be made a better world by assisting countries to integrate themselves to the international flows of goods and capital. The Bank, unlike any other international organization, is viewed by developing countries as being an honest broker, and it is therefore in the best position to offer them and the leaders of industrial nations a vision of the road to be traveled, to charter a course of action, and to mobilize the funding that is necessary to help move the world economy significantly closer to free trade, say within the next fifteen to twenty years. In the past much of this was achieved with the productive but informal linkage that the Bank maintained with the GATT Secretariat. Now there is a formal agreement with the WTO Secretariat, and we hope that the future linkage with this organization will serve to push, with even greater force than in the past, the advancement of the world economy toward free trade.

3   International Agencies and Cross-Border Liberalization: The WTO in Context

David Henderson

3.1   Introduction

This paper considers the role and functioning of the World Trade Organization (WTO) in the context of related international agencies. There are two main themes, general and specific. The former concerns the extent to which these agencies have contributed in the past, and might contribute in the future, to the process of cross-border liberalization across the world. The specific aspect is the current situation of the WTO, and the ways in which its prospective contribution could be strengthened. Under both headings, the treatment is comparative and institutional.

Six widely different agencies are initially included. In order of creation, they are the International Monetary Fund (IMF), 1945; the International Bank for Reconstruction and Development (World Bank), 1945; the General Agreement on Tariffs and Trade (GATT), 1947, and its successor agency (from 1 January 1995), the World Trade Organization (WTO); the Commission of the European Communities (the Commission for short), 1957; the Organisation for Economic Cooperation and Development (OECD), 1961 though with earlier antecedents; and the United Nations Conference on Trade and Development (UNCTAD), 1964. Following section 3.2 of the paper, however, the Commis-

David Henderson is an independent author and consultant, and a former head of the Department of Economics and Statistics at the Organization for Economic Cooperation and Development in Paris.

This paper has greatly benefited from information, ideas, and suggestions from Roderick Abbott, Jean Baneth, Douglas Irwin, Tony Killick, Geoffrey Lamb, Alan Oxley, Stanley Please, Jim Rollo, Tony Rottier, Karl Sauvant, and Alan Winters. The work for it was done during visits successively to the Institut d'Études Politiques de Paris, the International Economics Programme of the Royal Institute of International Affairs in London, and the Melbourne Business School, and the author is grateful for the facilities provided by all these centers.

sion is left out of the comparisons, and the final section focuses on three agencies only—the WTO, the OECD, and UNCTAD.

The emphasis here is on the part played by these organizations as such, with each of them treated as a special case. In each instance, the main question considered is the agency's influence on events in general, and external liberalization in particular: how history might have been different had it not existed, and how future developments could be affected by its current and potential role. A related and interesting topic, pursued here only incidentally, is the inner history of the various agencies—the ways in which their thinking, their approach to issues of international economic policy, has evolved over time.

Each of the agencies has its own character, administrative culture, ways of viewing the world, and sense of mission. With the possibly debatable exception of the WTO, none of them is exclusively concerned with external liberalization. Hence they are viewed initially in general terms, across the whole range of their respective portfolios: their concern with, and possible effect on, the liberalization of trade and capital flows is set in a broader institutional context.

To influence policies it is necessary to make an impact on national governments, either directly or by impinging on the general climate of public opinion, which in turn may affect what governments decide. For historical and institutional reasons, the channels and mechanisms of influence are different between the various agencies.

Answers to the questions posed here are bound to be in large part conjectural, largely because of the obvious difficulty of deciding what impact on events, past and prospective, is to be attributed to the agencies as distinct from their member states. International agencies are the creatures of national governments. It is their members that bring them into existence, decide their initial shapes and roles, finance their current activities (whether directly or indirectly), and exercise continuing control, though in varying degrees, over what they do and how they do it. Hence there is inevitably a question as to whether, how far, and through what channels these organizations, as the servants and instruments of governments, can affect the conduct of their masters. Where such influences can be detected, or reasonably anticipated for the future, a further problem arises as to the mix of causal elements that explains them—whether resourcefulness on the part of the agencies; inertia, inadvertence, tolerance, or conscious design on the part of the member governments; or sheer historical accident. On all this, what follows is no more than a minuscule dip into what has been aptly termed "the seething cauldron of history."[1] In part, it is a personal reading of events and relationships, colored by actual experience of a number of national and international agencies.

The scene is set in section 3.2. This gives a brief comparative review and description of all the six agencies, with particular reference to (1) their size, (2) the role and status of their staffs, (3) their relations with member govern-

---

1. The phrase comes from G. L. S. Shackle's fine essay on Hayek, published in 1989.

ments and the extent of their autonomy, and (4) the channels through which they may be able to exercise an influence of their own. In this first stage the Commission is brought into the comparison because including it makes for a more complete picture, a fuller inventory of cases and possibilities.

Section 3.3 is a historical sketch in two parts, with the Commission now left out on grounds of space and because of its special situation. The first part is historical: it considers some specific areas and episodes in which the other five international agencies appear to have played a distinctive role, and may have affected the balance between liberalism and interventionism in the trade and investment regimes of their member governments. The second part draws some lessons from these glimpses of the past.

Section 3.4 looks at future possibilities for furthering the cause of liberalization with reference to three of the agencies: in descending order of the space assigned to them, these are the WTO, the OECD, and UNCTAD. Consideration is given, not only to the agencies themselves and their interrelations, but also to the ways in which their member governments deal with them.

3.2   Six Agencies Compared

There are striking differences between the six agencies, which begin with the more obvious dimensions of membership, size, and makeup or identity.

3.2.1   Vital Statistics

Membership is easily determined, though in three cases (Commission, OECD, and WTO) there is scope for speculation as to the future, the more so since conditions apply to membership and these may become the subject of negotiation.

The Commission of course serves the member states of what is now the European Union, which at present number fifteen. Further applications for membership have been made, and others are in prospect. All the fifteen EU countries are members of the OECD, as are seven other European countries. Four of these latter—Iceland, Norway, Switzerland, and Turkey—are OECD members of long standing, while three are recent additions: the Czech Republic was admitted to membership in 1995, and Hungary and Poland in 1996. There are seven non-European members—the United States, Canada, Japan, Australia, New Zealand, Mexico (from 1994), and the Republic of Korea, which was admitted to membership in 1996. Hence the total OECD membership now stands at twenty-nine, with further additions likely.[2]

By contrast with these two limited-membership agencies, the IMF, the World Bank, and UNCTAD all have a common membership which is almost

2. For some twenty years, from the early 1970s to the early 1990s, the membership of the OECD remained stable at twenty-four countries, while the question of new accessions was not on the agenda. This situation has now changed.

universal, and which now comprises over 180 governments. The current figure for the WTO exceeds 120 countries, with further accessions in prospect. It seems likely that over time the membership will continue to increase, and hence come closer to that of the Fund and the Bank.

Relative size, which one might expect to be broadly correlated with influence, is more difficult to measure, because of questions of comparability that arise in interpreting the information that is readily and publicly available. A rigorous comparison would mean delving further below the surface: a few rough benchmarks only are offered here.

The most familiar indicator of size is staff numbers. By this criterion, much the largest of the six agencies is the Commission: the official figure for 1996 for the total numbers of those employed by the institutions of the Commission, in round terms, is not far short of 21,000.[3] This total has increased steadily over the years, and over the ten years to 1996 the increase came to some 45 percent. In part at least, this continuing rise in numbers has been linked to the admission of new member states. More broadly, the size of the Commission has to be considered in relation to its wide range of tasks and responsibilities; and it is worth noting the view expressed a few years ago—before the accession of Austria, Finland, and Sweden—by one informed observer, Peter Ludlow (1991, 104, 122) that "the Commission is a small institution relative to its responsibilities," and "will have to be considerably increased in size simply to perform the functions it already has."

The World Bank is by far the largest of the remaining five agencies, though in this case, and in contrast with the Commission, the number of staff employed is at present on a declining trend. In public discussion, a round total of 10,000 for current staff numbers is widely quoted, while a direct inquiry to the Bank yielded a figure of 9,405 for mid-1995. However, the Bank's annual report for 1996 gives for 30 June 1996 the figure of 5,681, and this may be closer to the totals given by other agencies as well as bearing the sanctity of the official printed word.[4] Compared with the corresponding figure for a year earlier, it represents a reduction of some 6 percent.

For the IMF, which comes third on the list, the corresponding total, quoted in the 1996 annual report for 30 April 1996, was 2,198. Although this is slightly higher than the 1995 figure, the current trend is downward: the report notes (p. 219) that "[t]he total authorized staffing of the Fund was reduced by 40 staff positions in 1995/96 and will be reduced by a further 6 positions in 1996/97." But in this case the total had been subject to a significant increase from the late 1980s, largely in response to the adoption by the Fund of programs for the countries of central and eastern Europe and the former Soviet Union. As a

3. The figure is taken from an official publication that the Commission calls its *Vade-Mecum Budgétaire*.
4. The difference is probably accounted for in large part by persons employed on temporary or short-term contracts, including for the World Bank consultants paid for out of trust funds.

result of this expansion, the Fund has now drawn well ahead of the OECD, to which it was formerly comparable in staff numbers. For the OECD, excluding the International Energy Agency which is effectively separate, a current round figure for secretariat numbers is 1,700; and in this case it is clear that some reduction will soon be made by the member governments.

Finally, much the smallest of the agencies on this measure, with not much at present to choose between them, are UNCTAD and the WTO. For the former, chapter 1 by Richard Blackhurst in this volume quotes a figure of 443. For the WTO, current staff numbers are rather more than 500. This reflects a recent increase of some 50 secretariat positions, following the decision by member governments to upgrade the status of temporary posts that had been created in connection with the Uruguay Round negotiations and the Trade Policy Review Mechanism. For 1997, it was decided that no new posts should be created; but in due course some further increase seems likely, in recognition of the wider responsibilities of the WTO as compared with the former GATT. Even if such an expansion were to be sanctioned by member governments, however, the WTO Secretariat numbers would be not much more than one-twelfth of what seems to be the corresponding total for the World Bank, and roughly one-fortieth of that for the Commission.

An alternative measure of relative size would be the operating budget of each agency, suitably adjusted in each case to allow for differences both in timing and coverage and in the purchasing power of the various currencies involved. Publicly available information does not in itself enable one to make such adjustments with confidence: some figures based on published sources are set out in table 3.1, but the extent to which these are comparable is not clear.

From the table, it is apparent that moving from staff numbers to total administrative budgets, though it leaves the ranking unchanged, gives a rather different impression of comparative size. If the comparison is made at current exchange rates, as in the second column of the table, the Fund and the Bank appear somewhat larger in relation to the four European-based agencies, and to the Commission in particular, than they do on the basis of staff numbers: this reflects the differences shown in the third column, for cost per staff member, where the Fund and the Bank show up as relatively "expensive" agencies and the Commission as the "cheapest." This effect is strengthened if the comparison of budgets is made using purchasing-power parity (PPP) rates, since the costs per staff member of the Fund and the Bank, as shown in the final column of the table, now appear substantially higher than the rest. It can be seen that from a comparison of staff numbers alone the World Bank appears to be not much more than one-quarter the size of the Commission, while from the figures for administrative budgets in PPP dollars, in the penultimate column of the table, it is shown as just over half as large. Of the four European-based agencies, the OECD appears to have the highest expenditures per staff member for both sets of exchange rates. If the comparison is made at PPP

Table 3.1   Six Agencies Compared: Staff Numbers and Administrative Budgets

Agency	Staff Numbers	Administrative Budget (millions of U.S. dollars, actual exchange rates)	Cost/Staff Member (thousands of U.S. dollars, actual exchange rates)	Administrative Budget (millions of U.S. dollars, PPP exchange rates)[a]	Cost/Staff Member (thousands of U.S. dollars, PPP exchange rates)[a]
Commission	21,000	3,400	162	2,700	129
IBRD	5,700	1,375	241	1,375	241
IMF	2,200	470	214	470	214
OECD	1,700	340	200	260	153
WTO	510	97	190	55	108
UNCTAD	440	80	182	45	102

Sources: Data for the Commission are from its *Vade-Mecum Budgétaire;* for the IMF, the IBRD, and the OECD from the respective annual reports (1996 for the Bretton Woods twins, 1995 for the OECD); for UNCTAD from Blackhurst (chap. 1 in this volume); and for the WTO from personal communication, relating to the situation in 1996.

Notes: Staff numbers and budget totals are rounded here. As emphasized in the text, these figures are no more than a starting point for interagency comparisons. Substantial questions of comparability arise, which cannot be resolved on the basis of readily accessible information.

[a]Purchasing-power parity (PPP) rates are those of the OECD for 1996, and are economywide. For the Commission, the rate for Belgium has been taken; for the OECD, the rate for France; and for UNCTAD and the WTO, the rate for Switzerland.

rates, the least "expensive" agencies are the WTO and UNCTAD, which are both based in Geneva: this reflects the large difference between the current exchange rate for the Swiss franc and the PPP rate.[5]

3.2.2   Staffs, Delegates, and Agency Identity

For many outsiders, it is natural to think of the agencies in terms of their staffs alone—the persons who work for the head of each agency, and whose salaries are paid through its budget. This is no more than a first approximation, however, and it remains so even if attention is focused on the whole administrative budget. For a truer picture, it is necessary to take account of the extent to which officials from member governments are actively involved in the day-to-day work of the agencies. In three at least of the six cases—the OECD, the WTO, and the IMF—the degree of involvement is such that the very conception of the agency has to be extended, at least for some purposes, so as to include national delegates as well as staff. In this respect, the three are in a different situation from that of the Commission and the World Bank.

5. It is worth noting that the PPP-based figures for administrative budgets and costs per staff member are not likely to be the "true" values, nor even necessarily closer to these than the totals based on current exchange rates. For this there are two main reasons. First, even for local expenditures, tailor-made PPP rates would be needed, rather than the economywide figures used here. Second, not all agency expenses are local—for example, both the Fund and the Bank spend substantial amounts outside the United States, on consultants, staff travel, and resident missions.

The point can be illustrated by comparing the Bank, which is at one extreme among the six, with the OECD and the WTO at the other. Alongside the 5,700 or so Bank staff members (9–10,000 on some counts), and overseeing their work, are the executive directors and their alternates, who are the nominees and representatives of member governments (though paid by the Bank, as are their counterparts at the IMF). At present, these number forty-eight. Allowing for their modest Washington-based staffing support might bring the total numbers in these "permanent delegations" to the Bank, as most other agencies would call them, to around 200. Hence the ratio of core Bank staff to resident national officials within the Bank is probably between twenty-five and thirty to one. The corresponding figure for the OECD appears to lie between three to one and four to one, while for the WTO it may well be close to unity.[6] If the Bank were constituted and run in the same way as the OECD, it would have some 1,500–2,000 national delegates attached to it in Washington, all of them continuously involved in its activities, while if the WTO were the model, the number might well exceed 5,000. Moreover, for the OECD in particular this comparison understates the difference between these two contrasting bureaucratic worlds, since it takes no account of the likewise heavy involvement in OECD meetings of visiting delegates from national capitals. As I have noted elsewhere, "The OECD is not just the Secretariat, with member governments watching over it but standing apart: it is *the combination—the Secretariat in conjunction with the delegates from member governments.* In the great bulk of OECD activities, Secretariat and national officials are jointly involved" (Henderson 1996, 14). This statement applies even more to the WTO, where as the numbers indicate the role of the permanent delegations—as distinct from visiting officials from national capitals, who play a smaller part than in OECD proceedings—is larger in relation to that of the secretariat than is the case for the OECD. In Geneva recently, in answer to my question, "What *is* the WTO?" one experienced delegate responded: "The WTO is a collegiate of Delegations serviced by the Secretariat"; and this is indeed a possible description, though in my view too unqualified. In both agencies, national officials from member governments are in effect the clients of the secretariat, clients who are both exacting and ever present; and for both, as also for the Commission, the costs to member governments of their involvement with the agencies go well beyond the figures that appear in the respective administrative budgets.

For the OECD and the WTO alike, this active and continuous participation of national delegates takes place through an elaborate structure of committees in which the member states (and normally, other international agencies as appropriate) are represented: in each of the two agencies, the proceedings of these committees form the core of its activities, and the principal role of the secretariat is to serve the committees. In the World Bank, by contrast, there is

---

6. In estimating the numbers of those attached to the permanent delegations in Geneva, Paris, and Washington, I have made use of the relevant telephone directories.

no such committee structure, and the main task of the staff is to design and manage the lending program and the financial operations that go with it.

The contrast between these two bureaucratic worlds extends also to the budgetary process. Aside from IDA replenishment funds, which have to be specifically and periodically voted by the group of donor governments, the Bank finances its own expenditures, from sources of revenue that accrue directly to it and which, though they derive originally from the paid-up capital subscriptions of the member governments, do not fall on their annual budgets. By contrast, the OECD and the WTO are financed almost entirely by direct contributions from member governments; and since these are items within national budgets, they are subject each year to prolonged and detailed scrutiny. In financing as well as in the conduct of its operations, the president of the Bank and his staff have greater leeway, and wider powers of initiative, than their counterparts in these other two agencies.

Both the OECD and the WTO are in fact classed as intergovernmental agencies; and so too is UNCTAD, which is financed from the budget of the UN Secretariat and hence depends on annual votes from member governments. But in the case of UNCTAD there is only a partial counterpart to the committee structures of the OECD and the WTO, and the continuous participation of national officials that these involve. Hence UNCTAD is more distant from its clients, and more closely identified with its secretary-general and staff, than are the OECD and the WTO.

The IMF is likewise an intermediate case, though in a quite different way. Not surprisingly, its situation is in most respects closely similar to that of its fellow "Bretton Woods twin," the World Bank. Like the Bank, it is international rather than intergovernmental; it has few permanent delegates (though more in proportion to staff numbers than the Bank); the concern of the staff is with its lending program, and its advisory and monitoring activities in member countries, and not with servicing a range of committees of national officials; and it has its "own" sources of finance. In this latter respect, it is possibly rather more independent than the Bank, since there is no full counterpart to the dependence on member governments that arises for the Bank from the periodic IDA replenishments: while the Fund's Enhanced Structural Adjustment Facility resembles IDA credits in being a soft-loan facility that is subject to periodic acts of renewal, its status is less subject to negotiation and debate. But the difference here is one of degree.

In one important respect, however, the Fund is unlike the Bank, in that it has always been subject to closer scrutiny and direction by its member governments, acting largely through the executive board (though sometimes, in the case of the largest countries, by bringing direct pressure to bear on the managing director). The contrast in this respect was noted a quarter of a century ago in the first official history of the World Bank. The authors remarked that "[t]he centerpiece of the Fund is the board of executive directors," whereas "[a] history of the Bank, on the other hand, must necessarily concentrate on management and staff" (Mason and Asher 1973, 538). Since then the difference has probably narrowed: governments in general, and the U.S. authorities in particular, now exercise more control than they used to over presidents of the Bank.[7] Nevertheless, the broad distinction still holds good today. Thus the best short answer to the question, "What *is* the World Bank?" remains "Its staff," while for the Fund, now as in the past, "The staff and the executive board" would be a better first approximation.

Finally, the Commission is in a different and special situation. Partly because of its much greater size, but still more in virtue of the extensive powers conferred on it by the Treaties relating to the European Communities, it stands alone among international agencies: the member states of what has now become the EU have deliberately created and maintained it as an entity that has explicitly assigned powers to put forward proposals affecting their future conduct, to monitor their actions and policies, even to the point of being able to take legal proceedings against them, and to represent and act for them in defined areas of external policy.[8] So wide are these differences from the other five agencies that its very inclusion here is open to question. All the same, the question raised about the other agencies, as to their influence on cross-border liberalization, is pertinent also to the Commission.

In this case too, one can pose the question, "What *is* the Commission?" As with the World Bank, a good first-approximation answer is "Its staff," the more so since (1) there is no close equivalent of the executive boards of the Bank and the Fund to exercise control over what it does, and (2) the numerous national officials of member governments, with whom the Commission staff have close and continuous contact, are best viewed as counterparts rather than (as with the OECD and the WTO) as clients. But in this case the commissioners—at present twenty in number—who are political appointments, are for the most part political figures rather than senior officials, and are formally enjoined from acting as national delegates or representatives, have to be viewed as an element in their own right, as distinct from the staff who work for them: indeed, in the treaties governing the European Union the term "the Commission" refers only to the commissioners. A fairly close analogy here is with the combination of ministers and officials within national administrations: the notion of a department of state embraces both.

In its relations with its member governments, the Commission can be viewed as bringing together the two contrasting features that I attributed to the World Bank, on the one hand, and the OECD and the WTO on the other. As compared with the two latter agencies, and like the Bank, it is much larger,

7. This may not be saying a great deal: Mason and Asher (1973, 63) observe of the Bank's executive board that "ever since Eugene Meyer's departure [in 1946], it has concerned itself primarily with the problems that the president chooses to put before it"—a remarkable situation for an international agency to be in.

8. A good source on the role and functions of the Commission is the essay already quoted, by Peter Ludlow. A general guide to EU institutions is Nugent (1994).

more independent financially, and far freer to take initiatives of its own—indeed, it has specified rights of initiative. At the same time, and unlike the Bank, it operates in close day-to-day conjunction with national officials—and with ministers too, at the level of the president and the other commissioners—in every aspect of its work, in part through its relations with the well-staffed permanent delegations of the member states. In this respect it shares the intergovernmental character of the OECD and the WTO.

3.2.3   Status and Support

In part, the capacity to influence events depends on the status of each agency, and the extent to which its role is well recognized and effectively supported by its member governments and public opinion. In this respect, there are again clear differences, and not surprisingly the relative situation of the six has been changing. The Commission has much the most assured status, because of its well-defined constitutional position and its close involvement in the everyday conduct of affairs in member countries in virtually all areas of economic and social policy: this makes a powerful combination. At the other extreme, for reasons to be summarized in section 3.3, is UNCTAD. As between the four remaining agencies, a number of points are worth noting.

First, the Bretton Woods twins are by no means identical from this point of view, while first appearances here are deceptive. Because of its much smaller size, together with the closer control that governments have always exercised over it, the IMF might seem to be in a chronically weaker situation than the World Bank. In my view this is not the case, since the Fund has two sources of strength that are lacking in the Bank. First, it has powerful friends in national capitals, since the ministers and officials who deal with it, and feel responsible for it, all come from ministries of finance and central banks. For them, the Fund is their agency: its attitudes and beliefs, its institutional and professional concerns, are theirs. Second, while changes in recent years have put in question the raison d'être of both agencies, the Fund has more clearly established its continuing relevance in the eyes of both governments and public opinion, largely because of what is seen by many as its role in "global governance."[9] By contrast, the revival of international capital markets has put in question the role and purpose of the Bank.

The Fund is also better placed than the OECD, thanks to a combination of more effective backing in capitals, a more clearly recognized role, and greater financial autonomy. When it comes to recognition and support, the OECD has a chronic problem because its activities are both low-profile and widely diffused. Like the Commission, but unlike the other four agencies, it is not at all a specialized agency: the agenda of its committees extends to pretty well every

9. A recent instance is to be found in the book by Fred Bergsten and Randall Henning (1996) on the role of the G7 group of countries, where it is argued that the group should make "conscious efforts to give the Fund a much more central role" (p. 10).

aspect of economic and social policies in its member countries, the only exceptions being defense, culture, and sport.[10] Although this is also a source of strength—a point to be taken up in section 3.4—it means that no one department of state feels closely identified with, and fully informed about, its activities as a whole, which are likewise not well known to a wider public.

From this point of view the WTO is better placed, and its situation is now much improved as compared with its predecessor, the GATT. John Jackson (1995, 24) has suggested that the establishment of the WTO marks "a watershed in the international economic system," resulting from "the mere fact of creating a definitive international arrangement, combined with the extraordinary expanse of the Uruguay Round negotiations." Aside from the Commission, the status of the WTO is in fact now the most secure of all the six agencies, in that few people, whether in government or outside, question either its right to continued existence or the recent and substantial widening of its responsibilities.

At the same time, however, the WTO like the OECD is still subject to constraints from which the Fund and (still more) the Bank remain much freer. It is not the case, as is sometimes suggested, that in creating the WTO governments have "transformed the GATT . . . into an international organization of equal standing to the IMF and the World Bank."[11] This can be seen by comparing—what is chiefly relevant here—the respective staffs of the agencies, both in numbers and available resources and in the extent to which they are able to exercise initiative and to respond to new developments. In these respects the GATT was manifestly weak in relation to the Fund and the Bank, and so far its successor has not become much—if at all—stronger. The more assured status of the WTO, and the extension of its portfolio, are indeed noteworthy; but they have not so far been reflected in a willingness on the part of member governments to increase significantly either the funds available to it or the scope for secretariat initiative. The contrast here with the Fund is instructive. The widening of the Fund's responsibilities, as a result of changes east of what had been the Iron Curtain, has gone together with an increase in staff numbers from (in round terms) 1,800 in 1989 to 2,200 today. The absolute increase over the period is thus not far short of the present and prospective total of secretariat numbers at the WTO. Such a response by the Fund was made possible by the combination of its solid backing in national capitals and its nonappearance in the budgets of its member states. In these respects, it was and remains in a different world from that of the WTO—as well as having a staff that is currently more than four times as large, and an administrative budget that appears to be a higher multiple.

10. Until quite recently, "law and order" would have been included in this list of exceptions; but the member countries have now set in train at the OECD a program of work on the problem of cross-frontier commercial bribery.

11. The quotation is from the publisher's announcement for the recent study by Hoekman and Kostecki (1995).

3.2.4   Sources and Channels of Influence

As to the ways in which the six agencies may affect what governments decide, there is an obvious distinction between the three that are intergovernmental and those that have operational or executive functions.

The OECD, the WTO, and UNCTAD are alike in having virtually no money to offer, and no power to instruct member governments (or indeed anyone else). Insofar as they exert influence, it is by one or more of four channels. (1) In committee proceedings and at other meetings that take place within these agencies, governments may bring arguments and pressures to bear on each other; and in the WTO particularly, but also on occasion within the OECD and UNCTAD, they can use the agencies as a venue for negotiations. (2) In both the OECD and the WTO, pressure can be exerted on nonmember countries that are seeking admission, and typically the main aim of this is to ensure compliance with accepted liberal norms: recent instances in the OECD are the liberalization measures that have been undertaken by Mexico, Hungary, Poland, and the Republic of Korea as part of the preparations for membership. (3) In both the OECD and (since 1989, when the Trade Policy Review Mechanism was instituted) the WTO, there is provision for the activity known as multilateral surveillance, in which governments systematically review each other's conduct and policies within specified areas of policy, drawing on secretariat documents that are normally published after revision in the light of committee discussions. (4) All of the three agencies are able to contribute to public information and debate through published papers and reports—though this aspect of the secretariat's role appears to be less fully accepted by member governments in the WTO than is the case in the OECD, and probably also UNCTAD, despite the fact that the trade policy reviews are published.

By contrast, both the IMF and the World Bank can exert direct pressure on the governments that borrow from them, through conditions formally attached to loans or credits that they extend; and these conditions may include specified moves in the direction of freer trade and capital flows. At present the list of borrowers is confined to governments of developing countries and former Communist countries—formally so for the Bank, and in practice for the Fund although its facilities are available to all member governments; and as a result, few of the OECD member states can be made subject to these forms of "conditionality." However, the Fund has some scope for influence at the margin on all its members, not just those that are current or potential borrowers, through its article IV consultations; and both the Fund and the Bank make substantial contributions to public discussion of economic policies across the world, including policies that would make for greater openness to trade and investment flows, through their respective publications programs. In what their staffs write about external economic policies, neither the Fund nor the Bank is restricted to looking at their borrowing countries alone; and the Bank in particular has done a good deal of work on the nature, extent, and consequences of protectionism in the OECD countries.

As to the EC, its channels of influence are extensive, and affect both member and nonmember countries. In relation to the latter, the Commission operates in three principal ways. First, and like the OECD and the WTO, it brings influence to bear on prospective applicants for membership, as also on those nonmember states that are members of the European Economic Area. In this, it acts with a view to (1) defining economic relations between these countries and the EU, mostly in the context of liberalization and closer integration, and (2) promoting the adoption of EU norms and standards. Second, the Commission in one of its many roles takes after the Fund and the Bank, in that it too acts as a development lending agency. It designs and operates the EU's development assistance program, as distinct from the bilateral programs that are still maintained by individual member governments: its development assistance programs are financed both through its main budget and through the mechanism of the European Development Fund (EDF). In this capacity, again like the Fund and the Bank, it can and does attach conditions to loans or grants, and these may include conditions relating to external liberalization. Third and especially significant, the Commission is responsible for giving effect to the EU's trade policies, including external aspects of the Common Agricultural Policy (CAP), and hence for the conduct of trade negotiations and trade diplomacy on behalf of its member governments. These common external policies are of course not just those of the Commission: they reflect the views, preferences, and decisions of the member governments. Even so, the Commission, here as elsewhere, is much more than a sounding board or instrument, so that there is scope for it to affect the balance between liberalism and interventionism in the EU's trade and investment regime.

Finally, there is the internal or intraunion aspect of international liberalization: the Commission has a strong and continuous influence, in accordance with the powers conferred on it in the treaties, over measures and policies affecting cross-border transactions within the EU. It is charged with the task of safeguarding and promoting freedom of intraunion trade and capital flows, and now also of internal migration, and hence with the oversight of domestic measures that may bear on this freedom; and it is concerned more broadly with the development of common policies and standards across all member states. Under both these headings, the Commission has helped to shape policies, so that it has influenced in its own right the extent to which economic integration has been taken within the EU. This influence has not been uniformly in one direction: there have been illiberal as well as liberalizing elements, chiefly arising from a tendency to view integration in terms of establishing uniformity as between member states, when in fact uniformity imposed by regulation may be a source of disintegration within economic systems. But on balance the role of the Commission in internal liberalization has been clearly positive.

The Commission's impact on events deserves a great deal more space than it can be assigned here, and in the section that follows only the other five agencies are considered.

3.3 Five Agencies and Cross-Border Liberalization: Episodes and Lessons

3.3.1 History

The Case of UNCTAD

Of these five agencies, UNCTAD has contributed least to cross-border liberalization, and indeed, it has arguably the least to show so far for its whole existence as an agency. In part, this is a matter of scale and input: as already noted, secretariat numbers are small in relation to all but the GATT/WTO, while there is only a partial counterpart to the close and continuous involvement in the GATT/WTO program—as also at the OECD—of national delegates: member governments are not prepared to put into UNCTAD proceedings the same sustained official time and effort as they give to those of the WTO and the OECD. Hence the total input, taking secretariat and delegates together, is limited, and in this respect UNCTAD has long been the weakest of these six agencies.

These chronic organizational limitations, however, are symptom as well as cause. The underlying reasons for UNCTAD's lack of weight are to be found in its history, including its origins and raison d'être. UNCTAD was created as an agency that would represent in particular the interests and concerns of the developing countries; and it was committed from the start to endorsing, and giving expression to, a particular conception of those interests, and of the working of the international economic system, which then prevailed in the developing countries (and had some support outside them). Within this view of the world, liberalization of trade and capital flows was a duty that the rich countries owed unilaterally to the poor, for whom such policies were inappropriate because of their stage of development. The interests of the developing countries lay (as it was thought) in (1) retaining full freedom to make use of administrative controls on cross-border transactions, and hence gaining exemption from international obligations that would restrict this freedom, while (2) putting pressure on the OECD countries not only to live up to these obligations, but also to offer a range of unilateral concessions—including higher flows of aid on less conditional terms, free or preferential access for manufactured exports from developing countries, "transfer of technology," and the financing of internationally agreed schemes to stabilize at "remunerative" levels the prices of commodity exports from those countries. To consider the resulting proposals, a series of discussions and negotiations was set in train, chiefly through UNCTAD or in the GATT, which became known as "the north-south dialogue"; and within these exchanges, most of the documentation embodying the viewpoint of the so-called Group of 77, established by the developing countries for negotiating purposes, was provided by the UNCTAD Secretariat.

Viewing the history of this process as a whole, there have been three main outcomes to note here. First, the results of the north-south dialogue were predictably slight. The OECD countries saw no reason to agree within it to changes which they perceived as being against their interests and unsupported by their own public opinion, all the more so since nothing tangible was offered in exchange. Such concessions as were made were unimportant, and the whole proceedings amounted to little more than a laborious twenty-five-year-long exploration of an intellectual and diplomatic blind alley.[12] Second, the UNCTAD Secretariat proved chronically unable to win the trust and confidence of OECD member governments, which saw it as lacking in objectivity and failing to meet the professional standards of the Fund, the Bank, the OECD, and the GATT. Third, the original mandate of UNCTAD gradually ceased to be relevant from the early 1980s on, because (1) it became evident that the prosperity of developing countries did not depend on securing unreciprocated favors from OECD member governments, favors that in any case were largely unforthcoming, and (2) a growing number of these countries decided on their own account to move toward more liberal trade and investment regimes, and hence to accept the disciplines of the GATT and the possibility of taking an active part in what became the Uruguay Round negotiations. As a result of these developments, UNCTAD's original vocation has been largely though not wholly undermined. It has been recognized that if the agency is to survive and develop it has to make substantial changes—a process that is in fact under way, and that was taken further in the 1996 UNCTAD IX ministerial meeting. Some possibilities for the future are touched on in section 3.4.

The GATT/WTO

By contrast with UNCTAD, the GATT's mission and raison d'être were and are more widely recognized, all the more so with the changes just noted in the developing countries, which among other things significantly broadened its membership and increased the degree of intergovernmental consensus within it. The creation of the WTO, with more extensive responsibilities than the GATT, is a clear mark of this recognition by governments across the world.

The most tangible evidence as to the past influence of the GATT, and hence the potential influence of the WTO as its successor, relates to the inception, conduct, and completion of the Uruguay Round over the period 1985–94. In part, this is because the process and its outcome can be viewed as successful from the agency's point of view, more so probably than any other episode dur-

---

12. It might be argued that the Generalized System of Preferences (GSP) has been a concrete outcome of the north-south dialogue, a feather in UNCTAD's cap, and furthermore a move in the direction of cross-border liberalization. But it is also possible to view the GSP, at any rate as it has been actually put into effect, as a backward step, because of its marked discriminatory features and the limited extent of market opening that it has brought.

ing its fifty-year life. A further factor is that in this case the sequence of events has been readably and informatively documented by an insider (now an ex-insider), John Croome, in his book *Reshaping the World Trading System,* which has been drawn on here. If one follows the story of the Uruguay Round with an eye to the contribution made by the GATT as an agency, three points in particular emerge.

First, and as one would expect, the contribution was limited. The dominant actors throughout the story were the member governments: it was their attitudes and decisions that decided at each stage the agenda for the officials working in the GATT in Geneva—secretariat and delegates alike—and largely determined what it was possible for them to achieve or even attempt. The clearest instances of this are to be found at the beginning and end of the negotiating process. In the early discussions, progress was held up by the opposition to negotiations that came from a group of twenty-four developing countries: their views were put forward to the June 1985 meeting of the GATT Council. By the following spring, however, "the 24 hardliners who . . . had opposed moves towards new negotiations had . . . shrunk in number to ten" (Croome 1995, 28), and soon afterward Argentina became another defector from the group. This remarkable change in the orientation of developing-country members, while it opened up new possibilities for the GATT, owed little to the agency itself: the governments concerned acted on their own account, unilaterally. Again, at the final stages of the Uruguay Round, the decisions that counted were made outside the GATT by the two largest trading entities: during this last phase, "it was always obvious that breakthrough agreement on the most difficult political issues could come only through some kind of settlement between the United States and the European Community" (p. 362). Such a settlement was indeed arrived at, but bilaterally and away from Geneva.

All the same, it is clear that at various points, and in a number of ways, what actually happened within the GATT, and through its procedures both formal and informal, helped throughout to give direction and impetus to the Uruguay Round negotiations. Various activities are involved here, all of them going well beyond the elementary secretariat functions of servicing meetings and keeping records of them. A process of this kind is dependent throughout on the creative response of those directly involved in it, all the more so when, as in this case, large new areas for negotiation have been opened up. In virtually every area, and in the negotiations as a whole, there were periods and stages at which further progress depended, in part at least, on the ability of the secretariat alone, or of the secretariat in conjunction with key committee members, to find ways of maintaining or restoring momentum. At the highest level, two notable instances of secretariat initiative, each of them at a critical juncture, are the actions taken by the two directors general successively involved—first, by Arthur Dunkel, in preparing the ground for a resumption of negotiations after the breakdown in Brussels at the end of 1990, and second, by Peter Sutherland, in the strong personal leadership that he gave during the final stages of the round.

The contribution thus made by the GATT as an agency was possible because the secretariat was able to define its role creatively. But in many if not most of the situations where this was called for, the actions undertaken took the form of a combined operation, with the secretariat acting not alone but in concert with national delegates. The individuals who emerge from the story of events in Geneva—as also, now and then, in other cities from Punta del Este to Marra-kesh—include not only the two directors general and their senior staff, but also the leading committee chairmen who were officials of member countries.

The OECD

As part of its assigned role, the OECD is clearly identified with the cause of external liberalization: this can be seen in article 1 of the convention that established the agency in 1961, where among other things it is enjoined "to contribute to the expansion of world trade on a multilateral non-discriminatory basis in accordance with international obligations." A wide range of its activities is related to this instruction. Among these, two quite different operations stand out as instances where the organization as such has had an influence of its own.[13]

The Freeing of Capital Flows, Direct Foreign Investment, and Trade in Services. From its earliest days, member governments have used the OECD as a forum for systematically reducing the extent of their restrictions on international capital flows of all kinds, as also on various categories of trade in services. Two committees have been chiefly involved, working in collaboration, together with three legal instruments that have been used within the committee mechanisms as a framework for systematically reviewing issues, possibilities, and new developments, and that have themselves been continually revised and extended in scope. The committees are the Committee on Capital Movements and Invisible Transactions and the Committee on Investment and Multinational Enterprises. The legal instruments are the two Codes of Liberalisation—one for capital movements, and the other for current invisible transactions—together with the National Treatment Instrument which gives expression to the principle of nondiscrimination as between domestically owned firms and those controlled from abroad.

During the OECD's lifetime, and more especially during the past fifteen to twenty years, far-reaching measures of liberalization have been undertaken across the whole OECD area in all these domains. Three leading instances are

- exchange controls, where there has been a continuing process of relaxing and removing restrictions, ending with the termination in 1994

---

13. The paragraphs that immediately follow are taken from Henderson (1996), which describes more fully the various ways in which the OECD is currently involved with issues of cross-border liberalization.

of the last two remaining exchange control regimes within the then OECD area (in Greece and Iceland);[14]

- direct foreign investment, where "the 1980s saw substantial progress by member countries as a whole in doing away with restrictions" (OECD 1992, 8); and

- financial services, where, in addition to widespread deregulation of domestic financial markets, consensus was reached in the early 1990s to introduce extensive new liberalization obligations concerning the provision of banking and financial services on a cross-border basis and through branching.

In relation to financial services, other OECD bodies have also been involved in work that bears on liberalization, including the Committees on Financial Markets and on Insurance.

Of course, the reforms that have been made cannot be credited solely, or even largely, to the OECD as such, just as parallel measures of multilateral trade liberalization cannot be credited solely to the GATT (or now, the WTO). The various measures listed above have reflected the wishes and judgment of member governments, which in part have been formulated and put into effect through the agency of the OECD. Moreover, the OECD has not been the only international organization closely involved in these particular forms of liberalization, since much of the progress, especially since the inception in 1985 of the Single Market, has taken place within the EU and with the Commission, not the OECD, as the venue and agent for the twelve countries then involved. But there is no doubt that the existence of the OECD, and the combined work within it by delegates and secretariat in the relevant committees, has contributed over more than three decades to the process of reform. Had the OECD committee structure not existed, it would have been necessary to invent something very like it.

The Reform of Agricultural Policies. The second instance is that of agricultural policies in the member countries. This aspect of the OECD's work is a more recent development. It is less formal, in that no question arises of conducting negotiations within the OECD; and the issues go well beyond trade liberalization although this is an important dimension. The committee mainly responsible is the Agriculture Committee, but the Trade Committee is also involved.

Initially, issues of agricultural policy were reviewed in the OECD in the context only of the Agriculture Committee. This situation changed in 1982—not without a good deal of debate and controversy among member governments and the Commission—when ministers collectively, through the Ministerial Council, gave the Organisation a broad mandate to analyze and review the forms and extent of agricultural support in member countries, including sup-

14. These developments, and the Organisation's role in relation to them, are reviewed in two OECD publications in particular (1990, 1993).

port through trade protection, and its effects on world trade. This reflected the explicit resolve of member governments, which since then has been regularly reaffirmed, that their agricultures should be made more subject to market disciplines and less dependent on official support. In response to this mandate, the secretariat, drawing in part on research that had been carried out elsewhere, developed and brought into use a comprehensive measure of the degree of agricultural support, the Producer and Consumer Subsidy Equivalents, together with a model designed to throw light on the worldwide effects of reductions in assistance. For member countries outside the EU, and for the EU itself under the CAP, comprehensive measures of support are now prepared annually, and used as a starting point for reviewing agricultural policies country by country. The final texts, including both the figures and the evaluations of policy, are published as secretariat reports.[15] Thus the OECD has become the standard source of authoritative data, and of informed and independent commentary, on the evolution of agricultural policies within its member countries; the locus for multilateral surveillance of those policies; and the main forum in which member governments consider and exchange views on the implications of possible reforms. All this helps to provide a firmer basis for reform, and with it for cross-border liberalization with respect to agricultural trade, even though only the member governments can decide how far they will actually move in this direction and such decisions are unlikely to be made in the OECD.

As with the WTO, what can be achieved within the OECD depends in most situations not only on the secretariat but also on the delegates involved—on the personal contributions of national officials, as well as international civil servants.

The Fund and the Bank

As noted, the main direct influence of both the Fund and the Bank is on their borrowing countries, through the dual though interconnected channels of reviews and discussions with the governments concerned ("policy dialogue"), and loans or credits that provide for specified changes in existing policies ("policy conditionality"). From the early 1980s, both agencies revised their lending strategies so as to place more emphasis on conditionality; and within these new strategies, cross-border liberalization has been given greater emphasis, so that conditions relating to it are now almost a standard feature of Fund and Bank programs. All this has formed part of a more general shift in thinking and practice, by which "the paramount need for the combined application of macroeconomic stabilization, structural adjustment, institutional reform (and, in the 1990s, good governance) became the accepted credo not only of the Bank and the Fund but also over time of the regional banks, the aid agencies of the industrial countries, and, most importantly, of an increasing number of developing countries" (Polak 1994, 8). Over time, Fund and Bank conditionality have been extended more widely, and one element within this process has

15. The latest in this series of reports is OECD (1996).

been a stronger insistence on external liberalization, as a leading element in "structural adjustment."

As to the Fund, the main emphasis in its programs has consistently been, and still remains, on the traditional aspects of its own conditionality, which relate to policies affecting monetary growth, fiscal deficits, and the exchange rate rather than to cross-border liberalization as such. However, alongside these central areas of concern, less prominent but equally traditional, is the objective of dismantling exchange restrictions which is referred to in the Fund's Articles of Agreement, and which enters explicitly into agreements with borrowers: "There is a standard clause in all programmes that the borrowing government will not introduce new restrictions, nor intensify existing ones, during the period of the programme; some programmes go further and include a liberalisation among their objectives" (Killick 1984, 236).

In recent years, Fund conditionality with respect to external policies has been taken further, through what Tony Killick describes as "an upgrading of the objective of trade liberalisation." As a result, it appears that "some countries have been refused programmes because of unwillingness to act in this area; and liberalisation is now sometimes written in as a performance criterion" (Killick 1995, 23).

On the Bank's side, involvement in issues of trade policy goes back a long way. From its earliest years, the Bank was concerned with general economic performance in borrowing countries, both for its own sake and because of the links between performance and creditworthiness; and external liberalization was seen as a means to improving performance. This theme enters into the ad hoc economic surveys that the Bank made of particular countries, starting with the report on Colombia in 1949; and in the mid-1960s it was a central element in a multivolume study of the economy of India. This latter report prepared the way for a proposed lending arrangement under which the Bank, together with other donors, would supply program assistance to India specifically linked to reforms. For various reasons this Indian operation did not evolve in the way that had been hoped, so that it did not become a precedent; and program lending remained a minor element in the Bank's total lending operations. But the thinking and influence of the Bank on trade and investment issues remained broadly liberal, possibly to an increasing extent over the 1970s.[16]

At the end of the 1970s, a major departure was made with the introduction of structural adjustment loans (and later and increasingly, sectoral adjustment loans), in which program lending has been linked to specified policy reforms. From the outset, trade liberalization was generally included in the list of agreed reforms, and from the early to mid-1980s it has become a standard feature of Bank conditionality.

---

16. In this connection, I take a more favorable view of the World Bank's record than Jeffrey Sachs (1996), who holds that "in the 1960s, the fad at the World Bank and among many donors was 'development planning.' In the 1970s, this gave way to 'basic needs.'"

It is worth noting that the idea of structural adjustment loans did not origi-
nate with the Bank's member governments, which indeed were initially resistant to the idea—developed and developing countries alike. It was conceived
and pushed through, in the face of general skepticism and even outright opposition among executive directors, thanks to the personal initiative of the president, Robert McNamara, and his senior vice president for operations, Ernest
Stern, who has been described as "the architect and inspiration" of the program. Only an agency that had established its own sphere of initiative and
autonomy could have carried through such a change: in the chillier world of
intergovernmentalism, where dwell the OECD and the WTO, the head of the
agency would have tested the water first, and then decided without hesitation
not to go ahead with any proposal.

To what extent cross-border liberalization in the borrowing countries has
actually been affected by this stronger emphasis on conditionality on the part
of aid agencies in general, and the Bretton Woods twins in particular, is very
much open to debate. It seems clear from studies that have been made that
conditional programs have had less effect on policies than had been hoped and
expected.[17] In a recent summary review, covering both the Fund and the Bank,
Tony Killick (1997) reaches three main conclusions: first, that "the high-
conditionality adjustment programmes of the IMF and World Bank have only
rather weak revealed ability to achieve their own objectives"; second, that the
extent to which reforms are made depends largely on the willingness of borrowing governments to act, for which conditionality is typically neither a necessary nor a sufficient condition; and third, that the Fund and the Bank, as also
other donors, "should recognise that their main contribution to policy reform
in developing countries has been through their influence on the contemporary
intellectual climate, and persuasion of governments through regular contacts."

Two further thoughts are worth adding to this in the context of the World
Bank. First, the point has been made, by Stanley Please in particular (1984,
1996), that at any rate in Africa the Bank has been able to influence effectively
the thinking and conduct of governments only when its conditional lending has
extended beyond projects to the central areas of economic policy: and indeed,
without this extra dimension of "conditionality" the Bank would have had less
influence on the climate of opinion in borrowing countries. Second, the Bank's
contribution to changing the intellectual climate in relation to trade and direct
investment policies has in large part been made through a substantial program
of publications and research, the scale of which has been made possible by its
relative financial independence. No intergovernmental agency, dependent on

---

17. Both the Fund and the Bank have carried out evaluations of their own. Outside reviews
include, for the Fund, Tony Killick's 1995 study, *IMF Programmes in Developing Countries;* and
for the Bank, the book by Paul Mosley and his colleagues (Mosley, Harrigan, and Toye 1991). For
the Fund, an analysis by a knowledgeable ex-insider is presented in Polak (1991). A recent paper
by Adrian Hewitt and Tony Killick (1996) reviews experience of conditional lending by bilateral
donor agencies.

annual votes from national budgets, could have established or sustained such a program.[18]

Currents of Agency Opinion

In part, the effectiveness of these five agencies in promoting cross-border liberalization depends on the extent to which their staffs (1) believe in it and (2) consider it to be important. Except in the WTO, the conjunction of these two elements over the organization as a whole is not to be taken for granted. However, there has I think been a gradual change in the microclimate of opinion within the agencies, with liberal ideas and presumptions gaining ground. Although published sources offer only limited evidence, the following tendencies can be detected.

In the World Bank, the extent of "project protectionism"—that is, favoring tariffs, quotas, tax concessions, or subsidies, where these would improve the perceived viability of projects—has fallen away to the point of insignificance.[19]

In the Fund, "revenue protectionism"—that is, the acceptance or advocacy of tariffs, or of higher tariff rates, on fiscal grounds—has likewise declined: in the 1995 annual report, the executive directors explicitly repudiated the notion.

In the OECD, issues of external liberalization are no longer the exclusive concern of specialized committees: ministries of finance and economics are also involved, through the Economic Policy Committee—though as will be argued below, there is room for this to go further.

In UNCTAD, as noted, the ideas of the secretariat and many of its client governments have moved on, so that cross-border liberalization is no longer presented mainly as an obligation owed by the rich countries to the poor.

In all these cases, part of the explanation for the change probably lies in the combined effect of (1) an increase in the numbers and influence of economists within the agencies, and (2) the evolution of mainstream thinking within the economics profession. Both these developments are to be seen also in many national administrations: tendencies in the agencies and in national capitals have reinforced one another.

3.3.2   Lessons of the History

In the events and processes sketched above, decisions as to external economic policies have remained firmly in the hands of national governments, which have likewise set the agenda for reviewing these issues in international

18. Of course, the Fund also has always conducted a substantial research program (from an earlier date in fact than the Bank), and here again this has been made possible by its relative financial autonomy; but for good reasons, the Fund, as compared with the Bank, has given less attention within this program to issues of trade liberalization and direct foreign investment.

19. Within the Bank, "project protectionism" was for the most part a local rather than a general phenomenon, to be found chiefly in the International Finance Corporation.

fora and largely determined the role and scope of the five agencies considered above. Yet as has been seen, the agencies have been more than mere instruments: in various ways they have been able to affect at the margin the balance between liberalism and interventionism in cross-border transactions, generally speaking by shifting it in a more liberal direction. A few broad conclusions can be drawn, with implications for the future, as to the factors that have made this possible, both within member governments and in the agencies themselves.

As to the member states, three main elements are to be seen. First, governments are sometimes willing to liberalize, and to take political risks in doing so, if they are acting in conjunction with others and as part of a wider agreement or understanding: an international agency can help in bringing this to pass. Second, governments are not monolithic, nor are their decisions predetermined: all of them are subject to the often conflicting pressures of interests and events, and to internal differences and divisions. In cases where the balance of arguments and forces is not too uneven, what happens within international fora, and the evidence and arguments that the agencies are able to bring to bear, often in published form, may influence the outcome. Third, many governments—and their number has been increasing—are ready to endorse liberal principles in a general way, as evidenced by the many official communiqués that make approving reference to freer trade and multilateralism. Rather explicitly in the case of both the OECD and the WTO, but also in relation to the Bretton Woods twins, member governments have in effect given the agencies a license, a mandate, to reflect this particular facet of their policies, and hence to promote cross-border liberalization. Just as the Commission can be viewed as the guardian of the treaties, so these five agencies, and the OECD and the WTO in particular, are recognized as custodians of the multilateral system.[20] Insofar as such ideas gain wider acceptance, the position of all the agencies, and their capacity to influence events in a liberal direction, will be strengthened.

For the agencies to live up to and develop such a role, a number of conditions have to be realized. First and foremost, the staff or secretariat must be respected and trusted by member governments. For both of these, recognized professional competence is a key element; and to achieve and maintain this is a considerable task, the more so because of the pressures that governments themselves, pretty well without exception, are liable to bring to bear when it comes to appointments. Continuing attention to recruitment, selection, career development, and promotion choices within the agencies is a necessary condition for keeping up professional standards.

Trust requires more than recognized competence. Agency staff have to be

---

20. This is consistent with allowing or encouraging other international agencies to think and act in different terms, reflecting other concerns or objectives on the part of governments: the International Labour Organisation is an instance of this, and arguably UNCTAD used to be.

seen to be objective and open-minded in their handling of evidence and situations, independent of individual governments, and resistant to politically driven pressures that virtually every member state is liable on occasion to exert. At the same time, they have to show themselves fully receptive to the views and sensitivities of members. Steering a balance here, and earning and keeping a reputation for being able to do so, is no simple matter. Professionalism in the agencies has several dimensions: it goes well beyond technical capacity in subject areas.

Respect and trust are the necessary basis for the agencies to be fully effective. But to exploit these assets requires well-judged initiatives, and a framework of relations with member governments that permits these. While the agencies cannot be too far ahead of governments, they need to be alert to new developments, new issues, and new possibilities, and ready to respond to these creatively. In this, they have to judge how far to await clear signals from governments and how far to anticipate these and even to help compose them. There are few rules to govern such decisions, and much depends, as always, on the calibre of leadership at the top.

One might suppose that the influence of an agency would depend on its size and degree of autonomy; but though pertinent, these are not dominant factors. Nearness to governments can be a positive as well as a constraining factor, and the reverse side of the close control that is exercised over the intergovernmental agencies is their ready access to national administrations. As well as providing channels of influence, this access enables them to draw on the professional knowledge and skills of national officials. Hence the OECD and WTO, as well as the less circumscribed Bretton Woods agencies, have been able to make their mark on events. At the same time, the Fund and the Bank have been able to use their relative freedom from detailed direction to take initiatives that have advanced the cause of liberalization.

3.4   Three Agencies and the Future

In this concluding section the focus is on the three intergovernmental agencies—the WTO, the OECD, and UNCTAD. I consider, first, the ways in which each of them could be made more effective and, second, some possibilities for closer collaboration between them.

3.4.1   The Dark Side of the Moon

All three agencies are currently under close scrutiny by their member governments. For the WTO, this is because it is a recent creation with responsibilities that go much wider than those of the GATT from which it sprang; new paths have to be marked out. In the case of the OECD, governments are carrying out a comprehensive review of its future, which has followed the arrival in mid-1996 of a new secretary general—the first non-European to hold the office. For UNCTAD, there are recurrent doubts and queries as to whether it should continue to exist as an agency, and a continuing debate as to its terms of reference and governance. A lot of official attention is therefore being given to the role and functioning of all the agencies, and to ways of improving their effectiveness.

In this, however, there is an important missing dimension. As noted, all three agencies are intergovernmental, so that member governments through permanent and visiting delegations are closely involved in their everyday activities: this is conspicuously true for the OECD and the WTO, and arguably it should become more true of UNCTAD. Yet proposals for change, both official and unofficial, typically refer to the secretariat alone, as though the agencies could be identified with their staffs. This gives only part of the picture. The effectiveness of these organizations depends on high professional standards and well-judged initiatives on the part not only of the secretariats, but also of national delegates and the departments of state that they represent.

This can be illustrated with reference to the OECD, where substantial changes are needed in governance and procedures. In particular,

1. the long-established practice of consensus in all things may need to be modified;

2. the principle of automatic representation of all member countries at (virtually) every meeting should be reexamined;

3. the staffing of permanent delegations should be made more considered and selective, with greater attention to background and experience in economic issues;

4. the question of which departments in national capitals are to be responsible for oversight and financing of the OECD needs to be reviewed: at present too much responsibility is typically assigned to ministries of foreign affairs, as distinct from departments with stronger economic interests and expertise; and

5. ministries of finance and economics need to become more broadly involved in the affairs of the Organisation.

A similar list could no doubt be given for the WTO and UNCTAD. In all three agencies, the same general principle applies: what they can achieve—or more strictly, what member governments can achieve through making use of them—depends on the degree of professionalism brought to bear not only within the respective secretariats but also in national administrations.

3.4.2 Strengthening the WTO: The Secretariat

A debate is now in progress among the member governments as to the proper role and functions of what has become the WTO Secretariat. Two schools of thought can be broadly discerned. The first favors a relatively active secretariat role, within a WTO that would be something more than a rule-making forum and a focus for negotiations, and would contribute substantially to public information and debate—rather as the OECD does. The second school takes a "strict constructionist" view: the WTO is seen as a place for negotiations and the implementation of agreements, and activities directly arising from these, with the secretariat's role confined accordingly to assisting delegations in their capacity as actual or prospective negotiators. A specific issue that divides the two parties is how far the secretariat should be involved in research.

On this, there is something to be said for the strict constructionist view, in two respects.

The perennial closeness of the WTO Secretariat to negotiations is bound to affect the nature and scope of its work, as was the case in the GATT. In this respect, there are differences between the OECD and the WTO. The OECD Secretariat is largely occupied with preparing substantial papers and documents for committee discussion, often with publication in mind; and only rarely are such agenda papers contributed by national administrations. By contrast, Croome's book on the Uruguay Round conveys the impression of a GATT/WTO staff that is engaged more in a process of (1) assembling data and information, and (2) working up first rough ideas, or refining drafts, which have originated either from member governments back home or in the course of committee proceedings in Geneva. With the important exception of the trade policy review documents, the initiative in preparing the agenda for committees lies more with delegates than is the case in the OECD, and the secretariat's work is less analytical and more operational.

It is indeed debatable how far "research" as such should be emphasized in an intergovernmental agency. Here again, the case of the OECD is pertinent. The Organisation is often described as a "think tank"; but this is misleading insofar as it conjures up a picture of the secretariat as a king-sized research institute whose mandate is to extend the frontiers of knowledge. It is true that preparing committee documents and subsequent publications often involves research; but this is a means only, not the end for which the work is undertaken. The chief mandate of the secretariat is to provide policy-related discussion documents that the clients will find relevant and useful.[21]

All the same, the strict constructionists are wrong. Even in relation to the conduct of negotiations, and in the GATT of ten or more years ago, the role of the secretariat, as is clear from the record of events, was an active and creative one. Since those days, and with the full acquiescence or support of member governments, three major developments have taken place: the WTO has been established, with its much broader responsibilities; the Trade Policy Review Mechanism has been created, and has now been confirmed as an integral and continuing part of the secretariat's work program; and a much larger and still growing number of member governments now accept the general case for moving toward a more liberal international economic order. In this new situation it

---

21. Within the OECD Secretariat, only the Development Research Centre has a clear mandate to undertake research as such.

is more logical, and more consistent with the way in which member governments now define their interests, for the secretariat to be assigned a role that is
more creative, not less, than in the days of the old GATT.

This implies an active publications program. The output of such a program
would not be limited to "research" as normally understood: what is involved
goes well beyond preparing the kind of article that gets submitted to refereed
professional journals (though this is not at all an activity to be ruled out). The
range of publications would include, as now, surveys, reviews, guides, com-
mentaries, and briefings of various kinds. Many of these would draw on the
results of inquiry and discussion, as well as research, within the WTO.

This aspect of the secretariat's potential role cannot be delegated to other
agencies, such as the OECD, in part because of the professional makeup of the
WTO Secretariat. The OECD is often referred to as "multidisciplinary," but in
fact it is the WTO that better deserves this description. This is because within
it both law and economics are well established as distinct but interacting disciplines, whereas in the OECD economics has no rival though it is not perhaps
consistently predominant.

A concrete example will serve to illustrate the argument. Since 1989 the
GATT/WTO Secretariat has been responsible for preparing and publishing reviews of trade policies in the member countries, within the Trade Policy Review Mechanism. The resulting reviews are lengthy and informative documents, which now in total run into scores of volumes. A fitting task for the
secretariat today would be to prepare, in the light of the reports, a summary
review and assessment study. Such a publication would cover, in a readable
and concise way, first, the evolution and present state of trade regimes across
the world, as revealed in the reports, and second, an appraisal of the working
of the review mechanism itself, and of the GATT/WTO experience with this
recently introduced form of multilateral surveillance. A document of this kind
would be a useful contribution to world understanding, which the WTO Secretariat is best qualified to make.

A broader secretariat role within the WTO, endorsed by governments, would
contribute usefully to public debate, since there are clearly topics on which, as
Croome's book makes clear, professionals at the WTO have something of their
own to offer. In doing so, it would help advance a cause to which permanent
delegations, as well as the secretariat, are giving their working lives—and indeed, one might hope that delegation members, along with the secretariat,
would be involved in some of this work. It is not only through negotiations that
the WTO can help to make the multilateral trade and investment system more
secure and effective, and the principles that underlie it more widely known
and understood.

All this has implications for the staffing and budget of the organization. The
case for strict constructionism is partly if not largely based on the recognition
by member governments that the WTO has new and wider responsibilities, as
compared with the GATT, together with a natural resolve that its budget should

not increase significantly: hence the wish to find economies by reducing to a minimum the role and functions of the secretariat in relation to its extended range of tasks. But this is the wrong direction in which to seek economies. For the effective conduct of current and prospective WTO business, the role of the secretariat needs to be more positive, rather than less; and the larger role of the organization, as compared with its predecessor, clearly points to some increase in resources, for secretariat and delegations alike.

To argue in this way does not imply that economies are not to be sought. On the contrary, the prospect of a larger WTO budget, even though the absolute amounts involved are small, underlines the continuing need, as in the case of the OECD also, (1) to ensure and to demonstrate that the secretariat is well managed and maintains high professional standards, and (2) for member governments to see to it that national delegations likewise are effectively staffed and run.

3.4.3   Interagency Aspects

UNCTAD and the WTO

Under this first heading, some tentative suggestions are offered.

It is sometimes argued, as for example by the 1995 report of the Commission on Global Governance (pp. 279–83), that because the original reasons for creating UNCTAD as a separate agency no longer apply, or have much less force than they used to, the time has come to wind it up. Such an argument is not conclusive, whether for UNCTAD or for the IMF to which it is also sometimes directed. Freed from the burden of sustaining the doomed "north-south dialogue," and propagating the highly questionable view of the international system on which it was based, UNCTAD may now be able to focus on more useful tasks.

It makes sense for UNCTAD to maintain its special role as a custodian of the interests of the developing countries in particular, including through technical assistance and advisory work. This role is recognized and accepted by the OECD countries; and it involves collaboration with the WTO, particularly though not only in relation to assistance for countries in Africa.

When seeking opinions on this subject, I was impressed by the spontaneous tributes that were paid to the quality of the UNCTAD Secretariat's work in specific areas. Examples of these were trade data (where a World Bank official remarked that "UNCTAD are our saviors"); tradable permits for carbon dioxide emissions;[22] private direct foreign investment;[23] and issues of debt management. There may be other areas in which the agency now has a distinctive role,

---

22. Cf. UNCTAD (1995), a survey in which reference is made to other work that the agency has carried out on this highly relevant subject.

23. Cf. UNCTAD's *World Investment Report,* among other related publications in this area.

and where its work can be viewed as complementary to that of others, including in particular the WTO.

As compared with the WTO and even the OECD, the UNCTAD Secretariat has in the past been freer to take initiatives, because it was less subject to close control and supervision by member governments. With the development of a closer consensus as between developed and developing countries, this situation may well be changing, with results that are likely to be positive on balance. UNCTAD could well gain from a more active and continuous participation by national officials, including some of those whose main concerns are with the WTO, and a closer involvement of member governments at working level rather than through ministerial meetings. More broadly, the whole question of UNCTAD's "governance" may need attention.

In UNCTAD even more than in the WTO, the extent to which the agency can become more identified with the cause of cross-border liberalization depends on how far liberal ideas are taken up by those developing countries where, as compared with ten to fifteen years ago, they have so far gained least ground: among the larger WTO member countries in this category are India, Pakistan, Bangladesh, Egypt, and Nigeria. Developments in both Russia and China will also bear on what can be done. For UNCTAD as well as for the WTO, much depends on how far governments across the world accept the case for liberalization within a multilateral framework, and direct their efforts accordingly.

Particularly in view of history, the UNCTAD Secretariat has to maintain, and be seen to maintain, professional standards that are fully in line with those of the other agencies covered in this paper.

The WTO and the OECD

The WTO and the OECD have roles that are in part related and complementary. Both are concerned with the global multilateral system of trade and investment, and with finding ways of making this system more complete, more secure, and more effective—in particular, by strengthening the body of rules and understandings in which the principle of multilateralism and nondiscrimination finds expression. In this they are allies, while no other international agency has the same express concern.

There is another and more prosaic reason why the two agencies should work in concert. In both of them, the secretariats are fully stretched and spread thin—the OECD because of its extended portfolio, and the WTO because of the smaller secretariat numbers, the much larger number of member countries, the proportionately larger numbers of those in permanent delegations, and its close involvement in the often intensive process of negotiation. Both secretariats need all the help they can get, including help from each other.

One suggestion has been that the OECD might become a "research arm" of the WTO. This, however, gives too much prominence to the idea of research as such; and in any case, it so happens that historically, and aside from particular areas such as financial services, the OECD Secretariat has produced little by way of research and publication on trade matters—for the valid though rather disturbing reason that this was not favored by its clients in the Trade Committee of the organization. The basis for a productive division of labor between the two agencies rests not on the superior research capacities of the OECD, but rather on two of its other attributes.

The first of these is its range. The OECD combines (1) a diverse portfolio of interests, concerns, and expertise, and (2) a dense and continuing network of contacts within member governments and other international agencies. These make it possible for the secretariat to handle subjects and issues that cut across administrative and professional dividing lines, and to do so in conjunction with teams of national officials who can be brought together as subject matter and occasion suit. A good recent instance of this capability is the *Jobs Study* (OECD 1994) and the (still continuing) activities associated with it: probably no other organization, national or international, could have undertaken this work. Among international agencies the OECD's distinctive contribution is to be found, not so much in particular areas of policy, but rather in the ways that it handles topics, its modes of operation. As noted, it is not especially "multidisciplinary"; but more than other agencies, it has the useful attribute that it can be "transdepartmental."

This transdepartmental aspect offers opportunities for the WTO, as well as member countries, to benefit from using the OECD as a venue for reviewing issues, including those that bear on cross-border liberalization, in a wider context and with the active participation of departments other than those that are represented in WTO permanent delegations. When it comes to international issues relating to minimum labor standards, environmental policies, competition policies, industrial subsidies, and agricultural support, an agency with an extensive portfolio and a correspondingly wide range of contacts has a natural role.

One aspect of this role is especially worth noting. The OECD is the only international agency in which officials from ministries of finance and economics are able, if they so wish, to review systematically questions of microeconomic policy, both with each other and, on special occasions, with representatives of other departments of state;[24] and the list of issues that can be considered includes all aspects of cross-border liberalization. The future prospects for the multilateral trade and investment system depend in part on how far these officials—and their ministers—keep a sustained interest in the sub-

24. In the OECD, the relevant discussions among these officials, who meet together with representatives of central banks, take place in the Economic Policy Committee (EPC) and its subsidiary bodies. As always in such proceedings, much depends on individual committee chairmen; and I would like here to pay a personal tribute to the leadership provided by Beryl Sprinkel, in the period when he was chairman of the U.S. Council of Economic Advisers and of the EPC.

ject, something that is by no means to be taken for granted, and that the mechanisms of the OECD can help to realize.

There is a second attribute which enables the OECD to act as a complementary agency to the WTO, in ways that have been seen on various past occasions. It is often useful for countries to be able to review and discuss issues, with the support of an independent secretariat, outside a negotiating context, and this remains one of the OECD's chief uses. Among other things, such meetings may help to prepare the ground for subsequent negotiations in the wider context of the WTO; and in relation to the Uruguay Round, this was the case in a number of areas. What is normally involved here is a prenegotiating process in three phases: defining issues and the ways in which they might be handled; detailed analysis and discussions, largely on the basis of secretariat documents; and arriving at a common understanding—not necessarily, or usually, a formal agreement—which OECD member governments take with them into the stage of negotiations in the wider arena. It is also possible, as in the case of the current discussions on the Multilateral Agreement on Investment (MAI), for actual negotiations within the OECD to be thought of as the first stages of a wider process—and in fact, the MAI is conceived as a free-standing agreement, to which non-OECD governments could adhere if they wished, with the possibility of agreed initial derogations.

It is precisely in relation to nonmember countries, and their economic relations with its members, that the OECD could now develop further its role, in parallel with the WTO. Alongside its established functions in relation to cross-border liberalization, it could increasingly become a venue for holding, or paving the way for, a wide range of discussions, exchanges, reviews, and even negotiations relating to trade, investment, regulatory, financial, and taxation issues where its members wish to include nonmembers and these latter countries are willing to take part. It is especially important that the governments of the three largest non-OECD countries—China, India, and Russia—should be drawn into such a process of systematic discussion and review, not necessarily linked to negotiation though with liberalization as its principal theme. The OECD is one of the vehicles for this, the more so because of its flexibility with respect to both subject matter and procedures.[25]

25. In such a process, there are potential advantages for nonmember governments even if membership is not in question. For a country such as India, which so far has had little contact with the OECD, there are several ways in which involvement in OECD activities could prove useful. First, the OECD would provide its officials, and on occasion private agents also, with direct access to ideas and information from both their OECD country counterparts and the secretariat. Second, the process of analysis and review could help to improve the content of, and the prospects for, economic reform in India, including the further liberalization of international transactions. Third, OECD meetings could provide an extra platform where the views and intentions of the government of India could be made known, explained, and defended. Fourth, OECD could likewise offer an additional channel through which Indian delegates could try to influence the thinking and actions of OECD member governments: India could be on the active side, as well as a recipient, in the process of multilateral surveillance—including, in particular, surveillance of protectionist mea-

Finally, as to the mechanics of collaboration between the WTO and the OECD, here are some specific suggestions.

Each agency should be well informed about the other, so as to have a good basis for judging what can be done or attempted in conjunction, and how work in one can be made use of within, or even perhaps designed for, the other. There should be adequate continuing contacts at working level, and a good well-diffused understanding of each other's roles. This applies in particular to the respective secretariats, but there may be scope also for contacts between the two sets of permanent delegations.

The whole question of representation and participation in each other's meetings should be looked at carefully and kept under review.

There should be as much joint involvement in projects—in published studies, for example, or even, now and then, the preparation of committee documents—as makes sense and can be reconciled with the basic constitutional point that the memberships of the two agencies are different.

There should be a flexible scheme by which staff members in each agency are actively encouraged to spend periods of service with the other. Ideally, the arrangements here should make it possible for WTO professionals who are nationals of countries that are not members of the OECD to work on assignment to the OECD Secretariat.

In order to enable it to make contact with ministries of finance and economics, the WTO Secretariat's involvement with the OECD should be extended to include its Economic Policy Committee, and hence within the OECD Secretariat the Economics Department which services that committee.

3.4.4   New Horizons

Cross-border liberalization is a complex and many-sided business. While it has always depended on, and reflected, the views and wishes of national governments, the international agencies, as has been seen, have exercised an influence of their own. Recent developments in the world economy, and in the attitudes of many governments, have strengthened their capacity to do so in the future.

Over the past decade or more, three developments have taken place, chiefly outside the OECD area, that have substantially altered the international economic scene. The first of these is the sustained high rates of growth, in both output and foreign trade, of a number of East Asian countries. The second is the trend toward liberalizing external economic policies. The OECD countries have themselves gone considerably further in this direction, despite continued resort to managed trade; and a large and growing number of developing countries, particularly though not only in Latin America and East Asia, and includ-

---

sures and tendencies on the part of the OECD member countries themselves. Hence it is not only its existing and immediately prospective member countries that have an interest in the effective working of the OECD.

ing most of the largest economies within the group, have moved decisively toward greater freedom of both trade and foreign investment flows. The third is the collapse of Communist economic systems, which has brought with it the prospect, and in some cases already the reality, of freer systems of external trade and payments in central and eastern Europe and the former Soviet Union. In effect, a large and still growing number of non-OECD countries, in a notable break with the past, have resolved to choose a path of closer integration into the world economy, within which some of them are becoming increasingly important elements.

All this is changing the pattern of international economic relations, and opening up new prospects. For the first time since the outbreak of World War I, the possibility has arisen of reestablishing a liberal international economic order, with virtually all governments moving toward substantial freedom for both trade and investment flows. Though the commitment to liberalization of governments everywhere is still heavily qualified, it goes wider than at any time in the previous half century. There has been convergence in attitudes and policies across the world, with a general shift, in domestic as well as external economic policies, in the balance between liberalism and interventionism.[26]

As a result of these changes, a broadly cooperative process of further cross-border liberalization can be envisaged. In this, the respective and long-established liberalizing vocations of the WTO and the OECD could be developed further, both separately and in conjunction, while new possibilities may have been created for UNCTAD to contribute in ways that could complement the activities of these two agencies. All three agencies need to equip themselves to meet changing tasks and responsibilities; and member governments themselves, in their dealings with them, are faced with a similar challenge.

References

Bergsten, C. Fred, and C. Randall Henning. 1996. *Global Economic Leadership and the Group of Seven*. Washington, DC: Institute of International Economics.

Commission on Global Governance. 1995. *Our Global Neighbourhood*. Oxford: Oxford University Press.

Croome, John. 1995. *Reshaping the World Trading System: A History of the Uruguay Round*. Geneva: World Trade Organization.

European Commission. 1996. *Vade-Mecum Budgétaire*. Brussels: European Commission.

Gwartney, James, Robert Lawson, and Walter Block. 1996. *Economic Freedom of the World, 1975–1995*. Vancouver: Fraser Institute.

26. Some interesting evidence on this is to be found in a recently published study by the Fraser Institute of Vancouver, Canada (Gwartney, Lawson, and Block 1996). A review of the changing balance between liberalism and interventionism in the OECD countries is to be found in Henderson (1995), where the case of Australia is considered in a wider context.

Henderson, David. 1995. The Revival of Economic Liberalism: Australia in an International Perspective. *Australian Economic Review* (1st quarter): 59–85.

———. 1996. The Role of the OECD in Liberalising International Trade and Capital Flows. In *The World Economy: Global Trade Policy 1996,* ed. Sven Arndt and Chris Milner. Oxford: Blackwell.

Hewitt, Adrian, and Tony Killick. 1996. Bilateral Aid Conditionality: A First View. In *Foreign Trade towards the Year 2000,* ed. Olav Stokke. London: Frank Cass.

Hoekman, Bernard, and Michel Kostecki. 1995. *The Political Economy of the World Trading System: From GATT to WTO.* Oxford: Oxford University Press.

International Monetary Fund. 1995, 1996. *Annual Report.* Washington, DC: International Monetary Fund.

Jackson, John. 1995. The World Trade Organization: Watershed Innovation or Cautious Small Step Forward? In *The World Economy: Global Trade Policy 1995,* ed. Sven Arndt and Chris Milner. Oxford: Blackwell.

Killick, Tony. 1995. *IMF Programmes in Developing Countries: Design and Impact.* London: Routledge.

———. 1997. Principals, Agents, and the Failings of Conditionality. *Journal of International Development* 9, no. 4: 483–95.

———, ed. 1984. *The Quest for Economic Stabilization: The IMF and the Third World.* London: Macmillan.

Ludlow, Peter. 1991. The European Commission. In *The New European Community: Decisionmaking and Institutional Change,* ed. Robert O. Keohane and Stanley Hoffman, chap. 3. Boulder: Westview.

Mason, Edward S., and Robert E. Asher. 1973. *The World Bank since Bretton Woods.* Washington, DC: Brookings Institution.

Mosley, Paul, Jane Harrigan, and John Toye. 1991. *Aid and Power: The World Bank and Policy-Based Lending.* London: Routledge.

Nugent, Neill. 1994. *The Government and Politics of the European Union.* 3d edition. London: Macmillan.

Organization for Economic Cooperation and Development. 1990. *Liberalisation of Capital Movements and Financial Services in the OECD Area.* Paris: OECD.

———. 1992. *International Direct Investment: Policies and Trends in the 1980s.* Paris: OECD.

———. 1993. *Exchange Control Policy.* Paris: OECD.

———. 1994. *Jobs Study.* Paris: OECD.

———. 1996. *Agricultural Policies, Marketing, and Trade in OECD Countries: Monitoring and Evaluation.* Paris: OECD.

Please, Stanley. 1984. *The Hobbled Giant: Essays on the World Bank.* Boulder: Westview.

———. 1996. Structural Adjustment and Poverty: Blunting the Criticisms. *Development Policy Review* 14: 185–202.

Polak, Jacques J. 1991. *The Changing Nature of IMF Conditionality.* Princeton Essays in International Finance no. 184. Princeton, NJ: Princeton University.

———. 1994. *The World Bank and the IMF: A Changing Relationship.* Washington, DC: Brookings Institution.

Sachs, Jeffrey. 1996. Growth in Africa. *Economist,* 29 June 1996, 25–27.

Shackle, G. L. S. 1989. Hayek. In *Pioneers of Modern Economics in Britain,* ed. D. P. O'Brien and John R. Presley, chap. 8. London: Macmillan.

United Nations Conference on Trade and Development. 1995. *Controlling Carbon Dioxide Emissions: The Tradeable Permit System.* Geneva: UNCTAD.

———. 1996. *World Investment Report.* Geneva: UNCTAD.

World Bank. 1996. *Annual Report.* Washington, DC: World Bank.

Comment on the Paper by David Henderson
Douglas Irwin

This paper has some similarities with Richard Blackhurst's. The focus here is more directly on a comparison of the WTO to other international economic agencies in terms of their influence in promoting external trade liberalization. The paper insightfully brings together information on these agencies. (David Henderson has firsthand knowledge of many of them.)

I must begin by raising the issue of whether these institutions are just a stage for members to achieve what they want to achieve, or whether they are more autonomous and can independently push policies in a more liberal direction. I do not propose to resolve this question, but it has to be on our minds in considering the effectiveness of these agencies. These institutions, of course, differ widely on this dimension: the WTO is much more of a forum for members, whereas the Bank and the Fund have some independent resources with which they can (in principle) affect policies in other countries.

Henderson makes mention of a very important point that I wish to highlight. He says that, aside from the EC, the WTO is the most secure of the major institutions in terms of its perceived legitimacy. This true statement is astounding in terms of where we were just a decade or two ago. In the early 1980s, after the failure of the 1982 GATT ministerial, we were told that the GATT was dead, that it was irrelevant, and that dispute settlement was a joke. In the late 1970s John Jackson published a paper in the *Journal of World Trade Law* about the "crumbling institutions" of liberal trade policy. The GATT/WTO has had a remarkable comeback over the past decade. This occurred largely because of the Uruguay Round, but also because the mandate of the WTO is exceptionally clear: enforce the rules of international trade policy. As such, the WTO serves a clear, distinct, widely recognized, legitimate purpose. We know what the institution does.

Contrast this with the other organizations Henderson considers. What does the IMF do? It was originally set up to provide balance-of-payments lending under a regime of fixed exchange rates. With the collapse of the Bretton Woods system, the IMF has turned to lending to support macroeconomic stabilization programs and other policy reforms, broadly construed and vaguely defined. What does the World Bank do? Some lending related to macroeconomic policy reform (similar to the IMF), some debt restructuring, some project lending, but otherwise it is not really clear what it does or what it is supposed to be doing (particularly when international capital markets are so well developed). As for UNCTAD, I won't even speculate as to what its supposed objectives are or should be. The point is that the WTO has a more assured status because its

Douglas Irwin is professor of economics at Dartmouth College and faculty research fellow of the National Bureau of Economic Research.

mandate is crisply defined and easily defended. This cannot be said of the other agencies.

One mild dissent I have about Henderson's paper is that, while he agrees that UNCTAD's original purpose has been "largely undermined," he cannot bring himself to propose abolishing it. I would argue that international institutions should be judged by a strict utilitarian calculus, that if it does not serve and cannot be made to serve a clear and useful purpose, the institution should not exist. I see no crying need for an UNCTAD. Henderson suggests that it could be remade to provide technical assistance to developing countries; but that is what the World Bank is for. Henderson suggests that it provides useful data; that it does, but those functions could easily be transferred to the Bank or another institution. Having said this, I fully doubt that UNCTAD will be abolished, because developing countries have an interest in perpetuating it.

I was particularly interested in Henderson's observations about the OECD. It might be useful for him to consider the Organization for European Economic Cooperation, which served a very useful purpose in the early 1950s in liberalizing exchange controls across Europe. While the OECD today is not a policy-setting body, it is a very useful forum for policymakers at various levels of government to meet on a regular basis on issues of mutual concern. (It would be wrong to judge the institution in terms of concrete achievements, because it was not set up with that in mind.) The OECD's informed, independent commentary on agricultural policies enabled the WTO negotiators to make significant progress on that issue. The OECD has served as the conscience of its members and has aided the cause of surveillance and reform of members' policies. I think this is an appropriate role for the OECD to play, although I would question Henderson's suggestion that the WTO become more active in this area of research. He mentions that the trust and respect an institution has is part of its capital, but if the WTO becomes perceived as an advocate, as pushing for certain policies, I think it will lose some credibility. If the WTO remains simply an entity for negotiations and oversight, it will have performed a great service to the world community.

4 International Institutions and Domestic Politics: GATT, WTO, and the Liberalization of International Trade

Judith Goldstein

While economic analysis can prove that nations will receive significant welfare gains from free trade, there is no consensus on the requisite political conditions to support such a policy. The problem is straightforward. Nations gain from trade in the aggregate, but those gains are not evenly distributed through society. This asymmetry leads to an organizational bias favoring those who lose from the economic policy. The result is the overrepresentation of protectionist interests and constant pressure on governments to close markets. Without some institutional support, liberal trade is a difficult policy for a democracy to sustain.

This paper examines how international rules and norms affect governments' interest in, and ability to sustain, an open trade policy. The empirical focus of the analysis is the GATT/WTO. The theoretical argument is in two sections, with the focus on the second.

First, I examine the general question of cooperation among nations in international economic affairs and the role played by formal international institutions in facilitating such cooperation. If we assume states to be rational and unified actors, international institutions such as the WTO play a critical role in reducing transaction costs, providing information, and monitoring behavior. All increase the probability of cooperation because they reduce the possibility of ex post "cheating" in a world in which trade is imagined to be an iterated prisoner's dilemma.

Second, I relax the assumption that nations are without domestic politics.

Judith Goldstein is associate professor in the Department of Political Science at Stanford University.

The author thanks all the participants at the conference and especially Jean Baneth and Richard Pomfret for their detailed and thoughtful comments on the paper. In addition, the paper has benefited from comments by Miles Kahler, Robert Keohane, Lisa Martin, Doug Rivers, Amy Searight, and the four anonymous referees.

Assuming that countries have competitive political systems, I argue that international institutions affect domestic politics in three ways. International institutions act as agenda setters, serving to "tie the hands" of domestic policymakers and undercut the power of proprotection interests; organizations such as the WTO facilitate the bundling or linking of issues within and across issue areas, increasing the probability of creating a majority in favor of free trade; and international institutions can cause a shift in domestic normative discourse.

The last section of the paper asks whether or not more detailed rules will foreclose cheating by WTO member countries. Although an expansion of the WTO's authority—especially to sanction—should increase cooperation among nations according to the logic offered in section 4.2, section 4.3 suggests that more legalization may do the opposite.

4.1   Coordinating International Economic Policy

The extent to which nations cooperate to attain mutually desired outcomes has varied over time and issue area. Often cooperation is the result of a situation of harmony: conflict is avoided simply because nations, acting in their self-interest, will facilitate the attainment of the goals desired by the other nation (see Keohane 1984, 51–52). As often, however, cooperation is not inevitable because it requires nations to coordinate their behavior in anticipation of the policies of other countries.

The degree of difficulty nations face in coordinating policies will vary depending upon the preference structure of actors. For example, coordination of standards may occur simply because one country's products already dominate the market or because of a technological advantage held in the production of a good. In such situations, countries prefer their own standard to become the common standard, but have a strong preference for a common standard over none at all. Institutions are helpful in such situations although their role need only be communicative; once a standard is accepted, no country has an incentive to use another.

In the area of trade politics, however, joint action is difficult in the absence of institutions to both provide information and monitor behavior. Even without consideration of domestic political variables, the structure of the international environment leads self-interested nations to pursue policies that are collectively irrational. Why? The international environment is anarchic. By this is meant less that it is a Rousseauian state of nature—there exists a nascent if still underdeveloped "international society"—but that there is no system of courts nor a system of enforcement apart from the individual actions of nations. Nations face a common dilemma. Cooperative behavior by their trading partners can never be assured—in the absence of an enforcement mechanism, even if nations can monitor "cheating" their only recourse is to mimic the behavior. In the absence of enforceable international law, the inevitability of ex post opportunism by others leads rational nations to act in their short-term self-interest. In the absence of a mechanism that assures compliance to a trade treaty, it is irrational to either negotiate or make such agreements.

The generic problem that characterizes trade relations among nations is captured in game theory by the prisoner's dilemma. The defining element of this game is a preference structure for nations in which they prefer unilateral defection to unrequited cooperation. The game is as follows: Two prisoners are suspected of a crime. The district attorney possesses evidence on a minor charge. If neither prisoner defects, that is, squeals on the other, both will only be convicted of the lesser crime. But the DA makes this difficult. He tells each that if he squeals on the other, he will go free and the other will get the heavier sentence. If both squeal, they both go to jail, but at least neither would be a sucker. The outcome, if played once, is that each player has a dominant strategy to defect, that is, squeal. If the other guy doesn't talk, then the player gets his best outcome; if he does, he is at least protected from his worst fear: being the sucker. Comparatively, if he fails to confess, he is confronted by less favorable outcomes. If his partner doesn't confess, he gets his second choice, that is, a short prison term. If he does, he gets the sucker's payoff—jail for him while his coconspirator goes free. The outcome is that they both confess and they both go to jail. If they could have either communicated or been able to assure the other that they would hold firm, they would both have been better off. In the absence of such assurance, the temptation to rat on the other is just too great.

Elements of trade policymaking among states are captured by the strategic situation of the prisoner's dilemma. When two countries consider whether to agree to lower barriers to trade, they are confronting a choice set identical to that above. Both would be better off with lower barriers, but each fears that the other will renege, making it the sucker.[1] In the absence of a system to monitor compliance to an agreement, neither side has an incentive to enter into a trade treaty. The problem, however, is not intractable.

First, the dilemma exists only if the game is played once (Axelrod 1981). If nations interact repeatedly, cooperation can occur, even given the potential of ex post opportunism. The easiest method is to play the game only with those you know will not cheat. Those who coordinate their behavior, as a group, do better than those who do not, creating the incentive for others to cooperate. Since players who maintain a reputation for honesty will do better than those without such a reputation, the key problem to be solved by an "institution" is how to accumulate and communicate information on the past behavior of players.

Milgrom, North, and Weingast (1990) take this insight to medieval Europe and demonstrate the importance of such an institution in the revival of trade in the early Middle Ages. In the absence of both commercial law and state

---

1. There are a number of ways in which trade liberalization deviates from the metaphor. Perhaps most important, economic theory suggests that unilateral free trade is better than protection, that is, each country should have a dominant strategy to cooperate, or lower barriers, even if the other does not. Historically, however, this is not how nations have behaved.

enforcement of contracts, long-distance trade was stymied. Traders could not monitor the behavior of those with whom they did business, and the distances, both geographic and temporal between the contract and delivery of goods, allowed merchants to cheat with minimal repudiation. Milgrom, North, and Weingast suggest that the institutional fix for this problem was the creation of the law merchant. Although powerless to punish offenders, law merchants together developed legal codes and supported an adjudication system. Traders adhered to their rules simply because the law merchant kept and made public records of the past behavior of individuals. Traders could break a contract once (and not make amends), but others would know and would be adverse to entering any future commercial relationships with the individual. Over time, trade occurred only between those who adhered to the "rules" and thus maintained a good reputation.

The law merchant was a functional response to the lack of a judicial system to enforce contracts. The environment dictated that some institutional support was necessary to allow individuals to garner the gains from trade. The problem of ex post cheating was dealt with through simply knowing what players had done in the previous round. Once traders found that cooperation led to a higher personal payoff, others adhered to the rules out of self-interest. This behavior is consistent with the tournament results conducted by Robert Axelrod (1981), who suggested that, in theory, the best strategy to pursue in an iterated prisoner's dilemma game was tit for tat, with players cooperating on the first move. Dyads who pursued this reciprocal strategy did far better than other players.[2] In essence, the law merchant recorded acts of reciprocal play.

Even if an institution is functional, its creation is still not guaranteed. If a free trade regime is assumed to be a collective good, the collective action problem of who will assume the costs for the creation of the regime must be solved. In the past, regimes have been created only when one member of the group chooses to provide the good out of self-interest (Olson 1965).[3] Assuming the necessity of some such benevolent great power, Charles Kindleberger (1973) explains the Great Depression as an artifact of the failure of the United States to take on hegemonic leadership. Kindleberger suggests that, at the close of World War I, one country was willing but unable to lead the world economy, Britain, and the other was unwilling but able, the United States.[4] As the world economy started to falter, there was no lender of last resort and no market for surplus commodities. The outcome was beggar-thy-neighbor policies, instability, and a depression that was in no nation's self-interest.

2. Axelrod suggested that, with a sufficiently long time horizon, tit for tat or reciprocity promotes cooperation by tying an actor's present behavior to anticipated future benefits. Assuming that players do not overly discount the future, the payoff of the game suggests that cooperation can emerge.

3. As well as one state, a small number of states may be able to jointly provide the good. The logic of the k or small number group is similar to that of one large nation paying the price on its own. See Olson 1965.

4. Similar arguments are made by Krasner 1976 and Gilpin 1981.

Similar to the law merchant example, great powers create rules and propagate norms that others have an incentive to adhere to. This is not to say that the international regime great powers create will have the same rules or will necessarily be optimal from an efficiency perspective. For example, the free trade era supported by Britain in the second half of the nineteenth century was far more laissez-faire than was that created by the United States after World War II. For a host of reasons, the United States pushed not classical but what has become known as "embedded" liberalism as the backbone of economic interchange (Ruggie 1982). Countries were encouraged to consider their social welfare needs and could protect their home markets when necessary.[5]

Once created, regimes affect the incentives of all member states and may be valued even without great power support. Using transaction cost economics, Robert Keohane (1984) provides a functional theory of international regime maintenance. Keohane observes that cooperation among nations is extremely difficult in situations where there is no legal framework that establishes liability, imperfect information, and high transaction costs. In *After Hegemony,* Keohane argues that international regimes are created by states in response to these three problems, that is, regimes are a response to the existence of unclear property rights, high uncertainty, and heavy transaction costs in international politics.

Of the three functions, international institutions are weakest in the area of establishing legal liability. Nations do not voluntarily give up their autonomy, and the rules that characterize the arrangements are almost never self-executing, that is, they are rarely automatically enforced. Instead of creating a common law that is designed to control the behavior of states, international institutions usually serve to establish expectations about the behavior of other nations. Nations adhere to codes of behavior not because they are binding but because they serve as focal points for all parties. Nations can renege at any time, but there are opportunity costs, notably foregone mutually beneficial deals.

International institutions have been more successful in providing information and lowering transaction costs. Making collective deals is difficult and time consuming. Regimes can make such contracting easier by creating links across issue area, by transforming the bargaining process so as to lengthen the "shadow of the future," and by taking advantage of economies of scale. Negotiations are easier because of the existence of common rules and expectations; the opportunity costs of leaving the regime increases directly with the degree of enmeshment in prior agreements. Perhaps the most important function an international institution can perform is to provide information to nations. Regimes monitor behavior. If nations disregard obligations, their reputa-

---

5. Many have suggested, and I essentially agree, that free trade, at least since World War II, should not be considered a collective good. Certainly, nations were excluded from the regime. See, for example, Gowa 1994.

tion is compromised, making further agreements more costly. Regimes level information asymmetries present in world politics. By making more and better information available, the regime reduces uncertainty and therefore encourages cooperation.

In sum, international institutions exist to perform explicit functions. They create principles and rules that reduce uncertainty, they provide information and monitor the behavior of other states, and they link issues, so as to expand the possible deals among nations. As Keohane (1984, 97) suggests, "[R]egimes make it more sensible to cooperate by lowering the likelihood of being double-crossed." Regimes are useful to sovereign nations in their attempt to increase the welfare of their citizens. They are not surrogate world governments nor should they be expected to command total compliance from members. They are convenient devices that serve a purpose to both nations and particular individuals.

Systemic analyses of the trading dilemma share a perspective: states are imagined to face a common problem to which they choose an institutional solution. Such analyses, however, can tell us little about the specific form that institution will take. The logic above suggests nothing about the process of collection and dissemination of information, what rules are chosen on even fundamental property rights or, for example, if reciprocity needs to be a regime's organizing principle. Rather, much about the nature of formal rules is underdetermined. The explanation for a particular solution to a coordination problem rests elsewhere, usually at a different level of analysis. Even if we assume that the most powerful nation is most likely to influence which rules and norms characterize a regime, we still need to ask why the nation chooses this, as opposed to any other, set of rules and then, as important, what is the effect of that rule choice on the domestic politics of participating nations. It is this question, and the case of the GATT/WTO, to which I now turn.

4.2   International Institutions and Domestic Politics

Nowhere is the interrelationship between domestic and international politics more evident than in trade policymaking. Groups affected by a country's trade policy are well organized and articulate. Whether it is farmers in France, auto producers in the United States, or computer companies in Japan, those whose interests will be hurt by either continued or expanded access to foreign goods and services are articulate spokespersons for specific policies. In most cases, these groups are veto players in society—leaders who would like to negotiate the opening of world markets find that fear of competition at home undermines their pro–free trade coalition.

This inability to mobilize and maintain a pro–free trade coalition is a problem that plagues all democracies. Although free trade is a policy in which the majority reaps efficiency gains, a trade barrier is a good with concentrated benefits and diffuse costs. Those who do better with higher barriers to trade have a great incentive to push for economic closure. Those who are hurt by higher prices suffer a relatively smaller loss and thus have less of an incentive to counter the proprotection forces. In some countries, this asymmetry is magnified because groups have been able to either assure their overrepresentation in the electoral process, such as agricultural producers in Japan and France, or because they have bureaucratic or corporatist support in government, biasing policy in their direction. Thus in the United States, for example, the existence of certain bureaucracies such as the Labor Department assures voice and thus representation for particular interests.

This political dimension of tariff setting offers a critique of systemic analyses of why nations desire to create and then adhere to a free trade regime. First, the literature cited above suggests that nations hold a preference for free trade agreements and it is the structure of the environment that precludes their conclusion. But if we consider the nation as a constellation of changing groups, some with a strong preference for closure, the problem with attaining the welfare-enhancing outcome of openness is found both within states and in the international environment. Even if the majority in a nation would benefit from liberal trade, the expressed preference of the country may be more reflective of the power of a few proprotection veto players.

Second, trade regimes themselves have varied by the character of politics in the lead economy. The British instituted free trade with the unilateral removal of tariff barriers. The United States, comparatively, lowered trade barriers reciprocally and then only under the condition that nations could renege under prespecified conditions. While the U.S.-inspired regime led to rounds of multilateral negotiations, the British opened up trade through specific bilateral accords. Although in both eras military politics greased the wheels of economic negotiations, the military dimension was far more central to postwar trade policymaking. This variation suggests that, even if systemic analysis is correct in its prediction that free trade occurs only in the presence of international institutional support, it can tell us little about the specific structures chosen. In fact, since in all iterated positive sum games there are an infinite number of possible equilibria, we shouldn't be surprised that the particular outcome of negotiations to form a trade regime is underdetermined. The choice of particular rules is the result of a historical, as well as functional, process.

Third, international trade regimes are not built in a state of nature. There do exist norms and values that characterize all international policymaking, and earlier agreements form the backbone of subsequent international accords. These norms and values are carried by both public and private actors and, although not always observed, are potential problems to central decision makers at home if they pursue opportunistic behavior. The existence of market "norms" is even more evident as trade has become increasingly global. Production occurs in a variety of national settings, capital flows freely searching for its most profitable home, and communications technology has linked issues, nations, and individuals in ways not easily captured by our standard game theoretical metaphors. Thus two additional assumptions of systemic analysis are questionable.

First, nations are not the only actors who exist to both monitor agreements and sanction deviant behavior. Other private actors may be as important in keeping nations from indulging in opportunism as are formal governments. Second, and related, norms, ideas, and values may exist even in competitive market situations which makes ex post opportunism less of a problem, even given the absence of international courts and laws. Nations may have an absolute preference for free trade for ideological reasons, suggesting a game theoretical metaphor of harmony, not prisoner's dilemma.

In sum, understanding trade policy entails asking not only what function does an international institution play for the state as a whole, but how does it influence the domestic political process. Instead of asking the more systemic question of how do international institutions help achieve Pareto-superior agreements among nations, I ask, how does an international regime help maintain support within its member nations? In particular, are there certain international structures that make it easier to gain a pro–free trade majority and, conversely, under what conditions do international agencies undermine their own purpose by pushing particular rules or sanctions?

Below, I examine how international trade institutions can influence domestic policy. Two arguments are offered. First, I address the general issue of sustaining a liberal trade policy in a democracy. Using the United States as example, I suggest that international institutions perform a function akin to that of domestic institutions—without some institutional fix, free trade coalitions are difficult to maintain. Second, I argue more broadly that international institutions are purveyors of ideas and norms. Where section 4.3 suggests that international rules influence coalitional patterns and formal domestic institutions, in section 4.4 I claim that international regimes influence the basic worldview of central decision makers.

4.3   Creating a Free Trade Coalition

Free trade majorities are always precarious. Because of the nature of protectionism, minorities who are hurt by trade policy or the potential of a change in policy have a great incentive to organize to gain increased protection and/or to become a veto player in attempts to liberalize policy. Those who benefit from low tariffs, either as consumers of final or intermediate imported products or as exporters, may be larger in number but accrue relatively less of a benefit from the low tariff (or a loss from higher tariffs) and thus have less of an incentive to organize in their own interests. In short, although a majority may exist for free trade, this asymmetry in benefits leads to the underrepresentation of free trade interests.

This problem exists most acutely in countries with small electoral units, like the United States. As districts increase in size, leaders are more willing to think about the "general" good, basically because they are able to make trade-offs between competing groups with cross-cutting interests. Thus the U.S. president with the largest constituency has historically been more willing to support free trade than has Congress. Among congressional representatives, the Senate is more free trade–oriented than is the House. With very small districts, House members have greater difficulty ignoring organized groups in their districts. Even though a majority may exist that will benefit from trade liberalization, it is more likely that it is the voice of import-competing groups that will determine the votes of these representatives. The outcome is a logroll in which all interests are accommodated; the cost is an irrational collective policy.[6]

Trade policy is not the only issue area in which leaders find that the democratic process leads to collective irrationality. Consider, for example, the American debate on military-base closings or social security payments. Everyone wants to close military bases and thus get the "peace dividend," yet no one wants a base closed in their district. Similarly, Congress cannot easily set benefit levels for senior citizens—found in every congressional district, their voice would lead to granting them more benefits than warrants their numbers. Left to its own devices, Congress would never close a base and the level of social security benefits would be fiscally unsound.

Congressional reaction in all three cases, trade policy, base closings, and setting social security benefits, has been to rely on an institutional solution to their collective action problem. In all three cases, Congress delegated responsibility to create a package of either cuts or benefits. In effect, Congress tied its own hands through the creation of structures—a blue-ribbon committee for base closings and indexing of social security—that allowed them to ignore the pressure of constituents.

Congress initially tied its hands in trade policymaking in 1934. Under the U.S. Constitution, Congress is granted the right to set tariff levels. For more than a century, it used this power with impunity. Then, in the wake of the Smoot-Hawley Tariff of 1930, Congress delegated the power to lower rates to the office of the president. Why in 1934? While revision of tariff schedules had never been a simple matter, the process in 1929–30 had degenerated into a frenzy of special-interest lobbying and deal making. Schattschneider (1935, 29, 36) wrote of the "truly Sisyphean labor" to which the legislation condemned Congress—11,000 pages of testimony and briefs in forty-three days and five nights of hearings. Destler (1992, 14) suggests that members of Congress chose to delegate in its aftermath to better "protect themselves from the direct one-sided pressure from producer interests that had led them to make

---

6. The textbook example of this is offered by E. E. Schattschneider (1935) of the 1929–30 Smoot-Hawley Tariff. No one wanted a huge tariff hike, but each representative wanted something for his constituents. The result was high tariffs and a rapid decline in trade.

bad trade law" (see also Pastor 1980). Whatever the impetus, delegation facilitated trade liberalization by granting the president agenda-setting power on trade matters. This allowed executive officials to mold "the agenda and policy process to their own ideological, bureaucratic and above all, international interests" (Haggard 1988, 91).

Presidential agenda control undercut the organizational bias held by proprotection groups in two distinct ways. First, after 1934 the president was able to craft bills that were immune from being "picked apart" by proprotection groups. Beginning in 1934, Congress delegated to the president the right to negotiate tariff cuts up to a specified amount, but under the "veil of ignorance" of exactly which industries would or would not be touched. These tariff agreements then became law without returning to Congress, or obtaining a super majority (as with other treaties). And because at least 51 percent of the districts benefited from tariff reductions, the negotiating authority was regularly renewed. As a result, American trade barriers declined dramatically. Attempts to renege on agreements through item-specific protectionism rarely passed the legislature under the threat of a presidential veto.[7]

After 1974, a second institutional fix was devised to deal with the same proprotection bias in the legislative process. By the mid-1970s, the key trade issues were about nontariff, not tariff, barriers (NTBs). As world tariff levels declined, other aspects of nations' trading practices—from procurement practices to subsidies—became the major impediments to world trade. While Congress had agreed to preapprove tariff reductions, thereby allowing the president to negotiate tariff treaties, such a procedure was impractical for NTBs. The nature of international agreements now entailed a treaty's explicit return to the legislature for approval of changes in domestic law. Although the general political problem was the same, that is, protectionist groups would have asymmetrical power to veto legislation, the solution of prestipulating the president's authority was now impractical.

The institutional fix was again an ex ante commitment, not to specified reductions but rather to a "closed" vote. Under the system known as fast track, the president would negotiate concessions in consultation with relevant congressional committees. Then, at least ninety days prior, he would give notice of intent to enter into an NTB agreement. Both houses of Congress would be required to act within sixty days of his submitting the implementing legislation. In return for consultation, Congress would vote under a closed rule—no changes would be allowed either in committee or on the floor.

In summary, American liberalization was facilitated by two institutional fixes that granted agenda power to the president and served to tie the hands of

---

7. The mandate to negotiate agreements was not open-ended. Rather, presidential agenda powers had to be regularly renewed, suggesting that the president was always constrained by congressional interests. The president still had to worry about gaining approval to continue to reduce tariffs, so he had to make sure that he could organize supporters. As section 4.4 argues, he did this through strategic bundling that enlarged his coalition.

Congress. Both forced a yes/no vote on trade agreements, thereby undercutting the ability of particularistic interests to pick apart legislation.

This strategy of Congress essentially hiding from powerful groups was successful only to the degree that an open trade policy was approved by a majority in the electorate. Agenda control and/or fast track can manipulate but not change the preferences of the legislature. Thus, as important in the explanation of liberalization of American policy is that presidents used their negotiating authority to make agreements that bundled export gains with import losses so as to keep 51 percent of Congress in the coalition. It is the president's bundling of international and domestic tariffs that led members of Congress to be more willing to trade-off the political risk of opening their home market for the political benefit of increased access to foreign markets. This preference change enabled the president to ask for and receive increasingly broader authority to negotiate tariff reductions. This preference change is both a cause and an effect of the internationalization of the world economy after World War II—initial U.S. efforts to lower its tariffs were sustained only because of the positive feedback effects of increased trade on the American economy (Bailey, Goldstein, and Weingast 1997).

The logic of presidential agenda control, the closed rule, and the bundling of agreements so as to expand the free trade majority have international analogs. First, the GATT/WTO facilitates the creation of complex agreements that are less likely to unravel when the treaty is ratified by individual nations. Obtaining and maintaining a free trade majority is easier when countries have the largest possible pool from which to make trade-offs among groups who benefit from export growth and those hurt by increased import competition. With a large number of nations willing to concede benefits, trade negotiators can more easily make these trade-offs, and thereby find a majority who will gain from increased trade. Thus the GATT, as a multilateral forum, facilitates the creation of interests that may otherwise not have cared about the liberalization process.

Less obvious but as important, GATT/WTO serves as an agenda setter for both the president and Congress. The power that derives from the American president's agenda control is his ability to force a yes/no vote on a set bill. International treaties also serve to bind Congress to a closed rule. Treaties that enter as a bundle of agreements force each representative to choose between the status quo and trade under the treaty. Given the generalized benefits of openness, each is more likely to choose the trade agreement.

Agenda control matters in a second sense. When elected officials fear that their party will not be in office long, they will try to lock in their policy preferences through changes in the political process. For example, the American civil service system exists because the reigning political party sought to undercut the ability of opponents to reward loyal party workers with government jobs. What resulted was the creation of a professional bureaucracy, the demise of thousands of political jobs, and the depoliticization of many aspects of policymaking. Similarly, legislation that moves the policymaking focus to any bureaucracy and out of the legislature will undermine future representatives' ability to manipulate policy.

In a like manner, international agreements serve to lock in the preferred policy of domestic leaders. In the case of the free trade regime, participating economies will adjust to changed prices of goods and services. Some of the import-competing producers will be wiped out; employment will transfer to sectors either unaffected by world trade or benefiting from continued openness. Over time, more groups are available to organize to maintain access to the world market. More producers will rely upon cheap imports of intermediate products to keep prices down. In short, the economic costs of undermining a trade agreement increases over time.

Similarly, the political costs of undermining multilateral agreements expand over time. Reneging by one nation becomes more difficult since small changes affect an increasingly larger number of sectors and nations. This interdependence is a constraint on policymakers of member countries who may otherwise think to defect from a GATT/WTO agreement. This constraint is not abstract but operates because of coalitional patterns in member countries. In particular, GATT/WTO rules increase the number of domestic actors hurt by a national decision to break an agreement, effectively providing decision makers with political support to counter the weight of proprotection groups.

For example, according to the GATT/WTO, if a nation reneges on an agreement, nations who are hurt by closure of the market to their goods are allowed to take reciprocal action to recoup economic loss. In practice, one country closes trade to another, and the response is an equal monetary loss through an increased tariff or other barrier to trade. The amount of gain is capped by the amount of loss, echoing the principle of reciprocity found throughout the GATT. The important part of this rule, however, is not the most touted, that is, the retaliation cap, but rather that ex ante no one knows who will be affected by the increased tariffs.[8] Thus, a country that decides it wants to aid one sector needs to consider who else will be effected. Certainly, the tariff will be placed on an export group, usually one that is competitive on international markets. Thus, before a nation decides to renege, it must consider not only the political clout of the import-competing group, but the potential force of the groups to be affected by the retaliatory tariffs. From the perspective of domestic politics, this creates an incentive for export groups to organize in defense of free trade and against particularistic protectionism, simply because there is some probability that they will be hit by the tariff hike. Where it was irrational for these groups to organize without the existence of the GATT/

---

8. According to logic, it should be better if the GATT/WTO allowed larger sanctions, that is, if we assume the function of sanctions is to assure that elected officials' hands are tied vis-à-vis proprotection groups. Even though this is logical, the founders of the GATT clearly worried more about a potential slippery slope in which the whole trade system could be undone than about rationality from the perspective of domestic elected leaders.

WTO, they now find it in their interest to counter the weight of proprotection groups.[9]

4.4   International Institutions and Free Trade Ideas

I suggested above that an international institution could facilitate free trade, first, by expanding the size and organizing potential of a pro–free trade coalition and, second, by using agenda-setting authority to undercut the relative power of protectionist groups. International regimes influence domestic coalitions in a second manner: institutions legitimate and disseminate ideas and norms. Even if we assume that individuals and nations maximize their self-interest, political action depends on the substantive quality of the ideas held by decision makers. Ideas clarify principles and conceptions of causal relationships and coordinate individual behavior (Goldstein and Keohane 1993). Proving the importance of a generalized belief in an idea such as free trade, however, is fraught with difficulty. Ideas are always available and can be merely hooks on which individuals or nations hang their interests. For example, both the United States and Great Britain could have embraced free trade ideas simply because of their resource endowments.

Still, without some attention to the ideas held by individuals, interest-based explanations of trade policy leave two key empirical puzzles unsolved. First, as argued above, trade is one of a number of issue areas in which an asymmetric organizational bias leads to suboptimal public policy. I suggested that this public policy problem has been solved in a number of ways. In the United States, trade liberalization is possible because the executive office has agenda control, military bases were closed through the creation of a blue-ribbon committee, and social security payments were held in check through the technical solution of indexing. All three are different solutions to essentially the same functional problem. Why is one selected rather than another?

Second, it was suggested that policymakers were able to maintain openness because, in the long term, the welfare of the majority in their districts benefited from the policy. But why would an elected official with a short time horizon, that is, two years in the House of Representatives, select a policy that will not reap benefits in a period in which he could claim credit? Given the distributional implications of entering world markets, short-term trade liberalization will more likely lead to substantial dislocation than economic gain. Why would elected officials pursue such a risky policy in the name of unorganized interests?

Both of these problems—of multiple equilibrium and time-horizon disjunc-

---

9. The extension of this logic is that the GATT/WTO should not fear authorized retaliation. Rather, authorized retaliation provides a credible commitment, making it rational for protrade groups to weigh in heavily to their domestic coalitions.

tion—suggest that other factors may explain trade policy choice. For liberalization to occur, officials must believe in the long-term efficacy of the economic doctrine. Without such ex ante belief, they would not lend support. This is not to suggest that a belief in free trade alone explains policy. If economic growth had not accompanied the opening of American borders to trade, the policy would have been long abandoned. Rather, economic vision plays a central role in interpreting outcomes and suggesting possible causal models of the economy. The association of protectionism with the Great Depression and war has played an important role in expanding the free trade coalition, even in the absence of constituency support.

Why are ideas about the economy central? People have incomplete information when they select strategies; elected officials who are trying to assure economic growth have far too little information to select with any accuracy the optimal strategy for their constituents. Thus individuals make decisions based on preconceived ideas, even if preferences are clear and actors are motivated purely by self-interest. If actors do not know with certainty the consequences of their actions, it is the expected effects of actions that explain them. Ideas help determine which of many means will be used to reach desired goals.

Saying that ideas are important says little about the transmission mechanism by which one set, rather than another, comes to influence policy. At least two avenues exist by which ideas have come to influence contemporary trade policy. First, there exists an epistemic community of economists, policymakers, and lawyers who share a common vision about economic growth (Haas 1992). This community acts as a transnational interest group, advocating trade liberalization and villainizing protectionism in their home countries. There are multiple reasons why members of a free trade epistemic community advocate trade openness. For those trained as neoclassical economists, and those who studied in universities with such professors, free trade is the most efficient way to organize world markets. Other policymakers may be less enamored by the theoretical defense for free trade but, rather, believe free trade and multilateralism to be the only means to avoid the devastation incurred by two world wars. Protectionism, by the United States and others, is often portrayed as the first step down a slippery slope toward war and economic depression. Whatever the origin of their beliefs, these advocates monitor government action and provide authoritative advice on the workings of the economy.

Second, free trade ideas are embedded in an extant group of international institutions. Regardless of how a particular set of beliefs came to influence politics, use of those ideas over time implies changes in existing rules and norms. Thus ideas have a lasting importance through their incorporation into the terms of political debate and through influence on organizational design. Embedded in institutions, ideas influence the incentive structure of those in the organization and those whose interests are served by that organization. Although rife with exceptions, both the GATT/WTO and the International Monetary Fund (IMF) essentially encapsulate and promote a model of market-driven economic development. These political institutions, through their laws, norms, and operating procedures, serve to promote a particular foreign economic policy both for members and those doing business with members. Over time, increasing amounts of trade activity have adhered to GATT rules. Even in arenas not explicitly covered, the general norms of reciprocity, open trade, and consultation among nations has permeated all aspects of trade relations. The GATT/WTO provides institutional support for free trade ideas both in promoting trade negotiations and in directing how nations may deviate from GATT principles.

To suggest that free trade ideas are important both because individuals believe in the precept and because the WTO has institutionalized free trade norms is not to argue that the trade vision found in the GATT or the WTO is akin to free trade models found in an economic textbook. The content of the trade policy ideas in the post–World War II period deviated from classical notions and is rather an "embedded liberalism" (Ruggie 1982). The ideological foundations of the trade regime are a hybrid, coupling trade openness with domestic stability—the liberalization of trade among nations was never a goal in itself but rather a means to domestic economic growth. Embedded liberalism meant that the formal trade system was expected to accommodate exceptions, explaining why far more detail exists on how to renege from an agreement than on how to negotiate the opening of markets. Indicative of this ideational compromise between politics and market efficiency, the post–World War II world trade system is characterized both by universal low levels of trade barriers and an increasing number of products regulated by some domestic safeguard or a negotiated agreement that undermines the "free" movement of the good.

The variation between the GATT vision and a more free trade set of beliefs is no better evidenced than through a comparison of the trade policies pursued by Britain and the United States when each "led" the world economy. Where Britain adopted a policy of unilateral tariff reductions, policy in the United States was always a hybrid of liberal ideals on the virtues of trade openness and older notions of the need for interventionist public policies. There was never a consensus that policy should be guided by economic orthodoxy, as was the case in Britain. In fact, until the 1960s, orthodoxy was suspect.

The original GATT vision reflected the status of liberal trade ideas in the United States. While the Roosevelt administration worked assiduously to create an international trade regime, that regime needed to accommodate an odd assortment of views on trade. Roosevelt, while associating himself with the Wilsonian international wing of the Democratic party, often sounded very much like a protectionist. In the 1932 presidential campaign he announced that his trade doctrine was "not widely different from that preached by Republican statesmen and politicians" and that he favored "continuous protection for American agriculture as well as American industry" (Haggard 1988, 106–7). In addition, many in the Roosevelt administration, including leading members of Roosevelt's "brain trust," considered America's problems to be domestic in nature, requiring domestic solutions. This made them inclined to use higher duties to insulate the domestic economy from the world economy in order to simplify the recovery program. Such sentiment manifested itself in provisions of the National Industrial Recovery Act (NIRA) and the Agriculture Assistance Act (1933), which allowed the government to limit imports if it were deemed that imports were interfering with the operation of the programs.

Further, the Great Depression did little to whet the appetite of these Democrats for lower tariffs. During the 1930s, efforts to unilaterally cut tariffs were dismissed as politically foolhardy. In 1931, Representative, and future Speaker, Henry Rainey (D., IL) claimed that a unilateral reduction of tariffs would trigger "a flood of imports" (Tasca 1938, 14). During the 1932 presidential campaign, Hull's proposal of unilateral reductions was roundly criticized by Roosevelt's advisers, and when Roosevelt was given a draft of a speech calling for a flat 10 percent reduction in tariffs, Democratic senators Pittman (NV) and Walsh (MT) advised him that support for such a measure was politically dangerous (Goldstein 1993, 142; Schatz 1965, 51). Even after the election, reciprocal cuts were so politically risky that Roosevelt delayed introduction of the Reciprocal Trade Agreement Act (RTAA) to Congress for a year due to fear that controversy over trade would derail high-priority items like NIRA (Tasca 1938, 24).

Thus when Congress passed the RTAA that would send the United States to Geneva, there was no common belief in the United States on an optimal trade policy. In the subsequent twenty-five years, however, a minirevolution in thinking occurred. By 1962 few in Congress did *not* count themselves among advocates of liberal trade. Where in the early years Congress followed the executive only to the extent that policy returned economic benefits, thereafter the association between postwar affluence and open trade made a pro-liberal-trade majority easy to assemble. Where partisanship explains much of what occurred in 1934, by 1962, trade was a bipartisan issue with few who criticized the general orientation. The vision, however, was always one that included a role for special cases; trade policy was not supposed to bring hard times.

In sum, those making trade policy in the postwar years came to share a vision. As opposed to earlier times, decision makers came to believe that nations do best when markets determine price and quantity. Markets were not seen as perfect, however; governments could and should intervene if markets fail and thereby cause economic and/or social disruption. In terms of trade policy, protectionism and autarchy were associated together, and both became anathema. But even while protectionism was being criticized, governments were justified in using other aspects of trade policy to assist domestic industry.

This consideration of the content of the ideas held by decision makers helps solve the puzzle posed at the start of this section. Elected officials wanted to increase economic welfare, for reasons of both their own and the collective interests. In the post–World War II period they came to believe that open markets lead to high levels of growth and closure to economic decline. Thus, to reap economic gain, they are willing to duck powerful groups, fearing that protectionism that results from political pressure will lead to a dismal economy and their certain political demise. Still, countries did not adopt a laissez-faire position. Protectionism, when administered in a "nonpolitical" manner, was deemed acceptable, explaining the detail in the GATT on the conditions under which countries may be excepted from the rules they agree to commonly. It was this combination of openness with a safety net that made the regime politically palatable in the United States and elsewhere.

4.5   Domestic Politics and the WTO

The creation of the WTO and the redesign of the dispute settlement procedures in the Uruguay Round of trade talks represent a high point in the legalization of the trade regime. These changes are noteworthy, given GATT history. The stepchild of the International Trade Organization (ITO), the GATT came into formal existence in January 1948. It had no independent bureaucracy and little funding—UN dollars and personnel provided its only support. In design, the GATT was to be a forum for making simultaneous bilateral reciprocal agreements. Unlike the ITO, the GATT did not aspire to be a multilateral mechanism for the formal control of all aspects of trade. Since its creation, the organization has grown in size and formality, and its rules increasingly provide discipline for international trading relationships. In short, the organization has attempted to depoliticize trade through the creation of more detailed and pervasive rules. Two results of this process are key. First, over time, increased legalization has led to a decline in uncertainty over the distributional affects of trade agreements. Second, the hub for dispute adjudication has moved away from participating nations to the trade regime itself (Goldstein and Martin 1997).

From the perspective of systemic logic offered in section 4.1, legalization in the WTO portends increased world levels of trade liberalization. If trade problems are due to either informational asymmetries or high transaction costs, the more efficient monitoring of behavior and better dissemination of information should lead nations to be more willing to expand access to their markets. Likewise, the new dispute settlement mechanism should provide a credible commitment—for the first time—that countries will be punished if they fail to adhere to their WTO obligations. If the problem that has stalled liberalization in the 1990s is captured by the prisoner's-dilemma metaphor, the solution of more explicit rules should change the nature of the strategic interaction among nations.

However, this systemic logic breaks down when we consider domestic politics. If trade liberalization is stalled, not because of a fear of ex post opportunism on the part of your trading partners, but either because liberalization imposes unacceptable domestic costs on political leaders or if the ideological foundations of the liberal regime is being challenged, then legalization will do little to increase trade among nations. In fact, more formal rules and frequent sanctions for violating rules and norms may be counterproductive to that purpose. Where some formalism is a helpful way to duck domestic resistance, too much may lead to the expansion of an anti–free trade majority.

Elected leaders find organizations such as the WTO helpful to the extent that they expand support for their preferred trade policy. For leaders who prefer trade openness, the WTO can be helpful in two respects. First, the trade organization acts as an agenda setter, undercutting the asymmetric power of proprotection domestic interest groups at home; second, the WTO facilitates bundled agreements that expand the size of the free trade coalition. Are either of these functions better served by an enlarged and more formal trade organization?

A more formal WTO should reduce uncertainty about the "winners and losers" of trade liberalization. Better information about the distribution of benefits, however, cuts two ways. As argued above, if export groups know with certainty that they will face foreign retaliation as a result of a protectionist act by their government, they will counter the rent-seeking efforts of import-competing groups. But while reducing the uncertainty of who will be affected by a retaliatory increase in a trade barrier may bolster free trade, good information on who will be affected by a reduction in a trade barrier may serve to undermine a nation's ability to sign free trade agreements. In the past, governments have claimed a "veil of ignorance" about which industries will and will not be subject to increased market competition in a round of trade talks. In the United States, for example, Congress has shielded itself from import-competing industries by specifying general but not specific tariff cuts. Individual industries never know, ex ante, how they would fare in negotiations. Given this uncertainty, industries often choose not to use scarce resources to lobby against tariff acts. Thus, in this instance, more and better information from a more formal trade institution could undermine trade liberalization. In sum, increased certainty about the distribution of benefits from trade mobilizes both those who seek new markets and those who will be hurt by competition.

The centralization of both the monitoring and punishment of trade violations suggests a different problem for the trade regime: enforcement of the more stringent rules agreed to during the Uruguay Round may undercut a precarious majority that exists for free trade. Without the ability to make "protectionist" side payments, political leaders will face increasing opposition at home. For example, since the 1960s, American leaders found it more convenient to respond to interest-group pressure for trade relief through use of voluntary-export-restraint (VER) agreements rather than use of a direct tariff, NTB, or subsidy. The choice was economically irrational and did little to bolster America's credibility as a trading partner. Still, VERs were functional from the perspective of politics at home. The U.S. government cannot ignore powerful industries whose economic well-being is hurt by imports. From the perspective of central decision makers, VERs were a compromise. The alternative, of unilateral protectionism, held the promise of unraveling trade policy as more and more groups demanded aid. In effect, VERs provided aid without closing the U.S. market. Without doubt, they were trade-restricting and they created global cartels. Still, they allowed elected leaders to stay committed to free trade ideals while placating powerful groups in Congress.

Under WTO rules, such arrangements are illegal, as are a number of other commonly used trade restrictions. Some analysts suggest that taking away the use of these trade-restricting tools will strengthen the trade regime. But taking away the tool has not eradicated the underlying problem. Democracies cannot ignore organized powerful resistance, and given the contemporary world economy, resistance to trade liberalization will probably increase. This means that, although the trade regime's rules were constructed as a means to discipline participating countries, circumvention may not reflect opportunistic behavior on the part of members. Deviations from rules may be a political necessity. The explanation for the longevity and stability of the post–World War II free trade regime may be, in fact, its inherent political nature; leaders could deviate from rules, give side payments, and renege on agreements without undercutting the fundamental norms of the regime. In that the regime is moving toward being more technical and less political, such deviant behavior is increasingly open to punishment. This represents a substantial norm change in the trade regime, one that may be difficult to maintain in hard economic times.

Formalism may be problematic for an additional reason. The ideological basis of the free trade regime has been located somewhere between the visions of a laissez-faire and a social welfare state. The general belief was that markets should make allocative decisions, unless the outcome was social and economic dislocation. In such cases, governments need to fix these "market failures." To the degree that WTO ideals have moved closer to economic orthodoxy, they have lost some of their political appeal. As was apparent in the U.S. debate over the Uruguay Round agreements, there is little support for a WTO that will undermine the ability of elected officials to intervene in their own economy. This is not to say that free trade beliefs have been abandoned—no U.S. leader has successfully used protectionism as a political platform. It is not this aspect of the WTO that became a political issue. Rather, it was the suggestion that WTO membership will undercut the freedom of governments to make social welfare policy that caused problems when the agreement went home for ratification.

The GATT has anchored free trade ideas in the postwar period. The organization has been instrumental in transmitting classical trade ideas around the globe and in creating international law to defend liberal world trade. To the degree that leaders believe in these ideals, they will find international law a helpful way to obtain their preferred policy, even in the face of domestic resistance. But, first and foremost, elected officials need to look toward the next election. To the degree that this international law constrains a leader's ability to obtain a majority, it will have lost its purposes at home.

References

Axelrod, Robert. 1981. The Emergence of Cooperation among Egoists. *American Political Science Review* 25:306–18.

Bailey, Michael, Judith Goldstein, and Barry Weingast. 1997. The Institutional Roots of American Trade Policy: Politics, Coalitions, and International Trade. *World Politics* 49, no. 3 (April): 309–38.

Destler, I. M. 1992. *American Trade Politics*. 2d edition. Washington DC: Institute for International Economics.

Gilpin, Robert. 1981. *War and Change in the International System*. Princeton, NJ: Princeton University Press.

Goldstein, Judith. 1993. *Ideas, Interests, and American Trade Policy*. Ithaca, NY: Cornell University Press.

Goldstein, Judith, and Robert O. Keohane. 1993. Ideas and Foreign Policy: An Analytical Framework. In *Ideas and Foreign Policy*, ed. Judith Goldstein and Robert O. Keohane. Ithaca, NY: Cornell University Press.

Goldstein, Judith, and Lisa Martin. 1997. Optimal Legalization in the GATT and WTO: Domestic Politics and Liberalization. Manuscript.

Gowa, Joanne. 1994. *Allies, Adversaries, and International Trade*. Princeton, NJ: Princeton University Press.

Haas, Peter. 1992. Introduction: Epistemic Communities and International Policy Coordination. *International Organization* 46:1–35.

Haggard, Stephan. 1988. The Institutional Foundations of Hegemony: Explaining the Reciprocal Trade Agreements Act of 1934. In *The State and American Foreign Economic Policy*, ed. G. John Ikenberry, David Lake, and Michael Mastanduno. Ithaca, NY: Cornell University Press.

Keohane, Robert O. 1984. *After Hegemony: Cooperation and Discord in the World Political Economy*. Princeton, NJ: Princeton University Press.

Kindleberger, Charles P. 1973. *The World in Depression, 1929–1939*. Berkeley: University of California Press.

Krasner, Stephen. 1976. State Power and the Structure of International Trade. *World Politics* 28:317–47.

Milgrom, Paul, Douglass North, and Barry Weingast. 1990. The Role of Institutions in the Revival of Trade: The Law Merchant, Private Judges, and the Champagne Fairs. *Economics and Politics* 2:1–23.

Olson, Mancur. 1965. *The Logic of Collective Action: Public Goods and the Theory of Groups*. Cambridge: Harvard University Press.

Pastor, Robert. 1980. *Congress and the Politics of U.S. Foreign Economic Policy*. Berkeley: University of California Press.

Ruggie, John Gerard. 1982. International Regimes, Transactions, and Change: Embedded Liberalism in the Postwar Economic Order. *International Organization* 36: 379–415.

Schattschneider, E. E. 1935. *Politics, Pressure, and the Tariff: A Study of Free Private Enterprise in Pressure Politics as Shown in the 1929–1930 Revision of the Tariff*. Hamden, CT: Archon Books.

Schatz, Arthur. 1965. Cordell Hull and the Struggle for the Reciprocal Trade Agreements Program, 1932–1940. Ph.D. dissertation, University of Oregon.

Tasca, Henry. 1938. *The Reciprocal Trade Policy of the United States*. Philadelphia: University of Pennsylvania Press.

Comment on the Paper by Judith Goldstein
Jean Baneth

I very much liked Judith Goldstein's analysis of the interplay of political processes and the pursuit of economic aims, of domestic and international institutions, and of sectional interests and the public good. I am also in broad agreement with the main points of her paper. This is much to my chagrin, because she has only modest expectations from democratic processes, and because she fears that the very improvements which the World Trade Organization (WTO) presents relative to the General Agreement on Tariffs and Trade (GATT) endanger free trade, rather than helping its preservation. My somewhat more favorable view of democratic processes is more than counterbalanced by greater concern that, in many industrial countries, experience will not bolster the free trade ideology in future, as it had bolstered it in the past. My comments will deliberately come from a European perspective, partly to complement the avowed Americanocentrism of Goldstein's political analysis.

I do not view western European politics with Panglossian optimism. I know corruption is widespread at many levels of politics, government, and business; and I also know that the people of Europe often hold unreasonable expectations. Even with open eyes, however, democratic politics seem less difficult to reconcile with the general interest in western Europe than in the United States.

This is partly related to institutional differences: Westminsterian parliamentary democracy, in its purest form, no longer prevails even in Westminster, but strong elements of it pervade western Europe. Their main characteristic is the ability of parliaments to compel the resignation of governments. This may, at first blush, appear a weakness. In fact, it increases the weight of the general interest, for this allows government to turn resistance to factional pressures into a showdown on a much broader issue, who will govern the country. Most governments that lose a vote of confidence can dissolve the dominant lower chamber of parliament. Representatives may be elected in small constituencies, but in parliamentary and quasi-parliamentary systems they cannot chiefly run on their defense of local interests, but mostly on their overall support or opposition to this or that government. Additionally, of course, even their ability to defend local interests greatly depends on their belonging to the government party.

Even when the government cannot dissolve the legislature, the very fact that a confidence vote concerns the survival of government rather than just a single issue greatly raises the relative weight given to the "general interest." This abil-

Jean Baneth has retired from the World Bank, where he occupied various positions, including director of the resident staff in Indonesia, of the Economics Analysis and Projections Department, of the International Economics Department, and of the Geneva office. In this last position, he represented the World Bank in the Uruguay Round. At present, he is *professeur invité* at Centre d'Études et de Recherches sur l'Économie Internationale, Université d'Auvergne, France, and concurrently visiting fellow of the Rajiv Gandhi Institute for Contemporary Studies, New Delhi, India.

ity to impose a central view is perhaps strongest under France's mixed presidential-parliamentary system and paradoxically, whether or not the parliamentary majority and the president belong to the same party; parliamentary discipline does not directly depend on presidential power, but on the knowledge that failure to keep discipline in key occasions would ensure defeat in both parliamentary and presidential elections.

The parliamentary process probably helps reinforce another, ideological difference between the United States and western Europe. Two different concepts of democracy are known under the names of *popular sovereignty* as opposed to the concept of *national sovereignty*. In the former, elected officials merely represent the will of the people, and as the will of the people evolves, the people's representatives must evolve with it. This concept is fairly close to prevailing in present-day American politics, with their frequent references to what the "people" of this district or that state want; and this is also what is reflected in Goldstein's analysis. Though it was strongly promoted by the extreme left in France during the immediate postwar constitutional discussions, this concept has nowadays little legitimacy in Europe.[1] Under the concept of national sovereignty the people designate representatives (parliamentarians and, in the majority of the republics, also the president); these are not supposed thereafter to reflect the people's evolving views on national matters; even less are they supposed to reflect the views and sectional interests of their constituents. They are elected to embody national sovereignty, and their constitutional responsibility is to determine policy as they see it best for the nation.

Just to complicate matters, while this is certainly the prevailing concept throughout western Europe, it is modified by increased recourse to the popular referendum. Through a referendum, for specific purposes the people resume the sovereignty normally delegated to their representatives. This tempers the embodiment of national sovereignty in parliament and president, and can override it. However, a referendum concerns the whole polity; it may not further the general interest, but by definition embodies the will of the majority, to the exclusion of regional subentities and other groups; it is quite unsuitable to the logrolling through which sectional interests are sometimes promoted in the United States. Switzerland makes the most ideologically coherent and most widespread use of the referendum: there, *the sovereign,* that is, the people, can take the initiative to override any law, and often does so. Thus in recent times, Swiss voters rejected membership in the United Nations and in the European Economic Area, while (interestingly enough) they overwhelmingly approved membership in the International Monetary Fund and the World Bank.[2]

Through habit and ideology both, the people of Europe generally adhere to

---

1. It was occasionally revived in France, mostly by the Right, when public opinion seemed to have shifted away from the Socialist president. However, the idea that such a shift should cause the president or parliament to change their policies or even to resign is now no longer heard of.

2. Any law voted by the federal parliament can be opposed by a petition that collects enough signatures in enough cantons; it must then be subjected to a referendum. Any law can thus be

the national sovereignty concept. They do not expect their representatives to anticipate and implement popular wishes, and apparently rarely want to punish them for not following such wishes. Thus, in Switzerland the sovereign regularly overturns parliamentary decisions, yet reelects the same parliamentarians and parties. Throughout Europe, the death penalty has been abolished by parliaments, even though (outside Scandinavia) it is generally strongly favored by the people.[3] Electorates may be no less interested in special favors and services than in the United States; but in addition, they demand from their representatives at least the appearance of good defenders of the national interest.

These tendencies make it easier for politicians to take free trade stances, as long as free trade seems to be in the national interest. In the 1950s all French and Italian lobby groups, labor unions as well as employers' federations, were strongly opposed to the Coal-Steel Community. It was nevertheless overwhelmingly approved by both parliaments, despite the well-known weakness of governments in those countries. More recently, GATT and WTO agreements and, in most cases, intra-European agreements were similarly approved.

This greater prominence given to the public interest enhances the role of ideology; everyone has some idea of his personal interests and of that of narrow groups to which he belongs; the public interest can be perceived only through an ideological structure. Interest groups themselves are often compelled to promote their self-interest through ideas that assimilate it to the public good. Thus the strength of, say, French or Swiss farmers does not come from a supposed overrepresentation in legislatures, but much more from the successful propagation of an ideology that presents them as the backbones of their respective nations. Such ideologies partly guide voters to support a supposed national interest against their own very clearly perceived self-interest: the same consumer who will every time prefer cheap imported tomatoes to expensive domestic ones (or Hollywood shoot-'em-ups to French comedy) will also approve of measures to limit such imports, in order to promote broader national aims he considers legitimate.

Ideology is therefore very important, and, by and large, it has hitherto worked in favor of trade liberalization, though in a way more complex than in the United States. Simplifying greatly, one can divide western Europe into three ideological areas: a group centered on Germany (but also including Ire-

---

challenged, but not initiated. However, constitutional changes can be initiated by a similar petition process; consequently, many constitutional proposals concern matters that are in reality more humdrum. In late 1989, the Swiss voted simultaneously on two constitutional proposals, one of which was to abolish (no less!) the army, the other to raise highway speed limits to the same level as in France. It is of more than anecdotal interest that all German-speaking cantons voted against raising speed limits and for keeping the army, all French-speaking cantons voted to abolish the army and raise speed limits, and the Italian-speaking canton voted to keep the army and raise speed limits.

3. Before the French presidential elections of 1981, Mitterrand clearly indicated his opposition to the death penalty, though opinion surveys indicated that the majority of the electorate was in favor of it: when the matter subsequently came to a vote in parliament, now President Chirac also voted for abolition, though his constituency was overwhelmingly in favor of keeping the guillotine. In neither case do these votes seem to have constituted electoral liabilities.

land) genuinely committed both to European integration and to free trade (in the sense of Goldstein's "embedded liberalism"); the United Kingdom, Denmark, and Sweden, also largely committed to free trade, but committed to the European ideal only grudgingly, as a means toward reciprocal access; and the remainder, which I shall misleadingly call the southern group (it includes Finland), mostly very committed to Europe but accepting non-European (and occasionally even European) free trade grudgingly, as the unavoidable concomitant of European integration.[4]

Germans or Britons will not reverse the march toward free trade: so it is this southern group that holds the deciding influence in the matter. Hitherto, this influence has been largely positive. European integration has been accompanied by external liberalization, no doubt in part because of American demands for reciprocity; and liberalization has been accepted as the unavoidable concomitant of Europe. If American administrations could, to some extent, hide behind GATT obligations (and more recently behind those of the North American Free Trade Agreement), southern European governments much more effectively could modernize and liberalize in the name of Europe, using the broad appeal to the public interest that Europe represented, to overcome not only sectional interests, but also many other things (like the protection of farmers, and most recently opposition to fiscal austerity) that also clothed themselves in public-interest garb.

This was all the more important as in the southern tier of Europe the ideological foundations of free trade were never as firm as in the English-speaking and Scandinavian countries, even in what Goldstein calls the "epistemic community." It is symbolic that France's only winner of the Nobel Prize in economics, Maurice Allais, has been a major source of rabid protectionist pamphlets. More generally, out-and-out protectionists, who would not fit into the academic mainstream in the United States or Britain, can comfortably fit into it in the southern countries.

The European ideal has long been enormously popular, a true symbol of the public interest. It was therefore overloaded as a motivator. When a few years ago, the French government reinforced the implementation of truck safety measures, its main argument was not the safety of road users but that it was required by Europe; and when one of my neighbors, a farmer's wife, told me she was taking an accountancy course, that was also to meet European competition. As a newspaper half-jokingly wrote a few years ago, there is not a municipal flower bed or drainage ditch put down in France without its being said

---

4. One should also mention the two western European countries still outside the union. Switzerland is deeply divided both about Europe and about free trade, but by and large those who want integration into the world, free-trading rules and all, want to do it through Europe; others want to preserve autonomy and Swiss traditions, including cartels and protectionism, only to be relaxed to the minimum extent needed to obtain reciprocal access for Swiss exports. Norway, apparently, just wants to keep its autonomy and oil money; the people are opposed to Europe, and neither enthusiastically in favor of global free trade nor particularly opposed to it.

to be in preparation for Europe 1992. Last but most prominently, the fiscal and privatization efforts now being accomplished would be clearly needed (though perhaps not on the same time scale) even if the union disintegrated, but they are all being pegged to Europe and Economic and Monetary Union (EMU).

The enormous driving force of the European idea originated in the pursuit of a political aim, that of reconciliation. However, to paraphrase Goldstein, if economic growth had not accompanied the opening of European borders to trade, the European ideal would have been long abandoned. For a long time, prosperity was there, and in the public eye it was clearly related to European integration. Europe and prosperity went hand in hand, thus reinforcing the European ideology; and it did not matter that they also went hand in hand with increasingly free extra-European trade. This association of prosperity with the European ideal perdured even after prosperity faltered. The Delors initiative of Europe 1992 was very widely seen as relaunching Europe both toward integration and, through it, toward greater prosperity and faster growth.

This association of European ideology with prosperity has by no means ended, but it has been dramatically weakened since the battles over the Maastricht Treaty, which unfortunately coincided with the last stages of the Uruguay Round. Trade liberalization has always been seen as Europe-driven, and the Uruguay Round's much publicized negotiations for further liberalization were conducted by European bureaucrats. Meanwhile, prosperity continued to falter. Unemployment not only was high and mounting throughout Europe, but was increasingly perceived as related to increased trade competition. An increasing segment of public opinion veered away, sometimes quite suddenly, from the perception of Europe (and through it, of freer trade) as a vehicle of general progress, to one in which Europe was seen as an obstacle to better alternative policies. Though these alternatives are ill defined at best,[5] they are mostly assumed to require more government intervention and greater protectionism.

Sectional interests obviously play a role in this, and they have been strengthened. More important by far, however, is changed perception of what constitutes the public interest. For example, the day before the referendum on the Maastricht Treaty I traveled through the vineyards of Beaujolais. No other French economic sector, with the possible exception of the strip-tease joints of Place Pigalle, has benefited so much from the outside world, has as little to fear from import competition, or as little need for subsidies. Yet I saw only anti-Maastricht posters, attacking Brussels both for its generally antiagricultural policies and for its surrender to American demands in the Uruguay Round: and the region voted strongly for rejection. Another French example, when public-sector workers went on strike last year in defense of various privi-

---

5. How ill-defined and how confused is illustrated by the heteroclite natures of the anti-Maastricht coalitions: and, more interestingly, by the violent anti-European campaign financed and run simultaneously in France and Britain by Jimmy Goldsmith, Europe's Ross Perot, who is a citizen of both countries.

leges, the public was enormously inconvenienced yet extraordinarily sympathetic; the strikers presented themselves, and were seen by many, not as defenders of sectional interests, but as a bulwark against the attack on the general interest conducted by the government in the name of Europe and EMU.

The reasons for this change of perception are obvious. Unemployment has been rising for twenty years, the rise in real wages has slowed down considerably, and there are widespread fears about the future of social insurance systems. Restructuring of a sector or a firm once meant rapidly finding a better job elsewhere; now it often means no hope for any future job at all. These problems obviously have many complex causes, but the most visible direct cause is often greater competition, foreign and even domestic, imposed by European rules, for the sake of European integration or under the WTO agreement also negotiated by the European Community.

In Europe, the inflexibility introduced by the WTO and its commitment to a purer form of economic liberalism is associated with the increasing area covered by European rules, also under a purer form of economic liberalism and financial orthodoxy. Thus, not only are there overall trade pressures and overall pressures for budgetary equilibrium; many previously widely practiced forms of intervention are now forbidden to national governments. Public services like communications and railways have to be opened to competition; so too must the financial sector, and government procurement in general; government subsidies to bail out public (or for that matter private) firms are subject to strict limits . . . A million rigidities and privileges remain, but they seem always to have been there, and public opinion does not focus on them, but on the novelty of their being attacked. In any case, these rigidities affect domestic competition more than competition from imports, perhaps because freedom of foreign trade is defended by the double tier of European and WTO institutional mechanisms. Academic purists may still complain of departures from theoretically free trade, and these no doubt remain numerous; but public opinion rightly views the dominant reality as that of fast increasing and very largely untrammeled foreign competition.

Whether or not European unemployment has the same causes as the fall in real wages in the United States, nothing in Europe yet matches the recent improvement in U.S. perceptions about the economy. Institutional safeguards ensure that Europe itself can never turn to protectionism; Fortress Europe will remain a myth. But the same forces are at work in Europe, and with greater strength, as those Goldstein has identified in the United States. They are contained and rolled back by an increasingly firm set of rules that establish an increasingly liberal economic environment. For the time being, the overall balance of ideas and perceptions is still in favor of respecting the rules. But if, despite further efforts toward financial orthodoxy and further advances toward European integration and free trade, prosperity remains elusive, the strains may increase. Then we might have to wish, both for the sake of Europe and for that of free trade, that the containment had been effected by more elastic rather than firm rules.

Like Goldstein, I see in rule-bound European integration and in rule-bound free trade clear dangers for the very objectives of integration and free trade that the rules are to protect. Yet I would be as reluctant to abandon the ambition for a rule-bound global trading system as I would be to abandon the ambition for a rule-bound integrated European Union. We should not look for the devil's portion, we should not seek flexibility in yielding to sectional interests or to misguided ideas, not even as a means for preserving a broader structure in the public interest. But even less should economists be content to rehearse old arguments in favor of free trade. We should instead intensify our search for policy mixes that would impel the public mind once again strongly to identify free trade with the public interest. Only through such policies can we hope to reconcile, in the long run, the international institutions of free trade and the domestic politics of democracies.

5 Designing and Implementing Effective Dispute Settlement Procedures: WTO Dispute Settlement, Appraisal and Prospects

John H. Jackson

5.1 Introduction and Review of the Policies of Trade Dispute Settlement Procedures

5.1.1 The Success of the Uruguay Round

On 1 January 1995 a new organization, the World Trade Organization (WTO), came into being for the purposes of assisting governments in the world to better manage problems of international economic interdependence. This event occurred fifty years after the establishment of the Bretton Woods system (with the World Bank and International Monetary Fund charters), and almost fifty years after the 1947 establishment of the General Agreement on Tariffs and Trade (GATT) and the later failure of the International Trade Organization (ITO) Charter, which would have been the institution to complete the Bretton Woods system.[1]

The WTO was one of the major results of the extended Uruguay Round negotiations on trade, under the auspices of the GATT. The Uruguay Round was the eighth major trade negotiating round of the GATT, and had been under way since September 1986. This massive undertaking resulted in a final act signed at Marrakesh, Morocco, on 15 April 1994, consisting of 26,000 pages (undoubtedly a record for a treaty length).[2] The length of time for the negotiation as well as the number of pages indicate the enormous complexity of the endeavor that had been undertaken. Although most of these pages are detailed schedules of tariff and service obligations, nevertheless about 1,000 pages of carefully negotiated treaty text covers subjects such as tariffs, financial ser-

John H. Jackson is the Hessel E. Yntema Professor of Law at the University of Michigan Law School, Ann Arbor.

1. The interested reader may also wish to see the following: Jackson 1990, 1989, 1969; Jackson, Davey, and Sykes 1995a.
2. WTO 1994, 1140. See also House 1994.

vices, intellectual property, antidumping measures, escape clause and safe-guard measures, textile trade, agricultural trade, and many more crucial questions of international economics. But perhaps the most significant measure included in the Marrakesh Final Act was the new "charter" for a "World Trade Organization," which would now replace the GATT as the central institution for international trade cooperation in the world.

5.1.2   The Institutional Problems of the WTO

The launch of the WTO is now obviously quite successful. After coming into force on 1 January 1995, the WTO after twenty months has 122 members, and the numbers are climbing (there are about 30 more nations in the process of negotiating for membership). It is also remarkable that, although the WTO and the Uruguay Round evolved from almost fifty years of GATT history, nevertheless, this new WTO institutional framework, arguably a relatively minimal change, does have some profound implications.[3] It embraces the so-called single-package idea, which requires every nation to accept the entire package (or at least 95 percent of it). This is in contrast to results under prior rounds, such as the Tokyo Round, whereby nations could pick and choose among a series of protocol agreements (a process called "GATT à la carte").

One of the central features of the new WTO institution (indeed some are calling it *the* central feature), is the new dispute settlement process. This paper focuses on these new procedures. In particular, section 5.3 discusses several significant and central issues concerning international dispute settlement procedures in the context of the WTO. Almost all of these issues relate to a broader question of "sovereignty" (whatever that means today). A number of the diplomats to the WTO have begun to realize the significance of the new procedures, and in some cases are worried or a bit fearful of them. The key attribute of the new procedures, as we will see below, is "automaticity." No longer will it be feasible for a nation to block the results of a dispute settlement procedure. In addition, during the U.S. congressional hearings on the implementing act for the Uruguay Round results, there was a considerable amount of debate about whether the intrusion on U.S. sovereignty by the WTO, and its dispute settlement process, was too great. I have testified on that subject (see appendix A). In my opinion, there are adequate checks and safeguards in the WTO against inappropriate incursions on "sovereignty," but it must be recognized that, even for the United States, the new procedures will effectively require some alteration in traditional thinking about diplomacy connected with international economic relations. Already there have been some effects (for example in the U.S.-Japan dispute concerning automobile exports to the United States.[4]

At the outset, it should be noted that there are some strong policy underpinnings for an effective dispute settlement process, which are often overlooked,

---

3. WTO 1994, 1140. See primarily the part devoted to dispute settlement, entitled "Dispute Settlement Understanding" (DSU); *see also* House 1994; Jackson 1995b, 11–31.

4. Both sides threatened to use the dispute settlement procedure, and the settlement was importantly influenced by the possibilities of the results of this procedure (GATT 1994).

or at least not often mentioned explicitly. Basically the goal is what has been termed a "rule-oriented system" (Jackson 1989, chap. 4), a system that gives guidance in the way of predictable and generally stable rules to millions of entrepreneurs around the world. Such guidance is very necessary for investment decisions, market opening decisions, technological decisions, and so forth. In economists' terms, this is a system that will reduce the so-called risk premium for some of those decisions.

5.2   The GATT, Its Birth Defects, and the New WTO Procedures

5.2.1   The GATT and the Uruguay Round

It is common knowledge that the GATT itself was never intended to be an organization. Rather, after the other Bretton Woods institutions were established (in 1945), world government leaders determined that it would be necessary to add another institution, one devoted to trade—the ITO. The GATT was merely designed to be a multilateral trade and tariff agreement that would depend on the ITO for its institutional infrastructure. When the ITO did not come into force because parliaments, particularly the U.S. Congress, would not approve it in the late 1940s, the GATT gradually became the central focus of coordinating activity among nations regarding trade.

Despite this inauspicious beginning, the GATT has been remarkably successful during its nearly five decades. Partly this is because of ingenious and pragmatic leadership, particularly in its early years. Nevertheless, because of this unfortunate history, the GATT endured a number of "birth defects" that proved increasingly troublesome in recent years as world economic affairs became more complex and harder to manage. These defects included

- provisional application and grandfather rights exceptions embraced by the Protocol of Provisional Application;
- ambiguity about the powers of the contracting parties to make certain decisions;
- ambiguity regarding the waiver authority and risks of misuse;
- murky legal status leading to misunderstanding by the public, media, and even government officials;
- certain defects in the dispute settlement procedures; and
- lack of institutional provisions generally, leading to constant improvisation.

The Uruguay Round, negotiated from 1986 to 1994, resulted in a new treaty text on dispute settlement, the "dispute settlement understanding" (DSU).[5] For the first time, therefore, we have substantial binding treaty text with respect to

---

5. DSU article 26. See Understanding on Rules and Procedures Governing the Settlement of Disputes, annex 2 to WTO agreement.

dispute settlement in the GATT/WTO system. The GATT clauses were very brief; three paragraphs essentially, embellished at the end of the Tokyo Round in 1979 by a so-called understanding. The DSU contains about forty pages. Beyond that, there are a number of specific provisions in various other texts of the Uruguay Round. The major change is the elimination of "blocking" of a final panel report. Blocking was a major defect of the previous system (Jackson 1990), which is no longer permitted. Thus the DSU provides "automaticity," whereby reports of a dispute settlement panel and the appellate panel (the final result of these processes) will almost always become binding in some sense, discussed below.

Some may ask what is the true relevance of "binding treaty texts." Skeptics may say that treaties are difficult to enforce and can often be evaded anyway, so that nonbinding treaty clauses, "hortatory" or "policy guidance," would be just as substantial. However, there is extensive commentary by both scholars and persons with considerable experience in international affairs that a binding treaty obligation under international law principles does have some important additional effects (Henkin 1994). In addition to the diplomatic advantages of being on the "right side" of international law, there are a number of potential domestic legal consequences of binding international law obligations compared to "soft law," which is not binding. For example, in some legal systems a binding treaty may have domestic law "statutelike" effect (Jackson 1992, 310; 1987, 141–70). Even in jurisdictions where such direct effect does not occur, a binding treaty can have various other legal effects in a domestic law system, such as influencing interpretation of statutes or other laws in such system.

In addition to the considerations above, the dispute settlement procedure resulting from the Uruguay Round is also a *unified* procedure. The previous system was fragmented, with eight or ten different dispute settlement processes. This change has very great implications, particularly for enhancing public understanding, including high government officials' understanding of the system.

The prior history of the GATT (see Jackson 1990, 1989, 1969, 1995a, 1995b) is related to the WTO by a very important clause in the WTO Charter, sometimes called the "guidance clause." Article XVI:1 of the WTO Charter explicitly says that the new organization and all of its component parts shall be "guided by" the practice and decisions, and so forth, of the GATT. That is a very significant clause that carries over what legal scholars would call the "jurisprudence" of the GATT as part of the underpinnings of a more stable and predictable system for the future in the WTO.

5.2.2 The WTO Dispute Settlement Procedures: Statistics and the "State of Play"

The new dispute settlement system has faced certain hurdles in its first years. The first hurdle was of course the U.S.-Japan controversy over automobiles, which was fortunately settled. The second was the selection of the appellate body itself, which was a very interesting process that turned out to take a half year longer than expected, but in the end worked out very well, with the establishment and swearing in of that body in December 1995. The third was the first case that went all the way through appellate body, the case against the United States on gasoline regulations (which now seems to be headed for a satisfactory resolution).[6] The fourth problem is the question of resource allocation needed for the dispute settlement process. As to the fourth point, there has been quite an encouraging amount of resources allocated to the dispute settlement process and to the appellate body within a secretariat that otherwise is very short of resources. But projections for the near future suggest the possibility of cases outstripping those resources.

As of 25 February 1997, there were a total of sixty-eight complaints initiated under the new dispute settlement process (WTO 1997a; see also Williams 1997; *WTO Focus*). That's two or three times the normal rate of application for dispute settlements, as witnessed and experienced in the later years of the GATT. Perhaps this is a tribute to the new process. These sixty-eight complaints involved forty-five discrete cases (because many complaints now have multiple complainants). Already, seventeen cases seem settled, which is a very encouraging aspect of the new process. Indeed, the tendency toward settlement is partly influenced by the "automaticity" of the system mentioned earlier.

Recently there were fourteen active cases with thirteen panels operating, and there are as many as thirty cases in operation, which will push the limits of resources for that activity. Three appeals were completed by the end of February 1997. The few appeals completed in 1997 is a relatively light load, and certainly in the future there may be many more. On the other hand, the first year of the appellate body has given its seven members a chance to study the processes and develop rules of procedure. Some of the members were not particularly expert yet in the GATT/WTO law and jurisprudence, so this has worked out reasonably well.

There are consultations going in the other disputes. By February 1997, the United States had brought twenty-five disputes—a really remarkable reliance on this new procedure, and it could represent confidence by the U.S. government in the new system (House 1996). The United States on the other hand is defending in eleven cases. Of all the cases brought by the United States, there already are settlements in five, and indications from the U.S. government that settlements in others are expected. The European Community (EC) has brought nine and is defending in thirteen, while Japan has brought four (one of which has been settled) and is defending in nine. But one of the most remarkable phenomena in this area is the fact that developing countries are using this process among themselves, namely, developing countries have complained

6. Appellate body reports include *United States: Standards for Reformulated and Conventional Gasoline* (WTO 1996b). See also WTO 1996a, 1997b.

against other developing countries. This was extraordinarily rare in GATT history.

5.2.3   The Procedures: GATT and WTO

A few words of explanation of the WTO dispute settlement procedures, with some comparisons to those of the GATT, might be useful (see, generally, Jackson 1989, chap. 4). Appendix B reproduces a WTO document that outlines the new procedures.

Under the old GATT, as indicated, the treaty clauses were sparse and the GATT developed through practice a relatively sophisticated set of procedures for dispute settlement. This practice was largely embodied in a 1979 understanding resulting from the Tokyo Round (GATT 1979). The practice under the GATT that led to these procedures included a shift in the late 1950s from the use of a "working party" to consider disputes, to that of a "panel of experts." This signaled a shift to a more juridical, rather than negotiating, procedure. The experts on a dispute panel were acting in their own right, and not as representatives of other governments. They had an obligation to be impartial and to apply careful reasoning to the cases brought before them.

In addition, the GATT language of dispute settlement focused on something called "nullification or impairment," in the language of article XXIII. This language did not necessarily require a breach of the international law obligations under the treaty, but merely a defeat of reasonable expectations for enhanced exports and trade, and a looser concept laid out in earlier documents. In a 1962 case brought by Uruguay, the panel introduced a revolutionary concept of "prima facie nullification or impairment." Under this panel's concept, a breach of the GATT would be "prima facie" nullification or impairment, and this would, if established, require the responding nation to carry the burden of proof for showing that there was no nullification or impairment. If it failed to fulfill this burden of proof, the responding nation would be required by the recommendations and findings of the panel report to change its law or practice to bring it into conformity with the treaty obligations.

As time went on, the GATT panels consistently cited the 1962 Uruguay case, and relied upon it for this principle. The principle was also embodied in the 1979 understanding resulting from the Tokyo Round. In the 1980s, as the procedures became more legally precise and juridical in nature, there developed the idea that there were two types of cases in the GATT: the violation cases (based on the prima facie concept), and certain "nonviolation cases," which did not involve a violation, but nevertheless alleged "nullification or impairment." In fact, the nonviolation cases have been relatively rare. One group of scholars has indicated that there are only from three to eight of this type of cases in the history of the GATT (Jackson, Davey, and Sykes 1995a, 362). Nevertheless, some of these nonviolation cases have been quite important (GATT 1990; Jackson, Davey, and Sykes 1995a, 357).

The procedure under GATT was for the panel to make its report and deliver it to the Council, which as a standing body met regularly and disposed of most of the business of the GATT. (This body was also not provided in the GATT text, but arose through practice.) The practice then became firmly established that, if the Council approved the report by consensus, it became "binding." If the Council did not approve, then the report would not have a binding status. The problem was "consensus." In effect, the nation that "lost" in the panel and might otherwise be obligated to follow the panel obligations, could "block" the Council action by refusing to participate in the consensus. Thus, the losing party to the dispute had a technique of avoiding the consequences of its loss. This was deemed to be the most significant defect in the GATT process.

Thus we see in the results of the Uruguay Round and as embodied in the WTO DSU (appendix B), that several important reforms have been established. For one, blocking is no longer possible. A panel report will be deemed adopted unless there is a consensus *against* it. As a sort of quid pro quo for this automaticity, however, a new appeal process was established so that a party to the dispute that was not satisfied with the basic panel report could appeal to an appellate panel of three persons, drawn from a relatively permanent roster of seven persons. The result of this appeal then is also a report made to the Council (technically to the Dispute Settlement Body, which is the Council acting as the DSB). Again, however, the report is deemed adopted unless there is a consensus *against* it. Therefore in the end, after either one step or two steps, depending on whether an appeal was taken, it will be virtually automatic that the parties are by treaty law obligated to carry out the recommendations.

There are a series of new clauses in the 1994 DSU regarding the case where a nation does not adequately fulfill its obligations after a dispute settlement process. The treaty text provides for "compensatory measures," which some would describe as retaliations. There are limits on these, however. They must be tailored to amount to approximately the same trade effect as that caused by the treaty violation, and only the country harmed can take the measures (this point is in contrast to the looser language in the GATT).

In addition, the DSU has a separate set of procedures for "nonviolation" cases. This is the first time that there has been this treaty-text separation between "violation" and "nonviolation" cases. Interestingly enough under the DSU, the end result of a nonviolation case is not to impose an obligation on the "losing party" to perform. This is logical, since they have not breached any obligation to do anything. However, they do have an obligation in good faith to negotiate some kind of compensatory measures. Thus, compensation becomes the prime remedy under nonviolation cases, but only a fallback remedy under the violation cases.

5.3   Several Significant and Central Issues about the WTO Dispute Settlement

We now turn to seven very significant issues about the dispute settlement process. These are not all of the issues that are important, by any means, but they do stand very high in any sort of inventory ranking of important issues. To some extent, most of these issues are central to problems of any legal system, including national government systems and the relationship of the courts to legislatures, and so forth. In addition, these issues were significant issues under the GATT, as well as now under the WTO. The key question, of course, is whether the WTO has improved some of the problems that lurk in these issues. It may have exacerbated others.

These problems include the question of incursions upon "sovereignty," and the questions of the appropriate allocation of power (both in the vertical and horizontal sense, that is, at what level of government—international, national, subnational—should power be allocated; and between what kinds of institutions on the same level—judicial, legislative, administrative). For some of these issues, we now have some important clues in the first few appellate panel reports under the WTO procedures, and these will be indicated.

5.3.1   Rule Orientation of the WTO Procedures

From the beginning of the GATT there was a certain bifurcation in the thinking about what the dispute settlement process was (Jackson 1989). Was it designed to be merely a procedure to assist parties to settle their disputes, and thus really to engage in diplomatic maneuvering with what is sometimes called a power-oriented approach? Or was it a system that was designed to be more rule-oriented in the sense of arriving at just results, in terms of the real obligations undertaken by parties through the negotiated treaty texts?

At the beginning of the GATT this was quite murky. To the very end of the GATT's history (at the end of 1995) there were differing attitudes about which was the true goal of these procedures. Even now in the WTO there is some dispute on that. However, the history of the GATT demonstrates a steady evolution toward a more rule-oriented approach. This was manifest even in the 1950s when the venue of disputes was shifted from "working parties" to "panels," then in the 1960s when the general concept of "prima facie nullification or impairment" was developed to apply to all violations of treaty obligations. In the 1970s the DSU developed in the Tokyo Round continued this development, and in the 1980s the GATT moved strongly toward a rule-oriented approach in the actual practice of the dispute panels.

With the new DSU text, the question is, what approach does it take? There are clauses that arguably go both ways, but if you read the DSU through carefully, and inventory the clauses that relate to this issue, you can easily come to the conclusion that the DSU opts for the rule-oriented procedure.[7] After several

---

7. See, for example, DSU article 3: 2, which in part reads "3.2 The dispute settlement system of the WTO is a central element in providing security and predictability to the multilateral trading system." Also see the speech of King Hassan II for the host government of the April 1994 Marrakesh ministerial meeting to conclude the Uruguay Round, where he said, "By bringing into being the World Trade Organization today, we are enshrining the rule of law in international economic and trade relations, thus setting universal rules and disciplines over the temptations of unilateralism and the law of the jungle" (*GATT Focus*, no. 107 [May 1994]: 4).

years of appeals, to an appellate body that obviously seems to lean toward that direction very strongly, this will likely be even more definitive.

The first appellate body report (see note 6) is extraordinarily interesting, even apart from the substance of what it was addressing (the environmental protection matters of U.S. regulation and how they related to at least three different clauses in the GATT, most particularly article XX). The flavor of that report is significant. Among other things, the report definitely says that this process, and the GATT and the WTO generally, are a part of "international law" as such. (There has been some dispute as to whether it was a "separate regime," sort of sealed off from normal concepts of international law, but the appellate body explicitly states that the WTO is part of international law, and it goes on to engage international law principles of treaty interpretation very deeply, referring to the Vienna Convention on the Law of Treaties.)[8] The appellate body report seems thus to embrace an even stronger endorsement of the rule-oriented concept.

5.3.2   The Legal Effect of a Dispute Panel Report: Obligation to Perform?

Second, what is the legal effect of a report? There are also contrary opinions on this (Jackson 1994a). Indeed, some statements by government officials on both sides of the Atlantic and elsewhere in the world have been misleading.

The alternatives are the following: At the end of a procedure, after the first-level panel report, or the appellate panel report, do the findings of the report mean that the nation that has lost the case, the nation to which the panel addresses a series of recommendations (usually recommending that the country concerned bring its practice into consistency with its international obligations under the Uruguay Round texts), has an international law obligation to conform its law practice to the recommendations? Or does it mean that such nation has a choice either to perform or to compensate? In other words, can you compensate and "get off"? (The word "compensation," incidentally, has some ambiguities in it also.)[9]

Government officials, including some in the United States who testified before Congress during 1994, have said that all a report requires is for a nation to "compensate," that it does not create a legal obligation of any kind to *per-*

8. Vienna Convention on the Law of Treaties (1969), entered into force 1980, article 31: 3(b). The Vienna Convention is deemed to express the general rules of international customary law, even for many nations who have not technically accepted the Vienna Convention itself. The convention clearly notes the obligation of "pacta sunt servanda," namely, the treaties will be fulfilled. It also sets up a series of principles for interpreting treaties (article 31), most notably the question of "preparatory work," in a way that is often different than such treatment in national legal systems. In the case of all of these principles, the appellate body's statement that GATT/WTO law is part of international law means that these general principles of international law apply to its work and that of the WTO generally. This could have the most significance with respect to principles of interpretation of treaties.

9. The word appears particularly in the DSU at article 22. Under GATT practice, compensation always meant trade measures and not any sort of liquid monetary compensation. It probably will be similarly interpreted under the WTO DSU also, although there is some ambiguity about that.

form. There are strong arguments that this is wrong. Unfortunately, the negotiators for the DSU did not quite nail that down explicitly. However, at least one of the negotiators that participated in that negotiation said they thought they had it nailed—that they discussed it for hours—and it was clearly meant that there was a legal obligation to perform. It turns out not to be quite that clear.

The DSU has at least twelve clauses that are relevant,[10] and all these add up to quite a strong propensity toward the legal obligation, including, and perhaps most interesting, a clause that says that, even if there is compensation, the matter remains on the agenda of the DSB until compliance occurs (DSU article 22:8). The idea is that compensation is only a temporary measure or a fallback measure as implied by the context of the other clauses, including the distinct preference expressed for bringing measures into consistency, and an interesting clause in a separate procedure that is now designed for "nonviolation cases."

In the nonviolation cases, there is no obligation to perform (DSU article 26), which is perfectly logical, as explained above. But expressing it there suggests that, in the violation cases, there *is* an obligation to perform.

Does this matter? Is compensation and/or retaliation the real underpinning of this system? I would suggest that the compensation retaliation measures are not what is really at the center of dispute settlement, and have not been so in the GATT historically. It is really the *credibility* of the judgment that is rendered that raises a series of diplomatic hurdles to a country that tries to ignore them. Even the most powerful trading entities in the world find it difficult diplomatically to ignore the results of the dispute settlement process, although in some sense, they could get away with it.[11]

5.3.3   The Standard of Review

The third issue to discuss here is the standard of review. This paper does not address the standard of review of the appellate body when it reviews the first-level report. Instead it addresses the degree to which the WTO dispute settlement process as a whole, both panel levels, should second-guess national government administrative decisions that relate to treaty clauses in the Uruguay Round.

National governments will inevitably be interpreting some of these broad clauses themselves; they will have to, because of the ambiguity mentioned earlier. So to what degree should the international dispute settlement bodies give deference to those national decisions on interpretation? This is the "standard of review" question. I and my colleague have recently published an article (Jackson and Croley 1996) about this very question, discussing in particular

---

10. See DSU articles and paragraphs 3:2, 3:7, 7:1, 11, 15:2, 15:3, 17:13, 21:1, 21:3, 22:1, 22:2, 26:1(b).

11. The United States, for example, has complied with most of the cases under the GATT that found the United States in noncompliance.

some of the efforts by certain negotiators, mostly those of the United States, who tried to achieve a very restricted standard-of-review treaty obligation in the Uruguay Round, especially in the context of the antidumping measures. The U.S. negotiators did not succeed entirely in their endeavor. They were trying to translate the domestic U.S. jurisprudence of the Chevron case into the international obligation in the treaties, but they did not succeed in doing that. There is, however, some very curious language in the antidumping text about the degree of deference that a panel should give to national governments.[12] Basically it says that if an analysis, according to normal interpretation procedures under international law, results in ambiguity and if a government has chosen one among "permissible options" for interpretation, the international panel should allow the government to continue with that option. There are numerous other problems with that approach, but without going into these it can be noted that the particular language of article 17:6 of the antidumping text applies only to antidumping decisions. It does not apply to the rest of the dispute settlement process, and regardless of what it means, therefore, in the other areas perhaps a different approach can be expected.

The DSU text, other provisions in the Uruguay Round text, and resolutions of the Marrakesh meeting provide for several possibilities that the antidumping standard-of-review text will apply more broadly than to antidumping decisions. For one thing, a Marrakesh decision notes, but does not require, the possibility that countervailing-duty decisions should be consistent and similar to antidumping decisions. In addition, a Marrakesh resolution provides for a review of this antidumping article 17:6 language at the end of five years.[13]

Nevertheless, this issue is an important one. It seems clear there should be *some* measure of deference to national government decisions at the international level in the dispute settlement process. There is support for that in other areas of international law, particularly in the European Convention of Human Rights (Macdonald 1993). At the very end of the 1996 first appellate body report, on the U.S. gasoline case, the panel includes this language: "WTO

12. Jackson, Davey, and O. Sykes 1995b, 194. "17.6 In examining the matter referred to in paragraph 5: (i) in its assessment of the facts of the matter, the panel shall determine whether the authorities' establishment of the facts was proper and whether their evaluation of those facts was unbiased and objective. If the establishment of the facts was proper and the evaluation was unbiased and objective, even though the panel might have reached a different conclusion, the evaluation shall not be overturned; (ii) the panel shall interpret the relevant provisions of the Agreement in accordance with customary rules of interpretation of public international law. Where the panel finds that a relevant provision of the Agreement admits of more than one permissible interpretation, the panel shall find the authorities' measure to be in conformity with the Agreement if it rests upon one of those permissible interpretations."

13. Decisions at Marrakesh: Decision on Review of Article 17.6 of the Agreement on Implementation of Article VI of the General Agreement on Tariffs and Trade 1994 (antidumping text); Declaration on Dispute Settlement Pursuant to the Agreement on Implementation of Article VI of the General Agreement on Tariffs and Trade, 1994, or Part V of the Agreement on Subsidies and Countervailing Measures (subsidies text). See Jackson, Davey, & Sykes 1995b, 435.

members have a large measure of autonomy to determine their own policies on the environment, including its relationship with trade" (WTO 1996b, 30).

This appears to be a declaration of intention by the first appellate report to give some measure of latitude to national governments in this respect. That raises a host of other issues. For example, how far should this go? What issues are more appropriately decided at the national level instead of the international level? Europeans sometimes call this the "subsidiarity" issue.

5.3.4   The Question of Panel "Judicial Restraint" Compared to "Activism"

The next "fundamental principle of WTO jurisprudence" discussed in this paper is the question of how much "judicial activism," or "judicial restraint" should be exercised by the international panel system. This question obviously relates to the standard of review, but there are other concepts and ideas that are involved, including how far an international body should "push the envelope" of interpreting ambiguous clauses to suit certain policy preferences, possibly preferences of the panel alone, or possibly policy preferences that the panel detects that the negotiators, or currently the governments, have. Again the DSU has some interesting clauses on this. Article 3:2 says: "The dispute settlement system of the WTO is a central element in providing security and predictability to the multilateral trading system. The Members recognize that it serves to preserve the rights and obligations of Members under the covered agreements, and to clarify the existing provisions of those agreements in accordance with customary rules of interpretation of public international law. Recommendations and rulings of the DSB cannot add to or diminish the rights and obligations provided in the covered agreements." What does that mean? Arguably it resonates in the direction of a caution to the panels to use "judicial restraint," and not to be too activist. Of course the U.S. Congress feels quite strongly about that, and in the Dole Commission proposal, the language "rights or obligations" is picked up again.[14] It is also included, incidentally, in the WTO Charter. So this notion of restraining changes in the rights and obligations of the nation states is quite prevalent in the system.

The United States arguably would be one of the most jealous about that, yet it seems that the United States wants to push the envelope in some of the disputes it is bringing. For example, with reference to the so-called nonviolation cases, almost uniquely in the GATT/WTO system, there is an opportunity to bring a case that does not involve any violation of treaty obligations. Instead, a case may involve what is called "nullification or impairment," which is a

---

14. This proposal was part of a compromise agreement between Senator Dole and President Clinton, just before the Senate vote on 1 December 1994. The agreement and the later bill introduced by Senator Dole (but not yet passed as of this writing) called for a special commission of U.S. federal judges to review the panel report of every WTO dispute settlement proceeding affecting the United States. The commission would give its advice to the Congress on the appropriateness of such report, in the light of four specified criteria in the Dole proposal. A description of the proposal is contained in Senate 1995.

very ambiguous phrase. These are termed "nonviolation" cases, as they have developed in the jurisprudence of the GATT. The DSU for the first time has an explicit separate procedure designed for those cases, as mentioned before.

When the United States or another country brings a case that does not involve a violation, but targets something like competition policy, or the Japanese Keiretsu, or something else that is not included within the current treaty texts, it is likely to be asking a panel to change the "rights and obligations." In other words it is saying to a panel, "we want you to interpret nullification or impairment to embrace some of these results that for policy reasons we would like to see in this case." That is risky—it is almost doing with one hand what the other hand was trying to prevent. Obviously this has longer-term fundamental implications.

5.3.5 Resources and Their Implications

An important issue for any institution, particularly a new one, is the allocation and adequacy of resources. The "judicialization" of the WTO procedures does not necessarily come cheap. Already, there is a considerably enhanced budget for dispute settlement compared to the GATT. Under the GATT, however, dispute settlement was almost always a "part-time affair," with virtually no specific allocated resources, except some secretariat lawyers to assist panels. Now there is an appellate body with significant staff and other resources, including retainers and per diems, as well as travel and support funds for staying in Geneva. There is a new legal staff devoted to the appellate body, consisting of a director and three staff lawyers, as well as some nonprofessional staff. Considerable and, one must say, very admirable space has been allocated for this effort in the secretariat building of the WTO on the shore of Lake Geneva. The regular legal staff continues from its former embodiment but is finding its work greatly increased, partly resulting from the large number of disputes that have been initiated.

So far, the resource allocation has been quite good. However, if disputes continue at the current rate, and there are not a larger number of settlements, we will shortly see some important strains on the resource possibilities. In addition, the issues that will need to be addressed by the dispute settlement system may incur special resource requirements. For example, some of the issues may be very technical (such as some of the financial services issues, or the intellectual property issues) and may require special expertise (some of which is allowed for in the DSU; see article 13). In addition, some issues may call upon a more serious examination of "facts" than the system has been able to provide in prior cases. This could be particularly true if "competition policy" type issues begin to flow into the WTO system.

5.3.6 Fact Examination

By and large the GATT dispute settlement process was not able and did not try to explore facts to any degree. Indeed, it was generally assumed that the facts would be brought to the attention of the international panel by written and oral arguments of the representatives of the disputing nations.

In the WTO procedure, this may also continue. Indeed, in the antidumping text on "standard of review," section 17.6, it is largely contemplated that the facts will be determined at the national level. However, this text applies only to the antidumping cases (so far), and may be difficult to sustain. Certain kinds of issues, such as environmental issues or financial services and other service issues, as well as intellectual property, may require some greater attention to facts. It has been noted that competition policy decisions in national legal systems tend to be very fact-oriented, with massive hearings and massive records to contend with. Indeed, in the potential dispute between the United States and Japan concerning film (Kodak and Fuji), the two private firms that are perhaps the major contenders in the dispute have produced very extensive fact accounts (most of which can be found on the Internet). A serious and prolonged fact-type hearing could easily bankrupt the resources allocated to the WTO dispute settlement system. (For example, one party told me of a hearing on environmental matters in Canada that lasted about 120 days! This would exceed all the hearing dates of all the procedures in a typical GATT dispute settlement year, and would probably involve budgetary allocation exceeding all the normal procedures for a year.)

Clearly some care will have to be taken about where the dividing line should be drawn between an essential examination of facts in order to determine how the law applies, and more extensive fact records.

5.3.7   Nonviolation Cases or "Nullification or Impairment"

One of the potentially very troublesome issues is involved in the unique attention given to "nonviolation" cases. Under the GATT, this attention developed through practice by the language in the GATT text, including the phrase "nullification or impairment" (as discussed above). This language has been carried into the WTO, and for the first time, a special separate procedure under the DSU has been designed, as the route to take when a nonviolation case is pursued. As indicated above, the problem with nonviolation cases is the generality of the language "nullification or impairment," which creates great ambiguity about what would be an appropriate way to analyze these cases and to determine when one nation had some sort of right of relief from another nation. It is interesting that, in the rules for nonviolation cases, there are no similar clauses to those in the violation cases that would suggest that there is an obligation to actually perform recommendations, that is, to bring one's law into consistency with the international rule. The relief allowed under the DSU is merely "negotiations for appropriate compensation." This makes sense, since the basis of a nonviolation case is *not* the alleged inconsistency of national laws or practices with an international rule.

One must hope that nations and the responding WTO institutions will be very cautious about entertaining nonviolation cases for new types of issue for which there are not adequate or adequately precise rules contained in the Uruguay Round treaty texts. This is an issue that has been discussed in connection with so-called competition policy. Competition policy is not centrally or explicitly taken up in the Uruguay Round and GATT treaty texts. Indeed, the fact that such policy was contained in the 1948 ITO Charter, which failed to come into force, has led the GATT itself to be very cautious about taking up these policy issues. On the other hand, there are a number of clauses in the new treaty texts for services and intellectual property, and so forth, which do relate to competition policy. If a country were to bring a nonviolation case that essentially would be based on competition policy considerations, it would seem that such approach would be truly law-making rather than law-applying. In essence the WTO panel would be asked to establish the rules of conduct concerning competition policy, so as to apply them in the particular case that was brought. This could be considered inconsistent with the clause in the DSU that is supposed to restrain panels from "changing the rights or obligations of parties."

5.4   Implications and Conclusions

Dispute settlement has now moved to the center stage of international economic diplomacy, as it is embodied in the Uruguay Round and WTO texts. In many ways this is a welcome step toward a more rule-oriented system that will hopefully allow better adjustment of frictions between nation-states, as well as greater predictability and reliability for entrepreneurs. It should to some measure reduce the "risk premium" of international trade and other economic transactions, such as investment. However, there are a number of problems lurking just under the surface of those waves. These shoals and boulders could, if not evaded carefully, cause considerable distress to the trading system. In the worst case, they could cause a general backlash by governments and public citizens, particularly international traders, against the WTO and bring it into disrespect. One will hope that the diplomats and statesmen involved in the international trade system will have the capability and perception to avoid these consequences.

Apart from these grave consequences, it is nevertheless clear that the new dispute settlement system is already having its effects on international economic diplomacy. The way negotiators negotiate has been considerably altered by the existence of the process as a fallback for a failed negotiation. In many of the press reports of disputes now, we see one side or the other "threatening to bring a case in the WTO." And it still seems the case that governments are very uneasy about being hauled before the International Trade Court of Justice as well as being very eager to avoid their nation from being "branded" as a rule breaker. All of this appears to bode well for this new development of international dispute settlement. It is likely to be seen in the future as one of the most important, and perhaps even watershed, developments of international economic relations in the twentieth century.

Appendix A
Excerpts from Testimony Prepared for the U.S. Senate Committee on Foreign Relations 14 June 1994 Hearing on the World Trade Organization and U.S. Sovereignty

A careful examination of the WTO Charter leads me to conclude that the WTO has no more real power than that which existed for the GATT under the previous agreements. This may seem surprising, but in fact the GATT treaty text contained language that was quite ambiguous, and could have been misused (but fortunately was not) to provide rather extensive powers. For example, in Article XXV of the GATT the Contracting Parties acting by majority vote were given the authority to take joint action "with a view to facilitating the operation and furthering the objectives of this agreement." This is very broad and ambiguous language. Under the WTO Charter, considerably more attention has been given to the question of decision making in a number of different contexts, and certain restraints have been added, such as increasing the voting requirements for certain actions (to three-fourths of the members for many waivers and for formal interpretations), and a provision in the amending clauses that a country will not be bound by an amendment which it opposes if the amendment would "alter the rights and obligations of the members." Likewise, the waiver authority is more constrained and will be harder to abuse. Furthermore, formal "interpretations" "shall not be used in the manner that would undermine the amendment provisions." Thus there are more legal grounds to challenge overreaching of the power of the WTO institutions.

Regarding the practice of "consensus," as established for several decades in the GATT, several characteristics are worth noting. In the GATT, there is no explicit indication of a "consensus practice," and the word "consensus" is not used. The reason that the consensus practice developed was partly the uneasiness of governments about the loose wording of GATT decision-making powers, particularly that in GATT Article XXV. Partly because of this uneasiness, the practice developed of avoiding strict voting. Instead, the Contracting Parties have for several decades taken virtually all of their decisions by "consensus." Even when a formal vote was required (such as for a waiver), there would generally be a negotiation for a consensus draft text before such text was submitted to capitals for the formal vote.

In the practice of GATT, however, the word "consensus" was not defined. In the legal sense, if some sort of "consensus" could not be achieved, the fallback was the loose voting authority of the GATT. In the WTO Charter, however, consensus is defined (at least for some purposes) as the situation when a decision occurs and "no member, present at the meeting when the decision is taken, formally objects to the proposed decision." It should be noted that this is not the same as unanimity, since consensus is defeated only by a formal objection by a member present at the meeting. Thus, those absent do not prevent a consensus, nor does an abstention prevent a consensus. Furthermore, the practice in GATT and surely also in WTO is that some countries who have difficulty with a particular decision, will nevertheless remain silent out of deference to countries with a substantially higher stake in the pragmatic economic consequences of a decision. Thus the consensus practice itself involves some deference to economic power. This has certainly been the practice in the GATT, and the WTO Charter provides that the WTO shall be guided by such "customary practices."

The WTO is considerably more explicit about the situation where consensus fails. In a few instances, a decision must be by consensus and there is no fallback to a majority vote. (For example, adding plurilateral agreements to Annex 4, Article X:9: and amendments to the dispute settlement procedures in Annex 2.) In many other situations, when consensus fails there is an explicit fallback vote, such as three-fourths of the membership. It is considered quite difficult to achieve such a heavy fallback vote as three-fourths of the membership (not three-fourths of those voting), since often 25 percent of the membership is not involved in a particular decision and may not show up at the meeting.

Thus the protections of national sovereignty built into the WTO Charter rules on decision making are substantially enhanced over that of the GATT.

The amending authority (Article X) is itself quite intricate and ingenious. It obviously has been carefully tailored to the needs of the participating nations related to each of the different major multilateral agreements (GATT, GATS [Services], and intellectual property). Amendments for some parts of these require unanimity. Other parts require two-thirds (after procedures in the Ministerial Conference and Councils seeking consensus for amendment proposals). In most all cases, as mentioned above, when an amendment would "alter the rights and obligations," a member which refuses to accept the amendment, is not bound by it. In such case, however, there is an ingenious procedure (partly following the model in GATT) whereby the Ministerial Conference can by three-fourths vote of the members require all to accept the amendment, or withdraw from the agreement, or remain a member with explicit consent of the Ministerial Conference. Quite frankly, it is therefore very hard to conceive of the amending provisions being used in any way to force a major trading country such as the United States to accept altered rights or obligations. As stated above the spirit and practice of GATT has always been to try to accommodate through consensus negotiation procedures, the views of as many countries as possible, but certainly to give weight to views of countries who have great weight in the trading system. This will not change.

Appendix B
The Uruguay Round and GATT/WTO Dispute Settlement Procedures[15]

One of the many achievements of the GATT, despite its "birth defects," has been the development of a reasonably sophisticated dispute settlement process. The original GATT treaty contained very little on this, although it did specifically provide (in Article 22 and 23) for consultation, and then submittal of issues to the GATT Contracting Parties. As time went on, however, the practice began to evolve more towards a "rule-oriented" system. For example, in the late 1950s the practice introduced a "panel" of individuals to make determinations and findings and recommend them to the Contracting Parties. Before that, disputes had been considered in much broader working parties comprised of representatives of governments.

In the Uruguay Round 1994 text, there is a major new text concerning dispute settlement procedures, the "Understanding on Rules and Procedures Governing the Settlement of Disputes."

The new text solves many of the issues that plagued the GATT dispute settlement system, although not all of them. It accomplishes the following:

1. It establishes a unified dispute settlement system for all parts of the GATT/WTO system, including the new subjects of services and intellectual property. Thus, controversies over which procedure to use will not occur.

2. It reaffirms the right of a complaining government to have a panel process initiated, preventing blocking at that stage.

3. It ingeniously establishes a new appellate procedure which will substitute for some of the Council approval process of a panel report, and overcome blocking. Thus, a panel report will automatically be deemed adopted by the Council, unless it is appealed by one of the parties to the dispute. If appealed, the dispute will go to an appellate panel. After the appellate body has ruled, its report will go to the Council, but in this case it will be deemed adopted unless there is a consensus *against* adoption, and presumably that negative consensus can be defeated by any major objector. Thus the presumption is reversed, compared to the previous procedures, with the ultimate result of the procedure that the appellate report will in virtually every case come into force as a matter of international law.

It should, however, be understood that the international legal system does not embrace the common law jurisprudence that prevails in the United States which calls for courts to operate under a stricter "precedent" or "stare decisis" rule. Most nations in the world do not have stare decisis as part of their legal systems, and the international law also does not. This means that technically a GATT panel report is not strict precedent, although there is certainly some

---

15. Based partly on the DSU (Jackson 1994b).

tendency for subsequent GATT panels to follow what they deem to be the "wisdom" of prior panel reports. Nevertheless, a GATT panel has the option not to follow a previous panel report, as has occurred in several cases. In addition, although an adopted panel report will generally provide an international law obligation for the participants in the dispute to follow the report, the GATT Contracting Parties acting in a Council or the Ministerial Conference, can make interpretive rulings or other resolutions which would depart from that GATT panel ruling, or even establish a waiver to relieve a particular obligation.

It is clear both that no system will be perfect, and that not all cases will be decided in the most appropriate way. There will be mistakes. There will be situations where the United States or other countries will lose cases which they should lose; but also there will be cases where the U.S. and others will lose cases they did not deserve to lose. This is not different from domestic legal processes. Nevertheless, in the broader context there is a great deal of utility in a creditable and efficient rule-oriented dispute settlement system that has integrity, and the U.S. is an important beneficiary of such system.

It is quite interesting how significant dispute settlement systems have become in major international trade agreements in the last decades. For example, they are a very intricate part of the European Union with its Court of Justice sitting in Luxembourg. They are also an important and enhanced part of the U.S.-Canada Free Trade Agreement, the NAFTA (North American Free Trade Agreement), and in other similar regional arrangements that are currently evolving.

References

General Agreement on Tariffs and Trade. 1979. *Understanding Regarding Notification, Consultation, Dispute Settlement, and Surveillance*. Geneva: GATT Document.

———. 1990. *EEC: Payments and Subsidies Paid to Processors and Producers of Oilseeds and Related Animal-Feed Proteins*. Geneva: GATT Document.

———. 1994. *Panel Report: U.S. Taxes on Automobiles*. DS31/R. Geneva: GATT Document.

Henkin, Louis. 1994. *How Nations Behave: Law and Foreign Policy*. New York: Columbia University Press.

Jackson, John H. 1969. *World Trade and the Law of GATT*. Indianapolis: Bobbs-Merrill.

———. 1987. United States of America. In *The Effect of Treaties in Domestic Law*, ed. Francis G. Jacobs and Shelley Roberts, 141–70. London: Sweet and Maxwell.

———. 1989. *The World Trading System: Law and Policy of International Economic Relations*. Cambridge: MIT Press.

———. 1990. *Restructuring the GATT System*. London: Royal Institute for International Affairs.

———. 1992. Status of Treaties in Domestic Legal Systems: A Policy Analysis. *American Journal of International Law* 86: 310–40.

———. 1994a. The Legal Meaning of a GATT Dispute Settlement Report: Some Reflections. In *Towards More Effective Supervision by International Organizations:*

Essays in Honour of Henry G. Schermers, ed. Niels Blokker and Sam Muller, 149–64. Deventer, The Netherlands: Kluwer Academic.

———. 1994b. Testimony Prepared for the U.S. Senate Committee on Foreign Relations, June 14, 1994. In *Hearing on the World Trade Organization and U.S. Sovereignty.* Washington, DC: Government Printing Office.

———. 1995a. The Uruguay Round, World Trade Organization, and the Problem of Regulating International Economic Behaviour. In *Policy Debates/Debats Politiques,* 1–33. Ottawa: Centre for Trade Policy and Law.

———. 1995b. The World Trade Organization: Watershed Innovation or Cautious Small Step Forward? *World Economy* 11–31.

Jackson, John H., and Steven P. Croley. 1996. WTO Dispute Procedures, Standard of Review, and Deference to National Governments. *American Journal of International Law* 90:193–213.

Jackson, John H., William J. Davey, and Alan O. Sykes. 1995a. *Legal Problems of International Economic Relations.* 3d edition. Minneapolis: West.

———. 1995b. *1995 Documents Supplement to Legal Problems of International Economic Law.* 3d edition. Minneapolis: West.

Macdonald, R. St. J. 1993. The Margin of Appreciation. In *The European System for the Protection of Human Rights,* ed. R. St. J. Macdonald, F. Matscher, and H. Petzold, chap. 6. The Hague: Martinus Nijhoff.

U.S. House. 1994. *Uruguay Round Agreements, Texts of Agreements, Implementing Bill, Statement of Administrative Action and Required Supporting Statements, Message from the President of the United States Transmitting These Matters to the Congress.* H.R. Doc. 316. 103d Cong., 2d sess.

———. 1996. *Testimony before the House Ways and Means Trade Subcommittee by Ambassador Michael Kantor, March 13, 1996.* Washington, DC: Government Printing Office.

U.S. Senate. 1995. *To Establish a Commission to Review the Dispute Settlement Reports of the World Trade Organization and for Other Purposes.* S. 1438, 104th Cong., 1st sess.

Williams, Frances. 1997. WTO: Sets Up Panel to Probe U.S. Shrimp Now. *Financial Times,* 26 February.

World Trade Organization. 1994. Final Act Embodying the Results of the Uruguay Round of Multilateral Trade Negotiations. Marrakesh. *International Legal Materials* 33:1140–67.

———. 1996a. *Japan: Taxes on Alcoholic Beverages.* Appellate Body Report and Panel Report. WT/DS8,10,11/AB/R. Geneva: WTO Document.

———. 1996b. *United States: Standards for Reformulated and Conventional Gasoline.* Appellate Body Report and Panel Report. WT/DS2/9. Geneva: WTO Document.

———. 1997a. Overview of the State-of-Play of WTO Disputes, [updated 25 February 1997]. From Web site <http://www.wto.org/wto/dispute/bulletin.htm>.

———. 1997b. *United States: Restrictions on Imports of Cotton and Man-Made Fibre Underwear, Complaint by Costa Rica.* Appellate Body Report and Panel Report. WT/DS24. Geneva: WTO Document.

6   The United States, the ITO, and the WTO: Exit Options, Agent Slack, and Presidential Leadership

John Odell and Barry Eichengreen

6.1   Introduction

Its allies and opponents have long complained that the United States is an unreliable partner in multilateral organizations. The hot and cold of U.S. entry into World War I and rejection of Wilson's league established this reputation, and recent events have revived it. The United States tended to shun the United Nations after the latter undertook initiatives (on Israel and the New International Economic Order) unpalatable to the American public. Today the country where the UN charter was signed and its headquarters is sited refuses to pay its dues in full. Its compliance with GATT panel judgments was the worst of any country (Hudec 1993). Washington's bilateral arm-twisting during the Uruguay Round irritated many partners. Some events since the end of that round have fueled doubts about the depth of the American commitment to the multilateral system. The Clinton administration continued down the bilateral track with high-profile complaints against Japanese auto companies, walked away from one multilateral deal in financial services, and in early 1997 declared that it would boycott WTO dispute settlement proceedings triggered by the U.S. Burton-Helms Act penalizing other countries' dealings with Cuba.[1]

U.S. leaders would counter that Washington did more than any other country to launch a new multilateral round of liberalization in the 1980s, that other countries were more responsible for impasses, and that even so the round yielded the most ambitious multilateral liberalization of trade and the most

John Odell is professor of international relations, University of Southern California. Barry Eichengreen is the John L. Simpson Professor of Economics and Political Science, University of California, Berkeley.

Odell is grateful for support from the USC Center for International Studies. The authors thank Nisha Mody for sterling research assistance.

1. David E. Sanger, "U.S. Rejects Role for World Court in Trade Dispute," *New York Times,* 21 February 1997.

significant strengthening of trade-related institutions in history. The United States was the principal demander behind arguably the most profound institutional change—the more automatic and unified dispute settlement and enforcement mechanism in the new World Trade Organization (WTO). The United States remains highly active in Geneva and responded to the first WTO panel judgment against it by affirming that it will comply.[2]

Either way, one undeniably central issue facing the new organization is the U.S. question. That is, to what extent will the United States abide by the spirit as well as the letter of the WTO's rules rather than going its own way de facto if not de jure? And what will shape the extent of U.S. compliance?

Isolating the critical factors requires us to identify what is distinctive about the historical context. In this chapter we do so by comparing the debate over the WTO with that surrounding the International Trade Organization (ITO) half a century ago. The United States negotiated and signed but failed to ratify the ITO Charter, while it did ratify the WTO agreement. The contrasting outcomes of the two debates are of more than historical interest even though ratification of the WTO is now history, for the same issues that surfaced in the context of ratification will also shape the willingness of the United States to acknowledge the authority of the new organization, abide by its rules de facto as well as de jure, and lead future negotiations.[3]

In analyzing the two episodes, we distinguish three stages in the process of reaching and implementing an international agreement: negotiation, ratification, and compliance. Our analysis of U.S. behavior in these stages emphasizes three factors: exit options; the slack between U.S. principals and their negotiating agents; and the presidential effort spent to build domestic support.

6.1.1   The Exit Option

A country's exit option is its best alternative to signing, ratifying, and complying with an agreement. Exit options can be institutional or regional—they can take the form of recourse to an alternative negotiating venue or the pursuit of regional trade liberalization. A key factor in the contrasting outcomes of the two ratification debates is that U.S. exit options deteriorated in value between the 1940s and 1990s. In both the forties and the nineties the General Agreement on Tariffs and Trade (GATT) was the institutional option.[4] The

---

2. Richard W. Stevenson, "U.S. to Honor Trade Ruling against It on Foreign Fuel," *New York Times,* 20 June 1996.

3. Here we do not address the question of whether the structure of the ITO and WTO agreements was desirable from the point of view of U.S. or world welfare. Their views informed by more than fifty years of hindsight, more than a few economists would question the efficacy of an ITO agreement that featured multiple exceptions from the commitment to liberalize trade. Similarly, the WTO has been criticized both for being too interventionist and for not being interventionist enough. Our focus here is on why the United States acted as it did, not on the actual or counterfactual welfare effects of the two agreements. After this essay was written, we discovered an article by Vernon (1995b) that adopted a similar approach but emphasized different factors and reached different conclusions.

4. The United States also possessed some ability to pursue its trade-policy goals bilaterally, as we will describe below.

GATT was more valuable to the United States as an alternative in the forties than in the nineties, given America's main objectives at each time. The superiority of the U.S. institutional alternative in the forties helps to explain why key principals spurned the ITO Charter while their successors supported the WTO. But thinking along these lines also raises the question why U.S. negotiators at Havana accepted so many departures from U.S. ideals. Part of the answer is that in the forties it was Europe—and the United Kingdom in particular—that could play the regional card. The United Kingdom possessed extensive trade relations with its Commonwealth and empire and a political infrastructure to support them. The story of the ITO negotiations is in part the story of U.S. concessions to keep Britain from exercising its imperial option. European regional cooperation was also a potential alternative to the ITO, increasingly so as the forties progressed. For its part, the United States did not have any obvious regional alternative for achieving its trade-related geopolitical goals. In the nineties, in contrast, regionalism was a serious option for neither the United States nor its principal trading partners. Japan could not credibly threaten to retreat into an East Asian trading bloc, given its dependence on the American market. The Single European Act did raise the specter of a Fortress Europe closed to exports from the United States, but Europe too was heavily dependent on the North American market and never regarded the European Community as a serious alternative to the multilateral trading system. After attempting to launch another GATT round in 1982 and being rebuffed, Washington seemed to head for the regional exit, negotiating free trade agreements first with Israel, then with Canada, and finally with Mexico. But in fact, these countries and even all of Latin America constituted too small a share of world trade to make a regional free trade area preferable to a significant, even if disappointing, Geneva package. Nor, in our judgment, was there ever much likelihood of Asia-Pacific Economic Cooperation (APEC), an entity spanning political economies as disparate as China and the United States, actually adopting and complying with liberalization measures as significant as those of the WTO. In neither period, then, did a regional exit option offer Washington sufficient reason to reject either multilateral agreement.

6.1.2   Agent Slack

While exit options shed light on the balance of concessions, they cannot explain why Congress agreed to the WTO pact but balked at ratifying the agreement signed at Havana fifty years earlier. To understand this we invoke a second consideration: principal-agent slack. In the forties, consultation among U.S. negotiators, domestic interest groups, and Congress failed to marshal a critical mass of domestic support for the package negotiated at Havana. In the nineties, in contrast, U.S. principals instructed their negotiating agents earlier, more often, and more precisely.[5] Negotiators, for their part, used these consul-

---

5. It is sometimes said that these institutional changes largely "privatized" the making of U.S. trade policy, effectively allowing the private sector to set the agenda.

tations to educate principals and move their preferences closer to provisions that could be negotiated internationally. As a result, the terms of the U.S. negotiating position and the final Uruguay Round package were closer to Congress's 1994 preferences. This reduction of agency slack was due to changes in the institutions of U.S. trade policymaking.

6.1.3   Presidential Leadership

Even so, a thorough domestic political campaign by the Truman administration still might have pushed the ITO Charter through to ratification. Because the gains from liberalization are widely distributed, they are also diffuse, so that political leadership is required for Congress to feel the preferences of the beneficiaries. The American presidency, representing the entire electorate, logically supplies the most forceful institutional voice on behalf of trade liberalization.[6] At the same time, the leverage of trade policy over the political economy remains relatively limited in the United States, and other issues often dominate the president's attention. His political capital is limited, and the White House must choose how to spend its scarce domestic bargaining chips. Truman and his lieutenants decided to expend fewer of the president's domestic political assets to win ratification of the ITO Charter than did Presidents Bush and Clinton for the WTO. Truman's decision to give priority to other objectives and Bush's and Clinton's stronger battles for the North American Free Trade Agreement (NAFTA) and the WTO played critical roles in the contrasting ratification outcomes.[7] A complete explanation will require accounting for the two administrations' contrasting priorities.

6.2   A Comparison of the ITO and WTO Negotiations

Before considering the evidence for these arguments, three parallels between these negotiations merit emphasis. First, the United States provided the strongest push to initiate each. Second, negotiation itself entailed compromises that added additional issues. Third, in neither case was ratification straightforward.[8]

6.2.1   The ITO

From the start, the ITO was an American idea. The proposal for a postwar trade organization was developed by a set of interdepartmental and interagency committees that met in Washington, DC, from the spring of 1943 to the summer of 1945. Its four foundations were (1) generalized most-favored-nation

---

6. See for example the discussion in Frendreis and Tatalovich (1994, chap. 6).

7. Our perspective suggests that the problem in the forties was not congressional overload, as many published accounts suggest, but executive overload: that the executive had so many other pressing draws on its scarce political capital. We return to this point below.

8. Standard sources for the two episodes, upon which we draw, are Brown (1950) and Schott (1994).

treatment, with exceptions only for long-standing preferences, (2) no increases in existing preferences, (3) a commitment to negotiate reductions in existing trade barriers, and (4) a ban on using quantitative restrictions except under exceptional conditions.

The Americans sprang an early version of their proposal on the British in December 1944 (Howson and Moggridge 1990, 14). James Meade described the British government's alarmed reaction thus: "[T]here is a very dangerous trend of thought in the USA, of which Will Clayton in the State Department may be taken as the symbol, that the way to cure unemployment is to have stable exchange rates and free trade rather than (what is much nearer the truth) that the only way to achieve the conditions in which one can establish freer trade and more stable exchange rates is for countries to adopt suitable domestic policies for maintaining employment" (Howson and Moggridge 1990, 106). Nonetheless, a prostrate Britain had little choice. As a condition for the 1945 Anglo-American loan, Britain committed to the restoration of current account convertibility and nondiscriminatory trade. In notes exchanged with the United States in 1945–46, Belgium, Czechoslovakia, France, Greece, the Netherlands, Poland, and Turkey, all current or prospective recipients of U.S. aid, committed to similar goals.

The first round of negotiations was convened in London in 1946. Participants agreed that quantitative restrictions should be removed and that all trade barriers should be applied in nondiscriminatory fashion. But the British and French emphasized the need for import controls to support their fragile balances of payments. The British further stressed the importance they attached to trade with the Commonwealth and empire. The Australians insisted that controls were needed to facilitate industrialization and the pursuit of full employment. The United Kingdom, Belgium, and the Netherlands opposed American proposals for sanctions against state trading and cartels.

The key issue in the next round of meetings in Geneva in 1947 remained the use of controls for balance of payments and development.[9] The United Kingdom and France succeeded in adding to the draft a clause specifying conditions under which their use would be permitted, and conceded to the United States an amendment requiring the trade organization, in deciding whether such measures were warranted, to accept the determination of the International Monetary Fund (IMF), in which the United States had dominant voting power.

Negotiators covered the same ground in Havana in early 1948. Dispute over the use of controls for balance of payments was settled by allowing countries to choose between the London and Geneva provisions while limiting their discriminatory application to a transitional postwar period, as specified by the IMF Articles of Agreement. Alternative methods of obtaining permission to use import quotas to promote the development of new industries were elabo-

---

9. At American insistence, delegates also discussed discrimination against foreign motion pictures and the treatment of private foreign investment.

rated, but the principle of prior approval was preserved. In return for what they considered significant concessions, the Europeans and Latin Americans obtained American agreement to a one-country, one-vote procedure for decision making within the ITO.

As Heilperin (1949) emphasizes, other countries were less interested than the United States in trade liberalization and were preoccupied with other economic policy goals.[10] The British were worried about their balance of payments and consequently sought exceptions and exemptions from free trade. Primary producers like Australia were preoccupied by the instability of their commodity prices. Developing nations were primarily interested in the right to use import quotas to protect their infant industries. India and Latin America were prepared to accept only a weak agreement riddled with exceptions. Their reservations about free trade forced the United States, when attempting to create an organization that could bring about the elimination of nontariff barriers, to offer concessions.

These dynamics were further reflected in the negotiation of provisions meant to protect foreign investments. These clauses were of interest mainly to the principal international creditor, the United States. But here too the United States was forced to offer concessions. The draft charter, by asserting that governments could not expropriate or nationalize such assets except under conditions that were "just," "reasonable," or "appropriate," could be interpreted as weakening the protection that U.S. foreign investments had previously enjoyed. Such terminology implied that the United States was prepared to recognize circumstances under which expropriation or nationalization was justified, something it had never done before.[11]

This discussion omits what turned out to be the negotiators' most significant achievement: the conclusion of the GATT. What is most relevant for our purposes is that states concluded this narrower tariff-cutting agreement early—before the ITO negotiations had been finished—and that they did not make the GATT conditional on ratification of the ITO. While the GATT was directly based on the chapter of the ITO Charter concerned with tariff cuts, its implementation did not require new authorization in U.S. law. Presidents could implement tariff cuts under the authority of the Reciprocal Trade Agreements Act (and similar subsequent legislation). The GATT, although designed to be part of the charter, was thus available as an alternative to the ITO as a whole. One can imagine that things might have turned out differently had the others made

10. Heilperin was an adviser to the International Chamber of Commerce and attended both the Geneva and Havana conferences.

11. Recent archival research finds that the deputy U.S. negotiator in Havana, Clair Wilcox, saw much opposition to a strong charter consistent with U.S. principles, and he preferred no agreement to accepting a "skeleton ITO" as a fallback. His superior, William Clayton, however, had identified himself with the charter and insisted on further bargaining, overriding Wilcox's reservations. From January through March Clayton made several additional concessions on the use of import quotas and on voting rules. See Dryden (1995, chap. 1).

the GATT conditional—part of a "single undertaking" that required countries also to accept the other elements of the ITO package.

Negotiations over tariffs commenced at the second Geneva Preparatory Meeting. Twenty-three countries bargained bilaterally on a product-by-product basis. Bargaining was confined to products for which one country was the other's principal supplier, and all concessions obtained were generalized to every member of this group. One hundred and twenty-three bilateral negotiations covering fifty thousand items were convened. The parties covered half of world trade and cut the average tariff by 35 percent. They completed the resulting document, called the General Agreement on Tariffs and Trade, before the Havana conference began. The GATT's "general clauses" prevented countries from using quotas and domestic impediments to trade to reduce the value of the agreed-upon tariff cuts. Otherwise, there was no discussion of import controls, cartels, foreign investment, commodity-price stabilization, or industrialization. Eleven more countries joined the GATT as contracting parties in the second round of negotiations at Annecy in 1949, and the concessions negotiated at Geneva were generalized to their economies.

6.2.2   The WTO

The protectionism associated with the oil shocks and international economic imbalances of the 1970s provided the impetus for the Uruguay Round. (This book's introduction provides a fuller account of the round.) Again the United States provided the initiative. It sought to enhance access to foreign markets for U.S. suppliers. More fundamentally, it sought to bring the GATT up to date by extending its coverage to agriculture and services and to remedy shortcomings in areas like intellectual property and foreign investment. But the U.S. proposal met with little support at the 1982 GATT ministerial. Europeans were leery about U.S. insistence on agricultural liberalization. Developing countries worried that the expansion of the GATT to new issues might deflect attention from the need for industrial countries to open their own markets to exports from the third world.

The Reagan administration therefore concentrated on issues like services that could be pursued outside the GATT. It negotiated bilateral trade agreements with Israel and Canada. In 1986, at Punta del Este, it overcame the lingering opposition of leading developing countries and initiated the Uruguay Round, whose expected concluding date was 1990.

William Diebold (1952) once said that the ITO had been squeezed between the protectionists and the perfectionists. The same was true of the Uruguay Round in the second half of the 1980s. The United States insisted on the elimination of all agricultural protection and subsidies, something to which the Europeans could not agree; they countered with a proposal for limited cuts. Other agricultural exporters (the Cairns Group) also insisted on reductions in farm subsidies and refused to accede to U.S. demands for the liberalization of services, in which they had relatively little interest, unless such reductions were forthcoming. The result was impasse at the final 1990 GATT Ministerial Conference in Brussels.

Canada's trade minister John Crosbie had proposed the creation of a World Trade Organization in April 1990 (Preeg 1995, 113), and in 1991 GATT director general Arthur Dunkel incorporated the suggestion into his comprehensive compendium of interim agreements (the Draft Final Act, or Dunkel draft).[12] In part, this initiative can be understood as an effort to bundle together the various issues and facilitate horse trading. By obtaining a credible commitment on services and intellectual property, the United States might be willing to compromise on agriculture. By obtaining concessions from Europe on agricultural trade, the Cairns Group might be willing to compromise on services. The "single undertaking," which bundled together treaties on these issues under the umbrella of the WTO, solidified the issue linkage.

The problem was that it was not clear that Europe stood to gain significantly. The European Community (EC) sought to limit U.S. recourse to "aggressive unilateralism" (its use of section 301, for example) and to raise the cost to America of ignoring panel rulings. Europe stood to benefit from protection for intellectual property and from liberalization of services trade, albeit less than the United States. But there was also significant resistance to a negotiated agreement. European farmers continued to block agricultural liberalization. The French government's concerns over "cultural imperialism" led it to oppose the liberalization of services if this left its domestic market vulnerable to American films. Thus, concessions by the Europeans were essential to bring the round to a successful conclusion.

Most accounts suggest that two factors combined to bring about the desired result. First, resistance was disproportionately concentrated in one European country, France, where the agricultural and cultural issues had special resonance. But France also had a particularly strong desire for monetary unification, negotiations over which were proceeding in parallel. The turmoil in the European Monetary System in 1992–93 underscored the extent to which reaching this goal was contingent on German support, strengthening the hand of German and other European governments that preferred concessions on these trade issues from France. Second, the Clinton administration signaled its readiness, like that of Bush, to walk away from the table if concessions on agriculture were not forthcoming. It committed to a binding deadline by requesting that fast-track authority be renewed only through 1994. It signaled its willingness to pursue the regional option by negotiating NAFTA and giving increasing prominence to APEC meetings.

Ratification met with some resistance in the U.S. Congress, for the agreement did more than bundle the GATT with other multilateral undertak-

---

12. Jackson (1990) had provided important intellectual support for this approach.

ings. Objections centered on the danger that WTO decisions might force the United States to change its laws, and on whether majority voting by WTO members would alter trade rules to the country's disadvantage. In the end other arguments carried the day. Congress ratified the agreement late in 1994.

6.3   Rival Arguments and Their Limitations

6.3.1   Declining Hegemony

One approach to explaining this ITO/WTO contrast might come from the hegemony theory of international economic stability.[13] Its more benevolent version treats international organizations as suppliers of global public goods, which facilitate the internalization of externalities that spill across borders. Trade is a case in point. At least some of the benefits of a country's decision to liberalize accrue to its trading partners, and a trade organization that promotes the exchange of commercial concessions can be thought of as internalizing such externalities. And large countries, like dominant firms in imperfectly competitive markets, should have the strongest incentive to invest in arrangements capable of internalizing such externalities.[14] Trade liberalization thus proceeds smoothly when there is a dominant power but slows in periods of hegemonic decline and rising multipolarity.

There are problems with this argument at the levels of both theory and history. Theoretically, while cheating means increasing volume in the cartel context, it means restricting it in the case of trade. While large firms might be thought to have the least incentive to cheat on a cartel agreement (since their incentive to increase output is partially offset by the induced decline in product prices), the opposite is true of large countries that cheat on an agreement to liberalize, for only large countries can significantly improve their terms of trade by restricting imports or exports.

Historically, by almost any measure the United States was more dominant in international markets soon after World War II than it is today. Other countries value access to the U.S. market today, but in the days of the postwar dollar shortage that access was more vital still. The hegemony theory taken alone, if it had any relevance for our question, would surely imply that the United States would have been more likely to ratify the ITO Charter than the WTO.

---

13. See Kindleberger (1973, 1981) for seminal statements of this view, Krasner (1976) for an application to international trade, and McKeown (1983), Snidal (1985), and Lake (1993) for critiques.

14. When a small firm reneges on its agreement to restrict output, this puts negligible downward pressure on prices and hence is relatively attractive. A small firm is presumably in the best position to avoid detection when it cheats. A small firm in an oligopolistic market has little capacity to punish producers who fail to restrict their output. The same logic is said to apply to small and large countries in international markets.

6.3.2   Fear of War

A second familiar argument holds that the fear of war between 1946 and 1950, when military conflict exploded in Korea, led the United States to pay a higher price to support the security of allied countries for military-political reasons—by lowering its own import barriers to their goods among other things. If so, then the decline of this U.S. fear especially after 1989 should have made the Americans less inclined to liberalize, other things equal. Again common wisdom leads us astray.

6.3.3   Congressional Overload

Many accounts of the ITO debate emphasize that Congress was overloaded with other international issues, straining the capacity of internationalists in the Senate and the House. These included the Marshall Plan, the North Atlantic Treaty Organization (NATO), and the Korean conflict, each of which shifted the ITO onto the back burner. But when is Congress not subject to overload? It is far from clear that this problem was any less severe in the 1990s, when Congress had to deal with NAFTA, Operation Desert Storm and Operation Provide Cover, the collapse of the Soviet Union, and potential eastward expansion of NATO, not to mention domestic issues.

6.3.4   Historical Memory

It is widely argued that memories of trade conflict in the thirties lent powerful impetus to the campaign for multilateral trade liberalization after World War II. The collapse of trade was associated with the Great Depression in the minds of both politicians and the public, legitimizing the campaign for liberalization. But these memories were fresher in the forties, when Congress refused to charter a multilateral organization, than in the nineties, when it did. In terms of the ITO-WTO contrast, this explanation too works in the wrong direction.

6.3.5   Openness of the U.S. Economy

The U.S. economy was more open in the nineties than in the forties, since it took decades to repair the damage to international markets inflicted by the Depression. More U.S. companies being oriented toward export markets, this argument goes, lobbying for trade liberalization must have been stronger. Of course, producers of tradables can favor either liberalization or protection, depending on whether they are in export-oriented or import-competing sectors. While the balance between these groups shifted over time, this explanation too works in the wrong direction. As the U.S. trade surpluses of the immediate postwar years gave way to deficits, presumably augmenting the scope of import competition relative to those with a vested interest in exporting, we should have seen stronger support for ratification in the forties than in the nineties. Admittedly, the emergence of multinational corporations as key contributors to both major parties' national political candidates, and hence their acquisition of privileged access, may incline U.S. policymakers toward liberalization. But, as the opposition of groups like the United Auto Workers to NAFTA reminds us, interests exposed to international competition by the increasing openness of the U.S. economy also pushed in the other direction.

6.3.6   Ratification Hurdles

Because joining the ITO required congressional ratification of an international treaty, Truman faced the formidable obstacle of marshaling a two-thirds majority. The WTO, in contrast, was adopted as a simple law, which required only 51 percent support. The United States failed to ratify the ITO, according to this view, simply because the ratification hurdle was higher; the WTO would not have passed either had a two-thirds majority been required. In fact, however, it is not clear in retrospect that the United States could not have joined the ITO through passage of a simple law. The United States accepted membership in the IMF and the World Bank on precisely that basis, by passing the Bretton Woods Agreements Act in 1945.

6.4   Poorer Exit Options

6.4.1   The Regional Alternative

The United States did not ratify the ITO but did join the WTO partly because its best alternative was more attractive in the first instance. The difference was not found primarily in the closing of regional exit options, however. Regionalism was not a better alternative for America in either period. It is true that in the 1980s the United States negotiated bilateral free trade agreements in part because the GATT contracting parties refused to initiate a multilateral negotiation (as argued by Schott 1989). Washington used North American free trade to concentrate the minds of other countries reluctant to embark on serious negotiations in Geneva. The Canada-U.S. Free Trade Agreement, signed in 1986, "provided the USTR with a credible threat to warn its trade partners that it could be forced by Congress to abandon the GATT system," and not coincidentally jump-started the Uruguay Round (Wiener 1995, 100). Negotiations acquired a new urgency in 1990 when U.S. trade representative Carla Hills warned that NAFTA might be extended into a hemispheric free trade agreement, the Enterprise for the Americas.[15] By the early nineties the NAFTA debate and not the Uruguay Round had come to dominate U.S. headlines.

In fact, however, even if other negotiators responded to these threats, NAFTA never was a truly credible substitute for the multilateral tariff negotiation. U.S. objectives in the Uruguay Round were to stem creeping protection-

---

15. Wiener (1995, 183). A knowledgeable commentator on an earlier draft reported that James Baker—successively President Reagan's chief of staff, treasury secretary, and secretary of state— seemed to believe regional economic deals were a serious alternative for the United States.

ism, roll back agricultural protection in Europe, and bring trade in services and intellectual property rights into the multilateral system, goals that could only be achieved in multilateral negotiations with the leading industrial countries. Exports to Canada and Mexico—indeed, exports to the Western Hemisphere as a whole—accounted for too small a fraction of the U.S. total to provide an attractive alternative to multilateral liberalization.

Some European policymakers were reported to be sufficiently alarmed by APEC to offer new concessions in Geneva in 1993 (see Destler 1995; Frankel forthcoming). By that summer, the Uruguay Round threatened to run aground again over the opposition of European farmers to agricultural liberalization. President Clinton therefore upgraded the November 1993 Seattle meeting of APEC ministers, adding a high-profile leaders' meeting. NAFTA had already demonstrated the administration's readiness to pursue the regional route; now the APEC meeting raised the possibility of its duplicating the NAFTA achievement. While APEC was a loosely structured organization that possessed neither the institutional infrastructure nor the political will to engineer a free trade agreement, it accounted for a much larger share of world trade (40 percent) than NAFTA and was by far the most rapidly growing share of the world total. When the president flew to Seattle the day after the key House vote approving NAFTA and posed for pictures with thirteen other APEC leaders, European policymakers grew concerned that the United States would again play its regional card. The result was German pressure on the French and concessions on agricultural liberalization by the Europeans. Thus, regional moves could affect the terms of a GATT agreement at the margin.

Still, given U.S. objectives, we find it difficult to imagine U.S. delegates walking away from Geneva, even absent those last concessions, because they regarded APEC or NAFTA or both combined as equivalent. The value of APEC as a vehicle for trade liberalization was far more symbolic than real. Can one really picture countries as diverse as China, Japan, the United States, and Mexico, lacking the institutional infrastructure of the GATT, not to mention its forty-five years of experience, rapidly reaching significant agreements? Nor was it obvious that extending NAFTA into South America would have been politically straightforward. The agreement with Mexico and Canada had provoked a firestorm of opposition in the U.S. Congress, partly because of the immediacy of free trade with contiguous and much poorer economies. It is not clear that negotiating free trade agreements including countries like Colombia, with its history as a source of drug traffic, and Brazil, with its history of dirigisme, would have been straightforward.

The United States lacked a credible regional alternative in the forties as well. As the cold war came to a boil, Washington sought to rebuild the trade and the economies of western Europe, Japan, and other parts of the world perceived as vulnerable to the Communist threat, as well as to benefit the U.S. economy through trade. No one regional arrangement could accomplish these goals in all of the relevant regions. From the standpoint of U.S. objectives, the GATT was a more efficient solution.

To the extent that a regional option existed, it belonged to the Europeans. The British had established an extensive set of imperial preferences starting with the Ottawa Conference in 1932. Trade with the Commonwealth and empire accounted for nearly half of the United Kingdom's merchandise trade in the second half of the forties. If Britain failed to obtain acceptable terms in the ITO negotiation, it could credibly threaten to walk away, and to fall back on trade with the Commonwealth. The British, dead set against liberalization, obtained a GATT clause that grandfathered pre–World War II preferences, allowing Britain to hold out against their removal.

While other European countries did not possess equally extensive imperial ties, they could look to the possibility of European integration. Much of Continental countries' trade was with one another. Additionally there was a strongly felt desire to lock a peaceful Germany into Europe by strengthening its trade links with its neighbors. This process commenced with a proposal in July 1947 for a Franco-Italian customs union, the First Agreement on Multilateral Monetary Compensation of November 1947, and the Agreement for Intra-European Payments and Compensations of October 1948, and culminated in the European Payments Union of 1950 and the European Coal and Steel Community of 1951. The EPU ultimately incorporated not only Britain but its overseas dependencies. While EPU members committed to freeing their trade with other EPU members, this agreement allowed them to continue restricting imports from other countries (Triffin 1957, 203).

The United States strengthened Europe's resistance to the nondiscriminatory multilateralism of the ITO by amending the GATT to facilitate the formation of regional customs unions (see Brown 1950, 242; Brusse 1996, 224 and passim). The 1947 drafting of GATT regulations coincided with the advent of the Marshall Plan, which capped the evolution of U.S. State Department opinion toward European integration as an engine of recovery. In the 1947 GATT draft, customs unions would be permitted if they freed "substantially" all trade among the members and if barriers to trade with the rest of the world were "on the whole no more restrictive" than before.[16] These ambiguous phrases further opened the door for Europe to pursue the regional option (see Dam 1970). For all these reasons, then, it was Europe rather than the United States that possessed the credible regional alternative in the forties.

These regional options go part way toward explaining bargaining outcomes in the two negotiations. Since in the forties it was the Europeans—especially the British—who possessed the most credible regional alternative to multilateralism, it was they who managed to extract concessions on such matters as the use of trade restrictions in the event of unemployment or payments problems. In 1993 the coincidence of NAFTA ratification, an APEC summit meeting, and the Uruguay Round final deadline evidently helped Washington to extract final agriculture concessions from the Europeans. In both periods, how-

16. The GATT further tolerated "interim agreements" leading ultimately to a customs union; in other words, the participating countries did not have to go immediately all the way to zero tariffs.

ever, the value of the regional option was significantly lower in reality than that of a multilateral deal for the United States.

6.4.2   The Institutional Alternative

The United States did have a better institutional exit option in the forties than in the nineties. This difference helps explain why key American principals decided to spurn the ITO Charter while their successors supported the WTO.

In both periods the GATT, supplemented in the second episode by the General Agreement on Trade in Services (GATS) and other multilateral agreements, was available as a fallback. In the forties U.S. officials were aware that drafting and ratification of the ITO Charter would not be quick. By 1946 they had less than three years of authorization to negotiate tariff reductions under the authorities of the Trade Agreements Act (TAA).[17] Hence the State Department decided to proceed with tariff negotiations before concluding ITO ratification. The GATT would be used to build on the TAA and generalize bilateral tariff cuts while completing the construction of the ITO, which would ultimately subsume the trade agreement (Aaronson 1996, 115–24).

The timing of the Geneva tariff round, prior to congressional consideration of the ITO, was dictated by Europe's worsening economic circumstances and tension with the Soviet Union. Shortages were pervasive, and the European economy threatened to grind to a halt in the winter of 1947. The reconstruction of intra-European trade lagged behind the recovery of the trade elsewhere. While the Marshall Plan was one response to these problems, the negotiation of mutual tariff reductions under the aegis of the GATT was another. The Truman administration's bargaining position with Congress might have been strengthened by delaying the effort to operationalize the GATT, but circumstances did not permit.

By the end of the forties, two GATT rounds had established the viability of the limited strategy of generalizing bilateral tariff cuts to all contracting parties. The Geneva Round reduced the tariffs applied by the contracting parties to one another's exports by more than a third, and the Annecy Round increased the number of GATT signatories by nearly a half. U.S. business and congressional opponents of the ITO could invoke the GATT as a proven alternative to a convoluted ITO Charter which some saw as a threat to U.S. sovereignty and others criticized as loophole- and exception-ridden.[18]

---

17. The TAA was scheduled to expire in June 1948. While it was renewed, this involved a considerable battle and could not be anticipated at the time.

18. The case should not be overstated: in 1950 there was still reason to worry about other countries' commitment to trade liberalization. Latin America was pursuing import-substituting industrialization. Other primary-commodity producers sought to support their export prices through the use of marketing boards and other trade restrictions. France and other European countries saw trade liberalization as incompatible with their programs of state-led investment in industrial modernization. Countries other than the United States had already displayed their reservations about tariff reduction in the course of the ITO negotiations, extracting a variety of other concessions in return for agreeing to negotiate tariff cuts. It was possible to dismiss the 35 percent cuts negotiated

In 1994 the GATT remained the obvious fallback option in the event of a failure to accept the WTO agreement. But the GATT had run its course: it was easy to foresee the day when the tariff cuts that were its bread and butter would reduce import duties to zero. Designed primarily as a venue for negotiating tariff cuts, the GATT had proven less adequate as a device for removing the nontariff barriers that remained. Among other things, the incidence of nontariff barriers was difficult to quantify, complicating the calculation of terms of trade between them. An agreement designed to reduce trade barriers at the border was of limited effectiveness in the age of deep integration, when liberalizing the market access meant modifying a variety of domestic practices over which the GATT had little authority.

Perhaps most important, the new issues around which efforts at trade liberalization now revolved—services, intellectual property, and trade-related investment—were covered not by the GATT but by parallel agreements like the GATS and the agreement on intellectual property. Participation in the GATT did not oblige countries to accept these agreements. They could opt out as they saw fit. The WTO, in contrast to the GATT alone, required its members to adhere not only to GATT rules but also to these other trade pacts, under the terms of the so-called single undertaking. The United States, particularly concerned with these new issues, thus stood to lose, probably disproportionately, if forced to fall back to the GATT alone.

6.5   Reduced Agent Slack and Stronger Presidential Leadership

While countries' varying exit options help to explain which issues were bundled together in these two negotiations and the resulting mix of concessions, they are not sufficient to explain why Congress agreed to U.S. participation in the WTO but balked at ratifying the ITO Charter, or why the U.S. negotiator in 1948 added concessions that later sank the charter at home. For these questions we must add two additional points. First, U.S. principals instructed their negotiating agents much more frequently, at more levels of government, and in much finer detail during the Uruguay Round than during the earlier episode. During the war U.S. trade negotiators lost touch with their principals, and especially during the Havana conference chief agent Will Clayton made several additional concessions that soured the opinions of powerful organized groups at home. In contrast, the final 1994 package and congressional opinion at that time were much closer together.

---

at Geneva and Annecy as nothing more than the removal of the most onerous wartime restrictions and to question whether they would have real effects in a Europe still riddled with quantitative trade controls. Contemporaries dismissed the results of the 1951 Torquay Round and the 1956 Geneva Round as "meager," "modest," and "not . . . a success" (Irwin 1995, 135–37). In retrospect, we know that the post–World War II GATT system was remarkably successful. But this could not have been known for sure in 1950.

Second, President Truman and his aides also spent less political effort mobilizing domestic support for ratification of the ITO than Presidents Bush and Clinton and their trade ministers spent on building support for NAFTA and the WTO. In the forties even with a split in the business lobby and substantial opposition, a comprehensive and sophisticated presidential political campaign might well have been sufficient to achieve ratification. Consider the analogy with the Bretton Woods Agreements Act of 1945. When that bill was submitted to Congress, the banking community opposed ratification, and prospects in the relevant congressional committees were quite bleak (Eckes 1975). Yet presidential leadership helped turn this situation around. The same might be said of the Marshall Plan. Relatively few thought at the time that an unpopular Democratic administration could push such an ambitious plan through an increasingly isolationist Republican Congress. But Truman launched a "full-court press." Over the fall and winter of 1947 and into the spring of 1948, Truman used messages and speeches to pound home the need for congressional action. He accommodated the desire of the senior senator from Michigan, Arthur H. Vandenberg, to depoliticize the issue and delink it from the 1948 election. He authorized giving Vandenberg continuous advice and support, including weekly briefings by Marshall.[19]

The American presidency, representing the entire electorate, typically supplies the most forceful institutional voice at home on behalf of trade liberalization (Goldstein 1993, 1996). At the same time, trade is only one of many issues on which presidents are asked to provide statesmanlike leadership. When will a president choose to expend his scarce political capital defending the general interest in a trade liberalization agreement against hostile special-interest lobbies? A superficial answer is "when he is not preoccupied by more pressing issues," but this only begs the question. Major foreign-policy conflicts tend to be identified as more pressing, and their presence (as in the forties) or absence (as, relatively speaking, in the nineties) is a powerful predictor of whether a president will provide a forceful institutional voice at home for trade liberalization. Prospect theory suggests that policymakers will focus their time and energies most on issues that pose major downside risks. A foreign policy conflict with potentially disastrous consequences (the cold war, the Korean conflict) poses just such risks. Hence, it was to these issues, and not ratification of the ITO Charter, that Truman chose to devote his political capital after 1948. President Clinton, in contrast, may have had to contend with Bosnia, Russia, North Korea, Iraq, and Iran, yet he faced no foreign-policy problem of comparable severity. He consequently retained the political capital needed to push through U.S. participation in the WTO. From this perspective, the problem in the for-

19. As Neustadt (1980, 41–42) puts it in his discussion of presidential leadership in support of the Marshall Plan, "Truman himself had sufficient hold on presidential messages and speeches, on budget policy, on high-level appointments and on his own time and temper" to "deliver [what his political allies and opponents] wanted in return."

ties was not so much congressional overload as presidential overload created by a series of pressing foreign policy crises.

6.5.1 The ITO: Greater Agent Slack and Weaker Presidential Leadership

During the planning and negotiation of the GATT and the ITO from 1941 through 1948, and especially before 1947, U.S. agents distanced themselves from their principals. The trade planners between 1943 and 1945 made a deliberate decision to give top priority to building international support for trade liberalization, over building domestic support (Aaronson 1993, chap. 3).[20] Not only was this attitude consistent with wartime planning; also in the 1934 Reciprocal Trade Agreements Act, Congress had delegated tariff setting to the executive branch precisely in order to insulate the process to a greater extent from constituency pressures that were difficult to resist.

Secretary of State Cordell Hull, his assistant Leo Pasvolsky, and Harry C. Hawkins envisioned the ITO as a critical component of a radically new U.S. foreign policy that would stand as a more hopeful legacy left by the generation that had fought this terrible second world war. Professor Clair Wilcox (1949, xvii), economist and chief trade planner who with William Clayton succeeded Pasvolsky and Hawkins in 1946, wrote: "The logic of our position allows us no alternative. We must go on, in international cooperation, from politics to economics, from finance to trade. World organization for security is essential; but if it is to succeed, it must rest upon continuous international participation in economic affairs. . . . If political and economic order is to be rebuilt, we must provide, in our trade relationships, the solid foundation upon which the superstructure of international cooperation is to stand."

State Department negotiating agents operated differently at home from Henry Morgenthau's Treasury, which planned the 1944 Bretton Woods Conference and secured passage of the implementing legislation,[21] and differently from the way UN planners concentrated on involving members of Congress and the general public. They kept Congress in the dark as to the essential details until 1946. They did not include representatives from either Congress or the public on their interagency trade planning committees. In 1944 some planners advocated creating a formal channel for business opinion, but after extensive internal debate, senior State officials rejected the idea explicitly (Aaronson 1993, 96). They made only vague public statements about plans for trade liberalization. During 1945 while they sought renewal of the 1934 TAA, their testimony never discussed plans for an international trade organization or spelled

20. Aaronson (1993, 1996) provides by far the most thorough available evidence on this process, going well beyond William Diebold's early and still valuable essay (1952).

21. On forming the Bretton Woods delegation and ratifying this agreement, see Eckes 1975 and Odell 1988. Vernon (1995a) detects a common pattern in all U.S. economic negotiations during the forties—executive officials launch bold institutional initiatives but in the end the United States rejects significant constraints on its own future policy choices.

out how they would use this authority in multilateral rather than in bilateral negotiations as before. This reticence was not attributable to lack of interest on Capitol Hill. On the contrary, expressed industry opposition to further liberalization was as plentiful as support. Members too had been sending signals that support for further liberalization would need to be cultivated (Aaronson 1993, 69). Hearings in 1946 on the loan to the United Kingdom can be seen as providing further warnings.

In 1946 Clayton and Wilcox continued to concentrate on the international level; Clayton rejected Wilcox's and Hawkins's suggestions to involve Congress and the public at home (Aaronson 1996, 65–67). After publishing the first version of their proposals in December 1945, they published the first complete suggested charter on 20 September 1946, just before the opening of the London meeting, the first multilateral conference on this proposal.

The strategic decision to keep the home front in the dark during these years would prove costly. By 1946 American public enthusiasm for new civilian multilateral organizations had passed its high-water mark. Strikes and inflation agitated the home economy, and just before the congressional elections a meat shortage drove President Truman to lift price controls on meat. Citizens were frustrated by higher taxes and insufficient housing and employment for returning veterans. American voters punished Democrats on balance and gave control of both houses to the Republican party. Republican leaders, foreshadowing 1994, then announced enthusiastically that voters must want fundamental change from the New Deal path. Some Republican leaders concentrated greater fire on the trade agreements program. That fall and winter State's trade planners privately voiced fears that they had missed their chance by largely disregarding congressional and other domestic opinion for so long (Aaronson 1996, 70–71). While polls showed no strong mass opposition to a new trade organization, neither did ordinary people care much about it.

In response to Republican and special-interest concerns, Truman in February 1947 modified the trade agreements program through an executive order that guaranteed an "escape clause" to any sector that might be affected by the coming GATT negotiations. During 1947 and 1948 State Department leaders finally held public hearings to collect views on the ITO, and they made some changes in their negotiating positions as a result. They invited private-sector and congressional representatives to advise the delegation at Havana. At the same time, however, they overestimated public support for their general plans and held to their earlier domestic tactics in some ways (Aaronson 1996, 71–78). At the Geneva trade conference in 1947, negotiators settled on the GATT and a provisional draft of an ITO, and the Havana conference completed the charter late that year and in early 1948.

After the negotiations, the U.S. administration did make some efforts to mobilize domestic support for ratification, but these efforts were long delayed and only lukewarm. Truman and Secretary of State George Marshall decided to spend most of their scarce Washington political resources on other issues. By this time, as is well known, continuing postwar frictions between the USSR and the West had escalated dramatically to proxy wars and even the brink of superpower war. From 1947 onward, trade negotiations had to compete for U.S. official and media attention with subversion and violence overseas and pleas for new foreign commitments to avoid World War III. During 1947 the European emergency especially seemed to demand measures that could make a difference quickly. Top leaders in State—Marshall supported by Robert Lovett and others—decided to give priority in Congress to winning ratification of their own expensive European recovery program and the North Atlantic Treaty. Efforts by Clayton and Wilcox to convince their new superiors of the ITO's continuing centrality and its need for greater support proved unsuccessful (Aaronson 1996, 86, 93–96). The wartime vision of international economic organizations as means of keeping allied capitalist and Communist governments joined in productive common endeavors began looking too optimistic. As for trade, Truman and Marshall evidently found the TAA plus the GATT a useful second-best. The GATT contracting parties completed their first round in 1947.

The TAA was due to expire in mid-1948. Early that year the Democratic administration, facing a Republican Congress and a general election, decided to concentrate on the safer course of seeking renewal of the expiring TAA, and to postpone submitting the more ambitious ITO Charter until the next Congress. Even then the TAA hearings were a platform for hostile Republican attacks on the State Department, revealing how much distrust its largely closed process had planted, as well as Republican determination to take charge of trade policy. Some politicians began to associate support for freer trade by their domestic rivals with being "soft" on communism. Still, a vigorous effort to round up supportive industries bore fruit, and Congress did extend the TAA—but for only one year, to 1949.[22]

In April 1949 the U.S. administration finally submitted the charter for congressional action, during yet another consideration of limited TAA extension. By then an informal coalition of U.S. protectionists and perfectionists had come out in opposition to ratification. While some business owners favored the ITO, organized groups that had supported earlier tariff liberalizations now split. Labor, the Farm Bureau, the Committee for Economic Development, the National Planning Association, and the Committee for the ITO called for approval. In addition to predictable protectionists, however, the U.S. Chamber of Commerce, the National Association of Manufacturers (NAM), the National

---

22. In 1949 State assigned some officials to monitor and influence elite opinion through speeches to and private lunches with representatives of the American Farm Bureau Federation, the National Association of Manufacturers, the U.S. Chamber of Commerce, and narrower interest groups. Junior staffers drafted articles for business journals. William Batt, president of SKF Industries, a manufacturer of ball bearings, agreed to head a private-sector Committee for the International Trade Organization, after two more prominent business leaders had declined. Batt secured endorsements from some one hundred leaders in business, unions, civic organizations, and universities (Aaronson 1996, 103).

Foreign Trade Council (NFTC), and the U.S. Council of the International Chamber of Commerce opposed ratification. The U.S. Chamber of Commerce and the NAM were the largest business organizations in the country, and the NFTC had been at the heart of earlier coalitions for liberalization. These, which Diebold dubs the perfectionists, objected mainly that the charter failed to implement the liberalizing principles it also included. Many critics concentrated on the exceptions that allowed continued use of quotas during balance-of-payments difficulties. Many corporate managers also felt hostile to the full-employment provisions, even though they went no further than U.S. law; these same individuals had opposed that law as well. They objected that the charter might sanction government commodity cartels, even though its provisions provided tighter controls on the use of commodity management than had ever been agreed before.[23]

These critics felt, in sum, that the ITO did not add much value because the United States would live up to its obligations but most other countries would use the charter's loopholes. But rather than saying that the charter was a package of compromises that fell short on balance, some organizations chose to denounce it as "a dangerous document" sanctifying principles utterly contrary to the American way, that "in effect commits all members of the ITO to state planning for full employment."[24] The administration had done relatively little to generate understanding and support in the public and Congress that could have offset the special-interest critics politically.

During this internal debate, Congress was investigating possible treason in the State Department. A jury convicted Alger Hiss of perjury in January 1950. On 25 June 1950 North Korea suddenly attacked southward across the thirty-eighth parallel, and thereafter American soldiers were dying in another hot war. This time the other side seemed to have atomic weapons. The president sent U.S. troops back to Europe as well and decided to abandon the ITO.

6.5.2 The WTO: Reduced Agent Slack and Stronger Presidential Leadership

Between the ITO and the WTO, the United States changed its institutions for making public trade decisions in ways that influenced U.S. negotiating positions and made ratification of signed trade agreements much more likely. Perhaps as a delayed reaction to the ITO experience, in 1962 Congress took

23. The charter's provisions on investment provoked some of the loudest corporate cries. Investors complained that once passages on compensation for expropriation had been qualified with adjectives such as "just" and "appropriate," they could actually end up with less protection than they had under the status quo (Diebold 1952, 18). Ironically it was these same business lobbies that had insisted that a reluctant State Department add the investment issue to the negotiations in the first place. The diplomats had warned that other countries might not accept a provision that would satisfy U.S. business. After business representatives had told Clayton they would "strongly support the ITO charter in toto in Congress" and "will swallow all other provisions" if it covered investment, Clayton had agreed (Aaronson 1996, 85). The NAM adviser in Havana did support the final charter text and labored, unsuccessfully, to persuade his organization to endorse it.

24. The Executive Committee of the U.S. Council of the International Chamber of Commerce, quoted in Diebold (1952, 414–15).

chief authority for trade negotiations away from the Department of State and created a new position, the special trade representative (STR), in the same legislation that authorized U.S. concessions in the Kennedy Round (Rightor-Thornton 1975). The STR was now the chief U.S. agent abroad as well as the chief manager of the related domestic politics. In 1974 Congress strengthened the STR by locating it in the Executive Office by statute and giving its leader Cabinet rank and salary. The title was changed in 1979 to United States trade representative (USTR). Therefore after 1962 the lead agency in trade diplomacy no longer had any responsibilities for other foreign policies. If military or political objectives came into conflict with trade guidelines, only the president could overrule the latter. This at least freed trade policy from compromises down inside the State Department like those that had weakened its domestic position in 1948 to 1950. To be sure, even if such institutions had been in place then, the dramatic events of the early cold war would probably have been sufficient to shift the Truman administration's priorities sharply toward immediate military-political dangers. Since then, hardly any USTRs have been among the most influential members of presidents' inner circles. Still, after 1962 U.S. commercial objectives were likely to dominate daily decisions to a greater extent on average.

The Trade Act of 1974, which authorized the president to participate in the Tokyo Round, also laid down new rules reducing agent slack. This law mandated quasi-corporatist consultations with the private sector and reporting to the key congressional committees throughout negotiations. It established an Advisory Committee for Trade Negotiations: forty-five citizens appointed by the president to represent all social sectors including labor and consumers, and to meet frequently with the USTR in Washington and Geneva. In practice, management representatives dominated overwhelmingly. At a lower level the act created three advisory committees covering industry, labor, and agriculture. Reporting to these in turn would be no fewer than twenty-seven additional, sectoral advisory committees, each composed of industry experts. Negotiators were required to provide access to confidential information to all these constituents and designated congressional staff. The law directed the private-sector advisers to publish an advisory opinion—in effect a report card—on the final agreement (Winham 1986, 133–37). Little opportunity was left for incomplete information about special-interest opposition to an agenda item.

Planners were concerned not only about the risk of ratification defeat but also the risk of Congress's simply delaying indefinitely or enacting conditions inconsistent with the agreement and impossible to negotiate—problems that had dogged the Kennedy Round's outcome. Thus came new rules creating a sui generis "fast track" for ratification. The 1974 act stipulated that once the president presents the results to Congress, it would then have no more than sixty days to vote. No amendments or delays would be in order after the president had formally submitted his bill. This rule created a strong incentive for the administration to involve key congressional leaders informally in writing the implementing legislation as well as in the negotiation itself. Equally, to the lobbyist seeking changes after the negotiation, it left only the possibility of entering the private process of crafting the president's bill, where negotiators have much greater autonomy to block entry. Five years later the U.S. House of Representatives and the Senate did ratify the Tokyo Round's complex set of compromises, by remarkable margins of 395 to 7 and 90 to 4, respectively (Winham 1986, 308).

Thus in sharp contrast to the pattern of 1943 to 1946, U.S. negotiators during the Uruguay Round reported to principals, heard their demands frequently and in detail, and in turn had opportunities to influence congressional expectations. They knew from the beginning—because the 1974 rules had been carried forward into later legislation—that the negotiation and the domestic ratification campaign would overlap in practice.

This institutional reality helps account for much U.S. behavior during the negotiating, ratification, and compliance stages. The very agenda of this round, launched in 1986 in Punta del Este, bore the clear fingerprints of a huge coalition of U.S. industries seeking better protection of intellectual property rights abroad, which had been meeting in Washington for a year under U.S. Chamber of Commerce auspices. To supplement the formal machinery, USTR Clayton Yeutter and his deputy Alan Holmer in 1987 also met secretly and regularly with an informal "insiders' group" of especially privileged corporate lobbyists (Dryden 1995, 338).

The binding constraint turned out to be agriculture, specifically the EC's refusal to accept dramatic reductions in agricultural production and export subsidies, matched by the equally intense determination of exporting countries including the United States to walk away from the entire round unless they accepted them. USTR Carla Hills, at the December 1990 Brussels Ministerial Conference just before the original deadline, did choose impasse over what had been offered, including significant gains outside agriculture. When her private-sector advisers in Brussels heard that she had walked away from a bad deal, they gave her a standing ovation (Dryden 1995, 368).

During the same period U.S. negotiators expended great additional energy in many bilateral fights with allied countries on behalf of particular industries. The long list of constituents benefiting included California and Florida citrus farmers, from agreements with the EC and Japan; corn farmers, from a 1986 near "war" with the EC over Spain's entry; cattle ranchers in Japan's market; and lumber producers regarding Canadian softwood exports. Cigarette makers saw USTR levering open doors in lucrative Asian markets for them. Boeing and McDonnell Douglas enjoyed Washington support for years in their rivalry with the European Airbus. The huge automobile industry got President Bush to push their interests to the top of his list during his first overseas trip after the Soviet Union's collapse—to Tokyo in January 1992. NAFTA was even more dear to Detroit's heart.

Pound for pound, the semiconductor industry achieved the most impressive Washington trade leverage. On its behalf President Reagan negotiated a bilateral agreement with Japan, and in 1987, in its name, he imposed the first economic sanction on Japan since the occupation. President Bush insisted on renewing this agreement despite Japanese resentment. President Clinton maintained the pressure and appointed high-technology executives to key Washington positions. His administration also managed to insert a new loophole into the final Uruguay Round subsidies agreement—running counter to the general U.S. position—to shelter research-and-development spending favored by high-technology producers.

The beleaguered U.S. steel industry, another political heavyweight, used its access to affect negotiations especially on dumping rules. While USTR Mickey Kantor managed in 1993 to negotiate some weakening of the multilateral agreement designed to discipline antidumping measures, some serious limits remained in the final agreements.

The Clinton administration then found technical ways in its implementing legislation to mute the new disciplines (Destler 1995, 240–44). In fact, "as it shopped for Congressional support for the pact, the Clinton administration agreed to do favors for a host of industries: steel, cars, wheat, lumber, cement, ball bearings, cellular telephones, civil aircraft, and apparel."[25] During the unseen drafting of the implementing bills, lobbyists for each of these sectors managed to insert new special provisions benefiting themselves.

After failing to win any commercially significant concessions for Wall Street securities firms, USTR Kantor neutralized their possible opposition with an agreement to continue financial services negotiations for an additional eighteen months. One of the last high-profile struggles took place on behalf of Hollywood's exporters of film services against EC protectionism.

The addition of the WTO itself to the bundle would also engage the presidency directly. U.S. trade diplomats had taken a lead in efforts to strengthen the GATT as an institution for exposing one nation's violation of another's rights. Their proposals attempted especially to limit the convention under which an accused state could prevent the parties from endorsing an unwelcome GATT expert panel report (Preeg 1995, 77–78, 103). U.S. officials had resisted creation of a WTO, however, partly because of fears of domestic opposition. The Americans did not agree, in fact, until the morning of the last day of the Uruguay Round, 15 December 1993. Because this institutional issue had been added to the bundle near the end of the process, Congress and U.S. constituents heard relatively little about it. This relative lack of consultation would come back to haunt advocates, just as it had in the forties (Destler 1995, 232).

Presidents Bush and Clinton, personally and through their White House trade representatives Carla Hills and Mickey Kantor, spent greater political resources to achieve ratification of the WTO than did President Truman for the ITO. Throughout the negotiation, as one close Washington observer noted just

---

25. Keith Bradsher, "The Deal-Making: Plenty of Favors Made," *New York Times*, 30 September 1994, C1.

after the round had concluded, "what Kantor sought above all was an agreement that could pass Congress" (Dryden 1995, 389). In February 1994 William T. Archey, vice president of the U.S. Chamber of Commerce, added: "The genius of the negotiation was that those who would have made the gravest problems [on Capitol Hill] were to some degree taken care of. There are a number of people who do not love this agreement but are not disposed to oppose it" (quoted in Stokes 1994, 353).

On 12 January 1994 the President's Advisory Committee for Trade Policy and Negotiations, chaired by James D. Robinson III and W. L. Lyons Brown, Jr., commended the negotiators for their gains and concluded, after balancing these against disappointments, that the president and Congress should implement the package. Only one member of thirty-seven, representing the AFL-CIO, dissented (U.S. Advisory Committee for Trade Policy and Negotiations 1994).

By this time, said the vice president of the Emergency Committee on American Trade, "it's not a question of whether or not the Uruguay Round implementing legislation will pass, but which year, how is it going to be paid for, and what is going to be attached to the implementing bill." While the AFL-CIO opposed ratification, one of its lobbyists confirmed this congressional forecast. "They will light up the braziers and incense will fill the air and it will blind the guys and they will vote for it" (Stokes 1994, 353–54).

Implementation turned out not to be a foregone conclusion, however, and it required further personal attention from the president. In May 1994 the *Financial Times* reported a warning from House Speaker Thomas Foley that Congress faced "a very real crisis" over ratification. Said the *Times:*

> Although President Clinton's power to pull off more victories ought not to be under-estimated, passage this year of the implementing legislation for the GATT agreement now seems almost as improbable as did the NAFTA victory last year. Mr. Foley and his colleagues see as the chief impediment the need to raise $10 billion to $14 billion over the next five years and perhaps as much as $40 billion over the next decade to compensate for the tariff revenue lost under the Uruguay Round deal. Budget rules require this to be done either by programme cuts or taxes.[26]

A second prominent argument raised by critics was the charge that creation of the WTO, together with its virtually automatic enforcement mechanism, would infringe U.S. sovereignty, including the authority to regulate pollution and consumer safety at home. Here the threat came from political rather than commercial entrepreneurs. Senator Bob Dole, the Republican Minority Leader, cited many constituency concerns about sovereignty as a reason to delay consideration.[27]

26. Nancy Dunne, "US Test for a 'Dead Fish' Theory," *Financial Times,* 25 May 1994, 5.
27. Keith Bradsher, "Dole Urges Postponement for Approval of Trade Pact," *New York Times,* 31 August 1994, cited in Destler 1995, 246.

The Uruguay Round agreements generated less grassroots opposition than had NAFTA the year before, but opponents were not absent.[28] Consumer advocate Ralph Nader on the Left and Patrick Buchanan on the Right were the most vocal. The Citizens Trade Campaign, which had worked against NAFTA the year before, also ran advertisements against the GATT.

On the other side, some twenty corporate chief executives lobbied Congress together on behalf of the GATT in June. Other elements of the three-level strategy of their Alliance for GATT NOW were grassroots campaigns and $2 million worth of advertising. The main organizations behind this alliance were the Business Roundtable, NAM, and the U.S. Chamber of Commerce.[29]

The process of writing implementing legislation lasted until 27 September 1994, when the Clinton bill finally went to the Capitol. This was the period during which Kantor and Clinton sealed all those special industry deals. After the November elections, however, Senator Jesse Helms, expected to become the chairman of the Foreign Relations Committee, and Senator Ernest Hollings attempted to delay the vote.[30] Senator Dole, despite his long history of advocating trade liberalization, held out until Thanksgiving before announcing that he would support WTO ratification. He then said he had extracted from President Clinton an agreement to support later legislation that would create a "WTO Dispute Settlement Review Commission." This group of five federal appellate judges would review all final WTO panel judgments adverse to the United States. If the commission found, during any five-year period, three such decisions in which a WTO panel "demonstrably exceeded its authority" or "acted arbitrarily or capriciously," then any member of Congress could introduce a joint resolution pulling the United States out of the organization.[31] This last deal was additional to the provision for a congressional vote again every five years, which Representative Newt Gingrich had negotiated earlier to provide his own political cover.

With Dole too now on board, and after further personal meetings and telephone calls by President Clinton, the Senate voted its approval by a margin of 76 to 24 and the House ratified by 288 to 146—with majorities of each party in each house voting in favor.[32] Senator Dole introduced legislation to enact his review commission, but no committee passed it during the 104th Congress.

28. Peter H. Stone, "GATT-ling Guns," *National Journal*, 2 July 1994, 1571–75; Keith Bradsher, "Foes Set for Battle on GATT," *New York Times*, 3 October 1994, C1. The definitive account of the NAFTA negotiation and ratification struggle is Mayer 1995.

29. Stone, "GATT-ling Guns," 1571.

30. David E. Sanger, "Helms Requests a Delay in Vote on Trade Accord," *New York Times*, 16 November 1994, A1; Destler 1995.

31. *Inside US Trade*, 25 November 1994, 23–24, quoted in Destler 1995, 253.

32. Kenneth J. Cooper, "House Passes GATT in Bipartisan Spirit," *Washington Post*, 30 November 1994, 1; Helen Dewar, "GATT Win Predicted as Senate Support Grows," *Washington Post*, 1 December 1994, A40; Helen Dewar, "Senate Approves GATT on Big Bipartisan Vote," *Washington Post*, 2 December 1994, 1.

Dole resigned his Senate seat in 1996. In the 105th Congress the review commission reappeared as part of a bill introduced in the House in January 1997 by Representative Ralph Regula, but it had still failed to pass any committee by July 1997.[33]

6.6   Speculations for the Future

These arguments may also help inform our thinking about the future. They point to the following conjectures.

U.S. exit options will remain limited. In the next half decade the United States will not have attractive international alternatives to the WTO for several issues it cares about. For the enforcement of U.S. trade rights provided by multilateral agreements, the WTO dispute settlement mechanism is now much more valuable to the United States than was the 1947 GATT. As for regional options, NAFTA accounts for less than a third of U.S. trade. APEC remains too heterogeneous a grouping to become more than a forum for periodic discussions and special negotiations.

For particular purposes, to be sure, plurilateral and bilateral agreements could appeal to Washington when U.S. initiatives run into strong opposition in Geneva. The former could be deployed as a lever for influencing negotiations in Geneva. The United States is likely to resort to bilateral negotiation to handle complaints about practices not covered by WTO rules. This option will seem attractive not only as a means of attaining immediate commercial gains but also, like the 1980s FTA negotiations, to prod partner countries closer to agreement on new multilateral rules to cover these issues.

There are some reasons to think that the regional option will grow more attractive over time. APEC and Western Hemisphere leaders hold annual summits. APEC has created a "wise men's" group. These institutions and interactions help to articulate a vision, build a consensus, and create a momentum regionally. The relative infrequency of WTO ministerial meetings as a counterweight is disturbing from this point of view. But working in the other direction is the increasing multilateralization of trade, as one country after another joins the ranks of those with outward-oriented trading systems. As the web of U.S. trade relations spreads increasingly wide, regionalism will probably become progressively less attractive as an alternative to multilateral negotiation.

Future "U.S. problems" will not take the form of failure to ratify agreements U.S. negotiators have signed. With hindsight, the ITO failure marked the end of an era. After each of the eight GATT rounds that began in 1947 and ended in 1994, the U.S. government essentially did what its negotiators had agreed it would do. One of the more important lessons of this history is that during the second half of the century, the United States became a more reliable partner in

---

33. U.S. Library of Congress, World Wide Web service, http://thomas.loc.gov.

the sense that it always implemented the trade agreements it signed.[34] The institutional changes of 1974 and later years ensure that U.S. negotiators and their key principals will remain locked in much closer interaction during negotiations, heightening the likelihood of ratification when agreements are reached.

Presidential leadership at home on behalf of the WTO will probably continue to fluctuate. This study suggests that a severe international political crisis coinciding with trade negotiations might again reduce the political capital devoted to trade liberalization. Otherwise, special interests inside the country will depend on a healthy world economy to a greater extent than during most of the twentieth century. Since calls for old-fashioned protection will fall on increasingly educated and globalized ears, national political leaders who attempt to ride such rhetoric to victory will probably lose—as did Richard Gephardt in 1988 and Patrick Buchanan in 1996—to rivals who appear more centrist or more ambiguous on this issue. The U.S. public continues to support multilateralism in general and specifically in the form, for instance, of participation in UN peace-keeping operations (Reilly 1995, 37).

On the other side, the U.S. economy also remains one of the most self-sufficient in the world. Selective resort to "sovereignty" as an escape from the obligations of multilateralism will probably continue to seem less risky there than in many small countries. Future presidents will probably find that trade policy still offers limited leverage for achieving key objectives. Trade specialists on all sides will probably continue to have difficulty holding the White House's attention for long. The distinctive division of national government authority plus federalism will continue to permit enactment of measures like the Burton-Helms Act even when they are unpopular with major U.S. interests.

At this writing, Washington remains divided with one party in the White House, its rivals controlling Congress, and the median voter less than fully satisfied with both. Assuming that U.S. institutions remain essentially unchanged, the degree and predictability of presidential leadership at home will probably also remain roughly what we have seen. Rather than shifting decisively away from multilateralism, America will continue to give it two, and only two, cheers (Keohane and Nye 1985).

References

Aaronson, Susan Ariel. 1993. For the People, but Not by the People: A History of the International Trade Organization (ITO). Ph.D. dissertation, Johns Hopkins University.

34. In 1975 Secretary of State Henry Kissinger proposed creation of a financial support fund in the Organization for Economic Cooperation and Development, as part of his strategy of preventing the oil crisis from splitting U.S. military alliances. After the presumed uncertainty of large-scale financial recycling seemed to diminish and the IMF staff strongly objected, the president decided not to submit this plan to Congress as well (Cohen 1996).

————. 1996. *Trade and the American Dream*. Lexington: University of Kentucky Press.

Brown, William Adams, Jr. 1950. *The United States and the Restoration of World Trade*. Washington, DC: Brookings Institution.

Brusse, Wendy Asbeek. 1996. The Americans, GATT, and European Integration, 1947–1957. In *The United States and the Integration of Europe: Legacies of the Postwar Era*, ed. Francis H. Heller and John R. Gillingham, 221–52. New York: St. Martin's Press.

Cohen, Benjamin J. 1996. When Giants Clash: The OECD Financial Support Fund and the IMF. University of California–Santa Barbara, February. Manuscript.

Dam, Kenneth W. 1970. *The GATT*. Chicago: University of Chicago Press.

Destler, I. M. 1995. *American Trade Politics*. 3d edition. Washington, DC: Institute for International Economics.

Diebold, William, Jr. 1952. *The End of the ITO*. Essays in International Finance, no. 16. Princeton, NJ: International Finance Section, Princeton University.

Dryden, Steve. 1995. *Trade Warriors: USTR and the American Crusade for Free Trade*. New York: Oxford University Press.

Eckes, Alfred. 1975. *A Search for Solvency*. Austin: University of Texas Press.

Eichengreen, Barry. 1993. *Reconstructing Europe's Trade and Payments: The European Payments Union*. Manchester: University of Manchester Press; Ann Arbor: University of Michigan Press.

Frankel, Jeffrey A. Forthcoming. *Regional Trading Blocs*. Washington, DC: Institute for International Economics.

Frendreis, John P., and Raymond Tatalovich. 1994. *The Modern Presidency and Economic Policy*. Itasca, IL: F. E. Peacock.

Goldstein, Judith. 1993. *Ideas, Interests, and American Trade Policy*. Ithaca, NY: Cornell University Press.

————. 1996. International Law and Domestic Institutions: Reconciling North American "Unfair" Trade Laws. *International Organization* 50:541–64.

Heilperin, Michael A. 1949. How the U.S. Lost the ITO Conferences. *Fortune* 40 (September): 80–82.

Howson, Susan, and Donald Moggridge. 1990. *The Collected Papers of J. James Meade*. Volume 4, *The Cabinet Office Diary, 1944–1946*. London: Unwin Hyman.

Hudec, Robert E. 1993. *Enforcing International Trade Law: The Evolution of the Modern GATT Legal System*. Salem, NH: Butterworth.

Irwin, Douglas. 1995. The GATT's Contribution to Economic Recovery in Postwar Western Europe. In *Europe's Postwar Recovery*, ed. Barry Eichengreen, 127–150. Cambridge: Cambridge University Press.

Jackson, John H. 1989. *The World Trading System: Law and Policy of International Economic Relations*. Cambridge: MIT Press.

————. 1990. *Restructuring the GATT System*. New York: Council on Foreign Relations.

Kahneman, Daniel, Paul Slovic, and Amos Tversky. 1982. *Judgment under Uncertainty: Heuristics and Biases*. Cambridge: Cambridge University Press.

Keohane, Robert, and Joseph Nye. 1985. Two Cheers for Multilateralism. *Foreign Policy* 60:148–67.

Kindleberger, Charles P. 1973. *The World in Depression, 1929–1939*. Berkeley: University of California Press.

————. 1981. Dominance and Leadership in the International Economy: Exploitation, Public Goods, and Free Rides. *International Studies Quarterly* 25:242–54.

Krasner, Stephen D. 1976. State Power and the Structure of International Trade. *World Politics* 28:317–47.

Lake, David. 1993. Leadership, Hegemony, and the International Economy: Naked Emperor or Tattered Monarch with Potential? *International Studies Quarterly* 37: 459–90.

Levy, Jack S. 1992. An Introduction to Prospect Theory. *Political Psychology* 13: 171–86.

McKeown, Timothy. 1983. Hegemonic Stability Theory and Nineteenth-Century Tariff Levels in Europe. *International Organization* 37:73–91.

Mayer, Frederick W. 1995. *Interpreting NAFTA: The Science and Art of Political Analysis.* Duke University. Manuscript.

Neustadt, Richard E. 1980. *Presidential Power: The Politics of Leadership.* 2d edition. New York: Wiley.

Odell, John S. 1988. From London to Bretton Woods: Sources of Change in Bargaining Strategies and Outcomes. *Journal of Public Policy* 8:287–316.

Preeg, Ernest H. 1995. *Traders in a Brave New World: The Uruguay Round and the Future of the International Trading System.* Chicago: University of Chicago Press.

Reilly, John E., ed. 1995. *American Public Opinion and U.S. Foreign Policy.* Chicago: Chicago Council on Foreign Relations.

Rightor-Thornton, Anne H. 1975. An Analysis of the Office of the Special Representative for Trade Negotiations: The Evolving Role, 1962–1974. In U.S. Commission on the Organization of the Government for the Conduct of Foreign Policy, *Report,* vol. 3, appendix H, 88–104.

Schott, Jeffrey J. 1989. *Free Trade Areas and U.S. Trade Policy.* Washington, DC: Institute for International Economics.

———. 1994. *The Uruguay Round: An Assessment.* Washington, DC: Institute for International Economics.

Snidal, Duncan. 1985. The Limits of Hegemonic Stability Theory. *International Organization* 31:1–23.

Stokes, Bruce. 1994. The Big Deal. *National Journal,* 12 February, 353–57.

Triffin, Robert. 1957. *Europe and the Money Muddle.* New Haven: Yale University Press.

United States Advisory Committee for Trade Policy and Negotiations. 1994. A Report to the President, the Congress, and the United States Trade Representative concerning the Uruguay Round of Negotiations on the General Agreement on Tariffs and Trade. 15 January. Washington, DC: Government Printing Office.

Vernon, Raymond. 1995a. The U.S. Government at Bretton Woods and After. In *The Bretton Woods GATT System,* ed. Orin Kirshner, 52–69. Armonk, NY: Sharpe.

———. 1995b. The World Trade Organization: A New Stage in International Trade and Development. *Harvard International Law Journal* 36:329–40.

Wiener, Jarrod. 1995. *Making Rules in the Uruguay Round of the GATT.* Aldershot, United Kingdom: Dartmouth.

Wilcox, Clair. 1949. *A Charter for World Trade.* New York: Macmillan.

Winham, Gilbert. 1986. *International Trade and the Tokyo Round.* Princeton, NJ: Princeton University Press.

II   Substantive Issues
and Challenges

7   Domestic Policy Objectives and the Multilateral Trade Order: Lessons from the Past

Frieder Roessler

7.1   Introduction

Trade issues are rarely discussed in isolation from other policy issues. The conference that led to the Havana charter for an International Trade Organization (ITO) was the United Nations Conference on Trade *and Employment.* Chapter II of the charter assigned to the ITO the task of resolving the most pressing economic problems of the late 1940s, including attaining full employment, eliminating *balance-of-payments disequilibria,* action against *inflationary or deflationary pressures,* and promoting *fair labor standards.* Chapter III committed the ITO's members to cooperation on economic development and reconstruction, and chapters III and V established the ITO as a forum for negotiating agreements on technology transfer, foreign investment, double taxation, and restrictive business practices, as well as commodity agreements (ICITO 1948).

While the Havana charter was never adopted, its chapter on commercial policy survived in the form of the GATT. Linkages taken over into the original GATT concerned *balance-of-payments disequilibria* and *competition,* to which a linkage between trade and *development* was subsequently added. Under the WTO, commitments on trade in goods have now been linked with commitments on *intellectual property rights* through an integrated dispute settlement mechanism.

When the Uruguay Round was brought to a close in April 1994 at the Marrakesh ministerial, the list of linkages with trade proposed by various speakers included *environmental policies, internationally recognized labor standards,*

Frieder Roessler, formerly director of the Legal Affairs Division of the WTO Secretariat, is now visiting professor at the Georgetown University Law Center, Washington, DC.

Thanks are due to Robert Hudec and Richard Snape, as well as Alice Enders, for their helpful comments on an earlier version of this paper.

competition policy, company law, foreign investment, immigration policies, development, political stability, and alleviation of poverty (GATT Document MTN.TNC/45 [MIN], 12). Only one of these proposals was accepted: the Decision on Trade and Environment provides for the WTO to continue the work of the GATT on environment (GATT 1994, 469). Efforts to link trade with labor standards did not succeed at the WTO ministerial meeting in Singapore in December 1996, but two working groups were established to study the relationship between trade and *investment* and the interaction between trade and *competition*, respectively.

As the preceding paragraphs demonstrate, linkages between trade and other policy areas have long been a feature of the multilateral trade order, and recent events suggest an intensification of the trend. The pursuit of domestic policy objectives through the multilateral trade order raises fundamental issues for the newly established WTO. Will such linkages be beneficial or harmful to the young institution? Will the attainment of domestic policy objectives be furthered or frustrated by their integration into the world trade order? Will the regimes established in disparate policy areas mutually reinforce or weaken each other when interacting in a single treaty with an integrated enforcement mechanism?

This paper attempts to shed light on these questions by examining the experience of the GATT with the linkages made between trade and balance-of-payments matters, development policies, and objectives of antitrust policies. The paper argues that the integration of these subject matters into the multilateral trade order undermined *both* the trade order *and* the attainment of the objectives in those nontrade policy areas. At least two important lessons can be drawn from this experience: first, the pursuit of domestic policy objectives through trade policy instruments is not judiciable and therefore leads to a delegalization of international trade relations; and second, exemptions from trade policy disciplines designed to permit the pursuit of domestic policy objectives attract protectionist forces that eventually subject that objective to their ends. The application of these lessons to the trade and environment linkage is considered in detail.

7.2   The Pursuit of Domestic Policy Objectives through the GATT

7.2.1   Trade and Monetary Policies

Within nations, trade policy and monetary policy are conducted in isolation. Trade policies are basically structural policies determined by legislators for long periods of time, while monetary policies are conducted on a daily basis by central banks, often politically independent of the executive and legislative branches. Trade and monetary policies are generally implemented with different instruments: trade policies with tariffs, quotas, and similar measures; monetary policies with interventions in the exchange and money markets.

The architects of the postwar economic system nevertheless considered that it was necessary to link these two policy areas. GATT contracting parties were permitted to impose import restrictions for the purpose of correcting a balance-of-payments deficit; in other words, to use trade policy instruments to achieve monetary objectives. According to article XII of the GATT, which applies to all WTO members, and section B of article XVIII, which applies only to developing countries (GATT 1994, 501, 512), a WTO member may impose import restrictions to safeguard its external financial position provided the restrictions do not exceed those necessary to prevent a serious decline, or achieve a reasonable increase, in its monetary reserves. The restrictions need not be withdrawn even if a change in monetary policies would make them unnecessary.

The 1979 Declaration on Trade Measures Taken for Balance-of-Payments Purposes of the GATT contracting parties recognized that "trade measures are in general an inefficient means to maintain or restore balance-of-payments equilibrium" (GATT 1978–79, 205). This statement is regarded by most economists as a truism. Since the fundamental cause for a balance-of-payments deficit is normally an excess of domestic consumption over domestic production, the solution lies in most cases in restrictive fiscal and monetary policies that help reduce the overall level of consumption. Imposing import controls on particular products will influence the *pattern* of domestic consumption but cannot have any predictable and durable impact on the overall *level* of domestic consumption. Like devaluations, import controls change the prices of internationally traded products, but only for imports and not exports, and therefore constitute at best "half a devaluation" (GATT 1983, 16).

In practice, the trade measures imposed under articles XII and XVIII:B of the GATT have not been applied across the board to all imports and have thus distorted the price relationships not only between imports and exports but between different categories of imports. Such distortions inevitably entail additional inefficiencies, widening the gap between domestic production and consumption. For these reasons, the only predictable consequence of an import restriction imposed under the GATT's balance-of-payments provisions is a worsening of the balance-of-payments deficit.

What practical use did the GATT contracting parties make of the balance-of-payments provisions? In the immediate postwar period, they were mainly invoked by European countries struggling to achieve the convertibility of their currencies. In the 1960s, when convertibility had been achieved, many European countries, eschewing devaluations, used the provision to justify import restrictions designed to maintain the exchange value of their currencies. In 1971, the United States invoked article XII to justify an import surcharge imposed to force its trading partners to accept a revaluation of their currencies in relation to the dollar. Since the replacement of the International Monetary Fund's (IMF) par value system by a system of flexible exchange rates in the early 1970s, industrialized countries ceased almost completely to invoke the GATT's balance-of-payments provisions (Roessler 1975).

These provisions then became the almost exclusive preserve of the developing countries, which invoked them, often for decades and longer, as a legal justification for their import substitution policies. By doing so, developing countries avoided the procedural strictures of GATT article XVIII:A and C, which were meant to be the legal basis for restrictive import measures imposed for development purposes. As import substitution policies became less popular and the pressure on the more advanced developing countries to liberalize grew, they began to disinvoke voluntarily the balance-of-payments provisions. In 1995 and 1996, seven WTO members ceased to apply article XVIII:B or gave undertakings to disinvoke it. In early 1997 the IMF found that India did not have a balance-of-payments problem justifying an invocation of article XVIII:B. The only members still consulting in the WTO Committee on Balance-of-Payments Restrictions (BOP Committee) are Bangladesh, Hungary, Nigeria, Pakistan, Sri Lanka, and Tunisia. Of these countries, all except Hungary have invoked article XVIII:B since their accession to the GATT.[1]

The determination as to what constitutes a serious decline or a reasonable increase in reserves is made by the BOP Committee on the basis of a determination by the IMF. According to article XV:2 of the GATT, the IMF's views on this matter must be accepted by the WTO (GATT 1994, 507). Under the current monetary system, however, the IMF faces an impossible task. The level of import controls necessary to resolve the reserve problem depends on the level of the exchange rate: the greater the devaluation, the less protection will be required to safeguard the external financial position. In the past, the IMF's par value system dictated the choice of the exchange rate, namely the exchange rate agreed with the IMF, but under the current monetary system, the choice of any exchange rate by the IMF would be arbitrary. If it chooses the exchange rate that prevails after the introduction of the import restrictions, its determination would only reflect what the market has already decided and automatically sanction the level of import controls actually applied. If it chooses the exchange rate that would be required to eliminate the need for the restrictions, it would effectively eliminate the right under articles XII and XVIII:B to impose restrictions. In short, the criteria that determine the level of restrictions have not been capable of rational application for more than two decades—except for the determination that a country has no balance-of-payments problems and therefore the level of restrictions should be zero—but the GATT, and now the WTO, have nevertheless not adopted any other criteria.

The linkage between trade and monetary matters has helped neither the GATT nor the IMF in the pursuit of their basic objectives. The right of all WTO members to impose import restrictions in the event of a balance-of-payments deficit creates significant legal uncertainty in international trade relations, and nourishes the illusion that import controls can reduce a deficit. It is disquieting that the United States could now, consistent with its WTO obliga-

---

1. Information supplied by the WTO Secretariat.

tions and section 122 of its Trade Act of 1974, impose a surcharge on a wide range of its imports, or that China could, once it becomes a WTO member, withdraw all the market-access commitments now painfully being negotiated in the process of its accession to the WTO simply by writing a letter to the director general of the WTO. In practice, the use of the balance-of-payments provisions by developing countries deprived them of the possibility to invoke GATT disciplines to ward off domestic protectionist pressures. The restrictions originally imposed in a payments crisis often created their own pressure groups, making their subsequent removal politically difficult or impossible. As a result, the countries disinvoking the balance-of-payments provisions generally required long transition periods to phase out the restrictions.

From the perspective of the monetary order, the balance-of-payments provisions of the GATT have also not had a favorable effect. Article IV:1 of the Articles of Agreement of the IMF states that "the essential purpose of the international monetary system is to provide a framework that facilitates the exchange of goods, services, and capital among countries" (IMF 1978, 6). However, the GATT balance-of-payments provisions allowed governments to postpone devaluations and therefore to mask the most visible sign of fiscal or monetary mismanagement. By helping governments postpone the political consequences of mismanagement, these provisions created a permanent moral hazard for governments, undermining the smooth operation of the international monetary system.

The right of GATT contracting parties to impose IMF-sanctioned trade controls in payments crises originally served to promote the goals of convertibility and of exchange rate stability, considered by the architects of the postwar international economic order to be of a higher priority than trade liberalization. Now the convertibility of the major currencies has been achieved and exchange rate stability as such has ceased to be a goal of the IMF. Nevertheless the IMF insisted throughout the Uruguay Round on the maintenance of GATT's balance-of-payments provisions and even on their extension to the General Agreement on Trade in Services (GATS).[2] One explanation is that the balance-of-payments provisions give the IMF the possibility to approve trade measures that permit its members in payments crises to use their scarce financial resources to reimburse their debts rather than to pay for additional imports. The provisions sought by the IMF thus give it the competence to approve measures designed to protect its own financial interests and those of its members.

The response to the above observations might be that the link between trade and monetary matters is a fact of political life, without which the world trade order would not be politically realistic. In reply, it could be pointed out that the world trade order should not pave the way to disaster but react appropriately when it occurs. Debt crises are also a political fact of life, but the creation of a

---

2. See the Declaration on the Relationship of the World Trade Organization with the International Monetary Fund (GATT 1994, 447), and articles XI and XII of the GATS (GATT 1994, 337).

formal legal framework for the rescheduling of debts has been wisely avoided. Rather than granting WTO members an almost unconditional right to impose trade controls for decades merely because of a payments deficit, the WTO should grant ad hoc time-bound waivers when grave crises arise, on conditions tailored to the circumstances of the case. The explicit and permanent linkage between trade and monetary matters incorporated in 1947 into the GATT has neither an economic rationale nor a political rationale and serves neither the purpose of the world trade order nor that of the international monetary system.

7.2.2   Trade and Development Policies

The central theme of international economic diplomacy in the 1960s and 1970s was third world development. The Charter on the Economic Rights and Duties of States, adopted by the United Nations in 1974, made all aspects of international economic cooperation subservient to the goal of development (General Assembly resolution 3281 [XXIX] of 12 December 1974). In the GATT decision on "Differential and More Favourable Treatment, Reciprocity and Fuller Participation of Developing Countries" (GATT 1978–79, 203), the principle of nonreciprocity in trade negotiations between developed and developing countries was recognized, developed countries were permitted to accord tariff preferences to developing countries under the Generalized System of Preferences (GSP), and developing countries were accorded the right to exchange preferences among themselves in the name of collective autonomy.

Today, the new international economic order is long forgotten, and the charter lies in the wastepaper basket of history. Declining tariffs eroded the commercial attraction of the GSP, and it never achieved its ethical mission—to create greater equality among nations—because the benefits were concentrated on a small group of highly advanced developing countries. The principle of nonreciprocity had on balance a negative impact on trade liberalization: rather than inducing developed countries to liberalize unilaterally imports in sectors of export interest to the developing countries, such as textiles and agriculture, the principle provided developing countries with a justification for refusing to make market-access commitments and to sign the agreements on nontariff measures concluded in the Tokyo Round. As a result of the principle of nonreciprocity, developing countries were deprived of the main benefit of GATT membership, namely the exposure to a system of rules and procedures that help correct the protectionist bias in trade policymaking, and of the benefits of adherence to codes of good government practice incorporated in the Tokyo Round agreements (Hudec 1987). The cause of development was manifestly not served by releasing developing countries from their GATT obligations.

The trade and development linkage eliminated the rule of law in north-south trade relations. The most-favored-nation rule was removed, but no other rule of conduct was put in its place. The beneficiaries of the principle of differential treatment were never defined. The GSP permits the donor countries to unilaterally determine the beneficiaries and to withdraw the preferences at any time, which led developed countries to impose numerous conditions on the grant of the preferences. Thus, the main preference donors, the United States and the European Community, each make GSP benefits conditional on the adoption of certain labor standards, cooperation in drug control, and many other policy conditions.[3] The nonreciprocal nature of the preferences thus turned out to be an illusion: rather than reciprocating in the field of trade, the developing countries were forced to make concessions in other policy areas without receiving legally guaranteed benefits in return. The new law of north-south relations consisted essentially of clauses enabling, but not obliging, developed countries to accord trade advantages under unilaterally determined conditions. What was hailed by some authors as "a new law of development" (Hubbard 1979, 92) consisted essentially of rules delegalizing trade relations between developed and developing countries.

The historical failure of the GATT in this area was the absence of an appropriate response to the genuine problems that low-income states may have had in applying GATT principles. For instance, certain countries with a fiscal infrastructure insufficient to raise revenue through domestic taxes could have been given the right to levy import duties for revenue purposes. Instead, the GATT responded to the broad political demands of the Group of 77, a coalition spanning the richest and poorest developing countries with no common trade interests. This group was able to formulate only the demand to exempt all of its membership from the rules of the GATT, and make them all eligible for GSP. None of the instruments the GATT adopted in response to the demands of the developing countries was therefore targeted to the real and definable problems of these states and to those of the poorest among them.

---

3. Under Title V of the United States Trade Act of 1974, a developing country cannot receive preferences if inter alia the country expropriates or otherwise seizes control of property owned by a U.S. citizen, including patents, trademarks, and copyrights; repudiates an agreement with a U.S. citizen; imposes taxes or other exactions with respect to property of a U.S. citizen; refuses to cooperate with the United States to prevent narcotic drugs from entering the United States unlawfully; aids or abets any individual or group that has committed an act of international terrorism; denies its workers internationally recognized rights, including acceptable minimum wages; refrains from enforcing arbitral awards; is a member of the Organization of Petroleum Exporting Countries.

Under articles 3:2, 7, 8, and 9 of Council Regulation (EC) 3281/94 of 19 December 1994 (Official Journal of the European Communities, 31 December 1994, no. L 348/1), the European Community makes GSP benefits available to countries that conduct a campaign to combat drugs; apply the conventions of the International Labor Organization on the freedom of association, on the protection of the right to organize and bargain collectively, and on the minimum age for admission to employment; apply standards relating to the sustainable management of forests; do not practice any form of forced labor; do not manifest shortcomings in customs controls on export or transit of drugs; comply with international conventions on money laundering; do not engage in unfair trading practices, such as discrimination against the European Community, comply with market-access obligations under the WTO agreements.

7.2.3   Trade and Competition Policies

At present, the only provision in the WTO agreements that links trade with competition is article VI of the GATT, which declares that dumping "is to be condemned if it causes or threatens material injury to an established industry" (GATT 1994, 493) and permits the levying of duties to offset such dumping.

Dumping and antidumping have been extensively analyzed in the literature on imperfect competition. At their origin, antidumping provisions in international trade agreements were intended to protect competition against anticompetitive practices, and in particular to combat predatory pricing (Hindley and Messerlin 1996). The general conclusion is that predatory pricing is only in exceptional situations a rational strategy of companies locked in a battle for control of a market and that, in most cases, the antidumping provisions have been used in circumstances in which predatory pricing cannot occur. Thus, it was found that "most antidumping cases involve products with a considerable number of producers at the global level, none of whom has a dominant share of global output" (Hindley and Messerlin 1996, 21). As a result, there is no economic rationale for the vast majority of antidumping cases.

Even on the assumption that predatory pricing may occur and will need to be suppressed by governments to safeguard competition, there would still not be any justification for special rules that differentiate between domestic and imported products. Article III, the GATT's national treatment provision, and article XX:d of the GATT's general exceptions allow WTO members to apply their competition policies equally to all sources of predatory pricing and to take in respect of imported products all measures necessary to secure compliance with those policies. The only function of the WTO antidumping provisions is therefore to permit WTO members to apply to imported products competition rules that are more onerous than those applied domestically.

Article VI of the GATT is supplemented by the WTO Agreement on Implementation of Article VI of the GATT 1994 (Antidumping Agreement), which regulates the application of antidumping measures at the national level in great detail. Such an agreement fosters the illusion that the rule of law applies in this area. In fact, however, the agreement leaves WTO members with an extremely wide range of discretion in determining whether injurious dumping has occurred, and its article XVII:6 explicitly exempts the exercise of this discretion from a full review by WTO panels and the WTO Appellate Body (GATT 1994, 193). The exercise of the right to take antidumping measures is consequently not submitted to judiciable criteria and effective multilateral control, notwithstanding the plethora of WTO rules on their application.

The origin of antidumping provisions in the GATT was innocuous, and such measures were rarely applied in the first two decades of the GATT's existence. As other authors have amply documented, however, the provisions became a safe harbor for protectionist domestic interests (Hindley and Messerlin 1996). Once GATT contracting parties were permitted to deviate from the basic trade policy principles, ostensibly to pursue competition policy objectives, the political forces that these principles are to control overwhelmed the competition policy objectives. There is near unanimity in the academic world now that the WTO's rules on antidumping operate to protect competitors rather than competition and consequently have acquired a rationale that is the complete opposite of the one they were originally meant to serve.

7.3   The Trade and Environment Link: Will History Repeat Itself?

The trade and environment debate raises novel issues and submits the principles of the world trade order to scrutiny from a new perspective. However, there are elements in the proposals to integrate environmental concerns into the multilateral trade order that so strongly resemble aspects of the unsuccessful linkages made between trade and other policy matters that a repetition of past mistakes is to be feared.

Technically, there is no conflict between environmental policies and trade policies. The rules of the WTO do not prescribe or prevent the attainment of any domestic policy goal in the field of the environment. They are merely "negative" rules prohibiting policies that distinguish, openly or in disguise, between products and services or service suppliers as to their origin or destination. Such distinctions are, however, normally not necessary to attain domestic environmental policy goals (Roessler 1996b). Why then do so many environmental organizations consider WTO law a threat to domestic environmental legislation?

Their opposition is based on the fear that many laws furthering environmental and other public interests may only be adopted with elements that are contrary to WTO law. The legal constraints imposed by WTO membership create in their view obstacles to the formation of domestic political coalitions between sectoral interests pursuing protectionist aims and public-interest groups pursuing environmental goals, and the rulings of WTO panels put into jeopardy existing domestic laws furthering legitimate domestic policy objectives for which there is, politically, no prospect of a WTO-consistent solution. As Ralph Nader stated in his testimony before the U.S. Senate Finance Committee on the results of the Uruguay Round (16 March 1994, photocopy): "Raw log export bans are one of the most trade restrictive means to attain the goal of conserving our nation's forests. Yet, after years of debate, raw log bans were the only politically feasible approach because they accommodated the interest of providing alternative lumber processing jobs to those who would no longer be cutting down forests. Laws with such mixed economic and social purposes, of which there are many, would likely fall before challenge under the World Trade Organization's rules."

Ralph Nader is no doubt right. And many other illustrations can be provided to substantiate his point. Take the case, for instance, of the introduction of a new clean-air standard for gasoline. Such a standard, by itself, can of course be introduced for all gasoline without any legal constraints under WTO law. A problem of WTO consistency would arise, however, if the domestic political constraints are such that a new standard would secure a parliamentary majority only if domestic gasoline is exempted from the standard for five years or, to put the issue in political-economy terms, if the cost of reducing pollution is initially borne only by nonvoting producers abroad. That discrimination would be inconsistent with the GATT's national treatment provisions of article III and would most likely not be justifiable under the GATT's public policy exceptions of article XX. The five-year exemption violating the GATT 1994 would thus not be *technically necessary* to implement a higher environmental standard (it would in fact reduce the new standard's environmental impact during the transition period), but would be *politically necessary* to adopt the higher standard.

Another example illustrating Nader's point is the phase-out mechanism for chlorofluorocarbons (CFCs) included in the 1987 Montreal Protocol on Substances That Deplete the Ozone Layer. In theory, the phase-out of CFCs could have been achieved through internal measures consistent with the national treatment principle, for instance, a system of sales licenses. However, such a system would have imposed only burdens on the producers of the chemicals and would probably not have won their support. The mechanism that was instead adopted provides for quantitative limits on the production of CFCs in the members, combined with a ban on imports from nonmembers, with the result that the consumption of CFCs is reduced. Under this mechanism, the decline in the domestic supply of CFCs combined with import controls generated rents for the domestic producers during the phase-out period, and the scheme therefore won their support. The import controls were thus not technically required to protect the ozone layer, but were politically necessary to win the support of the producers of ozone-depleting chemicals (Enders and Porges 1992).

How can the dilemma of groups pursuing environmental goals be accommodated in the WTO law? One approach would be to add a provision to the GATT 1994 permitting discriminatory trade measures if a legitimate domestic policy goal would not be politically attainable without that measure. However, such a "political necessity" clause would establish a license for unprincipled policymaking, and the market-access rights under the WTO agreements would therefore be submitted to the vagaries of the domestic political process of the WTO members. A provision with these functions, however drafted, would not mark a line between international trade interests and domestic policy constraints, and would therefore be incompatible with the rule of law in international trade relations (Roessler 1996a).

Environmental groups have also been concerned that a WTO member is, under the principle of unconditional most-favored-nation treatment, unable to offset through trade measures the economic consequences of the differences between its environmental policies and those of other WTO members. This concern is reflected in the following statement by Ralph Nader (16 March 1994):

> U.S. corporations long ago learned how to pit states against each other in a "race to the bottom"—to provide the most permissive corporate charters, lower wages, pollution standards, and taxes. Often it is the federal government's role to require states to meet higher federal standards. . . . There is no overarching "lift up" jurisdiction on the world stage. . . . The Uruguay Round is crafted to enable corporations to play this game at the global level, to pit country against country in a race to see who can set the lowest wage levels, the lowest environmental standards, the lowest consumer safety standards. Notice this downward bias—nations do not violate the GATT rules by pursuing too weak consumer, labor . . . and environmental standards. . . . Any . . . demand that corporations pay their fair share of taxes, provide a decent standard of living to their employees or limit their pollution of the air, water and land will be met with the refrain, "You can't burden us like that. If you do, we won't be able to compete. We'll have to close down and move to a country that offers us a more hospitable business climate."

The theoretical literature on interjurisdictional competition indicates that the problem described by Ralph Nader is largely a reflection of a desirable competition among jurisdictions and not a race to the bottom (Wilson 1996). Given that jurisdictions can be assumed to choose environmental quality to maximize the welfare of residents, they have no incentive to offer firms exemptions from taxes required to cover costs to the environment even when competing for scarce capital. However, second-best situations—unavailability of policy instruments or distortions in market structure or both—may give rise to the adoption of inefficiently low or *too high* standards; again, a case-by-case analysis is necessary.

Furthermore, if the race-to-the-bottom argument is accepted, it would apply not only to environmental policies but to all policies that affect the location of industries, including tax and subsidy policies, the provision of infrastructure, and production regulations of all kinds. Eliminating a race to the bottom only in the area of environmental policies would merely displace the race into other policy areas, for example in workers' safety. At the end of this process, there would no longer be local jurisdictions within federal states, and states would have to cede their policy autonomy to international authorities (Revesz 1992).

What would be the consequence of a new general rule in the WTO legal system that would permit WTO members to apply import taxes and restrictions designed to offset the competitive advantages that differences in environmental and other regulations accord to producers abroad?[4] With such a rule, the law

---

4. There is no provision in the WTO agreement that permits trade restrictions specifically designed to offset differences in domestic policies. WTO members may impose countervailing duties on products that benefit from a domestic production subsidy. However, a countervailing duty may be imposed even if the importing contracting party also accords a subsidy. Two WTO members

of the WTO would provide legal security only for the products and services traded between pairs of countries with identical domestic production regulations. This would be contrary to the principle of comparative advantage according to which nations are to exploit their differences, which are often reflected in their regulations (Bhagwati 1996). Moreover, the unconditional most-favored-nation principle would be lost, and with it the peace-engendering impact of that principle. With a general rule that permits WTO members to eliminate the external effects of the differences between them, the WTO legal system could therefore no longer fulfill its functions.

One legal method to take into account the domestic political constraints of WTO members and the fear of a race-to-the-bottom effect of trade liberalization would be to permit them to individually vary their market-access commitments in accordance with those constraints. That method is already available. The market-access commitments under the WTO agreements are made by product (GATT), by sector (GATS), or by entity (Agreement on Government Procurement). The schedules of commitments of WTO members therefore vary significantly. Moreover, WTO members are entitled to renegotiate their commitments. Both during the process of negotiating the commitments and after their acceptance, WTO members thus have the possibility to adjust their trade obligations in accordance with their domestic political constraints and the external impact of their policies. However, this adjustment takes place at the time when market-opening commitments are negotiated or after a renegotiation based on reciprocity, and therefore maintains the balance of rights and obligations among members.

From the perspective of WTO law, the issue is thus not whether domestic policy constraints should be taken into account or whether trade liberalization entails a healthy competition among jurisdictions or a destructive race to the bottom. Given the right of each member to adjust its market-access commitments to its perception of these issues, the real issue is whether WTO members should be able to react to the external repercussions of their own domestic policy choices by unilaterally withdrawing their market-access commitments or whether they should be able to do so only by renegotiating their commitments. A multilateral trade order based on the rule of law cannot but be based on the principle of renegotiation.

---

granting the same fiscal advantages to their steel industries may impose (and frequently impose in practice) countervailing duties on the steel products exported to each other. The countervailing-duty provisions of the WTO are therefore not provisions permitting measures designed to offset policy divergences, but are provisions permitting the protection of import-competing industries contingent upon the protection of an exporting industry in another country. This observation can also be made in respect of the provision of the GATT that exempts measures related to the products of prison labor from the obligations under the GATT (article XX:e). It is true that the domestic policies of another WTO member trigger in this case the right to impose import controls, but that right may be exercised independently of the prison-labor regulations of the contracting party imposing the import control. A WTO member could consequently permit the sale of products produced in domestic prisons while restricting the sale of those made in foreign prisons.

There are many proposals to use the market-access opportunities created by the obligations assumed under the WTO agreements as bargaining chips to induce other countries to change their environmental policies, and the withdrawal of these opportunities as sanctions against countries that do not cooperate in the protection of the environment. Thus, Steve Charnovitz (1993, 282) wrote:

> How can an agreement on minimum standards be achieved among a hundred countries with different values and resources? One approach is to devise a clever mix of carrots and sticks from a diverse enough issue garden to allow a cross-fertilization of concerns. The goal is not only to obtain an agreement, but also to maintain its stability. The carrots are the basic tool. Because countries face different economic trade-offs ... an assistance mechanism can be developed to enable gainers to compensate losers and rich nations to "bribe" poor ones. This assistance could be in the form of financial aid or technology transfer ... , or it could be trade concessions.

The proposal to use the world trade order as a source of carrots and sticks for the pursuit of environmental objectives is based on three illusions. The first is generated by the image of "carrots and sticks." "Carrot" suggests that you give something of value to you; "stick" suggests that you inflict pain without hurting yourself. However, such sticks do not exist in international economic relations. Here, nations can hurt others only by hurting themselves at the same time; a trade sanction inflicts costs both on the imposing nation and on the target nation, and the cost for the former can sometimes exceed that of the latter. The choice is thus not, as the image suggests, between costly subsidies and costless trade sanctions, but between subsidies that transfer resources from one nation to another and trade sanctions that destroy the resources of both (GATT 1991).

If the image of carrots and sticks has such currency in the trade and environment debate, it is probably because the costs of trade sanctions are generally so thinly spread across populations that they arouse little political opposition and are therefore not taken into account in the public debate. This is probably also the reason that a trade sanction seems to be the only stick seriously considered in the trade and environment literature even though the arsenal of economic sanctions contains many more sticks, such as the interruption of financial relations, telecommunications, transport services, and so forth. These other types of economic sanctions may be just as effective in obtaining commitments from other nations to cooperate in the protection of the environment as trade sanctions; however, they will cause concentrated and easily visible effects for a small group of producers and will therefore engender greater political opposition. If one has concluded that sanctions are required to achieve a negotiating goal, one still needs to decide that among the sanctions available the trade sanction is the most efficient one. The public choice on that issue, however, is likely to be distorted by the bias that distorts the public choice on trade policies generally. The focus of the trade and environment debate on trade sanctions, rather than economic sanctions generally, is an indirect reflection of this bias.

The second illusion is that the goals of trade liberalization and environmental protection can be obtained simultaneously in a single negotiation. In a reciprocity-based negotiation in the WTO, a nation will not obtain in return for its market-access commitment an equivalent market-access commitment *and* commitments in another policy area; it will obtain only one or the other and will therefore have to decide which of the two objectives to pursue. To propose that a multilateral negotiation cover market access issues *and* a raising of environmental standards is therefore to propose that nations with high environmental standards pursue their trade interests *or* their environmental interests.

The third illusion is that the trade and environment link is a one-way street toward better environmental protection. In any system in which the results of reciprocity negotiations are enforced through a right to retaliation, an issue linkage becomes a two-way street: if market access and the protection of endangered species were to be successfully linked in WTO negotiations, trade concessions could be withdrawn in response to the failure to protect an endangered species *and* vice versa. If environmentalists seek in the WTO the "trade weapon" to further environmental goals, they must therefore accept that other nations obtain the "environmental weapon" to defend their trade interests. However, it is totally inappropriate to make commitments on such essential matters as the protection of endangered species, where the withdrawal from obligations may have irreversible effects, dependent on the ups and downs of commercial policies. The main purpose of international bargaining is to create regimes, systems of rules and procedures making governmental actions more predictable. Each of these regimes cannot furnish predictability if it is constantly exposed to the need to adjust to a breakdown in other regimes. That is true for both the international trade order and international environmental law.

The inherent limitations of the cross-retaliation principle were recognized by the negotiators of the WTO agreements. Initially, the United States, mainly with its interest in protecting worldwide intellectual property rights in mind, proposed that there be an unbridled right of cross-retaliation under the WTO dispute settlement procedures. However, it subsequently revised its position to the effect that retaliation across sectors should be resorted to only if retaliation within the sector was not practical or effective. This change reflected the fear of the United States' banking sector that cross-retaliation resulting from failures to observe obligations in the field of trade in goods might upset the delicate balances of interest between nations in the field of financial services. Article 22:3 of the Dispute Settlement Understanding (DSU) therefore now contains eight subparagraphs which, while maintaining the principle of cross-retaliation, define meticulously the circumstances under which a WTO member may retaliate across sectors and the elements of the Uruguay Round package that constitute individual sectors, segregating—of course—financial services as a separate sector (GATT 1994, 423). If environmental groups did not have the illusion of the one-way street, they would, just like the U.S. banking community, make every effort to ensure that their important cause is not thrown into the crab basket of trade policymaking.

7.4   Conclusions

What do the linkages between trade and domestic policy objectives reviewed in this paper have in common? In each case, the linkage led to the creation of new rules permitting governments to depart from basic principles of the world trade order without, however, establishing effective new disciplines constraining the exercise of the resulting discretion. The reason was that the new rules enabled governments to pursue monetary, development, and competition policies with second-best policy instruments, and, as economic theory has amply demonstrated, one cannot define in the abstract and in advance under what circumstances the choice of the wrong instrument for the right policy raises welfare. Only a case-by-case analysis is appropriate in this situation. No generally applicable, abstract rule is therefore conceivable that would distinguish between permissible and forbidden second-best policies on economic efficiency grounds.

The choice of the second-best policy instrument was permitted essentially for political reasons, that is, to exempt from GATT disciplines the trade policy measures of governments politically unable to pursue their monetary, development, or competition policies with more direct and efficient policy instruments. However, a GATT rule that defines the domestic political circumstances that would justify the resort to a second-best policy instrument is impossible to craft. For instance, in the case of balance-of-payments policies implemented through trade measures, such a rule would have to provide for something like the following: "A WTO member incurring a serious balance-of-payments deficit may, instead of devaluing its currency, impose an import surcharge if it demonstrates that its government would, if it were to devalue, lose the next election/be toppled by riots/encounter serious problems in containing wage demands." It is obvious that such a rule would not be seriously considered even though it would precisely reflect the political purpose of the GATT's balance-of-payments exception. A fundamental lesson that can be drawn from the GATT's links with monetary, development, and competition policies is that, upon entering the realm of the second-best, the realm of the rule of law is left, and any such link therefore entails a delegalization of international trade relations.

Each of the linkages reviewed above was made to harness the instruments of trade policy for domestic policy objectives. In all three cases, however, the protectionist forces freed by the elimination of the trade policy disciplines seized the occasion and overwhelmed the domestic policy objective. Thus, the antidumping provisions, originally designed to protect competition, now operate exclusively to protect competitors. Another conclusion that can therefore be drawn from the experience under the GATT is that, if domestic policy objectives are not pursued in a trade-neutral manner, they attract protectionist interests that will tend to undermine the attainment of these objectives. As a result neither the world trade order nor the causes such linkages were meant to serve benefited from the link.

Many of the proposals to pursue environmental objectives through the multilateral trade order have features that resemble those of past failed linkages between trade policy instruments and domestic policy objectives. Again proposals are made that would permit the use of trade measures in the pursuit of policy objectives that cannot be attained efficiently with trade policy instruments. And, again, the hoped-for cross-fertilization is likely to turn into cross-contamination. The fundamental illusion that prompts these proposals is that the link between environmental policies and trade policies is a one-way street and that it is therefore possible to use the political pressures behind trade policy instruments for one's policy objectives without in turn being subjected to these pressures. In fact, however, that linkage, as the previous linkages of its kind, is likely to turn into a disservice to the important cause it is meant to advance.

References

Bhagwati, J. 1996. The Demands to Reduce Domestic Diversity among Trading Nations. In *Fair Trade and Harmonization: Prerequisites for Free Trade?* ed. J. Bhagwati and R. Hudec, 1:9–40. Cambridge: MIT Press.
Charnovitz, S. 1993. Environmental Harmonization and Trade Policy. In *Trade and the Environment: Law, Economics, and Policy,* ed. D. Zaelke, P. Orbuch, and R. F. Housman, 282. Washington, DC: Island Press.
Enders, A., and A. Porges. 1992. Successful Conventions and Conventional Success: Saving the Ozone Layer. In *The Greening of World Trade Issues,* ed. K. Anderson and R. Blackhurst, 130–44. Hemel Hempstead, United Kingdom: Harvester Wheatsheaf.
General Agreement on Tariffs and Trade. 1978–79. *Basic Instruments and Selected Documents.* Geneva: GATT Secretariat.
———. 1983. *International Trade 1982/1983.* Geneva: GATT Secretariat.
———. 1991. *International Trade, 1990–1991.* Vol. 1. Geneva: GATT Secretariat.
———. 1994. *The Results of the Uruguay Round of Multilateral Trade Negotiations: The Legal Texts.* Geneva: GATT Secretariat.
Hindley, B., and P. A. Messerlin. 1996. *Antidumping Industrial Policy.* Washington, DC: AEI Press.
Hubbard, D. 1979. The International Law Commission and the New International Economic Order. *German Yearbook of International Law* 22:80–99.
Hudec, R. E. 1987. *Developing Countries in the GATT Legal System.* London: Gower.
Interim Commission for the International Trade Organization. 1948. *Final Act of the United Nations Conference on Trade and Employment.* Lake Success, NY: ICITO.

International Monetary Fund. 1978. *Articles of Agreement.* Washington, DC: IMF.

Revesz, R. L. 1992. Rehabilitating Interstate Competition: Rethinking the "Race-to-the-Bottom" Rationale for Federal Environmental Regulation. *New York University Law Review* 67 (December): 1210–54.

Roessler, F. 1975. Selective Balance-of-Trade Payments Adjustment Measures Affecting Trade: The Roles of the GATT and the IMF. *Journal of World Trade Law* 9, no. 6 (November/December).

———. 1996a. "Diverging Domestic Policies and Multilateral Trade Integration." In *Fair Trade and Harmonization: Prerequisites for Free Trade?* ed. J. Bhagwati and R. Hudec, 2:21–55. Cambridge: MIT Press.

———. 1996b. Increasing Market Access under Regulatory Heterogeneity: The Strategies of the World Trade Organization. In Organization for Economic Cooperation and Development, *Regulatory Reform and International Market Openness,* 117–29. Paris: OECD.

Wilson, J. D. 1996. Capital Mobility and Environmental Standards: Is There a Theoretical Basis for a Race to the Bottom? In *Fair Trade and Harmonization: Prerequisites for Free Trade?* ed. J. Bhagwati and R. Hudec, 1:393–428. Cambridge: MIT Press.

8   Environmental and Labor Standards: What Role for the WTO?

Kym Anderson

During the past decade there has been a resurgence of interest in the links between trade and environmental and labor standards. Social standards in poor countries are being questioned by groups in richer countries concerned about resource depletion, environmental degradation, and abuses of human rights in the workplace. Many in developing countries perceive the entwining of these social issues with trade policy as a threat to both their sovereignty and their economies, while significant groups in richer countries consider it unfair, ecologically unsound, even immoral to trade with countries adopting much lower social standards than theirs.

After first summarizing the issues involved, this paper examines why these issues are becoming more prominent, why they are being entwined with trade policy, why this is a concern to liberal traders, and what roles if any the World Trade Organization (as compared with other multilateral fora) should play in providing international rules and other institutional support needed for ensuring adequate environmental and labor standards.

8.1   What Are the Issues?

Two separable but related sets of issues are involved. One is the concern in high-standard countries that some of their firms suffer a competitive disadvan-

Kym Anderson is professor of economics and foundation director of the Centre for International Economic Studies at the University of Adelaide, Australia, and a research fellow of the Centre for Economic Policy Research in London.

This paper draws on the author's earlier papers for the World Bank and the National Bureau of Economic Research. Thanks are due to Jagdish Bhagwati, Richard Blackhurst, Maureen Cropper, Jane Drake-Brockman, Bernard Hoekman, Robert Hudec, Takatoshi Ito, Anne Krueger, Deepak Lal, Will Martin, Rodrigo Prudencio, David Richardson, Dani Rodrik, and T. N. Srinivasan for helpful comments on this and those earlier papers, and to the World Bank, NBER, and the Australian Research Council for financial support.

tage because of lower environmental and labor standards abroad. The other has to do with international externalities.

8.1.1   Competitiveness Concerns

We should not be surprised that there are vast differences across countries in environmental policies and labor standards. These policy differences in part are a natural consequence of differences in national incomes: as communities become richer, they increase their demands for all normal goods, including higher environmental and labor standards. Environmental and labor policies differ also because of international differences in tastes and preferences. Indeed, one of the defining historical features of many countries was the bringing together of a group of people whose preferences were more similar to each other than to those of neighboring groups (Alesina and Spolaore 1995).

As international economic integration proceeds, pressure increases to reduce differences in domestic policies that have significant trade consequences. This pressure is driven not just by the desire to reduce administrative and conformance costs. More important are concerns in countries with high standards that costs of production for their pollution- or labor-intensive firms are higher than those in countries with lower standards, causing them to be less competitive. Such differences become ever more important as traditional barriers to trade and investment between countries fall (Bhagwati 1996). They lead to claims in the north of eco- or social dumping, and fears in the south of reduced access to their export markets in high-income countries.

In high-standard countries some groups fear a "race to the bottom" as governments compete to attract and keep investments in their territory by lowering standards. In poor countries, on the other hand, people fear being forced to raise standards at an earlier stage of development than they would otherwise choose, thereby reducing their comparative advantage in products whose production is intensive in the use of natural resources or unskilled labor.

8.1.2   International Spillovers

The issues are made more complicated by the fact that they also can involve some externalities that spill over national boundaries. The most obvious examples are physical spillovers associated with global environmental problems such as global warming and ozone depletion. Greenhouse gases contribute to climate change, and chlorofluorocarbons (CFCs) deplete the ozone layer, regardless of which country they are emitted from. Hence there is a concern that if one set of countries seeks to tax or otherwise induce less of these emissions by firms located in their region, the environmental benefits from those measures will be offset insofar as the activities responsible relocate to countries with lower standards. The freer are international trade and investment flows, the less effective will be subglobal regulation and hence the greater the need will be for international cooperation or coercion.

There are at least three difficulties that need to be addressed in coping with global environmental issues. One is the problem of free riding on the efforts of other countries in a many-country world without global governance. Another is that countries contribute to these problems unequally, with the richer countries tending in the past at least to have contributed most. And third, countries differ in the importance they place on reducing global environmental problems, depending on income, preferences, information as to causes, and so on. Hence a north-south divide also exists in seeking solutions to these global environmental problems.

To what extent is there a parallel claim with respect to labor standards? Many economists would say there is none, because they perceive no physical labor spillovers of the global-warming or ozone-depleting kind.[1] In addition to physical spillovers, though, people can be affected emotionally by and have humanitarian concerns for activities abroad. An example is that people may grieve if another country's activities threaten a particular animal or plant species in its jurisdiction, or involve abuse of worker rights or poor working conditions. Or they may grieve if they believe that the desires of another country's citizens for higher environmental or labor standards in their country are not being recognized sufficiently by their national government (a political market failure).

Some would argue that such emotional/humanitarian concerns are less worthy of consideration than physical spillovers, not least because they are less measurable, less objective, and hence offer more scope for "capture" by traditional protectionists. Others would counter that there is so much uncertainty about the extent and effects of physical spillovers that they too are subjective and hence are qualitatively no different from emotional/humanitarian concerns. Nor is there any reason a priori to presume that the latter are less important than physical spillovers in some "willingness-to-pay" sense. Again, though, richer people are able to afford to place a larger value on such emotional/humanitarian concerns than poorer people, adding to the gap between north and south in terms of perceptions about the need for international mechanisms to deal with these problems.

8.2 Why Environmental and Labor Standards Have Grown in Prominence

Fluctuate though they might with the business cycle (positively in the case of environmental issues, negatively in the case of labor standards), these concerns are likely to keep growing. In the case of the environment, one reason is that, even though uncertainties remain, the scientific basis for many of the con-

---

1. At least one minor spillover may be present in some times and places, though. It is the effect of high standards for low-skilled workers in attracting unwanted migrants from less-developed economies across borders that may be difficult to police. My thanks go to David Richardson for offering this suggestion. The first-best response to such a possibility may simply be to adopt measures to reduce illegal immigration.

cerns is perceived as becoming ever more solid. Another reason is that both the world's population and its real per capita income continue to increase at very high rates by historical standards, adding to demands on the environment. Unfortunately, though, the supplies of most natural resources and environmental services are limited, and markets for many of them are incomplete or absent (because of disputed, ambiguous, or nonexistent property rights, and/or because of the high cost of enforcing those rights).

It is true that the more advanced economies have established national institutional structures to help handle the tasks of arriving at a social consensus on what are appropriate environmental or sustainable development policies of allocating property rights, and of enforcing policies. The same is true in some traditional societies, before they begin to modernize and their resources come under pressure because of declining mortality rates. But these institutions are less common in the newly modernizing economies, where growth in the world's population and consumption is expected to be concentrated during the next few decades. And at the multilateral level, cooperative intergovernmental mechanisms for environmental policy have only recently begun to be formed and will take some time to become effective, especially where free-rider problems are rife.

Income growth and expanding knowledge also are factors in the case of labor standards: as people become more affluent, they can afford to demand both better working conditions for themselves and, should it concern them, more information on worker rights and conditions abroad (the cost of which is dropping as travel and communication costs fall).

In addition to these general trends, three other economic developments have heightened the prominence of these issues recently. One is the rapid spread of export-oriented industrialization to a growing number of developing countries. That has expanded the demand for natural resources and environmental services in general and the use of fuels in particular, which is adding to greenhouse gases. It has also expanded the supply of labor-intensive manufactures, depressing their relative price and hence eroding the demand for workers and capital in unskilled labor-intensive industries in high-income countries. That has contributed to other forces there that have resulted in high unemployment levels and/or a growing wage differential between skilled and unskilled workers in rich countries. There has been a tendency for trade from developing countries to be blamed disproportionately for the poor performance of labor markets in advanced economies, and for relatively low labor standards to be seen as part of the reason for low production costs in the newly industrializing countries.

The second economic development of significance is the accelerating economic integration of national economies regionally and globally. With the internationalization of the world economy, the decline in traditional trade barriers has ensured that any given cost-raising social standard is becoming *relatively* more important as a determinant of international competitiveness, and the deregulation of foreign direct investment abroad has increased the possibilities for firms to relocate their factories from high- to lower-standard countries.

And the third reason why environmental and labor issues have become more prominent at the global level is because they succeeded recently in penetrating regional integration agreements. Specifically, there is the Protocol on Social Policy annexed to the Treaty of Maastricht signed by European Union member governments in February 1992 (Sapir 1996). As well, these issues became the subject of side agreements to the North American Free Trade Agreement (NAFTA) in 1993—a price President Clinton paid to buy off opposition from environmental and labor groups to NAFTA's passage through the U.S. Congress. Having been encouraged by their success in those regional economic integration settings, and before that in some minor trade and investment agreements in the 1980s (see Lawrence 1995 for details), the advocates for those side agreements are now seeking to influence the multilateral trade system. In both situations, the desires of the GATT's contracting parties to conclude, ratify, and implement the Uruguay Round agreements on trade liberalization and to create the World Trade Organization (WTO) are simply being used opportunistically by these groups to further their own causes, despite the tenuous connection of those causes with trade. Their relative success to date is in large part because their causes have superficial popular appeal, while the downside in terms of the potential risk to the global trading system is far from obvious to the layperson.

8.3   Why Is Trade Policy Being Entwined with Social Standards?

In response to the above concerns, both North America and western Europe sought successfully to have a Committee on Trade and Environment set up at the outset of the WTO's establishment, and they have since been actively seeking a WTO working party on trade and labor standards. In the latter case, the concern in high-standard countries ostensibly is not so much the lower wage level in developing countries but rather such things as poor occupational health and safety standards, worker rights to form unions and seek a minimum wage level and other improved conditions of employment, the use of child or prison or forced labor, and the derogation from national labor laws in export-processing zones. For example, the United States, the European Union (EU), and Norway have been seeking the universal adoption of what they see as "core" labor standards: freedom of association and collective bargaining, elimination of exploitative forms of child labor, prohibition of forced labor, and nondiscrimination in employment. The United States and France were at pains to make clear at Marrakesh that their push for the WTO to consider trade/labor issues was very much focused on differences in labor standards other than wages. Like "green" groups pushing for tougher environmental regulations, human rights activists and development nongovernmental organizations

(NGOs) often add support to union calls for higher labor standards in developing countries, believing that would improve the quality of life there.

To more fully understand why concerns about environmental and labor standards are being entwined with international trade and investment policy, it is helpful first to ask what economic theory suggests might link them and then to look for empirical evidence that might support that theory.

8.3.1   What Does Economic Theory Suggest?

The standard theory of changing comparative advantages in a growing world economy has been developed without consideration of environmental concerns, but it can readily be modified to incorporate at least some of those concerns. As espoused by Krueger (1977) and Leamer (1987), this theory suggests that, when a developing country opens up to international trade, its exports initially will be specialized in primary products. This is because its stocks of produced capital relative to natural resources are comparatively low. Should those nonnatural capital stocks per worker (including human skills) expand more for this country than globally, the country's comparative advantage will tend gradually to shift to more capital- and skill-intensive activities (particularly manufactures and services). If such countries are relatively land-abundant, some of that produced capital and new or newly imported capital-intensive technology may be employed profitably to extract minerals or farm the land. But in most such countries the new capital will encourage the expansion of nonprimary sectors and shift these countries' comparative advantage away from primary products. Thus countries that are relatively lightly endowed with natural resources or that are densely populated will tend to industrialize at an earlier stage of economic development, and their nonprimary exports will tend to be more intensive in the use of unskilled labor initially. In the case of manufactures, the gradual process of upgrading to more capital-intensive production leaves room in international markets for later-industrializing, resource-poor countries to also begin with labor-intensive, export-oriented manufacturing.

If national boundaries were such that there were no international environmental spillovers and no global commons, the above determinants of comparative advantage need be complicated only slightly to incorporate labor standards and nonmarketed environmental services and pollution by-products. The complication required is simply to allow for the fact that, as a country's per capita income and industrial output grow, the values its citizens place on the environment and on labor conditions increase and with it their demands for proper valuation of resource depletion and environmental degradation, for the assigning and better policing of property rights, and for the implementation of costly domestic pollution abatement and labor policies—at least after certain threshold levels of income or pollution are reached. Beyond those threshold points the severity of abatement policies is likely to be positively correlated with per capita income, population density, and the degree of urbanization.

If all economies were growing equally rapidly but from different bases, the progressive introduction of national environmental taxes and regulations would tend to cause pollution-intensive production processes to gradually relocate from wealthier or more densely populated countries to developing or more sparsely populated countries. Those environmental policies would also slow or reverse the growth in demand for products whose consumption is pollutive, especially in wealthier or more densely populated countries, where taxes on such products would tend to become high. If more-advanced economies are net importers of products whose production is pollutive, as is likely, the imposition of these countries' optimal environmental policies would worsen their terms of trade to the benefit of poorer economies. Such policies would also worsen the terms of trade of more-advanced economies if they were net exporters of products whose consumption is pollutive (Siebert et al. 1980; Anderson 1992c). The extent of the benefit to developing countries would be greater the more their terms of trade improved as a result of rising standards in advanced economies.

In the case of labor standards, such things as shorter working weeks, higher overtime pay, longer annual leave, and safer and healthier working conditions may (but need not) ultimately raise worker welfare. They presumably raise the cost of employing labor though, otherwise they would have been adopted voluntarily and there would be no need for government or union action.[2] They are therefore similar to other taxes on production that differ across industries in that their *indirect* effects need to be considered as well (Ehrenberg 1994). Specifically, they effectively make (particularly low-skilled) labor scarcer. Their gradual introduction as living standards rise contributes to ensuring that the cost of production in labor-intensive industries rises even faster than it otherwise would in relatively rapidly growing economies, thereby reducing the capacity of those industries to compete with producers in low-standard countries while enhancing the capacity of other industries in high-standard countries to so compete, along Rybczynski (1959) lines.

Thus even countries without (or with unchanged) environmental and labor standards are affected through foreign trade and investment by the development of environmental and labor policies that accompany growth in *other* countries. Hence one country's environmental or labor policy choice is not independent of the choice of standards of other countries. The imposition of higher standards at home alters the international competitiveness of industries, in particular by harming the more pollution-intensive (or labor-intensive) industries in countries with higher standards. Unless they had been developing new, environmentally friendlier (or laborsaving) technologies, such industries would tend to lobby against the imposition of higher standards at home, partic-

---

2. So-called neoinstitutionalists argue that higher labor standards would raise worker productivity (see, e.g., Hanson 1983, 53–63), but it is reasonable to assume firms have already recognized any such possibilities and incorporated them in their work practices. If not, the first-best role for government is to subsidize the provision of information about those opportunities.

ularly if their competitors abroad were not being subjected to similar cost-raising policies and/or were equally able to access new technologies. Producers in the less-polluting (or less capital-intensive) industries at home, on the other hand, could benefit from the raising of a particular environmental (or labor) standard.

Environmental and labor groups in rich countries perceive that, since the loss of competitiveness of pollution- and labor-intensive industries could be offset by restrictions on imports from lower-standard countries, such restrictions could at the same time reduce such industries' opposition to higher standards at home and increase the incentive for foreign firms and their governments to adopt higher standards abroad to avoid being labeled a pollution or cheap-labor haven and subjected to duties aimed at preventing eco- or social-"dumping." Not surprisingly, those features make trade policy very attractive to environmentalists and unionists. But because such uses of trade policy are discriminatory and protectionist, they are equally unattractive to supporters of liberal world trade. For those concerned about the welfare of unskilled laborers in poor countries, it should be kept in mind that import restrictions in rich countries simply reduce the demand for such workers. So too would the raising of labor standards in the formal sector of poor countries: it simply drives employment into the informal sector (where labor standards are even lower), and/or lengthens the queues of unemployed people seeking high-paid, high-standard formal sector jobs.[3] In the case of young women displaced from their jobs by higher labor standards, they may to have to marry and bear children earlier than otherwise, or even to enter prostitution, in order to survive.[4]

As already mentioned, the demand for unilateral use of trade policy for the above reasons has grown with the internationalization of the global economy, in two ways. One is that the decline in traditional trade barriers (tariffs, transport and communications costs, and so on) is making any given environmental charge or labor standard relatively more important as a determinant of international competitiveness, ceteris paribus. The other is that, with the deregulation of financial markets and foreign direct investment during the 1980s, the possibilities for firms to disinvest in countries with high standards and relocate their factories in countries with lower standards have increased markedly. Environmental and labor groups fear this development will result in governments delaying the introduction or enforcement of stricter environmental policies or labor standards—and possibly even a lowering of standards in a "race to the bottom"—in their attempts to attract or retain investments and hence jobs (Wilson 1996). They also worry that greater relocation opportunities will re-

3. This could easily be shown using a Harris-Todaro type of model as modified, for example, by Corden and Findlay (1975). The consequences of raising labor standards in a multigood, multi-country world can be quite complex and sometimes counterintuitive, depending on the assumptions adopted. See the theoretical analysis of several possibilities by Brown, Deardorff, and Stern (1996).

4. I am grateful to Anne Krueger for suggesting this possibility.

duce the incentive for firms to develop more environmentally friendly technologies.[5]

The story becomes more complicated when important international environmental or labor spillovers are taken into account, be they physical or psychological. Controversial though they may be, many people perceive a need for multilateral action to reduce these spillover problems—and that is where trade policy again enters the debate. Trade measures are seen by environmentalists and unionists as providing powerful carrots and sticks for attracting signatories to multilateral environmental or labor agreements and for penalizing nonsignatories, as well as for encouraging other countries to adopt higher national standards for the sake of their own citizens and environment. Just the threat of trade sanctions (particularly if broadened to include unrelated products) may have a rapid and persuasive effect on raising national standards or encouraging a country to join an international environmental or labor agreement and subsequently to abide by its rules.

We know from the standard theory of distortions and welfare that if there is only one distortion in the global economy (for example, trade restrictions), then reducing the extent of that distortion will be welfare enhancing for the world as a whole. Not all groups need gain, but the extent of gain to those who benefit is more than enough to compensate all those who lose. That theory also tells us that if the world has more than that one distortion (for example, also environmental externalities that have not been addressed by optimal policies from a global viewpoint), then reducing only one distortion (trade restrictions) may not increase global welfare. For example, liberalizing trade between industrial and developing countries could lead to excessive felling of tropical forests if there were inadequate protection of forest property rights in the developing countries (Chichilnisky 1994). In such cases all other divergences must be reduced at the same time as trade is being liberalized in order to achieve unequivocal global welfare improvement. Even then, theory tells us that some countries may be made worse off and the environment may still be harmed (Copland and Taylor 1995). Thus it should be acknowledged by liberal traders that it is not possible to claim with certainty that trade liberalization will improve the environment and welfare for different groups of countries in the presence of significant environmental externalities without appropriately

---

5. Where the environmental damage caused by production is purely local, the calls by disadvantaged firms for trade restrictions or subsidies to offset the decline in their international competitiveness because of standards being raised has no economic logic: such assistance would tend to offset the desired effect of limiting by-product pollution. See, for example, Baumol (1971) and Siebert (1974). Such protection from import competition cannot be justified on economic efficiency grounds (or for that matter on environmental grounds) because the environmental policy is aiming to eliminate an unjustifiable (implicit) subsidy arising through undervaluation of environmental resources, rather than to add an unjustifiable tax (Snape 1992). Nor is it reasonable to conclude that other countries are engaging in "ecodumping" if the imports that they are able to supply are produced with laxer environmental standards, if those lower standards are consistent with the preferences and natural resource endowments of the exporting countries (for example, because those countries are poorer, less densely populated, or less urbanized).

offsetting environmental policies in place.[6] But equally it should be acknowledged by environmental groups that in many situations trade liberalization may actually help not only the economy but also the environment.

As with environmental standards, traditional protectionist forces in high-income countries are prompt to support any calls for import restraint by countries with high labor standards against goods from lower-standard countries. They sometimes bolster their case by quoting simple trade theory (the factor-price equalization and Stolper-Samuelson theorems) in support of their argument that liberal trade can lead to factor-price convergence and in particular to a drop in low-skill wages in high-wage countries (Brown, Deardorff, and Stern 1996)—even though those theorems have been shown to be not very robust when more than two countries, goods, and factors are involved.[7] As with the environment, it is an empirical question as to what extent if any trade has contributed to the poor labor-market performance of countries in the Organization for Economic Cooperation and Development (OECD) during the past couple of decades.

8.3.2 What Does the Empirical Evidence Show?

The reasons often given by environmental groups for their opposition to trade and investment liberalization tend to be based on one or more of the following grounds: freer trade means more output and income, which they presume would mean more resource depletion and degradation of the natural environment; freer trade and investment encourages the relocation of environmentally degrading industries to countries with lower environmental-protection standards or more fragile natural environments, and leads to greater transport activity, which contributes further environmental damage; and freer foreign investment reduces the incentive to develop environmentally friendlier technologies.

However, none of these assertions is unambiguously supported by empirical evidence. The first, that income increases mean greater damage to the natural environment, may be true initially for some developing countries (in which case any additional environmental damage has to be weighed against the marginal economic benefits of higher incomes for poor people). But once middle-income status is reached, people tend to alter their behavior in ways that reduce pressures on the environment. A key change is in family size: higher incomes lead in time to lower population-growth rates. This change is going to reduce the rate of environmental degradation due to population pressures in developing countries. In rural areas it means fewer people felling trees and denuding hillsides to eke out a subsistence income, while in urban areas it means fewer unemployed or underemployed squatters in shanty towns with poor water and

6. Even so, the first-best action is to overcome that political market failure so that trade reform *can* contribute to boosting welfare (Bhagwati and Srinivasan 1996).

7. See Falvey (1995). Markusen and Venables (1996) develop a model in which, while multinationals can increase the skilled-unskilled wage gap in rich countries, imposing import barriers does not protect their unskilled labor.

sanitation services. This no doubt is one reason for the empirical finding that many forms of pollution first increase and then decrease as per capita income rises (Grossman 1995; Grossman and Krueger 1993, 1995; Hettige, Lucas, and Wheeler 1992; Radetzki 1992; Seldon and Song 1994; Shafi and Bandyopadhyay 1992). That evidence suggests the demand for implementing and enforcing pollution-abatement policies is income-elastic, and that an inverted U-shaped environmental transition may be commonplace as stricter environmental policies are implemented and less-pollutive technologies are introduced.[8]

Another common behavioral change as economies open up and incomes rise is that the demand for education expands, and with more income and education comes more skillful management of all resources, including the environment, and more forceful demands on governments to improve the establishment and policing of private property rights and of more stringent environmental policies (as indicated by the inverted U-shaped or environmental transition curve mentioned above). As well, the political cost of implementing such policy reforms is reduced because of increased opportunities for businesses to meet stricter standards by acquiring more and cheaper environmentally benign production processes and products from abroad. One might therefore expect that, as trade and investment liberalization leads to upward convergence in incomes around the world, there would be an upward harmonization of environmental standards as well (Casella 1996).

As to the assertion by some groups that the relocation of production following trade and investment liberalization necessarily harms the global environment, we know from the law of comparative advantage that not all industries will relocate from rich to poor economies when trade barriers in rich economies are lowered: some industries will expand at the expense of industries in developing countries, and conversely. Recent preliminary examinations of the likely environmental effects of reducing government assistance to two of the most protected industries in industrial countries—coal and food—reveal that in both cases the global environment may benefit from trade liberalization, especially if complementary environmental policies are in place. That outcome is possible partly because production of those goods tends to have a higher environmental cost in industrial countries than elsewhere. Moreover, reducing coal-producer subsidies in Europe would raise the international price of coal, thereby discouraging its use elsewhere and so lowering global carbon emissions (Anderson 1992a, 1992b; Anderson and McKibbin 1997).[9]

---

8. See also Deacon and Shapiro (1975) on the correlation between income levels and voter attitudes toward environmental priorities. Studies aimed at explaining this transition (sometimes called an environmental Kuznets curve) are now beginning to emerge. Beltratti (1995) seeks to explain it in terms of transitional dynamics of endogenous growth models, while Jones and Manuelli (1995) provide a positive political-economy model. See also Dean (1996) for an econometrically testable simultaneous-equations model to measure the effect of trade liberalization on the environment, taking into account the income growth from liberalization.

9. The question of whether it is environmentally friendly to pursue broadly based liberalizations such as the Uruguay Round, as distinct from liberalization in individual product markets, requires large-scale formal global modeling analysis that as yet has barely begun to be attempted. Even if

The extent of international relocation of productive activities due to the raising and enforcing of environmental or labor standards should not be exaggerated. Recent studies suggest that the effects of such policies on comparative costs may be quite small (Leonard 1988; Low 1992; Jaffe et al. 1995; OECD 1996; Levinson 1996). They also indicate that multinational corporations tend to use cleaner technology than local firms in developing countries (Harrison and Eskeland 1996), and tend to provide higher labor standards than local firms. Japanese multinational corporations are in fact required to adopt the same environmental standards abroad as operate in Japan. Moreover, Tobey (1990) finds little evidence of actual changes in patterns of trade specialization in response to the imposition of environmental regulations since the 1960s— although as Hoekman and Leidy (1992) note, the absence of observed changes in trade patterns may be the result of import barriers that were raised to offset any decline in the competitiveness of affected industries. Technological changes induced by the raising of standards, and environmental and labor standards raised by the availability of new technologies also would reduce the likelihood of observing a correlation between rising standards and the international relocation of production.

Nor need the risk of environmental damage from transport activity increase with trade reform. The lowering of import barriers to processed primary products, for example, would allow more raw materials to be processed in resource-rich countries, reducing the bulkiness of shipments. And if there are negative externalities associated with shipping itself (such as the risk of oil spills), a more efficient course of action rather than reducing trade generally would be to ensure shippers pay more of the full cost of their activity (say, through an international agreement requiring a minimum standard of double hulls on oil tankers).

What of the argument that the opportunity for capital outflow breeds pollution havens abroad and thereby reduces the development of environmentally friendlier production technologies in countries with higher environmental standards? Some observers have argued that the opportunities for such innovations are so great that raising environmental standards could boost rather than retard a country's economy (Porter and van der Linde 1996). But that argument begs the question of why such investments would not have been made in an open economy without the imposition of stricter standards (Palmer, Oates, and Portney 1996). In any case, there is little empirical evidence to suggest that raising standards stimulates innovation, just as there is little theoretical or empirical support for the notion that raising standards has a significant impact on the competitiveness of firms in industrial countries or on their decisions to invest in developing countries (Jaffe et al. 1995; Wilson 1996).[10]

---

quantitative estimates of the various key environmental effects were available, a formidable task would remain in valuing those pluses and minuses and comparing the net value with the conventionally measured economic welfare gain from trade liberalization.

10. That does not mean, however, that developing-country firms would find it inexpensive to conform to the high environmental standards of industrial countries. The reason is that local firms in developing countries may be using older, less environmentally friendly technology that would

What evidence is there that trade liberalizations and/or differences in labor standards between rich and poor countries contribute, through trade's effects on factor markets, to the poor performance of labor markets in rich countries? At the outset it should be noted that, once allowance is made for differences in labor productivity, labor is not much cheaper in developing countries than in high-income countries (Trefler 1993). Also, in their recent simulation work, Francois, McDonald, and Nordstrom (1996) found real wages in all country groups are projected to increase as a result of implementing the Uruguay Round. Using a similar global computable general equilibrium (CGE) model, Tyers and Yang (1995) found through both backcasting and forecasting that increased imports from Asia do contribute to unskilled-skilled wage dispersion and possibly lower real wages and/or unemployment in the United States and EU, but only to a minor extent. Significantly, they also found that restricting imports from Asia would be an ineffective response since its impact through contracting the global economy would be to lower real rewards to *all* types of labor in industrial countries. Lawrence (1994) and Burtless (1995) also found that imports are at most only a minor contributor to poor labor-market performance in the United States, while the Commission of the European Communities (1996) found that the unemployment problems in the EU were mostly attributable to structural distortions within the union. Other contributors of much more importance to the changing demand for unskilled relative to skilled workers than trade with newly industrializing countries are the computer and information technology revolutions and the growth of the service sector (Wood 1994). The survey by the OECD (1996) concurred. Moreover, the OECD found little evidence that economies with low labor standards performed better than high-standard economies, or that economies with low labor standards attracted more foreign direct investment. It also found a positive correlation over time between sustained trade reform and improvements in labor standards.

8.4   Why Worry about the Entwining of Trade Policy and Social Standards?

The use of trade policy as a stick (or possibly a carrot) to influence unilaterally the social policies of other countries, and/or to increase the workability of multilateral environmental or labor agreements, raises potential conflicts of interest between rich and poorer economies. There is even dispute over what constitutes national sovereignty and the global commons. Some would argue, for example, that a country or region should not have to bow to international pressure to preserve endangered species in their territory (or at least not without adequate compensation), while others would argue that such countries are

---

be more costly to adapt. Indeed, the cost of conformance in industrial countries may be relatively low simply because the raising of legislated standards to some extent follows rather than precedes the development of cleaner technologies. That has been cited as one reason for the relative ease with which agreement was reached on reducing the use of ozone-depleting substances under the Montreal protocol (see Enders and Porges 1992).

merely the custodians of those resources for the benefit of humankind generally.

Such uses of trade policy should concern the world at large, and developing countries in particular. The reason is not so much because the latter may be required to impose higher environmental or labor standards in order to avoid seeing trade barriers raised against their exports. In fact, the competitiveness of some industries in middle-income countries with midlevel standards might well be enhanced if low-income countries with low standards were required to raise their standards more than them to reach minimum acceptable levels. Even the negative direct effect for low-income economies of having to raise their standards could be offset somewhat by a terms-of-trade improvement if many such countries were to raise their standards simultaneously. And such benefits would be greater the more developing countries taxed or otherwise restricted the export (or better still the production or consumption) of environmentally sensitive products rather than left the developed countries to tax imports of such products (the lesson from the Organization of Petroleum Exporting Countries). Still, people in developing countries are suspicious of the motives of high-income countries, and object to what they perceive as social imperialism and a denial of their national sovereignty.

While developing countries are not being singled out per se, the fact is that environmental and labor standards tend to be lower in developing countries simply because they are poorer. That, together with the fact that their comparative advantages often are in natural resource–intensive and labor-intensive industries, means those countries are vulnerable either to being pressured to enforce stricter standards or to facing less market access for their exports to countries with stricter standards and/or less foreign investment from such countries.

In addition, there are at least three other reasons why the world should worry about the entwining of trade policy with social standards. First, trade policy measures usually are not the best instruments for achieving social objectives. This is because trade sanctions do not directly affect the root cause of environmental or labor-market problems. Their use in place of more efficient instruments increases the use of global resources[11] and reduces unnecessarily the level and growth of global economic welfare as conventionally measured—and may even add to rather than reduce global environmental degradation.[12]

---

11. Even the *threat* of trade restrictions can be environmentally counterproductive. The talk of European import bans on tropical hardwood logs (together with tariff escalation on timber-product imports) has encouraged Indonesia to ban log exports. But since felling and timber-product exports have been allowed to continue, this policy has simply lowered the domestic price of logs and thereby raised effective assistance to Indonesia's furniture and other timber-using industries to extremely high levels (GATT 1991, 127). With lower log prices and lower-quality saw-milling techniques than in importing countries, it is not surprising that less of each tree is now used and little reduction in logging has been observed since the log export ban was introduced.

12. The ban on ivory trade provides a case in point. By lowering the value of elephant products, the ban reduces the incentive for rural Africans to tolerate elephants trampling their crops and so

The second reason for concern is that producer interest groups and some environmental groups are finding it mutually advantageous to use environmental and worker rights arguments to support their claims for unilateral import restrictions, particularly following the costly imposition of stricter standards on domestic producers (Hillman and Ursprung 1992; Hoekman and Leidy 1992). In this sense environmental and labor concerns can provide a convenient additional excuse for raising trade barriers—and one that is socially respectable (Steil 1994). However, such protectionist actions reduce real incomes not just at home but elsewhere, especially in developing and natural resource–abundant countries.

Third, insofar as this activity can lead to an escalation in trade disputes—as is almost inevitable, especially given the north-south dimension involved and the fact that environmental or labor uses of trade policy are inherently discriminatory—they could be followed by retaliatory and counterretaliatory action, the result of which would be an undermining of the global trading system.

8.5   What Roles for the WTO?

The demands for greater harmonization across countries of domestic policies, for competitiveness reasons, coupled with the greening of world politics and the growing interest in worker rights and conditions beyond national borders, are likely to put the WTO and trade policy under pressure to perform tasks for which they were not designed and are not well suited—and at a time when the WTO needs first to consolidate its role in the world and ensure the completion of unfinished business and implementation of the Uruguay Round.[13] Supporters of the WTO are therefore tempted to say the institution should resist all attempts to become involved in these issues.

That strategy is risky, however. While many developing countries might support it, reflect for a moment on its possible consequences. One is that we might see more aggressive unilateral use of trade measures against countries with lower social standards (as with the United States against Mexico regarding tuna fishing). Another might be a lesser willingness of advanced economies to maintain liberal trade policies and to participate in future multilateral trade

---

ultimately could result in more rather than less culling of elephants in some areas. In other areas with poor meat storage and transport facilities, the ivory-trade ban has reduced the value of the animal so much that it is no longer profitable to cull the herd. An unfortunate environmental consequence is that bushland in national parks is being decimated by the increased number of elephants, which is endangering other species (Barbier et al. 1990).

13. The suggestion has been made, for example, that the WTO become active in monitoring and enforcing agreed minimum social standards. That presumably would involve environmental and labor standards being reviewed as part of the WTO's Trade Policy Review Mechanism. Since that mechanism is already stretched to its limit in covering even the major trade policies of contracting parties, such an addition to its workload would require a substantial boost to its resources—not to mention the extra burden on those employed in national capitals when the reviews are under way. An even greater potential increase in workload would result for the WTO's dispute settlement mechanism.

negotiations.[14] A third possible consequence is that we might see more regional integration agreements with side agreements on these issues (as with NAFTA).

Hence some engagement in the debate by the WTO may be wise. At the very least, that could involve reminding the world of some of the nontrade measures and actions available. One is to encourage private actions by firms and consumers (eco- and social labeling, consumer boycotts, corporate codes of conduct).[15] Another is for nations to use unilateral aid as a carrot (greater Generalized System of Preferences [GSP] preferences, more development assistance in return for enforcing higher social standards).[16] Multilateral aid and World Bank structural adjustment loans also could be geared to reward developing countries that raise their standards. The WTO could participate in studies aimed at showing the extent to which trade and investment liberalization is accompanied or followed by a rise in social standards (i.e., showing that reform is part of the solution, not the problem). Studies identifying more-appropriate measures for addressing these issues also would be helpful.

How "green" are the GATT's rules at present, how have they been adapted over time, and should they be altered further? From the outset it could be claimed that the GATT has been a conservationist institution in the sense that its purpose is to reduce trade barriers and thereby the inefficiency in the use of the world's resources. The heart of the GATT, agreed to by twenty-three original contracting parties in 1947 and since then by another hundred or so countries, is the nondiscrimination requirements of articles I and III. These articles obligate parties to treat imports from any GATT contracting party/WTO member no less favorably than other imports (the most-favored-nation requirement) and no less favorably, after border taxes are paid, than similar domestic products (the national-treatment requirement). That is, they preclude any country's using trade measures as sticks to penalize other countries for having, for example, lower environmental or labor standards.

Article XX provides exceptions to these general rules, however, including provisions for some environmental and labor regulations. Specifically, parts b, e, and g of article XX allow trade restrictions "necessary to protect human,

---

14. Williamson (1996) warns of this possibility after examining the growth in wage inequality following the globalization of the latter nineteenth century.

15. Such codes have been suggested by multilateral institutions, such as the International Labor Office (ILO) in 1977 in its Declaration of Principles concerning Multinational Enterprise and Social Policy, and more recently the OECD in its Code on Multinational Enterprises.

16. Woolcock (1996) notes that the EU decided in 1995 that it will consider in 1998 ways to offer additional GSP preferences to those developing countries that meet the requirements of ILO conventions on forced labor, freedom of association and collective bargaining, and the minimum working age. He also notes that the U.S. 1984 Trade and Tariff Act provides for GSP preferences to be withdrawn (a stick rather than carrot approach) if similar labor standards are not met. Likewise, benefits are to be withdrawn (1) under the Caribbean Basin Initiative if the United States deems a country is not complying with those minimum labor standards, and (2) under section 301 of the 1974 and 1988 trade acts. The *threat* of withdrawal of benefits has in most cases been sufficient to induce changes satisfying the United States without its resorting to actual trade sanctions. Nonetheless, a carrot rather than stick approach would be more WTO-consistent.

animal, or plant life or health," "relating to the products of prison labour," and "relating to the conservation of exhaustible natural resources if such measures are made effective in conjunction with restrictions on domestic production or consumption," subject to the requirement that such restrictions "are not applied in a manner which would constitute a means of arbitrary or unjustifiable discrimination between countries where the same conditions prevail, or a disguised restriction on international trade." The environmental parts of this article have been interpreted to mean that the measure must be *primarily* for a conservation purpose (rather than for a mixture of motives) and must be *necessary* in the sense of being the *least GATT-inconsistent* measure available. These provisos have ensured that the article has been rather narrowly interpreted, which is partly why some environmental groups have felt that further greening of the GATT is required (Charnovitz 1991; Esty 1994). But there is nothing in the GATT that prevents a country from adopting the most efficient measures to offset environmental externalities, which typically are associated with production, consumption, or disposal activities. Nor is a country precluded from using a trade measure so long as it is prepared to compensate any trading partner harmed by that measure. But since trade itself is almost never claimed to be the root cause of an environmental problem, GATT supporters traditionally have seen little need to consider trade measures as part of the solution to environmental problems not involving international spillovers.

Trade policy actions are more likely to occur—and to be more difficult to dismiss as inappropriate—when there *are* international spillovers. Consider, for example, the U.S.-Mexico dispute over the use of dolphin-unfriendly nets for tuna fishing. In that case the GATT dispute panel ruled against the U.S. ban on imports of tuna from Mexico, partly because the ban did not discriminate according to which type of net was used. That kind of discrimination is difficult to achieve efficiently because what is considered objectionable is an aspect of the production process rather than the final traded product itself. Had the GATT panel ruled in favor of the tuna import ban by the United States, it would have set a major precedent. It would have opened a potentially huge loophole in the GATT for any country unilaterally to apply trade restrictions as a means of imposing its environmental standards on other countries. Such a loophole would work against the main objective of the multilateral trading system, which is to provide stable and predictable nondiscriminatory market-access opportunities through agreed rules and disciplines and bound tariffs on imports. This is why calls to amend article XX of the GATT to include environmental protection as an acceptable exception to the nondiscrimination principles of articles I and III should be resisted.

Environmental and labor groups perceive trade policy as useful not only as a means of raising national environmental or labor standards at home and abroad but also of inducing countries to become signatories to and to abide by international environmental and labor agreements where free-rider problems arise. One of the more obvious and possibly more cost-effective ways to reduce the free-rider problem is to write trade provisions into the agreements, as was done in the 1987 Montreal protocol on reducing the use of CFCs and halons to slow ozone depletion. To date no GATT contracting party has formally objected to that use of trade policy. Nor have they objected to the bans on trade in ivory, rhino horn, and tiger products that are part of the Convention on International Trade in Endangered Species, or to the trade provisions in the Basel convention on trade in hazardous wastes. Conflicts may well arise in the future, however, if trade provisions are drafted into more contentious multilateral agreements (say, an attempt to impose a global carbon tax or higher labor standards).

In assessing the appropriate role for trade policy in multilateral environmental or labor agreements, it is helpful to recall that supporters of trade liberalization and of environmental or labor standards share a common goal: to improve social welfare. They also share a common problem: the need to foster multilateral cooperation to fully achieve that objective, because in each sphere (the economy, the environment, and, indirectly, the labor market) there is considerable and increasing interdependence among countries. But the groups differ in the important respect that supporters of liberal world trade have understood its virtues for two centuries and have been active for more than fifty years in building institutions such as the GATT and the WTO to help achieve their goal. Widespread concerns about the environment, on the other hand, are relatively new, and supporters of environmental protection only recently became significant players in international policy arenas.

Understandably, supporters of liberal trade and the WTO resent the encroachment of these special-interest groups onto what they perceive as their hard-won territory, especially when they believe that reducing trade barriers is likely to be environmentally friendly and consistent with sustainable development and improved labor outcomes in the long run because it allows the world to use its resources more efficiently. But advocates of greater environmental protection are equally frustrated that international agreements as important as those resulting from the Uruguay Round can be implemented without being subject to environmental impact assessments or environmental safeguards.

Clearly there is scope for greater understanding and altered strategies on both sides. More than that, there is the distinct possibility that, by working together, all groups' objectives will be further enhanced—a win-win outcome. Some observers believe that it may ultimately require a world environment organization to set rules, incorporate existing international environmental agreements and negotiate new ones, monitor compliance, and settle disputes over environmental policies—in the same way that the GATT has presided over trade rules and policies for the past five decades (Esty 1994). And just as the GATT/WTO strengthens the capacity of governments to resist the demands of domestic vested-interest groups seeking higher import taxes, so a world environment organization may help governments resist interest-group demands to set low environmental standards (Deardorff 1995).

The advantage of a world environment organization for liberal traders, Esty argues, is that such an organization could redirect environmentalists' attention away from the use of trade measures and toward ensuring the implementation of more appropriate policy instruments for achieving environmental objectives, allowing both sets of policies to more effectively contribute, in mutually supportive ways, to the common goals of sustainable development and improvement in the quality of life.

However, a world environment organization is unlikely to be created in the near future, partly because governments in many countries are under pressure to downsize and some have a growing mistrust and even hostility toward international bureaucracies. In any case a world environment organization, like the International Labor Organization and other standards-setting international organizations, would lack the teeth to ensure enforcement of agreements.[17] Moreover, the issue of whether the rulings of the WTO or a world environment organization would have precedence would need to be resolved. We know from theory that, where the objectives of the two groups are in conflict, achieving the optimal welfare-maximizing outcome requires both to compromise somewhat (Corden 1997), but managing that tension would be difficult.

Thus the trade policy community needs to be involved in the negotiating of multilateral environmental agreements that are likely to include trade provisions, and to develop criteria by which WTO members can assess in advance the extent to which trade restrictions within such agreements are acceptable. The relevant criteria, some of which were enunciated clearly at the United Nations Conference on Environment and Development in Brazil, include the following: First, it is important to ensure that trade provisions are strictly necessary, in the sense that there are no alternative, more effective instruments than trade restrictions, and they need to be effective in achieving the environmental objectives involved. Second, where trade instruments are required in the absence of less costly policy measures, they should be used only in proportion to the size of the associated environmental problem. Finally, the measures ought to be transparent and not protectionist in impact, and where possible be consistent with both the GATT principles of nondiscrimination (most favored nation and national treatment) and key environmental principles such as the polluter pays and the precautionary principles. If those conditions were met, WTO members would be unlikely to object to the use of trade measures in multilateral environmental agreements. Hence even the possible need to use trade provisions in multilateral environmental agreements does not provide sufficient reason to amend GATT article XX to allow in the list of exceptions the use of trade measures for environmental protection.

Since the entwining of environmental and labor issues with trade and investment policy is more likely to tighten than to disentangle in the foreseeable

---

17. The ILO has been operating for more than seventy-five years, but has had little success in dealing with disputes (Charnovitz 1987; Woolcock 1996).

future, the question arises as to how developing countries ought to respond. One response is to point out that industrial countries had lower standards at earlier stages of their development and still have sweatshops operating illegally. Another is that, since developing countries have contributed a disproportionately small amount per capita to global environmental problems such as the greenhouse effect, they should be compensated for contributing to their solutions rather than have that contribution demanded of them under threats of trade sanctions. Compensation would be even more justified in cases where industrial countries are demanding responses by other countries to reduce the emotional/humanitarian concerns mentioned earlier. As Srinivasan (1996) notes, those in rich countries genuinely concerned about low labor standards in developing countries can always transfer income to such groups or lobby to allow such workers to migrate to the more-advanced economies.

Another response by developing countries could be to disseminate more widely the sound arguments for not using trade-restrictive measures to achieve environmental and labor objectives and hence for not amending article XX of the GATT to allow trade discrimination for those purposes. Those arguments are that

- differences in standards are a legitimate source of comparative advantage insofar as they reflect differences in resource endowments and societies' preferences and ability to afford the good things in life;

- standards rise with per capita income, and liberal trade promotes income growth;

- theory and empirical evidence provide little reason to expect that the raising of standards in industrial countries will contribute significantly to costs of production and hence to trade and investment patterns, nor that downward harmonization of standards (a "race to the bottom") is occurring;

- if freer trade were to worsen welfare because of inappropriate environmental or labor policies in some countries, nontrade measures such as ecolabeling and income transfers would be more cost-effective than trade policies because they allow consumers to exercise their preferences through the market;

- the GATT rules-based multilateral trading system is threatened by the risk of environmental and worker-rights groups being captured by traditional protectionist groups in countries with high standards, and will be at further risk if GATT article XX is amended to allow in its list of exceptions the use of unilateral trade measures for environmental or labor purposes; and

- if such an amendment were made for environmental and labor standards, there would be pressure to add ever more domestic-policy items to the list of exceptions, including health, education, and taxation.

More empirical analyses to support some of these arguments are sorely needed. The experiences of the Uruguay Round and of the Intergovernmental Panel on Climate Change made clear that empirical studies are far more powerful than abstract arguments in focusing attention on the need for policy reform and the shape it should take. Those quantitative exercises have provided the world with a suite of multisector, multicountry models that are capable of being modified to estimate the linkages between trade, labor standards, resource depletion, and environmental degradation. Modeling efforts are now being made in that direction, but there is great scope for further, high-payoff research in this area.

Such forward-looking modeling requires the inclusion of endogenous behavioral relationships not only for private households and firms but also for governments, so as to capture not just the demographic transition but also the transitions in trade, labor, and environmental policies that typically accompany per capita income growth. Government behavior needs to be included in the base case not to suggest that policy choices are inevitable but rather to represent what would happen if no further action is taken. Against that base case various alternative cases can be compared, with a view to using the results to convince governments of the wisdom of choosing a more appropriate set of policies. In particular, empirical estimates could be given of the contribution that trade liberalization in industrial countries in farm products, labor-intensive manufactures, and coal could make to raising wages and reducing environmental damage at the same time as improving the global economy.

Helpful though such argumentation and analysis could be, more dialogue and compromise between high-income and developing countries is likely to be needed. For example, if developing countries were to commit themselves to enforcing minimum standards and to raising those standards over time according to a specified schedule, in return for gradual improvements in access to developed-country markets, vocal interest groups in those high-income countries would be less able to deny that improvements in social standards are positively related to income and trade growth. That would be using trade policy as a carrot rather than a stick. Likewise, if developing countries were seen to be enforcing reasonable standards especially effectively on their foreign investors, concerns about capital outflows to "pollution havens" or "cheap-labor havens" and the consequent loss of jobs in high-standard countries would be less justifiable. Alternatively or additionally, developing countries could transfer the onus back to high-standard countries to insist their firms accede to the same high standards when they invest in developing countries as in more advanced economies. And anxiety over deforestation could be reduced if developing countries were able to demonstrate they can police restrictions on felling and are prepared to do so in return for adequate compensation in the form of greater access to OECD markets and/or aid (e.g., via the UNDP/UNEP/World Bank Global Environment Facility administered by the World Bank).

To conclude, it is instructive to examine the progress of labor policies in the subglobal arena of the EU. A recent assessment by Sapir (1996) concludes that in Europe there have always been the optimists who believe economic integration breeds greater economic growth and equality of social policies (led by the Ohlin report to the International Labor Office [1956] at the time of the formation of the European Economic Community), and the pessimists who believe upward harmonization needs to be imposed on lower-standard countries to improve citizens' conditions there and avoid "social dumping" through trade. In practice, relatively little has been imposed effectively on the poorer member countries of the EU; the most that has been agreed to is the adoption of some minimum standards and mutual recognition. Yet standards have risen rapidly with the acceleration of income growth in the poorer EU countries.

References

Alesina, A., and E. Spolaore. 1995. On the Number and Size of Nations. NBER Working Paper no. 5050. Cambridge, MA: National Bureau of Economic Research, March.

Anderson, K. 1992a. Agricultural Trade Liberalisation and the Environment: A Global Perspective. *World Economy* 15, no. 1: 153–71.

———. 1992b. Effects on the Environment and Welfare of Liberalizing World Trade: The Cases of Coal and Food. In *The Greening of World Trade Issues,* ed. K. Anderson and R. Blackhurst, chap. 8. Ann Arbor: University of Michigan Press; London: Harvester Wheatsheaf.

———. 1992c. The Standard Welfare Economics of Policies Affecting Trade and the Environment. In *The Greening of World Trade Issues,* ed. K. Anderson and R. Blackhurst, chap. 2. Ann Arbor: University of Michigan Press; London: Harvester Wheatsheaf.

Anderson, K., and W. McKibbin. 1997. Reducing Coal Subsidies and Trade Barriers: Their Contribution to Greenhouse Gas Abatement. CIES Seminar Paper no. 97-07, University of Adelaide, July.

Barbier, E. B., J. C. Burgess, T. M. Swanson, and D. W. Pearce. 1990. *Elephants, Economics, and Ivory.* London: Earthscan.

Baumol, W. 1971. *Environmental Protection, International Spillovers, and Trade.* Stockholm: Almqvist and Wiksell.

Beltratti, A. 1995. Can a Growth Model with Defensive Expenditures Generate an Environmental Kuznets Curve? Paper for a workshop, "Designing Economic Policy for Management of Natural Resources and the Environment," Venice, 12–13 May.

Bhagwati, J. N. 1996. The Demands to Reduce Domestic Diversity among Trading Nations. In *Fair Trade and Harmonization: Prerequisites for Free Trade?* vol. 1, ed. J. N. Bhagwati and R. E. Hudec, chap. 1. Cambridge: MIT Press.

Bhagwati, J. N., and T. N. Srinivasan. 1996. Trade and the Environment: Does Environmental Diversity Detract from the Case for Free Trade? In *Fair Trade and Harmonization: Prerequisites for Free Trade?* vol. 1, ed. J. N. Bhagwati and R. E. Hudec, chap. 4. Cambridge: MIT Press.

Brown, D. K., A. V. Deardorff, and R. M. Stern. 1996. International Labor Standards and Trade: A Theoretical Analysis. In *Fair Trade and Harmonization: Prerequisites for Free Trade?* vol. 1, ed. J. N. Bhagwati and R. E. Hudec, chap. 5. Cambridge: MIT Press.

Burtless, G. 1995. International Trade and the Rise of Earnings Inequality. *Journal of Economic Literature,* 33, no. 2: 800–816.

Casella, A. 1996. Free Trade and Evolving Standards. In *Fair Trade and Harmonization: Prerequisites for Free Trade?* vol. 1, ed. J. N. Bhagwati and R. E. Hudec, chap. 3. Cambridge: MIT Press .

Charnovitz, S. 1987. The Influence of International Labour Standards on the World Trading Regime: A Historical Review. *International Labour Review,* 126, no. 5: 565–84.

———. 1991. Exploring the Environmental Exceptions in GATT Article XX. *Journal of World Trade* 25, no. 5.

Chichilnisky, G. 1994. North-South Trade and the Global Environment. *American Economic Review* 84, no. 4: 851–74.

Commission of the European Communities. 1996. *Growth, Competitiveness, Employment: The Challenges and Way Forward into the 21st Century.* Brussels: Commission of the European Communities.

Copland, B. R., and M. S. Taylor. 1995. Trade and Transboundary Pollution. *American Economic Review* 85, no. 4: 716–37.

Corden, W. M. 1997. The Environment and Trade Policy. In *Trade Policy and Economic Welfare,* 2d ed., chap. 13. Oxford: Clarendon Press.

Corden, W. M., and R. Findlay. 1975. Urban Unemployment, Intersectoral Capital Mobility, and Development Policy. *Economica* 42:59–78.

Deacon, R., and P. Shapiro. 1975. Private Preference for Collective Goods Revealed through Voting on Referenda. *American Economic Review* 65:943–55.

Dean, J. 1996. Testing the Impact of Trade Liberalization on the Environment. CIES Seminar Paper no. 96–11, University of Adelaide, September.

Deardorff, A. V. 1995. International Externalities in the Use of Pollution Policies. Discussion Paper no. 383, School of Public Policy. Ann Arbor: University of Michigan, November.

Ehrenberg, R. 1994. *Labour Markets and Integrating National Economies.* Washington, DC: Brookings Institution.

Enders, A., and A. Porges. 1992. Successful Conventions and Conventional Success: Saving the Ozone Layer. In *The Greening of World Trade Issues,* ed. K. Anderson and R. Blackhurst, chap. 7. Ann Arbor: University of Michigan Press; London: Harvester Wheatsheaf.

Esty, D. C. 1994. *Greening the GATT: Trade, Environment, and the Future.* Washington, DC: Institute for International Economics.

Falvey, R. 1995. International Trade and Factor Price Convergence. Working Paper no. 290. Canberra: Australian National University, August.

Francois, J. F., B. McDonald, and H. Nordstrom. 1996. The Uruguay Round: A Numerically Based Qualitative Assessment. In *The Uruguay Round and the Developing Countries,* ed. W. Martin and L. A. Winters, chap. 9. Cambridge: Cambridge University Press.

General Agreement on Tariffs and Trade. 1991. *Trade Policy Review: Indonesia.* Geneva: GATT Secretariat.

Grossman, G. M. 1995. Pollution and Growth: What Do We Know? In *The Economics of Sustainable Development,* ed. I. Goldin and L. A. Winters. Cambridge: Cambridge University Press.

Grossman, G. M., and A. B. Krueger. 1993. Environmental Impacts of a North American Free Trade Agreement. In *The Mexico-U.S. Free Trade Agreement,* ed. P. M. Garber, 13–56. Cambridge: MIT Press.

———. 1995. Economic Growth and the Environment. *Quarterly Journal of Economics* 110, no. 2: 353–78.

Hanson, G. 1983. *Social Clauses and International Trade: An Economic Analysis of Labour Standards in Trade Policy.* New York: St. Martin's Press.

Harrison, A. E., and G. S. Eskeland. 1996. Playing Dirty? Multinationals and the Pollution Haven Hypothesis. Columbia University, New York, February. Mimeo.

Hettige, H., R. E. B. Lucas, and D. Wheeler. 1992. The Toxic Intensity of Industrial Production: Global Patterns, Trends, and Trade Policy. *American Economic Review* 82, no. 2: 478–81.

Hillman, A. L., and H. N. Ursprung. 1992. The Influence of Environmental Concerns on the Political Determination of Trade Policy. In *The Greening of World Trade Issues,* ed. K. Anderson and R. Blackhurst, chap. 10. Ann Arbor: University of Michigan Press; London: Harvester Wheatsheaf.

Hoekman, B., and M. Leidy. 1992. Environmental Policy Formation in a Trading Economy: A Public Choice Perspective. In *The Greening of World Trade Issues,* ed. K. Anderson and R. Blackhurst, chap. 11. Ann Arbor: University of Michigan Press; London: Harvester Wheatsheaf.

International Labor Office. 1956. *Social Aspects of European Economic Cooperation.* Report by a Group of Experts (the Ohlin report). Geneva: ILO.

Jaffe, A. B., S. R. Peterson, P. R. Portney, and R. N. Stavins. 1995. Environmental Regulation and the Competitiveness of U.S. Manufacturing: What Does the Evidence Tell Us? *Journal of Economic Literature* 33, no. 1: 132–63.

Jones, L. A., and R. E. Manuelli. 1995. A Positive Model of Growth and Pollution Controls. NBER Working Paper no. 5205. Cambridge, MA: National Bureau of Economic Research, August.

Krueger, A. 1977. *Growth, Distortions, and Patterns of Trade among Many Countries.* Princeton, NJ: International Finance Section.

Lawrence, R. Z. 1994. Trade, Multinationals, and Labour. In *International Integration of the Australian Economy,* ed. P. Lowe and J. Dwyer, 233–65. Sydney: Reserve Bank of Australia.

———. 1995. *Regionalism, Multilateralism, and Deeper Integration.* Washington, DC: Brookings Institution.

Leamer, E. E. 1987. Paths of Development in the Three Factor, n-Good General Equilibrium Model. *Journal of Political Economy* 95, no. 5: 961–99.

Leonard, N. J. 1988. *Pollution and the Struggle for World Product: Multinational Corporations, Environment, and International Comparative Advantage.* Cambridge: Cambridge University Press.

Levinson, A. 1996. Environmental Regulation and Industry Location: International and Domestic Evidence. In *Fair Trade and Harmonization: Prerequisites for Free Trade?* vol. 1, ed. J. N. Bhagwati and R. E. Hudec, chap. 11. Cambridge: MIT Press.

Low, P. 1992. Trade Measures and Environmental Quality: The Implications for Mexico's Exports. In *International Trade and the Environment,* Discussion Paper 159, ed. P. Low, chap. 7. Washington, DC: World Bank.

Markusen, J. R., and A. J. Venables. 1996. Multinational Production, Skilled Labor, and Real Wages. NBER Working Paper no. 5483. Cambridge, MA: National Bureau of Economic Research, March.

Organization for Economic Cooperation and Development. 1996. *Report to the Council at Ministerial Level on Trade, Employment, and Labour Standards.* Paris: OECD.

Palmer, K., W. E. Oates, and P. R. Portney. 1996. Tightening Environmental Standards: The Benefit-Cost or the No-Cost Paradigm? *Journal of Economic Perspectives* 9, no. 4: 119–32.

Porter, M. E., and C. van der Linde. 1996. Towards a New Conception of the Environment-Competitiveness Relationship. *Journal of Economic Perspectives* 9, no. 4: 97–118.

Radetzki, M. 1992. Economic Growth and Environment. In *International Trade and the Environment,* Discussion Paper no. 159, ed. P. Low, chap. 8. Washington, DC: World Bank.

Rybczynski, T. M. 1959. Factor Endowment and Relative Commodity Prices. *Economica* 22, no. 84: 336–41.

Sapir, A. 1996. Trade Liberalization and the Harmonization of Social Policies: Lessons from European Integration. In *Fair Trade and Harmonization: Prerequisites for Free Trade?* vol. 1, ed. J. N. Bhagwati and R. E. Hudec, chap. 15. Cambridge: MIT Press.

Seldon, T. M., and D. Song. 1994. Environmental Quality and Development: Is There a Kuznets Curve for Air Pollution Emissions? *Journal of Environmental Economics and Management* 27, no. 2: 147–62.

Shafi, N., and S. Bandyopadhyay. 1992. Economic Growth and Environmental Quality: Time Series and Cross-Country Evidence. World Bank Policy Research Paper WPS 904. Washington, DC.

Siebert, H. 1974. Environmental Protection and International Specialization. *Weltwirtschaftliches Archiv* 110:494–508.

Siebert, H., J. Eichberger, R. Gronych, and R. Pethig. 1980. *Trade and Environment: A Theoretical Enquiry.* Amsterdam: Elsevier.

Snape, R. H. 1992. The Environment, International Trade, and Competitiveness. In *The Greening of World Trade Issues,* ed. K. Anderson and R. Blackhurst, chap. 4. Ann Arbor: University of Michigan Press; London: Harvester Wheatsheaf.

Srinivasan, T. N. 1996. International Trade and Labour Standards from an Economic Perspective. In *Challenges to the New World Trade Organization,* ed. P. Van Dijck and G. Faber, chap. 11. Dordrecht: Kluwer Law International.

Steil, B. 1994. "Social Correctness" Is the New Protectionism. *Foreign Affairs* 73, no. 1: 14–20.

Tobey, J. A. 1990. The Effects of Domestic Environmental Policies on Patterns of World Trade: An Empirical Test. *Kyklos* 43, no. 2: 191–209.

Trefler, D. 1993. International Factor Price Differences: Leontief Was Right! *Journal of Political Economy* 101, no. 6: 961–87.

Tyers, R., and Y. Yang 1995. Trade with Asia and Skill Upgrading: Effects on Factor Markets in the Older Industrial Countries. Australian National University, Canberra, October. Mimeo.

Williamson, J. G. 1996. Globalization and Inequality Then and Now: The Late 19th and Late 20th Centuries Compared. NBER Working Paper no. 5491. Cambridge, MA: National Bureau of Economic Research, March.

Wilson, J. D. 1996. Capital Mobility and Environmental Standards: Is There a Theoretical Basis for a Race to the Bottom? In *Fair Trade and Harmonization: Prerequisites for Free Trade?* vol. 1, ed. J. N. Bhagwati and R. E. Hudec, chap. 10. Cambridge: MIT Press.

Wood, A. 1994. *North-South Trade, Employment, and Inequality: Changing Fortunes in a Skill-Driven World.* Oxford: Clarendon Press.

Woolcock, S. 1996. An Agenda for the WTO: Strengthening or Overburdening the System. Global Economic Institutions Working Paper no. 4. London School of Economics, October.

9   Greater Coherence in Global Economic Policymaking: A WTO Perspective

Gary P. Sampson

9.1   Introduction

When more than one hundred trade ministers adopted the results of the Uruguay Round in Marrakesh in April 1994, they stressed that growing interactions between national economic policies meant that cooperation in each aspect of economic policymaking—structural, macroeconomic, trade, finance, and development—was necessary for progress in other areas. In particular, if the origins of difficulties are outside the trade field, they cannot be redressed through trade measures alone.

There has been a long-standing perception on the part of the members of the General Agreement on Tariffs and Trade (GATT), and now of the World Trade Organization (WTO),[1] that due to interlinkages at the international level, policies relating to trade, money, and finance would be more coherent if there was a broadening and deepening of cooperation between the International Monetary Fund (IMF), World Bank, and GATT/WTO. While the desire for addressing these linkages institutionally has emerged at different times in GATT history, it received formal recognition as a result of the Uruguay Round. In particular, the Agreement Establishing the WTO states that one of the five basic functions of the WTO is to cooperate with the World Bank and the IMF to achieve greater coherence in global economic policymaking (see WTO

Gary P. Sampson is director at the World Trade Organization, Geneva.

Comments from anonymous referees are gratefully acknowledged. The views expressed are those of the author and not the organization for which he works.

1. The GATT no longer exists as an institution; its functions have been taken over by the WTO, which entered into force in January 1995. The WTO has the task of implementing the many agreements emerging from the Uruguay Round, one of which is the 1994 GATT, that is, the updated version of the original 1947 GATT. The texts of the agreements and other legal instruments for which the WTO is responsible—in particular those referred to in this chapter—can be found in WTO (1994).

1994, 7). Only the Bretton Woods institutions are singled out in this respect. This mandate is further elaborated in a ministerial declaration inviting the director general of the WTO to review with the heads of the Bank and the Fund how the institutions can cooperate to achieve this greater coherence (see WTO 1994, 442–43).

Notwithstanding the considerable discussion in the Uruguay Round based on national submissions and GATT Secretariat documentation, *coherence* emerged as a particularly vague concept. It could be argued that this vagueness reduces its usefulness, or that it opens the door to new possibilities. This paper opts for the second view. It is reasoned that the decision to formally address coherence represents a statement of political will on the part of trade ministers. As such, the term constitutes an umbrella under which a number of useful initiatives could be pursued. In identifying and elaborating these issues, past experience in the GATT, the Uruguay Round discussions leading to the adoption of the legal texts, and present practices within the WTO are all relevant.

It is important, however, to accept at the outset that a number of considerations circumscribe the extent to which the coherence mandate can be implemented—more particularly, the extent to which institutional relations can be broadened and deepened. First, the coherence mandate was the outcome of agreement between trade ministers. The extent to which future cooperation—in particular at the political level—is advanced will in large measure depend on the enthusiasm of finance ministers to do so. It will also depend on the seriousness with which trade ministers pursue the task they have assigned themselves when more than a political declaration is at stake. Second, the natures of the WTO and of the Bretton Woods institutions—and therefore their secretariats and staffs—differ greatly. Most importantly, the WTO agreements constitute legally binding contracts between WTO members that establish rights and obligations. The role of the WTO Secretariat is to service the needs of members in the implementation of these contracts, and not to interpret them. As a practical consequence, since the role of the WTO Secretariat does not extend to commenting on members' rights and obligations, any involvement in matters relating to policy is restricted for the WTO Secretariat. Third, a very practical consideration (and not unrelated to the second point) is that the size of the WTO (i.e., number of staff, budget, etc.) differs greatly from that of the Bretton Woods institutions.[2] This severely limits the possibilities for a number of activities such as joint inputs into country surveillance, joint research and seminars, staff exchanges, and participation in meetings.

Section 9.2 describes the basis for past institutional cooperation under the GATT with the World Bank and the IMF. Section 9.3 details how coherence was dealt with in the Uruguay Round, the issues raised, and the final outcome of the negotiations in this area. Section 9.4 provides an indication of what

---

2. The travel budget of the IMF is about the same size as the total WTO budget. The IMF has 2,200 staff members; the WTO has 200 professional staff.

could be considered as falling under the heading of coherence at present. Comments are made on how the subjects identified are presently dealt with in the WTO, and *practical* proposals are made for future cooperation.

9.2   Coherence: The GATT

That coherence should be sought among the areas of responsibility of the WTO, the IMF, and the World Bank should come as no surprise. The three institutions share the same basic philosophy and have very similar objectives. According to their articles of the agreement, they are all dedicated to, for example, expanding international trade, promoting high (or full) levels of employment, and increasing standards of living and real incomes while developing the full use of productive resources. Apart from these general objectives, each organization has specific objectives with respect to international trade. The IMF, for example, is to "facilitate the expansion and balanced growth of international trade" recognizing "that the essential purpose of the international monetary system is to provide a framework that facilitates the exchange of goods, services and capital among countries" (GATT 1986, 2). Thus, a former general council of the IMF has described it as an institution "in the service of international trade" (see Gold 1986). As far as the World Bank is concerned, it is to "promote the long range balanced growth of international trade . . . by encouraging international investment" (GATT 1986, 2). The trade-related objective of the bank is to promote trade, but its own role is limited to encouraging investment to contribute to this end.

While neither the Bank nor the Fund has any regulatory authority over trade, they both have important responsibilities in this area. The role of the Fund in regulating the use of exchange restrictions, in exercising surveillance over members' monetary and financial policies under article IV, and in negotiating the terms on which its resources are used by member governments gives it significant direct and indirect influence in trade matters. For example, a study carried out over the period 1990–93 to investigate trade policy conditionality in Fund adjustment programs revealed that over 85 percent of the seventy-eight arrangements reviewed envisaged trade policy action ex ante (Calika and Corsepius 1994b, 40–41). Similarly, most article IV country reports cover a wide spectrum of trade and trade-related measures, such as trade-distorting subsidies, antidumping measures, sectoral policies (such as textile and clothing protection in the United States, the Common Agricultural Policy of the European Union), and restrictive distribution systems such as the Keiretsu in Japan (IMF 1994a, 20). In encouraging liberalization of trade measures at the national level, the IMF is giving substance to a key objective of the WTO, namely, the reduction of tariffs and nontariff barriers to trade.

Similarly, for the World Bank, the growth of world trade, the level of barriers to trade, and the trade policies applied by its individual member countries may all influence the viability of specific projects financed by the Bank. In the case of nonproject lending, such as structural adjustment loans, trade developments and policies (including both the trade policies of the borrowing country and market access for its exports) may crucially affect the prospects for successful adjustment. It has been noted that cooperation between the Bank and the Fund in matters relating to trade reflects the crucial role played by sustained trade reforms in achieving macroeconomic and structural adjustment. Trade reforms supported by Bank operations need to be consistent with the macroeconomic framework of Fund-supported programs; and national trade liberalization measures initiated by the Fund are often dependent on other structural reforms in Bank programs (Calika and Corsepius 1994, 40).

Not only national trade measures but their interlinkages with those in the area of finance have been of long-standing interest to GATT members. From an institutional perspective, the international adjustment process and coordination between the IMF and the GATT has been on the GATT agenda since before the Tokyo Round. It figured prominently, for example, in the terms of reference of the Consultative Group of Eighteen established in GATT in 1975.[3] In this context, the trade/finance and GATT/IMF linkages related primarily to the functioning of the GATT provisions concerning trade measures taken for balance-of-payments purposes. This in turn was based on the recognition that exchange restrictions and trade measures can be substitutes.

In fact, the close institutional relationship between the GATT and the IMF has been based primarily on the GATT provisions on balance-of-payments restrictions and the role of the IMF in the GATT Committee on Balance-of-Payments Restrictions as provided for in article XV of the GATT. This long-standing "coherent" approach to trade and exchange restrictions results from the obligation that GATT (and now WTO) members must not, by exchange action, frustrate the intent of the provisions of the GATT, nor, by trade action, the intent of the provisions of the IMF.[4]

The GATT provides that members should cooperate with the IMF and pursue a coordinated policy with regard to exchange questions within the jurisdiction of the Fund and questions of quantitative restrictions and other trade measures within the jurisdiction of the WTO. In cases where WTO members deal with problems concerning monetary reserves, balances of payments, or foreign exchange arrangements, they are to consult fully with the Fund. WTO members are to accept the Fund's findings on statistical and other facts relating to foreign exchange, monetary reserves, and balances of payments, as well as the

---

3. The Consultative Group of Eighteen was established by the GATT Council in July 1975. The terms of reference of the group state that "[t]he task of the Group is to facilitate the carrying out, by the CONTRACTING PARTIES, of their responsibilities, particularly with respect to the international adjustment process and the co-ordination, in this context, between the GATT and the IMF" (Gold 1986, 157).

4. Six countries are currently involved in balance-of-payments consultations: Bangladesh, Bulgaria, India, Nigeria, Pakistan, and Tunisia.

Fund's determination as to whether the action of a WTO member in exchange matters is in accordance with the Articles of Agreement of the Fund.[5]

There has been no comparable basis for cooperation between the GATT and the World Bank; the Bank, for example, is not mentioned specifically in any of the articles of the 1947 GATT. Thus, while the relationship between the GATT members and the IMF was based on an arrangement for coordination and consultation, agreed by means of an exchange of letters in 1948, relations between the GATT and the World Bank have been maintained on an informal basis. As a result of the Uruguay Round, provisions relating to balance-of-payment restrictions have been extended to trade in services, and the special status of the Fund remains. As noted above, however, the World Bank is now identified in other WTO agreements.

9.3 Coherence: Uruguay Round

Trade and finance linkages were specifically addressed as one of the four objectives of the Uruguay Round: to "increase the responsiveness of the GATT system to the evolving international economic environment through facilitating necessary structural adjustment, and enhancing the relationship of the GATT with the relevant international organizations" (GATT 1986, 2). Another was to "strengthen the inter-relationship between trade, other economic policies and efforts to improve the functioning of the international monetary system and the flow of financial and real investment resources to developing countries" (GATT 1986, 2). As a result, the negotiating group on the functioning of the GATT system (FOGS) was created to, inter alia, "increase the contribution of the GATT to achieving greater coherence in global economic policy-making through strengthening its relationships with other international organizations responsible for monetary and financial matters" (GATT 1986, 7).

In the FOGS negotiations governments saw their task identifying "inconsistencies and contradictions" in policymaking in the areas of trade, money, and finance.[6] The inconsistencies and contradictions singled out by negotiators as being important included the simultaneous deployment of international efforts

5. The Fund also supplies confidential material for the consultations, particularly through Recent Economic Developments papers resulting from IMF missions to consulting countries; these papers are circulated to members of the Balance-of-Payments Restrictions Committee. The WTO is the only organization to which the Fund provides such findings. A Fund representative takes part in the meetings of the committee and, in the case of full consultations with a WTO member country, delivers a statement that has been approved by the Fund's executive board.

6. In an attempt to identify the relevant areas, a decision in 1988 of the Trade Negotiations Committee (the committee was established to oversee work in the various Uruguay Round negotiating groups) "invited the Director-General to approach the Heads of the IMF and the World Bank, as a first step, to explore ways to achieve greater coherence in global economic policy-making through strengthening the relationship of GATT with other relevant international organizations" (WTO 1994, 7). The report by the director general in 1989 on his meetings with the heads of the Bank and the Fund included matters relating to consultation by the Fund and the Bank with the

to overcome the debt problem and of trade measures that limit the opportunities of the indebted countries to pay their way through export earnings; the extension to developing countries of structural adjustment loans, which favor measures to reduce, inter alia, the antiexport bias of their economies while placing limitations on access to the markets for their exports; exchange rate fluctuations, which inhibit trade liberalization because of the uncertainties that they generate regarding conditions of competition; and the reliance by governments on trade restrictions to resolve economic difficulties for which the proper medium- or long-term remedy lies in adjustments in macroeconomic policies.

With respect to enhancing the relationship of the GATT with the Bretton Woods institutions, governments identified a number of needs as being important: procedures by which developing countries reducing their levels of protection in the context of IMF or World Bank programs could obtain, in return for this market opening, concessions in GATT negotiations from their trading partners; assurance to developing countries that if they join in multilateral efforts to liberalize trade they can count on support to overcome financial pressures that may arise while their economies adjust to the shifts in trade patterns that follow; addressing any lack of consistency between trade policy recommendations made by the World Bank in the context of lending programs and GATT requirements; and, more generally, reviewing the roles of the GATT, the IMF, and the World Bank in assisting governments to achieve a better coherence of their policies at the national level, as a precondition for a better global coherence of economic policies.

The result of these negotiations is the ministerial declaration adopted in Marrakesh in April 1994. While the subject matter addressed is far-reaching, there is a clear lack of specificity as to the initiatives to be pursued. For example, the declaration recognizes that the interactions between the economic policies pursued by individual countries (including trade and finance) continually grow; that the task of achieving harmony between these policies falls primarily upon governments at the national level, but their coherence internationally is an important and valuable element in increasing the effectiveness of these policies; that greater exchange rate stability should contribute to the expansion of trade; that there is a need for further efforts to address debt problems; and that the WTO, IMF, and World Bank should follow consistent and mutually supportive policies. The declaration also mandates the WTO to pursue and develop cooperation with the international organizations responsible for monetary and financial matters, while respecting their autonomy and avoiding the imposition on governments of cross-conditionality. Ministers in-

---

GATT in the formulation of trade-reform objectives in loan programs; the possibility for developing countries to obtain negotiating credit in GATT negotiations for trade policy reforms introduced by them under Fund or Bank programs; and financial support by the Fund and the Bank to assist the process of liberalization through multilateral negotiations in the GATT (see GATT 1989).

vite the director general of the WTO to review with the managing director of the IMF and the president of the World Bank the implications of the WTO's responsibilities for its cooperation with the Bretton Woods institutions, as well as the forms such cooperation might take, with a view to achieving greater coherence in global economic policymaking (see WTO 1994, 442–43).

9.4 Coherence: The WTO

A common theme in the FOGS discussions was that there is scope for further developing institutional cooperation.[7] Without a definition of coherence, advancing the practical implementation of the coherence mandate is more a matter of the institutions and/or their members deciding on the issues to address under the heading, rather than attempting to precisely define the term. This section provides some examples of issues that will be addressed, or could be addressed, in the future.

One general point is important for what follows. Merchandise trade between WTO members is now about $5,000 billion per annum. With its entry into force, the subject matter of the WTO of interest to the Bank and the Fund extends well beyond the traditional area of merchandise trade. For example, services trade—defined in the General Agreement on Trade in Services (GATS) to include commercial establishment (and therefore investment) as well as the cross-border movement of services and service suppliers—is certainly more than the $1,200 billion per annum usually cited for cross-border transactions. The sectors subject to GATS disciplines, and for which liberalizing commitments have been undertaken, include telecommunications, financial services, transport, professional services, tourism, and building and construction. In addition, unlike the Tokyo Round codes with limited membership, all WTO members are now subject to WTO disciplines on their use of subsidies, safeguards, and antidumping measures. Disciplines now exist for trade-related intellectual property rights, and since the Singapore ministerial meeting, the scope of WTO activities extend to investment and competition policy. There is also WTO surveillance of national trade policies via the Trade Policy Review Mechanism. The important point is that all these areas are of importance to both the Bank and the Fund, particularly in terms of country programs. In addition, the WTO is spreading its strengthened disciplines more widely. Twenty-eight countries are in the process of accession to the WTO (there are presently 130 members), and they include countries of considerable importance for all institutions, such as China, Saudi Arabia, and Russia.[8]

---

7. This is also the view of others. For example, it has been observed that the "IMF and GATT are supposed to work together but do so sporadically at best" (Bergsten 1994, 347–48).

8. The countries in the process of acceding to the WTO are Albania, Algeria, Armenia, Belarus, Cambodia, China, Chinese Taipei, Croatia, Estonia, Georgia, Jordan, Kazakhstan, Kyrgyzstan, Latvia, Lithuania, Macedonia (former Yugoslav Republic), Moldova, Nepal, Oman, Russian Federation, Saudi Arabia, Seychelles, Sudan, Tonga, Ukraine, Uzbekistan, Vanuatu, and Vietnam.

9.4.1 Institutional Considerations

Closer cooperation between the institutions can be achieved with or without the involvement of their members. One means to strengthen institutional linkages is through formal agreements, negotiated by the staff and adopted by the members. Another is through cooperation in staff-related matters—including the provision of technical assistance—that may well one way or another receive directions from governments. Both are discussed below.

Since the entry into force of the WTO, formal agreements have been concluded between the WTO and the Bank and the Fund.[9] Not surprisingly, the agreements are very similar. While the agreement between the WTO and the Fund is more far-reaching than that with the Bank, this relates largely to the special relationship determined by the balance-of-payments restrictions.

The agreements acknowledge the importance of cooperation between the WTO, the IMF, and the World Bank in achieving greater coherence, and stipulate that attention is to be given to identifying possible means for cooperation in specific policies followed by each institution within its respective area of competence. One area where a specific deepening of relationship is evident is the participation of the staff of each of the institutions in their respective meetings of members. The agreements provide for WTO Secretariat attendance at executive board meetings of the Bank and the Fund as well as the IMF Committee on Liaison with the WTO when matters of particular common interest or trade relevance are discussed. Participation in meetings of the executive board of the Bretton Woods institutions was not available to the GATT in the past, nor is it available to other organizations at present. For their part, the Bank and the Fund staff are offered observership in the vast majority of WTO bodies, including the Dispute Settlement Body provided certain conditions prevail (e.g., for the IMF when matters of jurisdictional relevance are considered). Among other things, the agreements provide for the exchange of information between the organizations for their confidential use (e.g., in WTO trade policy reviews of members), and staff consultations to ensure consistency between members' obligations under WTO agreements or the Articles of Agreement of the IMF.

The WTO view is that these agreements "lay the basis for carrying forward the WTO's Ministerial mandate to achieve greater coherence . . . and . . . establish new mechanisms by which the institutions can address each other" (WTO 1996). Thus, the agreements provide a framework within which the institutions can explore the precise mechanisms for intensifying institutional cooperation. In identifying these mechanisms, proposals in the FOGS group are once again instructive. They included the sharing of research efforts; joint production of a biennial report on coherence among trade, monetary, and finance policies; joint analysis of specific problems of interdependence among these policies, with

9. The agreement between the WTO and the IMF is described in IMF 1997, 8–9.

each organization analyzing the topic under discussion from its point of view; cooperation in the preparation of trade projections and joint research projects on subjects of common interest; a regular program of staff exchanges; and staff meetings at head and deputy level on a regular basis.

One specific area for institutional cooperation is the provision of technical assistance for developing countries, in particular building the institutional capacity in these countries to take full advantage of benefits that flow from a liberalized multilateral trading system. The GATT has for many years provided assistance for this purpose, both through training programs in trade policy and technical assistance activities (national and regional seminars, technical missions, provision of data on trade flows, etc.). According to the report to the FOGS group by the director general (GATT 1989), the Bank, which regards institution building as an important element in its lending, stood ready to finance technical assistance to build the capacity of governments to comply with GATT rules and to analyze multilateral trade policy issues. It was agreed that there is scope to further consolidate this shared interest by establishing joint technical cooperation projects.

In the past, technical assistance has been provided by the institutions in an uncoordinated manner. That the benefits of technical assistance, particularly for the forty-nine countries designated by the United Nations as "least developed" (thirty of which are members of the WTO), could be improved through cooperation has not gone unnoticed. The Group of Seven (G7) Halifax Summit Communiqué in 1995 notes that open markets are crucial to accelerate economic growth in developing countries; the WTO should monitor the impact of the Uruguay Round on least-developed countries; and the multilateral institutions should assist the integration of the poorest countries into the world trading system. The G7 Lyon Summit Communiqué in 1996 states that the leaders have "agreed on ways to help developing countries, especially the least developed, to benefit more fully from the Uruguay Round." What these "ways" are was not made known. Subsequently, however, Quad Ministers in September 1996 recognized the need for infrastructural improvement in least-developed countries to take advantage of trading opportunities and proposed that WTO member governments meet with "international financial institutions and least developed countries in an effort to increase coherence and efficiency in the provision of technical assistance."[10]

The acceptance of this view was multilateralized in the WTO, and at the WTO Singapore ministerial meeting in December 1996, ministers accepted the Comprehensive and Integrated WTO Plan of Action for Least Developed Countries. A large part of this plan involves the more efficient provision of technical assistance to build the capacity of least-developed countries to take

10. See Chairperson's Summary, Quadrilateral Trade Ministers Meeting, Seattle, 27–28 September 1996. Trade ministers from the Quad Countries—Canada, European Union (represented by the relevant European commissioner), Japan, and the United States—meet periodically to discuss trade issues and send out a communiqué on their meetings.

advantage of the multilateral trading system. A coordinated approach to the provision of technical assistance by the WTO and the Bretton Woods institutions is a key part of the plan.

9.4.2   Consistent and Mutually Supportive Policies

The ministerial declaration calls for the institutions to pursue "consistent and mutually supportive" policies. There are a number of areas where this objective could be pursued, and three examples are outlined below.

As in the fulfillment of requirements of the financial assistance packages of the Bank and the Fund, countries are required to adopt certain trade measures, such measures should be WTO-*consistent.* There have, in fact, been instances where Bank and Fund proposals for the adoption of trade measures (and indeed the implementation of measures) have involved a contravention of GATT obligations.[11] This has been a rare event. However, given the far broader coverage of the legal texts that create obligations relating to trade in services, intellectual property, and so forth, this need is most likely to increase. It would seem appropriate that there is close cooperation between the institutions to avoid possible inconsistency in the future. Such cooperation may also be useful in formulating the trade-reform programs of countries acceding the WTO, as most receive assistance from Bank and Fund facilities and are required to fulfill trade policy conditions.

It has been proposed on occasions that the WTO Secretariat should participate in selected Bank/Fund missions to comment on the conformity of measures proposed by the Bank or the Fund. In the past, this has met objections from WTO developing-country members because of concern over cross-conditionality. Indeed, the ministerial declaration specifically states that the "imposition on governments of cross conditionality is to be avoided." Many of these fears may have disappeared as an increasing number of developing countries are liberalizing their trade regimes. Even if this concern prevailed, the WTO could still provide *technical* information to the Bank and the Fund, for example, with respect to rights and obligations of WTO members.[12]

An example of *mutually supportive* policies stems from the WTO's being the appropriate body for the establishment of rights and obligations and the liberalization and binding of commitments. Many developing countries bind their tariffs well above the applied rates to maintain their negotiating coin for future rounds of trade liberalization. Unbound tariffs create uncertainty for foreign exporters and leave open the possibility for governments to renege on

---

11. One example is a World Bank structural adjustment loan for Egypt, parallel to an IMF stand-by arrangement; this provided for an increase in tariffs that involved the breaking of a number of tariff bindings; a waiver, which required a lengthy and uncertain process, had to be requested. A further example relates to advice on the use of import surcharges as a fiscal measure to achieve budget targets; the WTO allows their use only in the case of balance-of-payments problems.

12. Resourcewise, however, it is hard to imagine how the WTO could be active in the country visits of the Bank and the Fund, even if thought desirable.

past liberalizing reforms. Consequently, a number of governments consider it appropriate to create a mechanism whereby credit and recognition can be offered to developing countries for *binding* liberalization commitments in the GATT/WTO (not *liberalizing* per se) undertaken within the context of structural adjustment programs of the Bank and the Fund; no such possibilities exist outside the multilateral trade liberalizing rounds.[13]

Finally, the objective of the Decision in Favor of Least-Developed and Net Food-Importing Countries is to avoid adverse effects in developing countries (especially least-developed and net-food-importing developing countries) due to higher food prices following the implementation of the Uruguay Round results liberalizing trade in agriculture (WTO 1994, 448–49). The decision reflects a perceived need to ensure adequate supplies of basic foodstuffs from external sources on reasonable terms and conditions, including the granting of food aid. The decision states that countries with such problems should have access to the resources of international financial institutions under existing facilities, or through facilities that may be established, in the context of adjustment programs.[14]

9.4.3   Trade Finance Linkages

There has been a long-standing realization that exchange rate volatility and misaligned currencies may affect international trade flows and influence trade policy matters of relevance to GATT/WTO. In fact, the proposition that exchange rate fluctuations create uncertainty and inhibit trade liberalization was among the subjects identified in the FOGS group and addressed in the meetings between the director general of the GATT and the heads of the Bretton Woods institutions in 1989. They were not, however, prepared to associate themselves with the argument that exchange rate instability impeded liberalization, and considered problems of this kind to be among those "least amenable to improvement through action by the international agencies themselves" (GATT 1989, 8).

More commonly the case has been made that currency instability and misalignment gives rise to protectionist measures rather than inhibits liberalization. While evidence to support this proposition has not been particularly

---

13. This initiative is currently being pursued in the WTO Committee on Trade and Development.

14. In his report to the Development Committee in October 1994 in Madrid, the president of the World Bank noted that "[p]resent assessment indicates that the array of investment and policy-based lending in the Bank and the Fund are adequate to help countries reap the potential benefits of the post-Uruguay Round world. Existing financing facilities also appear adequate to meet financing needs that may arise in individual countries from the negative impact of the Uruguay Round." The managing director of the IMF stated at the same meeting: "We are mindful of the possibility that some countries may experience transitional costs in the implementation of the Uruguay Round, due to the erosion of preference margins and possible higher prices for food imports. . . . If balance-of-payments needs arise, the Fund stands ready to provide financial support for policy adjustments under existing Fund facilities, in conjunction with support from donors" (WTO 1994, 448–9).

convincing, the argument received a recent boost in the Bretton Woods Commission report (1994, A-4), which stated that "[e]xchange rate misalignment adds to protectionist pressures from vulnerable industries in one major country after another as their international competitiveness waxes and wanes." Similarly, Bergsten (1994) and others have promoted an initiative for "target zones" to reduce currency instability on the grounds that the trading system would function better, as currencies would be more stable and better aligned.

Additionally, it has been argued that currency realignments are a source of the increase in antidumping actions. In the view of Kenen (1995, 82), when a country's macroeconomic policies cause its currency to appreciate, domestic firms that face more foreign competition find it hard to lobby for a change in the macroeconomic policy mix. In frustration, they resort to lobbying for trade policy relief. When the policy mix causes the domestic currency to depreciate, foreign competitors try to preserve their export market shares by cutting their home currency export prices; this shows up as "dumping" and is, "no doubt, partly responsible for the striking increase in the number of anti-dumping actions in recent years. It is thus very clear that exchange rate instability is a continuing threat to a liberal trade policy regime" (Kenen 1995, 82).

It has been argued that there is a role for the WTO and the IMF in addressing problems that link, for example, fiscal deficits, trade deficits, exchange rates, and trade measures. It has even been suggested that the most comprehensive policy response to the linkage problem would be merger of the GATT and the IMF to force national governments to coordinate internally (Bergsten 1990, 10). More realistic proposals include providing a vehicle for a better appreciation by trade and finance policymakers of the interlinkages between the respective policies for which they are responsible. Understanding the source of protection pressures, for example, is important in a WTO sense, including evaluating the need for new rounds of multilateral negotiations, reacting appropriately to pressures for antidumping action, and so forth. Joint meetings of trade and finance ministers at the international level may be one means to promote a better appreciation of the nature and policy implications of trade/finance linkages.

9.4.4 G7, Ministers, and Joint Declarations

In fact, it was proposed in the FOGS negotiations that trade and finance ministers dialogue and coordinate much more effectively than is presently the case. As this was frequently not done nationally, it was considered all the more important to do so internationally. One practical obstacle to this proposal was identified in the Uruguay Round; while regular ministerial meetings were provided for in the context of the Bank and the Fund for finance ministers (Interim Committee, Development Committee, and annual meetings), this was not the case for trade ministers in the GATT. As ministerial meetings were convened only on an ad hoc basis in the GATT, it would have been difficult to exchange participation in meetings on a regular basis. This obstacle has been removed with WTO ministerial meetings formally provided for each two years, the first having been held in Singapore in December 1996.

Reaching agreement on the need for interaction between trade and finance ministers and establishing a mechanism whereby joint meetings could be held will not happen in the near future. A more practical approach may be to increase the exposure of each of the heads of the institutions to their respective ministerial constituencies. This proposal was also discussed in the Uruguay Round. In fact, exposure of the heads of the institutions to ministers has been a feature of recent ministerial meetings. The director general of the WTO addressed the fall session of the Development Committee in 1996 and the managing director of the IMF addressed the WTO Singapore ministerial meeting. Additional proposals included regular joint meetings of heads of institutions with ad hoc joint declarations when appropriate. A model could be the joint declaration of the three heads in September 1993, stressing the importance of trade, money, and finance linkages and encouraging trade and finance ministers to act jointly in mobilizing support to bring the Uruguay Round to a successful conclusion.

Various proposals have also identified a role for the institutions in the G7 context. It was also proposed in the Uruguay Round that there should be participation by the heads of the three institutions in the G7 summit meetings as part of a process of increasing the representativeness of the G7. This proposal has in fact been put into effect, as the three heads participated in the G7 Lyon summit. More far-reaching proposals involve the creation of a group at the prime minister, trade minister, and finance minister level to coordinate international economic issues, with members drawn from developing countries, economies in transition, and the Organization for Economic Cooperation and Development economies. It has been argued that no new bureaucracy would be required, as the IMF, World Bank, and WTO could provide the necessary support.[15]

9.5   Conclusions

The *breadth* of the subject matter on which the Bretton Woods institutions and the WTO can cooperate depends on their respective areas of competence. Cooperation has been a feature of the relationship between the GATT, the Bank, and the Fund in the past; with the broader responsibilities of the WTO, it would be natural for this to increase. This has indeed been the case since the establishment of the WTO. Just how far the existing cooperation can be extended depends on the very different nature of the WTO compared to the Bretton Woods institutions, in particular, the special contractual nature of the WTO agreements and the role of the WTO Secretariat in servicing them. The *depth*

15. Peter Sutherland, "Beyond the Market: A Different Kind of Equity," *International Herald Tribune,* 20 February 1997.

of cooperation will in many ways depend on the willingness of trade and finance ministers to identify specific areas where there is scope for cooperating and then to work together to bring greater coherence in global economic policymaking.

References

Bergsten, C. F. 1990. Trade Finance Linkages. Background paper prepared for a meeting of government officials and private experts, Institute for International Economics, Washington, DC, June.

————. 1994. Managing the World Economy of the Future. In *Managing the World Economy: Fifty Years after Bretton Woods,* ed. P. B. Kenen, 341–74. Washington, DC: Institute for International Economics.

Bretton Woods Commission. 1994. Bretton Woods: Looking to the Future. Commission Report, Staff Review, and Background Papers. Vol. 1 (July). Washington, DC: Bretton Woods Committee.

Calika, N., and U. Corsepius. 1994. Trade Reforms in Fund-Supported Programmes. In *International Trade Policies: The Uruguay Round and Beyond.* Vol. 2. Washington, DC: International Monetary Fund.

General Agreement on Tariffs and Trade. 1986. *Ministerial Declaration of the Uruguay Round.* MIN.DEC., 20 September. Geneva: GATT.

General Agreement on Tariffs and Trade. 1989. *Ways of Achieving Greater Coherence in Global Economic Policy-Making through Strengthened GATT Relationships with Other Relevant International Organizations.* Document MTN.GNG/NG14/W/35, 20 September. Geneva: GATT.

Gold, Joseph. 1986. Some Legal Aspects of the IMF's Activities in Relation to International Trade. *Österreichische Zeitschrift für Öffentliches Recht und Völkerrecht,* 36, no. 3: 157–217.

International Monetary Fund. 1994. *International Trade Policies: The Uruguay Round and Beyond.* Vol. 1, *Principal Issues.* Washington, DC: IMF.

————. 1997. IMF and WTO Sign Cooperation Agreement. *IMF Survey,* 13 January, 8–9.

Kenen, P. 1995. Agendas for the Bretton Woods Institutions. In *Fifty Years after Bretton Woods: The Future of the IMF and the World Bank,* ed. B. M. Boughton and R. Sarwar Lateex, 79–85. Washington, DC: International Monetary Fund and World Bank Group.

World Trade Organization. 1994. *The Results of the Uruguay Round of Multilateral Trade Negotiations: The Legal Texts.* Geneva: GATT Secretariat.

————. 1996. WTO and IMF Sign Cooperation Agreement. Press/62. Geneva: WTO.

Comment on the Paper by Gary P. Sampson   Jean Baneth

When I was invited to be a discussant of a paper entitled "Greater Coherence in Global Economic Policymaking," one of my first thoughts was for the Swiss constitutional revision of 1866 (completed in 1872), which removed legal discrimination against Jews. The relationship to the topic is obvious. But a discussant is not free to choose his statement, at least not in the rare instances (this being one of them) when he is actually shown several days in advance the paper he is to discuss.

Gary Sampson's paper is warningly subtitled "A WTO Perspective," and it is to that perspective that the first part of my discussion is addressed. I will, however, return to that Swiss constitutional change and to some broader issues of coherence of trade and other policies, globally and nationally.

Sampson gives us a very clear, complete, and concise presentation of the history of the relationships of the GATT and the WTO with other institutions, concentrating mostly on the IMF and (to a much lesser degree) the World Bank. This focus is justified both by the ancient history of the three institutions, conceived as the triple pillars of international economic relations, and by the recent focus on them in the GATT, the Uruguay Round, and the WTO, almost to the exclusion of explicit debate of relations with other international organizations. I can usefully add only a few details to that account; and if I summarize their conclusion, that will be merely to check whether my partial disagreement with some of them is not based on a misunderstanding.

Simplifying greatly, I will summarize Sampson's paper thus: The GATT had already developed fairly close relations with the IMF and useful ones with the World Bank. The former gave its binding opinion when payments restrictions were justified by balance-of-payments constraints; and all three organizations exchanged information within the constraints of their mandates. Nevertheless, in the context of the Uruguay Round and the creation of the WTO, new demands came for greater coordination to ensure better "coherence" in global policies; some of these demands will be met through greater staff cooperation, readiness of the financial institutions to address, through their existing programs, financing and adjustment issues with a trade background, and new institutional arrangements built into WTO, enhancing the formal presence of the financial institutions in WTO forums. Incidentally, Sampson does not mention that the World Bank inaugurated such closer staff cooperation by closing down the office that it had had in Geneva for the past fifteen years.

Going farther, the director general of the WTO has called for much more

Jean Baneth has retired from the World Bank, where he occupied various positions, including director of the resident staff in Indonesia, of the Economics Analysis and Projections Department, of the International Economics Department, and of the Geneva office. In this last position, he represented the World Bank in the Uruguay Round. At present, he is *professeur invité* at Centre d'Études et de Recherches sur l'Économie Internationale, Université d'Auvergne, France, and concurrently visiting fellow of the Rajiv Gandhi Institute for Contemporary Studies, New Delhi, India.

far-reaching cooperation, through "new structures," to meet "global economic challenges." Formal response to these far-reaching calls has been sparse, and Sampson's conclusion is dubitative as to "how far existing cooperation can be extended," though, on a more hopeful note, just before that he reminded us of the presence of the heads of the three economic institutions at the 1996 G7 summit meeting.

Having already said that concerning relations between the GATT/WTO and the Bretton Woods twins Sampson's statement is clear, cogent, and complete, I can only add a few nuances to it, partly from the vantage point of my having represented the World Bank in the Uruguay Round negotiations. I may just as well start near Sampson's conclusion, at the Lyon summit. I too feel that the three heads of institutions' participation in that meeting was symbolic. This statement should be put into the context of the meetings' greatest substantive achievement, which was to bring together the world's greatest leaders and the world's most outstanding haute cuisine.

It is noteworthy that initiatives for greater institutional cooperation have come almost exclusively from the GATT and the WTO. World Bank and IMF responses have mostly stated that "we do not need this," or "we have long been doing this already"; quite a few of the responses apparently combined both these statements. The absence of Bank and Fund initiatives is apparent in Sampson's paper, but it is interesting to add a little to some of his information.

Sampson refers to the GATT director general's visit to the heads of the World Bank and the IMF in 1989, to discuss economic policy "coherence." Four major issues were listed in his mandate: trade restrictions on two counts, implicitly by industrial countries against developing countries; the undue substitution of payment restrictions to structural adjustment, and "exchange rate fluctuations, which inhibit trade liberalization because of the uncertainties that they generate."

In retrospect, concerns about industrial country trade restrictions were exaggerated, at least in this context, because whatever industrial country protectionism then existed (and I have argued elsewhere that it was quite trifling), it clearly has not inhibited the success of vigorous export-oriented and other structural adjustment policies. It may seem ironic that the GATT should have drawn the financial institutions' attention to undue recourse to payments restrictions instead of structural adjustment, at the end of a decade when structural adjustment had been the financial institutions' watchword and clarion call. However, while urging adjustment and pushing for convertibility, the IMF had also continued routinely to certify to the GATT that payments restrictions by developing countries were justified by balance-of-payments considerations. The IMF was thus shielding developing countries from the pressure of GATT rules, even though those pressures went exactly in the same direction the IMF also favored. In recent years, however, much progress has been made in this field, as more and more developing countries have moved toward current account convertibility.

Most noteworthy is the financial institutions' reaction to the exchange rate fluctuation issue: the director general reported to the Trade Negotiations Committee that the Bank and the Fund "dissociated themselves" from that concern, a reaction all the more puzzling as there was little if any reaction to the other concerns.

One of Sampson's concrete examples of inconsistency or incoherence between the GATT and the Bretton Woods institutions relates to a World Bank structural adjustment loan to Egypt. One element of that program aimed at reducing the disparities in effective protection levels, by greatly reducing the higher tariffs and somewhat raising the lower ones. Bank staff dealing with Egypt either completely disregarded the country's legally binding GATT obligations, or at best acknowledged them grudgingly, saying only that it was up to the Egyptians to ensure compliance with them. Moreover, the Bank failed to acknowledge the nature of relations in the GATT. When addressing the issue at all, Bank staff kept noting that the overall effect of the program was to reduce Egyptian protectionism substantially, and that the GATT should therefore be happy. Behind this attitude lay a failure to note that the GATT was essentially its contracting parties, and that in that context Australia, for example, was not interested in the coming millennium of Egyptian trade liberalism, but in the fact that it was asked to tolerate a unilateral increase in a bound Egyptian tariff on Australian exports to that country. However, it is also relevant that the Egyptians showed admirable diligence in implementing the part of their tariff-harmonization undertaking that raised certain tariffs, but they pursued the other part of the undertaking much more cautiously, if at all.

The broad policy aims pursued by the GATT and the Bank toward Egypt were the same, but this episode clearly illustrates the inconsistency of some of the means toward that end. It also illustrates a certain reluctance to seek such consistency, or even to investigate whether it could be sought without excessive costs. I believe such attitudes are changing, mostly because developing countries themselves now appreciate that WTO rules often apply to them too.

I have already said that only in one, albeit important, respect do I consider the achievements of the Lyon summit to have been substantive and consequential; otherwise, the WTO director general's calls for better institutional arrangements and greater coherence have not been followed by much action. Progress has nevertheless been made toward better institutional coordination, with the aim of ensuring greater "coherence in global policymaking." However, this progress has occurred almost entirely in different frameworks, most notably through the inclusion of important developing countries in the Bank for International Settlements and the Organization for Economic Cooperation and Development (OECD). One might also think of talk shows like the recent Eurasian summit meeting at Bangkok, whose concrete achievements do not compare unfavorably with those of the G7 summit. In other words, there has been progress at the very technical end, where specific issues clearly require joint or coordinated treatment, and some progress at the other end, where leaders can meet and, if all goes well, generate goodwill toward all: an important prerequisite to bringing coherent solutions to common problems, when they are identified.

When they are identified: this last phrase may hold the key. If there has been little substantive progress toward institutional arrangements to tackle the big problems of global economic policy, this may well reflect the lack of consensus as to what constitutes such problems, and as to whether such problems are amenable to being solved through international or even national government action.

The experience of then GATT director general Dunkel's visit to Washington is symptomatic: it was predicated on the identification of four major problems. Two of these were the same one, and in reality did not constitute much of a problem; one was either largely technical or nonexistent; and the Fund and the Bank dissociated themselves of the mere mention of one of the issues of concern to the GATT. It is not that anyone thinks the world is devoid of economic problems; it is just that there is no consensus as to what they are, how they are to be solved, or even whether governments might have a proper role in solving them. The major reason for the lack of institutional arrangements to ensure greater policy coherence is the lack of consensus as to what policy coherence means, and what these institutions should do about it.

While it is unclear what coherence means at this lofty level, the coherence of trade policies and of the aim of free trade with other policies and aims constantly raises concrete issues. That trade policy does not stop at defining customs duties is well illustrated by the Swiss constitutional change of 1866 relative to the civil rights of Jews, which I mentioned earlier. This came as a direct consequence of the Franco-Swiss trade treaty of June 1864. France had not directly intervened in Switzerland's internal human rights through that treaty, but it had stipulated that certain rights of establishment, inherently needed for free trade, were to apply to all French traders, regardless of religion. It then struck the Swiss that it was incoherent for Switzerland to grant rights to French Jews that were not available to some Swiss Jews. There can be no free trade without reasonably free movement of people; once a country started to treat all its subjects as equals and insisted that they should also be treated as equals by its trading partners, even domestic religious discrimination showed up as inconsistent or incoherent with free trade.[1]

Trade rules and other policies and rules intersect in many other areas. Many such intersections and the consequent need for coherence arise out of the very

---

1. That free trade required free movement had long been recognized; it was already stipulated in the Anglo-Norwegian trade agreement of 1217 (the first ever concluded by England), which provided that "mercatores et homines qui sunt de potestate vestra libere et sine impedimento terram nostram adire possint, et homines et mercatores nostri simile vestram" (traders and people under your jurisdiction should be able freely and without hindrance to enter our lands, and in the same way, our people and merchants, your land).

nature of free trade, like in the Swiss example. One of the thrusts of the Uruguay Round was to identify the areas where nonborder rules interfered with free trade, and either to bring those areas under WTO jurisdiction or to ensure treatment coherent with free trade by other means. The negotiations and agreements concerning trade-related investment measures took the former track, by outlawing investment rules that effectively ensure trade discrimination. The preoccupation with quasi-automatic IMF certification of payments restrictions, supposedly for balance-of-payments purposes, reflect a similar preoccupation with incoherence: there is, of course, no point in eliminating duties and trade quotas if payments quotas are authorized; as demands for reciprocity by developing countries intensified, the WTO either had to bring these also under its own jurisdiction or ensure a more serious, one might say more coherent, treatment by the IMF.

The Uruguay Round also showed another set of new interfaces between trade and other policy areas. The treatment of intellectual property is a good example. Arguably, even the most blatant and complete disregard of intellectual property rights does not, by itself, restrict the freedom of trade. Intellectual property was not included in the Uruguay Round to remove a nonborder obstacle to trade; it was included to give legitimacy to the use of trade restrictions in retaliation against piracy. In this case, the route followed was different from the relationship with the IMF, whose authority over payments questions was not questioned; the World Intellectual Property Organization was, in effect, largely dispossessed of its jurisdiction, though it was not abolished.

In this case, the aims pursued through trade policy means were economic aims, though not trade aims. Trade policy means have also been already put to limited use in other areas, like the promotion of human rights not closely related to trade. Many more widespread uses have been proposed for them. Trade economists have generally not protested against the linkage between freedom to trade and respect for intellectual property, established by the Uruguay Round. However, they are generally viscerally opposed to other linkages. The instinctive tendency toward such negative reactions is, no doubt, much reinforced by some of the aims themselves appearing harmful, and not only the means used or proposed to bring them about. Yet this is a field where visceral reactions should be controlled, and certainly, it is a field where many issues need to be tackled. The question is whether there are other means to enforce international aims unrelated to trade that are desirable but not so important as to warrant war; and if there are no such other means, in which cases and under what conditions may trade policy be legitimately used for coercion.

A well-known case is that of so-called workers' rights. The aim itself is confused, and much of it is probably barely disguised protectionism. Some proposals appear to aim at giving the WTO the mandate to enforce the broad observation of workers' rights through trade policy and the menace of trade sanctions, in a way similar to the WTO's assumption of the mandate to enforce intellectual property rights. Whether one opposes this or not, it is important to know that the GATT has already recognized some workers' rights, for example, by allowing import discrimination against goods made by prison labor. Countries like the United States, which actually bans such imports in principle, define the term unilaterally. One of the oldest international organizations, the International Labor Organization (ILO), is mostly concerned with giving internationally acceptable definitions to workers' rights. There may well be a case for enhancing cooperation between the ILO and the WTO, in areas where trade and workers' rights intersect, if only to preclude the proliferation of unilateral standards imposed by individual countries (and even by private pressure groups) on selected trade partners.

Coherence is an issue in other areas, too, some of them not immediately obvious. Thus the draft treaty on the elimination of chemical weapons provides for the boycott by signatories of certain chemical exports by nonsignatories. In other words, signatory countries undertake to practice trade discrimination in a specific field against nonsignatories of a treaty that is far from being a trade agreement. To the best of my knowledge, nothing in the GATT or the WTO gives explicit authorization to such discrimination against countries that have violated no trade rules. Yet a challenge in the WTO by, say, the United States would most likely be rejected, because precedents have already been established for precisely such use of trade policy to enforce compliance with other rules. For instance, the Montreal protocol on the phasing out of gases that harm the ozone layer prescribes similar trade sanctions against nonsignatories. Similarly, as far as I know there has been no protect in the WTO against the worldwide ban on ivory imports, even though the biggest potential producers and exporters actively oppose it.

In other cases, and in different circumstances, trade sanctions against supposedly bad environmental practices have been condemned in the GATT: thus the U.S. ban on imports of tuna caught by methods deemed, by the United States, to endanger porpoises, and the Austrian attempt to impose logging standards on tropical wood imports. Unlike chlorofluorocarbons, poison gases, and elephants, no international treaty protects porpoises or tropical woods.

The evolving jurisprudence should help ensure that the interfaces of trade and other policies are reasonably coherent. Clearly trade-related measures, even when their impact is not felt at the border, are increasingly treated in a trade context, and increasingly in the framework of the WTO; this tendency will be amplified as negotiations on services progress. This seems logical and simple, but the consequences can be quite far-reaching and sometimes unexpected. This has been illustrated by that Swiss constitutional change; it is also illustrated by the important constitutional issues regarding state and provincial rights raised on both sides of the U.S.-Canadian beer wars, or by U.S. objections to European public health standards in the hormone-fed beef conflict.

When broad international agreement exists on a topic that is not directly trade-related, trade measures inscribed in it and closely related to the purpose of the agreement, as is the case for the treaties on poison and ozone-destroying gases, will be accepted by the WTO. Unilateral attempts to use trade retaliation against nontrade practices are likely to be condemned systematically by the WTO. This is certainly the case when the trade measure concerns things not closely related to the practice in question, like the use of trade measures to promote human rights. However, it is even likely to be the case when the trade measures and policy concerns are closely related. Thus, U.S. retaliation against companies investing in Cuba are likely to be condemned, tuna boycotts or restrictions against those not respecting unilateral logging standards are likely to remain illegal—though this may not prevent national governments from continuing to take such measures.

The issue is more uncertain when a wide agreement exists, but possible trade retaliation is not closely related to its object. For instance, will a link be established between minimal labor standards, agreed in the ILO, and trade under WTO rules?[2] Whether or not it is actually desirable to use trade policy as a means to enforce other desirable aims, I suspect this use will spread. Rejecting such use absolutely may not be an option. The realistic alternative may be between disorderly use of trade sanctions degenerating into a protectionist free-for-all, and orderly use under clearly defined conditions to help ensure compliance with broad international agreements and adhesion to them. Each agreement should then also take into account how much it may detract from trade policy aims. In other words, close institutional cooperation will be required, well beyond the WTO, IMF, and World Bank, to ensure greater coherence in global policymaking.

2. The establishment of such a formal link has been recently proposed by the director general of the ILO.

10   Reaching Effective Agreements Covering Services

Richard H. Snape

10.1   Introduction

That a general agreement on trade in services (GATS) was secured in the Uruguay Round of multilateral trade negotiations was a major achievement. There was considerable opposition from several key developing countries to including services trade in these negotiations at all. Agreement to include them was secured only by having the services negotiations on a different track from the GATT-based negotiations, with the negotiations strictly not being between contracting parties to the GATT, but between trade ministers representing their governments. The negotiations were serviced by the GATT Secretariat following GATT procedures and practices. The distinction between the two tracks became blurred over time, particularly after the midterm review (Croome 1995, passim).

While the GATT essentially concentrates on cross-border trade of goods, the GATS extends its coverage to all forms of trading services, or of obtaining access to foreign markets. It also explicitly encompasses regulations relating to access that do not discriminate against (or for) foreigners as such.

Thus the coverage of the GATS is in principle much broader than the GATT. In this sense it is a more general agreement. But this breadth of coverage has been secured at a cost in terms of the ease by which particular service sectors can be excluded from the major provisions of the GATS. Under the GATT all products are covered by the general provisions, and exclusion of products from

Richard H. Snape is professor of economics at Monash University and full-time associate commissioner at the Australian Industry Commission, Melbourne.

This paper draws in part on Snape and Bosworth (1996). The author is grateful to Malcolm Bosworth for discussions and his contributions. He is also grateful for comments from the appointed discussants of the paper, Robert Baldwin and Ron McKinnon, and other participants at the conference, particularly Ambassador Kesavapany, Geza Feketekuty, Frieder Roessler, Jaroslaw Pietras, David Vines, and Gary Sampson.

such coverage occurs only in special circumstances. Under the GATS, however, many of the most important provisions apply only to the service sectors that are specified in the schedules of members. For these provisions the sectors are negotiated in rather than out—a much less liberalizing procedure. And for the GATS, unlike the GATT, even the most-favored-nation principle can be implemented, in the first instance, on a conditional rather than an unconditional basis for specific measures affecting service sectors. From the perspective of product or sector coverage, the GATS at this juncture is much less a general agreement than the GATT.

The question then arises as to whether trade liberalization under the GATS would be more successful if its coverage were limited to that of the GATT—cross-border trade and measures that discriminate between domestic and foreign suppliers (between "us" and "them"). This would then leave measures that regulate access but do not discriminate between us and them, other aspects of competition policy, investment, and movement of people, to separate negotiations. In all these areas the negotiations could cover both goods and services; the relevant principles generally apply to both.

In the following sections I address with respect to both the GATT and the GATS the question of gaining access to foreign markets, the barriers to this access, the principles of product coverage and the extent of actual coverage, and the lessons that may be drawn.

10.2   Gaining Access to Foreign Markets

Access to foreign markets can be achieved in many ways; by trade across frontiers, production in the foreign market, licensing foreign production, and franchising.

The point has been made many times that, while most goods can be traded at arm's length so that there is no need for the producer and consumer of the good to be in physical proximity, this is not the case for many services (Bhagwati 1984; Sampson and Snape 1985). Of course, some goods do not travel: ready-mixed concrete and soufflés are two examples. And many services can be traded when the parties to the transaction are at a considerable distance from each other: all those services that can be traded through the electronic media and post, and the "servicing" of goods are examples.[1] Nevertheless, the option of arm's-length trading between the parties to a transaction is much more commonly available in goods trade than in services trade.

Because of this, those governments that were pressing for GATT-type rules to be developed for services pressed for all modes of supply to be covered by a services agreement: not only cross-border trade but also "commercial pres-

---

1. The distinction between what is trade in a good and trade in a service is not always clear. How much transformation in a good has to occur before it becomes a new good? How long does the rental of a movie have to be before the transaction becomes one in a good rather than in a service? And so on.

ence" and the movement of service consumers and of people to supply services.[2] The GATT itself has very little direct relevance to commercial presence or investment.[3] The one relevant provision relates to trade-related investment measures—that is, investment requirements tied to the cross-border trade in goods. These provisions received modest attention in the trade-related investment measures (TRIMs) agreement of the Uruguay Round. The GATT has no provisions relating to the movement of people whether as consumers or producers.

10.3   Barriers to Foreign Markets

Barriers to market access by foreigners can be imposed in many ways. First, they can be imposed at the frontier—tariff and nontariff barriers, regulations relating to establishing a foreign commercial presence and foreign investment (and to disestablishment and disinvestment), exchange controls and other restrictions on the transfer of funds, restrictions on the movement of people and their ability to visit or work in foreign countries, and so on. Second, barriers can be imposed internally, in the form of differential regulations or taxes imposed on foreign producers or products. Both these forms of barriers discriminate against foreigners, and in many cases the distinction between frontier and internal is quite blurred, for example, in some services such as beamed transmissions from abroad.

Third, foreign access can also be impeded in ways that do not in themselves discriminate against foreigners, but that impede all access whether it be by local or by foreign suppliers. These nondiscriminatory barriers—nondiscriminatory with respect to the nationality or the residence of the suppliers—fall under the heading of national competition policy where this term is interpreted broadly to embrace not only restrictive trade practices by firms but legislated barriers to entry to an activity as well as government regulation of access to essential facilities where "natural monopoly" elements are present.

Table 10.1 summarizes the broad coverage of the GATT and the GATS with respect to rules constraining the imposition of barriers to access, encompassing the modes by which access to markets may be secured, and the point and manner at which access may be denied for each mode. As in the previous two paragraphs a distinction is made between measures that discriminate between domestic and foreign supplies and those that limit supplies or suppliers from all sources. In the former category a distinction is also made between those measures that are applied at the frontier and those that are applied internally. Both the GATT and the GATS also have provisions that apply to discrimination

2. Commercial presence and investment are not identical, and regulations distinguish between them. But a substantial commercial presence will usually require investment, and the two are treated together in this paper.

3. Of course it has indirect relevance in so far as the existence of trade barriers influences investment-location decisions.

Table 10.1   **Coverage of GATT and GATS**

	Form of Market Access		
Access Barrier	Cross-Border	Investment/ Commercial Presence	Movement of People
GATT			
Discrimination against foreigners			
Frontier	(1) Main focus of GATT: MFN, proscription of quotas, etc.	(4) Covered by GATT only when related to cross-border trade	(7) No
Internal	(2) GATT national treatment	(5) No	(8) No
Barrier to both nationals and foreigners	(3) Little in GATT[a]	(6) No	(9) No
GATS			
Discrimination against foreigners			
Frontier	(1) Yes (including MFN, etc., and national treatment)	(4) Yes (including MFN, etc., and national treatment)	(7) Yes (including MFN, etc., and national treatment)
Internal	(2) Yes (including national treatment and market access and business practices)	(5) Yes (including national treatment and market access and business practices)	(8) Yes (including national treatment and market access and business practices)
Barriers to both nationals and foreigners	(3) Yes Market-access monopoly and business practices	(6) Yes Market-access monopoly and business practices	(9) Yes Market-access monopoly and business practices

[a]Nonviolation nullification or impairment (article XXIII) has relevance.

among foreign suppliers (most-favored-nation [MFN] and exceptions to it), but this form of discrimination is not included in the table.

The first part of table 10.1 applies this taxonomy to goods trade and to the GATT. The first two cells are of primary importance in the GATT. Thus in cell 1 the GATT proscribes all nontariff frontier barriers as a general rule, with exceptions in certain circumstances. For cell 2, the national treatment article of the GATT is of primary relevance. There is little of relevance to cell 3 in the

GATT, though the nonviolation provisions of the nullification or impairment article (see Hoekman and Mavroidis 1994) are at least of potential application. For cell 4, provisions relating to investment are covered by the GATT only to the extent that regulations governing international trade are tied to investment, as noted above. The GATT is not directly relevant to the other cells of the table.

As mentioned above, the distinction between a frontier and nonfrontier barrier is often quite unclear for services trade. In part reflecting this, the GATS concept of national treatment does not draw on a distinction between frontier and internal but embraces all policies that might discriminate between domestic and foreign suppliers (by all means of supply). (In contrast, the national treatment article of the GATT is headed "National Treatment on Internal Taxation and Regulation"). National treatment in the GATS requires that "each Member shall accord to services and service suppliers of any other Member, in respect of all measures affecting the supply of services, treatment no less favourable than it accords its own like services and services suppliers" (article XVII:1). If left at that, it would imply no discrimination at all against foreigners in all services—unlike national treatment in the GATT with respect to goods. But this liberality is conditioned by the first part of the same sentence in the article: "In the sectors inscribed in its schedule, and subject to any conditions and qualifications set out therein." Thus any form of discrimination against foreigners is in fact allowable, provided it is scheduled and does not discriminate among foreign sources of supply.

But that is not the end of the matter, for the principal demandeurs in the services negotiations were concerned with barriers to access that would apply to all suppliers whether they discriminated against foreigners or not. These barriers may be imposed by governments (for example, legislated barriers to entry to an activity) or by the owners of "natural monopolies" (whether they be government owners or not) or may be caused by other restrictive trade practices engaged in by enterprises. To address these other forms of barriers to market access, there is a "market-access" article (article XVI), and articles covering monopolies and exclusive service suppliers (article VIII) and business practices (article IX).

The market-access article provides that "[w]ith respect to market access through . . . [all] modes of supply . . . , each Member shall accord services and service suppliers of another Member treatment no less favourable than that provided for under the terms, limitations and conditions agreed and specified in its schedule." This article then partly overlaps the national treatment provisions, for national treatment covers any form of discrimination against foreign supplies. This overlap is a source of some confusion (Hoekman 1995, 347). But the provisions of the market-access article extend beyond those of national treatment to measures that restrict access but that do not discriminate against foreigners as such (Hoekman 1995, 334; Snape and Bosworth 1996). In this regard they extend into what, on a broad definition of the term, is part of competition policy—that part which relates to government regulation of competition in specific service sectors.

The article relating to monopolies and exclusive service suppliers provides that monopoly suppliers (or exclusive service suppliers) should not be allowed by a member to "act in a manner inconsistent with that Member's obligations" under the agreement, and that where a monopoly supplier is competing outside the scope of its monopoly, the member should ensure that the monopoly "does not abuse its monopoly position to act in its territory in a manner inconsistent" with the member's obligations under the GATS. The "business practices" article contains very weak provisions—consultation and information—regarding business practices that may restrict competition and trade.

Like national treatment, the market-access and monopoly provisions apply only to the service sectors for which specific obligations have been undertaken. (The monopoly provisions also relate to nondiscrimination among foreigners.) The market-access article also contains provisions that constrain the use of a number of quantitative restrictions on supply for all service sectors for which specific commitments are undertaken, and which, with one exception (this relating to foreign capital), appear to apply equally to national and foreign suppliers.[4]

Thus these three articles (and particularly the market-access and monopolies articles) take the GATS well beyond the provisions of the GATT with respect to barriers to supply that do not discriminate against foreign suppliers as such. The GATT is almost entirely concerned with relations between us and them; these provisions of the GATS are not concerned with us and them but between "some of us" on the one hand and "the rest of us and them" on the other.

Barriers to access can be applied directly—that is, on the product or service itself—or through the means of transacting, or through the means of payment for the transaction. For cross-border trade in goods, air, sea, rail, or road transport is essential. Means to pay for the products is also essential. In the above discussion I have focused on direct rather than indirect barriers. Barriers to means of transport or means of payment are indirect barriers to trade in goods. Similarly, barriers to these forms of transport, and to payment, also provide indirect barriers to trade in services as well as being direct barriers to the trade in transport or financial services in themselves. In addition, barriers to access to electronic transmission facilities also provide barriers to the cross-frontier "transport" of services as well as being barriers to telecommunications and other services in themselves. Viewed in this way telecommunications is just another form of transportation, though one that is particularly important for cross-border trade in services.

Transport services receive little attention in the GATT, apart from the national treatment provisions requiring that internal transportation charges should not discriminate against foreigners (article III:4), and provisions requir-

---

4. These apply to limitations on the number of service suppliers, on the value of service transactions or assets, on the total number of service operations or the quantity of service output, on the number of people employed, and on foreign capital or shareholding, and requirements for specific types of legal entity or joint venture.

ing freedom of transit for goods. Transport by air, sea, and basic telecommunications has proved to be a particularly difficult area for negotiation under the GATS and within regional trade agreements also, as have financial services.

10.4   Product Coverage

As table 10.1 illustrates, the coverage of the GATS is in principle very much broader than the GATT. In this sense it is a more general agreement. But this breadth of coverage has been secured at a cost in terms of the ease by which particular service sectors can be excluded from the major provisions of the GATS. Under the GATT all products are covered by the general provisions, and exclusion of products from such coverage occurs only in special circumstances (for example, the waivers for many agricultural products that were secured by the United States and European countries). Under the GATS, however, many of the most important provisions apply only to the service sectors specified in the schedules of members, and unlike the GATT, even the MFN principle can be implemented, in the first instance, on a conditional rather than an unconditional basis for specific measures. From this perspective the GATS is a much less general agreement than the GATT.

For the purpose of scheduled commitments for "products" under the GATS, services have been divided into 161 sectors, for example, legal, data-processing, research and development on natural sciences, real estate on a fee or contract basis, advertising, photographic, postal, rail transport, cargo-handling, and so on. Specific commitments are recorded in members' schedules for these sectors; if a sector is not scheduled, there are no restrictions on the forms or extent of the barriers to market access that can be maintained or imposed on that sector.

Any measure restricting access to service markets must be nondiscriminatory between foreign member suppliers unless it was listed as an exemption to nondiscrimination at the time the agreement came into force. This date was 1 January 1995 but because negotiations were extended beyond that date for many key sectors, the date was extended for these sectors. Such exemptions from unconditional MFN treatment do not exist under the GATT.[5] Under the GATS they are to be reviewed after no more than five years and "in principle" are to continue for no more than ten years.

Thus as far as MFN is concerned, the GATS applies a negative listing approach; all measures for all sectors are covered unless specifically exempted, and then in principle only for a limited time. On the other hand the national treatment and market-access provisions are on a positive list basis with respect to sectoral coverage; sectors are not covered unless they are listed. Once listed,

---

5. GATT exemptions from MFN were not possible (apart from free trade areas, customs unions, grandfathered preferences and for and between developing countries, and the nonapplication provisions of article XXXV) until the Uruguay Round, when limited selectivity for article XIX safeguard measures was introduced.

however, a mainly negative listing approach is adopted with respect to national treatment. Under the national treatment provisions there can be no discrimination against foreign supplies except in the manners specified for the scheduled sectors.

Under the market-access article, access (for each mode of supply) is to be no less favorable than specified in members' schedules—a positive listing approach. And for those sectors for which market-access commitments are undertaken (positive listing), a number of quantitative restrictions are prohibited unless scheduled (negative listing). The list of quantitative restrictions is not exhaustive (Hoekman 1995, 339); any other restrictions on access would have to be constrained on a positive-list basis.

The positive-listing approach to *any* constraint on restrictions on barriers is in part the price for the coverage of all modes of delivery. It is also due to the complexity of regulations in some service sectors—for example, telecommunications and financial services—and the protection of turf by regulators. But it greatly inhibits the transparency of the barriers that exist for services trade: this may contrasted with the North American Free Trade Agreement (NAFTA) and the Closer Economic Relations Agreement between Australia and New Zealand, both of which adopt a negative-listing approach. (In regard to positive and negative listing of sectors, the experience of the Canada-U.S. Free Trade Agreement, which had positive listing, as well as the GATS negotiations, influenced the negotiations for NAFTA [Hoekman and Sauvé 1994; Snape and Bosworth 1996].) If a sector or a part of a sector is not scheduled, then there is no disclosure at all with respect to the barriers to trade in that sector or subsector.

The possibility of MFN exemptions together with the positive listing of sectors and the practice of scheduling commitments by mode of supply for each sector (which as Sauvé [1995] and Hoekman [1995, 351], state, is not actually required by the GATS), introduces a very strong sectoral bias to the negotiations under the GATS. Sector-specific reciprocity, and even mode-of-supply sector-specific reciprocity is encouraged. The sectoral trade-offs which can remove major stumbling blocks are particularly difficult to secure when negotiations are sector-specific. Sector-specific negotiations are highly susceptible to being blocked or distorted (for example, to favor one mode of delivery over another) by vested interests (including regulators) who are able to mount effective campaigns designed to focus attention on the costs to the particular sector or mode of trade liberalization, rather than the gains to other sectors, and to the economy in general, of such reforms. The difficulties here have been accentuated by the stand-alone sector-specific negotiations that have extended into 1997.

On the other hand, the inclusion of particularly difficult sectors in cross-sectoral negotiations can impede liberalization in other sectors—the exclusion of much of agriculture and textiles and clothing from general GATT coverage and negotiations facilitated progress in liberalization in other areas. The difficult nuts of agriculture and textiles and clothing were only cracked in the context of negotiations much broader than those previously undertaken under GATT auspices, in the Uruguay Round. The optimum bundling of issues for successful negotiations—providing opportunities for trade-offs on the one hand and avoiding stumbling blocks on the other—is touched on by Judith Goldstein (chap. 4 in this volume).

Quite apart from the sector-specific nature of the negotiations, trade-offs are inherently more difficult to negotiate in services than goods (Hoekman 1995). First, tariffs on goods provide a continuum for negotiation—a 60 percent tariff is negotiable to all levels between 60 and 0. But barriers to trade in services, which are seldom in a price-based form comparable to tariffs on goods, are less quantifiable and are often subject to significant bureaucratic interpretation. They are frequently embedded in domestic regulations that restrict domestic as well as foreign access and often are justified on grounds such as consumer rather than producer protection. A second, and related point, is that some demandeurs in services are addressing negotiated reciprocity not in terms of the extent of market opening, as has been the tradition in GATT negotiations, but in terms of market openness. This interpretation of reciprocity places a particularly heavy political-economy burden on countries with closed service markets.

10.5   Negotiations and Commitments

While securing a services agreement was an achievement, the progress in actually liberalizing services trade under the auspices of the GATS has been very limited to date.[6] Little more than limited standstill commitments within sectors already open has been achieved even by those countries making significant commitments, though for some countries the telecommunications agreement, which was concluded in February 1997, involved significant commitments to market opening.

Most developed countries have made sectoral commitments in more than 70 sectors while the United States, members of the European Union (EU), Japan, Switzerland, and Austria have made commitments for more than 100 sectors, as compared with a maximum of around 150.[7] Transition economies made commitments in about half of all sectors, with developing countries only 16 percent (Low 1995; Altinger and Enders 1996, tables 2, 3). (These data and those in the next paragraph predate the conclusions of the telecommunications and financial services agreements.)

These overall sectoral commitment numbers are poor indicators of the coverage of services production. To illustrate the limited extent of the coverage of

---

6. This section in particular draws on Snape and Bosworth (1996).
7. This figure is less than the previously mentioned 161, as several financial sectors were combined.

commitments, reference can be made to Australia, not because it is out of step in its commitments, but simply because calculations have been made at the Industry Commission of the production coverage of its commitments. Australia has made commitments in more than eighty sectors. But it has been estimated that prior to the telecommunications agreement only one-fifth of its total production of services was covered by liberalizing obligations—bound commitments not to maintain nonconforming measures—and these commitments are biased heavily toward services already relatively open (Industry Commission 1995, 189–214).[8] Major sectors—at least some of which are known to have highly restrictive trade measures—were excluded from Australia's schedule, or subject to unbound commitments. Other countries' schedules have similar characteristics.

Analysis of GATS schedules for combined economies of the Asia-Pacific Economic Cooperation (APEC) indicates that well over two-thirds of possible service markets—defined as each mode of supply in each service sector in each APEC economy—may be impeded (APEC 1995, 72). Cross-border supply is the least restricted mode of supply within APEC economies as a group, while the presence of natural persons is the most constrained mode of supply.

When the WTO and hence the GATS come into operation on 1 January 1995, negotiations were largely incomplete in the key areas of telecommunications, financial services, maritime transport, and the movement of natural persons.[9] A timetable was established for extending these negotiations.

The results of the *financial services agreement*—concluded on 28 July 1995 with an interim agreement and then only after a one-month extension—were unsatisfactory. The United States insisted that offers from other countries were inadequate, and invoked an MFN exemption for the entire financial services sector, refusing to join the interim agreement, though leaving its offer on the table. Twenty-nine countries (counting the EU as one) of the seventy-six WTO members that made commitments in the financial services sector improved their offers during the extended negotiations and became members of the interim agreement.[10] Although some concessions were made to relax foreign equity participation and operational restrictions, these remain well below those needed to open financial markets significantly. Most developing countries still

8. A quarter of Australia's services production, including coastal shipping, was excluded outright from its specific GATS commitments, while those sectors scheduled for which no obligations were made to provide market access or national treatment—thereby allowing existing restrictions to continue and new ones to be introduced—represented a further 55 percent of Australian services production. Under the telecommunications agreement Australia committed itself to significant liberalization policies that had already been implemented or announced.

9. The EU, largely at the insistence of the French government, excluded the audiovisual sector from MFN treatment. The EU (along with some other members) thus made no sectoral commitments in this sector, and may impose discriminatory or nondiscriminatory measures in the entire audiovisual sector. However, it will be the subject of future negotiations.

10. These offers are to be implemented until 1 November 1997, after which members will have sixty days to negotiate further amendments to specific offers on financial services, or to take MFN exemptions.

have not scheduled all their financial services sectors, and thus many elements of financial services remain completely unbound.

Negotiations on the *movement of natural persons,* aimed at achieving better temporary entry of senior executives and professionals supplying services, also concluded unsatisfactorily on 28 July 1995. There are no plans to resume them.

Negotiations on *basic telecommunications,* initially due to conclude on 30 April 1996, were suspended in June of that year but then were brought to a successful conclusion in February 1997. The suspension occurred when the United States claimed that only ten out of the thirty-four country offers presented were acceptable, the United States being particularly concerned with "one-way bypass" or the ability of a monopoly supplier in another country to exploit the competitive conditions in the U.S. market to secure monopoly returns on the traffic between the United States and its own country (Hoekman, Low, and Mavroidis 1996). But with some significantly improved offers, sixty-nine countries, embracing over 90 percent of the basic telecommunications business of WTO members, reached an agreement, to be implemented on 1 January 1998.

A set of regulatory principles (including the establishment of independent regulators, terms for interconnection, and promises not to engage in anticompetitive cross-subsidization) were agreed, as were commitments to significant market opening by many countries. For some countries, including those of the EU, the United States, and Australia, the commitments largely involved the locking in of competition reforms that had already been implemented or announced. But others, including the Philippines, Thailand, and Singapore, made significant new commitments. Several developing countries and the United States lodged exceptions to MFN, the latter with respect to direct-to-home transmission and digital broadcasting by satellite.

No agreement on *maritime transport services* was achieved by the deadline of 30 June 1996. Negotiations have been suspended until 2000 when a further round of comprehensive negotiations on trade in services is scheduled. Of the forty-two governments participating in the negotiations, only twenty-four (including the EU as a single entity) tabled offers. The United States refused to make an offer in the negotiations.

10.6   Lessons?

It is arguable that the GATS is too general in one dimension—modes of delivery and forms of barrier to access—and not general enough in another—obligations. It is arguable also that reducing the former dimension of generality could increase what could be achieved in the latter.

10.6.1   Breadth of Coverage: Investment, Competition Policy, and People

International investment and competition policy (including under this latter heading government-legislated barriers to entry, provision of access to essential facilities, and regulation of restrictive trade practices) have proved to be particularly difficult areas for multilateral negotiation of binding commitments, and even difficult within the relative homogeneity of the Organization for Economic Cooperation and Development (OECD). Yet both of these subjects are embraced by the GATS. In many respects the problems to be addressed in investment and competition policies are not specific to services trade but are as applicable to goods trade as to services trade. Probably they are both more amenable to negotiation as separate agreements under the WTO, covering goods as well as services trade, rather than as parts of goods or services agreements. The movement of people also is probably best left to separate negotiations, involving as it does much broader social and political questions than are generally addressed in trade negotiations.

These excisions would then leave for services trade negotiations the same topics that are covered by the GATT—cross-border trade and measures that discriminate between domestic and foreign suppliers (between us and them). Thus referring to the lower panel in table 10.1, the GATS would cover cells 1, 2, and, to the same extent as the GATT, cell 4; an investment agreement would cover cells 4 and 5 in both parts of the table, the movement of people would cover cells 7 and 8, while a competition policy agreement (covering government regulations and enterprise behavior) would embrace cells 3, 6, and 9.

The reduction of coverage to measures that discriminate between domestic and foreign suppliers (and among foreign suppliers) would imply the removal of the market-access and other competition policy articles from the GATS. (The introduction of a nullification and impairment article similar to article XXIII of the GATT could be introduced to cope with government actions intended to frustrate liberalization commitments.) The market-access article does not appear to add anything to the provisions of the national treatment article insofar as discrimination between foreign and domestic supplies is concerned, and removing it would remove an overlap and confusion with respect to these discriminatory measures.

10.6.2   Breadth of Coverage: Difficult Sectors

As noted, there are two major areas in which the obligations under the GATS are less general and binding than under the GATT: MFN and national treatment. MFN exceptions can be taken, and have been taken, for measures applying to major service sectors—in particular financial services, basic telecommunications, shipping, and audiovisual. (The main part of air transport services is effectively excluded by an annex to the GATS itself.) Removing investment from the coverage of the GATS should facilitate multilateral agreement on those financial services that would still remain under its coverage, but for the other areas major difficulties would remain. As mentioned above, under the GATT, much of agricultural and clothing and textiles effectively remained out of the coverage of the general rules for decades, and they returned to the fold (though this has yet to be fully tested) only in the context of the very broad trade-offs that were achieved in the Uruguay Round. So under the GATS it may take considerable time, and possibly very broad trade-offs, to secure the application of MFN to the service sectors for which broad exceptions from MFN have been taken.

This implies that financial services, telecommunications, maritime and air transport, and perhaps audiovisual services may indeed best be negotiated separately from other services, being brought into cross-sectoral negotiations and trade-offs as part of a much broader set of negotiations than can occur under the GATS.

10.6.3   Cross-Border Trade

Perhaps more tractable, and important, is the lack of generality of national treatment and the positive listing of sectors for which specific commitments are made. As mentioned above, the lack of distinction between frontier measures and internal measures that discriminate between national and foreign supplies of services implies that full national treatment would imply free trade in services. Under the GATT, internal measures that so discriminate are proscribed; so also are all frontier measures apart from tariffs, except in stated circumstances. The effect of these proscriptions is that there is only one form of generally sanctioned discrimination against foreign suppliers—import tariffs—which then is the object of specific commitments (bindings) and negotiations. To secure national treatment as a general obligation under the GATS, a small set of sanctioned forms of discrimination against foreigners could be necessary, these being the subject of specific obligations, with national treatment as a general obligation for all other measures that would discriminate between domestic and foreign service supplies (Snape 1994; Hoekman 1995, 349–50). National treatment could then be addressed as a general obligation on a negative-list basis—all sectors would be covered and all measures that lay outside the "sanctioned" list could be applied only if they were explicitly listed (and accepted in negotiations) as exceptions. With respect to the sanctioned exceptions, they could be addressed in the same way as tariffs under the GATT—on a positive-list basis when bindings are negotiated. This approach would be greatly facilitated if the breadth of coverage of the GATS were to be reduced as suggested in sections 10.6.1 and 10.6.2.

The key question is what these sanctioned barriers should be. For cross-border trade in many if not most services, tariff-like charges would be quite feasible (Deardorff 1994; Hoekman 1995, 349–50). Examples would be taxes on foreign television programs transmitted locally (rather than quantitative limitations), taxes on life or health insurance placed abroad (rather than prohibition), taxes on data processing undertaken abroad, and so on. Of course there may be many implementation difficulties, but generally these would be no more difficult to police than quantitative restrictions or prohibitions on cross-border trade (UNCTAD and World Bank 1994, chap. 6).[11] But even if practical, the idea of converting all nonprice measures into price measures may be too bold for all cross-border service transactions. Thus the possibility of a limited number of sanctioned nonprice measures perhaps should be entertained, if that is what is required to secure negative listing for the coverage of service sectors and of nonsanctioned barriers and the advantages of relative liberalization and transparency that would accompany such listing.

10.6.4   NAFTA as a Model

Much of what has been suggested—other than the legitimization of a restricted number of frontier measures—is close to what has been adopted in NAFTA. In that agreement there are separate chapters for investment and competition policy (including monopolies and state enterprises), which cover both goods and services, for temporary movement of business persons, for telecommunications and financial services, and for cross-border trade in services. Special provisions also apply to air and maritime services. As noted above, the general approach in NAFTA to cross-border trade in services is one of negative listing, in contrast to the earlier Canada-U.S. Free Trade Agreement. NAFTA could provide the model for a substantial recasting of the GATS when it comes up for review. What has been achieved in telecommunications and financial services could stand as separate agreements; what has been achieved in investment commitments in services could provide the basis for more general investment agreement covering goods and services. And an agreement on competition policy would provide the basis for removing the market-access article from a services agreement—there is no market-access article in NAFTA.

References

Altinger, Laura, and Alice Enders. 1996. The Scope and Depth of GATS Commitments. *World Economy* 19, no. 3: 307–32.
Bhagwati, Jagdish. 1984. Splintering and Disembodiment of Services and Developing Countries. *World Economy* 7, no. 2: 133–44.
Croome, John. 1995. *Reshaping the World Trading System: A History of the Uruguay Round.* Geneva: World Trade Organization.
Deardorff, Alan. 1994. Market Access. In *The New World Trading System: Readings.* Paris: OECD.
Hoekman, Bernard. 1995. Assessing the General Agreement on Trade and Services. In *The Uruguay Round and the Developing Countries,* ed. Will Martin and L. Alan Winters, chap. 10. World Bank Discussion Papers no. 307. Washington, DC: World Bank.

11. While it is difficult to think of cross-border service transactions in which the difficulties of implementation of nonprice measures are not as great as price measures, it may be easier, for example, to detect the existence of equipment that can receive foreign transmissions, and restrict or tax its installation, than it is to monitor the receipt of transmissions themselves.

Hoekman, Bernard, Patrick Low, and Petros Mavroidis. 1996. Antitrust Disciplines and Market Access Negotiations: Lessons from the Telecommunications Sector. Paper presented at the Oslo Competition conference, "Competition Policies for Integrated World Economy," 13–14 June.

Hoekman, Bernard M., and Petros C. Mavroidis. 1994. Competition, Competition Policy, and the GATT. *World Economy* 17, no. 2: 121–50.

Hoekman, Bernard, and Pierre Sauvé. 1994. *Liberalizing Trade in Services.* World Bank Discussion Paper no. 243. Washington, DC: World Bank.

Industry Commission. 1995. *Annual Report, 1994–1995.* Appendix G. Canberra: Australian Government Publishing Service.

Low, Patrick. 1995. Impact of the Uruguay Round on Asia: Trade in Services and Trade Related Investment Measures. Paper presented at the Asian Development Bank conference, "Emerging Global Environment and Developing Asia," Manila, 29–30 May.

Pacific Economic Cooperation Council. 1995. *Survey of Impediments to Trade and Investment in the APEC Region.* Report by the Pacific Economic Cooperation Council for APEC. Singapore: APEC.

Sampson, Gary, and Richard H. Snape. 1985. Identifying the Issues in Trade in Services. *World Economy* 8, no. 2: 171–81.

Sauvé, Pierre. 1995. The General Agreement on Trade in Services: Much Ado about What? In *Trains, Grains, and Automobiles: Canadian Perspectives on the Uruguay Round,* ed. Daniel A. Schwanen. Toronto: C. D. Howe Institute.

Snape, Richard H. 1994. Services and the Uruguay Round. In *The New World Trading System: Readings.* Paris: OECD.

Snape, Richard H., and Malcolm Bosworth. 1996. Advancing Services Negotiations. In *The World Trading System: Challenges Ahead,* ed. Jeffrey J. Schott, 185–203. Washington, DC: Institute for International Economics.

United Nations Conference on Trade and Development and World Bank. 1994. *Liberalizing International Transactions in Services: A Handbook.* UNCTAD Programme on Transnational Corporations, with the World Bank, International Economic Department. New York: United Nations.

Comment on the Paper by Richard H. Snape
Robert E. Baldwin

As Richard Snape points out in his introductory sentence, the inclusion of a General Agreement on Trade in Services (GATS) as one of the WTO agreements was a major achievement. What is so remarkable is the scope of the agreement. Trade in services is defined not only as the supply of a service from one country to another (cross-border trade in services) but as the supply of a service to a consumer from another country who moves to the country supplying the service, as the supply of a service by a supplier from one country who establishes a commercial presence in another country, and as the supply of services by natural persons who move temporarily to another country. The

Robert E. Baldwin is the Hilldale Professor of Economics at the University of Wisconsin, Madison, and a research associate of the National Bureau of Economic Research.

rules in the agreement cover competition, investment, and access policies within countries as well as border policies that discriminate against foreigners. As Snape emphasizes, however, the broad nature of the policies covered comes at the cost of committing to liberalize only in those service sectors specifically listed in schedules of members and of permitting conditional most-favored-nation (MFN) status.

To date, I think all would agree that progress toward meaningful liberalization in the areas covered by the agreement has been disappointing. Snape illustrates this point with data on the extent of liberalization by Australia.

It is Snape's thesis that the very breadth of the coverage of the GATS is a major cause of the problem. He points out how difficult it has been to obtain binding commitments among even the developed countries in the areas of domestic competition and investment policies as they apply to goods and suggests that, because these policies are closely tied in the agreement to other aspects of liberalization in services, for example, liberalization of cross-border trade in services, we should not be surprised at the lack of progress in all aspects of the supply of services. His recommendation is to delink competition and investment policies as well as policies dealing with the temporary movement of people from the GATS and leave these topics for separate negotiations aimed at producing plurilateral rather than multilateral agreements and covering goods as well as services. This would leave the same subjects for services negotiations as are now covered in the negotiations on goods, namely, cross-border trade and other measures that discriminate between domestic and foreign suppliers. The stricter provisions in the GATT relating to MFN and national treatment could then be applied in the services sector.

This is a bold and imaginative proposal. However, while it might result in a stricter application of the MFN principle to the services trade covered by the narrower agreement, I wonder if it does not define away the key issues that were driving the Uruguay Round negotiations. As I understand the history of these negotiations, the business interests who pushed for negotiations on services were mainly concerned about restrictions that limited their ability to deliver services from facilities they established within other countries. Moreover, even those who supplied services on a cross-border basis were concerned about the ability of foreign governments to impose restrictions on the delivery of their services within the countries to which they were sent. In other words, all groups of service suppliers argued that it was impossible to achieve meaningful liberalization in services without including such matters as investment and competition policy. Moreover, it is not enough that discrimination against foreigners be eliminated. For example, it does not help new foreign suppliers of services to eliminate discrimination between foreigner and domestic suppliers with respect to investment if a government limits new investment in a market for both domestic and foreign suppliers or if it permits collusive business practices among a few existing domestic and foreign suppliers that can, in effect, freeze out all new suppliers. Consequently, I doubt if the groups that pressed for negotiations in this field would support Snape's proposal.

Dropping investment and competition policies from the agreement might also undermine the balance of concessions achieved across different issue areas that was so important in the Uruguay Round. Achieving a broadly framed agreement in services was one of the reasons that some of the advanced industrial countries were willing to make important concessions in the textile/apparel field and in agriculture. If services trade is now defined to cover only cross-border trade in services, these governments may be less willing to implement their agreements in these other issue areas.

I certainly agree with Snape that it has been very difficult to obtain binding agreements in the competition and investment areas, but I do not see why we cannot still keep the agreement as broad as it is, while focusing on liberalizing in those areas that are most feasible. Then, when we have liberalized the most feasible measures, we can move into these more difficult areas. If we take the difficult areas out of the agreement now, we may never get them back in. It may be true that simply having these provisions in the agreement is impairing feasible liberalization, but I would want to see more evidence on this point before drastically limiting the coverage of the GATS.

11   Imposing Multilateral Discipline on Administered Protection

Robert E. Baldwin

11.1 Introduction

In the last twenty-five years, the achievement of "fair" trade has become the centerpiece of trade policy in a number of advanced industrial countries. The following statement by President Reagan (1985, 1) typifies the view of political leaders in these countries: "I believe that if trade is not fair for all, then trade is 'free' in name only. I will not stand by and watch American businesses fail because of unfair trading practices abroad. I will not stand by and watch American workers lose their jobs because other nations do not play by the rules."

This paper examines two of the most important international rules designed to achieve fair trade: the antidumping (AD) and countervailing-duty (CVD) rules of the GATT/WTO. One purpose is to assess whether the current rules are being used not simply to address broadly supported concerns about fairness in international trade but for rent-seeking purposes that are inconsistent with generally accepted notions of fairness. A second objective is to recommend changes in these international rules if it appears that they are being used for purposes for which they were not intended.

As a means of better understanding both the intended purposes of these rules and how they might be misused, section 11.2 presents a brief history of the manner in which AD and CVD laws and administrative practices have developed over time both in the GATT/WTO and in the country that has become the leading proponent of tighter unfair trade laws, namely, the United States. Section 11.3 surveys the analytical and empirical literature concerning the motiva-

Robert E. Baldwin is the Hilldale Professor of Economics at the University of Wisconsin, Madison, and a research associate of the National Bureau of Economic Research.

The author is grateful for the helpful comments of his discussants, J. Michael Finger and Chong Hyun Nam, and other participants in the conference.

tions for dumping and subsidization, the economic impact of these practices, and the effects of AD and CVD. Particular attention is devoted to the recent insights gained by considering dumping and subsidization under imperfectly competitive market conditions. Section 11.4 first draws various policy-relevant conclusions from the previous two sections and then proposes specific changes in the current international AD and CVD rules. A final section summarizes the main conclusions and recommendations.

11.2 A Brief History of Administered Protection

11.2.1 Enactment of the Basic U.S. Laws

A political-economy framework is helpful in understanding the various changes over the years in both U.S. and GATT/WTO AD and CVD laws and rules, as well as in the degree to which they have been enforced.[1] In such a framework, public policies are viewed as determined through the political interactions between government officials and private common-interest groups. In making the final decisions concerning the nature of these policies, government officials are constrained by their desire to be reelected yet are also motivated by ideological concerns relating to various economic and social goals, whereas private-interest groups seek to maximize their own economic welfare. In lobbying public officials for economic policies that increase their economic welfare, interest groups pledge the campaign funds and votes needed to achieve the election goals of the politicians. Government officials then select the set of policies that best achieves the particular manner in which they weigh the relative importance of their election objectives and their ideologically based economic and social goals. If an international agreement, such as a new GATT/WTO trading rule, is being negotiated, the decision-making process also involves a bargaining process between the home country's officials and those of other countries.

A special feature of the protective actions taken under the AD and CVD laws is that the particular level of protection that can be imposed is determined by agencies of the executive branch of the government within broad guidelines set forth in these laws. Given the considerable leeway on the part of the administering agencies in deciding the extent of assistance warranted in a particular case, a significant part of the efforts of political pressure groups who hope to gain from this form of protection is directed at writing the laws and formulating the administrative rules and procedures in such a manner that administrators are forced to grant the protection they seek. These groups also direct their political efforts at placing in key administrative posts individuals who are sym-

---

1. The pioneering analysis of administered protection in political economy terms is Finger, Hall, and Nelson (1982). See Baldwin (1996) for an elaboration of the political-economy framework used here.

pathetic to their particular goals or at least to the general protective purposes of the relevant laws and rules.

Current U.S. trade laws dealing with unfair competition can be traced back to the CVD provisions in the Tariff Act of 1897 and the AD law of 1916. Enacted in reaction to foreign subsidization of sugar exports, the 1897 CVD provision states that "whenever any country . . . shall pay or bestow, directly or indirectly, any bounty or grant upon the exportation of any article or merchandise . . . , and such article or merchandise is dutiable . . . , there shall be levied and paid . . . an additional duty equal to the net amount of such bounty or grant."[2] The secretary of the treasury was charged with determining the net amount of the bounty and making various regulations needed to administer the law.

The 1916 AD law represented an effort to strengthen the enforcement of the antitrust laws in international commerce and, in particular, was aimed at the predatory pricing practices of certain foreign cartels.[3] It states that "it shall be unlawful for any person importing . . . any articles from a foreign country into the United States to . . . sell . . . such articles within the United States at a price substantially less than the actual market value . . . in the principal markets of the country of their production, or of other foreign countries to which they are commonly exported . . . : *Provided,* That such act or acts be done with the intent of destroying or injuring an industry . . . or preventing the establishment of an industry . . . or of restraining or monopolizing any part of the trade and commerce in such articles."[4] Individuals or businesses could sue those allegedly violating these provisions in federal court, seeking threefold the damage sustained. Thus, while the CVD law was established at the outset as a form of administered protection, the AD law was initially to be enforced through the court system in a manner similar to the antitrust laws.

In 1921 a new law was passed that turned AD enforcement into a form of administered protection. The background to its enactment is as follows. The U.S. Tariff Commission, which had been established in 1916, began a survey of U.S. businesses in that year to determine the extent of dumping by foreign producers, and in its 1919 report recommended an AD law patterned after a 1904 Canadian AD law that was administered by the executive branch of the government rather than being implemented through the courts. This recommendation was not adopted by the Wilson administration, but it appealed to the Republicans, who had regained control of the presidency in 1920 and had retained their majority in Congress. Because of their strong ideological commitment to protectionist policies, reversing the downward trend in tariffs that had taken place during the Wilson administration was an important goal of the new administration. A recession in 1921 that resulted in an especially sharp

2. Tariff Act of 1897, 55th Cong., sess. 1, 1897, chap. 11, p. 205.
3. See Finger (1993) for a discussion of the relation of the 1916 AD law to U.S. antitrust laws.
4. U.S. Statutes, vol. 39, 64th Cong., sess. 1, 1916, chap. 463, title VIII, p. 798.

decline in the prices of agricultural goods lent urgency to this task and caused President Harding to send a message to Congress urging "instant tariff enactment" (reported in Kelly 1963). Consequently, an emergency tariff bill was drawn up that significantly raised protection on agricultural products for a period of six months (later extended until the duties of the Tariff Act of 1922 entered into effect). In testimony before the House Ways and Means and Senate Finance Committees, many manufacturing firms also pressed for increased protection, but they were told that the lengthy hearings involved in a complete revision of the tariff schedule would prevent the agricultural sector from receiving the assistance it needed immediately (Senate 1921). However, hearings were also started for the permanent increases in tariff rates that took place under the Tariff Act of 1922. Since no one had received protection (and has not to this date received protection) under the 1916 AD act (mainly because of the difficulty of proving intent to destroy or injure an industry), it seems likely that an AD provision was added to the 1921 emergency tariff legislation not only to rectify this situation but also to mollify manufacturers for failing to increase their levels of protection at that time.

The AD act of 1921 differs from the 1916 AD act in four important ways. First, the secretary of the treasury rather than the federal court (under rules of evidence and due process) determines whether injurious dumping has occurred. Second, dumping is defined more precisely as selling an imported good domestically at a price less than its foreign market value or, in the absence of such value, less than its cost of production. Third, there is no requirement that the dumper must intend to destroy a domestic industry. For a favorable decision for a domestic industry, the secretary of the treasury need find only that the dumping is injuring or likely to injure the industry or preventing its establishment. Finally, instead of triple damages being imposed on importers, the action taken is to assess a special duty equal to the margin of dumping.

An important change in the CVD law also occurred in this early period of the new Republican administration. Section 303 of the 1922 tariff act broadened the group of foreign subsidies that could be countervailed from just export subsidies to subsidies to the manufacture or production of any article. The language of the 1922 CVD law was also included as section 303 in the Tariff Act of 1930. It should be noted that neither the 1897 nor 1922/1930 provisions required that a domestic industry be injured before the additional duty could be imposed.

11.2.2 Early Enforcement

Between 1897 and the Tariff Act of 1930 CVDs were imposed only twelve times, while between 1921 and 1934 there were fifty-four findings of dumping (an average of about four per year).[5] However, after the Democrats regained the presidency as well as both houses of Congress in 1932 and embarked on a

---

5. The CVD figure is from Hufbauer and Erb (1984, 15), and the source for the AD figure is testimony by O. R. Strackbein at the hearings on amendments to the Antidumping Act of 1921, (House 1957, 134).

trade liberalization program under the Trade Agreements Act of 1934, the number of successful AD cases declined significantly, even though the AD law was not changed. For the entire twenty-year period between 1934 and 1954 only seven findings of injurious dumping were made (House 1957, 15). Thus, of the 146 AD cases investigated during this time, only 5 percent led to additional duties being imposed. A finding of no dumping was made in about 60 percent of the cases, no injury was found in another 15 percent, and either a determination of negligible imports was made or the complainant's allegation was withdrawn in the remaining 20 percent.

These figures bring out a key point about administered protection. The extent to which protection is granted under laws administered in this manner depends largely on the protectionist versus free trade predilections of those administering the AD and CVD laws, in addition to the specific provisions in the statutes.

Republican legislators took action with this point in mind when they regained control of both houses of Congress in 1953. Long believing that the Treasury Department was much too lax in enforcing these unfair trade laws, they included a provision in the Customs Simplification Act of 1954 that transferred the determination of injury in AD cases from the Treasury to the International Trade Commission (ITC; then named the Tariff Commission), a semijudicial body. A 1958 amendment to the 1921 antidumping act increased the likelihood of affirmative injury decisions by stipulating that evenly divided votes by the ITC be deemed affirmative votes. The 1958 act also contained a number of technical amendments related to the definition and measurement of foreign market value and constructed value designed "to provide greater certainty, speed, and efficiency in the enforcement" of the 1921 act.

The number of AD cases filed with the Treasury Department following the shift of injury determination to the ITC rose to an average of about twenty-four per year during the rest of the 1950s (in contrast to an average of about seven per year for the previous twenty years), but only about 9 percent (in contrast to the 20 percent figure for the 1934–54 period) reached the injury determination stage (see table 11.1). Of the thirteen cases decided by the ITC, an affirmative determination was reached in only one instance—an injury determination rate even lower than during the previous twenty years. Thus, the efforts in the 1950s by the Republicans to enforce the AD law more vigorously were not successful.

Interestingly, it is only after the shift in political power from the Republicans to the Democrats as a result of the election of 1960 that we observe an increase in the number of AD cases reaching the ITC. Between 1960 and 1970, the number of AD cases filed with the Treasury was about the same as in the 1950s (twenty-three per year versus twenty-five per year) but 19 percent (in contrast to the 9 percent figure for the 1950s) went to the commission for injury determination, with thirteen (an average of slightly more than one per year), or 28 percent, of these cases being decided in the affirmative (see table 11.1). Records on subsidy investigations indicate that the Treasury Department imposed

Table 11.1   **U.S. Dumping Cases, 1954–79**

Year	Dumping Orders Issued	Petitions Initiated	Cases Closed by Department of the Treasury	ITC Investigations Cases Completed	Affirmative	Negative	Investigations Pending at the End of the Fiscal Year
1954	0	14	0	0[a]	0	0	0
1955	1	15	19	4	0	5	1
1956	1	18	28	3	1	2	0
1957	0	41	14	0	0	0	0
1958	0	13	25	2	0	2	0
1959	0	45	34	2	0	2	0
1960	0	33	33	2	0	2	1
1961	3	32	32	6	2	4	2
1962	1	16	16	4	1	3	0
1963	1	42	42	6	1	5	2
1964	2	27	28	8	2	6	3
1965	2	22	30	8	2	6	0
1966	0	16	16	2	0	2	2
1967	1	9	13	2	1	1	1
1968	1	13	11	1	1	0	2
1969	5	21	6	5	0	5	1
1970	3	23	23	5	3	2	1
1971	10	22	23	13	10	3	2
1972	15	39	36	18[b]	16	3	5
1973	8	27	42	23	8	15	7
1974	12	10	24	24	12	12	1
1975	1	10	N/A	7	1	5	2
1976	4	27	N/A	19	7	12	4
1977	4	19	N/A	22	15	7	N/A
1978	9	47	N/A	32	20	13	N/A
1979	15	30	N/A	26	19	7	5

Sources: "Petitions Initiated" (all years), "Cases Closed by Department of the Treasury" (all years), and "ITC Investigations" (1962–79) are from the *Annual Report of the Secretary of the Treasury* (various years) published by the Department of the Treasury. All other data are from the *Annual Report of the USITC* (various years) published by the ITC.

[a]Responsibility for injury determinations was transferred to the ITC via the Customs Simplification Act of 1954 and became effective 1 October 1954. Therefore, no cases were handled by the ITC in fiscal 1954.

[b]In 1972, investigation AA1921–85 (fishnets and netting from Japan) resulted in two decisions (affirmative for netting and negative for fishnets). As a result, "Cases Completed" does not equal the sum of "Affirmative and Negative" for 1972.

duties in only 12 of the 191 cases brought before this agency between 1934 and 1969 (Hufbauer and Erb 1984, 15; see also table 11.2 for the detailed record after 1954).

11.2.3 Early International Rules

Although officials within the Democrat administrations of the 1930s and 1940s placed a low priority on vigorous enforcement of the AD and CVD laws, they were instrumental in ensuring that the AD and CVD provisions in the ill-fated International Trade Organization (ITO) and its successor, the General Agreement on Tariffs and Trade (GATT), were patterned closely on U.S. law. Presumably they recognized that there was little chance of getting the ITO accepted by Congress unless rules similar to those in the United States were included. Moreover, although commercial treaties among nations with pledges of no subsidization were common, relatively few other nations (e.g., Canada, Australia, New Zealand, and South Africa) had AD laws, and U.S. negotiators may have wanted to ensure that other countries did not adopt laws on these matters less transparent than their own.[6]

The first major modification in GATT AD and CVD rules took place during the Kennedy Round of multilateral negotiations (1964–67), when an international AD code on the implementation of article VI of the GATT (the article on AD and CVDs) was successfully negotiated. More and more countries, including members of the European Union, were introducing AD measures, and U.S. officials wanted to ensure that these measures would not be used in an overly protectionist manner against U.S. exports. For example, they wanted to make sure that exporters accused of dumping had the right of access to all nonconfidential information bearing on their case and had a full opportunity to present evidence in rebuttal. In addition, they wished to tighten the "material injury" requirement in order to prevent countries from simply equating material injury with sales at less than the domestic price. Canada, in particular, did not have a formal "material injury" clause in its AD law.

At the same time, negotiators from a number of other countries were dissatisfied with the lengthy period required to process AD cases in the United States, especially the withholding of appraisement for customs purposes until a final decision on both dumping and material injury was reached. Even though only a very small number of dumping cases initiated resulted in the imposition of dumping duties, the uncertainty created during the period when the final duty rate was unknown acted, in the view of foreign exporters, as an unjustified nontariff barrier.

Both U.S. and foreign negotiators achieved their main objectives under the AD agreement negotiated. New provisions spelling out the manner in which evidence could be presented and examined met American concerns about the openness of the determination process, and a tightening of the material-injury clause required Canada to introduce an injury provision similar to that of other countries. Other countries' concerns about U.S. practices were satisfied by provisions stating that withholding of appraisement can be taken only when both a preliminary decision has been taken that there is dumping and there is sufficient evidence of injury. Furthermore, a period of ninety days was established as the time limit for withholding duty appraisement.[7]

---

6. See Seavey (1970) for a discussion of the history of formulating the AD and CVD provisions of the GATT.

7. Although executive branch officials believed that the president had the authority to negotiate the AD code without the approval of Congress, many members did not agree. As a consequence,

11.2.4   The Increasing Importance of Protection Based on
Unfair-Trading Grounds

From the time that the early AD and CVD laws were passed to the end of the Kennedy Round in 1967, unfair trade was not a major trade issue in the United States or in the GATT. The subject was rarely discussed by administration witnesses, either Democrat or Republican, in testimony on trade matters before congressional committees and was only raised occasionally by industry witnesses. Due to two developments, however, this situation began to change by the late 1960s. First, the United States, which had faced little competition in domestic and world markets in the late 1940s and the 1950s when most other industrial countries were struggling to regain their prewar productive capacities, began to encounter increasing competition from countries such as Japan and some of the newly industrializing economies. A surge of imports in the late 1960s adversely affected such industries as footwear, radios and television sets, motor vehicles and trucks, tires and inner tubes, semiconductors, earthenware table and kitchen articles, and even some steel items. The U.S. share of world manufacturing exports fell from 18.7 percent in 1959 to 13.4 percent by 1971.

The second development was the reduction in Cold War tensions. In the early postwar years, a liberal trade policy was justified by successive administrations as a means of strengthening the so-called free world and enabling countries better to resist the expansion of Soviet influence. For example, one of the listed purposes of the Trade Expansion Act of 1962 was "to prevent Communist economic penetration." Protectionists found it very difficult to resist continued trade liberalization when it was justified on national security grounds. However, while nuclear conflict with the Soviet Union was still a real threat in the late 1960s, the likelihood that the Communists could gain political control in a significant number of free-world countries seemed remote.

Thus, increasing import disruption in a number of important industries and the growing irrelevance of the traditional foreign policy argument for trade liberalization enabled protectionist pressure groups to become more successful in achieving their policy goals. Efforts to reintroduce traditional protectionism in 1970 through a system of import quotas (the Burke-Hartke bill) failed, but in the 1970s and 1980s the view that a significant part of the increasing competitive pressure on the United States was due to unfair foreign competition gradually gained the support of major public and private interests concerned with trade matters. Furthermore, both political parties, at the congressional and executive branch levels, adopted the view that greater protection against unfair trade actions by foreigners was desirable. Thus, as Krueger (1995) spells out

---

Congress enacted legislation prohibiting the Tariff Commission from following the code when it differed from existing U.S. legislation on AD.

in detail, we observe countries like the United States participating in efforts to reduce artificial barriers to what is considered to be fair trade, while undertaking actions that extend protection on grounds of unfair trade.

Under the leadership of key members of Congress, achieving fairness in international trade became a key goal of the Trade Agreements Act of 1974. One of its stated purposes is "to establish fairness and equity in international trading relations, including reform of the General Agreement on Tariffs and Trade" (Trade Agreements Act of 1974, 4). Besides providing the president with sweeping powers to deal with unfair trade practices under section 301, this act also contains amendments to the U.S. AD and CVD laws aimed at making it easier to gain protection via these laws. The most important change in the AD law was a provision that, in effect, finds dumping if a foreign exporter sells at prices below average total costs over an extended period. Other changes included the imposition of time limits on the decision-making process by the Treasury Department that significantly reduced its sometimes lengthy process of determining dumping or subsidization and a detailed specification of the deductions and additions permitted in calculating the exporter's sales price in AD cases. The CVD law was also broadened to cover duty-free articles as well as dutiable goods.

As a consequence of the Tokyo Round of multilateral trade negotiations (1973–79), in which the U.S. negotiators were authorized to participate under the Trade Agreements Act of 1974, both U.S. law and GATT rules on unfair trade were again changed in 1979.[8] Probably the most significant change was the U.S. acceptance of a material-injury clause in its CVD law. However, material injury was weakly defined in U.S. law as "harm which is not inconsequential, immaterial, or unimportant" (Trade Agreements Act of 1979). The term "material" injury and its definition were also included in the AD law of the United States.[9] One feature encouraging the more vigorous application of the CVD law was the enumeration in the amended U.S. law of a set of specific government actions that were to be regarded as actionable domestic subsidies. Other noteworthy changes were a further shortening of time requirements for dumping and subsidy investigations and the imposition of time requirements on the ITC for its injury determinations.

In the Tokyo Round agreements, the United States obtained acceptance by other GATT members of the notion that domestic subsidies may cause injury to domestic industries and that governments should seek to avoid such effects. But other language supporting the social and economic objectives of domestic subsidies weakened the effect of this provision. However, the United States was successful in weakening the language of the 1967 Antidumping Code re-

---

8. In the 1979 act, the AD and CVD laws were set forth as a new section (Title VII) of the Tariff Act of 1930. The original 1930 act did not contain a provision on AD.

9. Prior to 1979 just the term "injury" appeared in the law, although U.S. representatives at the GATT always maintained that the ITC interpreted this term to mean "material injury."

lating to the determination of injury. In return, the United States agreed to abide by the new code and to require a proof of material injury before imposing CVDs.

More important in accounting for the marked increase in the number of AD and CVD cases in the United States after 1979 than the specific provisions of the Trade Act of 1979 was a change in the manner in which the AD and CVD laws were administered that Congress pressured President Carter into accepting. The determination of dumping and subsidization was transferred from the Treasury Department, an agency traditionally in favor of liberal trade policies, to the Commerce Department, an agency that is more protectionist-oriented. In addition, Congress (specifically, the Senate Finance Committee and the Senate as a whole) began to use its confirmation powers to ensure that the top officials in the executive branch concerned with the administration of the AD and CVD laws as well as members of the ITC favored a more vigorous enforcement of these laws.

As noted earlier, the number of AD cases reaching the Tariff Commission in the 1960s averaged less than 5 per year, with only about one affirmative per year. The number of cases handled by the commission increased to an average of 20 per year from 1971 to 1979, even though the average number of cases initiated at the Treasury increased only slightly, from 23 to 26 annually.[10] More important, the number of cases in which material injury was found by the Tariff Commission increased to an average of 12 per year (table 11.1). The Treasury Department received 102 CVD petitions during this nine-year period and issued fourteen CVD orders (table 11.2). Beginning in 1980, the number of AD and CVD cases again increased significantly, with the number of AD petitions filed with the Commerce Department rising to about 43 annually from 1980 to 1994 (table 11.3). The number of cases on which the ITC reached an affirmative injury determination averaged 18 per year. Thus, while the volume of AD cases increased appreciably, the proportion of affirmative decisions to petitions filed fell somewhat, from about 46 percent to 42 percent. The number of CVD petitions filed rose to an average of about 26 per year over the 1980–94 period, with an average of 7.6 annually, or 29 percent, resulting in CVD orders (table 11.4).

Changes in U.S. AD and CVD laws in 1984, 1988, and 1994 indicate the continued successful efforts of sectors seeking protection through the unfair trade law to broaden the scope of the AD and CVD laws and prevent foreign exporters from circumventing the additional duties imposed.[11] Amendments in

10. The increase in AD cases investigated by the ITC may have been due in part to a provision of the Trade Act of 1974 directing the secretary of the treasury to forward to the commission within thirty days of receiving AD petitions those cases where the secretary has substantial doubt whether the affected industry is being injured. If, within thirty days of receiving the information from the treasury, the commission determines there is no reasonable indication that the industry is or is likely to be injured, the case is terminated.

11. For a more detailed description of the changes under these laws, see Nivola (1993) and Baldwin and Moore (1991).

Table 11.2   **U.S. Countervailing Duty Cases 1954–79**

Year	CVD Orders Issued	Petitions Initiated	Cases Closed by Department of the Treasury	ITC Investigations Cases Completed	Affirmative	Negative	Investigations Pending at the End of the Fiscal Year
1954	0	14	N/A	0	0	0	0
1955	1	17	7	0	0	0	0
1956	0	17	19	0	0	0	0
1957	0	12	13	0	0	0	0
1958	0	7	18	0	0	0	0
1959	1	6	5	0	0	0	0
1960	0	6	6	0	0	0	0
1961	0	0	2	0	0	0	0
1962	0	1	3	0	0	0	0
1963	0	1	2	0	0	0	0
1964	0	5	3	0	0	0	0
1965	0	2	3	0	0	0	0
1966	0	0	0	0	0	0	0
1967	1	0	0	0	0	0	0
1968	3	13	11	0	0	0	0
1969	3	14	3	0	0	0	0
1970	0	0	0	0	0	0	0
1971	2	0	1	0	0	0	0
1972	2	0	0	0	0	0	0
1973	3	0	3	0	0	0	0
1974	3	1	N/A	0	0	0	0
1975	3	32	N/A	0	0	0	0
1976	0	10	23	1	0	1	0
1977	0	16	N/A	0	0	0	0
1978	1	28	N/A	2	1	1	0
1979	0	15	N/A	7	0	7	0

Sources: "CVD Orders Issued," "Petitions Initiated," and "Cases Closed by Department of the Treasury" are from the *Annual Report of the Secretary of the Treasury* (various years) published by the Department of the Treasury. All other data are from the *Annual Report of the USITC* (various years) published by the ITC.

1984 included the requirement that the ITC cumulate the volume of imports from all sources in determining injury, making a product subject to CVDs if subsidized inputs bestow a competitive benefit to the foreign producer, requiring all agencies responsible for administering the trade laws to provide small U.S. businesses with technical assistance in preparing petitions under the unfair trade laws, and establishing an import monitoring system within the Commerce Department if this agency believes there is a pattern of persistent and injurious dumping. Changes in the Trade and Competitiveness Act of 1988 included permitting the Commerce Department to extend AD or CVD orders to the parts of a product as well as the product itself, permitting the Office of the U.S. Trade Representative to request third countries to take AD actions on

Table 11.3   U.S. Dumping Cases, 1980–94

Year	Petitions Initiated[a]	ITC Preliminary Investigations				Commerce Department Final Investigations				ITC Final Investigations				Total Suspended[e]	Dumping Orders Issued
		Completed[b]	Affirmative	Negative	Terminated[c]	Completed[b]	Affirmative	Negative	Terminated[c]	Completed[b]	Affirmative[d]	Negative	Terminated[c]		
1980	N/A	27	15	11	1	3	0	2	1	10	6	4	0	1	5
1981	(19)	14	9	2	3	7	5	2	0	5	4	1	0	0	4
1982	(71)	62	43	18	1	27	9	2	16	24	8	2	14	2	8
1983	31	41	33	7	1	25	N/A	N/A	N/A	23	14	7	2	1	14
1984	73	50	46	4	0	61	38	5	10	31	19	9	3	0	22
1985	63	89	73	16	0	53	28	5	20	48	11	7	30	0	11
1986	71	73	56	11	6	49	43	2	4	45	30	9	6	2	29
1987	15	20	17	2	1	43	39	3	1	51	39	9	3	0	38
1988	18	38	36	2	0	17	16	1	0	11	8	3	0	2	8
1989	13	25	20	5	0	38	36	2	0	38	23	15	0	0	23
1990	19	34	27	6	1	16	16	0	0	17	14	2	1	0	14
1991	24	55	31	22	2	29	28	0	1	32	19	13	0	0	19
1992	99	96	72	13	11	28	24	2	2	21	16	4	1	7	16
1993	42	43	30	5	8	77	76	1	0	73	41	32	0	0	41
1994	43	50	46	3	1	35	33	2	0	29	17	10	2	2	17

Sources: All data (except numbers in parentheses) are reported from the *Operation of the Trade Agreements Program* (1980–90) and *The Year in Trade: Operation of the Trade Agreements Program* (1991–94) published by the ITC. Numbers in parentheses are reported from the *Annual Report of the President of the United States on the Trade Agreements Program* (various years) published by the Office of the U.S. Trade Representative.

[a]"When a petition alleges dumping (or subsidies) with respect to more than one like product and/or by more than one country, separate investigations generally are instituted for imports of each product from each country and each such investigation may be given a separate number. For this reason, the numbers of investigations instituted and determinations made may exceed the number of petitions filed. Moreover, an investigation based on a petition filed in 1 calendar year may not be completed until the next year. Thus, the number of petitions filed may not correspond closely to the number of determinations made" (*The Year in Trade 1994*, 137, n. 24).

[b]"Completed" indicates cases completed and is the sum of affirmative and negative determinations as well as cases terminated.

[c]"Terminated" includes petitions withdrawn by the petitioner.

[d]ITC final affirmative determinations do not equal dumping orders issued in some years. This is because it is possible for a Commerce Department final determination to be made after the ITC final determination. In cases where the ITC final determination is affirmative and the Commerce Department final determination is negative, the number of ITC final affirmative determinations will be greater than the number of dumping orders issued.

[e]"An antidumping investigation may be suspended through an agreement prior to a final determination by the US Department of Commerce. An investigation may be suspended if exporters accounting for substantially all of the imports of the merchandise under investigation agree either to eliminate the dumping or to cease exports of the merchandise to the United States within six months. In extraordinary circumstances, an investigation may be suspended if exporters agree to revise prices to completely eliminate the injurious effect of the imports. A suspended investigation is reinstituted if LTFV sales recur (19 USC 1673c)" (*The Year in Trade 1994*, 137, n. 23).

Table 11.4   U.S. Countervailing Duty Cases, 1980–94

Year	Petitions Initiated[a]	ITC Preliminary Investigations				Commerce Department Final Investigations				ITC Final Investigations				Total Suspended[d]	CVD Orders Issued
		Completed[b]	Affirmative	Negative	Terminated[c]	Completed[b]	Affirmative	Negative	Terminated[c]	Completed[b]	Affirmative	Negative	Terminated[c]		
1980	(11)	9	2	3	4	16	14	2	0	53	2	51	0	0	5
1981	(14)	3	2	1	0	5	5	0	0	2	1	1	2	1	1
1982	(124)	111	62	49	2	90	38	22	30	13[e]	8	5	2	9	8
1983	(31)	8[f]	5	4	1	35	N/A	N/A	N/A	15	12	2	1	0	12
1984	52	17	13	3	1	39	18	6	5	7	5	2	0	3	12
1985	41	40	26	10	4	36	19	5	12	20	7	5	8	3	17
1986	29	26	22	4	0	24	18	3	3	12	7	2	3	1	13
1987	8	3	3	0	0	21	16	3	2	18	11	3	4	3	13
1988	8	10	10	0	0	11	5	5	1	2	1	1	0	0	3
1989	7	3	3	0	0	11	8	2	1	9	5	4	0	0	5
1990	5	5	3	2	0	4	2	2	0	0	0	0	0	0	2
1991	8	8	6	1	1	7	4	2	1	3	1	2	0	0	2
1992	43	49	43	6	0	8	4	2	2	5	2	2	3	0	2
1993	5	5	2	2	1	36	36	0	0	36	18	18	0	0	18
1994	7	7	6	2	0	1	1	0	0	1	1	0	0	0	1

Sources: All data (except numbers in parentheses) are reported from the *Operation of the Trade Agreements Program* (1980–90) and *The Year in Trade: Operation of the Trade Agreements Program* (1991–94) published by the ITC. Numbers in parentheses are reported from the *Annual Report of the President of the United States on the Trade Agreements Program* (various years) published by the Office of the U.S. Trade Representative.

[a]"When a petition alleges dumping (or subsidies) with respect to more than one like product and/or by more than one country, separate investigations generally are instituted for imports of each product from each country and each such investigation may be given a separate number. For this reason, the numbers of investigations instituted and determinations made may exceed the number of petitions filed. Moreover, an investigation based on a petition filed in 1 calendar year may not be completed until the next year. Thus, the number of petitions filed may not correspond closely to the number of determinations made" (*The Year in Trade 1994*, 137, n. 24).

[b]"Completed" indicates cases completed and is the sum of affirmative and negative determinations as well as cases terminated.

[c]"Terminated" includes petitions withdrawn by the petitioner.

[d]"A CVD investigation may be suspended through an agreement prior to a final determination by Commerce if (1) the subsidizing country or exporters accounting for substantially all of the imports of the merchandise under investigation agree to eliminate the subsidy, to completely offset the net subsidy, or to cease exports of the merchandise to the United States within 6 months or (2) extraordinary circumstances are present and the government or exporters described above agree to completely eliminate the injurious effect of the imports of the merchandise under investigation. A suspended investigation is reinstituted if subsidization recurs" (*The Year in Trade 1994*, 138, n. 32).

[e]In 1982, investigations 701-TA 150 (carbon steel wire rod from France) and 701-TA 148 (carbon steel wire rod from Belgium) were terminated after the ITC final decisions. As a result, ITC final investigations completed does not equal the sum of affirmative, negative, and terminated.

[f]In 1983, investigations 701-TA-201 (forged undercarriage components from Italy) resulted in three decisions: injury for semifinished links and rollers; no injury for semifinished segments; and no injury for finished articles.

behalf of the United States, and directing the Commerce Department not to reject CVD petitions simply because a subsidy was nominally available to many industries and enterprises.

The 1994 changes in U.S. AD and CVD laws were prompted by the need to approve the various agreements reached in the Uruguay Round of multilateral trade negotiations (1987–94). As these negotiations neared their end, the main objective of U.S. negotiators with regard to the AD agreement was to modify the text suggested by the secretary general of the GATT (the so-called Dunkel text) in a manner more consistent with U.S. law and practice. For example, they wanted an explicit statement permitting cumulation of imports from all sources, a strengthening of the anticircumvention provisions, a rejection of the five-year sunset provision for AD and CVD orders, and a weakening of the ability of dispute settlement panels under the World Trade Organization (WTO) to overturn U.S. decisions.[12] In contrast, a number of other countries believed that U.S. AD and CVD rules and procedures were biased in favor of U.S. firms and, therefore, sought procedural changes that would correct this perceived unfairness.

As would be expected, a compromise was reached between the two sides in the AD negotiations, but U.S. negotiators seem to have prevailed on the points of most concern to them.[13] For example, the new agreement permits the cumulation of imports from all sources. However, negotiators were unable to agree on a text covering anticircumvention measures, and a ministerial decision accompanying the agreement refers the matter to the Committee on Antidumping Practices for resolution. But the United States and certain other nations continue to apply the anticircumvention rules in their domestic law, although they remain liable to potential WTO challenge. Furthermore, a standard of review for dispute settlement panels in AD cases that was included in the agreement makes it clear that dispute settlement panels will have a very difficult time overturning an AD decision by any national government (Schott 1994, 83–84).[14] However, the five-year sunset provision was not changed, a 2 percent *de minimis* dumping margin was established, provisions insuring that petitioners represent a majority of the industry were put in place, minimum percentages for general and administrative expenses and for profit margins in constructed-value calculations were abolished, and the procedures for determining material injury were specified in greater detail. For example, the need to consider other possible causes of injury other than the dumped imports is stressed in the new agreement.

The Uruguay Round Agreement on Subsidies and Countervailing Duties

---

12. For a detailed discussion of the negotiations on these issues, see Cumby and Moran (1995).

13. For more detailed evaluations of the AD and subsidies and CVD agreements reached in the Uruguay Round, see Schott (1994) and Baldwin (1995).

14. Specifically, the AD agreement states: "If the establishment of the facts was proper and the evaluation was unbiased and objective, even though the panel might have reached a different conclusion, the evaluation shall not be overturned" (Final Act Embodying the Results of the Uruguay Round of Multinational Trade Negotiations).

also represents a compromise between opposing viewpoints—in this case between those who believe that almost all subsidies are unfair and should be countervailed and those who believe that most subsidies (other than direct export subsidies) promote important social and economic goals and should not be countervailed. The new agreement states that only specific subsidies—those specific to an enterprise or industry or group of enterprises or industries—are prohibited or countervailable. Furthermore, some specific subsidies, namely, those provided for research activities, those designed to assist disadvantaged regions within a country, and those given to promote the adaptation of existing facilities to new environmental requirements, are also not countervailable. All other subsidies are actionable in the sense that CVDs may be levied if they cause material injury to a domestic industry, nullify or impair benefits accruing to a WTO member under existing WTO agreements, or seriously prejudice the interests of a member. As in the case of the new AD agreement, the procedures for reaching decisions on these matters and for imposing additional duties are spelled out in more detail in the new agreement than in the Tokyo Round code.

Domestic interest groups favoring a wider use of the protection afforded under the AD and CVD laws used the occasion of writing the U.S. legislation implementing the WTO agreements both to ease further the requirements for gaining favorable decisions and to increase the likelihood of a higher offsetting duty. For example, the anticircumvention provisions were modified to make it easier to extend AD and CVD orders to products assembled in the United States from parts subject to such orders. At the same time, in determining market share and financial performance for injury determinations, the ITC was instructed to focus primarily on the merchant market for the upstream product rather than considering both this market and the sales of the product by domestic producers as an input for other products. The Commerce Department was also directed to deduct profits in the calculation of the exporter's sales price, thereby inflating dumping margins.[15]

As previously noted, an important feature of administered protection is that the extent to which protection is granted depends not just on the manner in which the laws are formulated but on the rules and procedures established by those administering the laws. There has been widespread criticism by foreign exporters that the rules and procedures formulated by the Commerce Department in determining dumping and subsidization have a protectionist bias. These practices include (1) calculating AD margins by comparing the average foreign market value with each sale in the United States, (2) throwing out negative dumping margins in calculating the dumping margin to apply to firms not investigated, and (3) imposing excessively harsh reporting requirements on foreign firms accused of dumping.[16]

15. See Cumby and Moran (1995) for a list of other changes that tend to make it easier to obtain a favorable AD decision or that tend to increase the margin of dumping.

16. See Palmeter (1991) and Cass and Boltuck (1996) for a more complete description of the various biases in the administration of the AD laws.

11.3   The Economics of Administered Protection

In evaluating WTO and national AD and CVD rules and laws, it is helpful to understand the motivations for dumping and subsidization and their economic effects and also the economic consequences of measures governments can take in response to these actions. Therefore, this section briefly reviews the economic literature on these subjects, including both the older literature in which trade economists examined behavior within either perfectly competitive or purely monopolistic market structures and modern analyses of dumping or subsidization under imperfectly competitive market conditions. Since both traditional and modern analyses of dumping and subsidization differ considerably, each is discussed separately.

11.3.1   Why Dumping Arises

As pointed out in section 11.2, there are two business practices on the part of foreign producers that can lead to petitions for the imposition of AD duties: sales in international markets by foreign producers either at prices less than they charge in their home markets or at prices below their costs of production. These, too, are best considered separately.

Price Discrimination

Traditionally, price-discriminating behavior has been analyzed by assuming that a foreign producer is the only supplier both in the domestic market and in the monopolist's home market or that, if there are domestic suppliers, they are organized in a perfectly competitive manner. To explore behavior in the latter situation, assume initially that producers in both the domestic and foreign market are organized competitively and, furthermore, that the domestic and foreign demand and upward-sloping supply curves for the product are identical. This implies that each country will supply its own demand for the good, and there will be no trade. However, now assume that the foreign producers organize and act like a single monopolist. In addition, suppose that the foreign country imposes a prohibitive duty on imports of the product into its home market. Under these circumstances, the foreign monopolist will divide any output produced between the two markets so as to equalize perceived marginal revenue in each and will select total output such that perceived marginal revenue in each market equals marginal cost. Since the demand curve that the foreign monopolist faces in the domestic market is equal to the domestic demand curve minus the domestic supply curve, this curve is more elastic than the foreign demand curve, thereby resulting in smaller inframarginal losses in revenue when export supply is increased compared to supply in the monopolist's own market. This, in turn, results in the price in the domestic market being driven lower than the price in the monopolist's home market, that is, in dumping.

This case illustrates the conflict between fairness and efficiency. Since the foreign producer sets a price in the domestic market that is lower than in the initial situation, domestic producers are forced to reduce output and therefore suffer a loss of producer surplus. In the case being analyzed, the foreign monopolist could not have exercised his monopoly power in the domestic market without the prohibitive duty on imports into the monopolist's home market, since, in the absence of any tariff, domestic producers would divert their output to the foreign market as long as the price was higher than in the domestic market. Understandably, domestic producers consider the existence of the tariff that enables the foreign monopolist to lower the price in the domestic market and raise it in the foreign market to be unfair and to warrant some type of retaliatory action by their own government.[17] However, while domestic producers lose from the price-discriminating behavior of the foreign producer, the gain in consumer surplus to domestic consumers because of the lower domestic price is greater than the producer surplus loss, and the domestic economy as a whole thus gains on balance under these circumstances.

A situation where this fairness-efficiency conflict does not arise is when the foreign monopolist undertakes predatory dumping, that is, the foreign producer lowers the domestic price to a point where all domestic producers are driven out of business and the foreign producer then raises the price to the optimum monopoly level in this market. While earlier trade economists thought such an outcome was highly unlikely, they did grant that some combination of the time it took to drive out domestic producers, the time it took them to reenter after the price increase, and the discount rates of foreign and domestic producers could reduce the long-term welfare of both domestic producers and consumers.

As modern trade economists have been broadening the framework for analyzing trade policy to include imperfectly competitive markets, there has been a significant increase in the number of analytical papers on dumping and an improved understanding of why dumping arises. Consider, for example, how the previous analysis is changed if there is a single producer in both the domestic and the foreign market, that is, a duopoly situation exists. More specifically, following Eichengreen (1982) and Eichengreen and van der Ven (1984), assume that the domestic and foreign demand curves are identical and that each firm possesses the same cost function (a given fixed cost and constant variable costs). However, a prohibitive tariff prevents domestic producers from exporting to the foreign market. Cournot behavior is followed by each firm, that is, each sets quantities under the assumption that its rival's supply to each market is fixed.

---

17. If there are no artificial barriers, such as tariffs, but transportation costs exist, a foreign monopolist can still dump by pricing the product in the domestic market so that the difference between the higher price in the foreign market and the lower price in the domestic market does not exceed the cost of transporting the product back to the foreign market. While domestic producers also regard this type of behavior as unfair, the margin of dumping is not likely to be very large for most products.

It is straightforward to show that in equilibrium the foreign firm will dump in the domestic market. This is because, in contrast to the foreign market, the foreign firm's share of the domestic market is less than unity and therefore its perceived export demand elasticity is greater than the elasticity of demand in its home market. Consequently, as explained above, in equilibrium the price will be lower in the domestic market than in the foreign market. Economic welfare in each country could be either greater or less than in the no-trade situation with each firm charging the monopoly price (Eichengreen and van der Ven 1984).

A drawback of the preceding analysis is its arbitrary assumption that the domestic firm is unable to export to the foreign country. The model formulated by Brander and Krugman (1983) does not have this disadvantage. In their framework, a single firm in each country faces the same constant marginal costs and behaves in a Cournot manner. Rather than there being a tariff on the good in one of the two countries, each producer faces similar transportation costs (of the iceberg type) in exporting the good to the other country. A possible solution in this model is what Brander and Krugman term "reciprocal" dumping, namely, each firm dumps in the home market of its rival. Because of the existence of transportation costs between the two countries, each country's share of its export market is less than its home market share, and each firm's perceived marginal revenue in the export market will, therefore, be less than in the home market. Consequently, each firm's markup over marginal costs will be lower in its export market than in its domestic market and dumping will exist. As the authors point out, compared to a monopoly situation in each market, welfare may be greater or less. Trade results in a waste of resources for cross-hauling purposes, but the lower prices resulting from the international competition increase welfare by reducing the monopoly distortion.

Pricing below Costs

Not only have the "new" trade theorists improved our understanding of why dumping in the traditional sense of discriminatory pricing occurs, but they have also provided new insights into the reasons for dumping in the sense of pricing below costs. Beginning with a pioneering article by Ethier (1982), a number of authors, for example, Davies and McGuinness (1982), Bernhardt (1984), Hillman and Katz (1986), and Das (1992), have demonstrated how the existence of uncertainty can lead at times to sales in foreign markets at prices below average and even marginal costs. In Ethier's model, for example, competitive producers must make decisions before knowing demand conditions but also must retain certain key personnel no matter what the state of demand. The consequence of these relationships plus the existence of sticky wages is that sales below variable costs may occur if realized demand is low. Other dynamic models have been developed to explain why foreign firms may price below variable costs periodically in order to attract customers who are unfamiliar with their product (Eichengreen and van der Ven 1984), why dumping below marginal cost may be employed as an entry deterrent (Davies and Mc-Guinness 1982), and why selling abroad at prices below marginal cost may arise if current production levels affect future production costs, that is, there are learning-by-doing effects in production (Clarida 1989).

11.3.2 The Effects of Antidumping Measures

Viner (1923) long ago made the case for AD duties as a response against short-run, predatory dumping. However, in the case of long-run price-discriminatory dumping by a foreign monopolist in a competitive domestic market, later economists showed that an AD duty had ambiguous national welfare effects: the producer surplus and tariff revenue gains might or might not offset the consumer surplus losses. As might be expected, more recent analyses of AD duties in response to long-run dumping in oligopolistic markets also yield ambiguous welfare outcomes (Webb 1992).

An important new line of research considers the strategic aspects of AD measures, that is, the use of the AD laws to influence price-setting behavior. Staiger and Wolak (1991) develop a model in which the filing of dumping suits by the domestic firm against foreign firms in periods of low demand serves as a means of deterring defection by foreign firms. This allows a greater degree of collusion (a higher price) to be sustained in low-demand periods. AD duties are never actually imposed, but the domestic firm obtains a greater market share in low-demand periods and expected discounted profits are greater for both the domestic firm and foreign firms. Prusa (1992) also demonstrates how the AD laws can be used to raise the profit levels of domestic and foreign firms. Under the legal principle termed the Noerr-Pennington doctrine, U.S. and foreign firms can engage in discussions to reach a settlement in an AD case without being subject to antitrust actions. Consequently, in Prusa's model, because of the increased coordination that this doctrine provides domestic and foreign firms, they are able to reach agreements that achieve cooperative levels of profits. The domestic firm then withdraws its AD petition. In another paper, Prusa (1994) points out another way in which the presence of an AD law can lead to collusive outcomes. With Bertrand price behavior by the domestic and foreign producer, the AD law has the effect of establishing a price floor in the domestic market for the foreign firm and causes it to raise its initial price. In addition, in some instances, the domestic firm will feign injury by lowering its initial price in order to improve the chance of receiving AD protection. Still another example of this line of research is the analysis by Hartigan (1995) of the use of AD investigations by domestic and foreign producers to exchange information and thereby influence the incentive of the foreign firm to engage in dumping.

11.3.3 Government Subsidies and Countervailing Duties

As in the case of dumping, there have been significant improvements over the last twenty-five years in our analytical understanding of the economic reasons for government subsidies and their economic effects. This subject was traditionally analyzed within a perfectly competitive framework in which it was assumed that resources were initially allocated in an optimal manner. Under these conditions, the government was regarded as "shooting itself in the foot" when it provided subsidies to domestic producers, since the consumer surplus loss was greater than the producer surplus gain. It was thought that such behavior could be explained only on noneconomic grounds.

The economic distortions literature of the late 1960s and early 1970s (see Bhagwati 1971, for example) led to a modification in this standard view. Stressing the widespread existence of economic distortions due to market imperfections or various government policies, the economists who developed this literature pointed out that, under these conditions, such measures as government subsidies and tariffs could raise economic welfare. They noted, for example, that knowledge spillovers associated with private research activities can create a situation where the marginal social costs of research efforts fall short of the marginal social benefits, thus justifying government subsidization of private research.

The new trade theory of the early 1980s brought about an even greater revision in the standard view about subsidies. As Brander and Spencer (1981, 1983) first showed, if imperfect competition prevails in international markets, it is possible that government subsidies to domestic exporters can shift profits from foreign to domestic producers and raise national welfare. The appropriateness of an export subsidy is, however, highly sensitive to the number of domestic firms, the assumed behavior conditions for the competitors, and the reactions of other governments.

As Spencer (1988) points out, in the case of a direct subsidy per unit of exports, imposing a CVD equal to the subsidy restores exports and profits to their levels prior to the export subsidy, regardless of whether the industry is purely competitive or has monopoly power. However, much more common than simple export subsidies are interest rate subsidies and grants toward the initial establishment of firms or for later expansion of plant and equipment. Spencer (1988) shows that, in these cases, CVDs can have very different effects. For example, if capital markets are operating efficiently, an interest rate subsidy that applies to existing capital facilities will not affect the price of capital to the subsidized firm and thus will have no effect on its level of exports. Consequently, by increasing the foreign firm's marginal costs, a CVD equal to the subsidy will reduce the firm's export and serve simply as a form of increased protection for import-competing firms in the countervailing country. In contrast, if the interest rate subsidy is given on the condition that it be used for the acquisition of new plant and equipment, a CVD equal to the subsidy may, in some circumstances, be insufficient to restore exports to their initial level, and import-competing firms end up being hurt on balance. Dixit (1988) also explores this topic and shows that only partial countervailing of foreign subsidies can be justified on national-welfare grounds.

11.3.4 Empirical Analyses

Given the wide variation in the economic effects of dumping, subsidization, and offsetting measures that the theoretical literature indicates are possible, empirical analyses in this field are especially important as guides to policy evaluation and formation. In particular, empirical estimates are needed not only of the effects of AD and CVDs on prices, imports, and output levels but of the effects on these variables of simply filing AD or CVD petitions as well as suspending an investigation. An especially important line of empirical research is to determine whether the AD and CVD laws are being used by producers for anticompetitive purposes rather than as a means of offsetting trade practices that most people would regard as unfair.

Although the extent of empirical analysis directed at such issues is still comparatively modest, research in this field is growing rapidly and there are now enough studies to reach some tentative conclusions about these matters. At the end of 1991, according to a recent ITC study (1995), there were 163 outstanding AD and 76 CVD orders in the United States, which affected $9.0 billion of imports, or 1.8 percent of total U.S. merchandise imports.[18] The ITC study ranks these AD/CVD orders behind only the Multifiber Arrangement and the Jones Act (which deals with maritime trade) in terms of significant U.S. import restraints. Of the 269 AD and 76 CVD cases for which there were affirmative final determinations from 1980 through 1993, the average margin of dumping found was 31.3 percent and the average subsidy margin was 5.4 percent.[19] In analyzing the impact of the imposition of duties in these affirmative AD cases, the ITC study found a 73 percent import decline and 33 percent price increase in cases where the dumping margins exceeded 50 percent but no significant import or price effect in cases where the margin was between 20 and 50 percent.[20] For those cases with margins below 20 percent, there also was no significant import effect, but prices declined about 10 percent, thus suggesting that the affirmative decisions on low margin cases are not effective in offsetting price decreases due to increasing competition.

In a study of AD cases covering manufactured products from 1980 to 1985, Staiger and Wolak (1994) estimate the effect on imports not just when a final affirmative injury determination is made and an additional duty is levied but, for example, when an affirmative preliminary injury determination is made but a duty is not imposed and when the case is suspended due to an agreement between the government and the foreign industry that stop the dumping. (See Harrison [1991] for a somewhat similar study.) The motivation for this latter analysis is to determine, as some of the new theoretical writings suggest,

18. These include all affirmative AD and CVD determinations prior to 1992 that had not been revoked, terminated, or suspended.

19. These weighted (by imports) margins were calculated from tables 3–1 and 3–1 in the 1995 ITC study.

20. The CVD cases are not analyzed in the study due to their relatively small number.

whether domestic firms gain from reduced imports during the investigation process, quite aside from whether an additional duty is imposed. In support of this literature, they find that petitioning firms gain import relief during the investigation that amounts to about half of what they might expect from a positive final determination and duty imposition. They also find that suspension agreements negotiated by the government result in import reductions comparable to the duty-imposition cases, whereas voluntary withdrawals do not lead to restricted trade.

Prusa (1995) has also undertaken a detailed study of the effects of AD actions from 1980 to 1988. Among his key findings are that imports are significantly curtailed from the named countries, especially when the duties are high, but that there is substantial trade diversion to nonnamed countries. Nevertheless, import prices rise substantially; for example, unit values rise more than twice as much when duties are imposed than when they are not. Moreover, they rise for nonnamed countries about 60–70 percent of the amount they rise for named countries. The observed price rise in low-duty cases despite a continued rise in imports is interpreted by Prusa as evidence that the AD law facilitates tacit collusion by providing coordination for the rivals.

An earlier analysis by Messerlin (1989) of AD cases initiated in the European Union between 1980 and 1985 produced results similar to those reached by later U.S. researchers. For example, although the volume of imports from countries against whom dumping in the EU is found drops by about 40 percent by the third year after the petition, increased imports from nondumping foreign countries is so substantial that total EU trade in these products actually increases somewhat. Messerlin also found substantial price increases for products in which dumping is found. After three years, prices of dumped products increase by 16 percent, which is approximately the same as the ad valorem equivalent of the AD measures imposed. However, one difference in the manner in which AD cases are settled in the United States and the EU is the much greater use of price undertakings, that is, agreements between the government and foreign exporters, in the EU. In the period investigated by Messerlin, price-fixing agreements represent about half of all the protective actions taken by the EU in response to dumping, whereas in the United States the Commerce Department can suspend investigations only in extraordinary circumstances.

11.4   Reforming Administered Protection

11.4.1   Policy-Related Conclusions

There are several conclusions to be drawn from the analysis in sections 11.2 and 11.3 that are helpful in suggesting ways in which the AD and CVD provisions of the WTO and the domestic laws of such countries as the United States should be modified. An important finding of the historical survey in section 11.2 is the wide variation over time in the proportion of cases in which findings of dumping or subsidization and of material injury were made, even though the AD and CVD laws did not change. This point is evident for the period from 1921 to 1954 as well as from 1958 to 1974. The conclusion to be drawn is that the determination of dumping and subsidization as well as of material injury is not just a matter of applying simple arithmetic and obvious economic criteria. Instead, there is an important judgmental component in these decisions that is influenced both by current views on what is fair and political pressures concerning enforcement of these views. The many technical amendments to the AD and CVD laws since 1974 are a manifestation of this interpretation, as protectionist pressure groups have sought to reduce the room for differences among government officials in what they consider to be injurious unfair trade.

Another conclusion reached in the historical survey is that the changes since the early 1970s in national AD and CVD laws and the manner in which they are administered seems to have been driven mainly by increased import competition faced by the United States and other advanced industrial countries. In particular, the tightening of the laws and their enforcement does not appear to have been the consequence of new forms of unfair trade practices by foreigners that require new legal and administrative provisions in order to maintain a given level of fairness. Instead, there has been an increase in the demand for import protection in these industrial nations as a consequence of global changes in comparative advantage patterns, and politicians have responded by permitting the unfair trade laws to become the means of providing this protection.

Recent theoretical analyses of dumping and subsidization within a framework of imperfectly competitive markets, which are summarized in section 11.3, also have provided important, policy-relevant insights. Replacing the traditional model of a foreign monopolist dumping in a perfectly competitive market with the more realistic framework of oligopolistically organized foreign firms dumping in a domestic market, in which domestic firms are also oligopolistically organized, not only changes the outcome of the dumping process but also the appropriateness of imposing offsetting duties. In the traditional framework, domestic firms initially behave in a socially optimal manner by setting price equal to marginal cost. Under these circumstances, the output reduction forced on the domestic firm by dumping by the foreign monopolist seems clearly unfair. In contrast, when domestic firms initially behave in a monopolistic manner themselves by setting price above marginal cost, the case for retaliation against foreign firms on grounds of fairness is much less clear. The injury they suffer as a consequence of foreign dumping could have been avoided if they had not been exploiting their monopoly power by pricing in an anticompetitive manner. For example, in a duopolistic situation where the fixed costs and constant marginal costs are the same for the domestic and the foreign firm, if the domestic firm initially sets its price at the lowest level at which its average cost equaled domestic demand, the foreign firm will be unable to dump in the domestic markets without pricing below average costs. If, however, the two producers are following Cournot or Bertrand behavior, the price of the good after foreign dumping can end up above the average costs of both firms so that each firm earns excess profits on its sales. In this situation, the material injury suffered by the domestic firm as a consequence of the dumping is artificial in the sense that it would not occur if the domestic firm did not exploit its monopoly power against domestic consumers. In these circumstances, it seems unlikely that the average citizen, who regards the act of dumping by a foreign monopolist in a competitive domestic market as unfair but also regards monopolistic behavior as unfair, would be willing to pay a higher price for the good in order to offset the artificial injury to the domestic firm.

Recent analyses of below-cost dumping also provide new reasons for rethinking the appropriateness of taking measures against this practice. For example, when there are strong learning-by-doing effects in producing a product so that firms' average costs decline as the cumulative volume of output rises, pricing below average costs in the early stages of the good's product life and above these costs near the end is necessary to introduce successfully a new, socially beneficial product. In this situation, AD authorities should take into account the life of the product in applying the below-cost standard rather than any fixed, short-term period, for example, six months. Similarly, in order not to misuse the basic notion of unfairness underlying the AD and CVD laws and rules, authorities must be careful not to prevent normal business practices such as pricing below variable costs temporarily in periods of low demand or to attract new customers unfamiliar with a product.

Perhaps the most important contribution of the recent analyses of dumping and subsidization in an imperfectly competitive framework is the demonstration that firms can use the AD and CVD laws and international rules to promote collusion between domestic and foreign firms. Thus, under the guise of offsetting the unfair practices of foreign firms, domestic firms can actually bring about greater monopolistic unfairness in domestic markets. As both theory and empirical evidence suggest, agreements between domestic and foreign firms under which the process of imposing AD duties is suspended are particularly likely to have this consequence.

11.4.2   Modifying the International Rules on Antidumping and Countervailing Duties

The Antidumping Agreement

Unfortunately, the Uruguay Round agreements on AD and on subsidies and countervailing measures take little account of the above policy-related conclusions. As will be argued, while the agreement covering subsidies and CVDs contains improvements that are consistent with some of the conclusions, the AD agreement was a major disappointment to those favoring greater trade liberalization.[21] As described earlier, a few procedural improvements were made,

---

21. Schott (1994), for example, gives it the lowest rating of the thirteen agreements he appraises.

but the basic problem of the misuse of the AD rules for protectionist and collusive purposes was not addressed in any serious manner. Moreover, a provision that protectionist interest groups were successful in introducing into the dispute settlement agreement seems likely to prevent successful challenges in the WTO to the misuse of the AD rules. Consequently, the only means of halting this misuse is by amending the Uruguay Round agreement.

The most important aspect of the AD agreements that need modification concerns the pricing behavior of foreign and domestic producers following the suspension of the injury determination process as a consequence of a voluntary agreement between these producers (termed "price undertakings" in most countries and "suspension agreements" in the United States) and following the imposition of an AD duty. Provisions must be added to prevent collusive actions that result in domestic prices ending up higher than they were prior to the foreign dumping. Not only are consumers hurt by such collusion, but employment in the industry may well decrease.

The provision in the Uruguay Round AD agreement specifying that price increases under undertakings shall not be higher than necessary to eliminate the margin of dumping does not protect consumers from ending up worse off than prior to the dumping. A profit-maximizing, noncolluding foreign firm that stops dumping and begins to sell at the same price in the domestic market in which the dumping takes place and in its own home market will typically set a uniform price by lowering the price in its home market and raising the price in the domestic market. Under collusion between domestic firms and the foreign firm, however, the margin of dumping is likely to be eliminated by setting the domestic and foreign price above these levels, for example, by raising the domestic price by the full margin of dumping, thus unfairly hurting consumers.

A provision should, therefore, be included in the AD agreement stating not only that price changes under price undertakings or suspension agreements should be no more than needed to eliminate the margin of dumping but also that the price increase in the market in which the dumping occurred should be no greater than is necessary to restore the domestic price to its predumping level, taking account of changes in cost and demand conditions since the dumping began. This is consistent with another existing provision of the agreement, namely, "It is desirable that the price increase be less than the margin of dumping if such increases would be adequate to remove the injury to the domestic industry" (Final Act Embodying the Results of the Uruguay Round of Multilateral Trade Negotiations). A similar provision that limits the extent of domestic price increases by domestic producers should also apply when AD duties are levied against foreign producers. The rationale for this proposal is simply that, when the government becomes a party to pricing agreements in imperfectly competitive markets, it has the responsibility for insuring that the producers involved do not use their monopoly power for purposes that unfairly injure the users of the products. Included as part of the change would also be language directing the AD or antitrust authorities to monitor price behavior after suspension agreements or the imposition of AD duties in order to ensure compliance with these new provisions.

A more modest proposal for dealing with the problem of collusive pricing after suspension agreements and after the imposition of AD duties is to require the antitrust authorities, in addition to the AD authorities, in the countries involved to approve any suspension agreement and to monitor price behavior after such agreements and after the imposition of AD duties. The agreement already permits authorities in the importing country to require any exporter from whom undertakings have been accepted to provide information relevant to the fulfillment of such undertakings. The authorities have also been given the responsibility of reviewing the need for the continued imposition of AD duties.

Another part of the AD agreement in need of reform concerns the determination of dumping when foreign firms sell in domestic markets at less than their costs of production. As noted in the analytical section, under various circumstances, such as the existence of strong learning-by-doing effects, below-cost sales are a part of normal business practices and would not be regarded as unfair by the typical citizen. Basically, a provision should be added, stating that foreign producers are permitted to price below average costs to the same extent that domestic producers are permitted to do so without being challenged under the country's own antitrust laws. Thus, if domestic firms are permitted to price their products so as to cover average costs over a good's product life rather than over some short time period or to price below average costs but above variable costs in recession periods, foreign firms also should be permitted to do so.

The provisions relating to the determination of material injury are a third important part of the AD agreement where reform is needed. As discussed in the theoretical section and first part of this section, when domestic as well as foreign producers possess monopoly power, the injury that domestic firms suffer as a result of foreign dumping may be due in large part to their own monopolistic behavior, in the sense that the injury would not have occurred or would have been much less if the domestic firms had not priced their products in a manner aimed at gaining excess profits. Their injury is not "material" or real in the sense of distorting trade that is based on comparative cost differences. Instead, it is due in part to the artificial pattern of trade associated with the monopolistic behavior of the domestic and foreign producers. The typical citizen supports action aimed at achieving "fair" trade but is not likely to support such actions when injury is the consequence of "feigned" trade.

A number of proposals have been set forth to deal with the monopoly problem in AD cases. One is to replace the AD provisions of the WTO by introducing competition policy into the WTO (see Nicolaides and Wijngaarden 1993). This would follow the practices of the EU and the Australian–New Zealand free trade area where trade within these regional groups is not subject to AD provisions but, instead, to competition rules. (See Kewalram 1993 for a discussion of the Australian–New Zealand arrangement.) Although, as Messerlin (1996) maintains, this approach has considerable merit as a long-run goal of the WTO, the considerable differences among members over the form that new rules on competition policy should take suggests that it will take a number of years to forge a comprehensive WTO competition policy for dealing adequately with dumping and AD issues.

As a short-term means of dealing with the various inadequacies of the current AD rules, Messerlin proposes the use of quantitative thresholds based on competition-oriented criteria. Under his proposal, reaching a threshold could lead to two possible outcomes: "either the antidumping case is automatically terminated because it is believed that any antidumping measure will hurt competition; or the case may proceed, but measures to be taken should follow the safeguard rules—in particular the fact that measures should last only four years, be degressive and be renewable only once" (Messerlin 1996, 13). The key component of his threshold standard is the requirement that the global market share of the complainants plus defendants should not exceed a certain percentage, for example, 85 or 95 percent. Cases in which these shares are exceeded would be terminated or processed through the safeguards route.

The appeal of the Messerlin proposal is its clarity and ease of implementation within a short period of time. The drawback is its implicit assumption that concentration per se leads to excess profits and socially welfare-decreasing behavior. However, we know that in the case of contestable markets the threat of entry forces average cost pricing even though the product is being produced by monopolistic firms. It is likely to be very difficult to obtain agreement on any simple quantitative threshold because such outcomes are possible.

An alternative approach is to place the burden on the domestic industry (when the degree of concentration within the industry exceeds some level) of demonstrating that it was not pricing in an anticompetitive manner prior to being injured by dumped foreign imports. To gain an affirmative material-injury finding, it would be required not only to meet the current injury requirements but to produce cost, price, and profit data for the injury-determining authority indicating that its prices only covered reasonable production, administrative, and selling costs plus a normal profit prior to the dumping. Since domestic firms already provide such data to the AD authorities for purposes of determining whether they are materially injured, it should be feasible to implement such a requirement without undue difficulty. If domestic prices prior to the period of dumping were found to exceed average costs plus a normal profit, the administering authorities would be required to reject the claim of material injury. The inclusion of this requirement has the disadvantage of increasing the bureaucratic red tape involved in AD decisions, but until feasible competition policies can be introduced to replace the AD rules, such a provision seems needed to safeguard the interests of consumers.

Subsidies and Countervailing Measures

The Uruguay Round agreement on subsidies and countervailing measures represents a considerable improvement over the Tokyo Round agreement, which was vaguely and ambiguously worded. In particular, it recognizes what economists have long pointed out, namely, that some subsidies are socially beneficial and other socially welfare-decreasing. Economists have also pointed out that net benefits or losses must be determined on an individual basis in most cases and that political pressures can result in the misuse of arguments for desirable subsidies. The provisions of the agreement that classify subsidies into those that are nonactionable (with limits on the extent of subsidization), those that are prohibited, and those that are actionable represent a reasonable approach to reconciling theoretical and practical considerations. However, the merits of including in the list of nonactionable subsidies those to disadvantaged regions within a country and those designed to assist in the adaption of existing facilities to new environmental requirements are questionable.

The agreement also does not deal with the issue of subsidies and CVDs being used to exploit monopoly power in an anticompetitive manner. It seems appropriate, for example, to include provisions aimed at preventing domestic industries that receive protection from CVDs or that reach agreements with their foreign competitors prior to the imposition of these duties from raising prices to monopolistic levels. The use of government subsidies simply as a means of diverting profits from foreign to domestic firms should also receive attention in any reform efforts.

11.5 Conclusions

Permitting governments to impose additional duties to offset the injurious effects both of dumping and of selective subsidization by foreign governments has long been widely accepted and supported as a basic rule of international commercial law. The extent to which this rule has been utilized, however, has varied greatly among countries and, as the historical analysis in section 11.2 of U.S. AD and CVD laws indicates, even over time within a country.

A disturbing development in recent years has been the successful effort by protectionist groups in some countries to use the AD and CVD laws for purposes other than those for which they were initially intended. In response to increased import competition due to shifts in comparative-advantage relationships, these producers have sought additional protection under the unfair-trading provisions rather than the safeguard provisions of the WTO because gaining protection under the former provisions require a finding only of "material" injury in contrast to "serious" injury under the safeguard laws. Using their political clout and capitalizing on widespread public support for "fair" trade, protectionists have, in effect, been able to capture a significant part of the process under which these laws are enforced. Technical provisions introduced into the relevant laws and administrative rules make it much easier to obtain findings of unfair trade, especially dumping, and material injury. In addition, protectionist interests have been quite successful in placing within the agencies administering the unfair-trade laws individuals who are sympathetic to their views.

Recent analytical and empirical work also provides evidence of the misuse of the AD and CVD laws for other purposes besides gaining protection against increased imports. In particular, there are both theoretical and empirical reasons for believing that the AD laws are being used to promote collusion between domestic and foreign producers that result in higher prices for consumers. Some government subsidies may also have the intent, or at least the effect, of shifting profits from foreign to domestic producers rather than promoting broad social and economic goals.

Since the Uruguay Round agreements do little to curtail these misuses of the AD and CVD laws, various changes in the international rules on dumping and subsidization are proposed in this paper. The long-run goal should be to replace the AD provisions of the WTO by rules on competition policy that can deal with legitimate concerns about unfair trading practices. However, even though a working party to study competition policy was established at the Singapore Ministerial Conference, the introduction of competition rules in the WTO is likely to be several years away. Consequently, as a short-run solution to dealing with current abuses, a number of proposals for amending the WTO AD agreement are made. They are aimed at preventing domestic firms who obtain AD duties or enter into suspension agreements with foreign firms from raising prices above their predumping levels, establishing the same below-cost pricing rules for foreign firms as for domestic producers, and tightening the material-injury provisions to prevent granting protection to domestic producers who are injured by foreign imports only because they are initially pricing in a monopolistic manner. These suggested reforms are also relevant to the WTO Agreement on Subsidies and Countervailing Duties.

Reform of the fair trade laws is needed not only to curb their misuse by some of the major advanced industrial countries but to prevent countries who have not used these laws extensively and the many new members of the WTO from adopting practices that seriously undermine the trade-liberalizing goals of the WTO.

References

Baldwin, Robert E. 1995. An Economic Evaluation of the Uruguay Round. In *The World Economy: Global Trade Policy, 1995,* ed. Sven Arndt and Chris Milner. Oxford: Blackwell.

———. 1996. The Political Economy of Trade Policy: Integrating the Perspectives of Economists and Political Scientists. In *The Political Economy of Trade Policy: Essays in Honor of Jagdish Bhagwati,* ed. Robert C. Feenstra, Gene M. Grossman, and Douglas A. Irwin. Cambridge: MIT Press.

Baldwin, Robert E., and Michael O. Moore. 1991. Political Aspects of the Administration of the Trade Remedy Laws. In *Down in the Dumps: Administration of the Unfair Trade Laws,* ed. Richard Boltuck and Robert E. Litan. Washington, DC: Brookings Institution.

Bernhardt, D. 1984. Dumping, Adjustment Costs, and Uncertainty. *Journal of Economic Dynamics and Control* 8:349–70.

Bhagwati, Jagdish. 1971. The Generalized Theory of Distortions and Welfare. In *Trade, Balance of Payments, and Growth,* ed. J. Bhagwati, R. Jones, R. Mundell, and J. Vanek. Amsterdam: North-Holland.

Brander, James, and Paul Krugman. 1983. A "Reciprocal Dumping" Model of International Trade. *Journal of International Economics* 15:313–21.

Brander, James, and Barbara Spencer. 1981. Tariffs and the Extraction of Foreign Monopoly Rents under Potential Entry. *Canadian Journal of Economics* 14:371–89.

———. 1983. International R&D Rivalry and Industrial Strategy. *Review of Economic Studies* 50:707–22.

Cass, Ronald A., and Richard D. Boltuck. 1996. Antidumping and Countervailing-Duty Law: The Mirage of Equitable International Competition. In *Fair Trade and Harmonization: Prerequisites for Free Trade?* ed. Jagdish N. Bhagwati and Robert E. Hudec. Cambridge: MIT Press.

Clarida, Richard H. 1989. Destructive Competition, Dumping, and Learning by Doing. Department of Economics, Columbia University. Manuscript.

Cumby, Robert E., and Theodore M. Moran. 1995. Testing Models of the Trade Policy Process: Do We Need a New Paradigm for the New Issues? The Case of Antidumping in the Uruguay Round: The Expansion of Trade Protection in the Midst of Trade Expansion. Paper presented at a conference, "National Bureau of Economic Research Conference on Effects of U.S. Trade Protection and Promotion Policies," Richmond, VA, 6–7 October.

Das, Satya. 1992. Market Uncertainties and Cyclical Dumping. *European Economic Review* 36:71–82.

Davies, Stephen W., and Anthony J. McGuinness. 1982. Dumping at Less than Marginal Cost. *Journal of International Economics* 12:169–82.

Dixit, Avinash. 1988. Antidumping and Countervailing Duties under Oligopoly. *European Economic Review* 32:55–68.

Eichengreen, Barry. 1982. The Simple Analytics of Dumping. Discussion Paper 943. Cambridge: Harvard Institute of Economic Research, Harvard University.

Eichengreen, Barry, and Hans van der Ven. 1984. U.S. Antidumping Policies: The Case of Steel. In *The Structure and Evolution of U.S. Trade Policy,* ed. Robert E. Baldwin. Chicago: University of Chicago Press.

Ethier, Wilfred J. 1982. Dumping. *Journal of Political Economy* 90:487–506.

Finger, J. Michael. 1993. The Origins and Evolution of Antidumping Regulations. In *Antidumping: How It Works and Who Gets Hurt,* ed. J. Michael Finger. Ann Arbor: University of Michigan Press.

Finger, J. Michael, H. Keith Hall, and Douglas R. Nelson. 1982. The Political Economy of Administered Protection. *American Economic Review* 72:452–66.

Harrison, Ann. 1991. The New Trade Protection: Price Effects of Antidumping and Countervailing Duty Investigations. Washington, DC: World Bank. Manuscript.

Hartigan, James C. 1995. Collusive Aspects of Cost Revelation through Antidumping Complaints. *Journal of International and Theoretical Economics* 151, no. 3: 478–89.

Hillman, Arye, and Eliakim Katz. 1986. Domestic Uncertainty and Foreign Dumping. *Canadian Journal of Economics* 19:403–16.

Hufbauer, Gary Clyde, and Joanna S. Erb. 1984. *Subsidies in International Trade.* Washington, DC: Institute for International Economics.

International Trade Commission. 1995. *The Economic Effects of Antidumping and Countervailing Duty Orders and Suspension Agreements.* Investigation no. 332–344, Publication 2900. Washington, DC: U.S. International Trade Commission.

Kelly, William B., Jr. 1963. Antecedents of Present Commercial Policy. In *Studies in*

United States Commercial Policy, ed. William B. Kelly, Jr. Chapel Hill: University of North Carolina Press.

Kewalram, Ravi P. 1993. The Australia–New Zealand Closer Economic Relations Trade Agreement: An Experiment with the Replacement of Anti-dumping Laws by Trade Practices Legislation. *Journal of World Trade* 27:110–24.

Krueger, Anne O. 1995. *American Trade Policy: A Tragedy in the Making.* Washington, DC: AEI Press.

Messerlin, Patrick A. 1989. The EC Antidumping Regulations: A First Appraisal. *Weltwirtschaftliches Archiv* 125:563–87.

———. 1996. Competition Policy and Antidumping Regulations. Paper presented at a conference, "The World Trade System: Challenges Ahead," sponsored by the Institute for International Economics, 24–25 June, Washington, DC.

Nicolaides, Phedon, and Remico van Wijngaarden. 1993. Reform of the Antidumping Regulations: The Case of the EC. *Journal of World Trade* 27:31–53.

Nivola, Pietro S. 1993. *Regulating Unfair Trade.* Washington, DC: Brookings Institution.

Palmeter, N. David. 1991. The Antidumping Law: A Legal and Administrative Nontariff Barrier. In *Down in the Dumps: Administration of the Unfair Trade Laws,* ed. Richard Boltuck and Robert E. Litan. Washington, DC: Brookings Institution.

Prusa, Thomas J. 1992. Why Are So Many Antidumping Petitions Withdrawn? *Journal of International Economics* 33:1–20.

———. 1994. Pricing Behavior in the Presence of Antidumping Law. *Journal of Economic Integration* 9:260–89.

———. 1995. The Trade Effects of U.S. Antidumping Actions. NBER Working Paper no. 5440. Cambridge, MA: National Bureau of Economic Research.

Reagan, Ronald. 1985. The President's Trade Policy Action Plan. U.S. Department of State, Bureau of Public Affairs, Washington, DC.

Schott, Jeffrey J., assisted by Johanna W. Buurman. 1994. *The Uruguay Round: An Assessment.* Washington, DC: Institute for International Economics.

Seavey, William A. 1970. *Dumping since the War: The GATT and National Laws.* University of Geneva, Thesis 205. Oakland: Office Services.

Spencer, Barbara J. 1988. Countervailing Duty Laws and Subsidies to Imperfectly Competitive Industries. In *Issues in US-EC Trade Relations,* ed. Robert E. Baldwin, Carl B. Hamilton, and Andre Sapir. Chicago: University of Chicago Press.

Staiger, Robert W., and Frank A. Wolak. 1991. Strategic Use of Antidumping Law to Enforce Tacit International Collusion. Manuscript.

———. 1994. Measuring Industry-Specific Protection: Antidumping in the United States. *Brookings Papers: Microeconomics,* 51–118.

U.S. House Committee on Ways and Means. 1957. *Hearings on Amendments to the Antidumping Act of 1921.* 85th Cong., 1st sess., 29–31 July.

U.S. Senate Committee on Finance. 1921. *Hearings before Committee on Finance.* 67th Cong., 1st sess. 18, 19, and 21 April.

Viner, Jacob. 1923. *Dumping: A Problem of International Trade.* Chicago: University of Chicago Press.

Webb, Michael. 1992. The Ambiguous Consequences of Antidumping Laws. *Economic Inquiry* 38:437–48.

12 Regionalism and the WTO: Is Nondiscrimination Passé?

T. N. Srinivasan

12.1 Introduction

The foundation of the architecture of the World Trade Organization (WTO) and its predecessor, the General Agreement on Tariffs and Trade (GATT), is the principle of nondiscrimination as enunciated in article I ("General Most Favoured Nation Treatment," or MFN) and article III ("National Treatment on Internal Taxation and Regulation," or NT) of GATT. Indeed, MFN and NT are incorporated in two of the major components of the Uruguay Round of multilateral trade negotiations (MTN) that led to the founding of the WTO, namely, the Multilateral Agreements on Trade in Goods and the General Agreement on Trade in Services (GATS).

Yet GATT was full of exceptions to MFN, many of them minor but a few major ones as well. At its very beginning, it "grandfathered" a number of preferential trading systems then in existence, allowed a prior contracting party to the agreement to "opt out" of its MFN obligations to a new contracting party at the time of the latter's entry into the GATT, authorized several actions on a discriminatory basis under some of its dispute settlement provisions, and included a procedure under article XXV for obtaining a formal waiver from the MFN clause. These have been carried over into the charter of the WTO. Nonetheless, almost all these authorized departures from nondiscrimination were really exceptions that proved the rule in the sense that recourse to them was meant to be (and mostly was sufficiently) infrequent and inconsequential (in terms of the volume of trade affected) so as not to undermine the principle.

T. N. Srinivasan is the Samuel C. Park, Jr., Professor of Economics, Yale University.

The author thanks Jagdish Bhagwati, Koichi Hamada, Anne Krueger, Philip Levy, and the two discussants, Sadao Nagaoka and Richard Pomfret, for their comments. The research for this paper was supported in part by the Ford Foundation under grant 950-1341 to the Economic Growth Center, Yale University.

However, the exceptions from MFN for customs unions (CUs) and free trade areas (FTAs) under article XXIV of the GATT (and its updated version in the WTO), under part IV of the GATT, relating to economic development adopted in 1965, and under the enabling clause of the Tokyo Round of MTN in 1979, "Differential and More Favourable Treatment, Reciprocity and Fuller Participation of Developing Countries," are much more serious, since any preferential and discriminatory trade agreements that were found consistent with these clauses could last indefinitely. The enabling clause in effect exempted the developing countries from many GATT obligations and allowed them to engage in preferential trade among themselves as well as to receive preferential treatment by developed countries. Far from helping developing countries integrate with the world economy, these departures from MFN in fact slowed such integration.

Interestingly, article XXIV reflects the positive view of CUs that prevailed in 1947 when the GATT was reached and the charter for the International Trade Organization (ITO) was adopted by the International Conference on Trade and Employment in Havana in 1948. As is well-known, the ITO did not come into being, and the GATT, which was to be subsumed under the ITO, governed world trade from 1947 until the WTO came into existence on 1 January 1995. Basically, two criteria were laid down in article XXIV for a CU or FTA to be granted waiver from MFN obligations: first, "substantially all trade" among members of a CU or FTA must be free, and second, postunion (or post-FTA) barriers on trade with nonmembers are not on the whole more restrictive than those that members had prior to their forming a CU or FTA. In his classic work on the charter of the ITO, Wilcox noted the logical inconsistency between being against any discriminating preferential trading arrangements (PTAs), even if only partial in coverage of trade, and being in favor of a CU, which is not only such an arrangement, but also one in which the discrimination against nonmembers is total. He explains the then dominant view in favor of CU:[1]

> A customs union creates a wider trading area, removes obstacles to competition, makes possible a more economic allocation of resources, and thus operates to increase production and raise planes of living. A preferential system, on the other hand, retains internal barriers, obstructs economy in production, and restrains the growth of income and demand. It is set up for the purpose of conferring a privilege on producers within the system and imposing a handicap on external competitors. A customs union is conducive to the expansion of trade on a basis of multilateralism and nondiscrimination; a preferential system is not. (1949, 70)

---

1. The possible reasons for this approach that favored 100 percent preferences but opposed lesser preferences have been discussed by Bhagwati (1991) and Snape (1993). Students of Meade's analysis know that he showed, within his model, that successive reductions of tariffs preferentially toward zero will, beyond a point, *lower* welfare and that 100 percent tariff removal preferentially may even lower welfare below the initial level; cf. the discussion of this model in Bhagwati and Panagariya (1996).

The thrust of Wilcox's argument in favor of a CU is the belief that any expansion of area within which all trade is free of barriers is desirable in the sense of improving welfare of one or more of its members while hurting no other country, as long as barriers to trade in the countries outside of the area are not raised. Indeed, this is the rationale for the two criteria laid down in article XXIV for a proposed CU or FTA to be consistent with the GATT. Recognizing, on the one hand, that the internal trade barriers will be gradually reduced so as to minimize adjustment costs and, on the other hand, that such gradualism may stop well short of the complete elimination of barriers, article XXIV also insisted on a plan and schedule for their complete elimination within a reasonable time. Although barriers (tariff and other measures) against nonmembers after the formation of a CU or FTA in fact meet the requirement that they are "on the whole" no higher or more restrictive than they were in the constituent territories of the CU (or FTA) prior to its formation, it is possible that the common external tariff of a CU could exceed some individual member's previously bound tariffs. For raising its previously bound tariff, such a member was to follow the procedures for withdrawal of any previously negotiated concessions, such as bound tariffs, as set forth in article XXVIII.

Any proposed CU or FTA agreement was required to be promptly notified to the GATT for examination by a working party. In all, ninety-eight agreements were notified under article XXIV during the life of the GATT from 1947 to the end of 1994, including the most enduring of all, namely the European Community (EC) and the European Free Trade Area (EFTA). A further eleven agreements were notified by developing countries under the 1979 enabling clause. Working parties were established to examine virtually all agreements. While fifteen working parties had not completed their examinations as of the end of 1994 and five did not report for various reasons, out of the sixty-nine that had submitted their reports, only six explicitly acknowledged conformity with article XXIV of the agreement, and this six does not include the EC or the EFTA, and only two of the six are still active! (WTO 1995, 16). In fact, "no agreement was reached on the compatibility of the Treaty of Rome with Article XXIV, and the contracting parties agreed that because 'there were a number of important matters on which there was not at this time sufficient information . . . to complete the examination of the Rome Treaty . . . this examination and the discussion of the legal questions involved in it could not be usefully pursued at the present time.' The examination of the EEC agreement was never taken up again" (WTO 1995, 11).

The main reason for failure to pronounce on compatibility was that required consensus to decide on the issue of compatibility could not be reached, with often strong opposition against declaring the notified agreements compatible with article XXIV. As the WTO report emphasized,

making no pronouncement on the key matters they were charged to examine has been the rule for Article XXIV working parties. The absence of such recommendations has been interpreted by several contracting parties as meaning that it must therefore be presumed that the agreement in question is in conformity with Article XXIV, while others have considered that, in the absence of any final decision by the contracting parties acting jointly on the conformity of a particular agreement with the provisions of Article XXIV, the legal status of such an agreement remains open. (WTO 1995, 17, emphasis in original)

As the chairman of the working party on the Canada-U.S. Free Trade Agreement put it, "One might . . . question what point was there in establishing a working party if no one expected it to reach consensus findings in respect of specific provisions of such agreements, or to recommend to the participants how to meet certain benchmarks" (WTO 1995, 11).

Whether or not a CU or FTA that is consistent with article XXIV would have increased global welfare, it is abundantly clear that the procedures laid down for examining such consistency have not worked. There are several reasons for this failure, apart from the consensus needed in the working party for a decision. The most important of these arise from the vagueness of the wording of article XXIV itself, in particular, the lack of a precise definition of the phrase "substantially all trade" in the requirement for liberalization within a CU or FTA, the lack of a well-specified procedure for determining whether the postunion FTA barriers on trade with nonmembers are not "on the whole higher or more restrictive" than those that member countries had prior to their forming a CU or FTA, and the absence of any explicit attempt to ensure consistency of the approach to permitted deviations from MFN under article XXIV, part IV on development, and the enabling clause of the Tokyo Round. Apart from specifying a tariff-averaging procedure to enable a comparison of pre- and post-CU or FTA tariff barriers and a period of ten years as a reasonable time within which internal barriers are eliminated within a CU or FTA, the understanding reached in the Uruguay Round relating to the interpretation of article XXIV did not substantially change the situation. The WTO report rightly concludes that

> [w]hile the purpose of the Understanding on Article XXIV is to clarify certain of the areas where the application of Article XXIV had given rise to controversy in the past, and particularly as regards the external policy of customs unions, it fell short of addressing most of the difficult issues of interpretation noted above. For example, no consensus emerged in the Uruguay Round Negotiating Group on GATT Articles concerning proposals made by several participants (notably Japan), to clarify the substantially-all-trade requirement. It is evident, therefore, that most of the problems that have plagued the working party process were not solved in the Uruguay Round. (WTO 1995, 20)

Article V of the GATS, which corresponds in many ways to article XXIV on goods trade, shares many of the unsolved problems of article XXIV.

In sum, the WTO articles and procedures as they are now are unlikely to succeed in the future in resolving, any more than GATT articles and procedures did, the tension, if not outright contradiction, between discrimination which is an inherent feature of CUs and FTAs and the fundamental principle of nondiscrimination.

This tension was not a serious practical issue as long as relatively few PTAs such as CUs and FTAs were proposed and implemented and fewer still endured. This was indeed the case until the final stages of the Uruguay Round. In all, sixty-eight agreements under article XXIV and six under the enabling clause were notified and came into force in roughly *four decades* between the birth of the GATT in 1947 and the Punta del Este conference that initiated the Uruguay Round of MTN in 1986. Of the significant ones, only the EC, EFTA, and the Australia–New Zealand agreement continue to exist. However, in *just one decade* between 1986 and 1 January 1995, when the WTO came into existence, thirty agreements under article XXIV and five under the enabling clause have been notified, and all but one have entered into force.[2] What is more, in just *one year* of operation of the WTO, *eight* more working parties were established under article XXIV.[3] An overwhelming majority of these agreements involve countries that are close geographically, and, as such, regional integration is an appropriate term in describing them. Not all of the proposed groupings, such as the Asia-Pacific Economic Cooperation (APEC), Hemispheric Free Trade Area covering all of the Western Hemisphere, and Transatlantic Free Trade Area, obviously can be described as regional groupings. Nonetheless the term "regionalism" has come to be applied to describe liberalization of trade and investment within such groupings.

The WTO report suggests that "[i]n the face of the wide range of views on whether the world is moving inexorably towards integration on a global scale or towards a geographic concentration of trade, with the attendant risk of trade conflicts among the regional groups, the only sensible course of action is to accept that there is movement along both tracks" (WTO 1995, 23). Its conclusion can hardly be overemphasized:

---

2. Pomfret, in his comments as discussant, suggested that the count of regional agreements in the 1990s may be inflated by the collapse of the Council for Mutual Economic Assistance to which the countries of eastern Europe belonged. I am not as optimistic that the new wave of regionalism will collapse just as most of the regional agreements of the 1960s and 1970s did.

3. Wilcox (1949, 69–70) noted that the distinction in the charter for the ITO between existing preferences, which were not to be increased and were to be reduced or eliminated through negotiation, and the prohibition of any new preferences (other than CUs and FTAs) was subject to much debate in the Havana conference. Some countries proposed the abolition of *all* preferences, and others proposed creation of several new ones! Burma (now Myanmar) proposed a Southeast Asian preferential grouping, arguing "[t]he tendency of the countries represented in this conference being to favor groupings on a regional basis and the manifestation of such tendencies being such that the whole world except South East Asia has been covered in such regional groupings, it is felt that countries of South East Asia should not lose by default and should have the right to form such groups if they desire to do so." Apparently the recent trend toward regionalism is more of a revival, and not something new.

the relative lack of success in enforcing the rules and procedures for customs unions and free trade areas is a concern, both as regards the specific issues involved and because of the implications it has for the broader credibility of the WTO system and its rules. This is especially true at a time when the number of actual or planned regional integration agreements, and the attention they are getting from third countries, is large. Moreover, even if there is an affirmative answer to the question of whether regional integration agreements have been complementary to the multilateral process, experience cautions against assuming that the post–Uruguay Round rules and procedures will be sufficient to guarantee that this will be the case with future agreements or, for that matter, with the evolution of current agreements. (WTO 1995, 23)

However, while credibility of the WTO will be certainly compromised if any of its rules, including those relating to CUs, are not enforced, it should also be noted that whether rules regarding PTAs, such as CUs, make sense is also an important issue.

The literature (relating to regionalism and multilateralism) is vast, and several volumes have appeared in which almost all conceivable issues have been discussed from several perspectives: economic theory; domestic and international political economy; systemic aspects, including legal aspects; and empirical evidence. A splendid survey of theory and models is available in Winters (1996b). The WTO report (1995), from which I have drawn extensively, also provides an excellent and balanced analysis.[4] The bibliographies in these two surveys list all the major contributions to the literature. I have little to add to these works and, instead, selectively focus on some issues. In section 12.2, I briefly discuss the recent literature on regionalism and multilateralism, focusing more on the issues raised than on the analytical models. In section 12.3, I critically examine the concept of "open regionalism," originally proposed by the Eminent Persons Group (EPG) of APEC and now embraced by the director general of the WTO, and find it problematic, if not altogether an oxymoron. Section 12.4 discusses how further progress toward the goal of a nondiscriminatory and liberal world trading and investment system could be achieved, even as regional liberalization initiatives proliferate.

12.2 Regionalism and Multilateralism

In his excellent survey, Winters (1996b) laments that while the topic of regionalism versus multilateralism is much discussed by trade economists, the literature is "surprisingly short on precise measures," by which he means quantitative indices of the extent of regionalism or multilateralism in the outcomes of trade policies of countries. But, as he himself recognizes, the more serious

4. A volume edited by Bhagwati, Krishna, and Panagariya (1997) collects the principal analytical contributions to the theory of PTAs since, and including, Viner's seminal 1950 work. The different contributions are distinguished and grouped by their analytical approaches.

problem is in defining the terms "regionalism" and "multilateralism." Bhag-wati (1993) and Winters (who points to the looseness of the definition, 1996b) define "regionalism" as *preferential* reduction of trade barriers among a subset of countries that might, but need not, be geographically contiguous. The em-phasis, presumably, is on the fact that preferences are restricted to a subset, and not extended to the whole set of countries of the world trading system. Thus, discrimination in liberalization is the essential feature of regionalism under this definition. As such, if multilateralism is to be viewed as the antithe-sis of regionalism, then it has to be defined as a nondiscriminatory reduction of trade barriers. But then *unilateral* reduction of trade barriers by one or more countries on a nondiscriminatory basis will also be deemed multilateralism.[5] However, one can distinguish MFN or nondiscrimination from multilateralism following Jackson (1992, 134). According to him, multilateralism "is an ap-proach to international trade and other relations which recognizes and values the interactions of a number, often a large number, of nation states. It recog-nizes the dangers of organizing relations with foreign nations on bilateral grounds, dealing with them one-by-one. MFN, on the other hand, is a standard of equal treatment of foreign nations." I return to this view of multilateralism as *a process* below.

It is instructive to view nondiscrimination and multilateralism from the per-spective of the fundamental objectives subserved by the WTO. The charter of the WTO is of course a constitution that enunciates the rules of the game, so to speak, for international trade in goods and services as well as trade-related investment measures and intellectual property rights. It also includes, most importantly, a mechanism for settlement of disputes among countries on the observance of rules. But all constitutions are frameworks for achieving more fundamental goals on the basis of accepted rules and for containing exercise of power by those endowed with it. In the case of the WTO, it is fair to say that the fundamental objective is a global trading (and presumably also investment) system that is free of policy-created barriers to flows of goods, services, and capital between countries. Arguably, even this is not the ultimate objective, which is global welfare in the sense of a Pareto optimum. Efficient allocation of resources through unimpeded trade in competitive international markets is an instrument to achieve it. Given that a global competitive equilibrium (over time and under uncertainty) will be a Pareto optimum only under a set of as-sumptions about the existence of a complete set of markets, absence of exter-nalities, and so on, I do not wish to pursue this line of argument, although not doing so leaves open the issue of noninstrumental justifications for a free trading system.

A system that is free of trade barriers is by definition nondiscriminatory with

---

5. Bhagwati (1993) distinguishes between multilateralism as a "process" (i.e., MTN) for liberal-ization, and multilateralism (i.e., MFN) as an outcome. Unilateral liberalization on an MFN basis, as with Peels's repeal of the Corn Laws, is then a multilateral outcome.

respect to the use of trade policy instruments. But, to the extent other nontrade, that is, purely domestic, policy instruments are effective substitutes for trade policy instruments in achieving discrimination in trade among a country's trading partners, eliminating trade barriers need not result in nondiscrimination in trade outcomes. Indeed, this issue has been highlighted in the debate about trade effects of domestic policies with respect to environment, labor standards, and market structure. Analogously, domestic corporate tax policies have effects on international flow of capital. The belief that labor, environmental, and competition policy standards in all countries of the global trading system have to exceed some internationally agreed minima, if not the same everywhere, for free trade to be beneficial has been politically powerful. Nongovernmental groups have been pushing these issues on the agenda of the WTO with only limited success so far. They have had greater success in influencing regional free trade agreements, such as the North American Free Trade Agreement (NAFTA). In fact, this success has been viewed by some as a strength of a regional approach to trade liberalization. Without delving into the burgeoning literature on the international effects of domestic policies, let me just assert (citing Bhagwati 1996, 24, in support) that GATT article XXIII on "nullification and impairment" could be used to address the problem arising from the deliberate use of domestic policy instruments by one or more countries to deny trading partners of benefits from their earlier nondiscriminatory liberalization.

One of the many issues raised in the recent literature is whether a regional or multilateral approach (or a combination of both) to reduction in preexisting barriers is superior for eventually achieving nondiscriminatory free trade for all. Bhagwati (1993), who is the originator of several felicitous phrases in this literature, has called this "the dynamic time-path question." In an earlier work (Bhagwati 1991), he raised the same question by asking whether trade blocs, that is, PTAs (regional and others), are "stumbling" or "building" blocks toward free trade for all. Of course, to be able to answer the question, a norm for establishing the superiority of one approach or path over another has to be specified.

A number of alternative norms are found in the literature, though not always in explicit form. For example, Summers (1991, vii) in his oft-quoted and criticized remark, took the "building block" view in saying that "[e]conomists should maintain a strong, but rebuttable, presumption in favor of all lateral reductions in trade barriers, whether they be multi-, uni-, bi-, tri-, plurilateral. Global liberalization may be best, but regional liberalization is very likely to be good." Implicit in this assertion is a norm for comparison, namely, global welfare (presumably in a utilitarian sense), so that global gains from Vinerian trade creation can be compared to global losses from trade diversion. As Barfield (1996, vii–viii) points out, "Summers and other proponents of regionalism base their case on a belief that total trade creation will outweigh trade diversion in most cases, that the multilateral process is too slow to produce substantial progress toward further trade liberalization, and that regional free trade arrangements will allow some nations to speed up liberalization and ultimately produce a self-reinforcing process toward more open markets."

Kemp and Wan (1976), on the other hand, explicitly use a partial ranking based on the Pareto principle, rather than the implicit complete utilitarian ranking of Summers, to show that as long as lump-sum income transfers among consumers within a CU are feasible, it is possible to choose the common external tariff for a CU of an arbitrary collection of countries in such a way that no consumer in any nonmember country is made worse off, and at least one consumer in the CU is made better off as compared to the pre-CU trading equilibrium. Thus, progressive Kemp-Wan-style enlargement *over time* of CUs ending up with the whole world within a CU, that is, global free trade, is a dynamic time path in which the trading equilibrium at each point of time Pareto-dominates earlier equilibria. In general, Kemp-Wan tariffs are not unique.[6] Being just a possibility and existence theorem, the Kemp-Wan result has no direct operational implication for the pursuit of regionalism in the real world.

An alternative way of assessing the entire time path of equilibria is to define a norm for the whole path. One admittedly extreme approach is to rank time paths according to the time each takes to reach a global free-trading equilibrium. Thus, the answer to another of Bhagwati's questions (1993), namely, "Is regionalism quicker?" is affirmative, if one can show that a time path, based on some version of regionalism, minimizes the time to global free trade among all other feasible time paths to the same goal, including ones based on multilateralism. However, an alternative welfare-oriented norm for a path of equilibria is the appropriately discounted sum of global welfare over the indefinite future along that path, whether or not it leads to global free trade in finite time or asymptotically. The presumption, however, is that a time path that maximizes intertemporal welfare in this sense will be one that achieves global free trade at least asymptotically.

It should be clear in comparing alternative time paths using the criterion of discounted sum of global welfare that any such path of multilateralism and regionalism could, in principle, be pursued in any sequence, for any length of time, or even simultaneously. Indeed, even the possibility that initial pursuit of one precludes the subsequent pursuit of the other is not ruled out. Thus, paths corresponding to what Bhagwati and Panagariya (1996) call independence and interdependence between the pursuits of multilateralism and regionalism are in principle included among the alternative time paths. Interdependence could arise in two senses. First, the pursuit of, say regionalism, could trigger and ease the pursuit of multilateralism. Second, the outcomes of the option pursued later in time could depend on that pursued earlier.

Instances of interdependence in both these senses are cited in the literature. For example, Winters (1996b) points to many commentators' having argued that the creation of the European Economic Community (EEC), that is, *region-*

---

6. I have elsewhere (Srinivasan 1997) characterized Kemp-Wan tariffs.

alism, led directly to the Dillon and Kennedy Rounds of *multilateral* trade negotiation, although Winters himself does not share this view. It is also said by some, though denied by others, that the Seattle APEC summit in November 1993 was perceived by the EU as a threat by the United States to go the route of regionalism and spurred it to compromise enough in those areas where it differed from the United States for the Uruguay Round negotiations to be successfully concluded in December 1993. These are two instances of interdependence in the first sense. WTO (1995, 54) flatly asserts that "[t]here is little question that the failed Brussels Ministerial in December 1990 and the spread of regional integration agreements (especially after 1990) were major factors in eliciting the *concessions needed* to conclude the Uruguay Round" (emphasis added). This is an example of interdependence in the second sense insofar as the *outcome,* that is, the failure or success of the multilateral negotiations of the Uruguay Round, was influenced by the prior spread of regional agreements.

The results from the analytical models so ably surveyed by Winters (1996b) are unfortunately extremely fragile and model dependent. A few examples will suffice. In the symmetric model of Krugman (1991a, 1991b) without room for comparative advantage to play a role, global welfare is minimized when the world consists of two or three blocs. Srinivasan (1993) and Deardorff and Stern (1994) show with different nonsymmetric models, in which comparative advantage plays a significant role, that Krugman's result need not hold.[7]

Levy (1997) examines whether incentives for multilateral trade liberalization are blunted by the possibility of concluding regional trade agreements in a median-voter-political-economy model of trade policy determination. More precisely, he considers two periods, during the second of which an opportunity for multilateral liberalization arises, and asks whether two countries concluding bilateral trade agreement in the first period will retain any interest in multilateral liberalization in the second period. In a standard Hechscher-Ohlin-Samuelson model with median-voter politics, the answer is affirmative, since the only effect of trade liberalization, bilateral or multilateral, is the Stolper-Samuelson effect on factor prices induced by terms-of-trade changes. However, if the model is one of differentiated product and monopolistic competition, there is an additional effect to consider, namely, the expansion of the varieties of the product available for consumption with trade liberalization. In such a model, concluding a bilateral agreement in the first period might result in the two countries losing interest in multilateral liberalization in the second period. Thus, the answer to the time-path question depends on the model of trade.

Krugman (1991a, 1991b) and several others have contended that countries

7. Hamada and Goto (1996) show that, in a symmetric world in which all trade is in differentiated products and market structure is one of monopolistic competition, the formation of a CU that is consistent with article XXIV in the sense that its common external tariff is no higher than the common (because of symmetry) tariff that each individual member had in place prior to the formation of the CU, worsens the welfare of nonmembers.

that trade with each other in larger volume than with other nations are "natural" trading partners and hence that PTAs among them are likely to be welfare-enhancing. It is further argued that countries that are contiguous are likely to trade more with each other and hence are "natural" partners to each other so that "regional" PTAs are welfare-enhancing. A related assertion is that regional PTAs are likely to improve welfare by minimizing transport costs. The models of Bhagwati and Panagariya (1996) challenge each of these assertions.

Bagwell and Staiger (1996a, 1996b, 1996c, 1997a, 1997b) have analyzed the dynamic time-path question using a repeated-game-dynamic framework, in which any deviation from cooperation (for example, maintaining low multilateral tariffs) is punished by reversion forever after to noncooperative Nash tariffs. Since they explicitly rule out enforcement of agreements by third parties and focus exclusively on self-enforcing contracts, their analysis assumes that any WTO enforcement mechanism is unlikely to be effective, and hence is not entirely relevant for assessing the relative strength of multilateralism. Be that as it may, the conclusion of Bagwell and Staiger (1996c, 1) is sufficient to illustrate the nonrobustness of the results of their model: "Our analysis suggests that the consequences of regional agreements for multilateral tariff cooperation need not be clear cut: Effects exist under which regional agreements complement multilateral liberalization efforts, and effects also exist under which regional agreements undermine the multilateral liberalization process."

There have been many attempts to evaluate empirically the likely effects of multilateral trade liberalization of the Uruguay Round. WTO (1995, 45) refers to numerous ex ante and ex post attempts to estimate the trade and other economic effects of regional integration agreements, principally those among developed countries. Again, because of differences in modeling, data used, degree of aggregation, and so forth, the estimated effects often differ not only in magnitude but even in sign. A brief survey of empirical evidence on regionalism versus multilateralism leads Winters (1996b, 24) to conclude, "Regrettably it seems as ambiguous as the theory, at least so far as issues of current policy are concerned." Thus, neither theory nor evidence provides a robust guide to the choice between regionalism and multilateralism. Obviously, merely counting a priori arguments in favor of one or the other is not much of a guide either. Inevitably, an overall judgment implicitly weighing all three has to be made.

12.3   Open Regionalism: An Oxymoron or a Fruitful Concept?

The United States under the Clinton administration has been actively pursuing the regional route.[8] The Council of Economic Advisers (CEA) to the presi-

---

8. Pomfret disagrees with this. He claims that the conclusion of NAFTA and the hosting of the APEC summit in Seattle in 1993 by the Clinton administration were in fact reversals of the earlier Republican administrations' aggressive unilateralism and pursuit of regionalism through the Caribbean Basin Initiative and free trade agreements with Israel, Canada, and Mexico. He argues that

dent in their annual report for the year 1995 claimed that "possibly the most distinctive legacy of this Administration in international trade is the foundation it has laid for the development of open, overlapping plurilateral trade agreements as stepping stones to global free trade. The Administration's plurilateral initiatives in North America, the rest of the Western Hemisphere, and Asia embody principles of openness and inclusion consistent with the GATT" (CEA 1995, 214–15). I have elsewhere (Srinivasan 1995) critically examined several of the arguments offered by the CEA in favor of plurilateralism and found them unpersuasive.

The CEA also defined the term "open regionalism" that had been earlier advocated by the EPG of APEC. According to the CEA (1995, 220),

> Open regionalism refers to plurilateral agreements that are nonexclusive and open to new members to join. It requires first that plurilateral initiatives be fully consistent with Article XXIV of the GATT, which prohibits an increase in average external barriers. Beyond that, it requires that plurilateral agreements not constrain members from pursuing additional liberalization either with non-members on a reciprocal basis or unilaterally. Because member countries are able to choose their external tariffs unilaterally, open agreements are less likely to develop into competing bargaining blocs. Finally, open regionalism implies that plurilateral agreements both allow and encourage non-members to join. This facilitates the beneficial domino effect described above.

In assessing these claims, it should be noted that by its very definition any plurilateral free trade agreement provides preferential market access to members and, as such, violates the MFN principle. Even if, in the face of experience to the contrary, such agreements are declared to be in conformity with the updated article XXIV, any extension of any liberalization among parties to the agreement to others, except on an MFN basis, cannot possibly be viewed as other than conditional and preferential market access. It is available to only those nonmembers who are willing to meet whatever conditions (e.g., reciprocity) are attached to such an extension. Viewed in such a perspective, open regionalism is nothing but an oxymoron.

Although the EPG recommended "unilateral liberalization to the maximum extent possible" and recognized that any individual APEC member can unilaterally extend its APEC liberalization to non-APEC members on an unconditional MFN basis, they do not think that either is likely or even desirable.[9] For

---

concluding NAFTA was essential to gain support for the Uruguay Round and the U.S. embrace of APEC was in fact a signal that the United States was not wedded to eastern Pacific regionalism. This is a very imaginative reading of the events! I prefer to rely on what the administration spokesmen have said or written.

9. Pomfret draws a distinction between the United States and western Pacific members of APEC. In his view, while the United States is wedded to reciprocity, governments of some western Pacific nations apparently have accepted that trade liberalization is good for the liberalizer even without reciprocity. Be that as it may, APEC leaders have disbanded the EPG, and its chairman, Fred

example they point out that "the largest members, including the United States, are unlikely to liberalize unilaterally when they can use the high value of access to their markets to obtain reciprocal liberalization from others. The same view applies in other economies in the region . . . we would note . . . that the region would give away an enormous amount of leverage . . . if its members, especially its largest members, were to liberalize unilaterally to any significant degree" (APEC 1994, 29). The EPG candidly admit that "[w]e rejected the concept of unconditional MFN treatment of non-members as the sole means of implementing open regionalism for the economic and political reasons" (APEC 1994, 34). The main reasons were the familiar free-rider problem and the claim that it is rare that benefits of politically negotiated trade liberalization, multilateral or regional, have been extended to nonparticipants on a non-reciprocal basis.

The "free-rider" argument and the demand for reciprocity reflect a mercantilist view (unfortunately enshrined in the GATT) of trade liberalization, namely, that a country's offer of liberalized access to its markets is a costly "concession" for which it has to be compensated by reciprocal liberalization by its trading partners. Except in cases where significantly adverse terms-of-trade effects are induced by liberalization (an unlikely event certainly for small countries, and most probably even for as large a grouping as APEC), this argument does not carry much weight. One would have thought that if indeed the goal of the EPG is globally free and open trade, far from bowing to political expediency, they should have used their prestige to educate the political leaders of APEC that their fears of unconditional MFN extension of their liberalization to nonmembers are unwarranted.

It is thus difficult to avoid the conclusion that "open regionalism," if not an oxymoron, is not a particularly fruitful new concept in the arena of trade liberalization. If the smaller developing countries of APEC, instead of pursuing their unilateral liberalization on an MFN basis, succumb to the open regionalism, they will be subjecting themselves to what Bhagwati (1995, 13–14) terms "a process by which a hegemonic power [often manages] to satisfy its multiple trade-unrelated demands on other weaker trading nations more easily than through multilateralism."

It is unfortunate that the regional route to liberalization and a version of open regionalism have been embraced by Renato Ruggeiro, the director general of the WTO. He recently suggested:

> The regional liberalizing impulse is not in itself cause for alarm among the upholders of the multilateral system. Regional initiatives can contribute significantly to the development of multilateral rules and commitments, and in

---

Bergsten, acknowledged that the disappointing results of APEC liberalization thus far threatened to make the Manila summit of November 1996 a failure, thereby undermining APEC's credibility (*Financial Times*, 18 November 1996).

regions such as Sub-Saharan Africa they may be an essential starting-point for integration of least-developed countries into the wider global economy. At the most basic level the real split is between liberalization, at whatever level, and protectionism. Viewed from this perspective regional and multilateral initiatives should be on the same side, mutually supportive and reinforcing. (WTO 1996, 10)

But he added:

However the sheer size and ambition of recent regional initiatives means we can no longer take this complementarity for granted, if indeed we ever could. We need a clear statement of principles, backed up by firm commitments, to ensure that regional schemes do not act as a centrifugal force, pulling the multilateral system apart.

The answer is to be found, I suggest, in the principle which some of the newer regional groupings have enunciated—*Open Regionalism.*

Ruggeiro contrasted two interpretations of open regionalism. The first essentially required that any regional PTA be consistent with article XXIV of the 1994 GATT and the understanding on its interpretation incorporated in the Uruguay Round agreements on trade in goods. In the second, "the gradual elimination of internal barriers to trade within a regional grouping will be implemented at more or less the same rate and on the same timetable as the lowering of barriers towards non-members. This would mean that regional liberalization would in practice as well as in law be generally consistent with the m.f.n. principle." He concluded: "The choice between these alternatives is a critical one; they point to very different outcomes. In the first case, the point at which we would arrive in no more than 20 to 25 years would be a division of the trading world into two or three intercontinental preferential areas, each with its own rules and with free trade inside the area, but with external barriers still existing among the blocs." He clearly expressed his preference for the second, arguing, in sharp contrast to the CEA, that it "points towards the gradual *convergence* of regionalism and multilateralism on the basis of shared aims and principles, first and foremost respect of the m.f.n. principle. At the end, we would have one free global market with rules and disciplines internationally agreed and applied to all, with the capacity to invoke the respect of the rights and obligations to which all had freely subscribed. In such a world there could and must be a place for China, Russia and all the other candidates to the WTO" (11).

Notwithstanding the director general's preference for the second interpretation, it seems odd: after all, if regional liberalization is to be extended *on the same timetable* "in practice as well as in law" to nonmember countries on an MFN basis, it would be multilateral and not regional. If that is the case, why would any group initiate it on a regional basis in the first place?

The concern of the director general that mere consistency with article XXIV is not enough to preclude the possibility of a world of trade blocs is well taken.

Whether a changed article XXIV would prevent such an outcome is an open question.[10]

12.4   Saving Nondiscrimination: Enhancing Credibility of WTO Processes Relating to Preferential Trading Arrangements

The dismal failure of the GATT working-party mechanism for examining the consistency of proposed PTAs with the conditions laid down in article XXIV and making recommendations to the governing council of the GATT was documented in section 12.1. The reasons for the failure, as noted earlier, were largely in the vagueness of the conditions in article XXIV itself. Under the circumstances, one approach to reform is to replace article XXIV by a better alternative that is precise, transparent, and predictable in its application.

An attractive alternative retains the notification requirements of article XXIV and lays down a precise time limit (say five years) within which, first, *any and all* preferences (tariff and nontariff) that are included in any existing or proposed PTAs are required to be extended to all members of the WTO on an MFN basis; second, in the case of CUs, if the common external tariff structure results in an increase in tariff relative to what prevailed in any country prior to its becoming a member, such increases are to be rescinded within the same period; third, in the case of FTAs, *any increase* in the applied external tariffs of a member following its formation, even if it is within its previously bound levels, is to be rescinded within the same period. Any disputes relating to the observance of these conditions would be resolved using the dispute settlement mechanism of the WTO. This alternative restores nondiscrimination within a set time limit and avoids having to examine whether PTAs satisfy specified conditions to be given a permanent waiver from MFN. It is extremely unlikely, however, that this proposal will attract support from countries that are members of existing PTAs such as EU and NAFTA. As such, one has to examine possible ways of strengthening article XXIV.

The imprecision of the requirement of article XXIV that duties and other regulations of commerce should be eliminated with respect to *substantially all the trade* between members in products originating in them has led to serious problems of interpretation (WTO 1995, 13): should the word "substantially" be interpreted qualitatively (i.e., no major sectors are excluded) or quantitatively (i.e., share of trade of the members covered)? Does exclusion from elimination of barriers with respect to trade among members in unprocessed agricultural commodities, as in most PTAs, violate the "all-the-trade" requirement? Are all types of nontrade barriers to be eliminated, whether or not such barriers are sanctioned under other articles, for example, those relating to safeguards,

---

10. Among recent contributors to the literature related to article XXIV are Bhagwati (1991, 1993), Bond, Syropoulos, and Winters (1995), Finger (1993), Jun and Krishna (1996), McMillan (1993), Roessler (1993), Serra et al. (1997), Snape (1993), Syropoulos (1995a, 1995b), and Winters (1996a).

antidumping, and national security? Are other members of a CU or PTA to be exempted when one member takes actions in the form of quantitative restrictions under the safeguard clause, actions that would otherwise have been nondiscriminatory?

The fundamental objective that prompted the inclusion of the "substantially all" trade condition was to "avoid a mass of protectionist oriented *a la carte* agreements that exclude a broad range of 'sensitive' sectors" (WTO 1995, 66). One way to achieve it while avoiding problems of interpretation is, first, to replace the phrase "substantially all trade" with "trade in *all* products and services except those explicitly exempted from MFN or NT requirements under other articles or understandings of WTO." Second, if a member of a CU or FTA avails of administered protection permitted under WTO articles that is required to be applied on a nondiscriminatory basis, other members should not be exempted from its application.

The second major problem of interpretation of article XXIV arises with respect to the requirement that the common external tariff and other restrictive regulations imposed at the time of the formation of a CU not be "on the whole higher or more restrictive" than those imposed by its members prior to its formation. The understanding reached in the Uruguay Round with respect to article XXIV clarified that, for purposes of comparison,

> the general incidence of the duties and other regulations of commerce applicable before and after the formation of a customs union shall in respect of duties and charges be based upon an overall assessment of weighted average tariff rates and of customs duties collected. This assessment shall be based on import statistics for a previous representative period to be supplied by the customs union, on a tariff-line basis and in values and quantities, broken down by WTO country of origin. For this purpose, the duties and charges to be taken into consideration shall be the applied rates of duty. (GATT 1994, 32)

The substitution of the vague phrase "general incidence" by a much more precise criterion for comparison of pre- and postunion tariff structures was a step in the right direction. However, no rationale for the proposed criterion was offered. Nor was it established that one can infer how the welfare of nonmembers is affected by the formation of CUs by using the suggested comparison.

Two of the proposals for reform of article XXIV in this context are by Bhagwati (1991) and McMillan (1993). Bhagwati proposed that a CU should be approved only when its common external tariff is set at the minimum of the preunion import tariffs of the member countries. An implication of this is that the CU will engage in free trade with *all* nonmembers, if at least one member had a zero preunion tariff for each of the traded commodities! Even if this were not the case, the Bhagwati proposal could *lower* welfare of some members of the CU and *raise* that of nonmembers (Srinivasan 1997). Since such a possibility could deter the formation of a union, the Bhagwati proposal may still be treated as a desirable reform that in effect sets a price or hurdle on WTO members who wish to enter a CU and thus compromise the MFN principle.

McMillan (1993, 300) suggests that "[a] proposed RIA [regional integration agreement], in order to get GATT's imprimatur, would have to promise not to introduce policies that result in external trade volumes being lowered. And, if after some years the RIA is seen to have reduced its imports from the rest of the world, it would be required to adjust its trade restrictions so as to reverse their fall in imports." Measuring trade volumes is certainly more workable. But changes in *aggregate* volumes of trade with nonmembers need not necessarily indicate changes in global welfare. Besides, by substituting *outcome* variables (viz., trade volumes for *instrument* variables, viz., tariff rates) when in fact outcomes are impossible to predict with any accuracy, the McMillan proposal runs into problems similar to those afflicting the malodorous "managed-trade" approach to trade policy.

The Kemp-Wan (1976) tariff structure by a CU, as mentioned earlier, is *sufficient* to ensure that the welfare of nonmembers is not adversely affected by its formation. It is certainly not *necessary*—after all, one cannot rule out the possibility that in spite of the change in the prices faced by nonmembers incidental to the adoption by a CU of a tariff structure that differs from a Kemp-Wan structure, welfare of nonmembers is not adversely affected. Even if a theoretically more satisfactory averaging of preunion tariffs could be specified, still the facts that tariffs are not the only barriers to trade, nontariff barriers cannot always be converted to equivalent tariffs, and most important, that preunion barriers could reflect expectations *then* about the *future* evolution of the world economy suggest that, whatever tariff-averaging procedure is suggested for comparing pre- and postunion barriers with respect to trade with nonmembers, it is difficult to ensure that it will guarantee that the welfare of nonmembers in the postunion future is no lower than what it would have been in the counterfactual world without such a union. Thus, from the only appropriate perspective, namely in determining whether a proposed CU or FTA adversely affects the future welfare of a nonmember relative to what it would have been in the absence of that CU or FTA, none of the proposed modifications of article XXIV is of much help.

A third and equally thorny issue that arises with respect to FTAs is their rules of origin (ROOs), which determine which products receive duty-free treatment when such products use intermediates imported from nonmember countries in their production. The Uruguay Round agreement on ROOs envisages a work program for harmonizing rules of origin and the establishment of a technical committee with responsibilities, inter alia, to examine technical problems in the day-to-day administration of ROOs and to prepare and circulate periodic reports on technical aspects of the agreement on ROOs. My reading of this agreement is that it can at best bring transparency and technical coherence to ROOs. But it does not come to grips with the crippling conceptual issue whether ROOs can ever be harmonized in a meaningful sense in a world where several countries are members of two or more overlapping PTAs.

I should also mention technical difficulties involved in determining the local (i.e., FTA) content for products when there is local production as well as imports of several intermediates from third countries. It is natural to consider using an input-output matrix for this purpose, thereby assuming that input coefficients are technological constants. A typical coefficient a_{aj} of the input-output matrix $\mathbf{A}$ represents the amount of *input* of commodity i needed to produce a unit of *output* of commodity j. But there is no way to decompose a_{ij} into domestically produced and imported quantities of i if there is import-competing domestic production of i. Besides, the constancy of the coefficients of matrix $\mathbf{A}$ is itself a strong assumption. Krueger's analysis (forthcoming, 1995) of ROOs and overlapping FTAs illustrates how, in establishing ROOs, nontransparent lobbying by protectionist interests is very likely. But the problem goes deeper and arises also in a CU. For example, the French apparently worry about and insist on value-added rules in determining whether an automobile *produced in the United Kingdom* in a Japanese-owned plant should be allowed duty free. Of course, if article XXIV is replaced by a time-bound phasing out of preferences, the problem of ROOs will become moot as well.

To the extent that PTAs are driven primarily by political objectives (e.g., the fundamental reason for the establishment of the European Coal and Steel Community and later the EC was to reduce the prospects of yet another European war) and those objectives are shared widely, the past "practice of looking the other way when Article XXIV runs up against overriding political goals" (WTO 1995, 65) will continue whether or not article XXIV is strengthened.[11] Nonetheless, requiring that any proposed PTA be notified prior to its being ratified member countries so that the WTO can weigh in with its recommendation, as suggested in WTO (1995), is a sensible idea even though the WTO's efforts could be wasteful in those cases where the proposed agreement is not ratified.

The recommendations in WTO (1995) on improving transparency and surveillance are also sensible. Indeed, the GATT had a biennial reporting requirement for developments within individual PTAs, but this was not met. A revised

---

11. Richard Pomfret was certainly right in his comments as a discussant in pointing out that the fundamental reasons for the formation of the European Coal and Steel Community, which later became the EC, were political, viz. to preclude a third European war in the twentieth century and to contain the Soviet Union, and not economic. As such, the EC had the strong backing of the United States. It is extremely unlikely that a finding by a GATT working party that EC was inconsistent with article XXIV would have prevented its coming about. More generally, there are political as well as economic motives for countries to form or join a CU or FTA. But the assertion that economic losses, if any, from departures from free trade must have been outweighed by political gains for members of a CU or FTA as well as nonmembers who supported or acquiesced in its formation is tautological. Carrying out a convincing empirically based analysis of the political economy of the formation, the success or failure once formed, of real-world CUs and FTAs is a complex task that has rarely been done.

and stricter enforcement of this requirement would be helpful. Perhaps instead of requiring CUs or FTAs to submit reports, a better procedure would be for the WTO itself to draw up such reports using the Trade Policy Review Mechanism.

There are also claims that recent regional agreements go beyond conventional trade arrangements, addressing not only trade in goods, but also the liberalization of trade in services, movements of labor and capital, the harmonization of regulatory regimes, and the coordination of domestic policies that influence international competitiveness. It is arguable that such harmonization is not always beneficial and, even if it is, that there are perhaps more efficient ways of achieving it. In any case, there is no convincing analytical argument establishing that trade or investment preferences of a PTA are either necessary or sufficient for a successful pursuit of regional integration in other areas. All said and done, in my judgment the adverse systemic and other effects of discriminatory PTAs far outweigh any beneficial effects.[12] Rather than try to reform article XXIV, a better approach, as suggested earlier, will be to ensure that all PTAs, regional or otherwise, are temporary features of the global trading system.[13] In fact, the best approach for WTO members could well be, first, to follow the advice of Nancy Reagan and "just say no" when presented with any proposed PTA for approval and, second, to follow the advice of Senator Robert Dole when he suggested to the proponents, "Just don't do it"!

References

Asia-Pacific Economic Cooperation. 1994. *Achieving the APEC Vision.* Second report of the Eminent Persons Group. Singapore: APEC.
Bagwell, Kyle, and Robert W. Staiger. 1996a. Preferential Agreements and the Multilateral Trading System. Columbia University. Manuscript.
———. 1996b. Reciprocal Trade Liberalization. NBER Working Paper no. 5488. Cambridge, MA: National Bureau of Economic Research.
———. 1996c. Regionalism and Multilateral Tariff Cooperation. Columbia University. Manuscript.
———. 1997a. Multilateral Tariff Cooperation during the Formation of Customs Unions. *Journal of International Economics* 42 (1/2): 91–123.

12. Pomfret argues that governments of member countries of CUs code sovereign power over external trade policy and tax revenue to the union and as such are inevitable precursors of some form of federation. To expect them to multilateralize their preferences is utopian in his view. While there is merit in his argument, it seems to be based essentially on the experience of the EU. Even in this case, as the saga of the implementation of social clauses and of steps toward a monetary union indicates, any form of federation is far from inevitable, and, if it is, it is a long way in the future.

13. It is for this reason that I am not persuaded that the recommendations of Serra et al. (1997) for improving the rules for regional trade agreements are appropriate. Besides, being Rube Goldbergian in their complication, the recommendations treat regional trade agreements as permanent and irreversible features of the global trading system.

———. 1997b. Multilateral Tariff Cooperation during the Formation of Regional Free Trade Areas. *International Economic Review* 38 (2): 291–319.

Barfield, C. 1996. Regionalism and U.S. Trade Policy. In *The Economics of Preferential Trade Agreements,* ed. Jagdish Bhagwati and Arvind Panagariya. Washington, DC: AEI Press.

Bhagwati, Jagdish. 1991. *The World Trading System at Risk.* Princeton, NJ: Princeton University Press.

———. 1993. Regionalism and Multilateralism: An Overview. In *New Dimensions in Regional Integration,* ed. Jaime de Melo and Arvind Panagariya. Cambridge: Cambridge University Press.

———. 1995. Foreword to Jagdish Bhagwati and Anne Krueger, *The Dangerous Drift to Preferential Trade Agreements,* vii–ix. Washington, DC: AEI Press.

———. 1996. The Demands to Reduce Domestic Diversity among Trading Nations. In *Fair Trade and Harmonization,* ed. Jagdish Bhagwati and Robert Hudec. Cambridge: MIT Press.

Bhagwati, Jagdish, Pravin Krishna, and Arvind Panagariya, eds. 1997. *Analyzing Preferential Trading Agreements: Alternative Approaches.* Cambridge: MIT Press.

Bhagwati, Jagdish, and Arvind Panagariya. 1996. Preferential Trading Areas and Multilateralism: Strangers, Friends, or Foes? In *The Economics of Preferential Trade Agreements,* ed. Jagdish Bhagwati and Arvind Panagariya. Washington, DC: AEI Press.

Bond, Eric, Costas Syropoulos, and L. Alan Winters. 1995. Deepening of Regional Integration and External Trade Relations: When Are Kemp-Wan Tariff Adjustments Incentive-Compatible? Pennsylvania State University, Department of Economics. Manuscript.

Council of Economic Advisers. 1995. *Economic Report of the President 1995.* Washington, DC: CEA.

Deardorff, Alan, and Robert Stern. 1994. Multilateral Trade Negotiations and Preferential Trading Arrangements. In *Analytical and Negotiating Issues in the Global Trading System,* ed. Alan Deardorff and Robert Stern. Ann Arbor: University of Michigan Press.

Finger, J. Michael. 1993. GATT's Influence on Regional Arrangements. In *New Dimensions in Regional Integration,* ed. Jaime de Melo and Arvind Panagariya. Cambridge: Cambridge University Press.

General Agreement on Tariffs and Trade. 1994. *The Results of the Uruguay Round of Multilateral Trade Negotiations: Legal Texts.* Geneva: GATT Secretariat.

Hamada, Koichi, and Junichi Goto. 1996. Regional Economic Integration and Article XXIV of the GATT. Yale University. Manuscript.

Jackson, John. 1992. *The World Trading System.* Cambridge: MIT Press.

Jun, Jiandong, and Kala Krishna. 1996. Market Access and Welfare Effects of Free Trade Areas without Rules of Origin. NBER Working Paper no. 5480, Cambridge, MA: National Bureau of Economic Research.

Kemp, Murray, and Henry Wan. 1976. An Elementary Proposition concerning the Formation of Customs Unions. *Journal of International Economics* 6:95–97.

Krueger, Anne. Forthcoming. Rules of Origin as Protectionist Devices. In *International Trade Theory: Essays in Honor of John Chipman,* ed. James Melvin, James Moore, and Ray Reisman. New York: Routledge.

———. 1995. NAFTA: Strengthening or Weakening the International Trading System? In Jagdish Bhagwati and Anne Krueger, *The Dangerous Drift to Preferential Trade Agreements.* Washington, DC: AEI Press.

Krugman, Paul. 1991a. Is Bilateralism Bad? In *International Trade and Trade Policy,* ed. Elhanan Helpman and Assaf Razin. Cambridge: MIT Press.

———. 1991b. The Move towards Free Trade Zones. In *Policy Implications of Trade and Currency Zones,* 7–42. Kansas City: Federal Reserve Bank of Kansas City.

Levy, Philip. 1997. A Political Economic Analysis of Free Trade Agreements. *American Economic Review,* forthcoming.

McMillan, John. 1993. Does Regional Integration Foster Open Trade? Economic Theory and GATT's Article XXIV. In *Regional Integration and the Global Trading System,* ed. Kym Anderson and Richard Blackhurst. London: Harvester Wheatsheaf.

Roessler, Frieder. 1993. The Relationship between Regional Integration Agreements and the Multilateral Trade Order. In *Regional Integration and the Global Trading System,* ed. Kym Anderson and Richard Blackhurst. London: Harvester Wheatsheaf.

Serra, J., G. Aguilar, J. Córdoba, G. Grossman, C. Hills, J. Jackson, J. Katz, P. Noyola, and M. Wilson. 1997. *Reflections on Regionalism: Report of the Study Group on International Trade.* Washington, DC: Carnegie Endowment for International Peace.

Snape, Richard. 1993. History and Economics of GATT's Article XXIV. In *Regional Integration and the Global Trading System,* ed. Kym Anderson and Richard Blackhurst. London: Harvester Wheatsheaf.

Srinivasan, T. N. 1993. Comments on Paul Krugman, "Regionalism vs. Multilateralism: Analytical Notes." In *New Dimensions of the Regional Integration,* ed. Jaime de Melo and Arvind Panagariya. Cambridge: Cambridge University Press.

———. 1995. APEC and Open Regionalism. Yale University. Manuscript.

———. 1997. The Common External Tariff of a Customs Union: Alternative Approaches. *Japan and the World Economy,* forthcoming.

Summers, Lawrence. 1991. Regionalism and the World Trading System. In *Policy Implications of Trade and Currency Zones,* 295–302. Kansas City: Federal Reserve Bank of Kansas City.

Syropoulos, Costas. 1995a. Customs Unions and Comparative Advantage. Pennsylvania State University. Manuscript.

———. 1995b. External Tariff Preferences in Customs Unions. Pennsylvania State University. Manuscript.

Wilcox, Clair. 1949. *A Charter for World Trade.* New York: Macmillan.

Winters, L. Alan. 1996a. Regionalism and the Rest of the World: The Irrelevance of the Kemp-Wan Theorem. CEPR Discussion Paper no. 1316. London: Centre for Economic Policy Research.

———. 1996b. Regionalism versus Multilateralism. World Bank Policy Research Working Paper Series, no. 1687.

World Trade Organization. 1995. *Regionalism and the World Trading System.* Geneva: WTO.

———. 1996. The Road Ahead: International Trade Policy in the Era of the WTO. Fourth Annual Sylvia Ostry Lecture, Ottawa, 28 May 1996. WTO Press/49, Geneva, 29 May 1996.

III Issues of Concern to Particular Country Groupings

13   The Role of the WTO for Economies in Transition

Jaroslaw Pietras

As the economies in eastern Europe and the former Soviet Union began their transition away from central planning toward a market orientation, the international economic institutions were a part of the international economy into which they intended to integrate. The economies in transition could not affect the structure of those institutions, nor could they influence the outcome of the Uruguay Round, which in any event was well advanced. The world trading system was simply a fact of life with which they were confronted.

This paper examines the ways in which the various features of the world trading system in general, and the World Trade Organization (WTO) in particular, affected and continue to affect the transition and economic prospects of central and eastern Europe and the former Soviet Union. Particular emphasis is placed on the situation of eastern European countries—Hungary, the Czech Republic, Poland—that were already members of GATT/WTO.[1] Those countries faced the task of altering their own trade regimes as part of the process of transition in the context of an ongoing set of international arrangements. As will be seen, many features of the international trading system helped facilitate the transition and the move toward a liberal trade regime, although some inhibited it.

For countries that were not members of the General Agreement on Tariffs and Trade (GATT) and then the WTO, the situation was more complicated still, as they had to negotiate entry into the organization. They were not automatically entitled to most-favored-nation (MFN) treatment or to having duties on their exports in importing countries set at the levels negotiated in the Uruguay

Jaroslaw Pietras is professor in the Department of Economics at the University of Warsaw and the undersecretary of state at the Office of the Committee for European Integration.
1. The Czech Republic was a founding member of the GATT but active membership was suspended under the Communist regime.

Round. The additional complications that arose as a result are covered in the comments on this paper provided by Constantine Michalopoulos.

Section 13.1 briefly sketches the economic conditions prevailing at the start of transition, and the key roles that the international economy and trade policy should have played in the transition. Section 13.2 reviews the ways in which the existing structure of the international economy and the WTO supported this transition. Section 13.3 examines the problems that policymakers encountered in opening up their transition economies because of features of the international economic system.

13.1   Background to Transition

The economies of Poland, the Czech Republic, Romania, and Hungary differed from market economies in western Europe and the rest of the world in a number of ways that were highly important for their transition. Not only were they centrally planned, but also they were virtually closed to the international economy. Trading ties were close with other parts of the former Soviet Union, but those trades were effected through arrangements between the responsible ministries in the countries that were members of Council for Mutual Economic Assistance (COMECON). For example, Poland's exports amounted to only 11.2 percent of GDP at the beginning of the Uruguay Round (1987), and of those exports, 24.5 percent were destined for the USSR and a further 16.2 percent for other eastern European countries (Central Office of Statistics 1991, 1992).

The distinguishing characteristic of economies in transition was the legacy from which they were attempting to become market-oriented economies. They had to cope, and are still confronted, with remnants of central planning and forty years of relative autarchy, vis-à-vis the industrialized market economies. While there was an advantage, at least to some extent, in not accumulating vested interests that resist trade policy shifts, it was nonetheless necessary to establish a new trade regime rapidly, before vested interests developed.[2]

Making the transition to a market economy entailed challenge enough, including the need to privatize existing state enterprises, to establish a viable commercial code, to enable prices to reflect relative costs and scarcities, to remove the monetary overhang, and to find new sources of government revenue.

But a central part of the transition had to be the integration of these econo-

---

2. There were also problems with those economic activities that had been overdeveloped under central planning, and those that had been highly neglected. Heavy industry, for one, had been overdeveloped, and there were significant problems involved in achieving a restructuring or a transition to a viable firm with a reasonable cost structure in many public-sector heavy-industry firms. Likewise, service sectors such as banking and insurance had been largely neglected under central planning, and there was a natural desire to provide protection for a period of time while these industries were developed.

mies with the international economy. It was well understood that many domestic industries were high-cost and needed restructuring, and that one reason for high costs was that there had been little or no competition for these firms. Introducing liberal trade policies was a major policy instrument for bringing competition into the domestic market.

Each of the economies in transition needed the WTO and the international economy for several things. First of all, adherence to the WTO ensured that trading partners would apply MFN treatment instead of protectionist measures. In practice, most trading partners have received MFN treatment. Second, the economies needed to provide a stable framework of incentives for economic activity in their own country, including a trading regime that would encourage individuals and firms to rely upon external as well as internal markets. To do that, stabilizing their trade policies along the lines and disciplines prevailing under GATT/WTO was important. The institutional constraints imposed by the WTO could be useful in establishing trade policies conducive to successful integration into the world economy.

13.2   Ways in Which the WTO Facilitated Transition

The WTO, and the structure of the international trading system resulting under its rules, conferred four key advantages for policymakers struggling to change the economies in transition. It goes without saying that the relatively open international economy, with the rapid growth of international markets, represents a strong plus for the economies in transition. Were the international markets stagnant, the difficulties associated with transition and integration with the world economy would be considerably more difficult. To the extent that the existence of internationally agreed-upon rules has facilitated or enhanced that growth, the economies in transition have clearly benefited from the presence of GATT/WTO rules.

But there are several more specific ways in which the WTO as an institution has facilitated the transition process. First, it is a forum where trade problems in bilateral or multilateral relations can be negotiated and the implementation of obligations undertaken and agreed upon by members can be monitored. Second, the dispute settlement mechanism is important for economies in transition. Third, the Trade Policy Review Mechanism has been important in contributing to policy formulation and execution. Finally, the tariff cuts and other trade arrangements negotiated in the Uruguay Round held advantages for the economies in transition. Each of these is discussed in turn.

Turning to the first function, there are a number of products in world trade where bilateral policies of large countries can have serious consequences for the exports of economies in transition. This is especially true for clothing, footwear, and agricultural products. There are significant trade barriers in the European Union (EU), the United States, and other countries. The economies in transition are relatively small and are unlikely to be able to affect their trading partners' treatments of those imports in bilateral negotiations. The WTO, as a multilateral forum, provides the representatives of the economies in transition with considerably more ability to raise these issues, and perhaps influence policy, than they would have had bilaterally. This was particularly important in dealing with the import practices of the EU.

More generally, the fact that large trading countries are bound by WTO rules provides protection for relatively smaller economies in the international market. Clearly, being entitled to MFN treatment saved the transition economies that were WTO members from difficulties they would otherwise have encountered with some of their trading partners. The very existence of monitoring makes policies of member countries more transparent, and raises the costs to them of protectionist measures or violation of the rules against other WTO members, even though they are small. Some difficulties that were significant, despite WTO MFN protection, are discussed in section 13.3.

The dispute settlement mechanism is also important for countries in transition. Policymakers in those economies are painfully aware of the fragility of their economic structures and their vulnerability to external shocks. The multilateral system offers obvious advantages in the presence of this very large asymmetry in economic power, and reduces the ability of larger and stronger economies to pressure weaker ones. Although the economies in transition have not yet referred any trade practice of a trading partner to the dispute settlement mechanism, the very existence of such an opportunity has considerable value.[3]

The Trade Policy Review Mechanism is valuable, both for what the reviews accomplish for the trade policies of the economies in transition and for what can be learned about policies of trading partners. The review of the policies of the economies in transition enables reflection and reevaluation of current trade practices. In some instances, measures addressing temporary needs or once-and-for-all circumstances have been adopted by policymakers without a long history of market-based trade policy, and the review process has enabled a critical reassessment of these policies. The review of trading partners' policies has enabled policymakers in the economies in transition to learn more about those policies and how they work. That in itself has been invaluable. In addition, the ability to ask questions about other countries' policies is useful. For example, during the review of Canadian trade policy, the Polish officials could request clarification as to why Canada maintained an antidumping duty on products from Poland that had not been exported since the 1970s.

Finally, members of GATT/WTO receive benefits from the relatively low protection levels that existed and were further reduced under the Uruguay Round. While negotiations were predominantly between the larger economies,

---

3. There is, however, a danger that countries in transition could be targets for complaints because of the inability of the relatively inexperienced policymakers to make trade policy instruments function properly. The administrators of trade policy in the economies in transition are not as knowledgeable and aware of the consequences of the use and misuse of trade policy instruments as are their counterparts in countries with a longer history of WTO membership.

Table 13.1   **Exports from Economies in Transition and Tariff Levels**

Country	Imports from Economies in Transition[a] ($ million)	Trade-Weighted Tariff Average[b] (percent)		
		Pre–Uruguay Round	Post–Uruguay Round	Reduction (percent)
Australia	72	18.2	12.5	31
Austria	750	4.5	2.8	38
Canada	159	13.6	8.1	40
European Community	5,835	5.3	3.0	43
Iceland	28	8.0	4.0	50
Japan	251	5.9	3.4	42
New Zealand	5	29.3	13.6	54
Norway	107	5.2	2.9	44
Sweden	433	3.8	2.2	42
Switzerland	185	3.2	1.9	41
United States	470	7.7	5.7	26
Western economies	8,313	5.5	3.3	40

Source: Economic Commission for Europe 1994, 22–23.

[a]Includes the Czech Republic, Hungary, Poland, and the Slovak Republic. Imports are from pre–Uruguay Round period (1986–88).

[b]Tariff averages exclude imports under tariff lines where duties were not available.

and certainly not focused on products of particular interest to economies in transition, those eligible for MFN treatment nonetheless benefited by tariff reductions and other Uruguay Round results.

Table 13.1 gives data on the exports of economies in transition to various Western countries,[4] with tariff averages on commodities exported from economies in transition weighted by their importance in exports.[5] As can be seen, tariff rates did fall, usually by 35–45 percent. In many instances, such as Sweden, initial tariff rates were quite low, so that the actual average tariff cut amounted to 1.6 percentage points. Nonetheless, these cuts were no doubt of benefit to the economies in transition. One estimate, made in Poland, was that the small amount of Polish exports would mean that the initial gain to Poland from lower tariffs might increase Polish exports by $14 million. That figure, of course, was based on relatively low export levels, and lower tariffs might enable more rapid growth of exports from Poland into those markets.

Then, too, a few countries in transition had negotiated tariff cuts under the Uruguay Round. The magnitude of reductions is reported in table 13.2. As can be seen, reductions were somewhat larger, especially for Poland, whose initial tariffs were higher. After the Uruguay Round, the average height of tariffs in

4. Between 15 and 25 percent of the exports of countries in transition are destined for intraregional trade with countries that were not members of GATT/WTO when transition started.

5. It should be recalled that the eastern European countries received and extended tariff preferences to some of these countries, so that actual tariffs were below the bound levels. There is further discussion of this phenomenon in section 13.4.

Table 13.2 **Tariff Reductions on Industrial Products by Countries in Transition**

Country	Imports from MFN Origin[a] ($ million)	Trade-Weighted Tariff Average (percent) Pre–Uruguay Round	Trade-Weighted Tariff Average (percent) Post–Uruguay Round	Reduction (percent)
Czech Republic	8,862	4.9	3.8	22
Hungary	9,468	9.6	6.9	28
Poland	7,477	16.0	9.9	38
Slovak Republic	8,862	4.9	3.8	30

Source: GATT 1994a, 71.

[a]Import values are for 1992. Data exclude petroleum and imports under tariffs where rates are not available in percentage terms.

Table 13.3 **Pre– and Post–Uruguay Round Bindings, for Agricultural Products**

Group	Value of Imports[a] ($ billion)	Tariff Lines Bound (percent) Pre–Uruguay Round	Tariff Lines Bound (percent) Post–Uruguay Round	Imports under Bound Rates (percent) Pre–Uruguay Round	Imports under Bound Rates (percent) Post–Uruguay Round
Western economies	84.2	58	100	81	100
Developing economies	30.4	18	100	25	100
Economies in transition[b]	4.8	51	100	54	100

Source: GATT 1994b, 9.

[a]Data for import values are for 1992.

[b]Total for countries in transition does not include Romania.

the countries in transition was below 10 percent in all four countries, and at 3.8 percent for the Czech Republic and the Slovak Republic.

Markets for agricultural products are of considerable interest to eastern European economies in transition. They are net exporters of agricultural products, and do not themselves have large domestic support schemes for agriculture. The countries participating in the Uruguay Round pressed hard for liberalization of agricultural trade, although only Hungary was formally a member of the Cairns Group. The final outcome in agriculture was determined by U.S.-European-Japanese interests, and involved difficult negotiations. On the positive side, a regime imposing discipline over agricultural policies was installed in the eastern European economies in transition. A simple average reduction of tariffs on agricultural commodities after the Uruguay Round was 39 percent on the exports from the economies in transition, not including Romania (table 13.3). On the negative side, tariffs on agricultural commodities in which the economies in transition seem to have a comparative advantage remain high, and there are still high domestic supports in place in many industrialized countries.

Progress in services and on other issues (trade-related intellectual property standards and investment measures, etc.) is also of potential benefit for economies in transition. In most regards, however, progress has not yet been substantial enough either to constrain the transition process or to provide significant benefits from services trade liberalization for economies in transition.

Clearly, the economies in transition benefit from the WTO as an institution, and will benefit more the greater the discipline it brings to bear on trade practices of their large trading partners. But this raises some issues of present practices in the international economy that have made the challenge of transformation even more difficult.

13.3   Aspects of the Current System Adversely Affecting Transition

When the eastern European countries began their transition, they tended to install very liberal trade policies, with low tariffs, and few other trade barriers beyond those associated with the legacy of central planning that could not be instantaneously removed. As already mentioned, there were few vested interests, so a shift toward a very open trade regime was not difficult.

But two aspects of the international economy have made the continuation and intensification of that move more difficult. The first is simply the protectionist practices of transition countries' trading partners. The second is the difficulties the desire to enter the EU creates for trade policy in the eastern European countries. Those difficulties, in turn, arise from the practices that are apparently legal under the WTO for customs unions.

Turning to the first issue, nearly all countries in transition have gone through a cycle that started with the attempt to create an open liberal market economy. They streamlined their laws and procedures both for domestic economic activity and for international trade. Barriers to trade were reduced sharply or removed as quickly as the authorities could act.

However, it was quickly discovered that, despite the spirit of the GATT/WTO articles, the trade practices of many of the large industrialized countries are protectionist and restrictive yet legal because GATT/WTO rules are loosely worded. These practices were not centered so much on customs duties as on nontariff restrictions involving quotas, voluntary export restraints, minimum import prices, licensing and monitoring of imports, technical requirements and standards, antidumping procedures, and so on.

This pattern of restrictionism was immediately evident to producers in the economies in transition who were attempting to expand their markets abroad. With relatively simple and open regimes in place, producers complained bitterly about the trade barriers they were discovering or encountering in their potential export markets. That pattern quickly prompted the authorities in the economies in transition to imitate the sorts of protective measures applied in the industrialized countries.

The pressure for protection in home markets intensified as domestic producers began to learn how to lobby, and their influence in the political process grew stronger. These lobbyists were very effective in giving examples of illiberal, complex, and highly protectionist policies pursued by other countries. National authorities in the economies in transition were highly vulnerable to such pressure.

The combination of political pressures and the sense that "other countries do it too" has led to a slow but visible retreat from the initial liberal trading policies of many of the economies in transition. The fact that the international economy is considerably less liberal than the ideals of the GATT articles is thus a factor leading to more protectionist policies in economies in transition than would otherwise be the case. It is very much in the interest of these economies, as well as the rest of the world, to find international disciplines to restrict these protectionist measures.

The second challenge for policy in the economies in transition has been even more difficult. Because of their natural trading ties with western Europe, because of the political imperatives to "rejoin Europe," and for other reasons, the eastern European economies have all been anxious to enter the EU as soon as possible. Indeed, that objective has been a key unifying force within the newly democratic bodies politic.

Ironically, preparation for entry into the EU required economies in transition to maintain (or at least declare for binding) higher tariffs and protection levels than they otherwise would have, because at a later date they would need to accept the EU levels. If tariffs had to be raised later to form the EU, compensation would have had to be paid. Moreover, for prospective entrants into the EU, worldwide reduction in EU tariff levels reduced the margin of preference that would be enjoyed once entry was achieved, which doubtless reduced the enthusiasm for tariff negotiations. This was especially important for negotiations over liberalization of trade in textiles and apparel, where there appeared to be more to gain (at least in the short run) for Poland, the Czech Republic, the Slovak Republic, and Hungary, with higher EU tariffs on imports of textiles and clothing, as the margin of preference for economies in transition would be larger. In the event, the trade-weighted tariff average was reduced from 11.0 to 9.1 percent for the EU, and by even larger percentages for many other importing countries. At the same time quotas are supposed to be phased out. These moves will benefit the economies in transition later on, when their own economies have advanced sufficiently so that they become textile and apparel importers, rather than exporters, so the loss to them is temporary.

The economies in transition naturally wanted to press for deep cuts in the levels of agricultural protection (and of producer subsidy equivalents) in industrialized countries in the Uruguay Round. But their position was influenced by the prospect of becoming a part of the EU and its agricultural economy. This meant that the negotiators in the Uruguay Round for the eastern European countries felt they had to maintain their committed tariff levels no lower than those that would be accepted when they do enter the EU. The outcome is that economies in transition have much lower actual tariffs than the levels bound under GATT/WTO, thus giving them the latitude to raise tariffs again when they gain entry. But the cost is that they could place less pressure on industrialized countries for lowering their own tariffs and subsidy equivalents to agricultural trade.

13.4 Conclusions

The transition economies benefit more the more open and liberal the international trading order is. Therefore, the existence of the WTO and its disciplines is a net benefit for them. A healthy international economy greatly facilitates the transition process, and an international discipline supports that healthy economy.

The economies in transition are net beneficiaries of strengthening of WTO disciplines and their extensions to new areas. As relatively small economies, their international bargaining power is small, and they are much better off with an open multilateral system than they are attempting to negotiate bilaterally.

Ironically, however, their need for closer ties with the EU constrains their willingness to reduce their own trade barriers, as they will have to adopt the EU's protection measures. Similarly, the prospect of EU entry makes them somewhat schizophrenic about the desirability of lowering EU tariffs and trade barriers: their margin of preference will automatically fall as external EU protection falls. Thus, the WTO permission for excepting preferential trading arrangements from WTO disciplines has questionable effects on the economies in transition.

Finally, continued resort to nontariff measures (antidumping, voluntary export restraints, domestic subsidization of agriculture, etc.) makes the task of maintaining open trade regimes in eastern Europe all the more difficult. Lobbyists are given an excellent argument for protection, namely, that their products are discriminated against abroad. In newly democratic countries, when those arguments capture the attention of the electorate, extreme pressures for backsliding in efforts to open trade regimes takes place. When the WTO can achieve agreement on rules to limit these practices, the economies in transition, along with other trading nations, will benefit.

References

Central Office of Statistics. 1991, 1992. *Yearbook of Central Office of Statistics: Foreign Trade.* Warsaw: Central Office of Statistics.
Drabeck, Zdenek, and Alasdair Smith. 1995. Trade performance and trade policy in central and eastern Europe. London: Center for Economic Policy Research. Discussion Paper no. 1182. May.
Economic Commission for Europe. 1994. The impact of the positive conclusion of

the Uruguay Round on intraregional trade with special reference to the countries in transition. Geneva: GATT.

General Agreement on Tariffs and Trade. 1994a. The results of the Uruguay Round of Multilateral Trade Negotiations. Geneva: GATT Secretariat.

———. 1994b. News of the Uruguay Round Deal (April), 9. Geneva: GATT.

Kawecka-Wyrzykowska, Elzbieta. 1995. *Trade in sensitive products between Poland and the European Union under the Europe agreement and the Uruguay Round agreements.* Warsaw: Foreign Trade Research Institute.

Michalek, Jan J. 1994. *Polish exports of non-agricultural products after the Uruguay Round: Simple estimate.* University of Warsaw. Manuscript.

Organization for Economic Cooperation and Development. 1993a. *Assessing the effects of the Uruguay Round: Trade policy issues.* No. 7. Paris: OECD.

———. 1993b. *Foreign direct investments in selected central and eastern European countries and new independent states.* Paris: OECD.

Schultz, Siegfried. 1996. Transition economies and the multilateral trading system: The need for faster integration. *Economic Bulletin,* German Institute for Economic Research, no. 3, March.

Comment on the Paper by Jaroslaw Pietras

Constantine Michalopoulos

Pietras's paper makes two fundamental points about the role of the WTO in economies in transition that are worth emphasizing: the WTO, (1) ensures MFN treatment which has been denied for years, and (2) imposes a discipline on domestic policies.

The paper focuses on the problems of the economies in eastern Europe that had been members of the WTO and have had to essentially reactivate their membership. For many of the countries future ties with the EU have been probably of greater importance than the WTO disciplines and benefits. This has created some interesting dilemmas: countries have had to maintain greater protection than they wanted, especially in agriculture, so that they can bring their policies in harmony with the EU. A very difficult problem has been faced by Estonia, which has adopted a very liberal trade regime with the support of the World Bank and the International Monetary Fund but where EU argued for them not to bind their tariffs at the very low level they were proposing, because to do so would have raised the possibility that the EU would later have to compensate third countries once Estonia became a member.

Unfortunately the paper is not correct in stating that most of the countries in transition are close to becoming members. Among countries of the former Soviet Union, only Estonia and one or two others might expect to conclude negotiations by the end of 1997. The others, including Russia, will take longer.

Constantine Michalopoulos, currently special economic adviser at the World Trade Organization, wrote this comment when he was senior adviser, Europe and Central Asia Region, at the World Bank. The views expressed are solely those of the author and should in no way be attributed to the World Trade Organization or the World Bank.

China is obviously a different case. The countries that are not members face various problems.

First, so far they have relatively liberal trade policies in part facilitated by sharply devalued exchange rates. As the power of the new elite is consolidated and stabilization leads to exchange rate appreciation, protectionist pressures mount. We in the Bank and the Fund are urging governments to make all efforts to accede to the WTO and to hold the line against protection. The main argument we use is that accession will be facilitated by a liberal trade regime unimpeded by preferences and based on private-sector rather than state trading. Our biggest challenge is with regard to what level these countries should bind tariffs at entry as many governments argue that holding out for higher bound levels would give them a better bargaining opportunity later on.

The second issue is the pressure that Russia has been exerting on several of the smaller countries to join its so-called customs union with Belarus and Kazakstan. We feel that these countries would not benefit from joining, not so much because of the trade diversion/creation effects, but rather because a customs union would strengthen the links with antiquated industrial technology, which they need to break if there is to be effective restructuring. We have also been arguing that establishing a customs union is going to delay the countries' entrance into the WTO. So far even the members of the existing customs union have applied to the WTO as individual countries.

A third issue is that as long as these countries are not members of the WTO they are treated by the United States and the EU as state trading countries for purposes of antidumping and in the EU for countervailing as well, although they have basically privatized the bulk of their economy. This designation results in the use of even more opaque procedures, in the determination of whether dumping has occurred, with greater potential for mischief through the provision of unwarranted protection. Their accession to the WTO would make it more difficult, but not impossible, for the EU and the United States to continue to use these designations and procedures.

It seems to me that the international community has a responsibility to assist these countries to become members as quickly as possible. The WTO has organized some support for this purpose, but it is not enough. Additional resources are needed to help these countries develop the detailed information needed to process an application. And it obviously must reach a conclusion over the issue of China.

14   What Can the WTO Do for Developing Countries?

J. Michael Finger and L. Alan Winters

We begin from the widely accepted premise that the integration of many developing countries into the world economy has been an important source of their recent success. This integration has ensued from two factors: (1) the access to international markets that was available to them, and (2) reforms of developing countries' policies that integrated their industries into international markets. The criterion then for answering the question that is the title of our paper is obvious: how can the WTO continue to help developing countries to integrate themselves into the international economy? We deal minimally with access to international markets for products of export interest to developing countries, however, and focus instead on how the WTO supports reform of developing countries' own policies. Given that access to major markets does not vary substantially across developing countries, while trade performance and integration do, we infer that the latter plays a fundamental if not a predominant role.

The WTO assists the process of reform of developing countries' policies in several ways. GATT/WTO sponsors multilateral negotiations through which countries agree to reduce and to bind their restrictions, particularly tariffs, against unilateral increases. It provides rules that specify what restrictions are not allowed, what restrictions a country may retain or newly put in place (safeguards, antidumping, etc.), and how trade restrictions are to be administered (e.g., customs valuation).

J. Michael Finger is a lead economist in the International Trade Division, International Economics Department of the World Bank. L. Alan Winters is division chief of the same division.

The authors are grateful to Alan Hirsch, their official discussant, conference participants, and some anonymous referees for comments on an earlier draft of this paper. The authors gratefully acknowledge skillful assistance from Ulrich Reincke and Francis Ng. The views expressed here are those of the authors alone. They do not necessarily represent those of the World Bank or any of its member governments.

Our emphasis is on the WTO and GATT rules, particularly on how these rules influence *unilateral* trade policy decisions by developing countries. While post–World War II liberalization among the industrialized countries has been mostly reciprocal, liberalization by the developing countries has been much more a matter of unilateral decisions by individual countries.

In the context of multilateral, reciprocal liberalization, GATT rules such as those that condition when a safeguard, antidumping, or other trade-remedy decision can be applied can be reasonably viewed as pressure valves designed to let off a bit of protectionist steam from time to time, while the engine of reciprocal liberalization keeps rolling on. In the context of unilateral liberalization, however, the GATT's policy rules have a different meaning. They become guidelines for determining which trade restrictions to impose or retain, and which to avoid. Particularly for countries whose small economies make it impossible for them to integrate the domestic politics of liberalization into the reciprocal GATT process,[1] GATT rules that relate to unilateral actions are the most influential part of the agreement. Governments will interpret these rules as guidelines for good policy.[2] Perhaps more important, international rules provide a basis for a government to resist domestic pressures for protection, and in this way what the GATT/WTO rules allow or disallow serves as a mold for unilateral policy choices.

Section 14.1 reviews developing-country participation in the reciprocal tariff negotiations of the Uruguay Round. We go on in later sections to examine three important sets of GATT/WTO rules. We argue that antidumping and other rules that specify when a country may unilaterally restrict troublesome imports are not good policy advice—they do not separate those interventions that will augment the national economic interest of the country that intervenes from those that will not. In the case of regional arrangements—currently popular among developing countries—we argue that the GATT/WTO requirements are less incorrect than incomplete. We also examine the good deal of special and differential treatment that remains in the GATT/WTO system. On market access, GATT/WTO rules ask the developing countries to meet the same standards as the industrialized countries—reciprocity in the tariff negotiations and the elimination of quantitative restrictions to defend the balance of payments are examples. In other areas such as customs valuation procedures or technical standards, areas shaded by their technical nature from the spotlight of political accountability, special and differential treatment remains substantive. Section 14.4 presents our conclusions and recommendations.

---

1. In a negotiation in which all foreign liberalization is most-favored-nation (MFN), the government of a small country will have trouble convincing exporters that their access to foreign markets depends on their convincing local producers to allow foreign access to the domestic market.

2. In governments' dealings with other multilateral institutions, e.g., the World Bank and the International Monetary Fund (IMF), the objective, if not always the result, of the relationship is to determine policies that best serve the national economic interest of the country.

14.1   Tariff Negotiations and the Developing Countries

From the perspective of an individual country, the multilateral negotiation of tariff reductions provides opportunities of different sorts:

- to bargain for lower tariffs in markets of interest,
- to use the multilateral negotiation as leverage against domestic interests that resist tariff reductions, and
- to negotiate bindings that will provide defenses against future domestic pressures to increase rates or to provide protection by other means.

Binding has the effect not only of putting a cap on unilateral increases of tariffs; it also restrains a government from providing protection through other means that could be interpreted as nullification or impairment of that tariff binding.

In this section we examine how extensively developing countries agreed at the Uruguay Round to reduce their tariffs. We also examine how extensively they agreed to bind their tariffs, and to what extent those bound rates are above presently applied rates. Finally, for a sample of developing countries that introduced extensive unilateral tariff reductions during the 1980s and early 1990s, we examine the extent to which they have bound these unilateral reductions at the Uruguay Round.

Table 14.1 provides summary results from a tabulation of the concessions agreed on at the Uruguay Round. This tabulation covers only those countries that have supplied data to the WTO Integrated Data Base (IDB).[3] According to the WTO Secretariat, the IDB covers all industrial and transition economies that participated in the Uruguay Round, plus twenty-six of ninety-four developing-economy participants. The countries covered are listed in the notes to table 14.1. This data base provides post– and pre–Uruguay Round bound rates, as reported by the member countries.

Measuring applied rates was more complicated. From several alternative measures[4] we chose the best proxy for the applied rate that reflected unilateral changes made just before or during the Uruguay Round, but excluded any

3. The IDB includes countries that account for 100 percent of nonpetroleum imports of North America, western Europe, and WTO members (at the time of the Uruguay Round) in central and eastern Europe. The IDB covers 90 percent of Asia's nonpetroleum imports, 80 percent of Latin America's nonpetroleum imports, but only two sub-Saharan African countries (Senegal and Zimbabwe), which together account for 30 percent of sub-Saharan Africa's nonpetroleum imports.

4. Various of the countries whose applied rates are below their bound rates provided different measures of applied rates. Some of these are labeled in the IDB as the "MFN applied rate," the "MFN Uruguay Round base rate," or the "MFN statutory rate." As our proxy for MFN applied rates before the Uruguay Round cuts, we used the MFN applied rate whenever it was available. If the MFN applied rate was not available, we used the lower of the MFN base rate and the MFN statutory rate. A number of countries, particularly in Latin America, introduced substantial unilateral reductions of their tariff rates before or during the years of the Uruguay Round. These unilateral changes were in some cases not reflected in the MFN applied rate. In those cases we updated

Table 14.1   **Bindings of MFN Tariff Rates before and after the Uruguay Round, and Uruguay Round Tariff Reductions for Selected Countries and Country Groups**

Country or Group	Percentage of Imports GATT Bound				Average Uruguay Round Tariff Reduction[a]	
		Post–Uruguay Round				
	Pre–Uruguay Round	Total	At Applied Rate	Below Applied Rate	Across Reduced Items Only	Across All Imports
High-income countries[b]	80	89	38	30	3.2	1.0
European Union	98	100	43	39	3.1	1.5
Japan	73	83	42	38	2.7	1.0
United States	92	93	41	37	2.9	1.4
Hong Kong	1	28	28	0	—	—
Lower- and middle-income countries[c]	31	81	13	29	8.1	2.3
South Asia[d]	11	52	10	23	16.5	3.9
East Asia[e]	16	77	14	40	9.4	3.8
Korea	21	83	13	64	8.5	5.5
Philippines	9	61	27	17	7.9	1.3
Eastern Europe[f]	55	96	28	41	2.4	1.00
Latin America[g]	50	100	3	1	2.4	0.02
Argentina	17	100	0.2	0	4.2	0.001
Brazil	16	100	6.0	1	1.1	0.007
Mexico	100	100	2.0	0	0.9	0.004
Senegal and Zimbabwe[h]	26	40	22.0	1	5.8	0.05

Source: Finger, Ingco, and Reincke 1996.

[a]Weights are based on 1988 import values.

[b]Australia, Austria, Canada, European Union, Finland, Hong Kong, Ireland, Japan, New Zealand, Norway, Singapore, Sweden, Switzerland, and the United States.

[c]All countries covered below plus Tunisia and Turkey.

[d]India and Sri Lanka.

[e]Indonesia, Korea, Macao, Malaysia, Philippines, and Thailand.

[f]Czech and Slovak Customs Union, Hungary, Poland, and Romania.

[g]Argentina, Brazil, Chile, Colombia, El Salvador, Jamaica, Mexico, Peru, Uruguay, and Venezuela.

[h]Senegal and Zimbabwe are the only sub-Saharan African countries that have submitted tariff data to the WTO IDB.

changes that were the results of the round. We then measured the post–Uruguay Round applied rate (tariff line by tariff line) as the lower of this applied rate and the Uruguay Round bound rate. The figures provided in the tables are averages across all merchandise imports, including agricultural prod-

the MFN applied rate with data from the United Nations Conference on Trade and Development (UNCTAD) TRAINS data base.

ucts. For all sectors, including agriculture, where the Uruguay Round requires the conversion of all nontariff barriers (NTBs) to tariffs, our data do not include tariff equivalents of NTBs.[5]

14.1.1 Tariff Reductions

The right-hand columns in table 14.1 report the degree of tariff reduction agreed on at the Uruguay Round. In interpreting these numbers, the reader should be aware that we have measured tariff change as the reduction of the ad valorem rate (or ad valorem equivalent rate) divided by unity plus the ad valorem rate, as $dT/(1 + T)$, expressed as a percentage. For a country whose imports do not affect world prices, $dT/(1 + T)$ measures the percentage by which the domestic price of imports will fall as a result of the tariff cut. In this way, we take into account that halving a 20 percent rate will have a larger effect on imports, other things given, than halving a 2 percent rate. The second-to-last column in table 14.1 provides an average over only those tariff lines on which the tariff was reduced. The last column measures the overall tariff cut, an average cut across all tariff lines. Zero reductions are included in the second average, but not in the first.[6]

Our tabulations of Uruguay Round tariff reductions and bindings are presented in detail in Finger, Ingco, and Reincke 1996. Here we highlight only a few of our findings.

Looking first at the amounts by which tariffs were reduced, the table reports that the developing and transition economies agreed at the Uruguay Round to reduce their tariffs by an average 8 percent on 29 percent of their imports. These reductions come to a 2.3 percent reduction of their overall tariff. By comparison the industrial and other high-income countries agreed to reduce their tariffs by an average 3.2 percent on 30 percent of their imports, for an average reduction of 1 percent across all tariff lines. Among developing countries, the Asian countries agreed to relatively large reductions. Tariff reductions agreed on at the Uruguay Round by Latin American countries were quite small, but as we shall see below, the Latin American countries introduced large unilateral reductions in the 1980s and 1990s. For them, the relevant issue is the extent to which they bound these reductions at the round.

14.1.2 Tariff Bindings

Until the Uruguay Round, insistence on special and differential treatment was an important part of many developing countries' policy toward the multilateral negotiations. One result was that few developing-country tariffs were

---

5. We measure a reduction of tariffs on agricultural products only when the post–Uruguay Round bound rate is below the pre–Uruguay Round applied tariff rate. Likewise, elimination of voluntary export restraints under the safeguards and clothing-textiles agreements are not taken into account by these figures.

6. The last column is arithmetically the product of the two immediately preceding, divided by 100.

Table 14.2   **Average Tariffs, Post–Uruguay Round Applied and Bound Rates for Selected Countries and Country Groups**

Country or Group	Applied Rates	Bound Rates
High-income countries[a]	2.6	3.7
European Union	2.8	3.2
Japan	2.8	3.7
United States	2.8	3.3
Hong Kong	0.0	0.0
Lower- and middle-income countries[b]	13.3	25.2
South Asia[c]	30.4	50.8
East Asia[d]	11.9	21.0
Korea	7.7	16.4
Philippines	19.0	21.9
Eastern Europe[e]	6.7	13.3
Latin America[f]	11.7	32.7
Argentina	10.3	31.0
Brazil	11.7	29.0
Mexico	10.4	34.1
Senegal and Zimbabwe[g]	9.0	19.4

Source: Authors' calculations based on UNCTAD TRAINS data base.

Note: Weights are based on 1988 import values.

[a]Australia, Austria, Canada, European Union, Finland, Hong Kong, Ireland, Japan, New Zealand, Norway, Singapore, Sweden, Switzerland, and the United States.

[b]All countries covered below plus Tunisia and Turkey.

[c]India and Sri Lanka.

[d]Indonesia, Korea, Macao, Malaysia, Philippines, and Thailand.

[e]Czech and Slovak Customs Union, Hungary, Poland, and Romania.

[f]Argentina, Brazil, Chile, Colombia, El Salvador, Jamaica, Mexico, Peru, Uruguay, and Venezuela.

[g]Senegal and Zimbabwe are the only sub-Saharan African countries that have submitted tariff data to the WTO IDB.

bound—in table 14.1, less than one-third of imports were under bound rates. Note, however, that at the Uruguay Round the developing and transition economies agreed to significant bindings. The major Latin American countries have agreed to bind all of their tariffs; the extent of bindings is as high now in many developing and transition economies as in the industrialized countries.

Table 14.2, which compares post–Uruguay Round applied and bound rates, focuses on this point.[7] While developing countries' tariff reductions, as we have measured them, have been rather large, their tariff rates are still high, as compared with those of the industrialized countries. Many developing-country bindings are at ceiling rates, above applied rates. India's post–Uruguay Round

7. Generally, Uruguay Round agreed rates will be effective no later than 1 January 1999, but some countries have, for some commodities, negotiated later deadlines. The bound rates we report are final rates, after all stages are completed. We measure the post–Uruguay Round applied rate, tariff line by tariff line, as the lower of the current applied rate and the post–Uruguay Round bound rate. Average applied rates cover all tariff lines, but average bound rates cover only those tariff lines that are bound.

average bound rate is 52 percent; its average applied rate is 31 percent. Latin American countries' bound rates average around 30 percent (with minimal dispersion, most rates are near 30 percent); their applied rates average 10 to 12 percent.

As noted above, a ceiling binding provided a government a basis for resisting pressures to backslide on the liberalizations it had already made. Nontariff measures other than the kind of restrictions allowed under the "rules" part of the GATT would likely be considered nullification or impairment of the tariff binding. Any restriction other than a tariff increase or a GATT-legal "trade remedy" would open the possibility of complaints through GATT enforcement processes from trading partners.

14.1.3   Binding of Unilateral Concessions

The Uruguay Round also provided countries that had unilaterally liberalized the opportunity to bind these concessions. Such binding might be useful in two ways: as "coin" for buying concessions from trading partners and as a basis for resisting domestic pressures to raise the rates again.

Table 14.3 reports calculations for selected countries of the percentage of recent tariff reductions that have been bound. (The sample is limited to the countries for which suitable data are available.) In these calculations we used the IDB "Uruguay Round base rate"—as of 1986—as our measure of tariff

Table 14.3   Percentages of Unilateral Tariff Reductions by Selected Countries That Were Bound at the Uruguay Round

Country	Total Reduction[a]	Bound Reduction[b]	Percentage of Total Reduction Bound[c]
Argentina	16	9	57
Brazil	25	12	47
Chile	19	8	39
Mexico	27	8	30
Peru	20	9	46
Uruguay	6	3	41
Venezuela	19	2	12
India	27	22	82
Average, weighted by import value			39

Source: Authors' calculations based on the WTO's Integrated Database.

[a]Import weighted average of changes calculated by tariff line. The change is from the rate before unilateral reductions and before reciprocal (Uruguay Round) reductions to the rate after both. Reduction is defined as $dT/(1 + T)$.

[b]Import weighted average of changes calculated by tariff line from the rate before unilateral reductions and before reciprocal reductions to the post–Uruguay Round bound rate. Reduction is defined as $dT/(1 + T)$. In calculating the averages, in those tariff lines for which the bound rate was above the initial rate, the bound reduction was set equal to zero.

[c]Bound reduction as a percentage of total reduction.

rates pre–Uruguay Round and pre–unilateral concessions. We measured the "total reduction" as the change from this base rate to the lower of the 1992 applied rate[8] or the IDB post–Uruguay Round bound rate. The "bound reduction" is the change from the base rate to the post–Uruguay Round bound rate.

Overall, our calculations indicate that the countries in the group have bound somewhat less than half of the unilateral concessions that they have implemented since 1986. Measured as we have measured tariff cuts, that comes to a bound cut of 8 to 12 percent for a number of Latin American countries and 22 percent for India. Comparing these figures with those in the last two columns of table 14.1, we find that, except for India, these countries have added little to their tariff reductions through the reciprocal negotiations. At the Uruguay Round Latin American countries agreed to reciprocal reductions that averaged only 0.02 percent across all of their imports.[9] Even so, the 5 to 6 percent bound cut compares favorably with the 1 to 2 percent reduction agreed to by the higher-income countries at the round.[10]

14.2 GATT Rules

Some eleven of the GATT's twenty-five functional articles provide rules about what trade restrictions a country can and cannot impose—nine of the eleven providing for the application of certain kinds of measures—safeguards, antidumping, general exceptions, national security exceptions, and so forth.[11]

The historical reason that the many provisions allowing trade restrictions are in the GATT is most likely that protectionist interests have been strong enough to insist that such restrictions be provided for. To those seeking to create an open international trading system, the provisions are part of their losses, not of their victories. The familiar rationale for the provisions is that, had they not been included, protectionist interests would have prevented the tariff reductions that have been the core of the GATT. In figurative language, allowing for a possible step backward was part of the price of achieving two steps forward. A related and more forward-looking version of the latter rationale is that any government that maintains a liberal trade policy must have ways to deal with constituent pressures for exceptions—pressures for protection of particular domestic sectors. We build our evaluation of such provisions on that view.

8. These data were taken from the UNCTAD TRAINS data base.

9. It is tempting to think that the bound reduction plus the reciprocal reduction equal the total reduction, but they do not. The bound reduction plus the "unbound reduction" (not presented) would equal the total reduction; the reciprocal reduction is a part of the bound reduction.

10. The results indicate that on the whole these countries' bound rates are about halfway between their initial applied rates and the rates to which their unilateral reforms have brought them. For only a few tariff lines is the Uruguay Round bound rate below this unilateral rate. Since the Latin American countries' bindings are more or less uniform at 30 percent, these few tariff lines are likely the ones for which the unilateral rates are relatively high, above 30 percent.

11. Finger (1996) lists these articles and reports the frequency with which GATT members have used them.

14.2.1   GATT Pressure-Valve Provisions

Any government that strives to maintain an open trade regime must have mechanisms for managing domestic pressures for protection. In a system such as the GATT/WTO system, part of the discipline built into such domestic mechanisms is the international commitment not to impose new trade restrictions. Within the international system, the latitude the domestic mechanisms have to acquiesce to domestic pressures are in the rules the GATT/WTO provides as to when new restrictions may be imposed.

In reviewing the criteria that underlie the pressure valve provided by the GATT, we will evaluate them against two standards. (1) Good trade restrictions versus bad: Do the criteria make economic sense? Do they isolate actions that have greater economic benefits than costs for the country that takes the action, or for the world economy? Do these rules provide a basis for a developing-country government to resist domestic pressures for actions that would not serve the national economic interest? (2) Less trade restrictions versus more: Do the criteria provide an objective basis for saying no? On the presumption that most trade restrictions would not pass the economic sense criteria, fewer trade restrictions would make more economic sense than more.

Emergency Actions under Article XIX

GATT article XIX begins: "If, as a result of unforeseen developments and of the effect of the obligations incurred . . . under this Agreement, including tariff concessions, any product is being imported . . . as to cause or threaten serious injury to domestic producers . . . of like or directly competitive products . . . the contracting party shall be free . . . to suspend the obligation . . . or to withdraw or modify the concession." This sentence obviously authorizes import-restricting actions, but what limits are there on such actions? The following two subsections discuss two possible sources of constraint: the article's statement of the conditions under which pressure-valve actions can be taken, and the relation between this article and the notion of reciprocity that underlies the GATT tariff-cutting process.

Conditions. As the quoted sentence states, emergency action is conditioned on (1) injury from imports that results from (2) a concession (liberalization) *and* from (3) "unforeseen developments." The intent of conditioning import relief on "unforeseen developments" seems obvious: without this qualification relief would be available each time a liberalization had its probable effect—to increase imports—and the emergency-action provision would provide for the undoing of all the liberalization negotiated.

Early on in the GATT's history, in the hatters' fur case of 1950, a GATT working party interpreted "unforeseen developments" in a way that eliminated it as a constraint on emergency actions. As Gary Sampson concludes (1987, 143): "What this [interpretation] meant in practical terms was that any increase in imports, even if through normal changes in international competitiveness, could therefore be considered actionable under Article XIX."

Other interpretations further weakened article XIX as discipline against emergency actions. The hatters' fur working party also concluded that the country taking emergency action is entitled to the benefit of the doubt in determining injury: the exporting country has to actively disprove injury (to importing country producers) in order to overturn an action. Near the same time as the hatters' fur case, another working party concluded that a determination of serious injury from imports does not require even that imports be *increasing* before injury can be determined (Sampson 1987, 143).

The import of these decisions is that the condition "unforeseen developments" was nullified as a constraint on article XIX actions to restrict imports. At the same time, the capacity of the condition "injury" to constrain was weakened by allowing the importing country the benefit of the doubt in determining its operational meaning.

Reciprocity. While article XIX's conditionality has not restrained its use, the other constraint, reciprocity, has provided discipline. Article XIX explicitly calls for consultations with exporters and explicitly provides for retaliation— suspension of "substantially equivalent concessions or other obligations." Compensation (to buy off retaliation) is implicit in these provisions.

In the early years of its application, most invocations of article XIX were accompanied by either mutually agreed compensation or retaliation. Of the twenty-five actions taken under the escape clause between 1948 and 1962, compensation was offered in fourteen cases and retaliation took place four times, including three cases in which compensation had been offered (GATT 1994, 500–516).

The Uruguay Round Safeguard Agreement. The major elements of the Uruguay Round on an agreement on safeguards are described below.

Phase out of voluntary export restraints (VERs) must be completed within four years, with the exception that each member may retain one VER until 31 December 1999. Only the European Union has notified an exception, its VER on Japanese cars and trucks. Likewise, existing article XIX measures (GATT-legal measures) must be phased out eight years after application or by 31 December 1999, whichever comes later. Quantitative restrictions are explicitly recognized, however, and after a formal determination of injury, an import quota applied as a safeguard measure may, by mutual agreement, be administered by the exporting country.

Actions under article XIX are subject to several limits. The key ones are progressive liberalization and limits on the duration of safeguard measures.

Two major changes that make article XIX more usable by interests seeking protection are the explicit allowance of discriminatory quantitative restrictions and the removal of the exporting country's right to retaliate against a safeguard

measure for the first three years. The latter change removes the burden to negotiated compensation, that is, it allows an article XIX action to be unilateral,
disciplined only by the condition that injury must be determined.

The 1994 agreement contains many explicit procedural requirements for
transparency and openness that were not in the original article XIX. First, a
member may apply a safeguard measure only after an investigation and a determination of injury.[12] The investigation must be carried out according to procedures previously established and made public; it must include public notices
to all interested parties and public hearings for the presentation of evidence,
views, and comments from all sides.[13] The determination must demonstrate a
causal link between imports and injury.[14] The agency that conducts the investigation and makes the determination must publish a detailed analysis, setting
out its findings and conclusions, and how these relate to the facts developed
and to the applicable law.[15]

The economic criteria that conditions when an import restriction may be
imposed is *serious injury* to domestic producers of like or competing products.
Injury is more or less a translation into administrative terms of the economic
concept of comparative disadvantage; hence it is not a criteria that will isolate
those restrictions that serve the national economic interest. Indeed, the gains
from trade are likely to be larger when the cost advantage of imports over
domestic production is large, and injury is of significant magnitude. Injury,
simple or serious, fails the economic sense criterion.

Likewise, unless there is injury (i.e., displaced domestic production) from
imports, there will be little motive for petitions for import restrictions. Hence
"injury" will not provide a basis for rejecting a significant share of petitions
for relief. For the criterion to provide a basis to reject some petitions (i.e.,
provide less import restrictions rather than more) will depend on there being a
politically convincing basis for separating serious injury from less serious. In
practice, this has not been the case.[16]

The public notice and transparency requirements the Uruguay Round safeguards agreement adds to article XIX procedures—like similar requirements
for antidumping procedures—are laudable on their own terms, but they do not
correct the bad economics of article XIX. To do the wrong thing the right way
is still to do the wrong thing. Because the requirements do nothing to bring
out the costs of protection or to enfranchise those interests that will bear these
costs, they are not likely to change the domestic political balance in favor of
fewer restrictions.

12. The familiar details of article XIX are retained, e.g., "serious" injury, "cause or threaten."
13. Information and views may be presented to show the safeguards measure is in the public interest.
14. The "unforeseen circumstances" requirement of article XIX has been removed.
15. Extension of a safeguard measure has the same requirements as the initial action.
16. Administratively operational criteria for distinguishing degree of injury have often been
arbitrary. Finger (1992) examines the issue. Note that a negative finding is described in news
releases and in political rhetoric as a finding of "no injury," not as a finding of "not serious" injury.

Restrictions to Protect the Balance of Payments. GATT article XVIII permits developing countries to introduce trade restrictions either to support infant industries or to protect their balance of payments. Neither makes economic sense. In practice, developing countries' use of the balance-of-payments exception has far exceeded their use of the infant-industry exception. Table 14.4 reports almost 3,500 restrictions declared under the balance-of-payments exception, less than 100 under the infant-industry exception.[17]

Why have there been so few actions under the infant-industry provision? The procedural requirements of the balance-of-payments provision are easier—developing countries find it easier to obtain GATT "cover" for infant-industry protection under the guise of "balance-of-payments" reasons.

The facts of usage bear out this interpretation. Anjaria (1987, 680) reports that in almost three-fourths of the developing countries that declared article XVIII:B measures, the measures covered less than half of import categories. If these restrictions were truly for balance-of-payments purposes, they would cover all import categories.

Before the Uruguay Round began, the increased commercial presence of developing countries had provoked industrial countries to press for market-opening actions by the developing countries. The industrial countries applied this pressure both through the GATT Committee on Balance-of-Payments Restrictions and the Trade Committee of the Organization for Economic Cooperation and Development (OECD). One of its focal points was reduced use by developing countries of article XVIII:B restrictions.

At the same time, the demonstration effect of the Asian model of export-led development changed developing countries' view of trade policy. Realistic exchange rates had been an important element in this experience, and there was a growing realization that an unrealistic exchange rate buttressed by trade control was bad development policy. Hence developing countries were more willing to give in on use of article XVIII:B. As of June 1996, only three developing countries (Tunisia, India, and Pakistan) maintained import restrictions declared under GATT article XVIII:B that are of major concern to potential exporters.

Uruguay Round Balance-of-Payments Understanding. During the Uruguay Round, OECD countries—the United States and Canada in particular—were strong proponents of strengthening GATT balance-of-payments provisions to more accurately reflect changes in economic ideas about the interrelation of trade and development. The Uruguay Round understanding has added statements to encourage use of price-based measures rather than quantitative restrictions, and to encourage phasing-out of balance-of-payments measures.

17. Article XVIII:A and D also provide in slightly different ways for import restrictions to support industry development. As of March 1994, article XVIII:A had been invoked nine times, while section D had not been invoked at all. For details on the use of section A, see GATT 1994, 465.

Table 14.4	Number of Customs Cooperation Council Nomenclature Items on Which Developing Countries Notified Quantitative Restrictions under Different GATT Articles, 1974–87	
GATT Article Cited as Justification		Number
VIII	Fees and formalities connected with importation and exportation	316
XI:2	Restrictions in order to apply standards or classifications, to manage short supplies, or to complement agricultural or fisheries support programs	108
XVII	State trading enterprises	15
XVIII:B	Balance-of-payments measures for developing countries	3,437
XVIII:C	Industrial development	91
XX	General exceptions	131
XXI	National security	4

Source: OECD 1992, 100.

The understanding also adds detailed documentation requirements.

The Uruguay Round understanding thus earns high marks as a guide to sensible economic policy—it reflects the growing realization that an unrealistic exchange rate that must be buttressed by trade control is bad development policy.

Antidumping

Antidumping was a minor instrument when the GATT was negotiated, and provision for antidumping regulations was included with little controversy. Since then, antidumping has become the industrial countries' major safeguard instrument, and is gaining increasing popularity among developing countries. As of July 1996, fifty-eight developing and transition-economy countries have notified antidumping laws or regulations to the WTO, and sixteen had notified antidumping actions to the WTO.[18]

Several features of antidumping explain its popularity.

- Discriminatory action is permitted.

- In national practice, the injury test for antidumping action tends to be softer than the injury test for action under article XIX.

- The rhetoric of foreign unfairness provides a vehicle for building a political case for protection.

- Antidumping and VERs have proved to be effective complements; that is, the threat of formal action under the antidumping law provides leverage to force an exporter to accept a VER.[19]

18. Since 1985, GATT member countries have notified over 150 antidumping cases per year. Article XIX notifications have been less than 3 per year.

19. Finger and Murray 1993 report that over 1980–88, 348 of 774 U.S. antidumping cases were superseded by VERs.

- Suspension agreements are provided for in the 1989 Tokyo Round anti-dumping code and in the Uruguay Round agreement.[20]
- The investigation process itself tends to curb imports. This is because exporters bear significant legal and administrative costs, importers face the uncertainty of having to pay, once an investigation is completed, backdated antidumping duties (Finger 1981; Staiger and Wolak 1994).

The Uruguay Round Agreement. The negotiations were a pitched battle between victims and users of antidumping. The only clear victory for the victims was the introduction of a sunset clause requiring that all antidumping actions be terminated after no more than five years—unless a review determines that termination would lead to continuation of recurrence of dumping and injury. The agreement considerably increases documentation requirements, but they do not change its economics.[21]

The Economics of Antidumping. National regulations allow antidumping action in a broad range of circumstances. This point, supported by considerable research, is stated by different authors in different ways, for example, that such regulations are biased toward finding dumping and toward overstating dumping margins (Bierwagen 1991; Litan and Boltuck 1991) or that antidumping is ordinary protection with a good public relations program (Finger 1993a).

An important detail of these findings is that, in practice, the criteria of what constitutes dumping are so broad that the dumping standard is met in virtually every case.[22] Without the injury standard, all antidumping cases would reach affirmative outcomes; that is, the criterion that distinguishes an affirmative antidumping finding from a negative one is the same as the criterion of an article XIX safeguard action: injury to competing domestic producers.

Its rhetoric aside, neither legal nor economic analysis finds a link between antidumping investigations and the detection of anticompetitive practices. An OECD study, for example, has found that imports posed no threat to the existence competition in more than 90 percent of the cases in which the U.S. and EU imposed antidumping duties in the 1980s (de Jonquieres 1995, 5).

As economics, antidumping is an injury test, nothing more. Thus the eco-

---

20. Stegemann (1992, 8) reports that from July 1980 through June 1989, of 384 antidumping actions taken by the European Community, 184 were price undertakings. Though the Tokyo Round code does not explicitly provide for such settlement, both U.S. and EC antidumping regulations allow for suspension through acceptance by the exporter of a quantity limit (Jackson and Vermulst 1989, 52, 116).

21. The agreement is examined in some detail by Finger (1996), who points out that the victims were in large part successful only in adding documentation requirements to the practices that they wanted removed.

22. Quantitative evidence for this conclusion is based on U.S. experience only, the United States being the only country that separately publishes outcomes of dumping and of injury determinations. Finger 1993a, chap. 3, reviews the evidence.

nomic evaluation presented above of article XIX actions as a pressure valve applies equally to antidumping. Its sorting of restrictions that are authorized from those that are not makes no economic sense, and it serves minimally as an influence for fewer restrictions than for more. While antidumping may not score a zero by the criterion "fewer restrictions rather than more," the inflammatory rhetoric that antidumping supports and the weaker injury test that it embodies suggest that it should receive a lower score than article XIX. This, as noted above, is why the protectionists prefer it.

14.2.2   Conclusions about GATT Pressure Valves

This brief review of pressure valves allowed by the GATT leads to the following conclusions.

1. GATT pressure valves make no economic sense. The conditions under which the GATT allows a country to take emergency actions or antidumping actions, or to impose trade restrictions to protect the balance of payments are not the conditions under which such action would serve the national economic interest of the country. In economics, pressure valves are just ordinary protection, with sufficient political influence that antiprotection forces cannot overcome it.

The rationale for these mechanisms remains political. Their nonsense economics raises the following question, however: might there be processes that served as a pressure valve for protectionist pressures and at the same time make economic sense? One of the major disappointments of the Uruguay Round is that this question was never addressed.

2. GATT rules provide little discipline over use of pressure valves. This proposition follows from the following two.

3. Trade restrictions are fungible. The GATT provides a long list of apparently special-purpose restrictions, but the type of restriction that a country imposes is not determined by the nature of the "problem" that the country faces. It is determined by the relative ease of qualifying for one or another type of GATT coverage for the restriction. In the GATT's first decade, article XIX actions, renegotiations, and negotiations were impossible to distinguish from each other. At present, antidumping is the instrument of choice of protection-seeking interests. In the 1970s and 1980s, VERs were the favorite form of protection of the industrial countries, article XVIII:B balance-of-payments actions the favorite GATT cover for developing countries' import restrictions.

4. Safeguard action is always possible under the rules. "Injury" is the economic concept that underlies article XIX actions and antidumping. Each of these pressure valves includes a second factor, "dumping" for antidumping and "unforeseen developments" for article XIX action. But in practice, the meaning of "dumping" is so broad that the injury test is the only constraint on antidumping action. And the "unforeseen developments" condition on article XIX action was rendered ineffective the first time it was challenged. Thus, "injury"

is the sole condition that restrains article XIX or antidumping action, and "injury," as economics, is identical with comparative disadvantage. Any time imports displace or threaten to displace domestic production, pressure-valve action is GATT-legal. The GATT chain is as strong as its weakest link, and antidumping is at present the protectionists' favorite means.

5. GATT pressure-valve processes make little political sense. Only in the cheap sense of bowing to political reality are the GATT's pressure valves defensible. They do nothing, however, to empower the good guys—the interests that would be hurt by the imposition of an import restriction.

Worse, the GATT's pressure valves empower the bad guys. An investigation of injury—on which pressure-valve actions are premised—provides a tribune from which the interests that will benefit from an import restriction can make their case. An antidumping investigation adds the opportunity to accuse exporters of unfairness. Given the proprotection logic and structure of the pressure-valve process, reasons to refuse protection are arbitrary[23]—free trade, not protection, depends on exploiting the loopholes in trade law.

14.2.3   Customs Unions and Free Trade Areas

Article XXIV of the GATT seeks to specify circumstances under which countries may violate the most-favored-nation (MFN) clause by forming free trade areas or custom unions. It imposes three principal restrictions, that the free trade area or customs union (1) cover "substantially all trade" (par. 8); (2) reduce internal tariffs to zero and remove internal quantitative restrictions other than those justified by other GATT articles (par. 8); and (3) not raise the average level of protection against excluded countries (par. 5).

Mercantilist Sense. These provisions were written in a pre-Vinerian world which did not recognize the concepts of trade diversion and trade creation, and which held that liberalizing trade with a subset of partners was a good thing.[24] They are also, of course, part of a document whose primary focus is the mercantilist one on the rights of trading partners rather than the economist's one on the benefits of policy for the member country itself. From these perspectives there is some logic to conditions 2 and 3. Condition 3 may be viewed as preserving the sanctity of tariff bindings by ensuring that forming a customs union does not provide a wholesale way of dissolving previous bindings. There is also a convention that compensation is due to individual partners (in terms of other tariff reductions) for increases induced by the customs union if the

---

23. For example, antiprotectionists oppose "cumulation," the adding-up of injury from each of many exporters, no one of which is large enough to cause "serious" injury. But is it reasonable to provide protection to an industry that has been devoured by a shark, while denying protection to an industry nibbled to death by piranhas? Finger (1992) takes up in detail the point that the constraints on safeguards actions are arbitrary.

24. In fact, Viner first defined the concepts in 1931—in Swedish—but they were not widely known. We are grateful to Richard Snape for this observation.

corresponding reductions to keep the average constant are not adequate. Together, these provisions offer reasonable assurances about the barriers facing nonmembers.

Condition 2 is best seen as a means of defending the MFN clause by making it subject to an "all-or-nothing" exception. If countries were free to negotiate different levels of preference with each trading partner, binding and nondiscrimination would be fatally undermined—no member could be sure that it was receiving the benefits it expected from a bound tariff negotiation. Moreover, one might view customs unions as a first step toward deeper integration—ultimately nation building—and feel it inappropriate that an international trade treaty should stand in the way of such progress. If so, internal free trade, such as one (usually) achieves within a single country, would be an acceptable derogation of MFN, whereas preferences would not be. Condition 1 does not lie within the GATT tradition of tariff-line by tariff-line negotiation, but does reinforce 2 by requiring a serious degree of commitment to a free trade area or customs union before sanctioning it under the GATT.

Economic Sense. The conditions of article XXIV also make some, albeit incomplete, sense when viewed from a more modern and economic perspective. The requirement not to raise barriers against nonmembers not only honors the latters' market-access rights under the GATT but also heads off one otherwise available route to increased protectionism. This is desirable on any account, but in the context of free trade areas and customs unions the danger and costs of trade diversion will be greater if the members can increase their external tariffs. It is also useful that the Uruguay Round Understanding on the Interpretation of Article XXIV offers instruction on how to assess whether this condition has been met.[25]

Condition 2 is, from an economic point of view, unnecessary. Trade theory is now quite clear that, from the point of view of the free trade area or customs union, a small tariff on trade between members is better than free trade if there are positive tariffs on nonmember countries (Ethier and Horn 1984). However, its rationale in defending MFN seems sufficiently strong both systemically and individually to create a net benefit overall. The benefit to an individual country of preserving the condition is that, if partial preferences are permissible, governments may come under increased pressure internally or externally to use them, and could have to expend considerable effort resisting proposals for degrees of preference that did not generate Ethier-Horn-type benefits.

---

25. It is worth noting that this instruction refers to the applied rates of duty, not the bound rates. The exact impact of this is not clear yet. On the one hand it may be seen as effectively binding an average of the previously applied rates—at least for so long as the conditions applicable to the *creation,* as opposed to the operation, of a customs union remain in force. On the other hand, it may imply a lack of discipline on the relationship between the preintegration bound rates of the members and those of the customs union.

Political Sense. Condition 1 does have an important role from a welfare point of view. Recent advances in political-economy modeling—for example, Grossman and Helpman 1995—have suggested that, if governments are susceptible to lobbying by sectoral producer groups, political pressures will tend to favor trade-diverting regional arrangements. Trade diversion unambiguously generates gains for partner exporters, so when two countries swap trade-diverting concessions, both sets of producers gain. On the other hand, if they swap trade-creating concessions, producers lose some sales in their home markets and may or may not gain overall. Lobbies increase the weight of producer gains and losses in overall decision making, so that it is perfectly possible that trade diversion is politically more powerful than trade creation and that the option of regional liberalization undermines the incentives for first-best non-discriminatory liberalization (Krishna 1994; Levy 1994). Condition 1 means that governments cannot select only commodities that are likely to feature trade diversion, and this in turn seems likely to encourage more efficient free trade areas and customs unions.

This argument makes obvious the case that the GATT/WTO generates welfare less through disciplining a country's trading partners than through bolstering the country's government against pressures to pursue inappropriate policies at home. Not only does condition 1 constrain the government's response to such pressures, but it also, one hopes, reduces the frequency with which such pressure is applied.

Does Article XXIV Ensure Good Policy?

The previous paragraphs suggest that article XXIV is generally an aid to rational policymaking. However, they do not suggest that it is sufficient for good policy. The rules prevent a given group of countries from limiting a free trade agreement to those products on which trade will be diverted, but they do not prevent a free trade agreement among countries for which elimination of internal barriers will be entirely or predominantly trade-diverting.

In fact, article XXIV has not provided as much discipline as it might have, for it has been notoriously weakly enforced. WTO (1995) reports that of sixty-nine working parties reporting up to and including 1994, only six had been able to agree that a free trade area or customs union met the requirements of article XXIV. However, the remainder did not conclude that the agreement under review was not in conformity, but merely left the matter undetermined.

The reluctance of the GATT as an institution to decide on the consistency of regional agreements with the rules does not mean that the rules have had no effect—we do not know which potential arrangements they discouraged—but it is not an encouraging record. There have been clear breaches of condition 1 (e.g., the European Coal and Steel Community), breaches of condition 2 (e.g., the European Economic Cooperation's monetary compensatory amounts on intra-EEC agricultural trade), and, on some interpretations, breaches of condition 3 (e.g., the EEC, of which the GATT executive secretary[26] expressed "the view, with which he thought there was no disagreement, that the incidence of the Common Tariff was higher than that of the rates actually applied by the Member States at the time of entry into force of the Treaty of Rome" [GATT Document C/M/8, 6; cited in GATT 1994, 750]).

The Enabling Clause

A further complication for developing countries is the enabling clause—the Decision on Differential and More Favorable Treatment, Reciprocity, and Fuller Participation of Developing Countries of 1979 (see GATT 1994). This significantly relaxes the conditions for creating free trade areas or customs unions that include only developing countries. It drops condition 1, on the coverage of trade, and dramatically relaxes condition 2, allowing developing countries to reduce tariffs on mutual trade in any way they wish and NTBs "in accordance with criteria which may be prescribed by the CONTRACTING PARTIES." It then supplements condition 3 by requiring that the arrangement not constitute a barrier to MFN tariff reductions or cause "undue difficulties" for other contracting parties.

In practice, developing countries have had virtual carte blanche. Twelve preferential arrangements have been notified under the enabling clause, including the Latin American Integration Association (LAIA), the Association of Southeast Asian Nations (ASEAN), and the Gulf Cooperation Council (GCC). These have made liberal use of the scope allowed by the enabling clause. Internal preferences of 25 percent and 50 percent figured in ASEAN's trading plans and in many of the arrangements concluded in the LAIA and the GCC. There is little sign that internal preferences have undermined MFN agreements with other trading partners in the sense of causing a reversal of previous conditions. Until the late 1980s, however, the Latin American countries' frequent use of regional arrangements and weak participation in the multilateral rounds might suggest a substitution of one form of liberalization for the other. Probably more pernicious have been the sectoral agreements that have abounded in Latin America. For example, Argentina and Brazil signed seventeen such agreements in 1986; there was little doubt that they generated a fair measure of trade diversion (Nogués and Quintanilla 1993). Similarly, ASEAN's trading arrangements were, for some time, partial in their coverage of products, although they are probably better categorized as ineffective than as harmful (DeRosa 1995).

Overall, the enabling clause serves to dilute even the weak discipline that article XXIV imposes. Even if article XXIV does not actually stop many harmful practices, at least it does not give them the respectability of legal cover as a matter of course. Thus, as Finger (1993b) notes, while the GATT knowingly

26. Before 1965, the director general of the GATT was called the executive secretary.

and willingly permitted the earlier manifestations of the LAIA (the Latin American Free Trade Agreement, 1960) and the initial notification of ASEAN (in 1977) to violate article XXIV, it at least left open the possibility of challenge in the dispute settlement process.

14.3   Special and Differential Treatment

One of the most profound institutional changes that the conclusion of the Uruguay Round induced in the world trading system was the advent of the so-called single undertaking. This entailed that all members of the WTO should adhere to nearly the same set of agreements on trading rules, in contrast to the situation prior to the round, in which members adhered to the GATT plus whatever subset of codes on trading rules that they chose. However, while the Uruguay Round agreements reduced the scope of the special and differential treatment that the GATT system had offered the developing countries, they did not eliminate such treatment completely. In many instances, the agreements common to all members permit or prescribe different treatment for developing countries. This section considers how much special and differential treatment has slipped through into the post–Uruguay Round trading system.

Hindley (1987) suggests five areas in which developing countries received special and differential treatment prior to the Uruguay Round: one from the 1947 GATT (article XVIII, the right to infant-industry and balance-of-payments trade restrictions); one from part IV of the 1964 GATT (exemption from making reciprocal tariff concessions); and three stemming from the enabling clause (the right not to sign the Tokyo Round codes, exemption from article XXIV, and the legitimization of the Generalized System of Preferences [GSP]). We have already dealt with articles XVIII and XXIV above. The remainder of this section comprises subsections on special and differential treatment for developing countries as victims of trade policy, special and differential treatment for developing countries as perpetrators of trade policy, and some conclusions.

14.3.1   Special and Differential Treatment for "Victims"

The Generalized System of Preferences

Perhaps the developing countries' most significant exceptions from other countries' trade policy arise from the GSP, which permits industrial countries to exempt some of their exports from MFN duties. These exemptions are autonomous policies (i.e., granted unilaterally by the industrial countries), which continue quite independently of the outcome of the Uruguay Round, under the cover of the enabling clause. The reductions in tariffs in the Uruguay Round agreements eroded GSP margins of preference, but, with a few exceptions, not very significantly. For example, the average reduction in margin was below two percentage points for sub-Saharan Africa (Amjadi, Reincke, and Yeats 1996).

At first sight, there seems little to object to in the notion that industrial countries should exempt imports from developing countries from tariffs. Even if the exceptions are not much of a basis for industrial development—because many are subject to quantitative limits and all are unbound and hence reversible—at least they transfer some tariff revenue to developing-country producers. Moreover, it might be argued that, since developing countries have little bargaining power in reciprocal negotiations, this is the only way that they will obtain relatively free access to the world's major markets.

There are four problems with these arguments. First, preferences essentially transmit to developing countries the production distortions inherent in developed countries' tariff structures. That is, they permit—perhaps encourage—producers to have costs above those in nonpreferred countries. Second, and closely related, current GSP schemes are so hedged with exclusions, quantitative limits, and rules of origin that they have only limited coverage.[27] The excluded imports are typically the most important from the point of view of development (e.g., clothing, footwear, leather) and the effect of the scheme is to divert resources away from them.

Third, the fact that the preferences might be withdrawn at any time encourages a degree of short-termism on the part of entrepreneurs. Their decisions are likely to be biased toward the quick fix rather than the long haul. Fourth, both for entrepreneurs and for their governments the desire to keep and exploit the rents inherent in preferences distract from longer-term and ultimately more productive activities. For example, the wish to maintain preferences could undermine developing countries' willingness to invest in rounds of negotiated trade liberalization, or even devalue their stake in the world trading system itself.

Special Treatment under the Rules

Developing countries also formally receive a measure of special and differential treatment in the ways in which they are treated by other countries' trading rules. In the case of countervailing duties and safeguards this is explicit and mandated. A developing country's exports to a market cannot be countervailed if its share of total imports of the product is 4 percent or less and if the sum of all such small suppliers' shares is 9 percent or less. Similarly, developing countries are exempt from safeguards actions if their share is 3 percent or less. There are no such limits for developed suppliers. Also, in the countervailing-duty agreement, whereas the *de minimis* limit is 1 percent for developed suppliers, it is 2 percent for developing countries (and 3 percent for least-developed countries until 2003).

In addition to these concessions, the WTO texts are handsomely endowed with exhortatory rather than mandated suggestions of special and differential

27. UNCTAD (1994) reports that in the European Union only 68 percent of dutiable imports from beneficiary countries qualify for preferences under the Generalized System of Preferences, of which only 33 percent (slightly below half) actually take them up. The corresponding figures for Japan are 35 percent and 16 percent and for the United States 36 percent and 18 percent.

treatment. For example, for antidumping, active countries are urged to seek "constructive remedies" when "essential interests of developing countries" are at stake and generally to pay regard to the "special situation" of the developing countries. In import licensing, members are asked to give "special consideration to . . . developing country members" in allocating new licenses. The Agreement on Technical Barriers to Trade (TBT) and the Agreement on the Application of Sanitary and Phytosanitary Measures have several special and differential treatment clauses urging, inter alia, special recognition of the needs of developing countries and their difficulties in formulating, implementing, and testing standards. Whether such exhortations amount to anything concrete remains to be seen.

14.3.2 Special and Differential Treatment for Perpetrators

Of much greater significance to their economic performance is the special and differential treatment that developing countries receive as perpetrators of trade policy. While the advent of the single understanding removes some aspects of special treatment, several instances remain in which general obligations under the GATT are relaxed for developing countries. If the relaxed obligations are constraining and harmful, this is indeed the "more favorable treatment" that the formal terminology for special and differential treatment implies, but if the obligations have the effect of encouraging countries' progress toward better economic policy, the exemptions are harmful. We quote those specific examples here.

Part IV

Superficially among the most important aspects of special and differential treatment is part IV of the GATT. Its article XXXVI:8 states baldly that the developed countries do not expect reciprocity from the developing countries. This exemption took quite concrete form for the former colonies of member countries, which could use it to avoid providing schedules of tariff concessions (bindings) when they assumed membership (see Hoekman and Kostecki 1995). This privilege no longer pertains: every WTO member has to submit schedules of bindings in goods and services.

The broader form of nonreciprocity embodied in part IV—the absence of need to negotiate and offer concessions in order to win them—was modified but not revoked by the Uruguay Round. Part IV was exhortatory rather than binding and has been replaced by equally nonoperational language. The Punta del Este declaration stated that developing countries were not expected to make concessions inconsistent with their "development, financial and trade needs" and the Marrakesh Decision on Measures in Favor of Least-Developed Countries continued this for least-developed countries.

Practice was quite different from these exhortations. In the Uruguay Round, developing and industrialized countries each agreed to cut their tariffs on about 30 percent of their imports. The cuts by the industrialized countries will reduce the prices of those imports by an average of 3 percent, those by the developing countries by an average 8 percent.[28] Thus, many developing countries made significant concessions. But the Marrakesh agreement provides at least legal cover for those who wish to be left out as a matter of principle.

Technical Barriers to Trade

The TBT agreement offers special and differential treatment to developing countries on both their exports and their imports. On the latter, they are not expected to "use international standards as a basis for technical regulations or standards, including test methods, which are not appropriate to their . . . needs." This concession is intended to allow the preservation of indigenous technology and technologies appropriate to countries' development needs. While the general terms of the TBT agreement restrict the use of standards for protectionist purposes, and developing countries are not exempt from its provisions, this particular piece of language seems to grant the right to use idiosyncratic standards. If so, it could put a substantial brake on the modernization and competitiveness of developing-country industry.

Subsidy/Countervailing Measures

The Uruguay Round Agreement on Subsidies and Countervailing Measures substantially revised the corresponding Tokyo Round code, linking together for the first time the concepts used in the two parts of the agreement. The agreement imposes significant discipline on specific subsidies, identifying prohibited, actionable, and nonactionable classes and providing far readier action against the first class than against the second. Unfortunately it then goes on to use special and differential treatment to dilute the disciplines significantly for developing countries and even further for least-developed countries (defined as the UN list plus countries with per capita income below $1,000). For example, whereas export subsidies are banned almost immediately for developed countries, they are banned in eight years for developing countries and never (subject to a condition on quantities) for least-developed countries. Similar differentials impose tighter conditions on WTO members before they can take action against developing-country exports, and give more generous definitions of "de minimis" for the latter. The overall impression is that subsidies do not matter much for least-developed countries so long as they do not disrupt other countries' markets, and this view is significantly enhanced by the statement that "subsidies may play an important role in the economic development programs of developing country members" (article XXVII:1 of the Agreement on Subsidies and Countervailing Measures). In sum, the agreement offers governments of least-developed countries virtually no cover against lobbies seeking subsidies (Winters 1994).

28. Abreu (1996) and Finger, Ingco, and Reincke (1996) provide details of developing country concessions.

Among other areas in which special and differential treatment dilutes developing countries' obligations to liberalize are customs valuation (longer transition periods), agriculture (smaller tariff cuts), safeguards (longer-lasting restrictions), trade-related investment measures (restrictions available for balance-of-payments purposes), and services (similar special and differential rules as for goods).

14.3.3   Conclusions on Special and Differential Treatment

It is impossible to make a simple quantitative assessment of the extent of special and differential treatment, but some qualitative conclusions are possible. In terms of market access for developing countries' exports, special and differential treatment is quite extensive—if not very effective economically—in offering tariff reductions on a wide variety of exports. In terms of market access to their own markets, developing countries have successfully managed to avoid the obligation to make tariff concessions, but have, at least in industrial products, frequently made them anyway. In the area of rules, special and differential treatment is de facto no longer very extensive in the visible high-profile cases. Thus, for example, balance-of-payments restrictions are coming under increasing pressure in the WTO Balance of Payments Committee and are fading away quite rapidly, and antidumping and countervailing-duty rules are the same for developed and developing countries. In the lower visibility areas, however, shrouded in technicality, special and differential treatment appears to continue unchecked. Least-developed countries have virtually free rein to subsidize exports, and, apparently, a great deal of latitude in both standards and, for several years, in customs valuation. Arguably, the least-developed countries need the most, not the least, support of the multilateral system in devising satisfactory policies.

14.4   What the WTO Can Do for Developing Countries

We second, but have not repeated, important points about market access, such as assuring that liberalization of agricultural trade and trade in clothing and textiles and other products of export interest maintain the schedules agreed on at the Uruguay Round.

Our focus instead has been on the GATT/WTO system as a guide for unilateral decisions. From this perspective we offer two broad guidelines: Pay attention that its guidelines make economic sense; they often do not.[29] Avoid the temptation to view immunity from rules that make sense as a benefit.[30]

We provide below more specific recommendations in three issue areas.

---

29. "But our policies are GATT-legal" is an argument we often hear against our recommendations for reform.
30. Hudec (1987) shows why this view is a snare and a delusion.

14.4.1   A Better Pressure Valve

Some may comment that a pressure valve cannot make economic and political sense at the same time. Not true. A pressure valve or trade-remedy process that truly enfranchised all the economic interests affected by a proposed import restriction would be more honest and more transparent politics than the obfuscation and misdirection politics of the present antidumping system.

Here are some of the general guidelines on how a government might meet its need for a means to evaluate requests for exceptions to a basically liberal trade policy.

Identify the costs and the losers. Procedures should bring out the costs of the requested exception, and the identities of the persons or groups who will bear these costs. More expensive imports will cost somebody money and—if the imports are needed materials—eliminate somebody's job. These costs, and the people in the domestic economy who will bear them, should have the same standing in law and in administrative practice as the other side already enjoys. The process of considering the request for an exception should be used to help fortify the politics of not granting it.

Be clear that the action is an exception. Procedures should establish that the requested action would be an exception to the principles that underlie the liberalization program. Admitting to political weakness is better than admitting that the exception is a good idea.

Don't sanctify the criteria for the action. Procedures should not presume that there is some good reason for granting an exception—procedures that compare the situations of the petitioner with preestablished criteria for granting an exception should be avoided. Procedures should stress that the function of the review is to identify the benefits and the costs—and the domestic winners and domestic losers—for the requested action.

The last guideline is more important than it might seem. The history of antidumping and other trade remedies shows that clever people will always be able to present their situation exactly as the criteria describe. If you start out to find just the few exporters who are being unfair to Australia or the United States or Mexico, you will soon be swamped by evidence that everyone is.

At the technical level, useful concepts for review procedures—such as transparency and automatic expiration for any exception that is granted (a sunset clause)—can be gleaned from procedural changes made at the safeguards negotiations of the Uruguay Round.

14.4.2   Regional Arrangements

The guidelines presently provided suffer more from incompleteness than from error. Indeed, given their necessarily sui generis nature, it may be impossible to write GATT-style rules to cover all of the dimensions that distinguish an economically beneficial regional arrangement from a bad one. The WTO and, perhaps, other international organizations should sponsor economic analyses of regional arrangements—as was done by the European Commission for the European Union's Single Market initiative—but taking pains *not* to limit the review to criteria provided in article XXIV. As we have pointed out, the latter was written even before the basic concepts of trade creation and trade diversion were widely available to guide thinking.

Such reviews should be useful for the partners to a potential regional arrangement to identify their own interests. They should also identify effects on excluded countries—an obvious area of concern to the WTO—but not just in terms of the potential changes in their exports to the integrating countries. As we have argued elsewhere (Winters 1997), this is an inappropriate yardstick and must be supplemented at least by information on excluded countries' imports and their terms of trade. Moreover, such reviews should be done ex ante and used as a guide to the renegotiation of the free trade area's or customs union's instruments of trade policy. There is no virtue to McMillan's suggestion (1993) that ex post adjustments be made to maintain excluded countries' exports at preintegration levels: this is both the wrong criterion and redolent of managed trade.

14.4.3   Special and Differential Treatment

Special and differential treatment as commonly interpreted in the WTO agreements does not do much for developing countries. Special access to developed-country markets transfers revenue to them but at the expense of discouraging effective efforts to integrate into the world economy. Exemptions from WTO rules—inadequate as some of these are—and exemption from the need for reciprocal trade liberalization merely exacerbate the difficulties of pursuing satisfactory policies at home. They should be phased out as soon as possible.

The one element of special and differential treatment that does seem to us potentially beneficial is to offer assistance in the business of being a WTO member. Meeting the full procedural requirements of the WTO is very burdensome and can absorb disproportionate amounts of human capital. To the extent that they can be implemented without compromising substance or transparency, the elements of special and differential treatment that permit developing countries to use streamlined procedures and/or lighter notification burdens seem, to us, desirable. By the same token, the actual delivery of the technical assistance referred to so frequently in the Uruguay Round agreements would be beneficial, especially if it can be devoted to training and capacity building rather than just to producing a product.

References

Abreu, M. 1996. Trade in Manufactures: The Outcome of the Uruguay Round and Developing Country Interests. In *The Uruguay Round and the Developing Countries,* ed. W. Martin and L. A. Winters, chap. 3. Cambridge: Cambridge University Press.

Amjadi, A., U. Reincke, and A. Yeats. 1996. Did External Barriers Cause the Marginalization of Sub-Saharan Africa in World Trade? Policy Research Working Paper no. 1586. Washington, DC: World Bank.

Anjaria, S. J. 1987. Balance of Payments and Related Issues in the Uruguay Round of Trade Negotiations. *World Bank Economic Review* 1, no. 4: 669–88.

Bierwagen, R. M. 1991. *GATT Article VI and the Protectionist Bias in Antidumping Law.* Kluwer Studies in Transnational Law, vol. 7. Deventer: Kluwer.

de Jonquiers, Guy. 1995. Report Counts Cost of Antidumping. *Financial Times,* 2 September, p. 5.

DeRosa, Dean A. 1995. Regional Trading Arrangements among Developing Countries: The ASEAN Example. Research Report no. 103. Washington, DC: International Food Policy Research Institute.

Ethier, W. J., and H. Horn. 1984. A New Look at Economic Integration. In *Monopolistic Competition and International Trade,* ed. H. Kierzkowski, 207–29. Oxford: Clarendon Press.

Finger, J. M. 1981. Policy Research. *Journal of Political Economy* 89:1270–71.

———. 1992. The Meaning of "Unfair" in United States Import Policy. *Minnesota Journal of Global Trade* 1, no. 1: 35–56.

———, ed. 1993a. *Antidumping: How It Works and Who Gets Hurt.* Ann Arbor: University of Michigan Press.

———. 1993b. GATT's Influence on Regional Arrangements. In *New Dimensions in Regional Integration,* ed. J. de Melo, and A. Panagariya, 128–48. Cambridge: Cambridge University Press.

———. 1996. Legalized Backsliding: Safeguard Provisions in the GATT. In *The Uruguay Round and the Developing Countries,* ed. W. Martin and L. A. Winters, chap. 8. Cambridge: Cambridge University Press.

Finger, J. M., M. D. Ingco, and U. Reincke. 1996. *The Uruguay Round: Statistics on Tariff Concessions Given and Received.* Washington, DC: World Bank.

Finger, J. M., and T. Murray. 1993. Antidumping and Countervailing Duty Enforcement in the United States. In *Antidumping: How It Works and Who Gets Hurt,* ed. J. M. Finger, 241–54. Ann Arbor: University of Michigan Press.

General Agreement on Tariffs and Trade. 1994. *Analytical Index: Guide to GATT Law and Practice.* 6th edition. Geneva: GATT.

Grossman, G., and E. Helpman. 1995. The Politics of Free-Trade Agreements. *American Economic Review* 85:667–90.

Hindley, B. 1987. Different and More Favorable Treatment—and Graduation. In *The Uruguay Round,* ed. J. M. Finger and A. Olechowski, 67–74. Washington, DC: World Bank.

Hoekman, B., and M. Kostecki. 1995. *The Political Economy of the World Trading System: From GATT to WTO.* Oxford: Oxford University Press.

Hudec, R. E. 1987. *Developing Countries in the GATT Legal System.* Aldershot: Gower.

Jackson, J. H., and E. A. Vermulst. 1989. *Antidumping Law and Practice: A Comparative Study.* Ann Arbor: University of Michigan Press.

Krishna, P. 1994. Regionalism and Multilateralism: A Political Economy Approach. Brown University. Photocopy.

Levy, P. I. 1994. A Political Economy Analysis of Free Trade Agreements. Economic Growth Centre Discussion Paper no. 718. New Haven: Yale University.

Litan, R. E., and R. Boltuck, eds. 1991. *Down in the Dumps: Administration of the Unfair Trade Laws.* Washington, DC: Brookings Institution.

McMillan, J. 1993. Does Regional Integration Foster Open Trade? Economic Theory and GATT's Article XXIV. In *Regional Integration and the Global Trading System,* ed. K. Anderson and R. Blackhurst, 292–309. New York: Harvester Wheatsheaf.

Nogués, J., and R. Quintanilla. 1993. Latin America's Integration and the Multilateral Trading System. In *New Dimensions in Regional Integration,* ed. J. de Melo and A. Panagariya, 278–313. Cambridge: Cambridge University Press.

Organization for Economic Cooperation and Development. 1992. *Integration of the Developing Countries into the International Trading System.* Paris: OECD.

Sampson, G. 1987. Safeguards. In *The Uruguay Round,* ed. J. M. Finger and A. Olechowski, 143–52. Washington, DC: World Bank.

Staiger, R. W., and F. Wolak. 1994. The Trade Effects of Antidumping Investigations: Theory and Evidence. In *Analytical and Negotiating Issues in the Global Trading System,* ed. A. V. Deardorff and R. M. Stern, 231–61. Ann Arbor: University of Michigan Press.

Stegemann, K. 1992. *Price Undertakings to Settle Antidumping Cases.* Ottawa: Institute for Research on Public Policy.

United Nations Conference on Trade and Development. 1994. *Review of the Implementation, Maintenance, Improvement, and Utilization of the Generalized System of Preferences.* Geneva: UNCTAD.

Winters, L. A. 1994. Subsidies. In Organization for Economic Cooperation and Development, *The New World Trading System,* 129–34. Paris: OECD.

———. 1997. Regionalism and the Rest of the World: The Irrelevance of the Kemp-Wan Theorem. Oxford Economic Papers.

World Trade Organization. 1995. *Regionalism and the World Trading System.* Geneva: WTO.

Comment on the Paper by J. Michael Finger and L. Alan Winters   Alan Hirsch

This is an intellectually stimulating paper, addressing first principles and conventional thought about the role of multilateral trade rules. It has the deceptive simplicity and clarity of thought that has often characterized previous works by the same two authors. However, does it address the whole question as posed? The question appears to ask about the role of the WTO, which is an organization, not simply about the rule environment for multilateral trade agreements. But the authors say early on that their "emphasis is on the WTO and GATT rules, particularly on how these rules influence *unilateral* trade policy decisions by developing countries."

If I had been asked the question posed, I would have attempted to answer it not only by looking at the rules of the GATT, but also by looking at the *functioning* of the WTO in relation to developing countries.

Alan Hirsch is chief director for industrial and technology policy in the Department of Trade and Industry in Pretoria, Cape Town, South Africa.

There are questions about the role of the WTO in relation to developing countries that South African policymakers constantly ask as regards our own domestic policymaking, and as regards our relations to other developing countries. While there are questions about the rules themselves, many questions revolve around the implementation of GATT agreements and procedures. Most of the recent discussions about the WTO and the GATT undertaken between developing countries, for example at the United Nations Conference on Trade and Development (UNCTAD) IV meeting in South Africa and at the recent conference "The World Trade Organization: Perspectives from the South" in Kuala Lumpur, have focused on quite a different set of issues from those addressed in this paper. One of the elements of special and differential treatment for developing countries is the provision of training and technical assistance," but this issue is considered only briefly in the text; whereas in the report on the proceedings of the Kuala Lumpur conference, this issue is highlighted as the single most important obstacle to the implementation of the Uruguay Round agreements (*Report* 1996, 1).

The paper, as I have already noted, has great merit in its own right, and the issues raised are extremely pertinent for developing countries. Therefore, I will attempt to respond, first by treating the paper on its own terms, and then by raising some of the key issues prominent in the discourse of developing countries on the role of the WTO.

The guiding logic of the paper is clear and simple: trade liberalization is good for economic development; the WTO is designed to support trade liberalization; the domestic forces against trade liberalization are generally stronger or more vocal than the supporters and beneficiaries; and the key role of the WTO is, therefore, to assist governments in counteracting the forces opposed to liberalization. The underlying thesis is reiterated from time to time, and the authors also make reference to the discrediting of the Singer-Prebisch thesis, which supported import substitution industrialization policies and often acted as a crutch for protectionist interests and governments.

Whether or not the thesis itself, about relative price trends, is utterly discredited is still a matter of debate, though there is little debate on the suitability of ISI, especially for small developing countries. More important, though, is the question of whether governments can assist in economic development in any direct ways, or whether our role as economists and the WTO is simply to protect the markets from government interference. Perhaps I am mistaken, but the logic of this paper seems to include such an assumption.

This debate has progressed a great deal since the early 1950s, when the implementation of the GATT rules was first framed, as in the hatters' fur case mentioned by Finger and Winters. ISI policies clearly have very little value, particularly in small developing countries, and this is now widely accepted, as shown by the mode of participation of many less developed countries in the Uruguay Round. At the same time, a new institutionalism, based on the perceived experience of East Asian development, is considered in some quarters to have shown that, within certain parameters, government intervention to support economic development has had powerfully positive effects. For example, one can address the antiexport bias in developing countries in several ways, of which only one essential element is the removal of distortions in the domestic market caused by protectionism.

Successful developing countries today, with the exception perhaps of tiny city-state-type economies, do not assume that government intervention is damaging per se; rather, they have redrawn the line between acceptable and unacceptable interventions, ruling out many of the accepted interventionist tools of the ISI era. In South Africa, for example, we have delineated measures into unacceptable "demand-side interventions" and acceptable "supply-side support measures."

The Finger-Winters paper does not seem to take the evolution of the debate sufficiently into account, partly perhaps as it fails to differentiate among the so-called developing countries. Indeed, when asking about the role of the WTO in relation to developing countries, one surely needs to differentiate more carefully within an extremely heterogeneous category.

With this reservation in mind, the political-economy argument put forward by the paper is sound. Governments do need protection against the powerful and vocal lobbies against liberalization, which block the real objective underlying liberalization: economic restructuring, growth, and greater welfare. Examining whether or not the basic rules of the GATT and the existence of special and differential treatment assist or hinder governments is therefore a valuable exercise. In many cases, Finger and Winters have shown how both the rules and special and differential treatment may not have the positive effects they should have, and it may well be true that the reasons are rooted in the history of the postwar world economy and its policy legacy.

One specific point that needs stronger argument to fully convince is the critique of what the authors call the "pressure-valve" options. I have no doubt that the existence of provisions for antidumping and countervailing duties had positive effects during the crucial domestic negotiations that led to South Africa's relatively liberal offer in the Uruguay Round. Without the existence of these potential tools, it would have been a great deal more difficult to achieve sufficient domestic consensus to allow South Africa to enter its current crucial liberalization process.

In addition, the reluctance of the South African government to continue to pursue costly subsidy programs for exporters was not only assisted by our being treated as a developed country in the Uruguay Round negotiations. It was also supported by the fact that, if we had to continue such programs, or introduce new subsidies, it was more likely that we would be punished by one of our major trading partners using antidumping or countervailing-duty measures than that we would be blocked by a GATT/WTO action.

The problem with this in the paper is that, while it recognizes the role of administrative measures in allowing for the formation of a liberalization coalition, it rejects these measures on economic grounds, and offers no political alternative. All we are given are guidelines that may or may not be implementable. This leaves us with little option but to continue to attempt to refine untenable provisions, in ways such as those suggested by Robert Baldwin's paper (chap. 11 in this volume) and by his commentators.

Much as I agree with Finger and Winters's treatment of regionalism, it understates the importance of two problems. The first is the difficulties that rules of origin create. The second problem is a more practical, political one. Regional integration is about much more than trade integration. At its best, it is about economic development, of mutual value to its partners, and it is designed to lock in liberal economic and political reforms. The past, especially in Africa and Latin America, is littered with failed regional integration programs, often because they were considered consciously or unconsciously as substitutes for domestic economic reform. They were seen as expanding the scale and scope of inward-looking competition. The structure of the positive alternative could be subject to a great deal of variation, because of the variety of regional circumstances as recognized by Finger and Winters. The complexity of southern Africa, for example, has already led to discussions with the secretariat about bending the rules, but the secretariat, while understanding and sympathizing with our objectives, is not free to offer any advice beyond the guidelines of article XXIV. Perhaps this is another field in which the advocacy and policy advice role of the WTO could be expanded, even beyond the review procedures suggested by Finger and Winters.

This suggestion is offered with some trepidation as so many decisions to enter regional arrangements today appear overdetermined by the fear of being left out of the powerful economic alliances such as the European Union and the North American Free Trade Agreement, entirely contrary to the spirit of the GATT.

South Africa is not considered a developing country in the GATT environment. It participated in the Uruguay Round as a developed country, and conforms to developed-country rules; it has little if any recourse to "special and differential treatment," in spite of its per capita income of less than $2,900 per annum. The critique of Generalized System of Preferences (GSP) by Finger and Winters is generally true, particularly recently, when it has generally not significantly altered the terms of trade. We have found that South African firms have been slow to take up our newly awarded GSP status with the United States, for example, and the uncertainty (and arbitrariness) of such arrangements is certainly a negative factor.

Equally accurate is the critique of the negative effects of allowing weaker obligations on developing countries, which could disarm economic reform coalitions. My view now, though it was not four years ago, is that South Africa was fortunate to be treated as a developed country, by and large, for the purposes of the Uruguay Round negotiations.

It remains for me to identify some of the issues concerning the role of the

WTO as regards developing countries (drawing largely from *Report* 1996) that have not been addressed by the paper. Most of these issues relate to the concern that, without sufficient assistance and encouragement, some developing countries could be left behind in the development of a freer world trading system. There are two main themes in this discussion: the first concerns technical assistance; the second concerns the credibility of the Marrakesh agreement and the WTO. In some proposals these concerns are both present.

- Some developing countries have difficulty with the notification process; both technical support from the WTO and rationalization of the requirements are suggested.

- In addition, technical assistance is required to help developing countries and least-developed countries exploit the advantages of the Uruguay Round.

- The WTO should address least-developed and developing countries' concerns about back-loading of the Multifiber Arrangement and agriculture reforms through policy support, as well as helping poor food importers prepare for the future.

- Developing countries are seeking support studies to establish the gains and losses and distribution effects of the Uruguay Round.

- Growing out of such studies is the possibility of suitable compensation for losers, especially if the losses are short- to medium-term (though "compensation" can be understood too many different ways).

- The WTO should facilitate access of developing countries to information and analysis of Uruguay Round compliance requirements, and the effects of Uruguay Round reforms. The Malaysian conference preferred that such activities were not undertaken by the secretariat itself, which "is perceived to be biased against developing countries in its methodological assumptions" (*Report* 1996, 2).

The Malaysian conference appeared to consider UNCTAD the probable suitable vehicle for policy research activities, while the WTO might provide technical support. It urged greater cooperation between the two organizations. What the conference missed, I believe, was the possible additional role of the World Bank, particularly when it comes to the issue of addressing the short- to medium-term costs of liberalization, and the development of appropriate compensatory programs. This would close the loop opened earlier when I complained that the authors only saw the need to protect the market from the state, and not to provide suitable medium-term adjustment policies and programs.

Clearly, the perceptions of developing countries as expressed at the Malaysian conference, an odd mixture of commitment to the Uruguay Round and suspicion of the WTO (suggesting that countries participate for the wrong reasons), indicate the need for an urgent review of the role of the WTO Secretariat and its relationship with both UNCTAD and the World Bank.

The danger of ignoring these issues is that new converts to the GATT cause could soon be lost. This is worrying to such countries, but even more so to their slightly more advanced neighbors. Hence the role of some of the newly industrialized countries in advocating on behalf of the least-developed countries.

While incorporation of these latter points in the Finger and Winters paper might disrupt the clear focus of the current version, consideration of the issues should be reflected somewhere in the collection of papers.

Reference

Report of the Conference Proceedings. 1996. Proceedings of the World Trade Conference "Perspectives from the South." Kuala Lumpur: ISIS.

IV Conclusions

15   An Agenda for the WTO

Anne O. Krueger

The papers included in this volume were presented and discussed at a conference held at Stanford University in late September 1996. That was less than two months before the Singapore ministerial meeting of trade ministers, in which progress in implementing the Uruguay Round was assessed, and ministers had an opportunity to take further actions.

It seems appropriate, therefore, to provide some assessment of the events that have taken place since the papers were presented, including not only the Uruguay Round but several key agreements that have been reached under it since September 1996.

Section 15.1 provides an account of the conclusions emerging from the conference regarding organizational concerns about the WTO. Section 15.2 examines some of the threats to the organization that were discussed during the conference. Section 15.3 briefly reviews the substantive challenges. Section 15.4 assesses the outcome of the Singapore ministerial meeting and other developments that took place in the half year subsequent to the conference.

15.1   Challenges to the WTO as an International Organization

There are two remarkable phenomena, noted in the introduction, that must be repeated as a starting point for an assessment of the WTO's prospects as an international organization. The first is that progress in liberalizing international transactions since the Second World War has been remarkable, especially in light of the absence of a strong international organization. The second is that,

Anne O. Krueger is the Herald L. and Caroline L. Ritch Professor in Humanities and Sciences and director of the Center for Research on Economic Development and Policy Reform at Stanford University.

especially taking into account the rhetoric that preceded and accompanied it, the Uruguay Round was highly successful.

Indeed, with hindsight, one could almost argue that the range of issues that were brought within the scope of the new international organization was too ambitious. Whereas the GATT Secretariat focused primarily on a fairly well defined range of issues pertaining to trade, its very success left the dismantling of tariffs (at least among industrial countries, although developing countries are moving in the same direction) as a minor part of the remaining challenge of global liberalization. The GATT's very success therefore raised a host of new issues, and the WTO's extended mandate also covers trade in services, agreements on intellectual property rights and trade-related investment measures, brings agriculture more firmly into the WTO's domain, liberalizes trade in textiles and apparel, and generally provides for mechanisms with which international transactions can be still further liberalized.

15.1.1   The WTO Secretariat and Its Role

Any group of people, working together in a given location and assigned particular tasks, would have difficulty in being told that they are a different institution, still working together in the same location. For the WTO, that difficulty is compounded by a number of factors.

Consider first the challenges facing the staff. First of all, they have to carry out the complex negotiations for the admission of a large number of new members—China and those from eastern Europe and the former Soviet Union. The work is difficult and demanding, and in itself places a considerable additional burden on WTO staff.[1] Second, the dispute settlement mechanism is strengthened, and the number of cases that have been brought before the WTO has mushroomed (see chap. 5). While that is a sign of success, it too places large additional demands on the secretariat. Third, there are the various services codes to be moved from broad statements of intent to implementable arrangements. Fourth, working parties are already assigned to consider furthering some issues, continuing negotiations on some particular services (financial services is the most publicized of these), and other items.

Yet to handle all this, the WTO Secretariat's staff was permitted to increase by only 10 percent. It remains very small—around four hundred—relative both to the staffs of many other international organizations and to its workload (see chap. 1). There are significant dangers that the increased workload will simply overwhelm the secretariat, leading to political backlash against the organization and to delays or failures in implementation of the Uruguay Round results. On the basis of its increased workload, a very strong case can be made for a considerable expansion of the WTO budget and staff.

But there are other questions. As pointed out in Henderson's and Vines's papers and by participants at the conference, an international organization's

---

1. See the contributions by Pietras, Michalopoulos, and Hirsch on this point.

capability is in part determined by its in-house analytical work. As shown by Henderson (chap. 3), the Organization for Economic Cooperation and Development (OECD) provides a good example of staff influence through the quality of its analytical work. The scarcity of in-house capacity at the WTO can constrain the ability of the secretariat to undertake some of its functions, quite aside from the need for increased personnel to handle ongoing operations. In the general discussion, it seemed clear that strengthening the staff and that capability at the WTO, in addition to expanding the staff for undertaking the tasks listed above, would be invaluable in enabling the organization to fulfill its role.

Related to the need for in-house analytical capability, there is a broader question as to whether the traditional, fairly passive, role of the GATT Secretariat—being there simply to serve the signatories to the GATT articles—is adequate for the WTO. While the WTO Secretariat, as a rules-based organization, clearly must have a different relationship with its members than, for example, the World Bank or IMF staff do with theirs, one can advocate a large increase in the secretariat's overall size, as well as its analytical and research capacity, without believing that it should become a major policy initiator.

There are a number of considerations pertaining to the degree to which the director general and WTO Secretariat could or should become more active. The questions raised by Goldstein are highly relevant. As she points out, the trade policies of the large trading nations in Europe, North America, and Japan are in large part driven by domestic concerns over trade issues. There are significant questions as to the degree to which international norms or rules can be negotiated that go against those domestic interests. One can question whether the development of formal rules helps or hinders the process of global liberalization when those rules are not entirely consistent with the domestic political concerns of major players.

Of course, there is much middle ground: research undertaken by a strengthened WTO staff could inform discussions leading to an agreement among major countries that rules governing preferential trading arrangement would be strengthened without any WTO Secretariat advocacy; the director general of the WTO could hold private and unpublicized meetings with officials in key countries in an effort to achieve a consensus on strengthening the rules; and so on.

From the discussion at the conference, a consensus emerged that increasing the WTO staff and budget significantly is highly warranted. The case is clear-cut, and the real question is only how much the secretariat should be strengthened. One does not have to take the view that the WTO Secretariat should become activist in order to conclude that additional personnel are needed even to carry out their presently assigned tasks.[2] Keeping an organization "lean and

---

2. It was noted at the conference that delegations to the WTO from member countries can in effect be part of the "staff," or the resources, available to carry out assigned tasks. But it was also

mean" need not imply stretching it so thin that the quality of work suffers. Moreover, expanding the research staff and analytical capabilities would appear desirable.

Many conference participants also believed that, as the WTO evolves, the secretariat will inevitably become less passive. The real question was the extent to which deliberate efforts to move the secretariat in that direction, as contrasted with its gradual evolution, were likely to accelerate the process, and might indeed even retard the evolution of a more active stance.

The issue, and the challenge, to the WTO as an international organization is clear. Finding ways to strengthen the secretariat's capacity to carry out the workload consistent with the sensitivity of members in a traditionally participatory framework will be an important task for the director general of the WTO and for those concerned about the open multilateral trading system. How much the secretariat can and should go beyond that role and seek to take initiatives with respect to advancing the cause of an open multilateral trading system is a question that will require political judgment, as well.

While the emergence of the WTO as an international organization has been recognized, little attention has been paid to these organizational issues. They are important, and deserve more attention than they have received. If the papers in this volume induce more attention to these matters, they will on that count alone have served the world well.

15.1.2   Linkages to Other International Organizations

Another issue that is important for the future is the relationship to other global economic organizations, especially to the World Bank and the International Monetary Fund (IMF). As shown in Sampson's paper, and discussed further by Nogués, trade ministers assigned the WTO lead responsibly in achieving "coherence" between the Bank, the Fund, and the WTO. There are some obvious issues, such as the consistency of individual Fund and Bank programs with members' obligations under the WTO. But at a more basic level, there are important challenges. Even within national governments, consistency between economic policies across different ministries is not always achieved. And when trade ministers deal at the GATT, while finance ministers govern the IMF and they or aid ministers govern the World Bank, the degree of economic policy coordination internationally can be problematic. But whether anything beyond informal cooperation between the staffs of the organizations can make a significant difference is an open question.[3]

---

noted that many of the delegations to Geneva are overwhelmed by the increased workload, and many believed that these resources, too, are inadequate to the task.

3. The strength of the WTO Secretariat may also be an issue here. At its present size, the professional staff of the WTO is a small fraction of that of the World Bank or the International Monetary Fund; the extent to which WTO staff can participate may be limited simply on that account. A strengthened WTO Secretariat might offer more opportunities for meaningful cooperation and interaction.

15.1.3 Decision-Making Modes in the WTO

Traditionally, decisions in the GATT and now the WTO have been taken by "consensus," and delegates have been welcome to participate in any working group they wished to. As the membership of the WTO has increased, the consensus rule and the voluntary participation arrangements may become more cumbersome. Mechanisms for giving a somewhat larger voice to key countries may be necessary, along the line of the European Union's "qualified majority," or through formal designations of country groups to name representatives to working parties.

Likewise, the present plan is for trade ministers to meet every other year. Whether that will suffice to maintain the degree of contact between the WTO staff and their constituents that is desirable for an international organization is a question. The IMF and the World Bank have annual meetings and, halfway through the year, have meetings of the Interim and Development Committees, as well. Finding arrangements that permit greater contact and exposure of the WTO senior staff and officials in key member governments is another challenge for the fledgling institution.

15.2 Threats on the Horizon

Four key issues can be identified as dangers to the WTO: (1) the tendency to go to sector-by-sector and issue-by-issue negotiations; (2) the emergence of preferential trading arrangements; (3) efforts to link trade issues to a variety of other international concerns; and (4) the proliferation of antidumping regulations and enforcement.

15.2.1 Sector-Specific Trade Negotiations

Two developments since the September 1996 conference have been the telecommunications agreement and the agreement to achieve free trade in information technology. These are discussed in section 15.4 from a substantive viewpoint, but a key issue that applies more generally arises from them. That is, the arrangement in services is that negotiations will be carried on sector by sector. That decision was driven in part by the distinctive characteristics of a number of service sectors. But that practice is diametrically opposed to the earlier successes in multilateral trade negotiations. Under the GATT, the ability of governments to reach agreements depended in part on the support of their export sectors, which were gaining from the reduction of foreign protection, to be able to overcome protectionist pressures from import-competing sectors.

The argument has been advanced that trading relations have become so complicated that there should be no more multilateral rounds with broad coverage, and that future negotiations should be conducted on specific issues. The concern about this approach is that policymakers may be unable to cut "cross-sector" deals, and that the political support for further trade liberalization may diminish. Trade liberalization is naturally supported more enthusiastically in cases where there are export interests. If negotiations become sector-specific, this probably biases trade liberalization toward items of interest to large trading nations. Certainly, information technology is a sector in which the United States currently has a comparative advantage, and the impetus for negotiations came from the United States.[4]

While agreement to move to free trade in a new economic activity is always desirable because it prevents the imposition of protection on products as yet undeveloped, the tendency toward sector-specific negotiations is worrisome for the future of trade liberalization. The director general and secretariat of the WTO will need to find ways to broaden negotiations and to offset the bias inherent in the big-country, sector-specific initiatives.

15.2.2   Preferential Trading Arrangements

Quite clearly, there are important concerns about the proliferation of preferential trading arrangements. The issues raised by Srinivasan clearly point to the need for strengthened WTO rules.[5] Preferential trading arrangements can be liberalizing and building blocks toward a more open trading system, but they can also be stumbling blocks, diverting trade from the rest of the world toward partners included in the preferential arrangement.

WTO rules regarding preferential trading arrangements (article XXIV) are sufficiently imprecise that panels have not found that any preferential trading arrangements were in violation of article XXIV, although they have in fact not reached any conclusion at all!

Srinivasan and others at the conference made a strong case that present practices may lead to undesirable outcomes. Pietras and Michalopoulos, for example, pointed out that trade liberalization by eastern European countries and others is constrained by the need to have tariffs as high as the European Union in order to prepare for entry. Otherwise, compensation would later have to be paid. As such, less trade liberalization is undertaken than it would be if European Union rules did not exist. There are therefore good reasons for altering WTO rules in ways that would prevent the trade-restricting by-products of preferential trading arrangements, and for bringing criteria for rules of origin, accession, and other arrangements under some agreed-upon WTO discipline.

However, whether the domestic politics of key countries are such as to make it advisable to proceed with rewriting the rules and whether the WTO Secretariat should take any initiatives in that direction are more difficult questions.

---

4. In the information technology deal, it is also perhaps significant that the United States sought to exempt optical fibers, television monitors, capacitors, and photocopiers. See *Financial Times,* 4 December 1996, 4. Presumably these were the subsectors in which U.S. domestic industry was sensitive to foreign competition.

5. The descriptions by Pietras and Michalopoulos also point to some of the ways in which the presence of a preferential trading arrangement can curb liberalization.

15.2.3   Linkages

Roessler's paper made a strong and well-reasoned case against linkages between trade liberalization and other global concerns, such as the environment and labor standards. As Roessler demonstrated, linkages in the past have resulted in double defeats: trade was less liberal than it otherwise would have been, and the linked objective was not achieved. Tying other objectives to trade weakens trade and the other objective.[6]

A key policy issue is, once again, the role of the WTO itself in achieving the desirable delinkages between policy issues. This raises the questions discussed in connection with the role of the secretariat. For supporters of the open multilateral trading system, it seems clear that finding means to keep other objectives delinked from trade is crucial to the future health of the trading system. How proactive a role the secretariat should play in assuring a desirable outcome is a question subject to the considerations discussed above.

15.2.4   Antidumping Abuse

Antidumping legislation is permissible under the WTO. The rationale is that there can be legitimate concerns about the possibility of predatory pricing. But antidumping measures can in practice be used as protectionist measures, even when there is no predatory pricing.

One of the areas in which the Uruguay Round made less progress than had been hoped was with respect to standards to be used in national antidumping laws and administration. In many instances, the procedures and standards used have little or no relationship to criteria for an efficiently functioning market or international economy.

A variety of alternative approaches could be taken to this issue. On one hand, it could be required that national firms be subject to the same behavioral tests as are foreign firms when subject to antidumping complaints. Another alternative would be the development of an international competition (antitrust) code that might replace antidumping provisions at the national level. Yet another, weaker alternative would be to increase the requirements for findings of antidumping (for example, to impose a *de minimis* standard of at least 10 percent).

15.3   Substantive Issues

The papers presented on substantive issues and included in this volume are mostly self-explanatory. Clearly, achieving substantive agreement on trade in

---

6. This is quite aside from the obvious point that many of those attempting to make a linkage between trade and another desirable goal are in fact not concerned with that goal, but rather with achieving protection in their own self-interest.

services is crucial, and Richard Snape's paper covers the key issues in that dimension. Achieving progress in liberalizing services is crucial for the WTO's future as well as that of the open multilateral trading system, and the telecommunications agreement (discussed in section 15.4) is therefore greatly to be welcomed.

There were two additional substantive issues, however, which were discussed extensively at the conference, but for which there are no papers in this volume. They deserve at least brief mention here.

15.3.1   Agriculture

One key issue is agriculture. The Uruguay Round enabled a great step forward in providing for the tarification of existing barriers to trade in agricultural commodities; it was only a first step, and protection levels will remain high even after agreed-upon measures are fully implemented. Liberalization of trade in agricultural products lags well behind that in manufactures.

In order to achieve further progress, protection to and subsidization of agriculture will have to be reduced further. It was deemed highly desirable that preparatory analytical work on trade in agriculture be undertaken to provide a basis for negotiations to start on further liberalization in 1999.

15.3.2   Intellectual Property Rights and Investment

Progress with respect to implementing the agreement on intellectual property rights was not a subject of discussion, as the implementation of the Uruguay Round appeared to be proceeding satisfactorily. And, while the same could be said for trade-related investment measures (TRIMs), a key issue is arising with respect to a general investment code.

Under the Uruguay Round, the TRIMs agreement dealt with issues such as the tying of export conditions to foreign investment agreements. It did not cover many of the more general issues governing investment in one country by nationals of another. As of the fall of 1996, industrialized countries were meeting under OECD auspices to develop an investment code. The relationship of the developing countries to this code was a major concern. On one hand, if the OECD-developed code were simply turned over to the WTO, developing countries would naturally feel left out and be unlikely to embrace it. If, on the other hand, the code were administered by the OECD, the developing countries would be left out, and, moreover, the WTO would be charged with overseeing international trade relations, but not investment relations.

Achieving an investment code agreed upon by industrialized and developing countries alike is clearly a desirable objective. Moreover, given that the WTO is a rules-based organization and that many of the issues that arise with respect to treatment of foreign investment also arise with respect to trade, it would appear natural that the WTO be the organization administering an international investment agreement. Bringing the developing countries into the agreement therefore appears to be highly desirable.

15.4   Outcome of the Singapore Ministerial Meeting and Other Developments

At the time of the conference, the press voiced considerable pessimism over prospects for progress at the Singapore ministerial meeting scheduled for December. Indeed, conference participants generally concluded that the Uruguay Round should focus on accelerating the implementation of Uruguay Round agreements, rather than addressing new issues.

In fact, the Singapore ministerial was more of a success than anticipated in the press. The key headline was the agreement to eliminate tariffs on information technology products, which was widely publicized and, in fact, seemed to signal "progress" toward freer trade. As already indicated, this mode of tariff reduction raises questions as to the desirability of sector-specific bargaining, but nonetheless the information technology agreement enabled delegates to Singapore to announce a successful outcome.[7]

In addition, it was agreed that four working groups would be formed to analyze competition policy, trade-investment links, transparency in public procurement, and simplification of customs procedures. Interestingly, no working group was established on agriculture. Of these, the ones on competition policy and on trade-investment links may be important and influence significantly the agenda for future trade negotiations on new issues.

With respect to linkages, the Singapore meeting can be regarded as having been largely successful. While the ministerial declaration backed "internationally recognized core labor standards," it did not establish a working group or any other provision for follow-up activity. Developing countries, of course, were vocal in their opposition to labor standards, since establishing those standards can so readily become a veil for protection against unskilled-labor-intensive imports.[8]

A number of observers and delegates to the Singapore ministerial had hoped that some action would be initiated with respect to preferential trading arrangements, arrangements to strengthen provisions to make them compatible with the open multilateral trading system. Although ministers did affirm the primacy of the open multilateral system, no measures were taken to initiate discussion of a strengthening of those measures.

Thus, as with progress in the WTO itself, the Singapore ministerial can be judged to have moved the open multilateral trading system forward, albeit slowly. While one could wish there had been more impetus with respect to

7. There was also an agreement among the United States, the European Union, Japan, Canada, Norway, Switzerland, and the Czech and Slovak Republics to abandon tariffs on about 450 pharmaceutical products. In this instance, negotiations were single-sector and did not even cover all members of the WTO.

8. There was also criticism from developing countries that the Uruguay Round agreement to dismantle the Multifiber Arrangement was being implemented slowly. Delegates expressed disappointment that no measures were authorized at the Singapore ministerial to accelerate implementation.

agriculture, the Multifiber Arrangement, preferential arrangements, and expansion of the secretariat, there were steps forward and linkages, such as labor standards, were not endorsed.

Since the Singapore ministerial, a telecommunications agreement was reached, and Richard Snape has discussed that agreement in the revised version of his paper. As the first key agreement in services, the telecommunications agreement marks an important step forward for the WTO. A case can be made that telecommunications was the "easiest" services sector for reaching agreement. This is because it was primarily developing-country markets that were opened and they desperately need good telecommunications if they are to attract foreign investment. Nonetheless, the fact that agreement was reached marked a milestone for the WTO.

A partial offset was the abandonment of negotiations with respect to maritime services. This may be an illustration of the difficulties with sector-specific negotiations: the United States strongly protects its maritime services, and was the country that finally declared the negotiations unsuccessful.

A key test for the WTO will be the outcome of the financial services negotiations, for which the deadline is the end of 1997. On one hand, most countries signed the earlier agreement, but the United States failed to sign. Achieving greater success with the subsequent negotiations will be important as a next major step in achieving liberalization of trade in services.

Thus, one must conclude that both the Singapore ministerial and subsequent developments have been moderately positive for the WTO. Over the first two years of its life, international trade grew at twice the rate of growth of world GDP, continuing the earlier trend toward increasing importance of trade in the international economy. As links between countries increase in importance, the imperative from those linkages to liberalization will provide momentum for the WTO.

It is to be hoped that governments in the key trading nations provide support for a strengthened secretariat, for maintaining an open multilateral system and disciplining preferential agreements to conform with it, and for continuing liberalization of trade, especially in new areas. Based on the record of the past fifty years, it seems reasonable to conclude that the momentum for a liberalized and open multilateral system will continue, while resistance will simultaneously prevent progress from being as rapid as might be desirable. But that momentum should, over time, work to strengthen the WTO as an international organization and to elevate it to a status commensurate with the importance of the global trading system.

Conference Participants

Kym Anderson
Centre for International Economic
  Studies
Adelaide, South Australia 5005
Australia

Robert E. Baldwin
University of Wisconsin
1180 Observatory Drive
Madison, WI 53706

Jean Baneth
10 Avenue de New York
75016 Paris
France

Richard Blackhurst
World Trade Organization
Rue de Lausanne 154
1211 Geneva 21
Switzerland

Barry Eichengreen
Research Department
International Monetary Fund
Washington, DC 20431

J. Michael Finger
World Bank Group
Room N5–043
Washington, DC 20433

Judith Goldstein
Stanford University
MC:2044
Stanford, CA 94305

David Henderson
c/o Ms. O'Flynn
Chatham House
10 St. James's Square
London SW1Y 4LE
England

Alan Hirsch
Industrial and Technology Policy
Department of Trade and Industry in
  Pretoria
Cape Town
South Africa

Douglas Irwin
Department of Economics
Dartmouth College
Hanover, NH 03755

John H. Jackson
University of Michigan
625 South State
Hutchins Hall
Ann Arbor, MI 48109

Anne O. Krueger
Stanford University
MC:6072
Stanford, CA 94305

Constantine Michalopoulos
World Trade Organization
Rue de Lausanne 154
1211 Geneva 21
Switzerland

Julio J. Nogués
World Bank
1818 H Street, NW
Suite D13051
Washington, DC 20433

John Odell
School of International Relations
University of Southern California
VKC 330
Los Angeles, CA 90089

Jaroslaw Pietras
University of Warsaw
Department of Economics
UL DLUGA 44150
00–241 Warsaw
Poland

Frieder Roessler
Law Center
Georgetown University
600 New Jersey Avenue, NW
Washington, DC 20001

Gary P. Sampson
World Trade Organization
Rue de Lausanne 154
1211 Geneva 21
Switzerland

Richard H. Snape
Industry Commission
Locked Bag 2, Collins Street East
45 Collins Street
Melbourne, Victoria 3000
Australia

T. N. Srinivasan
Economic Growth Center
Yale University
27 Hillhouse Avenue
New Haven, CT 06520

David Vines
Balliol College
Oxford, OX1 3BJ
England

L. Alan Winters
World Bank
1818 H Street, NW
Room N5043
Washington, DC 20433

Name Index

Subject Index